DEUTERONOMY
1–11

VOLUME 5

THE ANCHOR BIBLE is a fresh approach to the world's greatest classic. Its object is to make the Bible accessible to the modern reader; its method is to arrive at the meaning of biblical literature through exact translation and extended exposition, and to reconstruct the ancient setting of the biblical story, as well as the circumstances of its transcription and the characteristics of its transcribers.

THE ANCHOR BIBLE is a project of international and interfaith scope. Protestant, Catholic, and Jewish scholars from many countries contribute individual volumes. The project is not sponsored by any ecclesiastical organization and is not intended to reflect any particular theological doctrine. Prepared under our joint supervision, THE ANCHOR BIBLE is an effort to make available all the significant historical and linguistic knowledge which bears on the interpretation of the biblical record.

THE ANCHOR BIBLE is aimed at the general reader with no special formal training in biblical studies; yet, it is written with the most exacting standards of scholarship, reflecting the highest technical accomplishment.

This project marks the beginning of a new era of cooperation among scholars in biblical research, thus forming a common body of knowledge to be shared by all.

William Foxwell Albright
David Noel Freedman
GENERAL EDITORS

THE ANCHOR BIBLE

DEUTERONOMY
1–11

♦

A New Translation
with
Introduction and Commentary

MOSHE WEINFELD

VOLUME 5

THE ANCHOR BIBLE

Doubleday

New York London Toronto Sydney Auckland

The Anchor Bible
PUBLISHED BY DOUBLEDAY
a division of Bantam Doubleday Dell Publishing Group, Inc.,
666 Fifth Avenue, New York, New York 10103.

LIBRARY OF CONGRESS CATALOGING-IN-PUBLICATION DATA

Bible. O.T. Deuteronomy I–XI. English. Weinfeld. 1991.
Deuteronomy 1–11: a new translation with introduction and commentary / Moshe Weinfeld. — 1st ed.
p. cm. — (The Anchor Bible ; v. 5)
Includes bibliographical references.
ISBN 0-385-17593-0
1. Bible. O.T. Deuteronomy I–XI—Commentaries. I. Weinfeld, Moshe. II. Title. III. Series: Bible. English. Anchor Bible. 1964 ; v. 5.
BS192.2.A1 1964
[.G3 vol. 5]
[BS1273]
222′.15077—dc20 90-31508
CIP

ISBN 0-385-17593-0

Printed in the United States of America

First Edition

10 9 8 7 6 5 4 3 2 1

October 1991

CONTENTS

CONTENTS

CONTENTS

CONTENTS

Preface

◆

The decision to allocate a separate volume for Deuteronomy chapters 1–11 was motivated by three reasons. The first was the specific nature of these chapters, which contain history and homily, in contrast to chapters 12–26, which are comprised of legal material. Second, the Decalogue, included in this part of Deuteronomy (chapter 5), deserves special and comprehensive treatment (indeed, more than one hundred pages), especially because the book of Exodus in which the Decalogue first appears has not yet been published in the Anchor Bible series. Finally, the partition permits the provision of a long introduction to the book, which reflects its special importance. Deuteronomy serves as an Archimedean point for biblical criticism: it enabled scholars to date the Pentateuchal sources and the editorial framework of the historiography of the books of Joshua and Kings, the so-called deuteronomistic history.

The INTRODUCTION covers all aspects of the book: literary-critical, legal, historical, and theological. Only the section on Text and Versions has been postponed for the second volume, because research into the Qumran versions of Deuteronomy is still in process of publication. The Index to all of Deuteronomy will appear at the end of Vol. 5A.

The author owes special thanks to the editor of the Anchor Bible, Professor D. N. Freedman, for his critical comments and sharp observations. They were most helpful in the shaping of the commentary.

I am very grateful to Moshe Benowitz for his help, especially for his assistance in the textual notes. John W. Carnahan of University of California, Berkeley, was very helpful in preparing the material for the first chapters of the COMMENTARY. Special thanks are due to Edwin Firmage and Roy Gane for their assistance in preparing the final draft of chapters 6–11. Many thanks also go to Beverly Fields for typing the material of the Decalogue, to Dr. Sidnie Ann White for allowing me to use her dissertation on seven manuscripts from Qumran (4Q Dta, 4Q Dtc, 4Q Dtd, 4Q Dtf, 4Q Dtg, and 4Q Dtn), as well as to Dr. Julie Ann Duncan for her permission to use her dissertation on the other six manuscripts from Qumran (4Q Dtb, 4Q Dte,

4Q Dth, 4Q Dtj, 4Q Dtk, and 4Q Dtl). Special thanks to Dana Ben-Or and Rachel Yaniv for their help in matters of Bibliography, Textual Notes, etc.

The translation of Deuteronomy and of other books of the Bible is that of the author, unless indicated otherwise.

Jerusalem, August 1990

Abbreviations

♦

AASOR	Annual of the American Schools of Oriental Research
AB	Anchor Bible
AfO	*Archiv für Orientforschung*
AHW	W. von Soden, ed., *Akkadisches Handwörterbuch* (Wiesbaden, 1959–81)
AJS Review	*Association for Jewish Studies Review*
ANEP	J. B. Pritchard, ed., *The Ancient Near East in Pictures Relating to the Old Testament* (Princeton, 1954)
ANET	J. B. Pritchard, ed., *Ancient Near Eastern Texts Relating to the Old Testament* (Princeton, 1955)
AOAT	Alter Orient und Altes Testament
AOF	*Altorientalische Forschungen*
ARAB	D. D. Luckenbill, *Ancient Records of Assyria and Babylonia* (New York, 1926)
ARM	Archives royales de Mari
AS	Assyriological Studies
AThANT	*Abhandlungen zur Theologie des Alten und Neuen Testaments*
BA	*Biblical Archaeologist*
BASOR	*Bulletin of the American Schools of Oriental Research*
BBB	Bonner biblische Beiträge
BDB	Brown, Driver, Briggs, *Hebrew English Lexicon of the Old Testament*
BHK	Biblia Hebraica edidit Rudolf Kittel
BHS	Biblia Hebraica Stutgartensia
BHT	Babylonian Historical Texts
BJPES	*Bulletin of the Jewish Palestine Exploration Society*
BK	Biblischer Kommentar
BWANT	Beiträge zur Wissenschaft vom Alten und Neuen Testament
BWL	W. G. Lambert, *Babylonian Wisdom Literature* (Oxford, 1960)
BZ	*Biblische Zeitschrift*

BZAW	Beihefte zur *Zeitschrift für die alttestamentlische Wissenschaft*
CAD	*The Assyrian Dictionary of the Oriental Institute of the University of Chicago,* ed. L. Oppenheim et al. (Chicago, 1956)
CB	Cambridge Bible
CBQ	*Catholic Biblical Quarterly*
CH	Code of Hammurabi
CRAIBL	*Comptes rendus de l'Académie des inscripions et belles-lettres*
CTA	A. Herdner, *Corpus des tablettes en cunéiformes alphabétiques,* 2 vols. (Paris, 1963)
DJD	Discoveries in the Judaean Desert
EA	El Amarna Tablets According to Knudtzon
EI	*Eretz Israel*
EM	*Encyclopedia Miqra'it,* 9 vols. (Jerusalem, 1952–88)
EncJud	*Encyclopaedia Judaica* (Jerusalem, 1971)
FRLANT	Forschungen zur Religion und Literatur des Alten und Neuen Testaments
GKC	*Gesenius' Hebrew Grammar,* ed. E. Kautzsch, tr. A. E. Cowley, 2d English ed. (Oxford, 1910)
HAT	Handbuch zum Alten Testament
HKAT	Handkommentar zum Alten Testament
HSS	Harvard Semitic Studies
HL	Hittite Laws
HTR	*Harvard Theological Review*
HUCA	*Hebrew Union College Annual*
ICC	International Critical Commentary
IEJ	*Israel Exploration Journal*
IOS	*Israel Oriental Studies*
JAOS	*Journal of the American Oriental Society*
JBL	*Journal of Biblical Literature*
JCS	*Journal of Cuneiform Studies*
JEA	*Journal of Egyptian Archaeology*
JJS	*Journal of Jewish Studies*
JNES	*Journal of Near Eastern Studies*
JPOS	*Journal of the Palestine Oriental Society*
JPS	Jewish Publication Society of America, Translations to the Holy Scriptures
JQR	*Jewish Quarterly Review*
JSOT	*Journal for the Study of the Old Testament*
JSS	*Journal of Semitic Studies*
JTS	*Journal of Theological Studies*
KAI	H. Donner and W. Röllig, *Kanaanäische und aramäische Inschriften* (Wiesbaden, 1962–64)

KAT³	Die Keilinschrifte und das Alte Testament, eds. E. Schrader, H. Winckler and H. Zimmer (Berlin, 1903)
KB	L. Koehler and W. Baumgartner, *Lexicon in Veteris Testamenti libros* (Leiden, 1958)
KBO	Keilschrifttexte aus Boghazköi
KEH	Kurzgefasstes exegetisches Handbuch zum Alten Testament
KS	*Kleine Schriften*
KTU	M. Dietrich et al., eds., *Die keilalphabetischen Texte aus Ugarit* (Neukirchen, 1976)
KUB	Keilschrifturkunden aus Boghazköi (Berlin, 1939–44)
LXX	Septuagint
Maarav	*Maarav: A Journal for the Study of the Northwest Semitic Languages and Literatures*
MGWJ	*Monatsschrift für Geschichte und Wissenschaft des Judentums*
MDOG	*Mitteilungen der deutschen orientalischen Gesellschaft*
MT	Masoretic Text
MVAG	Mitteilungen der vorderasiatisch-ägyptischen Gesellschaft
NEB	The New English Bible
NEchB	*Die Neue Echter Bibel*
NJPS	The New Jewish Publication Society of America, Translations to the Holy Scriptures
OBO	Orbis Biblicus et Orientalis
OBS	*Oriental and Biblical Studies*
OIP	Oriental Institute Publications
OLA	Orientalia Lovaniensia Analecta
OLZ	*Orientalistische Literaturzeitung*
OTS	*Oudtestamentische Studiën*
PEQ	*Palestine Exploration Quarterly*
PRU	*Le Palais royal d'Ugarit*
RA	*Revue d'assyriologie et d'archéologie orientale*
RB	*Revue biblique*
RevQ	*Revue de Qumrân*
RevSém	*Revue sémitique d'épigraphie et d'histoire ancienne*
RHA	*Revue hittite et asianique*
RIDA	*Revue internationale des droits de l'antiquité*
RLA	*Reallexikon der Assyriologie (1928–)*
RS	Field Numbers of the Tablets Excavated at Ras Shamra
RSO	*Rivista degli studi orientali*
RSV	Revised Standard Version
Shnaton	*An Annual for Biblical and Ancient Near Eastern Studies*
SJT	*Scottish Journal of Theology*
SPB	Standard Prayer Book

SSAW	Sitzungsberichte der Sächsischen Akademie der Wissenschaften zu Leipzig
StBogT	Studien in den Boğazkoy Texten
Syr	Syriac version
TCL	Textes cunéiformes du Musée du Louvre
TDNT	G. Kittel and G. Friedrich, eds., *Theological Dictionary of the New Testament,* 10 vols. (Grand Rapids, 1965–78)
TDOT	G. J. Botterweck and H. Ringgren, eds., *Theological Dictionary of the Old Testament,* 5 vols. (Grand Rapids, 1974–86)
ThWAT	G. J. Botterweck and H. Ringgren, eds., *Theologisches Worterbuch zum Alten Testament,* 6 vols. (Stuttgart, 1970–88)
UF	*Ugaritische Forschungen*
UT	*Ugaritic Textbook*
VAB	Vorderasiatische Bibliothek
VAS	Vorderasiatische Schriftdenkmäler
VT	*Vetus Testamentum*
VTE	D. J. Wiseman, *The Vassal Treaties of Esarhaddon* (London, 1958)
VTSup	*Vetus Testamentum,* Supplements
Vg	Vulgate Bible
WMANT	Wissenschaftliche Monographien zum Alten und Neuen Testaments
WZKM	*Wiener Zeitschrift für die Kunde des Morgenlandes*
ZA	*Zeitschrift für Assyriologie und vorderasiatische Archäologie*
ZAW	*Zeitschrift für die alttestamentliche Wissenschaft*
ZDMG	*Zeitschrift der deutschen morgenländischen Gesellschaft*
ZDPV	*Zeitschrift des deutschen Palästina-Vereins*

DEUTERONOMY
1–11

INTRODUCTION

♦

1. THE NAME AND ITS MEANING

Both the Greek appellation of the book, *To deuteronomion* (hence Latin *Deuteronomium),* and the Hebrew appellation, *Mishneh Tôrah (Sipre,* §160, based on Deut 17:18; Josh 8:32), mean 'repeated law' or 'second law'[1] and allude to the fact that Deuteronomy is a (revised) repetition of a large part of the law and history of the Tetrateuch (the first four books): compare Naḥmanides to Deut 1:1 and Ibn Ezra to Deut 1:5. Although the words *mšnh htwrh hzʾt* in Deut 17:18 may mean 'a copy of this Torah,' it is true that Deuteronomy constitutes a second covenant besides the Sinaitic one (cf. 28:69) and thus may have been rightly considered to be secondary. In fact, according to 5:28, though all of the laws were delivered to Moses at Sinai, the people received them only at the plains of Moab, and a covenant was established there in addition to the covenant concluded at Sinai (28:69).

As will be shown below, Deuteronomy is dependent on the previous traditions of the Pentateuch but was revised according to the principles of the Hezekianic–Josianic reforms. Thus, for example, the laws of tithe, of *šĕmiṭṭāh* (the year of the release of debts, 15:1–11), and the rule of the release of slaves (15:12–19), of the firstborn animal (15:19–23), and of the three festivals (16:1–17) are all ancient laws (cf. Exod 21:1–11; 22:28–29; 23:10–11, 14–19; 34:19–26). They appear, however, in Deuteronomy in a new form, adjusted to the principles of centralization of cult as well as to the social-human tendency that is characteristic of Deuteronomy (see below). There was thus an awareness of this book being secondary.

A similar categorization of stabilized canonical tradition versus extraneous or secondary, later added, tradition is found in Mesopotamia. There we find the term *šanû* 'second/another' for sacred literary material distinct from the original

[1] Philo names Deuteronomy *epinomis* (=appendix/addition); cf. (the king will write) *tēn epinomida . . . kefalaiōde typon* 'the appendix in the form of a summary' *(The Special Laws* 4.160; cf. also *Who Is the Heir?* 162, 250).

canonical one (see recently Rochberg-Halton 1984). An Akkadian term that overlaps *šanû* is *aḫû* (external; ibid., 140–44), an expression that equals late Hebrew *ḥîṣôn,* for which one is to compare the expression *sĕfārîm ḥîṣônîm* 'extraneous books', which defines noncanonical literature (see *m. Sanh.* 10:1). In the Qumran literature we find the term *sefer haTôrāh hašenît,* referring apparently to a noncanonical Torah.[2]

Alongside the Hebrew name *Mishneh Tôrāh (Deuteronomium),* the prevalent name for the book was *Dĕbārîm* 'the Words', taken from the incipit of the Hebrew book, as was the case with the names of the other books of the Pentateuch: *Bĕrēshît* 'In the beginning' for Genesis, *Shemôt* 'The names' for Exodus, *Wayikrā* 'He called' for Leviticus, and *Bamidbār* 'In the desert' for Numbers. As with the name of Deuteronomy so with the other books of the Pentateuch, there existed thematic appellations side by side with the nomenclature taken from the opening words of each book: Genesis (= Creation), Exodus (= exit from Egypt), Leviticus (Levitic = priestly laws, cf. Hebrew *tôrat kōhanîm* 'priestly law'), Numbers (= the census of the Israelites, cf. Hebrew *ḥômeš hapĕqūdîm* 'the fifth (part of the Pentateuch) of "census" ': cf. *m. Yoma* 7:1, *Sôṭā* 7:7).

The system of naming a literary creation after its incipit is very ancient: compare the Babylonian creation epic named after its opening: *enūma eliš* 'when above', and the so-called "Righteous Sufferer," the ancient title of which was *ludlul bēl nemēqi* 'I will praise the lord of wisdom', after the opening words of the work.

2. Outline of Contents

1:1–5 consists of a title that indicates the place and the time of Moses' farewell speech.

1:6–4:40 contain Moses' first discourse, which consists of (a) a historical introduction (1:6–3:29) describing the incidents of the Israelites' journey from Horeb (= Sinai) till they arrive at the plains of Moab at the valley opposite Beth-Peor (3:29); and (b) a sermon *4:1–40* that inculcates loyalty to the one true God who revealed himself to the Israelites at Sinai and gave them the Ten Commandments. The sermon stresses the uniqueness of God and his chosen people.

4:41–43 provides an account of Moses' assignment of the three cities of refuge in Transjordan (cf. 19:1–10 and Num 35:9–34).

4:44–49 consists of a superscription to the second introduction to the code. It indicates, like the title in 1:1–5, the place and the time of Moses' speech.

[2] DJD 5.177, l.14 Catena A, pp. 67ff.; and see Weinfeld 1978–79a, p. 233.

5:1–11:32 are a paraenetic discourse that contains the Decalogue and the basic command (*hamizwāh*, cf. 6:1) of loyalty, which draws on the first two commandments of the Decalogue. A special section in the discourse is dedicated to the story about the worship of the golden calf and its sad consequences (9:7–10:11). The discourse ends with the episodes of the foundation ceremony at Mount Gerizim and Mount Ebal (cf. the NOTES to 11:26–32), which comes to stress the blessing for obeying the commandments of God and the curse for disobedience (cf. chap. 27).

12:1–26:15 comprise the code of the laws: (a) sacred injunctions (12:1–16:17), which refer to the centralization of cult (12:1–28); repression of idolatry (12:29–13:19); the prohibition of defilement that violates the holiness of the people (14:1–21); and sacred dues and sacred seasons (14:22–16:17); (b) the main institutions of Israel as a nation and state (16:18–18:22): judges (16:18–20, 17:1–13); the king (17:14–20); priests (18:1–8); and prophets (18:9–22); (c) criminal law (19:1–21): homicide (19:1–13); removal of boundaries (19:14); false witness (19:15–21); (d) war regulations and expiation of an uncertain murder (20:1–21:9); (e) family law and civil life (21:10–25:19): the captive woman (21:10–14); primogeniture (21:15–17); the wayward son (21:18–21); execution and burial of the criminal (21:22–23); lost property (22:1–3); miscellaneous laws connected with social and religious behavior (22:4–12); laws concerning marriage, seduction, and rape (22:13–32); prohibited marriages (23:1–9); purity of the military camp (23:10–15); the fugitive slave (23:16–17); prohibition of religious prostitution (23:18–19); prohibition of interest (23:20–21 = 24–25 E); laws about vows (23:22–24); laws against seizure of the neighbor's crop (23:25–26); on divorce (24:1–4); exemptions of newly married men from public-military obligations (24:5); hand mill not to be taken as pledge (24:6); against man-stealing (24:7); on leprosy being subject to priestly directions (24:8–9); on pledges (24:10–13); on justice toward hired people (24:14–15); against communal-familial responsibility for crimes of the individual (24:16); against injustice to the underprivileged (24:17–18); gleaning to be left to the underprivileged (24:19–22); limit of corporal punishments (25:1–3); humanitarian behavior toward animals (25:4); law of levirate (25:5–10); against immodesty in women (25:11–12); against false weights and measures (25:13–16); and a ban of the Amalekites (25:17–19); (f) ceremonies in connection with the offering of first fruits (26:1–11) and completion of triennial tithe (26:12–15).

26:16–27:26 recount the founding of Israel before the entrance into the promised land: (a) the proclamation of Israel's peculiar mission (26:16–19); (b) the cultic ceremony at Israel's entrance into the land: erecting stone monuments and inscribing the law upon them, and building an altar on Mount Ebal (27:1–8); (c) proclamation of Israel's establishment as the people of God (27:9–10); (d) the ceremony of blessings and curses on Mount Gerizim and Mount Ebal (27:11–13); (e) imprecations for sins done in secrecy (27:14–26).

Chapter 28 lists blessings and curses of two different categories: (a) 28:3–7, 16–19, which belong to the Shechemite ceremony of chap. 27 (see below); and (b) 28:1–2, 8–15, and 20–68, which reflects the Deuteronomic character of the material, namely, curses of the Assyrian vassal treaty type.

Chapter 29 is a covenantal scene in the land of Moab, introduced by a short historical discourse (29:1–8).

Chapter 30 gives a promise of return to the land after the Exile provided Israel sincerely repents (30:1–10); the choice given to Israel between the path of life and the path of death (30:11–20).

In *Chapter 31,* Moses commands his successor Joshua, who will conquer the land (31:1–8). 31:9–13 gives the Deuteronomic law written by Moses and to be read by Joshua (cf. Josh 8:34–35) before the people every seventh year; there follow the commission of Joshua by God (31:14–15, 23), an introduction to the Song of Moses (31:16–22), and an epilogue to the Deuteronomic book of the law (31:24–29).

32:1–43 is the Song of Moses.

32:44–47 is an epilogue to the Song of Moses.

32:48–52 contains God's command to Moses to ascend Mount Nebo and to die there (a priestly inclusio corresponding to Num 27:12–23).

Chapter 33 is the blessing of Moses.

Chapter 34 gives the account of Moses' death.

3. The Literary Form of Deuteronomy

Farewell Speech of Moses

Deuteronomy is presented as a farewell speech delivered by Moses shortly before his death. The form of the "testament" given to the book looks peculiar but has its antecedents in the Egyptian method of diffusing moral teaching. Most of the Egyptian wisdom instructions were dressed in the form of testaments of kings and viziers to their successors (see Lichtheim 1973–76, 1.5–9, 58–82, and 134–92). This technique may have exerted its influence on Israel's literature, especially because there exist affinities between Deuteronomy and the didactic wisdom literature (see below). Indeed, the book of Deuteronomy is a kind of manual for the future kings of Israel (cf. 17:14–23) written by scribes (see below), just as were the instructions for the Egyptian and Mesopotamian kings.[3] As will be shown below, the valedictory speeches in the Deuteronomic corpus are linked to a ceremony of succession bound by covenant, a ceremony

[3] Compare the so-called "Advice to the Prince" in Mesopotamian literature, *BWL,* pp. 110–12.

attested in the neo-Assyrian Empire in the *vassal treaties of Esarhaddon* (cf. *VTE,* pp. 1–99). This concept of covenantal succession is reflected in the Greek rendering of biblical *bĕrīt: diathēke* 'testament', though not all of the words *bĕrīt* in the OT could be understood as 'testament'.

It seems that the basic sense underlying *diathēke* in the LXX is 'imposed obligation', which is semantically true for the Hebrew *bĕrīt* (cf. Weinfeld 1973d; and for the usage of the LXX, cf. Tov 1987, p. 249). It is hard to decide whether the valedictory speeches were modeled on the ethical wills of the Egyptian type or rather belong to the covenantal scene of royal succession of the Assyrian type. At any rate, Deuteronomy adopted the form of speech as a literary device for disseminating its message. The practice of ascribing religious-ethical valedictories to leaders and kings was also used by the editors of the Israelite historiography who were influenced by the book of Deuteronomy. Thus the Deuteronomic writers end the period of the conquest with a farewell speech of Joshua (chap. 23), the period of the Judges concludes with a valedictory speech of Samuel (1 Sam 12), and the description of David's life in the Deuteronomic edition ends with a religious-ethical will of David (1 Kgs 2:3–4; see Weinfeld 1972a, pp. 10–14). Besides the valedictory speeches, the Deuteronomic school used to ascribe to national leaders speeches of prophetic nature, liturgical orations, and military addresses (ibid.).

A similar literary method is found in Greek historiography. Numerous speeches are cited in the works of Herodotus and Thucydides, supposedly delivered by national heroes. Thucydides himself declares that it was his habit to make the speeches say what, in his opinion, was demanded of them by the various occasions (1.22.18; cf. Weinfeld 1972a, pp. 51–53).

Expressing ideology by means of programmatic speeches put into the mouths of leaders and great personalities continued in Israelite historiography of the Second Temple period. Thus the Chronicle puts into the mouth of King Abijah, the son of Rehoboam, a speech that emphasizes the eternity of the Davidic dynasty and the sole legitimacy of the Jerusalemite Temple (2 Chr 13:4–12) in order to show that the Northern Kingdom's objection to the Davidic Kingdom and to the Jerusalemite Temple is a rebellion against God.

The same pattern is found in the apocryphal literature. Two speeches are ascribed to Judith, the heroine, before she acts against the enemy. The first speech (8:11–27) comes to implant faith and confidence in her action by citing the tests to which God put Israel in the past, while the second (9:2–14), which is a prayer, invokes the greatness of the God of Israel and his deeds in the past. Similarly, we find in the farewell speech of Mattathias, the Hasmonean, an enumeration of the faithful ancestors and their pious deeds in order to encourage his sons to give their souls for keeping God's covenant (1 Macc 2:48–67). This system of programmatic speeches can be traced down to the speeches of Peter and Stephen in Luke's Acts of the Apostles (2:14–36, 7:2–53). These speeches survey Israel's past,[4] and thus serve a didactic purpose.

4. The Covenant at the Plains of Moab

A change of leadership in the ancient Near East was accompanied by a pledge of loyalty on behalf of the people. The so-called vassal treaties of Esarhaddon *(VTE),* which have so much in common with Deuteronomy (see below), are simply fealty oaths imposed by the retiring king on his vassals with respect to his successor (Ashurbanipal). The covenant in the land of Moab, which is concluded at the time that Moses nominates Joshua as his successor (Deut 3:23–29; 31:1–8), resembles then formally the situation found in the *VTE.* The difference is only that the contents of the Mosaic covenant are divine law and the sworn pledge refers to God, whereas the *VTE* are concerned with stipulations of a political nature, referring to the human suzerain. Formally, however, the two documents are very similar. Especially striking are the covenantal scenes in the *VTE* and in Deuteronomy. Both scenes have the entire population gathered, young and old (Deut 29:9–11, cf. 2 Kgs 23:1–3, and *VTE* 4–5; see Weinfeld 1979b, pp. 392–93). In both scenes those gathered take the pledge not only for themselves but also for future generations (Deut 29:14, *VTE* 6–7, cf. Sefire treaty 1.A.1–5).

In fact, even before the discovery of the Esarhaddon treaties the particular formal structure of the book of Deuteronomy had been recognized. G. von Rad inquired into the significance of the peculiar structure of Deuteronomy:[5] history (chaps. 1–11), laws (12:1–26:15), mutual obligations (26:16–19), and blessings and curses (chaps. 27–28); he suggested that the structure reflects the procedure of a formal cultic ceremony. According to von Rad, this ceremony opened with a recital of history, proceeded with the proclamation of law, was accompanied by a pledge, and ended with blessings and curses. Because, according to Deut 27, the blessings and curses have to be recited between Mount Gerizim and Mount Ebal, von Rad identified Shechem as the scene of periodic covenant renewal in ancient Israel (cf. Josh 24). Although no real evidence for a covenant festival has been discovered so far, the observation made by von Rad that the literary structure of Deuteronomy reflects a covenantal procedure has been confirmed by subsequent investigations. It has become clear that the covenant form as presented in Deuteronomy was in use for centuries in the ancient Near East. G. E. Mendenhall in 1954 found that the Hittite suzerainty treaties have a

[4] See M. Weinfeld, *From Joshua to Josiah,* (in print).

[5] G. von Rad, *The Problem of the Hexateuch* (Edinburgh, 1966), pp. 1–78.

structure identical with that of the biblical covenant.[6] The basic elements are titulary; historical introduction, which served as motivation for the vassal's loyalty; stipulations of the treaty; a list of divine witnesses; blessing and curses; recital of the covenant; and the deposit of its tablets.

The treaties of Esarhaddon (dated 672 B.C.E.), discovered in 1956, provided new material and a better understanding of the Deuteronomic covenant. It transpires now that, like the *VTE,* Deuteronomy is not a covenant between two parties but a loyalty oath imposed by the sovereign on his vassal. The demands for loyalty are expressed in Deuteronomy and in the *VTE* in identical terms. "Love" stands in both sources for loyalty, and the subjects in both documents are commanded "to love" their suzerain "with all your heart and all your soul" (cf. Deut 6:5; see Weinfeld 1976b, pp. 384–85). The standard terms for being loyal to the sovereign in both documents are "to go after" (= to follow), "to fear," and "to hearken to the voice of." Furthermore, even in the contents there is identity between the Assyrian oath and that of Deuteronomy. The whole series of curses in Deut 28:23–35 is paralleled in the *VTE,* and even the order of curses is the same in both documents (see COMMENT). While the order of the curses, as for example leprosy and blindness, in the Assyrian treaties can be explained—the order follows the hierarchy of the gods Sin and Šamaš, who are each associated with a specific curse (leprosy and blindness, respectively)—the order of the same curses in Deuteronomy cannot be explained, which shows that the curses originated in the Mesopotamian tradition. Indeed, Frankena has suggested that the Deuteronomic covenant was a substitution for the Judean loyalty oath to the king of Assyria (the time of Manasseh) and hence the identity in the curses.[7]

After the discovery of the *VTE* it became clear that distinction should be made between a covenant between two equal parties and an oath of loyalty imposed by the suzerain on his vassals. The latter corresponds to the form of Deuteronomy, which is a loyalty oath imposed by God on his vassal, Israel. Such loyalty oaths were prevalent from the days of the Hittite Empire in the fifteenth and fourteenth centuries through the Assyrian Empire down to the Roman Empire (see Weinfeld 1976b, pp. 381–83). The Hittites included in their oath a historical introduction in which the benevolence of the suzerain toward the vassal was stressed, which came to justify their demands for loyalty. A similar element is found in Deuteronomy, which has a long historical introduction (chaps. 1–11), an element not attested in the usual Assyrian treaties. (An exception may be found in a fragment of the treaty between Ashurbanipal and Yauta, king of the Qedarites [cf. Deller and Parpola 1968, and Buis 1978], but the historical reference there does not function as an apology, the way the Hittite

[6] G. E. Mendenhall, "Covenant Forms" (1954):49–76.

[7] R. Frankena, "The Vassal Treaties of Esarhaddon and the Dating of Deuteronomy." *OTS* 14 (1965):153.

historical prologue does.) It seems that the Assyrian emperor, who saw himself as king of the universe, felt that it would be both unnecessary and humiliating to justify his demand of loyalty by referring to the benevolence of the suzerain to the vassal in the manner of the Hittite kings. This assumption may also explain the lack of the blessings in the Assyrian treaties on the one hand and the long list of curses on the other. The Hittites felt it necessary not only to justify their demands for loyalty but also to give promises of help in time of danger, as well as to bestow divine blessings for loyal service. The Assyrians neither gave promises to the vassal nor bestowed blessings but, on the contrary, increased and expanded the list of threats and curses in order to terrorize him.

The arrogance of the Assyrian king may also explain the lack of any sign of the sovereign's affection for his vassal. In the Hittite treaties and in the Israelite covenant (see the NOTE to 7:6), along with the demand of "love" (loyalty) on the part of the vassal come expressions of affection from the side of the sovereign. The Assyrian king, however, demands scrupulous "love" (loyalty) from the vassals but no sign of affection on the king's side. In this matter of affection Deuteronomy follows the Hittite line and not the Assyrian one.

Another parallel feature between the Assyrian oath of loyalty and the one in Deuteronomy is the theme of self-condemnation in connection with the violation of the oath. The end of Deuteronomy 29 reads, "And the generations to come . . . will ask: Why did YHWH do thus to this land? and they will say: 'because they forsook the covenant of YHWH' " (vv 21–24). The same motif is found in the neo-Assyrian texts concerning the breach of the oath. Thus the annals of Assurbanipal state, "the people of Arabia asked one another saying: why is it that such evil has befallen Arabia? and they say 'because we did not observe the obligation sworn to the god of Ashur.' "[8]

The pattern that served a political need in the ancient Near East came to serve a religious need in Israel. The religious use of this pattern was especially possible in Israel, for only the religion of Israel demanded exclusive loyalty to the God of Israel, a jealous God, who would suffer no rival. The religion of Israel therefore precluded the possibility of dual or multiple loyalties, such as were permitted in other religions in which the believer was bound in diverse relationships to many gods. So the stipulation in political treaties demanding exclusive loyalty to one king corresponds strikingly to the religious belief in one single, exclusive Deity.

The idea of the kingship of God also seems to have contributed to the concept of Israel as the vassal of YHWH the King. It is true that the idea of the kingship of God was prevalent all over the ancient Near East (cf. Frankfort 1948). There was, nevertheless, an important difference between the Israelite notion of divine kingship and the corresponding idea in other nations. Israel adopted the idea of the kingship of God a long time before establishing the

[8] Streck 1916, 2.9.68–72, p. 75; for an additional example see Weinfeld 1972a, p. 115.

human institution of kingship. As a result, for hundreds of years the only kingship recognized and institutionalized in Israel was the kingship of God. According to Israelite tradition during the period of the Judges (cf. Crüsemann 1978 and the review by Weinfeld: 1981a), YHWH was actually the King of Israel (Judg 8:23; 1 Sam 8:7; 10:19).

Because of the concept of the kingship of God, relations between the people and their God had to be patterned after the conventional model of relations between a king and his subjects, a written treaty. It is no wonder, then, that the pattern of the vassal treaty found a permanent place in the Israelite religion; nor is it a coincidence that this treaty pattern was adopted in its entirety precisely by the book of Deuteronomy. The pattern of a state treaty based on the demand for exclusive allegiance is well suited to a book in which the concept of the unity of God reaches the apogee of expression. E. W. Nicholson's skepticism about the ancient Near Eastern parallels to the covenant of God with Israel (1986) is based on a misunderstanding. The covenant of God with Israel is not to be paralleled to political pacts between states in the ancient Near East but is to be compared with the loyalty oaths of vassals to their suzerains, as I have indicated above.

Deuteronomy is actually dependent on two models of covenant: the Hittite one and the Assyrian one. The Hittite model is old and seems to underlie the old biblical covenantal tradition.[9] Deuteronomy shows connections with both sets of loyalty oaths: one of the second millennium and the other of the first millennium. The Hittite model pervaded the old biblical tradition, which Deuteronomy used and reworked in accordance with the prevalent covenantal pattern reflected in the *VTE*.

5. Composition and Structure

In spite of its apparent formal unity, the book is not a homogeneous piece of work. It has two introductions (1:1–4:40, 4:44–11:32), two different kinds of blessings and curses (27:11–13 with 28:3–7, 16–19, and the curses in the rest of chap. 28; see below). In addition, we find appendixes of various kinds: the Song of Moses (32:1–43) and the Blessing of Moses (chap. 33), which are old poems ascribed to Moses and appended to the book by the editor of Deuteronomy. Similar appendixes were added by the Deuteronomic historiographer to the stories about David in the books of Samuel. The Song of David (2 Sam 22) and his last prophetic blessing (2 Sam 23:1–7) were appended to the books of Samuel after they had assumed their basic structure (see Weinfeld 1972a, pp. 11–12). The Deuteronomic redaction of the Davidic stories ended the account of

[9] See Mendenhall, 1954, "Covenant Forms."

David's life with a farewell address (1 Kgs 2:3–4), which was incorporated into the old Davidic testament (1 Kgs 2:1–2, 5–9).

The Song of Moses (32:1–43) was preceded by an Elohistic introduction (31:16–22) that presented the song as a written prophetic *witness (ʿed)* for the next generations when troubles might befall Israel as a result of violating the covenant. This stimulated the author of Deuteronomy to present also the Deuteronomic Torah as a prophetic *witness* for the future generations (31:26–29). Both the Song and the Torah were said to be written by Moses (cf. 31:9 with 22) and taught by him to Israel (31:22, 32:46).

The composite nature of the book of Deuteronomy has been dealt with by many modern scholars, but no final solution has been reached. There is a general agreement in regards to Deut 4:44–28:68. It is believed that these chapters constituted the original book, which was later supplemented by an additional introduction (1:6–4:40) and by varied material at the end of the book (chaps. 29–30). The rest of the book is usually divided into two categories: first, the Deuteronomic material dealing with the commissioning of Joshua (31:1–8), the writing of the Torah, its use in the future (31:9–13), the depositing of it at the Ark (31:24–29; 32:45–47), and the death of Moses (chap. 34); and, second, ancient material appended to the book—as indicated above—such as the Song of Moses (32:1–43) with its Elohistic introduction (31:14–23), the Blessing of Moses (33:1–29), and the priestly passage in 32:48–52, which recaptures the priestly tradition about the death of Moses in Num 27:12–14, in order to connect it with chap. 34, the account of the death of Moses. It should be recognized, however, that chaps. 5–28 are not homogeneous either. The law code that constitutes the main part of the book was originally put into a framework of the ceremony of blessings and curses of Gerizim and Ebal. The theme of this ceremony appears at the opening of the code (11:26–32) and at its conclusion (26:16–27:26). It undoubtedly adds significance to the code of laws. The old Shechemite ceremony, which is an act of foundation (see Weinfeld 1988) and which parallels the Gilgal tradition, which also has a ceremony of erecting monuments (Josh 3–5), was linked by Deuteronomy to the covenant of the plains of Moab. Moses' proclamations about Israel becoming a nation "this day" (26:16–19; 27:9–10) are thus interwoven with the ceremony at Mount Gerizim and Mount Ebal. The first proclamation, in Deut 26:16–19, comes before the command about the erection of the stones and building the altar at Ebal, while the second proclamation, in 27:9–10, comes before the blessings and the curses at Gerizim and Ebal (27:11–26). By this combination the author makes it clear that the establishment of the people of Israel at the plains of Moab cannot be dissociated from the foundation ceremony at Mount Ebal. Moses' farewell address in Deuteronomy is a kind of preparation for the ceremony at Gerizim and Ebal.

Deuteronomy 27 preserved a very old tradition about the establishment of the nation at Shechem, the capital of the house of Joseph. Foundation stories of the Greek world (see Weinfeld 1988) indicate that settlers whose colonization was based on divine instigation used to perform ceremonies accompanied by blessings and curses by writing the sacred laws on stelae and by building an altar and sacrificing. Deuteronomy 27 indeed revolves around the following elements: (1) erecting stones on Mount Ebal in order to write upon them the words of the covenant (vv 1–4, 8); (2) building an altar and offering sacrifices on it (vv 5–7); (3) the proclamation of the act of foundation (vv 9–10); and (4) blessing and curses (vv 11–13). In addition, we find there curses for transgressors who perpetrate crimes clandestinely (vv 14–26).

The blessing and curses in vv 11–13 actually refer to Deut 28:3–6 and 16–19:

> Blessed shall you be in the city and blessed shall you be in the country:
>
> Blessed shall be the fruit of your womb, the fruit of your soil and the offspring of your cattle, the calving of your herd, and the lambing of your flock.
>
> Blessed shall be your basket and your kneading bowl.
>
> Blessed shall you be in your comings and blessed shall you be in your goings.

Their reversal—in other words, the curses—occurs in 28:16–19: "Cursed shall you be in the city," and so on.

That the ceremonies of blessing and cursing on Mount Gerizim and Mount Ebal, respectively, refer to the series of blessings and curses in Deut 28:3–6 and 16–19 was already observed by Ibn Ezra. It was also Ibn Ezra who saw that the curse proclamations in Deut 27:14–26 apply to transgressions perpetrated in secrecy.

It is indeed interesting that both types of public anathema—cursing the violators of the oath and banning transgressors—are attested in Greek amphictyonic oaths concerning the temple of Apollo of Delphi. Thus, for instance, in the oath taken by the members of the amphictyony against Cirrha (the first "holy war," 590 B.C.E.), we read, "If anyone should violate this, whether city, private man or tribe let them be under the curse . . . that their land bear no fruit; that their wives bear children not like those who begat them, but monsters; that their flocks yield not their natural increase; that defeat await them in camp and court and their gathering place" (Aeschines 3.109–11). Similarly, in the Greeks' oath at Plataeia before the battle with the Persians (479 B.C.E.), we find, "If I observe what is written in the oath my city will be free of disease: if not it shall be sick . . . ; and my (land) shall bear (fruits): if not it shall be barren; and the women shall bear children like their parents; if not they shall bear monsters; and the flock shall bear like the flock; if not (they shall be) monsters" (Siewert 1972, pp. 5–7). These blessings and curses are strikingly similar to the series of blessings and curses in Deut 28:3–6 and 16–19 quoted above.

As in the Greeks' oath at Plataeia, every blessing in Deut 28:16–19 has its corresponding curse. And the content of the series is identical with that of the Greeks' oath: fertility of the soil, women, and the flock. The element of coming and going in Deuteronomy is identical with the element of success and failure in camp, court, and agora in the Greek' oath. Furthermore, the element of sickness that occurs in the oath of Plataia appears in an identical series of blessings and curses in the ancient epilogue to the covenant code in Exod 23:25–26:

> I shall remove illness from your midst.
> None will miscarry or go barren in your land.

This idea is elaborated in Deut 7:13–15 in a chapter that depends on the peroration in Exod 23:25–26. Here we read, "He will bless the fruit of your womb and the fruit of your soil . . . the increase of your herd and the lambing of your flock, . . . there shall be no sterile male or female among you or among your livestock. YHWH will remove from you all sickness." To all appearance, this genre of blessings and curses has its origin in the tribal confederation based on covenant; hence the similarity to the blessings and curses of the amphictyonic oaths in Greece. The stereotyped series of blessings and curses in Deut 28:3–6 and 16–19 thus belongs to the ancient Shechemite covenant ceremony, which is elaborated by the Deuteronomic author of 28:7–14, 20–68. These Deuteronomic expansions have a lot in common with the Assyrian and Aramaic treaties of the eighth and seventh centuries B.C.E. and thus are clearly later than the short stereotypic blessings and curses, which have their parallels in the Greek tribal milieu.

The "curses" in 27:14–26 represent a different genre. These are not threats of punishment, like those in 28:16–19, but legal proclamations accompanied by a curse and addressed to those who commit crimes clandestinely, which cannot be punished by the authorities. Such "curses" are also attested in Greek tribal culture. In Greece those who violated the law were reviled by the leaders and priests of the polity and were made "accursed" *(eparatos).* So, for example, it is related of Alcibiades (Plutarch, *Alcibiades* 22) that he was found liable at law for desecrating the sacra of Demeter. After placing his property under the "ban," his judges decided that the priests and priestesses should curse him. Aristides is said to have suggested that the priests should cast curses on anyone who abandoned the war treaty with the Greeks (Plutarch, *Aristides* 10). As in Greece, so in Israel, it is the sacred group (the Levites) who have the authority to "revile," that is, excommunicate the transgressors.

Early Israel's affinities to the Greek tradition are most clearly expressed, however, in the foundation ceremony found in Deut 27. As indicated above, oath taking, erecting stones during foundation ceremonies, inscribing sacred laws on stelae, and building an altar and sacrificing on it are attested in Greek colonization. Indeed, the Greeks as well as the Israelites had elaborate foundation traditions. Israel nurtured divergent traditions about their first settlements in the land. Besides the Shechemite tradition recounted in Deut 27 we find other versions describing foundation ceremonies linked to other places. According to a cycle of traditions crystallized at Gilgal, the children of Israel crossed the Jordan at Gilgal and erected stones there (Josh 3–4). Instead of a written covenant we find there the ceremony of circumcision, which is considered the sign of the covenant in Gen 17, and the celebration of the Passover, which is the oldest ritual connected with the Exodus.

The mentioning of Gilgal in Deut 11:30 in connection with the ceremony of Gerizim and Ebal might be a reflection of the divergent Benjaminite tradition about the foundation of Israel at its beginning (see the COMMENT to 11:22–32).

In the light of all this, it is clear that two different traditions are combined in chaps. 27–28. Deut 27:1–26, 28:3–6, 16–19, though slightly reworked by the Deuteronomic author (Weinfeld 1972a, pp. 164–277), constitute an ancient Shechemite tradition of the premonarchic period, while 28:7–14, 20–68 reflect the neo-Assyrian period. The neo-Assyrian period is also reflected in Deut 29:9–28. The scene of the covenant in vv 9–14 resembles the Josianic covenant in 2 Kgs 23:1–3 and the neo-Assyrian covenantal gatherings (see above), while the punishments for violation of the covenant in vv 19–28 have much in common with the neo-Assyrian loyalty oath to the Assyrian king (ibid., pp. 114–16). It seems that the exile referred to in 29:27 reflects the fall of the Northern Kingdom, which serves as an example for the punishment of Judah in case of a violation of the covenant.

6. DEUTERONOMY AND THE DEUTERONOMIC HISTORIOGRAPHER

According to M. Noth, Deuteronomy is a part of the Deuteronomic historiography, which started with Deut 1:1 and concluded with 2 Kgs 25 (1943, pp. 12–18). Deuteronomy 4:44–30:20—in his view—were incorporated en bloc by the Deuteronomic historiographer into his work. Deuteronomy 1–3 comprise—according to M. Noth—a historical account that has nothing to do with the code of law of Deuteronomy. Just as the book Joshua is concerned with the conquest of the promised land in Cisjordan, so are Deut 1–3 concerned with the conquest of Transjordan by Moses. Indeed—as will be shown in the COMMENT on 2:24–3:22—for the Deuteronomic historiographer the beginning of the realization of the promise of the land is the crossing of the Arnon River (2:24–25) and not just the crossing of the Jordan, as in the old conventional sources. Furthermore, Deut 1–3 are linked to 31:1–8, and both form a deuteronomistic framework for 4:44–30:20. The central concern of this framework is the succession of Joshua. The commissioning of Joshua for the conquest of the land beyond the Jordan is repeated several times in Deut 1–3 (1:38; 3:21–22, 28) as well as in 31:3, 7–8, and this topic opens the book of Joshua. In Deut 1–3 and 31:1–8 we encounter the same phrases that occur in Joshua chap. 1; compare especially the phrases in Josh 1:5–6, 7, 9 with those of Deut 1–3 and 31:1–8: 'be strong and courageous' *ḥzq wʾmṣ* (Josh 1:6, 9; Deut 3:28; 31:6, 7, 23); *lʾ tʿrṣ* 'have no dread' (Josh 1:9; Deut 31:6); *lʾ ʾrpk wlʾ ʾʿzbk* 'I will not fail you and not forsake you' (Josh 1:5; Deut 31:6, 8); *lʾtyrʾ wlʾ tḥt* 'fear not and be not dismayed' (Josh 8:1, 10:25; Deut 1:21, 31:8); *ʾth/hwʾ tnḥyl/ynḥyl ʾt hʾrṣ* 'You/he (Joshua) will give them the land as an inheritance' (Josh 1:6, 7; Deut 1:38, 3:28, 31:7). By the same token the conquest of Transjordan by the two and a half tribes in Josh 1:12–18 corresponds to Deut 3:12–20; compare especially Deut 3:18–20 with Josh 1:14–15.

The deuteronomistic framework of the book should not, however, be limited to chaps. 1–3 and 31:1–8. Also of deuteronomistic nature are 4:1–40 and 30:1–10. Just as Deut 1–3 correspond to Deut 31:1–8, so does Deut 4:1–40 and especially 4:25–31 correspond to Deut 30:1–10 (see COMMENT to 4:1–40). Both sermons foresee the repentance of Israel and the return to its land (4:25–31). This is actually envisaged in the deuteronomistic prayer ascribed to Solomon in 1 Kgs 8:44–53 (Wolff 1964).

One should, however, take account of the fact that chaps. 1–3, in spite of being historical in nature, are styled in the first person (as a discourse of Moses), just as are the other chapters of Deuteronomy. Besides, unlike the historiographic accounts of the Deuteronomist in Joshua 1:1–18, which mainly narrate events, Deut 1–3 are homiletic in character and have much in common with the paraenesis of chaps. 5–28. Thus we find here, as in chaps. 5–28, admonitions (compare 1:26, 43 with 9:7, 23–24), examples of divine care (compare 1:31 with 8:5), divine blessing (compare 2:7 with 12:7, 14–24, 29; 15:4, 6, 10, 14, 18, etc.) and distinctive vocabulary of different kinds, which is also found in the second introduction, such as "great, numerous, and tall" (compare 1:28, 2:10, 21; 4:38 with 9:1–2; 11:23), 'large cities fenced into heaven' *(ʿrym gdwlt wbṣrwt,* compare 1:28 with 9:1), 'it is forty years' *(zh ʾrbʿym šnh,* compare 2:10 with 8:2, 4), and 'so much as foot can tread' *(mdrk kp rgl,* compare 2:10 with 11:24).

One must admit, therefore, that although Deut 1–4 are to be dated in the Exilic period, that is, the period of the crystallization of the deuteronomistic literature, from the point of view of genre it belongs to Deuteronomy and not to the historiography of the former prophets.

7. "Singular" and "Plural" Layers

The book's composite nature is recognizable not only in its framework but also in the code that forms the basic section of the book. Thus in chap. 12, two parallel sets of prescriptions about the centralization of the cult are found: vv 1–12 and 13–25. The two sets are distinguished by their styles: in the former the people are addressed mainly (exceptions: vv 12:1aβ; 7b) in the second-person plural, while in the latter the address is mainly (except v 24a) in the second-person singular. The distinction between the singular and plural addresses was observed and used as a criterion for establishing different layers in the book already in 1861 (see Begg 1979). This theory was systematically applied by W. Staerk (1894) and by C. Steuernagel (1894) and later by G. Minnette de Tellesse (1962). Indeed, one must admit that there are duplicates and overlapping in Deuteronomy that can be explained by the existence of two separate sources, the "singular" and the "plural"; compare Deut 6:7–9 with 11:18–20, 12:1–12 with 12:13–25. Nevertheless, not all of the interchanges of second-person singular and plural in Deuteronomy can be explained on literary-critical grounds. The change may simply be a didactic device to impress the individual or collective listener, or it may reflect the urge for literary variation (see the Notes to chap. 4). Certain changes in stylistic addresses can be explained by the supposition that an expression is being quoted (cf. Begg 1980): for example, 11:19b, singular in a plural context, which seems to be a quotation from 6:7b. Shifts from singular to plural and vice versa come often in order to heighten the tension, as for example in 4:19, where after the reference in the singular to the apostate nations comes the address in the plural to Israel, which was chosen from other nations (v 20). The author shifts to the plural in order to create a contrast between Israel and the nations (see Note to 4:19–20).

The change in the form of address may be recognized also in the pre-Deuteronomic sources such as Exod 22:19–23: "a stranger shalt *thou* not wrong, neither shalt *thou* oppress him, for you were strangers in the land of Egypt . . . if *thou* dost afflict him . . . I will surely hear . . . his cry and my anger shall blaze forth and I will kill you with the sword." The shift from plural to singular and vice versa is also found in the ancient Near Eastern covenantal documents, such as the Aramaic Sefire treaties 3.4, 16, 23: *šqrtm* '*you* will trespass' and in the continuation 3.9, 14, 20 and 27: *šqrt* '*thou* wilt trespass' (Fitzmyer 1967, pp. 96–100). Even in places wherein the distinction between singular and plural forms of address seems to indicate layers, like the repetition in chap. 12 (see above), there are still interchanges that cannot be explained by the literary-critical criterion. Repetitions are encountered within units of common style. Thus in the plural section of chap. 12, vv 11–12 repeat vv 4–7. Steuernagel considered these to be two different sources and therefore maintained that there were three strands in the chapter. In truth, a repetition appears also within the singular section itself: vv 15–16 equal vv 20, 22–24; one may, therefore, postulate the existence of four layers in chap. 12.

Furthermore, within the plural sections of Deut 12 singular address may be found at 12:1aβ and 7b, and the reverse is also true: the passage with singular forms (vv 13–25) contains an address in the plural (v 16a).

Similar inconsistencies are to be found in the parallel passages of 6:7–9 and 11:18–20, as indicated above: in the plural passage of 11:18–20 a singular address is attested in 19b, which might be seen as a quotation from 6:7b.

In some instances the verse would lose its sense completely if one isolates sources, as, for example, in 4:25: "Should *you,* (sing.) when *you* (sing.) have begotten children and children's children and *[you]* are (pl.) long established in the land, act destructively." The singular without the continuing plural does not make any sense. The singular of the first clause seems to be influenced by the previous verse, which is styled in singular.

In sum, although in some cases the interchange of singular and plural address may indicate the existence of different layers, in general the interchange reflects stylistic variations introduced by the same author.

8. Deuteronomy: The Archimedean Point in the History of the Pentateuchal Literature

The existence of sources in the Pentateuch has been established since J. Astruc in 1753, but no clue for the date of the composition of the sources had been found. The one who supplied the clue was W. M. L. de Wette in his work of 1805. Trying to trace the historical circumstances underlying the book of Deuteronomy, de Wette found a correspondence between the reforms of Hezekiah and Josiah (see below) and the legislation of Deuteronomy. Hezekiah was the first to centralize worship in Israel (2 Kgs 18:4, 22). Before the time of Hezekiah, places of worship throughout the land were considered indispensable for the religious life of Israel, so that, for Elijah, destroying altars of YHWH was almost tantamount to slaying his prophets (1 Kgs 19:10, 14). In the legislative literature in Israel, the demand for cult centralization occurs for the first time in Deuteronomy. This book would therefore be a model or inspiration for the reforms of Hezekiah and Josiah or a reflection of them. These reforms are reflected in Deuteronomy not only in the law of centralization but also in (1) the prohibition against pillars in the worship of YHWH (16:22), which according to the older sources is legitimate and even desirable (e.g., Gen 28:18; 35:14;

Exod 24:4; Josh 24:26); (2) the references to "astral worship" *(ṣbʾ hšmym,* Deut 4:19; 17:3), which is not mentioned in the earlier parts of the Pentateuch and seems to have been introduced into Judah through Assyrian influence in the eighth century B.C.E. (cf. Weinfeld 1972b); and (3) the correspondence between the manner of celebrating Passover in the days of Hezekiah (2 Chr 30) and Josiah (see below) and the prescription in Deut 16:1–8. According to 2 Kgs 23:22, Passover had not been celebrated in such a manner since the times of the judges.

No less important for the date of Deuteronomy is the unique style of this book, both in its phraseology and in its manner of discourse (rhetoric). Style such as that found in Deuteronomy (see below) is not found in any of the historical and prophetic traditions before the seventh century B.C.E. Conversely, from the seventh century onward almost all of the historical and the prophetic literature is permeated by this style. Theologically and stylistically, Deuteronomy has become the touchstone for dating the sources in the Pentateuch and the historical books of the OT. The legal codes that do not presuppose centralization of cult must therefore be from pre-Hezekianic times. By contrast, the editorial passages of Kings that evaluate the kings of Judah in accordance with their observance of centralization of cult and the passages in Joshua and Judges that are styled in Deuteronomic phraseology cannot be from before the time of Hezekiah. An objective clue has thus been established for fixing the date of the editorial parts of the historic literature.

A new dimension has been added to the dating of Deuteronomy by the discovery of the *VTE* of the year 672 B.C.E. Many affinities between the *VTE* and the Deuteronomic covenant have been established (see above), and they support the dating of Deuteronomy in the seventh century B.C.E.

9. The Book of Law (Torah)

The term "book of the Law" *(seper haTorah)* as a sanctified, authoritative work that contains all of the divine law is encountered for the first time in Israel's history in the account of the reform of Josiah (2 Kgs 22–23). In the Pentateuch the term is attested only in Deuteronomy (17:19–20, 28:58, 29:19, 31:11–12), and from there it passed to the Deuteronomic editorial framework in the former prophets (Josh 1:8, 8:34, 23:6; 2 Kgs 14:6). There it is also designated as "the book of the law of Moses" *(seper Torat Moshe,* Josh 8:31, 23:6; 2 Kgs 14:6). Deuteronomy is, in fact, the only book of the Pentateuch to be ascribed to Moses (Deut 31:9) and the first book to have been sanctified publicly (2 Kgs 23:1–3). Only after the other books were appended to Deuteronomy was the term "Torah" applied to the whole Pentateuch. In the Tetrateuch the term "Torah" designates specific instructions such as "the Torah of the burnt offering/meal offering/sin offering" (Lev 6:2, 7, 18), "the Torah of the guilt offering/well-being offering" (Lev 7:1, 11), "the Torah of the woman in confinement" (Lev 12:7), "the Torah of the leprosy/leper" (Lev 13:9, 14:2, 32, 54), "the Torah of jealousy" (Num 5:29), and "the Torah for the Nazirite" (Num 6:13, 21); compare also the *tôrôth* as general instructions in Gen 26:5; Exod 16:28, 18:20; and Lev 26:46. The transition from Torah as a specific instruction to the sacred "book of the Torah" of the Josianic period marked a turning point in Israel's spiritual life. The ritual instructions, which had been kept in priestly esoteric circles, were now written by scribes and wise men (cf. Jer 8:8) and became part of the national lore. This permitted the transfer of the Torah from the priest to the scribe and the sage, as was the case in the Second Temple period. Indeed, Ezra, who introduced the book of Torah into Judah of the Second Temple period, functioned as a scribe *(Sofer;* Ezra 7:6, 11, 12; Neh 8:1, 4; etc.). In spite of being a priest he is named a scribe, and he performs his religious functions as such. But one should keep in mind that Ezra's function as "scribe of the Torah" (Ezra 7:6, 11) is not a new phenomenon in Israel's life (as Schäder 1930 contends) but rather an intensification of the process already started at the time of Josiah. It was the sanctification and publication of "the Book of the Torah" in the time of Josiah that gave rise to scribes with the ability and competence to handle Scripture. Although the real turning point in Torah teaching took place in the period of the Second Temple, it had its roots in the time of Josiah, when the process of canonization of Scripture started.

There is a further analogy between Josiah and Ezra. Josiah enforced the law of the "Book of the Torah" both by his royal authority and by means of a pledge taken by the people (2 Kgs 23:1–3). Likewise in the period of Ezra and Nehemiah "the law of Moses" was enforced both on behalf of the Persian crown (Ezra 7:12–26) and on the authority of a pledge, to which the people had agreed in a formal ceremony *(ʾamanāh,* Neh 10).

The Discovery of the Book of the Torah

Discovery of ancient sacred documents in a temple, like that which happened in the time of Josiah (see below), was always a thrilling event. Thus we read in the Hittite accounts of the fourteenth and thirteenth centuries B.C.E. that King Muwatalli presents a prayer of confession for negligence in observing the laws of divinity as written in the law of covenant *(išḫiul)* in the ancient scripture and promises to do his utmost to rediscover the written covenant of the gods, and to fulfill it:

> Whatever I . . . now find from written records, this I shall carry out and [what] I have [not] brought into correspondence with the ceremonial rites *(šaklai-)* of the gods, you, O storm-god, my lord, know it. And whenever I shall examine *(punušk-)* a venerable old man, as they remem-

> ber a (certain) rite and tell it, I shall also carry it out. . . . I shall follow the (covenantal) bond *(išḫiul)* of the gods that I am rediscovering, and it shall be henceforth carried on. (KBO 11.1)

The written instructions of the gods that the king is to rediscover are defined here as *išḫiul,* which, like Hebrew *bĕrit,* represents the covenantal law imposed on the people.

Furthermore, just as Josiah, king of Judah, in the seventh century B.C.E., when he rediscovers the ancient law, promises to fulfill it and asks for forgiveness for the violations of the covenant written in the rediscovered book (2 Kgs 22:13), so also does Muwatalli, saying, "I ask for forgiveness of the sin of the country."

Very instructive from the point of view of comparison with Hebrew traditions is the king's declaration that he will carry out whatever had been referred to him through the recollection of a venerable old man. This corresponds to the tradition preserved in *m. ʿEd.* concerning the collection of testimonies given by sages on legal matters and not attested to in the conventional written lore.

10. Relation of Deuteronomy to the Tetrateuch

Critical work in Deuteronomy has indicated that this book depends on the preceding books of the Pentateuch, especially the so-called Elohistic source. An exception, however, has to be made in regard to the priestly code, which did not influence Deuteronomy (see below). This is to be explained not by the lateness of the priestly literature, as is commonly argued, but by its specific, almost esoteric nature, in contradistinction to the so-called JE source, which, like Deuteronomy, reflects the general national milieu. Deuteronomy shows dependence especially on the book of the covenant (Exod 21–23); Deuteronomy itself also contains "the words of the covenant" (28:69, compare 2 Kgs 23:2–3). This, however, does not mean that the author of Deuteronomy sees his code as of lesser value. On the contrary, he makes it quite clear that at Sinai the Decalogue was proclaimed, whereas the law proper was given to Israel by Moses on the plains of Moab. In other words, Deuteronomy would be seen as replacing the old book of the covenant and not as complementing it. It cannot be known whether the author of Deuteronomy had before him "the book of the covenant" in its present form or used a legal source in which laws of the type found in Exod 21–23 were incorporated. What is clear is that Deuteronomy used laws identical in formulation with those of the book of the covenant and revised them according to its ideology.

The parallels mainly pertain to the moral-religious section of the book of the covenant, the so-called apodictic law (Exod 22:17–23:19). The civil section of the book of the covenant, the so-called casuistic law (Exod 21:1–22:16), is not represented in Deuteronomy except for two laws (Exod 21:1–11, 22:15–16); compare Deut 11:12–18, 22:28–29). This may be explained in the following way: the civil-law section in Exod 21:1–22:16 constitutes the common law of the ancient Near East and has strong affinities to the Mesopotamian law codes (cf. Paul 1970). As in the neighboring codes, this section in the book of the covenant is mostly concerned with offenses against property, and even when dealing with human rights (injury, slaves, etc.) it is the compensation for the damage that stands at the center of the discussion. Deuteronomy ignored these laws because the author's purpose was not to produce a civil-law book like the book of the covenant, treating of pecuniary matters, but to set forth a code of laws securing the protection of the individual and particularly of those persons in need of protection. Conversely, it was anxious to incorporate into its legal corpus laws concerning the protection of the family and family dignity (22:12–29), which are not included in the book of the covenant.

The only laws from the civil section of the book of the covenant employed by Deuteronomy are the law of the Hebrew slave (Exod 21:1–11 = Deut 15:12) and the law of the seduction of a virgin (Exod 22:15–16 = Deut 22:28–29). These two laws, which are located at the beginning and at the end of the section, respectively, were incorporated by Deuteronomy because they contain moral implications aside from their civil aspect. Moreover, by the way these two laws are presented, Deuteronomy actually deprived them of their civil-financial character and turned them into purely moral-social laws. In Exod 21:1–11 the rights of the master are protected no less than those of the slave (cf. the provision about the slaves born in the master's home belonging to the master, the master's right of keeping the slave in perpetuity, etc.), the main concern of the legislator there being to define the status of the slave. Deuteronomy, however, is concerned with only the slave, and, therefore, the obligations of the master to this slave (to bestow gifts, etc.) are stressed. By the same token, the law of the seduced virgin in Exod 22:15–16 is discussed from the pecuniary point of view (the loss of the bride price), whereas Deuteronomy is concerned with the humiliation or moral degradation of the virgin and therefore does not deal explictly with the bride price *(mohar)* and does not grant the man who violated the virgin the right to refuse to marry her, but compels him to marry her forever (cf. Weinfeld 1972a, pp. 282–88).

In a similar way the author of Deuteronomy revised all other laws in accordance with the new reality and its unique humanitarian approach. There follows a brief review of the principal changes.

(1) In the law of the slave and maidservant in Deut 15:12–18, there is a stylistic dependence on Exod 21:1–11, though in Deuteronomy the law underwent a very basic revision (see above). The casuistic section of this law in the

covenant code (Exod 21:3–4, 8–11), which deals with the owner's rights in regard to the wife and children of the slave as well as the personal rights of the maidservant, was totally omitted from Deuteronomy, because Deuteronomy does not view the slave and maidservant as a property (chattel) belonging to the master's house, as does the covenant code (Exod 21:1–11). Their status is defined as hirelings (Deut 15:18; cf. Lev 25:40) who sell their labor. Their personal affairs, such as the problem of the slave's wife or maidservant's husband, are not at all subject to negotiation with their masters. The word "master *(ʾādôn),*" which is mentioned six times in the covenant code, is not mentioned even once in the law of the slave in Deuteronomy, which is not insignificant. The slave is here called the "brother" of his employer (cf. Lev 25:35), who thus cannot view himself as a "master." The maidservant in the Deuteronomic code is not sold by her father as in Exodus but, like the slave, the "brother," is instead independent and sells her labor. Thus there is no difference between the law of the slave and that of the maidservant.

The Deuteronomic lawgiver obligates the owner to reward the slave and the maidservant who are liberated from his service with generous grants, mentioning the Israelites' liberation from Egypt in this connection. No mention of this is made in the book of the covenant. A significant change of a different type is the section on taking the slave, whose ear is pierced with an awl, "before God" (Exod 21:6), which was omitted from the parallel law in Deuteronomy. The reason for the omission stems from the centralization of the cult, which excludes the existence of "houses of God" throughout the land.

(2) The law of kidnapping found in Exod 21:16 does recur in Deut 24:7, but the general style of the covenant code had undergone a national reformulation: "kidnapping a fellow Israelite." The parenthetic phrase "you will sweep out evil from your midst," which is unique to Deuteronomy, is appended to the law.

(3) The casuistic laws dealing with injuries, theft, and damage to property (Exod 21:18–22:16) were omitted from Deuteronomy because they are not the concern of a religious-moral code (see above). The only laws from this section that remained in Deuteronomy are the *lex talionis* 'punishment in kind' (Exod 21:23–25) and the law of seducing a virgin (22:15–16). The *lex talionis* was utilized by Deuteronomy in the law of the conspiring witness (19:21), while the law of the seducer of a virgin, which in the covenant code embodies only a financial matter (loss of the bride price to the father), became in Deuteronomy a moral problem (Deut 22:28–29) and was included in the code for this reason (see above).

(4) The law of the sorceress in Exod 22:17 was broadened and developed in Deuteronomy (18:9–13), while the ban of the idolater (Exod 22:19) merited a separate chapter in Deuteronomy (chap. 13; also 17:2–7).

(5) The covenant code forbids the Israelite to wrong or afflict the resident alien (Exod 22:20–22; 23:9). The author of Deuteronomy, in contrast, not only enjoins the Israelite to refrain from discriminating against the resident alien, but

also exhorts the Israelite to love him (10:19; cf. Lev 19:34) and to be solicitous for his welfare (14:21, 29; 16:11, 14; 24:17, 19, 20).

(6) The covenant code commands the creditor who has taken a debtor's garment as surety to restore it to the debtor by sundown so that he may cover himself with it at night (Exod 22:25–26). According to the Deuteronomic law, however, the creditor is also denied the right to select what article he wishes as surety (24:6, 17) and is even forbidden to enter the debtor's house to collect it (24:11).

(7) The covenant code ordains that anything that has been torn by beasts, *ṭĕrefāh,* which Israelites are forbidden to eat for sacral reasons, should be cast to the dogs (Exod 22:30). The Deuteronomic law, by contrast, ever attentive to the needs of indigent persons, enjoins the Israelite to give the carcass *(nĕbelāh)* to the resident alien (14:21). The humanistic tendency becomes clear in the light of the juxtaposition of the resident alien and the foreigner. The author enjoins the giving of the carcass to the resident alien, but *the selling of it* to the foreigner, who was usually involved in trade and commerce.

(8) Exodus 23:14 ordains that a stray animal must be returned to its rightful owner. The Deuteronomic legislator, however, extends this law to garments and all types of lost articles (22:3) and exhorts the finder not to ignore the lost object but to take it home with him and keep it until it is sought by its owner (22:2–3).

(9) The laws of just judgment (Exod 23:1–3, 6–8) were developed in Deuteronomy (16:18–20; 17:8–13; 19:15–21; 24:17–18; 25:1–3), though in Deuteronomy 16:19 there are still signs of dependence on the covenant code. Deuteronomy changed the *pqḥym* 'the clear-sighted' of Exod 23:8 into *ḥkmym* 'wise men' (16:19; see below).

(10) In the old codes we find three types of firstborn dedications: the firstborn of man, of a pure animal, and of an impure animal (Exod 13:1, 11–16; 22:28–29; 34:19–20; cf. Lev 27:26–27; Num 18:15–18). Deuteronomy, however, does not mention the firstborn of man or of impure animals, but only the firstborn of pure animals (Deut 15:19–23).

It seems that Deuteronomy omits the laws of the human firstborn and the firstlings of impure animals because they are rooted in mythical and magical concepts not shared by the author of Deuteronomy (see below).

Furthermore, even the firstborn of an animal is differently treated in Deuteronomy. According to the other codes, the firstborn of an animal has to be set apart for the sacral sphere (Exod 22:28; 34:19; Lev 22:26–27; Num 18:17–18); Deuteronomy, however, enjoins the eating of the firstborn *by the owner* in the precincts of the central temple (Deut 15:19–20).

(11) Concerning the sabbatical year, the covenant code commands that the land shall not be worked during that year and that its fruits be left ownerless so that the poor and even the beasts of the field should be able to eat from them (Exod 23:10–11; cf. Lev 25:1–7; see below). Deuteronomy does not mention the law of releasing the land but only release of debts (see below).

(12) Deuteronomy and JE are similar as regards the absence of exact dates for the festivals, for both are popular sources, unlike the priestly literature, which represents the priestly institution and must therefore be especially concerned with calendrical and other matters pertaining to the implementation of cultic ceremonies. The same is the case with the laws concerning the New Year Day and the Day of Atonement, which are mentioned in neither Deuteronomy nor JE. These are temple festivals in which the people do not play any active role.

The laws in Exod 23:15, 18 (= 34:18, 25) connected with the Feast of Unleavened Bread and the Paschal sacrifice may be traced in Deut 16:1–4, but they are formulated there according to Deuteronomy's particular approach. In the covenant code and in the priestly literature there still exists a separation between the Feast of Unleavened Bread and Passover (cf. 23:15 with 18; Exod 34:18 with 25; in the priestly source: Exod 12:1–14 with 15–20 and Lev 23:5, "a Passover offering to YHWH," with 23:6, "the Feast of Unleavened Bread to YHWH"). In contrast, Deuteronomy combines both festivals and attempts to create a single one. For this purpose it interpolates the section on the law of unleavened bread in the middle of the law of the Passover offering, which appears very artificial. The phrase "you shall not eat anything leavened with it" at the beginning of 16:3 refers to the Passover sacrifice, and from the parallels in the covenant code it can be learned that this prohibition goes with that of leaving the flesh of the sacrifice until morning (Exod 23:18; 34:25), repeated in Deut 16 at the end of v 4. Indeed, if this part dealing with unleavened and leavened bread (from "seven days you shall eat unleavened bread" to "no leaven shall be found with you . . . seven days") is taken out of vv 3–4, there remains a consecutive account of the Passover sacrifice that parallels the passages in the covenant code. The section on unleavened bread is taken from the covenant code (Exod 23:15), while the section on leaven is from Exod 13:7, and is perhaps influenced by Exod 12:15, 19 (= the priestly school).

(13) Deuteronomy and JE both enjoin pilgrimage to the holy sites (Exod 23:17; 34:23; Deut 16:16), with the difference that Deuteronomy adds the phrase "in the place that he will choose." This law is not found in the priestly literature. This omission too can be explained by the special nature of that literature. This commandment is directed only toward the common people as against the priests, who dwelled in the temples all year long. Therefore, the sources intended for the common people stress this precept, while the author of the priestly source, who is concerned primarily with temple rituals and their procedures, does not speak of the pilgrimages, which are, by their very nature, a concern of the masses. He talks instead about the ceremonies and sacrifices connected with these festivals (see Lev 23:9–21; Num 28–29).

(14) JE and Deuteronomy command "the instruction of the children" (Exod 12:26–27; 13:8–15; Deut 6:20–25), which bears the character of a catechism aimed at inculcating in the younger generation a national religious educa-

tion by means of recounting the event of the Exodus from Egypt. There is a significant difference between the two sources, however. In JE the "instruction" is connected with the Passover ceremonies and the sacrifice of the firstborn, the ceremony serving as both educational motive and means. The child is aroused to question by the uniqueness of these ceremonies, and the ceremony serves as a fitting opportunity for an educative answer. In Deuteronomy the "instruction" is divorced from all ceremony. The child asks not about the Passover service or the firstborn sacrifice but about the "precepts, laws, and rules" that the Israelites were commanded to fulfill (Deut 6:20). The question is not connected with the festival. It can be asked on any occasion.

(15) With regard to the scope of the promised land, Deuteronomy follows JE and speaks of a land that extends from "the wilderness and the [Red] sea to the Euphrates" (Gen 15:18; Exod 23:31 [= JE]; Deut 1:7; 11:24). The priestly literature fixes the northern boundary at Lebo-Hamath (Num 13:21; 34:8) and excludes Transjordan from territory of the promised land (see below and the COMMENT on 2:24–3:22). In the historical documents of the periods of territorial expansion both types of border designations are found (2 Sam 8:3 = 1 Chr 18:3; 1 Kgs 5:4 on the one hand, and 1 Kgs 8:65 and 2 Kgs 14:25 on the other). Under consideration here is not a historical development but rather versions that stem from different circles.

(16) In the episode of the spies' sin and the rebellion of Korah (Num 13–17), Deuteronomy follows JE. According to JE, the spies reached Wadi Eshcol in the vicinity of Hebron. The faithful one among the spies was Caleb, who indeed received Hebron as a reward (Num 14:24; cf. Josh 14:6ff.). In Deut 1:24, 36 a similar picture is portrayed. The priestly source, however, extends the reconnoitered area to Lebo-Hamath (Num 13:21) and, accordingly, joins Joshua, conqueror of the entire land, to Caleb, thus promising both of them entry into the land (14:30).

JE records the rebellion of Dathan and Abiram against Moses and their punishment: the earth swallows them up (Num 16). Deuteronomy also mentions Dathan and Abiram in 11:6, along with the ground that opened up its mouth to swallow them. In contrast, the priestly literature, which notes here a sacral offense and not a civil rebellion, speaks about Korah and his group who opposed the Aaronide priesthood and about their being burned by a fire from God because they sacrificed incense illegally (Num 16:35; 17:5). This recalls the episode of Nadab and Abihu in Lev 10:1–2.

11. Deuteronomy and the Priestly School

Two schools of crystallized thought are to be discerned in the Pentateuchal literature: the priestly school, which contains the priestly literature and the holiness code (Lev 17–26), and the Deuteronomic school, reflected in the book of Deuteronomy. Distinction should be made between the holiness code and the priestly school, and, as has been recently demonstrated by I. Knohl,[10] the priestly literature antedates the holiness code and not vice versa. For our purpose, however, we may refer to both as to a common school of priestly nature. In order to understand properly the theology of Deuteronomy, we must juxtapose it with the theology of the priestly literature. These two schools differ from each other in their concept of religion, their mental climate, and their mode of expression. Let us start with the analysis of the priestly source.

The bulk of the laws found in the priestly source centers on the divine Tabernacle and all that relates to its construction and to the ministrations performed in it. It is the pervading presence of God in the midst of Israel (i.e., the Sanctuary) that gives meaning to the Israelite scene. Remove the divine immanence, and the entire priestly code collapses. Not only would the worship of God cease, but laws relating to the social sphere would become inoperative. The laws of asylum, for instance, are inconceivable without a high priest (Num 35:25); the laws of warfare are unimaginable without the participation of sacral persons who march forth with their holy trumpets in hand (Num 31:6; cf. 10:9); the law of suspected conjugal infidelity could not be implemented without a sanctuary (Num 5:11ff.); military operations could not be conducted without the presence of the high priest bearing the Urim and Tummim (Num 27:21); and so forth. These laws do not presuppose the post-Exilic theocracy, as Wellhausen believed, because post-Exilic Judea did not conduct wars, nor were its leaders appointed by the congregation *(ʿadat Yiśrāʾel)*. Nor was it possible to speak of the presence of God in a temple when the Ark, upon which the Glory of God dwelled between the cherubim and to which the ritual of the Sanctuary was oriented, no longer existed.

The reality reflected in the priestly code accords more with the ancient life of Israel, grounded on sacral dogma and prescriptions, which continued to mold the life of the Israelites even after the establishment of the monarchy. The reality depicted in the ancient narratives, which are not tendentious, is, indeed,

[10] I. Knohl, "The Priestly Torah Versus the Holiness School: Sabbath and the Festivals," *HUCA* 58 (1987), pp. 65–118.

similar to that reflected in the priestly document. Thus, Saul and David conduct their military campaigns according to the instructions provided by the Urim and Tummim (1 Sam 14:18, 36–41; 23:2–3, 6, 9, 10–11); holy wars resound with the blast of trumpets and horns (Josh 6; Judg 7:18); the priestly class participates in military expeditions (Josh 6; Judg 20:26–28; 1 Sam 4); and the booty is brought to the house of God (Josh 6:24; 2 Sam 8:11; 2 Kgs 12:19; cf. Num 31:50–54).

The regime of holiness and taboo underlying the priestly document is not the product of the theological ruminations of priests of the post-Exilic period but derives from the Israelite reality prevailing during the time of the Judges and in the monarchical period. The sacral institutions, which occupy a central place in the priestly theology, are known to us from early biblical literature. Thus the Sabbath, for example, or the New Moon, the "days of solemn rest" *(shabbaton)*, and the "holy convocations *(miqra᾽ qodesh)*" are not peculiar to the priestly document. Like that document, the early sources also speak of days on which one refrained from work (Amos 8:5), days on which one partook of holy meals (1 Sam 20:24–32), made pilgrimages to holy men (2 Kgs 4:22–23), gathered in sacral assemblies and holy convocations (Isa 1:13), offered sacrifices and poured libations (Hos 9:4–5).

Matters affecting purity and defilement, concerning which the priestly document provides such detailed regulations, are also known to us from early biblical literature. The participants in a sacral event must purify themselves and cleanse their garments (Gen 35:2; Exod 19:10; 1 Sam 16:5); Israelite warriors must observe sexual continence and consecrate their vessels before departing for war (1 Sam 21:6, cf. Num 31:21–24); women must clean themselves of menstrual impurity (2 Sam 11:4, cf. Lev 15:19–24); lepers are ejected from the city (2 Kgs 7:3ff., cf. Lev 13:45–46); and persons defiled by contact with the dead are forbidden to enter the house of YHWH (Hos 9:4, cf. Num 19). The same is true of matters concerning the temple and holy taboos. The danger that ensues from approaching the divine sanctum, which is so frequently mentioned in the priestly document, is also alluded to in the early sources (1 Sam 6:19; 2 Sam 6:6–9).

These old sources, furthermore, contain regulations for sacrifices and alimentary offerings to God (Exod 23:18; 34:25; 1 Sam 2:13–17; 21:7 [the bread of the Presence]; Amos 4:5, cf. Lev 7:13) and describe cultic practices, which also figure as an essential part of priestly teaching. The early sources also contain references to holy consecrations, communal sacrifices, and sin and guilt offerings (2 Kgs 12:17; 16:15). The institution of the Nazirite, which is one of the most ancient in Israel (Judg 13:4–5; 1 Sam 1:11; Amos 2:11), is treated, remarkably enough, only in the priestly document (Num 6) and nowhere else in the Pentateuch. Nonsacrificial slaughter, which is prohibited by the holiness code (Lev 17) and which is designated as "eating with the blood" (Lev 19:26), is mentioned in 1 Sam 14:32–35: "Behold the people are sinning against YHWH by eating with the blood," in other words, by eating without first sprinkling the blood upon the altar.

While much can be learned about the character of the priestly literature from a knowledge of what it contains, much more can be discovered about its world view by considering what is missing from this source. Most astonishing is the marked absence from the priestly documents of civil-social ordinances and regulations pertaining to conjugal life, which occupy so great a place in the book of Deuteronomy. Even when we do encounter laws dealing with such matters in the priestly schools, they always appear in a sacro-ritual light. Thus the incest prohibitions are set forth in the same context as the prohibitions concerning menstrual uncleanness, bestiality, Molech worship (Lev 18:21–23), necromancy, and clean and unclean animals (20:6, 25). Incest, then, is conceived as a distinct sacral matter and not as one that concerns civil law.

The sabbatical year, which in the book of Deuteronomy has a patently social character, figures in the holiness code as a sacral institution: "The land shall keep a Sabbath of YHWH" (Lev 25:2), which is to say that the obligation to rest falls upon the land, so that if the land does not fulfill this duty while the nation dwells thereon, it must pay back this obligation during its years of desolation when the people are in exile: "Then shall the land make up for its sabbath years . . . throughout the time that it is desolate it shall observe the rest that it did not observe in your sabbath years while you were dwelling upon it" (Lev 26:34–35). Here, in contradistinction to the book of Deuteronomy, which makes mention only of the remission of debts (Deut 15:1–11), there is no reference to the year of release, which cancels the debts of the poor. It must be pointed out that as far as actual practice was concerned, the two laws were not mutually exclusive, which is to say that it is quite likely that both were observed or, at any rate, that both were regarded as obligatory, and that nevertheless there was a connection between them. The way in which the two laws appear in the sources, however, sheds light on the ideology of the respective writers. Thus, for example, the priestly writer is concerned with the taboo of the seventh year and with the sacral implications of this taboo, while the author of Deuteronomy is concerned with the social aspect of this law and completely ignores the sacral side.

This recalls the manner in which the Sabbath is presented in each of these two sources. In the priestly source the rationale for the Sabbath is that God worked six days in creating the world and rested on the seventh (Gen 2:1–3; Exod 20:11, 31:17), which is to say that man, by his Sabbath rest, reenacts, so to speak, God's rest on the seventh day of creation—a point of view appropriate to the priestly circle, which, by means of its ritual in the Sanctuary, reenacts what takes place in the divine sphere (Weinfeld 1981b). In contrast, Deuteronomy supplies another reason for the Sabbath: the Israelite is obligated to rest on the Sabbath not because God rested on this day but rather to provide a respite for his servants: "so that your male and female slave may rest as you do" (Deut

5:14). Alongside the social motivation there appears the religious one: "Remember that you were a slave in the land of Egypt and YHWH your God freed you from there with a strong hand and outstretched arm; therefore, YHWH your God commanded you to observe the Sabbath day" (Deut 5:15). Thus Deuteronomy derives the Sabbath not from creation, as in the priestly literature, but from the Exodus. As in the case of the sabbatical year so in the case of the Sabbath, it is possible that the social motivation existed alongside the sacral and that they were both able to coexist. It is a fact that the Sabbath is given a social motivation in Exod 23:12. Still, there is no doubt significance to the fact that the author of the priestly source specifically selected the sacral motivation and developed it in his own way, while the book of Deuteronomy chose the social motivation and formulated it in its own unique way, that is to say, humanistically.

Another example that demonstrates the different theologies of the two compositions under consideration is the law concerning going forth to war. According to the priestly literature, when the people go forth to battle, the priests are to blow trumpets (Num 10:9). At the end of the war the soldiers must undergo purificatory rites (Num 31:19–20) and must give an offering to the sacral domain from the booty (Num 31:50–54). The book of Deuteronomy, by contrast, makes no mention of the blowing of trumpets or of purificatory rites; it speaks rather of a priest who, before the war, speaks to the people to encourage them and to implant in them the spirit of valor (Deut 20:1–9). Regulations as to conduct within the battle line contain provisions that are bound up with the maintenance of cleanliness no less than they are with the preservation of the sacral state of the camp (Deut 23:10–15).

Another matter that provides information about the different theologies of these compositions is the law of retaliation. This law, the *lex talionis,* which stands by itself in the covenant code (Exod 21:23b–25; cf. Alt, *KS* 1 [1953]: 278ff.), appears in various contexts in the holiness code and Deuteronomy. In the holiness code it appears in connection with the law of the blasphemer (Lev 24:16–22), while in Deuteronomy it is found in connection with the law of the false witness (Deut 19:21), in other words, in the context of civil and criminal legislation.

Just as the priestly code concerns itself with codifying sacral legislation, so Deuteronomy occupies itself with laws belonging to the civil-secular sphere. Not only do we encounter institutions of a manifestly secular character such as the judiciary (Deut 16:18–20; 17:8–13), the monarchy (17:14ff.), the military (Deut 20), and civil and criminal law, which treat of the family and inheritance (21:18–23; 22:13–19; 24:1–4; 25:5–9), loans and debts (15:1–18; 24:10–13), litigations and quarrels (25:1–3, 11–12), trespassing (19:14), false testimony (19:15–21), and the like, but even institutions and practices that were originally sacral in character have here been recast in secularized forms. Thus, for example, the piercing of the slave's ear, which, according to the covenant code, must be done "before God" (i.e., in the temple; Exod 21:6), is to be done near any door without any connection to a sanctuary, according to Deuteronomy (15:17). Similarly, the cities of refuge, which, according to the priestly school, are levitical cities, in other words, cities that belong to the sacral realm, are transformed in Deuteronomy to serve the pragmatic purpose of holding the manslayer in protective custody from the avenger of blood, and nothing more. In the priestly literature, by contrast, the manslayer, who is required to dwell in the city of refuge until the death of the high priest (Num 35), achieves the expiation of his sin by dwelling in the city of refuge.

The absence of sacral institutions in the book of Deuteronomy is no less surprising than the absence of socio-legal institutions in the priestly document. The very book that makes "the chosen place" such a central concern completely ignores the sacral institutions that the chosen place must necessarily imply, and without which the conduct of sacral worship is unimaginable. The holy ministrations, which involve the presentation of the shewbread, the kindling of candles, the burning of incense, the offering of the suet, the daily and seasonal sacrifices, and the reception and disposal of the holy donations (Exod 25:30; 27:20–21; 30:7; Lev 1–7; Num 28–29; 18:1–32)—in short, the most essential charges and rites of the Israelite cult—are scarcely mentioned in Deuteronomy. The exhortations regarding the awe and reverence with which the sanctity of the Temple must be treated (Lev 19:30b; 26:2b) and the restrictions imposed to avert the desecration of the sanctum are familiar to us from the early Israelite literature and figure prominently in the priestly document but find no mention whatsoever in the book of Deuteronomy. Even if the author of Deuteronomy presupposed these regulations, he should still have given some intimation of their existence when setting forth the ordinances concerning the chosen place. Particularly obvious is the absence from Deuteronomy of the sacral law (Latin *fas),* to which such an important place is dedicated in the priestly writings. In Deuteronomy there is no warning whatsoever against blasphemy, the most heinous of sins in Israel, which is dealt with in the covenant code (Exod 22:27) and in the priestly literature (Lev 24:15–16; cf. 1 Kgs 21:13).

Sorcery, the worship of Molech, and necromancy, which, according to the holiness code and the testimony of the historical books, were punishable by death (Exod 22:17; Lev 18:21; 20:1–6, 27; 1 Sam 28:3, 9), are, of course, forbidden by Deuteronomy (18:9–12) but without any particular punishment specified. Instead, in the book of Deuteronomy capital punishment is prescribed in two cases in which the other codes had not called for it. These are the cases of the rebellious elder (Deut 17:12) and of the one who instigates idolatry (Deut 13:2–12). The nonsacral character of the legal conception of Deuteronomy is also manifest in the fact that severe religious and cultic offenses, which are punishable, according to the priestly literature, by *kāret* ("the soul shall be cut off from its kin") do not even appear in Deuteronomy, for all of these offenses are connected with the sphere of sacral legislation (Latin *fas),* while Deuteronomy deals with the sphere of civil legislation (Latin *jus).* These religious and cultic offenses include the eating of fat or blood (Lev 7:25–27), the consumption of the flesh of sacrificed animals in a state of impurity (Lev 7:20–21), the defilement of the Sanctuary and its appurtenances (Lev 22:3; Num 19:13, 20), the breach of the covenant of circumcision (Gen 17:14), failure to offer the Paschal sacrifice (Num 9:13), and failure to practice self-denial on Yom Kippur (Lev 23:29).

Laws Common to the Priestly School and Deuteronomy

Although the sources of the priestly literature and of Deuteronomy differ, as has been shown, in their purpose and methods of presentation, they have in common several matters that do not occur in JE at all. When these matters are considered, especially the institutions and laws common to both, it can be seen that in most cases the priestly literature is the primary and original source. There follows a brief survey of these laws.

Rituals. (1) Deuteronomy 24:8 commands that a leper be dealt with according to the instructions of the priests and Levites. It is doubtless referring to the instructions relating to the various forms of leprosy as they appear in Lev 13–14. There is no reason to assume that the laws, as such, did not exist at the time of the formulation of Deuteronomy, though it is not certain that they existed then in their present form.

(2) The section on pure and impure animals in Deut 14:3–21 is paralleled in Lev 11, and Deut 14:13–18a has been shown to have been borrowed from the priestly source (Moran 1966). But while in Lev 11 there is also a detailed description of impure swarming things and the manner in which they transfer impurity (11:24ff.), Deuteronomy comprises mainly matters relating to eating and does not place special emphasis on the impurity of a carcass, with which the priests were particularly concerned.

(3) The laws of hybrid species in Lev 19 include hybrid cattle, hybrid seeds, and hybrid clothing (19:19). Deuteronomy includes these laws and even presents and explains them in detail (22:9–11). The lateness of these laws in Deuteronomy may be indicated by the explanation of the word *shaʿatnēz.* In Leviticus this word is not explained because, apparently, it was well known, while Deuteronomy found it necessary to add the explanatory phrase "wool and linen together."

(4) A law that in Deuteronomy is close to the law of hybrid species is that of *gĕdilīm* (22:12), which in the priestly literature are called *ṣiṣīt* ('fringes'; Num 15:37–14). Both expressions are identical in meaning and refer to the threads woven into the hem of the garment in the shape of a flower, or the like (cf. 1 Kgs 6:18, 29, 32, 35: *ṣīṣīm;* 1 Kgs 7:17: *gĕdilīm,* both of which are intended to

beautify and embellish the Temple; cf. also Akkadian *gidiltu* and *ṣiṣitu).* The priestly source dwells on the religious significance of this custom. The "fringes" are considered a "sign" that will serve as a reminder to fulfill the commandments (Num 15:39, 40), and indeed the "sign for remembrance" is very characteristic of the priestly school's theology; note the "sign of the covenant of the Sabbath" (Exod 31:13), the rainbow (Gen 9:12, 17), circumcision (Gen 17:11), Passover (Exod 12:13), and others (e.g., Num 17:3, 25).

(5) In relation to the festivals, Deuteronomy is apparently dependent on the holiness code, for it enjoins the observance of Sukkot for seven days and enjoins the Israelites to rejoice on these days, as does Lev 23:39–40. Like the holiness code, Deuteronomy also names the festival "the Feast of Tabernacles [Booths]." The name is explained in the holiness code by the commandment appearing there regarding dwelling in booths (23:42), which is not mentioned in JE. The author of Deuteronomy preserved the name of this festival but ignored the commandment about dwelling in booths and the ceremonies with the decorative flora (Lev 23:40), which are connected with cultic observances in which he was not interested. Deuteronomy also commands the "counting" of seven weeks from the beginning of the harvest to the festival of Shavuot, which covers—according to the holiness code—the period between the waving of the *ʿomer* at the beginning of the harvest and bringing the "new offering," the two baked loaves, at its end (Lev 23:9–21). While Deuteronomy does preserve the period of seven weeks, it does not mention the ceremonies that are the basis for this counting.

(6) The pagan institutions such as the Molech (or, in Deuteronomy, "he who passes his son and daughter through fire"), divination and soothsaying, ghosts and familiar spirits (Lev 18:21; 19:26, 31; 20:1–6, 27) are prohibited in Deuteronomy too (18:10–11), but to these are added the magician, one who casts spells *(ḥbr ḥbr),* and the one who inquires of the dead *(drš ʾl hmtym).*

Social Matters: The Resident Alien. Like the holiness code (Lev 19:10, 33–34; 23:22), Deuteronomy also enjoins helping and loving the stranger (Deut 10:19). There are differences, however, in regard to obligations devolving on the stranger in the priestly school and Deuteronomy. According to the priestly school, the resident alien and the native Israelite alike are required to observe the regulations of the Torah, because it is the person's residence in the land that subjects him to the religio-cultic ordinance (Exod 12:19; Lev 16:29; 17:8, 10, 12, 13, 15; 18:26; 20:2; 24:16; Num 15:30; 19:11; 35:15). Residence in the land is deemed to be an automatic recognition of the God of the country on the part of the resident and thus also entails the obligation to worship him (cf. 2 Kgs 17); conversely, an Israelite who resides outside the land of YHWH is deemed to dwell in an unclean land and to be the worshiper of foreign gods (1 Sam 26:19; cf. Josh 22:16–19 [= priestly source]; Hos 9:3–5; Amos 7:17). The resident alien and the native Israelite both draw their sustenance from a common sacral source; both, consequently, are required to observe the code of holiness that it entails.

This is not the view of the book of Deuteronomy. According to Deuteronomy, the laws of the Torah apply only to those who are related to the Israelite people by blood, while the resident alien is not regarded as an Israelite and, consequently, is not required to observe the sacral laws of the congregation even though he dwells in the land and is willing to subject himself to them. He does enjoy, to be sure, the full protection of the laws and the same political and economic rights that all Israelites enjoy. As he is not a true Israelite, however, he is not required to assume the special sacral obligations imposed on the "holy people." Deuteronomy intentionally differentiates, then, between the Israelite and the resident alien in all matters pertaining to religious obligations, the fulfillment of which it regards as exclusively binding only on the holy people. In Deut 14:21 we read, "You shall not eat anything that has died a natural death; give it to the stranger *(ger),* who is within your towns, that he may eat it, or you may sell it to a foreigner *(nkry),* for you are a people holy to YHWH your God." The holiness code (Lev 17:15), by contrast, ordains, "and every person who eats what dies of itself or has been torn by beast *(nĕbelāh u-ṭĕrepāh)* whether he is *a native or a stranger (ger)* shall wash his clothes and bathe himself in water." The two passages thus stand in open contradiction to each other. The source of the contradiction is the divergent viewpoints of the documents. The holiness code is only concerned with the ritual problem of impurity involved: all who eat *nĕbelāh,* whether Israelite or resident alien, carry impurity upon them. The land is unable to bear impurity no matter who the carriers of the impurity may be (cf. "lest the land vomit you out when you defile it," Lev 18:28). The book of Deuteronomy instead regards the prohibition only as a matter of *noblesse oblige.* Israel must abstain from eating *nĕbelāh* because it is an act unbecoming to a holy people, not because it causes impurity from which one must purge oneself by ritual bathing (Lev 11:40; 17:15). It does not, consequently, impose this on those who are not of the holy people.

Care of the Poor. The holiness code and Deuteronomy contain laws in connection with leftovers from the harvest and the grape harvest for the poor (Lev 19:9–10; 23:22; Deut 24:19–22). The outstanding differences between the two laws are as follows. First, Deuteronomy does not enjoin that one leave "the edges" *(peʾah)* of the field or of the vineyard (Haran 1968), as does the priestly literature, but rather commands about the gleanings from the ingathering of the crops: the fall of the wheat *(leqeṭ)* and the remainders of that which falls during the harvest of the grapes and olives. In contrast, the holiness code does not include the law about the sheaf *(ʿomer)* forgotten in the field, which should be left for the poor. Second, Deuteronomy prescribes separate laws for olives, which are not mentioned in the holiness code. The term "vineyard *(kerem),*" however, also includes olives (cf. Judg 15:5), and it may thus be possible that the holiness code is referring to olives as well. It is difficult to establish which is early and late in this instance, but here too Deuteronomy's formulation is more pragmatic, that is to say, it presents the law in a more tangible manner and, characteristically, adds a religio-moral justification (Deut 24:22). The fact that it does not mention the leftover of the corner of the field *(pe'ah)* may be explained in that the *pe'ah* is a remnant of ancient magical beliefs (being intended for spirits of the field and demons) and does not conform to the specific liberal attitude of Deuteronomy. Perhaps for the same reason, it does not accept the taboo of the sabbatical year—the abandonment of the field during the seventh year, found in JE and the holiness code—but enjoins only the remission of debts during this year (see above).

Finally, laws of weights and measures are also found only in the holiness code and Deuteronomy (Lev 19:35–37; Deut 25:13–16). On the one hand, the law in Deuteronomy does not explicitly mention scales and liquid measures (the *hin),* but it is difficult to draw chronological conclusions from this. On the other, it is clear that Deuteronomy incorporates into this law idioms from wisdom literature (Prov 11:1; 20:10, 23; see below) and the concept of "an abomination to YHWH," which is also found only in wisdom literature. The dependence on the law of the holiness code is evidenced in the expression "deals dishonestly *(ʿśh ʿwl)*" (Deut 25:16), which is apparently influenced by Lev 19:35 *(l' tʿśw ʿwl bmšpṭ).*

Laws of Asylum. In the covenant code, the altar and "the place" *(mqwm)* are the original places of asylum for the accidental manslayer (Exod 21:13–14), while in the priestly literature the cities in which the Levites resided (Num 35; cf. Josh 20–21) serve as places of refuge. The premise underlying these laws of asylum is that the accidental manslayer must atone for the shedding of innocent blood and must therefore undergo the punishment of forced residence at a sacral domicile. According to the priestly school, the homicide is compelled to reside in a city of refuge until the death of the high priest—the person who bears "the iniquity of the holy offerings of the children of Israel" (Exod 28–38) and whose death alone might serve as the expiation of blood guilt (Greenberg 1959). The city of refuge, according to this conception, does not necessarily perform the protective function of safeguarding the accidental manslayer from the avenger but serves as the place in which he atones for his sin. The book of Deuteronomy, however, with the abolition of provincial altars and sanctuaries, removes the institution of asylum from sacerdotal jurisdiction. It retains the numerical principle of three cities of refuge on each side of the Jordan (Deut 4:4–43; 19:1–10), but strips it of its sacral character. The assignment of cities of refuge is no longer dependent on sacral factors (levitical cities) but is decided by rational and geographic considerations. The land must be measured and subdivided equally into three sections and cities of refuge assigned at equidistant locations, so that the fleeing manslayer may reach the place of asylum with the maximum speed. The asylum is not the place in which he serves his punishment, but the place that protects him from the vengeance of the blood redeemer: "Lest the avenger of blood in hot anger pursue the manslayer and overtake him" (Deut 19:6). Therefore, the Deuteronomic law does not prescribe the period of time that the homicide must reside in asylum (i.e., until the death of the high priest); he is to remain there until the rage of the avenger subsides.

Priestly Donations. The priestly literature and Deuteronomy have preserved the laws defining the priests' portion of the well-being offering. According to the priestly school, the priest receives the breast and the thigh of the sacrificial animal (Lev 7:28–34), while according to Deuteronomy, he receives the shoulders, the cheeks, and the stomach (Deut 18:3). Regarding the firstfruits, the two agree in defining the gifts: "All the best of the new oil, wine, and grain" (Num 18:12; cf. Deut 18:4). In addition, the priestly source commands setting aside a loaf "from the first yield of your baking" (Num 15:18–21), while Deuteronomy commands that the first shearing of the sheep shall be given to the priest (Deut 18:4). JE apparently alludes to the firstfruits of grain and wine in Exod 22:28: *(mĕleʾ atkhā we-dimʿakhā).* The priestly school associates the rites of the firstfruits with festivals as follows: the sheaf *(ʿomer)* is waved by the farmer at the beginning of the harvest (Lev 23:9–14), and the two loaves of bread with the addition of two lambs are given to the priest at the end of the harvest (23:15–20). Deuteronomy also enjoins the ceremony of the bringing of the firstfruit (Deut 26:1–10), but neither fixes a date nor defines the amount given to the priest. JE also includes the firstfruit offering, which is brought to the House of God apparently during a feast (Exod 23:19; 34:26), but its nature is not sufficiently clear. According to the priestly literature, the tithe is given to the Levites (Num 18:21–24) who set aside "a tithe of the tithe" from it for the priest (18:25–32). According to Deuteronomy, the owners bring the tithes with them to the central temple and eat them there, and every third year they leave the tithe in their towns, where it is eaten by the Levites as well as by the stranger, the orphan, and the widow (Deut 14:22–29; 26:12–15). An ancient law incorporated into the holiness code deals with the tithe given to the deity from the "seed from the ground, the fruit from the tree, as well as from the herds and the flocks" (Lev 27:30–32). It is not known whether, according to this attitude, these tithes were transferred to the temple treasury or were given to the priest (Weinfeld 1971).

The general impression gained from the laws of gifts to the priesthood according to the various sources is that (1) JE does not define either the firstfruit gifts or the other types of sacral donations. (2) The priestly school clearly defines the gifts but preserves two different traditions in relation to the tithe (Lev 27:30–32; Num 18:8ff.). (3) Deuteronomy defines the gifts, but in its treatment they undergo a process of liberalization. The gift from the sacrifice is of far less worth than that obligated by the priestly school. The firstfruits are not associated with particular dates or with fixed quotas. The tithe (like the firstfruits) was expropriated from the Levites and priests and given over to the owner, who would eat it in the central temple. This liberalization apparently originated in a reform, namely, the centralization of the cult from the time of Hezekiah–Josiah (see below).

The Priestly Literature and Deuteronomy: Comparison of Tradition and Style

The Peroration. At the end of the holiness code (Lev 26), as at the end of the Deuteronomic law code (Deut 28), there is a section comprising blessings and curses, but there is a distinct difference between these two sections. In Lev 26 the setting is local and agricultural in character: the threshing and vintage (26:5), the vicious beasts in the land (26:6, 22; cf. Gen 37:33; 2 Kgs 17:26), deserted sites (Lev 26:30–31; cf. Amos 7:9), and the desolation of the land (Lev 26:32ff.). There are also special literary signs that can be noted here, such as the repeated refrain: "But if you do not obey . . . and if you remain hostile to me" (26:14, 21, 23, 27), as well as the typological numbers seven (26:18, 21, 24, 28) and ten (26:26). The parallel section in Deuteronomy contains no material bearing a local character of the type indicated, but rather emphasizes global catastrophes alluding to an Assyrian conquest, such as plague, pillage of property, and exile of children by a cruel nation that comes from afar (28:30–34, 48–51), a harsh siege of all towns (28:52–57), and the king's exile (28:36). An analysis of the arrangement of curses indeed shows that it manifests the distinct influence of seventh-century B.C.E. Assyrian treaties (Weinfeld 1965).

Levitical Priests. The priestly literature makes a clear distinction between priests and Levites, while Deuteronomy speaks of one class: "levitical priests." There is no basis to assume that the priestly code was the first one to form the distinction between the two classes, priests and Levites. On the contrary, it is clear that Deuteronomy already recognized the two classes (cf. Deut 18:3–5 with 6–8), but it rather deliberately identifies the status of the Levite (18:6–8) and creates the single status of the "levitical priests." The Levites who served in the provincial towns until the reform lost their status after the reform, and for this reason the Deuteronomic legislator displays concern for them in two ways: by giving them the opportunity to receive the rightful holy dues (see 18:6–8), and by including them in holy feasts and gifts (12:12, 18; 14:27, 29; 16:11, 14).

Stylistic and Idiomatic Differences

The two theological schools each adopted separate forms of expression and linguistic usages. It is impossible to determine priority or lateness on the basis of these expressions because it is impossible to differentiate strata in the biblical language of the First Temple period. Certain differences can at least point to differences of sociological approach and attitude. The following list the main differences:

Deuteronomy	Priestly Literature
šaʿareŷkem	mōšĕboteŷkem
haʾāḥ wehagēr	haʾezraḥ wehagēr
šebeṭ	maṭṭeh
qāhāl	ʿedāh
pādāh	gāʾal
šāmar	zākar
šāmar wĕʿāśah	zākar wĕʿāśah
hālak bĕdarkeŷ	hālak bĕḥuqōt
hālak ʾaḥareŷ	zānāh aḥareŷ
gĕdilîm	ṣîṣīt
šĕnat sĕmiṭṭāh	šĕnat šabbattôn
heʿebîr baʾeš	nātan mizarʿô lamôlek
gēr yatôm wĕʾ almanāh	heʿāni wĕhagēr
bibĕli daʿat	bišĕgāgāh
šem YHWH	kĕbôd YHWH
šikkēn sĕmô	šākan
ʾarôn habĕrît	ʾarôn haʿēdût
luḥôt habĕrit	luḥôt haʿēdût
ubiʿartá harʿá	wĕnikrĕtāh hanepeš
miqirbekā	meʿameŷhā
hāyā bô ḥeṭʾ	naśaʾ ḥeṭʾ

Some of the differences can be explained on a theological basis, for example, "Glory of God *(Kĕbôd Y.)*" in contrast to "name of God *(šem Y.)*" and "[God] dwelled *(šākan)*" as opposed to "caused God's name to dwell *(šikkēn)*" (see below). Others can be explained on a sociological basis, as in the use of *môšab* 'settlement', *ʿedāh* 'congregation', *geʾullah* 'redemption, acting as a kinsman', or *nkrt mʿmyw* 'be cut of its kin', which indicate a patriarchal background, in contrast to *šaʿar* 'gate', *qāhāl* 'assembly', *pidyôn* 'ransom', *bʿr myśrʾl* 'be extirpated of Israel', which indicate a more socially urban background. The provincial background of the priestly literature becomes evident in comparing Lev 26 with Deut 28 (see above). In this regard it is significant that Deuteronomy makes no mention of not working the land during the sabbatical year, which is so basic in Lev 25–26 (Japhet 1986). In contrast, it places special emphasis on the release from debts, which is important in an urban society. Another significant fact in this connection is the role played by the foreigner *(nkry)* in Deuteronomy. As is known, foreigners acted as traders in ancient Israel, and it is against the background of buying and selling that they are portrayed in Deuteronomy (14:21; 15:3; 23:21; 29:21; see Weinfeld 1968a).

12. Deuteronomy as Turning Point in Israelite Religion

The Josianic reform revolutionized all aspects of Israelite religion. The centralization of the cult was in itself a sweeping innovation in the history of the Israelite cult, but its consequences were—as we shall see—decisively more revolutionary in nature, in that they involved the collapse of an entire system of concepts that for centuries had been regarded as sacrosanct. The elimination of the provincial cult permitted the transformation of Israel's religion into a more abstract religion, one that minimized external expression (see below). Indeed, the very purpose of the book of Deuteronomy was to curtail and circumvent the cult and not to extend or enhance it. The Deuteronomic conception of cult is vastly different from that reflected in the Tetrateuchal sources; it represents a turning point in the evolution of the faith of Israel.

Let us start with the concept of the divine abode. Deuteronomy defines the Sanctuary as "the place where YHWH chose to cause *his name* to dwell there." It has been rightly observed (von Rad 1963, pp. 38–39) that the expression "to cause his name to dwell *(lškn šmw)*" reflects a new theological conception of the Deity, and that the repeated consistent employment of this and similar expressions *(śwm šmw/hyh šmw/qrʾšmw/bnh lšmw/hqdyš lšmw;* see Weinfeld 1972a, pp. 324–25) by the author of Deuteronomy and his followers is intended to combat the ancient popular belief that the Deity actually dwelled within the Sanctuary. The Deuteronomic school used this "name" phraseology in a very consistent manner and never made the slightest digression from it. There is not one example in the Deuteronomic literature of God's "dwelling in the temple" or the building of a "house of God." The temple is always the "dwelling of his name," and the house is always built "for his name." This consistency is seen most clearly when a Deuteronomic text is interwoven with an earlier text, which does not know the "name theology." Thus, for example, in the authentic part of Nathan's prophecy the main issue is the building of a house for God's dwelling *(lšbtw,* 2 Sam 7:5, 7), while the Deuteronomist (v 13a; Driver 1913, p. 276 n. 1; McCarter 1984, 2.205–6) speaks about building a house for "his name." Similarly, the account of the temple's construction and the ancient story of dedication of the temple speak plainly about building a house for God (1 Kgs 6:1, 2;

8:13), while the Deuteronomist, whenever he mentions the building, describes it as being built "for the name of God" (1 Kgs 3:2; 5:17, 19; 8:17, 18, 19, 20, 44, 48).

The most definite expression of this theology is to be found in the Deuteronomic litany of Solomon in 1 Kgs 8.[11] According to the deuteronomistic prayer (vv 14–69), the temple is not God's place of habitation but serves only as a house of worship in which Israelites and foreigners alike may deliver their prayers to the God "who dwells in heaven." The idea that God's habitation is in heaven is here expressed most emphatically in order to eradicate the belief that the Deity sat enthroned between the cherubim in the Temple. Whenever the expression "your dwelling place *(mkwn šbtk)*" is employed it is accompanied by the word "in heaven" (vv 30, 39, 43, 49). The Deuteronomist is clearly disputing the view implied by the ancient song that opens the prayer (vv 12–13) and designates the temple as God's exalted house *(byt zbl)* and a dwelling place *(mkwn šbtk)* forever. The Deuteronomist in the prayer ascribed to Solomon consistently appended to the expression *mkwn šbtk* the word *hšmym* 'in heaven' in order to inform us that it is heaven that is meant here and not the temple, as the ancient song implies. In fact, however, the term "your dwelling place *(mkwn šbtk)*" in early sources as well as in Solomon's song (vv 12–13) denotes the Sanctuary, and it is the Deuteronomist who is here attempting to alter this meaning and thereby wrests the song from its original sense.[12]

The theological corrective, that is to say, the addition of "heaven" to the phrase "holy habitation" occurs in Deuteronomy itself. In Deut 26:15 the Israelite in his prayer says, "Look down from your holy habitation *(mʿwn qdšk)*, from heaven." The words "from heaven" seem to be an explanatory gloss intended to prevent misconstruing the expression "holy habitation" as referring to the Sanctuary. Indeed, the fact that the earlier prevailing conception was that God's habitation *(mʿwn)* was in Zion may be inferred from Ps 76:3: "His abode has been established in Šalem, his habitation *(mʿwntw)* in Zion." This abstract view of the heavenly abode is also reflected in the Deuteronomic account of the Sinaitic revelation. In contrast to the account in Exod 19 of God's descent upon Mount Sinai (19:11–20), we read in Deut 4:36, "From heaven he let you hear his voice . . . and on earth he let you see his great fire; and from the midst of that fire you heard his words." Deuteronomy has, furthermore, taken care to shift the center of gravity of the theophany from the visual to the aural plane. In Exod 19 the principal danger confronting the people was the likelihood that they might "break through to the Lord to gaze" (v 21); it was to prevent this that there was need to "set bounds for the people round about" (v 12) and to caution them not to ascend the mountain. Indeed, the pre-Deuteronomic texts invariably speak of the danger of seeing the deity: "For man shall not see me

[11] On the deuteronomistic nature of this prayer see Weinfeld 1972a, pp. 35–36.
[12] In Exod 15:17, *mkwn šbtk* may refer to the heavenly temple.

and live" (Exod 33:20), and similarly in Gen 32:31: "For I have seen God face to face, and yet my life is preserved" (cf. Judg 13:22; Isa 6:5). The book of Deuteronomy, by contrast, cannot conceive of the possibility of seeing the Divinity. The Israelites saw only "his great fire," which symbolizes his essence and qualities (4:24: "for YHWH your God is a consuming fire, an impassioned God," cf. 9:3), whereas God himself remains in his heavenly abode. The danger threatening the people here, and the greatness of the miracle, is that of hearing the voice of the Deity: "Has any people heard the voice of God speaking from the midst of a fire, as indeed you have, and survived?" (4:33; cf. 5:23).

This attempt to eliminate the inherent corporeality of the traditional imagery also finds expression in Deuteronomy's conception of the Ark. The specific and exclusive function of the Ark, according to the book of Deuteronomy, is to house the tablets of the covenant (10:1–5); no mention is made of the Ark's cover *(kprt)* or of the cherubim that endow the Ark with the semblance of a divine chariot or throne (compare Exod 25:10–22 = the priestly text). The holiest vessel of the Israelite cult performs, in the Deuteronomic view, nothing more than an educational function: it houses the tablets upon which the words of God are engraved, and at its side the book of the Torah is laid, from which one reads to the people so that they may learn to fear the Lord (Deut 31:26; cf. vv 12 and 13). The Ark does not serve as God's seat upon which he journeys forth to disperse his enemies (Num 10:33–36), but only as the vessel in which the tablets of the covenant are deposited. This becomes quite clear when we compare Deut 1:42–43 with Num 14:42–44, a tradition on which the Deuteronomic account is based. In Num 14:44 we read that after the sinful incident of the spies "the Ark of the Covenant of YHWH departed not out of the camp," and this was the reason for the Israelites' defeat in their subsequent battle with the Amalekites and Canaanites. The Deuteronomic account, conversely, completely omits the detail of the Ark and ascribes the Israelite defeat to the fact that God was not in their midst.

The author of Deuteronomy similarly relates that it was God who went before the people to seek out new resting places (1:33), whereas the earlier source, on which Deuteronomy is dependent, relates that it was the Ark that journeyed forth before the people to seek out new resting places for them (Num 10:33). The absence of the Ark is especially striking in the Deuteronomic law of warfare (23:15). One would expect a passage that speaks of the presence of the Divinity within the military encampment to make some mention of the Ark, which accompanied the warriors on their expeditions, as in 1 Sam 4:6–7, "And when they learned that the ark of YHWH had come to the camp . . . they said, the gods have come into the camp." The Deuteronomic law, however, speaks of YHWH as moving about the camp (23:15) but does not make the slightest allusion to the Ark or the holy vessels.

A similar conception is encountered in the book of Jeremiah, for instance at 3:16–17, "They shall say no more, 'The ark of the covenant of YHWH,' it shall not come to mind. . . . At that time Jerusalem shall be called the throne of YHWH." In other words, the Ark of the Covenant shall no longer serve as God's seat, as the people were previously accustomed to believe, but all of Jerusalem shall be "the seat of YHWH," that is, in a symbolic sense (Weinfeld 1976a). In another passage the prophet declares, "Do I not fill heaven and earth? says YHWH" (23:24), recalling the words of Deutero- (or Trito-)Isaiah when he expressly repudiates the notion of the Sanctuary as the place of God's habitation: "Heaven is my throne and the earth is my footstool, what is the house which you build for me? and what is the place of my rest?" (66:1). This view is also met with in the Deuteronomic prayer of Solomon: "Behold, heaven and the highest heaven cannot contain you; how much less this house that I have built" (1 Kgs 8:27). The Sanctuary is here conceived as a house of prayer and not as a cultic center. This tendency to minimize the cult is already manifest in the book of Deuteronomy and signifies a religious turning-point that occurred following the abolition of the high places and the provincial sanctuaries.

The first thing that strikes our attention when endeavoring to grasp the significance of sacrifice in the book of Deuteronomy is that we do not find sacrifice practiced for its own sake. The Deity, in the Deuteronomic view, has no need of the "pleasing odor *(ryḥ nyḥḥ)*" of sacrifices, and no mention is made of the "food of God," which is amply attested in the priestly code (cf., e.g., Lev 1:9, 13, 17; 21:6, 8, 17, 21). Neither is there any mention of the sin and guilt offerings designed to atone for involuntary sins, ritual impurity, perjury, theft, and deception (Lev 4–5). The author's view seems to be that spiritual purification and repentance—consisting of confession and prayer—and not sacrificial offerings expiate sin. The sole instance in which the book of Deuteronomy does mention a rite analogous in character to the sin and guilt offering is in the law of unsolved murder (Deut 21:1–9). Yet, interestingly enough, it is precisely this law that reflects Deuteronomy's special attitude to sacrifice. The rite conducted here does not consist of a sacrificial offering complete with ceremonial slaughter and blood sprinkling, but calls only for the breaking of the heifer's neck in an uncultivated valley. The priests are present during this act, not because they play any part in the execution of the ritual, for this is carried out entirely by the elders, but merely to guarantee the religious aspect of the ceremony by presiding over it. The entire act has a symbolic value: the heifer's neck is broken at the scene of the crime, as it were, and the elders cleanse their hands only as a purificatory expression of their innocence (cf. Pss 24:4; 26:6–10; 73:13; etc.). There is no laying of the hands on the heifer or a transference of the sin to it, as in the case of the ritual scapegoat (Lev 16:21), because its beheading as such does not atone for the sin; expiation is effected only by the confession and prayer uttered at the close of the ceremony (vv 7–8). It is true that the custom itself originated in a rite of elimination, as shown by D. P. Wright (1987). In the present formulation, however, nothing is said about removal of impurity or sin by the priest, as in Lev 14:53 and 16:22, or about the transferral of the evil to the open country, as in Lev 16:22 and in the Mesopotamian incantations (cf. ibid., p. 402). In this rite, God absolves the sin himself without recourse to any intermediary, whereas in the priestly literature all expiatory sacrifices are executed by the priests, whose mediation alone effects the expiation of the sin (cf. the common priestly expression in the book of Leviticus: "and the priest shall make atonement for him"). In the Deuteronomic law, atonement is possible only through the confession of the elders of the city, who, as representatives of the guilty city, beseech absolution through prayers; in the priestly school expiation is effected through ritual sacrifice and incense burning, which are mostly not accompanied by prayer on the part of the penitent.

Deuteronomic sacrifice consists primarily of offerings that are consumed by the offerer in the Sanctuary and are designed to be shared with the poor, the Levite, the alien resident, the orphan, and the widow. The constant emphasis on the obligation to share the sacrificial repast with indigent persons creates the impression that the principal purpose of the offering is to provide nutriment for the destitute elements of Israelite society. The author of Deuteronomy alludes to this himself when, after prescribing that the joyful nature of the festival be shared with the *personae miserabiles,* he goes on to say, "You shall remember that you were a slave in Egypt; and you shall be careful to observe these statutes" (16:22). It is indeed remarkable that the very book that promulgates the law of centralized worship at the "chosen place" has not so much as a word to say about the presentation of communal sacrifices (the daily and seasonal offerings) that constituted the principal mode of worship at this exclusive Sanctuary.

Sacrifice, according to Deuteronomy, is not an institutional practice but a personal one, which has two principal objects: the first is humanitarian, to share the sacrificial repast with the poor, as noted above; and the second is private, to fulfill a religious obligation and express one's gratitude to the Deity by means of votive offerings (12:6, 11, 17, 26; 23:22–24). God has no need of the sacrifice itself; it is only an expression of gratitude to the Deity, and this constitutes its entire significance. We may perhaps note in passing that the expression "to pay a vow *(šlm ndr),*" found in wisdom literature (Prov 7:14; Eccl 5:4), is not found in any book of the Pentateuch except Deuteronomy (23:22).

The same attitude is revealed in the only passage in Deuteronomy (12:27) that describes the manner in which the sacrifice is to be offered. The verse differentiates between nonburnt offerings and burnt offering *(ʿôlāh),* and ordains that the flesh and blood of the burnt offering be offered up entirely on the altar, whereas the blood of the nonburnt is to be poured upon the altar and the meat eaten. It is most surprising that the author makes no mention of the burning of the suet, the fat piece that is set aside for God and which thus renders the meat permissible for priestly and lay consumption (1 Sam 2:12–17). The blood and fat were deemed to be the food of God (cf. Ezek 44:7), which is why the priestly literature forbids the eating of the fat, just as it forbids the "eating" of blood

(Lev 7:22–27). Yet the author of Deuteronomy not only fails to mention the interdiction concerning the eating of the suet, he completely ignores the fact that the suet was to be offered upon the altar, the very reason for which the sacrifice had to be offered at the Sanctuary. Ritual detail, then, is of no importance to the author of Deuteronomy, and it is possible that he deliberately ignored it because it did not accord with his own religious frame of mind.

Sacrifice, however, is not the only rite to be conceived differently by the book of Deuteronomy, for all laws pertaining to cult and ritual are here conceived more rationally than in the earlier sources. This is particularly evident in the laws contained in chaps. 12–19, which are a direct consequence of the implementation of cult centralization and form the legal basis of the religious reformation. These laws clearly mirror the change in religious beliefs and attitudes that occurred in the wake of the reform.

Chapter 12 promulgates the law of centralized worship at the chosen place, but alongside this law, or as a result of it, we find the authorization permitting nonsacrificial slaughter. Whereas before the reform all slaughter—except that of game animals—was deemed to be a sacral act and was prohibited even for nonsacrificial purposes unless the blood was sprinkled upon the altar (Lev 17:1–7; cf. 1 Sam 14:32–35), it was now permissible to perform nonsacrificial slaughter without being obliged to sprinkle the blood upon an altar (Deut 12:15, 16, 20–24). It need hardly be said that the sanctioning of profane slaughter freed a significant aspect of Israelite daily life from its ties to the cultus. The more crucial import of the law, however, is that by sanctioning nonsacrificial slaughter it repudiates the hallowed Israelite dogma that ascribed a sacral quality to the blood and prohibited one from pouring it upon the ground. According to the priestly document or, to be more precise, the holiness code, the blood of slaughtered animals potentially valid for sacrifice must be sprinkled upon the altar, whereas the blood of game animals—which are invalid for sacrifice—must be covered with dust (Lev 17:13): for all spilled blood, even of fowl and beasts of prey, cries out for vengeance and satisfaction, and if the shedding of blood cannot be atoned by offering it upon the altar, then it must be covered up. Uncovered blood begs, as it were, for an avenger (Job 16:18, "O earth, cover not my blood," cf. Isa 26:21; Ezek 24:7–8), a role that, in the case of homicide, is assumed by the Deity. The author of Deuteronomy, by contrast, declares that the blood of all animals slaughtered for nonsacrificial purposes may be poured upon the ground like water (12:16 and 24), thereby asserting that blood has no more a sacral value than water has. He does, to be sure, retain the interdiction on the eating of blood (compare Deut 12:23 with Gen 9:4; Lev 17:11), but he absolutely repudiates the concept that the spilled blood of animals requires satisfaction.

The book of Deuteronomy also contains a less sacral conception of the tithes than do the other Pentateuchal sources. The tithe, which the priestly document designates as "holy to the Lord" (Lev 27:30–33) and which, according to a second tradition, accrues to the Levites (Num 18:21–32), remains by Deuteronomic legislation the property of the original owner (14:22–27). Furthermore, it may be secularized and employed for profane purposes on payment of its equivalent monetary value (without the addition of the fifth part required by the priestly school; cf. Lev 27:31). This provision seems to be yet another expression of the liberation of the cultus from its intimate ties to nature. The sanctity of the tithe is not conceived as an inherent quality of the grain or animal, as in the priestly document (Lev 27:30–33), for it is man who consecrates it and may, if he wishes, secularize it through redemption. In the Deuteronomic view, sanctity is not a taboo that inheres in things that by nature belong to the divine realm, but is rather a consequence of the religious intentions of the person who consecrates it.

The wording of the Deuteronomic law of firstlings makes this conception particularly clear. The author of Deuteronomy instructs the Israelite to consecrate (*tqdyš*) the firstborn of his animals to YHWH (Deut 15:19), a command that openly contradicts the injunction in Lev 27:26: "But a firstling of animals, which as a firstling belongs to YHWH, no man may consecrate (*lʾyqdyš*), whether ox or sheep; it is YHWH's." According to the priestly law the sanctity inheres in the animal by virtue of its birth (cf. "which as a firstling belongs to the Lord," *ʾšr ybkr lYHWH);* it is not man who makes it holy. Thus Num 18:17 expressly forbids the redemption of the firstling of clean animals: "But the firstling of a cow . . . you shall not redeem; they are holy." Man can neither make the firstling holy nor secularize it by redemption. The author of Deuteronomy, in contrast, by ordaining that the owners consecrate their firstlings with the alternative of redemption if they find it too difficult to bring them to Jerusalem (14:23ff.), shows that he does not recognize automatic sanctity but only sanctity that derives from the express will of the consecrant.

Like the tithe, the firstling is also taken from the possession of the priest and is restored to the owner. According to JE (Exod 22:29; 34:19) and the priestly school (Num 18:15–17), the firstling is "holy to YHWH" whether it is given to the Lord (Exod 22:29) or presented to his servants (i.e., the priests, according to the priestly text, Num 18:17–18); while according to Deuteronomy it remains in the possession of its original owner, though he is obliged to consume it at the chosen place. Indeed, it is the law of the firstlings that informs us of the author's negative attitude regarding holy taboo. In the earlier laws the regulations pertaining to the redemption of the firstlings of clean animals are always accompanied by regulations concerning the firstborn of humans and the firstlings of unclean animals (Exod 13:2, 12, 15; 22:28–29; 34:19–20; Lev 27:26–27; Num 18:15–18). The book of Deuteronomy, however, omits the laws of the human firstborn and the firstlings of unclean animals because these regulations in no way advance its humanitarian purposes (the participation of the *personae miserabiles* in the consumption of the firstlings) and because they are based on mythical and magical conceptions not shared by the author of Deuteronomy (see above).

The severance of these laws from the realm of myth and magic finds its clearest expression in the Deuteronomic ordinances concerning the Paschal sacrifice. According to the JE and priestly documents the Paschal sacrifice is a domestic celebration accompanied by apotropaic rites of an animistic nature: the Paschal blood is daubed upon the lintel and doorposts (Exod 12:7 [priestly], 22 [JE]); the animal must be roasted together with its head, legs, and inner parts (v 9); it may not be removed from the house; no bone may be broken (v 46); and a special dress is prescribed for the celebrants (v 11). In the Deuteronomic law, however, not the slightest reminiscence of these magical prescriptions has been preserved. The Paschal ritual has instead been converted into a communal sacrifice, which must be offered up at the central Sanctuary like all other sacrifices. The Paschal offering—which is the most ancient sacrifice in Israel's tradition and which apparently originates from the tribes' former nomadic life—succeeded in preserving its early primitive character until it was here divested of its original import and recast in a form more consistent with the spirit of the times. Even the earliest features of the sacrifice, such as the requirement that it be selected only from sheep or goats, or that it be roasted by fire—which attest to the nomadic origin of the ritual—have been completely obscured by the Deuteronomic law. The new provision allows the Israelite to select the animal from cattle as well as sheep and goats (Deut 16:2) and permits it to be boiled like any ordinary sacrifice (v 7).

13. Deuteronomy and Its Northern Roots

I have already dwelled on the importance of the Shechemite tradition (the ceremony of Gerizim and Ebal in the framing of the Deuteronomic code; see above), which shows a predilection for the northern heritage. I shall now check the northern influence on the code and on its basic principles.

The Purification of the Cult

The purification from Israel's cult of pagan elements, including the abolition of the high places, associated with the Hezekianic–Josianic reforms, has its roots in northern Israel.

The struggle with Baal worship started in the north in the period of Ahab, and in the time of Jehu the Baal was extirpated from Israel (2 Kgs 10:28). From the struggle with the Baal apparently evolved the polemic against the golden calves, which is expressed by Hosea (10:5; 13:2). As is well known, the sins of the Baal and of the golden calves are, in Deuteronomic historiography, the two decisive sins of Israel. Both sins were condemned in northern Israel (see especially Hosea) before the rise of the Deuteronomic movement.

Furthermore, it seems that the condemnation of astral worship so characteristic of the Deuteronomic writings has its roots in the north. Amos 5:26 refers vaguely to this sin (cf. Weinfeld 1972b, pp. 149–50), but the assault is more clearly expressed in the LXX version of Hosea. In the framework of the admonition against pagan worship in Hos 13:1–4 we find in the LXX a short doxology at the end of v 4, which reads as follows: "I am YHWH your God who forms *(stereōn)* the heavens and creates *(ktizōn)* the earth, whose hand created all the host of heavens and I did not fix them for you to go after them. I am the God who brought you out of Egypt. . . ." (The pair *stereō* and *ktizō* is found only in Amos and Hosea, and the Greek of the doxology in Hos 13:4 is very similar to Jer 8:2, which is also concerned with astral worship.)

We find here affinities with other scriptures that condemn astral worship and specify that the worship was assigned by God to other nations and was forbidden to the Israelites (Deut 4:19; 17:3; 29:25). It seems that, like Amos, Hosea incorporated doxologies into his prophecies in the context of admonitions concerning foreign worship (for the authenticity of the doxologies in Amos, see Crenshaw 1975). Similar hymnic affirmations are attested in Job (5:9–16; 9:4–10) and in Deutero-Isaiah (40:22, 42:5; 44:24; 45:18). The fact that in the Hoseanic passage reflected in the LXX, hymnic elements are found like the ones in Job and Deutero-Isaiah may teach us that doxologies like those of Amos were interwoven in the admonition of Hosea.

Another interesting short doxology in Hos 12:6 polemicizes against popular religious views. As H. L. Ginsberg recognized,[13] Hos 12:4–5 contains criticism of the notion of Jacob wrestling with the angel (cf. Gen 32:25f.). Hosea seems to imply in 12:6 that one should not rely on angels because God himself is the savior and none else: "Yet YHWH the God of Hosts, must be invoked as YHWH" *(NJPS)* (and not any of the angelic hosts). The same attitude is to be recognized in the book of Deuteronomy. Deuteronomy chap. 7 purposely omits the angel encountered in the old Exodus traditions of Exod 23, on which it relies (see the COMMENT to Deut 7). A similar omission occurs in Deut 26:8, which is verbally dependent on Num 20:15–16, where the angel appears as bringing the people out of Egypt. This antiangelologic view comes clearly to expression in Deut 4:37: "He himself *(bpnyw)* led you out of Egypt." For this meaning of *pnym* cf. Exod 33:14–15; 2 Sam 17:11. It seems that aversion to belief in angels as mediators is a characteristic feature of Deuteronomy. This accords with the facts that the Urim and Tummim are not mentioned at all in

[13] H. L. Ginsberg, "Hosea's Ephraim, More Fool Than Knave" *JBL* 80 (1961): 339–47.

Deuteronomy and that the Ark in Deuteronomy does not function as the seat of the Lord but only as a receptacle for the tablets (cf. above).

The polemic against the worship of stone and wood, which is so salient in Deuteronomy and the Deuteronomic literature (4:25; 27:15; 28:36, 63; 29:16; 31:29), is already found in Hosea and appears there in phraseology identical with that of Deuteronomy. In Hos 13:2 we find "craftman work *(mʿśh ḥršym),*" which is identical with *mʿśh ydy ḥrš* in Deut 27:15. Similarly, the expression "handiwork of man" in Hos 14:4 is most characteristic of Deuteronomic literature. It seems that we ought to speak not only about the influence of Hosea on the Deuteronomic school but also about an iconoclastic tendency originating in the north, which pervaded Judah after the destruction of Samaria. It was this tendency that caused Hezekiah to smash the bronze serpent in Jerusalem (2 Kgs 18:4). The chronicle that recounts this event speaks also about the removal of the high places, the breaking of the pillars, and the cutting down of the Asherah: it is not by chance that all of these are mentioned together. We have to do here with deeds intended to purge pagan elements from Israelite religion. As is well known, the Canaanite cult was based on high places, which contained stone pillars and wooden symbols, and it seems that the inconoclastic stream that started in the north developed the struggle not only against the golden calves but also against high places, pillars, and Asherim. In the final stage all provincial altars were prohibited, as the doctrine of centralization of the cult reflects. This process too finds its echo in the book of Hosea. Let us adduce the evidence.

Like Deut 12:2, which prohibits worship on high places because this is the way the pagans worship their gods, "on lofty mountains and on hills or under any luxuriant tree," Hosea admonishes his generation for worshiping "on mountaintops, on hills . . . and under trees whose shade is pleasant" (4:13). The condemnation of trees in worship joins the condemnation of stone worship, as in the Deuteronomic literature: "he made altars a plenty, cult pillars abounded . . . their heart is divided, they feel guilty, he will pull apart his altars, he will smash his pillars" (Hos 10:1–2). There is no reference here to idolatry but to the multiplying of altars and pillars. Israel is guilty because of serving God with divided heart—false and insincere—in contrast to the "wholeheartedness" much stressed in the Deuteronomic writings. The same tendency is reflected in Hos 8:11–13:

> For Ephraim . . . has multiplied altars
> altars have become his sin . . .
> they love sacrifices,
> let them slaughter and eat meat *(yzbḥw bśr wyʾklw),*
> YHWH has not accepted them.

(For a similar critique in an Aramaic text in Demotic script from Egypt, concerning hypocrisy in sacrificial worship, cf. Weinfeld 1985b).

This kind of reservation about altars and sacrifices is also found in Amos. He says,

> Come to Bethel and transgress
> Come to Gilgal and multiply transgressions,
> present your sacrifices every morning,
> and tithes every three days . . . for that is *what you love,* o Israelites.
> (4:4–5)

The sacrifices are seen here as transgressions, and their multiplication means multiplying sin, as Hosea sees in the multiplication of altars multiplication of sin. Hosea and Amos see the sacrifices as means for the gratification of the desire to eat flesh; therefore the proclamation "Let them slaughter and eat meat, YHWH has not accepted them." A similar phrase is found in Jer 7:21: "Add your burnt offerings to the other sacrifices and *eat meat.*" It is this very language that Deuteronomy uses (12:15) when allowing profane slaughter: "wherever (or whenever) you desire you may slaughter *(tzbḥ wʾklt bśr)*" (Ginsberg 1982, p. 21). This is the view that took root in Judah during the days of Hezekiah and paved the way for the reform.

True, it was not ideology alone that brought about the revolutionary change, the political circumstances also played a prominent role in this matter (Weinfeld 1964a). But the northern opposition to multiplying sacrifices could well have served as the ideological support for the centralization. One must add that the fact that Jerusalem was saved by a miracle from Sennacherib's assault added a glorious dimension to the centralization (see below).

The objection to provincial sites created the proper atmosphere for spiritualization of worship. The temple in Jerusalem in the Deuteronomic school was conceived not as the physical house of the Lord but as the house in which God established his name (see above).

We do not know whether this spiritualized understanding of the religion existed in northern Israel or is the outcome of inner development in Judah in the time of Hezekiah-Josiah. One thing is clear: it confines the line of development that started in Israel during the time of Ahab and continued until the period of Hosea the prophet. This brings us to the feelings of guilt and the expression of repentance that are so characteristic of the Deuteronomic movement but have their incipits in the book of Hosea.

The Return to God

The exile of the Israelite population, which started in 732 with the invasion of Tiglath Pileser III into Galilee (2 Kgs 15:29), deeply shocked the nation of Israel. It seems that at this time the faithful of the nation began to ponder

Israel's destiny. They saw in the national catastrophe divine punishment for their syncretism: the worship of the Baal and the golden calves. Because of these sins Hosea indeed predicts dispersion into Egypt and Assyria (8:9–13; 9:3; 11:5). Especially striking in these predictions are the phrases "they will go back to Egypt," "and Ephraim will go back to Egypt," which reminds us of the conclusion of the threats in Deut 28:68, "and God will bring you back to Egypt with ships." At the time of Hosea, the prophet, when the kingdom of Samaria disintegrated, Israel as well as Judah had a close relationship with Egypt (2 Kgs 17:4; Isa 18:2; 30:1ff.; 31:1ff.), and as the Assyrian danger approached, Israelites sought asylum in Egypt. The Israelite diaspora in Egypt in this period is mentioned in Isa 11:11, which is about an exile in Egypt, Patros, and Cush. We have no right to see this verse as post-Exilic—as some assume—because these three territorial units appear in the same order in the Esarhaddon inscriptions and this topographical combination does not occur elsewhere (cf. Parpola 1970). It seems that the Jewish diaspora in upper Egypt—*p-t3-rśy* = the land of the southerner (Patros)—started in this period and continued there until the time of Jeremiah (Jer 44:1, 15). Hosea, who lived and acted before the fall of Samaria, speaks therefore about the descent to Egypt no less than about the ascent to Assyria (8:9). In general he speaks about wandering among nations (9:17; 7:8; 8:8).

The phenomenon of exile brought with it naturally the longing for return to the homeland and hence the current term for return *(šwb šbwt),* which is prevalent in the Deuteronomic literature but is first mentioned in Hosea (6:11). In fact, the idea of returning from exile or returning from captivity is not particular to Israel and Judah. It is also attested in Aramaic texts of this period, in the Sefire inscription: "And now the gods have brought the return *(hšbw šybt)* of my father's house . . . and the return of Talayim" (3.24–25).[14] In Hosea[15] and in the Deuteronomic writings, however, the return to the land is combined with the return to God. Hosea speaks about God who brings about the return of his people and heals Israel: "When I would bring about the restoration of my people, when I would heal Israel" (6:11–7:1). Similarly, we read in 14:2–5, "Return, O Israel, to YHWH your God, for you have fallen because of your sin. . . . I will heal their apostasy. I will take them back in love." The return to God is then conditioned by healing caused by God out of generous love, an idea that occurs in Deut 30:1–10 and 4:29–30. This, like Hos 14:2–10, comes after a list of threats (28; 29:9–28). As in Hos 14:2, in Deut 30:2 we find the expression "to return to God" as well as the expression *šwb šbwt.* Here, also, it is accompanied by the idea of divine help in enabling the people to repent: "The Lord will circumcise your heart . . . to love YHWH your God" (v 6). Circumcision of

[14] Cf. Fitzmyer 1967. For the other minorities in Syria striving to return to their homeland, see Ephal 1977.

[15] For a thorough analysis of the theme of repentance in Hosea see Biram 1955.

heart here parallels the healing of apostasy in Hosea 14:5, *ʾrpʾ mšwbtm.* The same idea appears in Jeremiah:

> Return to me apostate sons. I will heal your apostasy *(ʾrpʾ mšwbtykm)* (3:22).
>
> I will heal and cure Judah and Israel . . . I will restore their fortunes, I will cleanse them of all the wickedness and sin (33:6f.).

In another instance dealing with restoration and repentance we find more verbal congruence between Deuteronomy and Hosea:

Hos 5:15–16:1	*Deut 4:29–40*
In their distress *(bṣr lhm)* they will seek me. "Come let us return to YHWH."	You will seek the Lord . . . when you are in distress *(bṣr lk)* . . . you will turn back to YHWH.

As indicated above, Deut chaps. 30 and 4 are of the post-Exilic period. But one has to admit in the light of Hosea that the ideas of repentance and return started to crystallize in northern Israel and were later adopted in Judah and applied to the exile of Judah (cf. Jer 29:13–14; 1 Kgs 8:47f.).

The affinities between Hosea and Deuteronomy may also be found in other areas of theology: thus the concept of the love of God for Israel is very clearly expressed in Hosea as well as in Deuteronomy: Hos 11:1–8; 14:5; Deut 1:31; 10:15; and cf. Jer 31:2. The same applies to the concept of *bĕrīt* connected to Torah, which is central in the Deuteronomic literature but is clearly attested in Hosea (8:1, cf. 6:7; 8:12). There is no justification for denying the authenticity of these verses in Hosea, for the concept of despising the Torah of YHWH occurs also in Isa 5:24 and 30:9, undisputed Isaianic verses.[16]

The most striking point of contact between Hosea and Deuteronomy is the formulation of the idea of hubris. The concept of forgetting YHWH out of affluence and satiety, which also occurs in other biblical sources (Deut 32:10f.; cf. wisdom literature, Weinfeld 1972a), is expressed in Hosea and Deuteronomy in a particularly idiosyncratic manner: man eats his fill, and his heart grows haughty and forgets God.

[16] L. Perlitt argues that *mʾs twrt YHWH* in Isa 5:24 as well as in Amos 2:4 is deuteronomistic (1969, p. 147). But this phrase is not attested in Deuteronomic literature. Cf. the list of idioms and indexes in Weinfeld 1972a, pp. 320ff.

Hos 13:6	*Deut 8:12–14*
They were filled, their heart was lifted up, therefore they forgot me. *(śbʿw wyrm lbmʿl kn skḥwny)*	Lest, when you have eaten and are filled . . . your heart be lifted up and you forget YHWH your god. *(pn tʾkl wśbʿt . . . wrm lbbk wškḥt ʾt YHWH ʾlhyk)*

The verbs are identical in both sources: *śbʿ, rwm lb, škḥ*. The idea as such occurs in the Song of Moses (Deut 32:10ff.), in the framework of the description of leaving the desert and coming into the affluent land. It is interesting to note that Hosea 13:6 follows a mention of God guiding the Israelites in the desert.

How are we to explain the contact between northern prophecy and the book of Deuteronomy, which became the basis for Jerusalemite theology in the period of Hezekiah–Josiah?

The National Renascence at the Times of Hezekiah and Josiah

After the fall of Samaria, Hezekiah, king of Judah, made efforts to draw the northern population toward Jerusalem, as may be learned from 2 Chr 30. Although the Book of Chronicles is a tendentious work, we have no right to see the event itself as fiction. The flow of northerners to Jerusalem in those days is now attested archaeologically. At the end of the eighth century B.C.E. Jerusalem underwent an expansion never encountered before; the same applies to the territory of Judah. As shown by N. Avigad,[17] Jerusalem at that time included the western hill of the city, now the Jewish quarter. By the same token, the settlement of Judah grew immensely at this period, and the population doubled (cf. Kochavi, ed., 1972, pp. 20–21). The only explanation for this situation is that after the fall of the Northern Kingdom, Israelites began to migrate to the south to the territories under the control of their brethren (cf. Broshi 1974, pp. 23–26). That people from the north were attached after the fall of the Northern Kingdom to Jerusalem and its cult may be learned from the fact that after the destruction of the Temple of Jerusalem, people from Shechem, Šiloh, and Samaria made pilgrimages to the temple site (Jer 41:5). It seems that in this period the hatred between Judah and Israel vanished, and some kind of symbiosis between the sister nations was established. This is reflected perhaps in Isaiah's consolation oracle of this time: "Ephraim's jealousy shall vanish and Judah's enmity shall end, Ephraim shall not envy Judah and Judah shall not harass

[17] N. Avigad, *The Upper City of Jerusalem* (Jerusalem, 1980), pp. 23ff.

Ephraim" (11:13). In the continuation of this oracle we read about the expansion of Israel and Judah toward the Philistine territory in the west on the one hand and toward Ammon, Moab, and Edom in the east on the other (v 14). The period of Hezekiah was indeed a period of great expansion. In 2 Kgs 18:8 we hear about Hezekiah overrunning Philistia as far as Gaza, and from 1 Chr 4:41–43 we learn about his incursion toward Seir in the south. It is in this period that "the remnant of Israel . . . and the house of Jacob" return to the Lord and to "the mighty God" *(ʾl gbwr;* Isa 10:20–21).[18] As has recently been seen by H. Cazelles, the remnant that returns *(šʾr yšwb)* represents the Israelites from the north who join Judah and accept the authority of Hezekiah, styled (among other things) "El Gibbor" (cf. Isa 9:5).[19] The same imagery is found in Mic 5:1. Micah speaks about the youngest of the clans of Judah, who will rule Israel: "then the rest of the brethren will return to the children of Israel" (5:1–2). This rectifies the earlier situation, when Judah was cut off from the other tribes (cf. Deut 33:7: "Hear, O YHWH, the voice of Judah and bring him back to his people"). Micah goes on to say that the leader of Judah "will stand and shepherd by the might of YHWH . . . Assyria with the sword" (vv 3–5). This suits Hezekiah, who rebelled against the king of Assyria and expanded the territory of his kingdom (before the invasion of Sennacherib).

This period of national revival may explain the nationalistic and patriotic atmosphere prevailing in Deuteronomy and Deuteronomic literature. The book of Deuteronomy abounds with military speeches aimed at strengthening the people in their future wars with their enemies (Weinfeld 1972a, pp. 45–59). These in fact reflect the national fervor of the times of Hezekiah–Josiah. Remarks such as "be strong and courageous *(ḥzq wʾmṣ)*"; "no man shall be able to stand against you *(lʾ ytyṣb ʾyš bpnykm)*"; "every spot on which your foot treads shall be yours"; and "YHWH your God will put your dread and fear of you over all the land in which you set foot" (11:24–25) seem to express the national enthusiasm of the period of Hezekiah–Josiah. I refer to the Hezekianic or Josianic period because it is very hard to date the various layers of Deuteronomic literature. As the book of Deuteronomy was discovered in the days of Josiah (622 B.C.E.) we must suppose that the main layout of the book existed long before that time—that is, at the time of Hezekiah. But we still do not know what belongs to later Josianic elaboration and what existed before (see below).

The idea of the ban on all Canaanite population also seems to have crystallized at this time. According to Deuteronomy the Israelites are commanded to exterminate all of the Canaanites and not to leave a soul of them living (Deut 7:1–2; 20:16–17). Such a policy, obliging the extermination of the whole population of the land whether fighting or passive, is utopian and is indeed unheard of

[18] This equals *ḥzqyh* and seems to allude to King Hezekiah.

[19] H. Cazelles, "Le Nom de Shear Yashub etc.," in *Proceedings of the Eighth World Congress of Jewish Studies,* Division A (Jerusalem 1982), pp. 47–50.

in the historical accounts of Israel. On the contrary, from 1 Kgs 9:21 we learn that the Israelites were unable to annihilate the inhabitants of Canaan, and Solomon subjected them to corvée labor. Rabbinic sources[20] preserved a tradition according to which Joshua sent out three messages to the Canaanites: "Whoever wants to make peace let him make peace, whoever wants to evacuate let him evacuate and whoever wants to fight let him fight"; Judaism could not conceive a massive slaughter by command of God. The command of Ḥerem of all the Canaanites in Deuteronomy is a utopian program that reflects the ongoing bitter struggle with the Canaanite religion and culture from the time of Elijah until the time of Josiah. Indeed, the reason for the annihilation of the Canaanites in Deut 20:18 is one of *Kulturkampf:* "lest they [the Canaanites] lead you into doing all the abominable things that they have done for their gods and you shall be sinful to YHWH your God." One should acknowledge that the Ḥerem as such was practiced in ancient Israel, as it was elsewhere in the ancient world (see the COMMENT to chap. 7). It is found in connection with Jericho (Josh 6:17) and Amalek (1 Sam 15), and is also applied to apostate or treacherous cities within Israel, such as the city condemned for idolatry in Deut 13:16 and the cities of Benjamin, which were banned because of the sin at Gibeah (Judg 20:40, 48). It seems that Deuteronomy adopted the ancient doctrine of Ḥerem from the north (cf. also 1 Kgs 20:42) and applied it theoretically to the seven nations of the land of Canaan. The original Ḥerem referred to hostile cities, banned by means of votive proclamations (Josh 6:17; Num 21:2–3), whereas Deuteronomy conceived Ḥerem as an automatic decree, which applied to a whole country and its inhabitants. This sort of Ḥerem is not dependent on any vow or dedication, but is an a priori decree that belongs more to theory than to practice.

The national patriotic attitude of Deuteronomy may also be recognized in its conception of the extent of the promised land. According to the ancient sources of the Pentateuch, and especially the list of boundaries in Num 34:1–15, Transjordan was not part of the land of Israel. The request of the Gadites and Reubenites to settle in Transjordan was considered by Moses as a sin (Num 32:14), and from Josh 22:19 we may deduce that Transjordan was considered impure land. The stories of the conquest in Josh 2–9 also make it clear that the conquest started with the crossing of the Jordan: the passage of the Jordan and the erecting of the stones at Gilgal actually commemorate the entrance into the promised land (Josh 3:10; 5:1; etc.). This old conception about the Jordan being the border of the land was not accepted by Deuteronomy. According to Deut 1–3, the conquest of the land started with the crossing of the river Arnon (Deut 2:24) at the border between Moab and the Mishor, the territory of King Sihon. In accordance with this view the Israelites apply the law of Ḥerem to these territories (2:34; 3:6) just as they are commanded to do to the peoples of the

[20] Cf. Y. *Šeb.* 6:1, 36c; *Debarim Rabah, Šopĕtim* 14 (ed. Lieberman 1955–, p. 101).

western side of the Jordan (Deut 20:16–17). The conquered territories of the eastern side of the Jordan are divided among the tribes, as are the other parts of the promised land, and are not just a gift on condition, as in Num 32. The author of Deuteronomy accepted the ideal borders of Gen 15:18, which reflected the borders of the Davidic kingdom, as binding borders (see Deut 1:7; 11:24); for him, therefore, Transjordan was an integral part of the land (cf. Deut 34:1). In this manner, the author of Deuteronomy affords Transjordan a status equal with that of Cisjordan; this looks like an endeavor to restore Israel to its ideal borders of the Davidic–Solomonic period (see Weinfeld 1983c).

The national resurgence of the period of Hezekiah and of Josiah explains the feelings of superiority expressed in Deuteronomy. Israel is promised exaltation above all nations of the earth (26:19), to be always at the top and never at the bottom (28:13); people who hear the laws of Israel will say "that great nation is a wise and discerning people" (4:6); "Israel will rule many nations but they will not rule it" (15:6). The book of Deuteronomy depicts Israel as a proud nation, unfearful but feared. In accordance with this, it changes and reworks old sources. In Numbers, the Israelites asked permission from Edom to cross its territory. The Edomites refused and went out against the Israelites in force (Num 20:14–21). In the book of Deuteronomy, the opposite happens: not only do the Israelites pass Edom and buy food there (2:6, 29), but the Edomites fear the Israelites, and the Israelites are asked not to exploit this fact in order to provoke the Edomites (2:4–5; see Weinfeld 1967, pp. 412ff.).

The national pride prevailing in Deuteronomy comes to bold expression in the account of Moses' appointing officers for judging the people. According to Exod 18, the appointment arose from the advice of Jethro, the priest of Midian. In Deut 1:13–17, Moses appoints the officers on his own initiative. Jethro is not mentioned at all because—as A. B. Ehrlich says—"in the Deuteronomist's days it was not glorious to tell the people that a foreigner contrived such a plan" (1909, s.v. Deut 1:9).

Deuteronomic Historiography

The national consciousness that developed in the period of Hezekiah and Josiah set in motion the work of Deuteronomic historiography that pretends to present the nation's history from the Exodus to the end of the monarchic period. The alleged restoration of old Israel at this time awakened a new interest in the past of the nation. In order to implement the task it was necessary to collect various traditions from the great Israel in the north, and this was done with the help of the people from the north who migrated to the revived capital (see above). The scribes who were engaged in this work divided the history into three periods—conquest, judges, and monarchy—a division accepted until our days. This schematic division, however, is the product of the systematic thought of the scribes. The material was presented in a way that would suit the tripartite division of the history of Israel in its land; the material itself, however, cannot be subjected to such division. The conquest—as is well known—continued during the time of the Judges and was not limited to the days of Joshua.

In order to present the period of the conquest, these scribes collected traditions from northern sanctuaries such as Gilgal, Shechem, and Šiloh (not from Bethel or from Dan, which were associated with the cult of the golden calves) and these were preferred to the Judaic tradition of Judg 1. I have tried to show elsewhere that Judg 1 constitutes a tendentious Judahite document about the conquest, which ignores the achievement of the Ephraimites under the aegis of Joshua. This tradition was not incorporated into the original Deuteronomic historiography, which completes the conquest with the farewell speech of Joshua in Josh 23 and opens the period of the Judges with the sermon in Judg 2:6ff. Judges 1:1–2:5 contains, by contrast, ancient material that was added as an appendix in later times.

The Deuteronomic scribes utilized northern traditions in order to render an ideal picture of total conquest of the land under Joshua, the leader of the house of Joseph. The traditions themselves do not draw such a picture, for the wars described are limited to the area of Benjamin and to the valley of Ayalon southwest of Mount Ephraim on the one hand (chaps. 2–10), and to the battle of the waters of Merom on the other (chap. 11). The scribes, however, arranged the traditions in such a way as to create the impression of a systematic military operation: a battle in the center with its ramification to the south, which permitted the conquest of the center and the south (Josh 10); and a battle in the north, which completed the conquest of the whole land from Baal Gad in the valley of Lebanon down to Mount Halaq at Seir in the south (Josh 11:16–17). The individual traditions themselves utilized by the author do not feature such a blitz.

In order to describe the settlement of the tribes in the various parts of the land, the Deuteronomic scribes utilized various administrative lists from various periods and retrojected them to the time of Joshua. Thus, for example, the list of settlements used to present Joshua's allotment of Judah (chap 15) is actually an administrative list of Judah from the time of Josiah (for the Josianic background of this list see Alt 1959). Analysis of the list shows that it could not have been composed before the times of Josiah. Thus, for example, the city of En Gedi mentioned in the list (v 62) was nonexistent before the seventh century (cf. Mazar 1975a, pp. 65–90). Most of the lists are from the time of the monarchy, and the delineations of the tribes' borders as well as the list of the levitical cities are from the time of the united monarchy (cf. Kallai 1986). They were used by the scribes anachronistically as descriptions of settlements at the beginning of the Israelites' settlement in the land of Canaan.

It is hardly necessary to mention that the presentation of the period of Judges is mainly based on documents and traditions from the north. For the period of David and Solomon the scribes drew from the Jerusalemite archives, but for the Israelite kingdom they were dependent on northern material, including prophetic stories. Only when they reached the period of Hezekiah and Josiah did they use Judean material again (2 Kgs 18–25). The large proportion of northern material in the Deuteronomic historiography teaches us that the writers availed themselves of contacts with the north in their work. In fact, the bulk of Tetrateuchal traditions also originated in the north; but these had already crystallized before the Deuteronomic movement started its activity. The author of Deuteronomy used these traditions and reworked them according to his proclivities.

The School of Scribes

The character of the circle involved in the Deuteronomic creation emerges from the fact that the school could not conceive a regime without a king. In contrast to the other law codes in the Tetrateuch, in which no indication of a monarchic regime can be found, Deuteronomy presents laws that reflect a typical monarchic rule. We find here not only the law of the king but a whole set of legal pericopes reflecting a monarchic state: laws about courts of justice and the supreme court, about priesthood and prophecy, and about the military. It is true, all of these laws still preserve the old premonarchic reality, as has been seen by M. Noth;[21] but their manner of presentation reflects the Hezekianic–Josianic period.

The cultic laws in chaps. 12–18 are all presented in a revised form, in the light of the centralization that was put into practice by royal initiative in the period discussed here. The laws about the tithe, the firstborn, Passover, and the festivals are in fact brought up in order to stress the innovation following the reform (see above).

On the whole the Deuteronomic code constitutes a manual for the king and the people. Sacred matters are dealt with here insofar as they touch the religious-social aspect of national life. Methods of sacrifice and performance of the sacral service, which are so extensively discussed in the priestly code, are altogether missing in Deuteronomy (see above). This is not the concern of the author of the book, whose main interest is the education of the king and his people. The educational vein stems from the scribal circles, which were interested in those days not only in secular, but also in religious education (cf. Weinfeld 1972a, pp. 298–306). Confirmation is to be found in Jer 8:8, where wise men and scribes are mentioned as being involved in the Torah of YHWH. It is interesting to note in this context that the verb "to learn *(lmd),*" which is so characteristic of wisdom literature, is not found at all in the Tetrateuch and yet

[21] M. Noth, *Die Gesetze im Pentateuch, ihre Varaussetzungen und ihr Sinn,* Schriften der Königsberger Gelehrten Gesellschaft, Geisteswissenschaftliche Klasse 17 (Königsberg, 1940), part 2: *Gesammelte Studien zum Alten Testament* (1957), pp. 9–141.

is prominent in Deuteronomy. Furthermore, the Torah is here defined as wisdom and understanding (4:6); it is no wonder therefore that this book speaks so often about writing on stones (27:1–8), door frames (6:9; 11:20), books (31:9), and the like. Deuteronomy is the only book of the Pentateuch that refers to a written Torah as comprising the divine will (see above).

The most interesting item in this context, however, is the copy of the law that the king is obliged to write for himself in Deut 17:18–19. Recently I have had the opportunity to study the so-called *peri basileias* literary genre, that is, the type of educational literature designed for kings (Weinfeld 1978–79a). It has become clear to me that this type of literature, so prevalent in the Hellenistic period, has its roots in the cultures of the ancient Near East. In Mesopotamia as well as in Egypt, we find instructions (some kind of Torah = *sb3yt* in Egyptian) for the king written by court counselors and scribes. Prominent topics in this instruction were just behavior and warnings against greediness and against the oppression of his subjects. Most instructive is the so-called "Advice to the Prince" *(Fürstenspiegel)* in the Mesopotamian literature from the library of Ashurbanipal (the seventh century B.C.E.). Here the king is warned to listen to his counselors, not to covet money, and not to mobilize into the army people of Nippur, Sippar, or Babylon. As has been most recently shown by E. Reiner (1982), this text was canonical in Mesopotamia; we find it quoted in a middle Babylonian text from the twelfth century B.C.E., which says that the ancestors handed down these tablets whereon it is written that people of Nippur, Babylon, and Sippar should not be mistreated (Weidner 1935, pp. 141–42). In this text allusion is made to a foreigner *(nakru)* who is named king, which brings to mind the commandment not to appoint a foreigner as king (Deut 17:15). In a recently discovered letter to Esarhaddon, king of Assyria (see Reiner 1982), the author cited the rights of the cities Sippar, Nippur, and Babylon and says, "let the Lord of Kings . . . look up the tablet: 'if the king does not give heed to justice,' " which is the beginning of the *Fürstenspiegel;* the writer goes on to say that the tablet is true *(tuppu kīnu)* and that they should read it to the king.

What is more, the colophon to the *Fürstenspiegel* says on behalf of the king, "I wrote it in tablets . . . and put it in my palace to my constant reading."[22] Similar colophons are attached to other ritual texts, which may indicate that the Assyrian king was obliged—as it were—to read texts pertaining to religious behavior and apparently having to do with national cultic-religious policy. The Hittite kings also had to comply with the instructions written in the books. Thus we hear Muwatalli, the Hittite king, saying, "whatever I find written in the tablets . . . I will do," and similarly Muršili: "what concerns laws/covenants of the temple . . . the scribes started to violate them and I have written them anew" (see above). This reminds us of Josiah's eagerness to fulfill the words

[22] *ina tuppāni aštur . . . abrēma, ana tamarti šitassiya qereb ekalliya ukîn,* cf. Hunger 1968, no. 319.

written in the book of the Torah discovered in the Temple. In Egypt too we hear about the king being subjected to instructions written in a book. Hecataeus of Abdera (300 B.C.E.) tells us that the Egyptian king had to obey instructions written in the books and that he had to listen to recitations from holy books in order to practice the fear of god.[23] This reminds us of the law of the king in Deut 17:19: "and he shall read out of the copy of the Torah all his days of life so that he will learn to fear the Lord." From Deut 31:10–13 we learn that the leader—according to the *M. Soṭ* 7:8 the king—ought to recite the Deuteronomic code every seventh year before the assembled people. It is thus clear that the same book that the king read for himself was also recited before the people. This means that the book of Deuteronomy was a manual for both king and people, which seems to be a particularly Israelite phenomenon. Would it be legitimate to suppose that the scribes of the courts of Hezekiah and Josiah are responsible for this transition, from a book for the king to a book for the whole people? One thing is clear: this book turned out to be the binding law code for the next generations—not the priestly or holiness code—perhaps because Josiah put it into practice by means of a solemn covenant in Jerusalem (2 Kgs 23:1–3).

14. The Land in Deuteronomy

The land plays a most important role in the book of Deuteronomy. According to Deuteronomy the laws could be implemented only in the land of Israel, as may be learned from the opening sentence of the code, which states that the laws to be presented are designated for the people after they enter the land (12:1). In the desert, where the Israelites live in the Mosaic period, there is a lawless situation: "everyone doing what he pleases" (12:8). This view is in opposition to the priestly author of the holiness code, who opens like Deuteronomy's author with the law of sacrifice (Lev 17) but designates it for the people "in the camp" of the desert (vv 2–7); contrast also Num 28:6, where the regular whole offering *(ʿôlat tāmīd)* is made at Mount Sinai (contrast Amos 5:25; Jer 7:22). The difference between the priestly author and the Deuteronomic one is also reflected in their view concerning the time and place of the delivery of the laws to the Israelites. According to Lev 26:46 (compare Lev 27:39), the laws were given to the Israelites at Mount Sinai, while according to Deuteronomy the laws were given to the people in the plains of Moab on the verge of crossing the Jordan (1:1; 4:45–46; 28:69). In accordance with the Deuteronomic principle the laws were inscribed on stones at Mount Ebal (27:1–8; cf. Josh 8:30–35),

[23] Diodorus Siculus 1.70. For this source and its parallels in Deut 17:19 and the Temple Scroll from Qumran (Yadin 1977, 57:1ff.), see Weinfeld 1980.

while in the previous sources the erection of the stone monuments as well as the writing of the laws take place at Mount Sinai (Exod 24:4).

The Land Is Given on Condition

The gift of the land to Israel, according to the old sources, is a perpetual, unconditional gift (Gen 13:5; 17:8; 48:4). It was promised to the Patriarchs by God because of their devotion and loyalty to him (Gen 22:16, 18; 26:5). Similarly, David was given a dynasty forever (2 Sam 7:13, 16; 23:5; Ps 89:30; etc.) because he served God with loyalty (1 Kgs 3:6; 9:4; 11:4; etc.). As I have shown elsewhere (1970–72, pp. 184–203), the promises to Abraham and to David belong to the type of "grant" to royal servants who have devoted themselves to their master, the king. These "grant" documents were common in the ancient Near East from the middle of the second millennium onward and, like the biblical promises (Gen 17:8; 48:4), contained the phrase "I grant it to you for your descendants after you throughout the generations" (Gen 17:7–8) or "for your descendants forever *(lzrʿk ʿd ʿwlm)*" (Gen 13:15); compare Deut 1:8.[24] In contrast to the vassal treaty, which constitutes a vassal's obligation to his sovereign, the royal "grant" constitutes a sovereign's obligation to his vassal.

Following the fall of the Northern Kingdom, however, an explanation was sought for the failure of the promise, and the explanation given was that the realization of the promise to the Patriarchs was conditioned a priori by the fulfillment of the obligatory covenant of the Israelites at Sinai, in which they committed themselves to keep the laws of God. Two covenants, which existed separately—the covenant of God with the Patriarchs on land (grant type) and the covenant of Israel with God on law (vassal type)—were thus combined and were seen as dependent one on another (cf. 4:25–27; 8:19–20; 11:8–10, 13–17, 22–25; 28:63; 29:24–27; 30:17–18). The same thing happened with the Davidic covenant. After the fall of Jerusalem, the divine promise for an eternal dynasty to David, which was originally unconditional (2 Sam 7:13–15), was understood as conditional by the fulfillment of the Sinaitic covenant (1 Kgs 2:3–4; 8:23–25).

Although the loss of land is a punishment for the violation of the covenant, which means abrogation of the law in general, principal sins are specified for which the people will go into exile. Thus according to the holiness code the land will be desolate and people will go to exile because of not keeping the laws of land release (Lev 26:34–35). Deuteronomy, however, specifies idolatry as the principal sin for which to lose the land: "Beware lest your heart be seduced and you turn away to serve other gods. . . . For YHWH's anger will flare up against you, and he will shut up the skies and there will be no rain and the land

[24] For these legal formulas in Alalach, Ugarit, and Elephantine, see Weinfeld 1970–72, pp. 199–200.

will not yield its produce; and you will perish quickly from the good land that YHWH is giving you" (11:16–17; cf. 4:25–28; 29:23–27; 30:17–18).

Going into exile and desolation of the land are also specified as punishment for betrayal in the vassal treaties. Thus we read in *VTE,* lines 538–44, "may your seed and the seed [of your sons] and daughters perish from the land (if you violate the treaty)" (see Weinfeld 1972a, p. 133). Similar threats occur in the Hittite treaties with their vassals: "may they break you like reeds, may your name and your seed . . . perish from the land" (Weidner 1923, pp. 34–35 lines 64–66). The latter two curses, "breaking like a reed" and "perishing from the land," are found together in Deuteronomic historiography: "YHWH will strike Israel . . . like a reed in water and will uproot Israel from this good land that he gave to their fathers" (1 Kgs 14:16).

The whole Deuteronomic corpus actually revolves around the fate of the land of Israel. As has been indicated above, the Deuteronomic law is given to the people for observance after the entrance into the land (Deut 12:1). The promised land and the occupation of the land are dependent on the observance of the law (4:26; 11:17; 28:63; 30:19). The aim of the Deuteronomic historiography is to describe the fate of the land of Israel following the sins of the nation. The sins of the period of the Judges caused the curtailment of the land within its ideal borders. The "remaining land" *(hʾrṣ hnšʾrt,* Josh 13:2), namely, the coastal area and the Lebanon (Josh 13:2–5; Judg 3:3), were taken away from the Israelites forever because of their sins after the conquest (Josh 23:12, Judg 2:21–29). By the same token, the sin of the northern Israelites caused the loss of the territories of the north (2 Kgs 17:7–23), while the fall of Jerusalem and the exile of Judah were caused by the sins of Judah (2 Kgs 21:12–15; see Weinfeld 1984a, pp. 120–22). It is this consciousness of sin on the part of the Israelites from the conquest to the exile that motivated the writing of the Deuteronomic historiography.

It should be remarked, however, that the loss of land is not presented in Deuteronomy as final. If Israel returns to God in the exile, God will recall the promise to the Patriarchs and will bring them back to their land (Deut 4:27–31; 30:1–10). True, these are late texts (cf. above), but the idea itself may be of early origin (compare Hos 14:2–8, and see above).

The Good Land

In Deuteronomy the land is depicted not just as "a land of milk and honey," as in the previous sources (Exod 3:8, 17; 13:5; 33:3; Lev 20:24; Num 13:27; 14:8) but as a rich land in every respect: a land of grain, wines, and all sorts of fruits as well as of natural resources such as iron and copper (8:7–9). Unlike Egypt, which is flat and rainless, with only the Nile incessantly flowing through a monotonous landscape, the land of Israel has a nice variegated landscape: "hills and vales" through which brooks spring forth (8:7), soaking water from heaven (11:11). The comparison is a theological and not a real empirical one: the rain from heaven expresses divine providence. The Egyptians developed a theology of opposite nature. According to their view, the barbarians and the animals depend on the water from heaven, whereas the water for the Egyptians comes from the underground (see the NOTES to 11:10–12). Moreover, Deuteronomy's view of Egypt stands in opposition to the other sources of the Pentateuch, where Egypt is represented as a most fertile land: "as the garden of YHWH" (Gen 13:10; cf. Exod 16:3; Num 16:13; 20:5).

Inheritance of the Land

The idea of the inheritance of the land *(yrš hʾrṣ)* is most prominently expressed in the book of Deuteronomy (see Weinfeld 1972a, pp. 341–42). It refers not only to the conquest of the land but also to its possession after the conquest, as for example in 16:20: "Justice, justice shall you pursue, that you may live and occupy [= keep] the land *(wyršt ʾt hʾrṣ)*." The root *yrš* is to be understood here as habitation and possession of the land, as in Pss 25:13; 37:11, 22, 29, 34; compare also Isa 57:13; 60:21; 1 Chr 28:8, and not the occupation by conquest. "Life" in the full sense of the word (cf. Weinfeld 1972a, pp. 306–13) is possible for Israel only in its land. The Deuteronomic expression "to lengthen one's days *(hʾrk ymym)*" is usually accompanied with "upon the land" (4:40; 5:30; 11:9; 25:15; 32:47), and conversely "to perish" is accompanied with "from the land" (4:26; 11:17; 28:63; 31:18; cf. Josh 23:13, 16).

15. THE IDEA OF THE ELECTION OF ISRAEL

The particularity of Israel was expressed in the ancient Israelite sources by expressions such as "know *(ydʿ)*" and "separate *(hbdyl)*." Thus Abraham was "known *(ydʿ)*" by God, which means singled out in order that his descendants might do justice and righteousness (Gen 18:19). The same expression is found in Amos 3:2: "Only you have I known [= singled out] of all the families of the earth." In the holiness code the particularity of Israel is expressed by the phrase separate/set apart *(hbdyl)*: "I have set you apart from other peoples to be mine" (Lev 20:26). In Deuteronomy this idea is for the first time expressed by the verb "elect *(bḥr)*." It is linked here (7:6; 14:2; 26:18) to the idea of *segullah* ("special possession," *sigiltu* in Akkadian), which is rooted in the ancient Near Eastern political sphere, in which the sovereign singles out his vassal by giving him a status of *sglt*,[25] which means *peculium* 'special property'. Theologically, the peculiar status of the people was defined as "holy people *(ʿm qdwš)*" (Deut 7:6,

[25] *PRU* 5, no. 60:7–12; see the NOTE to 7:6.

14:1, 21). In Exod 19:5–6, the *segullah* is linked to *gôy gdwš* 'holy nation', but there the special status of the people serves as a reward for being loyal to the covenant (19:5a), while in Deuteronomy the election serves as a motivation for observing the laws, especially laws of purity and rejection of pagan practices: "You shall not eat *nĕbelāh* . . . because you are a holy people to YHWH your God" (14:21; cf. 14:1–2 [against self-mutilation] and 7:1–5 [against idolatry]).

A distinction should also be made between the holiness-code concept of holiness and the Deuteronomic one. While the holiness code urges the people to sanctify themselves and to be holy—"you shall be holy *(qdšym thyw)*" (Lev 19:2) or "you shall be holy to me" (Lev 20:26), "you shall sanctify yourselves and be holy *(whtqdštm whyytm qdšym)*" (Lev 11:44), and hence not to contaminate their souls with impurity—Deuteronomy reverses the order and urges the people not to contaminate themselves because *they are holy to God* by virtue of their election because "you are a holy people to YHWH your God *(ky ʿm qdwš ʾth lYHWH ʾlyhk)*" (7:6; 14:1, 21). In the holiness code, holiness depends on observing purity (compare also Exod 22:30: "You shall be holy to me, you should not eat flesh torn by beasts"), whereas according to Deuteronomy observance of purity is bound to the holiness of the people, which is an established fact. It is true that from the point of view of piety the concept of holiness in the holiness code is more intense: Israel has to deserve to be holy and is not holy automatically (cf. Milgrom 1973, p. 158), whereas in Deuteronomy the holiness is inherent in the people and is not conditioned by preserving purity. One should admit, however, that in both cases the privilege of being holy involves obligation *(noblesse oblige).* This applies also to Gen 18:19 and Amos 3:2, where the singling out of the people means responsibility and self-perfection.

It should be added here that there was an awareness of the moral danger that the election might involve. The consciousness of election is apt to foster a superiority complex; therefore the author of Deuteronomy, when speaking about election, is eager to add that it is not the virtue and strength of the nation that caused the election, but God's love for the Patriarchs is the main reason for choosing their descendants (Deut 7:7–8; 9:4–5, see the COMMENT and NOTE there).

In the Second Temple period, the election of Israel was interpreted as God's giving of Torah and Sabbath to Israel. God's bestowal of Torah and Sabbath upon Israel was seen as a graceful act and a sign of election (Neh 9:7–14). This idea is also attested in a passage from the book of Jubilees of liturgical nature (2:31–32) and constitutes an important element in the festive prayers of Qumran (4Q 503:24–25, Baillet, DJD 7) and in the conventional Jewish liturgy for Sabbaths and festivals (SPB, p. 339).[26] The declaration of election opens also the benediction before the recital of the Torah *(SPB,* p. 84; see below).

[26] See M. Weinfeld, "Prayers and Religious Practice in the Qumran Sect," in *Symposium on the Dead Sea Scrolls* (Haifa, 1988).

Besides Deuteronomy, the doctrine of election is amply attested in the prophecy of Deutero-Isaiah (41:8, 9; 43:10; 44:1, 2; 45:4; 48:10; 49:7). There is, however, a substantial difference between the function of election in each of these works. In Deuteronomy, the concept of election comes to intensify the peculiarity of Israel. To foreign nations God assigned the luminaries for worship, while Israel was chosen as an inheritance by the one true God; therefore they are warned not to worship the sun and moon, as the nations do (4:19–20; cf. 29:25). In contrast, for Deutero-Isaiah the election does not serve only as a means for distinction of Israel; rather it is conceived as a vehicle for spreading the faith of the God of Israel among the nations: "It is too little that you should be my servant so that I raise up the tribes of Jacob. . . . I will make you a light of nations that my salvation may reach the ends of the earth . . . to the honor of YHWH . . . to the holy one of Israel *who elected you*" (49:6–7; cf. also 42:1–4; 43:10; 44:1–5). Thus the election was seen not as an instrument for the preservation of Israel's particuliarity but as a medium for bringing the nations to the true faith of Israel (cf. Zech 2:14–15; 8:20–23). In the times in which there was no longer danger of pagan influence on Israel, Israel could think of influencing other nations by monotheism (see Weinfeld 1964b).

16. Deuteronomy and Wisdom Literature

The book of Deuteronomy has many verbal and conceptual affinities to wisdom literature. Thus, for example, the term "abomination of YHWH *(twʿbt YHWH),*" which is found in the OT only in Deuteronomy and in the book of Proverbs, has its parallels in Sumerian wisdom literature, in the Akkadian proverbs (cf. Hallo 1985–86), and in the Egyptian wisdom instructions of Amenemope (cf. Weinfeld 1972a, pp. 265–69). As R. Yaron has demonstrated,[27] many abomination proverbs are structured as tricolons, as for example Prov 17:15:

> he that justifies the wicked
> and he that condemns the just
> both are an abomination for YHWH,

which is to be compared with the Mesopotamian proverb:

> the one who perverts justice
> the one who loves an unjust verdict
> it is an abomination to Utu [Šamaš]. (See Young 1972.)

[27] R. Yaron, "The Climactic Tricolon," *JJS* 37 (1985): 153–59.

Especially relevant for our purpose is Prov 20:10:

> alternate weights *(ʾbn wʾbn)*
> one alternate measure *(ʾyph wʾyph)*
> both are abomination to YHWH.

The latter has been legally reformulated by Deuteronomy:

> You shall not have in your bay alternate weights *(ʾbn wʾbn),* great and small
> You shall not have in your house alternate measures *(ʾyph wʾyph),* great and small . . .
> for abomination to YHWH is everyone who does such things. (25:13–16)

In order to adjust the matter to the spirit of the book, Deuteronomy adds the motive clause of retribution (v 15).

There are other significant overlappings in contents between Deuteronomy and wisdom. Laws that have no parallels in the Tetrateuch have their parallels in wisdom literature. Thus the injunctions about "neither adding to nor subtracting" from the word of God is found only in Deut 4:2; 13:1 and in Prov 30:5–6 (cf. Eccl 3:14; Weinfeld 1972a, pp. 261–65). The injunctions about removal of boundaries (Deut 19:14; cf. 27:17) and falsification of weights and measures (25:13–16) have their verbal parallels in Prov 22:28; 23:10; 11:1; and 20:10, 23, and in Egyptian wisdom (Amenemope 18.15–19.3, Lichtheim 1973–76, 2.157). Furthermore, as in Deuteronomy and in Proverbs, the Amenemope exhortations about falsifying weights and measures are motivated—as indicated above—by the same rationale: "for it is an abomination to YHWH" (Deut 25:13–16; Prov 11:1; 20:10, 23) and "abomination of Re" in the Egyptian wisdom of Amenemope (18.15–19.3).

The warning against vows and cultic commitments in Deut 23:22–26 has its parallel in Eccl 5:1–5. Although Ecclesiastes is a late book, it contains a great deal of early material (cf. 9:7–9 with the Gilgamesh epic, *ANET,* p. 90 and with the Egyptian Song of the Harper [Lichtheim 1973–76, 1.193–97] and cf. the Mesopotamian parallel to Eccl 4:9–12.)[28] Warnings against rash declarations and vows are a frequent topic of Israelite wisdom (Prov 20:25; 12:13; 18:7) and non-Israelite wisdom alike; compare the Babylonian injunction "guard your lips, do not utter solemn oaths . . . for what you say in a moment will follow you afterwards" *(BWL,* pp. 104, 131–33). The motivation for restraint in this area is distinctly utilitarian, typical of sapiential literature. There is consequently no reason to see Pentateuchal influence on this passage in Ecclesiastes. The style of

[28] A. Shaffer, "The Mesopotamian Background of Lamentations 4:9–12," *EI* 8 (1967): 246–50; idem, "New Light on the 'Three-Ply Cord,' " *EI* 9 (1969): 159–60.

the exhortation in Eccl 5:4: "It is better *(ṭwb)* that you should not vow than that you should vow and not pay," is sapiential and is characterized by the gnomic dicta that begin with the word "better *(ṭwb)*."[29] While using this maxim, Deuteronomy reworked it in order to accommodate it to the religious aims of the book. In place of the neutral sapiential rationale: "for [God] has no pleasure with fools" (5:3), the author of Deuteronomy has supplied it with a religious rationale: "for YHWH your God will surely require it from you" (23:22).

Another law that parallels a sapiential exhortation is Deut 23:16: "You shall not surrender a slave to his master," which corresponds to Prov 30:10: "do not slander a servant to his master" (cf. LXX, Syriac; Weinfeld 1972a, pp. 272–73). Such prescriptions of humane nature are characteristic of wisdom literature, and it is quite strange to find them in a legal code, which by nature is concerned with stabilizing interclass relationships rather than with prescribing laws that would undermine them.[30]

The predilection for wisdom in Deuteronomy is recognizable in several other places. First, observance of the commandments equals wisdom and understanding (4:6), and the people of Israel, who observe the laws and the commandments, are considered "a wise and discerning *(ʿm ḥkm wnbwn)*" people (4:6b). (The same term is applied to Joseph [Gen 41:39] and to Solomon [1 Kgs 3:12].) This equation implies some kind of identification of wisdom with law, which took place in Israel during the seventh century B.C.E., the period in which scribes and wise men began to take an active part in the composition of legal literature (cf. Jer 8:8, see above; cf. Weinfeld 1972a, pp. 150–51).

Second, according to Deut 1:9–18, Moses appoints "men who are wise, discerning, and experienced *(ḥkmym, nbwnim, ydʿym)*" in order to judge the people. In the old tradition of Exod 18:13–27, the appointed judges are to possess different qualities: "capable men who fear God, trustworthy men who hate gain." According to Deuteronomy, leaders and judges must possess intellectual qualities, wisdom, understanding, and knowledge, traits that characterize the leader and judge in wisdom literature (Prov 8:15–16). The same attitude is revealed when Deut 16:19 is compared with Exod 23:8. While Exod 23 reads, "You should take no bribes for bribes blind them *that have sight (pqḥym),*" the parallel in Deut 16 reads, "You shall take no bribes, for bribes blind *the wise (ḥkmym).*" The author of Deuteronomy believes that the qualification of a judge must be intellectual in character.

The same conception is met in the Deuteronomic historiography. Solomon is given wisdom and understanding so that he might judge the people (1 Kgs 3:4–15; see Weinfeld 1972a, pp. 246–47). Like Moses, who complains of the burden of governing a people who are "as numerous as the stars in the sky"

[29] On the *ṭwb* sayings see W. Zimmerli, "Zur Struktur der alttestamentliche Weisheit," *ZAW* 51 (1933): 192–94.

[30] For the duty to extradite slaves cf. CH 15–20; HL 22–24.

(Deut 1:9–10), Solomon speaks of the difficulty to judge a people "who cannot be counted . . . for multitude" (1 Kgs 3:8–9). Like the author of Deut 1:9–18, the Deuteronomic editor in 1 Kgs 3:4–15 regards wisdom and understanding as the principal requisite for the competent functioning of the judiciary.

All of this might support my thesis that scribes and wise men were engaged in the composition of Deuteronomy (see above).

17. Deuteronomy and the Reform of Josiah

The reign of Josiah, son of Amon, king of Judah (640–609 B.C.E.), signified a great national revival, and the author of the Books of Kings writes in his estimation of Josiah, "No king before him had turned back to YHWH as he did, *with all his heart and soul and might,* following the whole law of Moses; and after him no one arose like him" (2 Kgs 23:25). We find a similar estimation in connection with Hezekiah: "He put his trust in YHWH the God of Israel; there was nobody like him among all the kings of Judah who succeeded him or among those who had gone before him. He clung to YHWH and did not turn away from following him; *and he kept the commandments which YHWH had given to Moses*" (2 Kgs 18:5–6). But in contrast to the estimation of Hezekiah, in which his faithfulness to the Commandments of Moses is referred to in a general way, the appreciation of Josiah is specifically connected with the book (Deuteronomy) that was discovered during his days. The measure of the appreciation of Josiah is formed according to the ideal precept found in Deut 6:5: "You shall love YHWH your God with all your heart and with all your soul and with all your might"; and, indeed, it is explicitly said of Josiah that he followed "the whole Torah of Moses *(kkl twrt Mošeh),*" an expression that points to the book of Deuteronomy.[31] In contrast, the expression in the estimation of Hezekiah—"He kept the commandments *(mṣwtyw)* which YHWH had given to Moses"—is taken, not from the book of Deuteronomy, but rather from the priestly literature; compare: "These are the commandments *(hmṣwt)* that YHWH commanded Moses . . . on Mount Sinai" (Lev 27:34). Indeed, the decisive difference between the reform of Hezekiah and that of Josiah lies in the fact that the former was not authorized by a book, whereas with the latter it is emphasized several times that the actions were performed in accordance with the book found in the House of YHWH (2 Kgs 23:3, 21, 24).

Josiah holds an important place in the history of Israel, not only because he

[31] Cf. 2 Kgs 14:6, "as it is written in the Torah of Moses," and that refers there to Deut 24:16.

succeeded in freeing himself from the yoke of Assyria and in making "the law of Moses" predominant throughout his kingdom, but also because he succeeded in expanding the border of the kingdom at the expense of the Assyrian provinces in northern Israel. According to 2 Kgs 23:19, Josiah removed the shrines of the high places *(bty bmwt)* in the cities of Samaria after having destroyed the altar at Bethel (v 15), whereas, according to 2 Chr 34:6, he even reached as far as the cities of Naphtali in the north. From the description of Josiah's encounter with Pharaoh Necho (2 Kgs 23:29–30; 2 Chr 35:20–24), it is difficult to know whether Megiddo was in the hands of Josiah before Pharaoh Necho arrived at the place, or whether it was still an Egyptian base during the expedition of Psammetichus I in 616 B.C.E., and in the year 609 B.C.E. Josiah arrived at the place in order to curb the expedition of Pharaoh Necho, who was coming from the south to assist Assyria in its war with Babylon (cf. the discussion of Malamat 1979, pp. 205–9). In any case, the fact of Josiah's daring to stand against pharaoh, king of Egypt, teaches us not only of his courage, but also of the political campaign on an international dimension initiated by this king; and perhaps he aligned himself with Babylon, in an action similar to Hezekiah's (2 Kgs 20:12–15; cf. Malamat 1983, pp. 228–34).

We can also learn of the ramified military enterprises of Josiah and of the extension of his dominion in the land of Israel from archaeological finds unearthed in recent years. It appears from archaeological excavations that Josiah established feudal properties along the coast of Philistia. In the so-called stronghold of Ḥašabyahu, a coastal fortress situated fifteen kilometers south of Yavneh-Yam, an ostracon containing the complaint of an Israelite hired workman to the superintendent appointed over him was discovered along with Greek ceramic wares, revealing the existence of a Greek mercenary force in the army of Josiah (see Naveh 1960 and 1962, pp. 27–32). We also learn of this mercenary force from the Arad inscriptions, which speak of Kittim (of Aegean stock) who received supplies for the needs of their stay in the various fortresses at the borders (cf. Aharoni 1975, pp. 12–13). A Greek ceramic attesting the existence of Greek mercenaries in the area was found at Tel Melḥatah, which is south of Arad (cf. Kochavi 1977, p. 774). Unwalled settlements from the period of Josiah were discovered southeast of Gaza (Gofnah 1970), and in addition it has become clear that Josiah ruled over Gezer (Lance 1971, p. 330), and that in the south his sovereignty extended as far as Kadesh-Barnea, where he established a great fortress (Cohen 1981).

It is also possible to draw a conclusion on the extent of the expansion of Judah during this period from the list in Ezra 2 (= Neh 7), in which we find that the cities of Bethel and Jericho, which had belonged to the kingdom of Ephraim, as well as the cities of the coastal plain, Lod, Hadid, and Ono, were now considered to be part of Judah (vv 28, 33). The borders of Judah, as they are represented in this list, undoubtedly go back to the period of Josiah and remained unchanged until the destruction of Jerusalem (cf. Kallai 1960, pp. 74–75).

It appears that Josiah also extended his sovereignty over parts of the Gilead in Transjordan (Ginsberg 1950), an occurrence that ties in with the point of view embodied in the book of Deuteronomy, which considered that Transjordan was an integral part of the land of Israel and that it should be treated the same way as Canaan (see above).

The dominion of Josiah over extensive areas in the land of Israel is also reflected in the tradition of the author of the Books of Chronicles: "Josiah removed all the abominations *from the whole territories of the Israelites (mkl hʾrṣwt ʾšr lbny yśrʾl)"* (2 Chr 34:33) and, as I indicated above, the author of the Chronicles was describing Josiah's rule as extending as far as Naphtali in the north. Although it is true that there exists in the Books of Chronicles a tendency to describe the territorial expansion of Judah at every opportunity (the periods of David and Solomon, of Asa, Hezekiah, and Josiah; cf. Japhet 1977, pp. 244–77); one nevertheless need not necessarily see in these descriptions pure invention. The fact that the author of the Books of Chronicles specifies an enlarged dominion in relation to Josiah in particular shows that he had before him traditions and evidence of the greatness of this king.

We learn of the expansion of Josiah's kingdom northward and of the hopes for a renewal of the whole kingdom of Israel from Jeremiah's prophecies of consolation, which concern northern Israel (Jer 3:14–16; chaps. 30–31) and, as scholars since P. Volz (in his commentary *KAT,* 1922) have already understood, these prophecies belong to the period of the expansion of Josiah. The prophecy in Jer 3:6ff. begins with the words "The Lord said to me in the days of King Josiah" in the course of a plea for the cause of Israel and an arraignment of Judah. In the continuation we find Jeremiah's appeal to the northern tribes to return to Zion:

> "Return, faithless people," declared the Lord,
> For I am your husband.
> I will choose you—one from a town and two from a clan
> and bring you to Zion." (v 14)[32]

An entreaty such as this was certainly not proclaimed in a vacuum but, rather, against the background of appropriate political circumstances, such as the liberation of the northern tribes from Assyrian subjugation.

The same background can be discerned in Jer 30–31. Here we find clear allusions to the throwing off of the yoke of Assyria and to the renewed unification of the community of Israel as it was in the time of David. Thus we read in Jer 30:7–10,

[32] For the historical background of the prophecy see Cazelles 1968, pp. 147–58.

Ah, that day is awesome
There is none like it!
It is a time of trouble *for Jacob,*
But he shall be delivered from it.
In that day . . . I will break the yoke from off your neck,
And I will rip off your bonds,
strangers shall no longer make slaves of them,
Instead they shall serve YHWH their God,
And David, the king whom I will raise up for them.
But you,
Have no fear *My servant Jacob*—declares YHWH
Be not dismayed, *O Israel!* I will deliver you from far away
Your folk from their land of captivity,
And *Jacob* shall again have calm
And quiet with none to trouble him. (Cf. 46:27–28)

What is being referred to here is Jacob or Israel, that is, the northern tribes of Israel, who are in trouble but are about to be delivered from it. This deliverance will be accompanied by a breaking off of the yoke and a ripping off of bonds *(šbr ʿwl wntq mwsrwt),* the concrete meaning of which is release from subjugation to Assyrian imperialism (see Isa 9:3; 10:27; 14:25; Nah 1:3; Jer 28:2ff.).[33] As one can also learn from the continuation of the verse, "strangers shall no longer make slaves of them," it appears that Josiah embodied Israel's hopes for a renewal of the Davidic dynasty, and accordingly the prophet says that instead of serving foreigners, they will serve God and *David their king* (cf. Hos 3:5; Ezek 34:23–24).

The prophecy of consolation contained in the verse, which states that the descendants of Jacob will come from the land of their captivity and that Jacob shall have calm and quiet with no one to trouble him, should be understood according to its plain meaning: the Israelite exiles will return to the land of their birth. The same is true of the following prophecy:

I will restore the fortunes of *Jacob's tents* . . .
His children shall be as of old,
And his community shall be established by My grace . . .
His chieftain shall be one of his own;
His ruler shall come from his midst.
I will bring him near, that he may approach me . . .
You shall be My people,
And I will be your God. (Jer 30:18–22)

[33] For the terms *ʿwl* (= Assyrian *nīru)* and *mwsrwt* (Assyrian *abšanu)* in the sense of subjugation to Assyria, see Weinfeld 1972a, p. 84 n. 4.

Here is expressed the hope that the community of Israel will be established as of old and that their ruler will no longer be a foreigner, but rather a leader from their midst (cf. Weinfeld 1976a, pp. 47–48) who will be close to God; and as a result the covenant between God and Israel will be renewed (for the formula as covenantal, see Weinfeld 1972a, pp. 80–89). This prophecy could be a reference to the covenant of Josiah.

In the prophecy of Jer 31 we find a still clearer reference to the connection that was created at that time between the northern tribes and Jerusalem. Jeremiah envisions watchmen on Mount Ephraim who say, "Come, let us go up to Zion, / To YHWH our God!" (Jer 31:6), a proclamation that contains a sort of acceptance of Jerusalem as the exclusive place for the worship of God (in the wake of the reform). In the continuation we read of the glad tidings to the remnant of Israel: that YHWH will bring them from the northland, and that they will come and shout "on the heights of Zion *(bmrwm Ṣywn)*" and "be radiant over the bounty of the Lord *(wnhrw ʾl ṭwb YHWH)*" (v 11). The latter expression reminds us of the prophecy of Hosea (which might have influenced Jeremiah): "And they will thrill over YHWH, and over His bounty in the days to come *(wpḥdw ʾl YHWH wʾl ṭwbw bʾḥryt hymym)*" (Hos 3:5). The nostalgic descriptions of Rachel weeping for her children and God comforting her by saying that her children will return to their country from the land of their enemy (Jer 31:5ff.), along with the longings and yearnings for Ephraim, the dear son (vv 18–20)—both of these can be understood only against the background of the period of Josiah and the expansion to the north that took place during his days. After the death of Josiah and the frequent troubles that overtook Judah from the period of Jehoiachin onward, there was no longer any place for hopes such as these for the inhabitants of the north.

The Reform

The reform, the crowning achievement of Josiah's activities, is described in 2 Kgs 22–23 and its parallel in 2 Chr 34–35. According to the description in 2 Kgs 22, Josiah's reform began with the discovery of the book of the Torah in the eighteenth year of Josiah, that is, in the year 622 B.C.E. In contrast, we find three stages in the course of the reform in the description in the Book of Chronicles:

1. In the eighth year of his reign, 632 B.C.E., Josiah began "to seek the God of his father David *(ldrwš lʾlhy dwyd ʾbyw)*" (2 Chr 34:3).
2. In the twelfth year of his reign, 628 B.C.E., he began with a purge on traces of idolatry—the high places *(bmwt)*, the sacred poles *(ʾšrym)*, the idols *(pslym)*, and the molten images *(mskwt)* in Judah and Jerusalem (34:3–5) and in other regions of the land of Israel (34:6–7).

3. Finally, in the eighteenth year of his reign, 622 B.C.E., the year in which the book of the Torah was discovered, he made a covenant with God (34:29–33) and celebrated the Passover (35:1–18).

Although one should not generally rely on the dates of events specified by the author of the Books of Chronicles, one can give credence to the chronological schema that is before us here, for it is difficult to suppose that he was likely to invent a sequence of times such as this and even more difficult to understand what his motive for inventing it would have been.[34] In addition, this course of events fits in well with the concatenation of political events of those days, for the twelfth year of Josiah's reign (628/27 B.C.E.), which, according to the author of the Books of Chronicles, was the year in which this king initiated his reform, was also, it appears, the year of the death of Ashurbanipal (cf. Borger 1959 and 1965; Oates 1965; von Soder 1967; and Reade 1970), an incident that undoubtedly caused a ferment in the west (as was generally the case with the death of an emperor). The eighth year of Josiah's reign (632 B.C.E.) also apparently marked a turning point in the history of the Assyrian Empire. It seems that this was the year in which Ashurbanipal abdicated the royal throne—an opportune time for rebellion (cf. Cross and Freedman 1953). Josiah began at this time to eradicate idolatry—in particular in astral worship, which was characteristic of the Assyrian religion—when the collapse of the Assyrian Empire already appeared on the horizon.[35]

At first sight the description in the Books of Chronicles seems to contradict that of 2 Kgs 22–23, according to which the reform was the direct outcome of the discovery of "the book of the Torah." But a closer scrutiny of the text of 2 Kgs 22–23 reveals that there is no substantial contradiction between the two descriptions. It is the arrangement of the material by the editor of the Books of Kings that creates the impression that the discovery of the book led to the reform. In fact, there are actually two sources, each having a different character,

[34] It is true that the dates of the Chronicles are tendentious and cannot be trusted (see M. Cogan 1985); in the present case, however, it is hard to explain why the author would invent three stages of activities were it not for the traditions that lay before him.

[35] I agree with those who contend that Assyria did not enforce its worship on its vassals (cf. M. D. Cogan 1974 and McKay 1973). We must admit, however, that Assyrian and Aramaic religion influenced the local population even without coercion; see Weinfeld 1972b, pp. 144–54. It is true that the Assyrians inclined to exhibit their divine symbols and statues in their occupied territories regardless of the feelings of the native population, and thus it appeared as if they were forced to accept foreign worship. The reasons adduced by H. Spieckermann (1982) for religious coercion by the Assyrians are not convincing. What he interprets as coercion can be seen as a demonstration of the Assyrians' religion in the vassal's state against the will of the local population. By doing this the Assyrians did not intend to uproot the religion and beliefs of the vassal. The fact is that exiled gods were returned to the vassal the moment he acknowledged Assyrian suzerainty.

which are interwoven here: the first source (2 Kgs 22; 23:1–3, 21–25 = account A) is pragmatic and was composed by the editor of the book, as can be inferred from its style and phraseology (this is the deuteronomistic editor); whereas the second source (2 Kgs 23:4–20 = account B), which has a dry and factual character, was undoubtedly taken from the archives of the court of Josiah.[36] In contrast to account A, which is primarily concerned with the glorification of the name of Josiah and does not spare superlatives in order to exceed in his praise (22:2; 23:22, 25), account B presents the bare facts and is not concerned with evaluation and embellishment. The course of events according to account B is more reliable than that of account A, which is later and was written according to the dictates of its ideology, based entirely upon the idea of "the book of the Torah." Account B does not mention the "book of the Torah" even once, in contrast to account A, which entirely revolves around this book found in the House of YHWH and which finds it necessary to stress several times that the activities of Josiah were carried out in accordance with what was written in the "book of the Torah" (23:3, 21, 24). It also contains phrases that we do not find elsewhere apart from the book of Deuteronomy, such as *bkl lbbw wbkl npšw wbkl m'dw* 'with all his heart and soul and might' in v 25, which should be compared with Deut 6:5. In account B there is no reference whatever to the year in which the activities were carried out, in contrast to account A, which takes the trouble to emphasize that the Passover was kept in the eighteenth year of Josiah (23:23). In fact, the editor introduces into his description of what took

[36] Hoffmann 1980 regards 2 Kgs 23:4–20 as a deuteronomistic description and, in his opinion, this is a fictitious collection of passages of the reforms as described by the Deuteronomist on previous occasions. But his arguments are not valid. In the account of 2 Kgs 23:4–20 we find phrases unattested elsewhere in the Deuteronomic historiography. Compare the expressions "environs of Jerusalem *(msby Yrwšlm)*" in v 5; "objects [made for Baal] *(klym)*" in v 5; "shrines of the gates *(bmwt hšʿrym)*" in v 9; "coverings for the Ashera *(btym lʾšrh)*" in v 7; and "the shrines for the male prostitutes *(bmwt hqdšym)*" in v 7. The term "idolatrous priests *(kmrym)*" in v 5 is not attested in the Deuteronomic frame of the Book of Kings and the same is the case with phrases like "put out of action *(hšbyt)*" in vv 5, 11, as well as "defiled *(ṭmʾ)*" in vv 8, 10 and the verb "crushed *(rṣṣ)*" in v 12. The account in 23:4–20 is then not of Deuteronomic stock but an official chronicle of the court of the Temple. The chronicle does not use at all the key terms characteristic of the Deuteronomist, such as the "book of the covenant," "the book of the Torah," or "the Torah of Moses," which are many times repeated in the pragmatic story of 22:1–20 and 23:1–3, 21–25. Hoffmann's eagerness to deny the authenticity of the account in 23:4–20 has caused major distortions. Thus, for example, he argues that the details of the "shrines of the gates which were at the entrance of the gate of Joshua, the city perfect" (v 8) were invented by the deuteronomistic author in order to make us believe that the story is true. This is a very strange argument. On the contrary, such details point to the writer's personal acquaintance with the installations in the city and are a sign of contemporaneity; see Cogan and Tadmor, 1988, 2 Kgs AB p. 287, NOTE to v 8.

place in the eighteenth year of Josiah's reign, the chronicle of 2 Kgs 23:4–20—which appears to survey an undertaking of several years in duration—in order to create the impression that all of the activities of this king were carried out in the year of the discovery of the book of the Torah, which was the eighteenth year of his reign.

The author of the Books of Kings was interested in creating the impression that it was the book of the Torah that stood behind this important enterprise of Josiah and therefore dovetailed the section on the discovery of the book with the account of the purification of the cult and its centralization in order to create an association of ideas between the discovery of the book and the facts of the reform. Likewise, the author of the Books of Chronicles intentionally arranged the material according to a purpose. Out of the seventeen verses that are devoted to the purification of the cult and its centralization in the Second Book of Kings, the author of the Books of Chronicles included only five (2 Chr 34:3–7). His motives are clear. He omitted the known facts of the eradication of astral worship in the Temple because, according to this view, toward the end of his days Manasseh had repented and purified the Temple from alien gods, primarily the astral images (cf. Gressmann 1924, pp. 315–16), and therefore it remained for Josiah only to destroy the rest of the abominations, not only in Jerusalem and Judah, but also in the whole territory of the Israelites (34:33). In addition, the ceremony of the Passover was most important for the author of the Chronicles —cult ritual stands at the center of his work (cf. Japhet 1977, pp. 370–74)—and accordingly, he developed the subject so that it comprised a complete chapter. The two historiographers, therefore, worked each according to his particular tendency and perspective, although one should note that the author of the Book of Kings did not add things, as the author of the Books of Chronicles was accustomed to do, but rather arranged the sources in such a way that it would appear as though Josiah began to purify the city and the land from foreign cults as a result of the discovery of the book of the Torah.

The account of 2 Kgs 23:4–20 has a unified literary structure. It opens with the liquidation of the cult objects in Jerusalem (v 4) and concludes with the king's return to Jerusalem (v 20). From this we learn that the writer of the account collected the facts and put them down in writing according to literary criteria (for an analysis of the structure of chaps. 22–23 as a whole, see Lohfink 1987). It is unreasonable to suppose that the activities included in this account were carried out in the same year, for it relates the following: (1) the purification of the cult in the capital city and its surroundings (vv 4–7, 8b–14); (2) the unification of the cult in the area of Judah "from Geba to Beer-Sheba" (v 8a); (3) the destruction of the cultic center at Bethel (v 15); and (4) the extirpation of the high places in the area of Samaria (v 19).

These are undertakings in which the diversified activities related to extensive areas beyond the bounds of the original dominion of Josiah were involved. It appears, moreover, that this activity was carried out in stages, as it is described in the Books of Chronicles. The first actions were undertaken without connection to the book of the Torah, whereas the later ones, especially the making of the covenant and the celebration of the Passover, were performed in accordance with what was written in the book of Deuteronomy.

My proposal, that the eradication of alien cults preceded the discovery of the book of the Torah, can be supported by the following arguments.

1. The reforms of the other Judean kings—Asa (1 Kgs 15:12–14), Jehoshapat (1 Kgs 22:47), and Joash (2 Kgs 11:17–18)—were carried out without the sanction of a written book. In fact, the struggle against idolatry was ancient, with a history as old as the existence of the people of Israel, and Josiah did not require the authorization of a written book to know that it was necessary to root out idol worship from Israel.

2. It is difficult to suppose that Josiah would conclude a covenant in the Temple in Jerusalem (2 Kgs 23:1–3) while the image of Asherah was still standing there (cf. 2 Kgs 21:7), male cult prostitutes were still frequenting the place, and women were weaving vestments for Asherah there (2 Kgs 23:6–7). Before every covenant ceremony of renewal of relations between God and his people, it was necessary for the people to purify themselves and to rid themselves of alien gods (Gen 35:2–4; Josh 24:23; Judg 10:16; 1 Sam 7:3–4), and it is inconceivable that Josiah, of all people, would make a covenant in the Temple at a time that all of these idolatrous practices were still to be found there.

3. Josiah sent a delegation to inquire of YHWH, not in order to learn what should be done in the future, but rather to ascertain whether the wrath of YHWH, which was kindled against Israel because *their fathers* had not obeyed "the words of this scroll to do all that has been prescribed," would indeed fall upon them (2 Kgs 23:13). From this it follows that he himself did not have feelings of guilt, for if he had, he would immediately have set about purifying the city and its surroundings from idolatry on account of which the calamity was to come upon the people. He would not need a prophecy by Hulda, the prophetess, in order to know that idols should be removed. His behavior can only be explained by the shock he received from the book containing the reproof, which was discovered *only after he had purged the land.* The discovery of the book was considered to be an omen, the meaning of which only a prophet could understand. Indeed, he sent the delegation to the prophetess Hulda in order to inquire of YHWH on behalf of himself and his people, that is to say, so that she would offer up a prayer for him and for the people requesting from God the annulment of the divine punishment. This incident is similar to Hezekiah's sending a delegation to "Isaiah the prophet, the son of Amoz" during Sennacherib's siege, requesting him to offer up a "prayer for the surviving remnant" (2 Kgs 19:4), also to Zedekiah's sending a delegation to Jeremiah at the time of Nebuchadrezzar's siege. This delegation was commanded to say to Jeremiah, "Please inquire of YHWH on our behalf, for King Nebuchadrezzar of Babylon is attacking us" (Jer 21:2). After reading the harsh rebuke in the book of Deuter-

onomy, which related all of the evils that would befall the people if they did not obey YHWH (chap 28), Josiah became conscious of the grievous sins of Manasseh and asked the prophetess to seek YHWH on behalf of himself and his people, in other words, to seek an annulment of the verdict. The answer was that, although the calamity was most certainly coming, the king and his contemporaries would nevertheless be saved from it, and Josiah would be laid in his tomb in peace (2 Kgs 22:20; cf. Weinfeld 1972a, p. 26). This is certainly the viewpoint of the editor of the Book of Kings (2 Kgs 23:26) as well as of Jeremiah (Jer 15:4); who imputed to Manasseh and the sins he committed the punishment of the destruction of Jerusalem.

The prophecy of Hulda, therefore, was not proclaimed against the background of Josiah's reform and was not dependent on it at all. Rather, it was uttered against the background of a history of burdensome sin that weighed upon the nation and its king, for which the reform could not atone.

4. The book was discovered in the course of renovations of the Temple, which, it appears, took place following the removal of idolatrous objects that had been introduced into the Temple by Manasseh. The Books of Chronicles report the fact that extensive repairs *(ḥzq bdq)* were being made to the Temple because earlier kings had allowed the structure to deteriorate: "They put it out to the artisans and the masons to buy quarried stone and wood for the coupling and for making roof beams which the Kings of Judah had allowed to fall into ruin" (2 Chr 34:11). It appears, therefore, that Josiah began his activity of purification even before the eighteenth year of his reign and that the book was discovered in the course of the Temple's purification and renovation.

The Eradication of Alien Cults

Josiah's undertaking to eradicate alien cults was radical in the extreme. What is distinctive about his action is not the fact that he eradicated idolatry—that had been done by other reforming kings before him, especially Hezekiah—but that he rendered it inoperative by rooting out established idolatrous institutions that had been in existence many years before his time, and by abolishing the positions that were dependent on these institutions. Thus Josiah destroyed both idolatry and syncretism in Israel once and for all. He deposed the idolatrous priests who had been appointed by the kings of Judah before him to serve in the high places in the cities of Judah, along with those who offer incense to Baal and to the host of heaven (2 Kgs 23:5). He tore down the houses of the male cult prostitutes (v 7) and the high places of the gates at the entrance to the city (v 8). Likewise, he defiled the Valley of Tophet, which had served as a place for passing the sons and daughters through the fire to Molech (2 Kgs 16:3; 21:6; Jer 7:31; 19:11–13; cf. Weinfeld 1972b), and also abolished the cult of the sun god, which was bound up with the dedication of horses and chariots to this deity (v 11; for this type of cult in Assyria see Weinfeld 1972b, p. 151 n. 142).

Additionally, Josiah destroyed the altars of the rooftops that the kings of Judah had made in order to offer incense on them, a ritual that was extremely widespread in Judah at that time (Zeph 1:5; Jer 7:18; 19:13; 32:29; 44:17; Weinfeld 1972b, pp. 151–54). But his most daring action was the desecration of the high places that King Solomon had built facing Jerusalem to the south of the Mount of Olives. These high places had been in existence in Judah for more than three hundred years, and no king had dared to touch them. Even Hezekiah, who removed the high places and pulverized the brazen serpent that Moses had made, did not have the courage to desecrate these high places because of the eminence of King Solomon. Notwithstanding, Josiah did just this (cf. Weinfeld 1972a, pp. 168–69).

A most audacious action was also carried out by Josiah in the area of the Kingdom of Israel in the north. He completely demolished the altar and the high place at Bethel (v 15), a place that had formerly been the king's sanctuary (Amos 7:13) and was considered to be the gate of heaven (Gen 28:17); he also removed the shrines at the high places in the towns of Samaria (v 19). It appears that he had a bitter struggle with the priests of the high places and accordingly was forced to act with ruthless force (see above).

Idolatrous ritual had taken root in Judah primarily in the period of Manasseh, but in actual fact it had already begun to be introduced during the reign of Ahaz, the king of whom the Scripture testifies that he passed his son through the fire, following the detestable practices of the nations (2 Kgs 16:3), and that he built an altar according to a model of one he had seen in Damascus, when he went there to meet Tiglath Pileser (v 10). We read about Tophet and the preparation of a fire there in Isaiah (30:33), and in 2 Kgs 23:12 we read about the "altars which had been erected on the roof near the upper room of Ahaz." One must presume that these altars had been built by Ahaz himself, though this is not necessarily so.

Even if there were political motives for this ruthless eradication of syncretistic religious institutions, one must nevertheless acknowledge that the zeal of the king in this matter, and in particular his resolution in destroying every remnant of pagan manifestation—including that which had been in practice for three hundred years, such as the high places of Solomon—is evidence of a monotheistic religious fervor the like of which had not been seen in Israel before. It is not without reason that the Scripture notes that "There was no king like him before who turned back to the Lord with all his heart and soul and might" (v 25). Although this verse contains several superlatives, there is nevertheless no justification for seeing in it the invention of an editor. His zeal for the God of Israel, which found expression in the eradication of idolatry from the land, shows us the veracity of this sentence.

Josiah's destruction of all of the installations that served the idol worship and the syncretizing ritual, including the institutions of sorcery and magic of every kind (v 24), points, as I have said, to an extirpation, once and for all, of all cultic practice alien to the religion of Israel, and it appears that this is just what Josiah succeeded in doing. After Josiah's time, there is no further mention in the Books of Kings of a king who reintroduced idolatry and the high places, and it appears that this fact is in accord with the historical reality, for if idolatry and the high places had been renewed, the historiographer would not have been compelled to impute the destruction of Jerusalem precisely to Manasseh. It would have been easier to ascribe this event to the kings who were closer to it. The evidence of the prophecies of Jeremiah (7:16–19, 30–34; 19:1–15; 32:34–35) and of Ezekiel (chap. 8) indeed tended to refer to the sins of the past (cf. Weinfeld 1972a, pp. 29–32). Even if we do not accept this, however, we must acknowledge that these prophetic Scriptures contain a generalization, for it is not the kings who were involved in sin that are spoken of, as in earlier periods, but rather, individuals who sin in secret (Ezek 8:12) or women (Ezek 8:14 cf. Jer 44:15ff.).

If idolatry ceased from Israel and was not resumed even in the period after the destruction of Jerusalem, one must credit Josiah, and the same holds true for the eradication of worship at the high places.

The Destruction of the High Places from Israel

Hezekiah was the first king who began to destroy the high places (2 Kgs 18:4, 22), though his enterprise was reduced to naught during the days of Manasseh. Josiah took up Hezekiah's work, only just as he had acted with extremity in connection with the eradication of idolatry and succeeded in uprooting it from Israel entirely, so also he acted in connection with the unification of the cult: he was not content with merely destroying the high places, he also annulled the position of the priests who served at them in Judah and transferred the entire priesthood to Jerusalem (2 Kgs 23:8). Henceforth, these priests of the high places could maintain themselves from the gifts that were given to the priests in Jerusalem, but they had no right to serve at the altar of YHWH in Jerusalem (v 9).[37]

[37] Since the reform the Zadokites were therefore the only ones privileged for service at the altar (cf. Ezek 44:15). Hilkiah, the high priest, was the son of Shallum of the family of Zadok (Ezra 7:2; Neh 11:11; 1 Chr 5:38–39) and, as has been observed by B. Mazar on the basis of the genealogical lists of the high priesthood (cf. Ezra 7:1–5; Neh 11:10–11; 1 Chr 5:28–40), the family of Zadok was ousted from the high priesthood from the times of Solomon till the times of Josiah. This might link the reform to the priests of the family of Zadok (according to Katzenstein 1961). The Zadokites returned to service at the time of Hezekiah (see 2 Chr 31:10). The connection between the discovery of the book of Deuteronomy and the Zadokites may be reflected in the Covenant of Damascus, where it says that David multiplied his wives because he had not read in the sealed book "that was inside the Ark, because it had not been opened since the days of Eleazar and Joshua . . . and it was hidden until the Zadokites arose" (Rabin 1954, 5:2–5, p. 19).

That Josiah succeeded in extirpating cultic practice at the high places in Israel we learn from the fact that the exiles who returned from Babylon did not even attempt to renew worship at the high places in Judah. For them it was already clear, according to the laws prescribed in the book of Deuteronomy discovered in the days of Josiah, that one could worship God by means of the offering of sacrifices only in the Temple of Jerusalem. Likewise, the attempts of the exiles in Babylon to erect an altar there were unsuccessful. As M. Greenberg has observed (1983, COMMENT on Ezek 20), the prophecy in Ezek 20 turns on the high place that the elders of Israel were trying to erect in Babylon, which the prophet opposed vehemently with the sanction of the law concerning the unification of worship in the book of Deuteronomy. Ezekiel reproves the people for the sins of the high places in the past: "When . . . they saw any high hill or any leafy tree, they slaughtered their sacrifices there" (20:28) and mocks the shrine that they visited with the wordplay *šmh bmh* (v 29),[38] regarding this as idol worship and as the passing of children through the fire (v 31), in a similar manner to that of the author of the book of Deuteronomy in his juxtaposition of the law prohibiting high places with the mention of the shameful practices of the nations, including the burning of sons and daughters in the fire (Deut 12:29–31). At the beginning of the chapter on the prohibition of high places, the author of Deuteronomy opens with the demolition of sites and altars of the nations who worship their gods there and requires that the sons of Israel do not serve their God in like manner, but rather worship him *at the site that YHWH will choose* (12:2–5). Thus he compares the worship at the high places with the worship of idols. Ezekiel also speaks of the idols with which the Israelites defiled themselves, considering themselves to be like the nations worshiping wood and stone (20:31–32), and closes with the cry, House of Israel, serve YHWH "on My holy mountain, on the lofty mount of Israel" (v 40), that is, on the Temple Mount in Jerusalem, as opposed to their worshiping on every high hill (cf. 6:13). The worship at the high places "on every high hill" is consequently regarded by the prophet as identical to idol worship, and the matter was also understood in this way by the returned exiles, for it never entered their minds to renew the high places. In all of this one must acknowledge the radical activity of Josiah and the ideological movement that came into being as a result of the revolutionary centralization of the cult at Jerusalem.

[38] There is wordplay here between *bmh šmh* 'a shrine there' and *bʾym šmh* 'they come there'; see Greenberg 1983.

The Transition from Worship at the Temple and the High Places to Worship in the Synagogue, from Sacrifice and Offering to Prayer and the Reading of the Book

Until the reform of Hezekiah–Josiah, the worship of God had been attached to the temple and the high places. Even prayer was offered in these holy places. So, for example, we read in Isa 16:12, "And when Moab wearies himself upon the high place *(hbmh)*, he comes to his sanctuary *(mqdšw)* to pray, and does not prevail." The high place *(bmh)* and the sanctuary *(mqdš)* in Moab served as a place of prayer, and so it was also in Israel before the reform. It goes without saying that as the sanctuary and the high place were places of sacrifice and offering, prayer was considered subsidiary to them (cf. Haran 1988). And so the poet says: "Take my prayer as an offering of incense, my upraised hands as an evening offering" (Ps 141:2), that is to say, he requests that his prayer and the lifting up of his hands be considered in the eyes of God as incense and an evening offering, which were the customary offering to God, causing a "pleasing aroma to YHWH" (cf. Weinfeld 1984d, 4.998–1000). Even in the Second Temple period, during which the synagogue had already become an autonomous institution, the public still saw in the offering of incense the most important ritual act, to which prayer should be attached (Ezra 9:5; Jdt 9:1; Luke 1:9–10; *m. Tamid* 6:3; *Kelim* 1:9), and from this mode of thought comes the concept *tplt mnḥh* 'minhah prayer'. In general, prayer was regarded as a sort of substitute for sacrifice.

Nevertheless, one must add that after the destruction of the high places and the establishment of the cult in one unique sanctuary in Jerusalem, the link between prayer and concrete ritual was severed, and prayer was changed into an independent institution connected with the synagogue and having no relation to the sanctuary or sacrifices. This institution appears in its full tangibility in the description of prayers from the period of Ezra and Nehemiah. In Neh 8–9 we read of the assembling of the people at the time of the festivals "to the square before the Water Gate" (Neh 8:1) in order to read the Torah and utter prayers and confess sins. The order and content of these assemblies reminds us of the arrangement of prayer and the reading of the Torah as they are conventionally practiced up to this day in the synagogue. Ezra stood on a wooden platform (Neh 8:4), opened the book, apparently raising it, then all of the people stood on their feet (v 5). All of these actions are customs anchored in the ritual of the synagogue. Afterward, Ezra blessed the Lord, and the people all responded with Amen (v 6). The reading of the Torah was accompanied by a translation and commentary (v 7; for the ritual involved in the recital of the Torah see Elbogen

1931). The chapter goes on to relate that during the days of the festivals of Sukkot, the Torah was read day after day, from the first day to the last (v 18).

On the twenty-fourth day of the seventh month, the people again assembled and read the Torah for a quarter of the day, and for a quarter of the day they confessed and prostrated themselves before the Lord (Neh 9:1–3). The prayer opens with praise for the greatness of God in his creation of everything in the universe, for his preservation of all created beings, and for the host of heaven who worship him, and it continues with the election of Israel and the giving of the Torah and Sabbath. All of these elements are congruent with the structure of Sabbath and the festivals in the conventional Jewish liturgy "Amidah":

(1) the first blessing of the Amidah in which God is praised for his supremacy in creation: "the great mighty and awesome God, the most high God creator of heaven and earth *(hʾl hgdwl, hgybwr whnwrʾ, ʾl ʿlywn qwnh šmym wʾrṣ)" (SPB,* p. 173);[39]

(2) the benediction of the great acts of God *(gĕburôt),* which includes praise for keeping in life the created beings *(mḥyh ʾt klm);*

(3) the benediction of the sanctification of the Name, which includes praise of the angels (= Kedusha); and

(4) acknowledgment of the election of Abram and his being called Abraham, the election of Israel, the Exodus from Egypt, the giving of the Torah and Sabbath (9:14–17)—elements that comprise the principal content of the Amidah for Sabbaths and festivals.[40] At the end we find confessions and supplications, which generally accompany all prayers *(taḥanûn).*[41]

Here, we do not find a single reference to the Temple or to temple worship, even though it was precisely on festival days of the seventh month that the people made a pilgrimage to the Temple and made offerings for the festivals (cf. Ezra 3:4–6). This lack of reference to the worship of God in the Temple can be explained by the fact that the author was describing prayer and the reading of the Torah as they were practiced in the assemblies of the people (the synagogues), and these had no connection with worship in the Temple, which was conducted by the priests. In this way one can also explain the absence of any mention of the Day of Atonement. As is known, the ritual of the Day of Atonement was mainly performed in the Temple by the high priest while the people remained passive. The author of the description under discussion in Neh

[39] For this as the original benediction see Wieder 1976.

[40] Compare my article in the forthcoming volume of University of Haifa Symposium, *Forty Years of Research in the Dead Sea Scrolls,* March 20–24, 1988.

[41] Ibid.

8–9, whose subject matter is the worship of God apart from the Temple, did not find it necessary to refer to events and ceremonies connected with the Temple and thus did not mention the Day of Atonement. In the same way, he omitted to mention the sacrifices of Rosh Hashanah and the festival of Sukkot.[42]

This liturgical framework, which has no link whatever to the Temple but is, rather, characteristic of the synagogue, is apparently the outcome of the destruction of the high places. The destruction of the high places and the provincial sanctuaries created a vacuum, which was filled by the institution of the synagogue. After the reform, the people who, until this point, had entered into their religious experience in a sanctuary close to where they lived or in a high place situated in their town, needed to find a substitute. The abolition of the high places without any provision of a replacement for them would have been tantamount to the destruction of daily religious experience, a thing that, unlike in our own times, would have been impossible in the ancient world. This substitute was found, therefore, in prayer and reading of the book of the Torah, which comprised the worship of God in the synagogue.

We have evidence of the building of synagogues beginning from the third century B.C.E. in Hellenistic Egypt.[43] But synagogue worship certainly cannot have begun in Alexandria in Egypt. As we saw above, liturgical customs of synagogue worship in Palestine were already crystallized in the middle of the fifth century B.C.E., and it would appear that these customs may be traced even further back, to the time of Josiah's reform. The unification of worship in the days of Josiah was bound up with the discovery of the book of the Torah, and the reading of the Torah was indeed the most important part of formal prayer in the Second Temple period. Alongside the reading of the Torah, there existed prayer, which has two basic components: the Ten Commandments and the recitation of the Shemaʿ, which actually appear juxtaposed to each other in Deut 5–6. The Ten Commandments and the Shemaʿ were read daily in the Temple (*m. Tamid* 5:1), and it appears that this custom is anchored in the book of Deuteronomy itself, which juxtaposed these two portions. The book of Deuteronomy is conspicuous for its liturgical elements and forms, which are recognizable to us in the prayers from the time of Ezra and Nehemiah onward. Declarations on the uniqueness of God and his dominion over creation, the mighty acts and wonders of God, his election of Israel, and the like are found in the prayers of the Deuteronomic literature and in the prose sermons of the Book of Jeremiah (cf. Weinfeld 1972a, pp. 32–45). A very reasonable hypothesis is that it was scribes from the family of Shaphan who, after the destruction of Jerusalem, settled in Mizpah, where the survivors who were under the leadership of Gedaliah ben Ahikam the son of Shaphan lived (2 Kgs 25:22–26, 40–41). These

[42] Contrast the description of the temple ritual in Ezek 3:1–7 at the time of Zerubabel.
[43] See the inscription on the dedication of a synagogue for Ptolemy III and Berenike (246–221 B.C.E.) in Frey 1952, no. 1440.

scribes gave a permanent shape to the Deuteronomic literature, which contained liturgical forms that reflect the prayer formulas that were conventional to the Jews after the destruction of the Temple. Indeed, it is even possible to assume that after the destruction of Jerusalem, the institution of the synagogue was founded in the town of Mizpah in Benjamin, and that it continued to develop with increasing momentum after the arrival of the exiles from Babylon in the time of Ezra and Nehemiah. It is also possible that the "house of YHWH *(byt yhwh)*" to which men from Shechem, Šiloh, and Samaria came after the destruction, bringing grain offerings and incense with them (Jer 41:5), is the place of prayer and worship at Mizpah, as has already been suggested (see Giesebrecht 1930, p. 42). As is known, Mizpah was a place appointed for cultic assemblies from ancient times (Judg 20:1; 21:1, 5; 1 Sam 7:5; cf. 1 Sam 10:17) up to the period of Judas Maccabaeus (1 Macc 3:46). In the story of Judas Maccabaeus in the first book of the Maccabees it is also stated explicitly that the people gathered at Mizpah because this was formerly a place of prayer *(topos proseuchēs)* in Israel; possibly the author is alluding, not to the days of the Judges in Samuel (Judg 20:1; 1 Sam 7:5; 10:17), but rather to the period after the destruction of the First Temple, when the center of the survivors was at Mizpah (Jer 40–41). In the story from 1 Maccabees, the spreading out of the scroll of the Torah is mentioned (3:48), which is an allusion to the reading of the Torah on this occasion.

The Discovery of the Book of the Torah

We shall now pass to the problem of the discovery of the book of the Torah. The central question concerning this matter is, what was the nature of the book that was discovered then? Already in traditional rabbinic literature we find the opinion that the "book of the Torah" that was found in the Temple is the book of Deuteronomy (Ginzberg 1959, 6.377, no. 116), and, in fact, the tradition that the reading of the "Portion on the King *(pršt hmlk)*" at the end of the sabbatical year *(m. Soṭa* 7, 2, 8) is based on the idea that "this Torah *(htwrh hzʾt),*" what was to be read in the presence of the "assembled people" (Deut 31:11–12), is none other than the book of Deuteronomy, for it was only sections from the book of Deuteronomy that were to be read before the assembled people.

In his commentary on Ezek 1:1, Jerome also voices the opinion that the discovered book is Deuteronomy (and cf. Targum Jonathan on Ezek 1:1), and the hypothesis was given a scientific basis by de Wette (see above). The main reasons are as follows:

1. The term "*the* book of the Torah *(spr htwrh)*" with the definite article is not found in the first four books of the Pentateuch. Rather, it occurs only in the book of Deuteronomy, thus signifying the book of Deuteronomy itself (see above).

2. In the Second Book of Kings, the concluding of the covenant is carried out according to the formulated obligations found in the book of Deuteronomy: "that they would follow the Lord and observe his commandments, his precepts *(ʿdwtyw),* and his laws with all their heart and soul" (2 Kgs 23:3). Such a combination of formulas (mark especially *ʿdwt)* is found only in Deuteronomy (cf. Weinfeld 1972a, p. 338).

3. The agitation of the king on hearing the reading of the book is comprehensible only in the light of the rebuke in Deut 28:36 in which not only the people but also the king are referred to: "YHWH will drive you, and the king you have set over you, to a nation unknown to you or your fathers."[44]

4. The celebration of the Passover by all of the people in Jerusalem, that is, "in the place which YHWH will choose *(bmqwm ʾšr ybḥr YHWH),*" corresponds to the Passover law as it is formulated in the book of Deuteronomy (16:1–8). According to the regulations in the other sources of the Pentateuch (see Exod 12), the Passover was a household sacrifice, and even if it did have a connection with the sanctuary or the high place (cf. Haran 1978, pp. 343–48), it was not a public sacrifice that was to be offered only in the capital city, as is required in the book of Deuteronomy. Indeed, the Scripture itself in the Book of Kings attests that *such a Passover* had not been performed since the days of the Judges. Also, the wording, "make a Passover to YHWH your God *(ʿśh psḥ lYHWH ʾlhyk),*" is congruent with the precept in Deut 16:1, "and you will make a Passover to YHWH your God *(wʿśyt psḥ lYHWH ʾlyhk).*"[45]

5. The magical terms *ʾwbwt* 'mediums' and *ydʿwnym* 'spirits' mentioned in 2 Kgs 23:24 are found in Deut 18:10–11, even though we find prohibitions against these things also in the legislation of the holiness code in the book of Leviticus (19:26; 20:6).

6. The stylistic influence of this book is recognizable in Israelite literature, beginning from the end of the seventh century B.C.E. In the prophetic literature from before the seventh century B.C.E. we do not find this style, whereas in the prophecies of Jeremiah[46] and Ezekiel, Joel, Zechariah, and Deutero-Isaiah,[47] the influence of the book of Deuteronomy is considerable.

[44] The rabbis speculate that when the king opened the book it was this verse that captured his eyes *(y. Šeqal.* 6:1, 6d; *b. Yoma* 52b).

[45] On the change in the Passover law in Deuteronomy and its implications, see above.

[46] The Deuteronomic style in Jeremiah is discernible not only in the prose sermons but also in the poetry of the book; see Weinfeld 1972a, pp. 359–60.

[47] The influence of the Deuteronomic style is recognizable in the dogmatic phraseology: (a) the foreign worship "under every leafy tree" (Isa 57:5; Ezek 6:13); "fetishes *(glwlym)*" and "detestable things *(šqwṣym)*" in Isa 66:3 and Ezekiel (passim); (b) monotheism *(ʾyn ʿwd)* cf. Isa 45:5, 6 et al.; 46:9; Joel 2:27; and (c) loyalty (love of God) and observing the Torah: Isa 56:6; Zech 3:4; and Mal 3:14: "to walk in the ways of YHWH and keep his guard"; "to turn away from evil" (Ezek 13:22; 33:11; Jonah 5:8; Zech 1:3).

When was the book written? Two answers have been given to this question. According to the first, the book was written in the time of Josiah, and its amazing discovery was nothing but a pious fraud. This opinion, which was prevalent among scholars of the nineteenth century and the beginning of the twentieth, claims that the priests of the period of Josiah wrote the book and were interested in conferring on it an aura of holiness so that it would be accepted by the people. They therefore put it is a hidden place in the Temple. In recent years, no one has supported this view.

The second answer claims that the book was written during the time of Hezekiah, was concealed in the time of Manasseh, and was only rediscovered during the period of Josiah. This opinion is accepted today by the majority of scholars.

One should note that the very purport of posing such a question concerning the time of the composition of the book is out of place from a methodological viewpoint. The concept of "composition of a book" is meaningless with regard to the Israel of ancient times and, indeed, with reference to the entire ancient eastern world. Today when we speak of a book, we mean a composition written by a certain person at a specific place and time: every line is impressed with the personality of the author and the period and milieu in which it was written. Such was not the case in Israel or in the ancient East. Even in the book of Ecclesiastes, which comes closer to the concept of a modern book, we find sections of which similar examples can be found in Babylonian and Egyptian literature from the first half of the second millennium B.C.E. (see above). The author of ancient times was generally a collector and compiler of traditions rather than a creator of literature, and was certainly not an author in the modern sense of the term. Even if the book of Deuteronomy had been put into writing in the days of Hezekiah–Josiah, that does not mean to say that all of its contents reflect that period, for in the book of Deuteronomy there have been preserved for us very ancient laws, especially in sections that have no connection with the subject of the centralization of the cult, such as chaps. 21–25. Even the laws that have as their basis the idea of the centralization of the cult, such as the regulations of the firstfruits, the firstborn animals, and tithes, the festival of the Passover, and other festivals are not in themselves within the category of an innovation, for they comprised some of the most ancient precepts of Israel; only, during the period of Hezekiah and Josiah, they were adapted to the principle of the centralization of the cult and were written anew. We can comprehend this process of adaptation by way of a comparison of these laws with the other collections of ancient laws (see above). It is impossible to come to a decision concerning the date of Deuteronomy without comparing every individual law included in it with the same law as it appears in the other collections, in the book of covenant and the holiness code. If we conduct a comparison and an examination such as this in a systematic and consistent manner, it becomes clear that although the regulations in the book of Deuteronomy were adapted to the new orientation, nevertheless we have essentially before us the selfsame laws, such as the Sabbath, the three pilgrimages, firstfruits, firstlings, tithes, sabbatical year, gifts for the priests, the law of the cities of refuge, and so on.

It is beyond doubt that the book of Deuteronomy contains ancient laws from the period of the Judges or even from the time of Moses. But it also contains an element from the period of Hezekiah–Josiah, and this is the element connected with the centralization of the cult. Finally, there is also a Josianic element that finds expression in the final literary edition of the book. After all, we deal here with a period in which books were not yet considered to be sacred in every letter, as was the case in the Second Temple period and onward: what is sacred is the principal content of the books. In view of the double framework found in the book of Deuteronomy, two introductions (1:1–4, 40; 4:44–11:32) and also two epilogues (27–28; 29–30), we are entitled to assume that it passed through many stages in the circles of scribes during the period of Josiah. It is not necessary to assume that the book that was discovered was literally identical with the book of Deuteronomy as we have it before us today; for, indeed, Shaphan the scribe read the book twice through the same day, once before Hilkiah the priest and once before Josiah, and it appears that also on the same day, the delegation was sent to Huldah the prophetess. One cannot suppose that it was possible to read through a book of the extent of Deuteronomy as we have it today twice or three times on the same day and then to undertake further activities concerning it on the selfsame day.

In conclusion, the period of Josiah is typified as the period of the "book," and in fact it commenced the process of the canonization of the Scripture, a concept that also penetrated Christianity and Islam: revelation of YHWH embodied in the written word of a book. Josiah sanctified the book of the Torah of Moses, that is, the book of Deuteronomy, and obligated the people to keep it (2 Kgs 23:1–3). As a result of the sanctification of this book, other written traditions began to be sanctified. Already in the period of Josiah and especially after him, in the period of the destruction of Jerusalem, there arose scribes who collected and edited the traditions connected with the period of the settlement and the monarchy, while making use of the ideology of the sacred book of Deuteronomy and its style (see above). After them there were other scribes who collected other literary treasures, chiefly Ezra the Scribe, who collected the scrolls that had apparently been preserved by the priests. The primary impetus for the crystallization of the sacred Scripture, however, was the sanctification of the book of Deuteronomy, and it was this impulse that changed the religion of Israel into the faith of the Book.

Bibliography

♦

Abel, F. M.
1933–38. *Géographie de la Palestine,* 2 vols. Paris.
Aberbach, A. and L. Smolar.
1967. "Aaron, Jeroboam and the Golden Calves." *JBL* 86: 129–40.
Abou Assaf, A., P. Bordreuil, and A. R. Millard.
1982. *La Statue de Tell Fekherye et son inscription bilingue assyro-araméenne.* Paris.
Abramsky, S.
1968. "Matakhot." *EM* 5.644–62. (Hebrew)
———.
1985. "The Attitude Toward the Amorites and Jebusites in the Book of Samuel." *Zion* Jubilee Volume 50: 27–58. (Hebrew)
Abudarham ha-Shalem, (ed. S. A. Wertheimer), Jerusalem, 1963.
Aharoni, Y.
1975. *Arad Inscriptions.* Judaean Desert Studies. Jerusalem. (Hebrew)
———, V. Fritz, and A. Kempinski.
1975. "Excavations at Tel Masos (Hirbet el Meshash)." *Tel Aviv* 2: 97–124.
——— and A. Rainey.
1979. *The Land of the Bible: A Historical Geography.* 2d ed. London.
Aḥituv, S.
1971. "Ezion Geber." *EM* 6.332–33. (Hebrew)
———.
1982. "Tophel," *EM* 8.895. (Hebrew)
———.
1984. *Canaanite Toponyms in Ancient Egyptian Documents.* Jerusalem and Leiden.
Albertz, R.
1978. "Hintergrund und Bedeutung des Elterngebot im Dekalog." *ZAW* 90: 348–74.
Albright, W. F.
1940. *From Stone Age to Christianity.* Baltimore.

———.
1968. *Yahwe and the Gods of Canaan.* London.
Alp, S.
1947. "Military Instructions of the Hittite King Tuthaliya." *Belleten* 11: 403–14.
Alt, A.
1934. "Die Ursprünge des Israelitischen Rechts." SSAW, Philologisch-hist. Klasse 86.1. Leipzig. = *KS* 1.278–332. Munich. Also = Alt 1970. *Grundfragen der Geschichte des Volkes Israel,* pp. 203–57. Munich.
———.
1959. "Judas Gaue, unter Josia." *KS* 2.276–88. Munich.
———.
1963. "Das Verbot des Diebstahls im Dekalog." *KS* 1.333–40. Munich.
———.
1968. "Josua." *KS* 1.176–92. Munich.
Altman, A.
1981. "On the Question of the Designation of the Land of Israel as māt Amurri (the Land of the Amorites)." *Tarbiz* 51: 3–22. (Hebrew)
Amir, Y.
1985. "The Ten Commandments According to the Teachings of Philo of Alexandria." In *The Ten Commandments as Reflected in Tradition and Literature Throughout the Ages,* ed. B. Z. Segal, pp. 95–126. Jerusalem. (Hebrew)
Anbar, M.
1975. "Aspect Moral Dans un Discours "Prophetique" de Mari." *UF* 7: 517–18.
Anderson, F. I. and D. N. Freedman.
1980. *Hosea.* AB 24. New York.
Anderson, G. W.
1951. "A Study of Micah 6:1–8." *SJT* 4: 191–97.
André, G.
1982. " 'Walk' and 'stand' and 'sit' in Psalm 1:1–2." *VT* 32: 327.
Artzi, P. and A. Malamat.
1971. "Shibtu, Queen of Mari." In *Bible and Jewish History, Dedicated to the Memory of J. Liver,* ed. B. Uffenheimer, pp. 169–83. Tel Aviv. (Hebrew)
Astour, M.
1966. "Some New Divine Names from Ugarit." *JAOS* 86: 277–84.
Astruc, J.
1753. *Conjectures sur les mémoires originaux dont il paroit que Moyse s'est servi pour composer le livre de la Genèse.* Brussels (Paris).
Avigad, N.
1980. *The Upper City of Jerusalem,* Jerusalem. (Hebrew)

Avishur, Y.
1975. "Phoenician Topoi in Proverbs 3." *Shnaton* 1: 13–25. (Hebrew)
———.
1984. *Stylistic Studies of Word Pairs in Biblical and Ancient Semitic Literatures.* AOAT 210. Neukirchen.
Baillet, M., J. T. Milik, and R. de Vaux.
1962. *Les 'Petits Grottes' de Qumran,* DJD 3. Oxford.
Barkai, G.
1986. *Ketef Hinom, a Treasure Facing Jerusalem's Walls.* Jerusalem.
Beckman, G.
1982. "The Hittite Assembly." *JAOS* 102: 435–42.
Begg, C. T.
1979. "The Significance of the *Numeruswechsel* in Deuteronomy—The 'Prehistory' of the Question." *Ephemerides Theologicae Lovanienses* 55: 116–24.
———.
1980. "The Literary Criticism of Deut. 4:1–40: Contributions to a Continuing Discussion." *Ephemerides Theologicae Lovanienses* 56: 10–55.
———.
1985. "The Destruction of the Calf (Exodus 32:20; Deuteronomy 9:21)." *Das Deuteronomium,* ed. N. Lohfink, pp. 208–51. Louvain.
———.
1987. *Contributions to the Elucidation of the Composition of Deuteronomy with Special Attention to the Significance of the Numeruswechsel.* Ph.D. diss. Louvain.
Ben-David, A.
1967. *Leshon miqra uleshon ḥakhamim,* vol. 1. Tel Aviv. (Hebrew)
Bengtson, H.
1960–69. *Die Staatsverträge des Altertums,* vols. II, III, Munich.
Ben Hayyim, Z.
1957. *The Literary and Oral Tradition of Hebrew and Aramaic Amongst the Samaritans.* Jerusalem. (Hebrew)
———.
1967. "Observations on the Hebrew and Aramaic Lexicon from the Samaritan Tradition." In *Hebräische Wortforschung. Festschrift W. Baumgartner.* VTSup 16, pp. 12–24. Leiden.
———.
1974. "Word Studies." *H. Yalon Memorial Volume,* pp. 46–58. Ramat Gan. (Hebrew)
Ben-Zevi, I.
1953–54. "ʾeben mezuza Shomronit mekĕfar Bilu." *BJPES* 18: 223–29. (Hebrew)

Bergsträsser, G.
1926–29. *Hebräische Grammatik.* 2 vols. Leipzig.
Biram, A.
1955. "Hosea 2:16–25." In *Festschrift E. Urbach,* pp. 116–39. Jerusalem. (Hebrew)
Blau, J.
1956. "Zum Hebräisch der Übersetzer des Alten Testaments." *VT* 6: 97–99.
———.
1977–82. *An Adverbial Construction in Hebrew and Aramaic.* Jerusalem. (Hebrew)
Blidstein, G.
1975. *Honor Thy Father and Mother: Filial Responsibility in Jewish Law and Ethics,* Ktav. New York.
Boling, R.
"Levitical Cities: Archaeology and Texts," *Biblical and Related Studies Presented to Samuel Iwry,* Eisenbruns, Winona Lake, pp. 23–32.
Bordreuil, P. and D. Pardee.
1982. "Le Rituel funéraire ougaritique." *Syria* 59: 121–28.
Borger, R.
1956. *Die Inschriften Asarhaddons König von Assyrien. AfO* Beiheft 9. Graz.
———.
1959. "Mesopotamien in den Jahren 629–621 v. Chr." *WZKM:* 62–76.
———.
1965. "Der Aufstieg des neobabylonischen Reiches." *JCS* 19: 59–78.
Boyarin, D.
1986. "Voices in the Text: Midrash and the Inner Tension of Biblical Narrative." *RB* 93: 581–97.
Boys, D. J. H.
1961. "The Creed and Hymns of the Samaritan Liturgy." *London Quarterly and Holborn Review* 186: 32–37.
Braulik, G.
1978. *Die Mittel deuteronomischer Rhetorik.* Analecta biblica 68. Rome.
———.
1985. "Das Deuteronomium und die Geburt des Monotheismus." In *Gott der einzige. Zur Enststehung des Monotheismus in Israel,* ed. E. Haag, pp. 115–60. Freiburg, Basel, and Vienna.
Brettler, M. Z.
1982. "The Promise of the Land of Israel to the Patriarchs in the Pentateuch." *Shnaton* 5–6: 7–24. (Hebrew)
Breuer, M.
1990. "The Division of the Decalogue into Verses and Commandments." In *The Ten Commandments in History and Tradition,* ed. B. Z. Segal, pp. 291–330. Jerusalem.

Brichto, H. C. H.
1963. *The Problem of "Curse" in the Hebrew Bible.* Philadelphia.
Broshi, M.
1974. "The Expansion of Jerusalem Under Hezekiah and Menasseh." *IEJ* 24: 21–26.
Brunner, H.
1958. "Was aus dem Munde Gottes geht." *VT* 8: 428–29.
Buber, M.
1950. *Israel und Palästina.* Zurich.
Buber, M. and Rosenzweig, F.
Die Schrift, 4 vols., Köln, 1954–62.
———.
1964. *Darko Shel Miqra.* Jerusalem. (Hebrew)
Buis, P.
1978. "Un Traité d'Assurbanipal." *VT* 28: 469–72.
Cagni, L.
1969. *L'Epopea di Erra.* Studi semitici 34. Rome.
Caloz, M.
1968. "Exode 13: 3–16 et son rapport an Deutéronome." *RB* 75: 5–62.
Cassin, E.
1938. *L'Adoption a Nuzi.* Paris.
———.
1968. *La Splendeur divine.* Paris.
Cassuto, M. D.
1954. "Dagon." *EM* 2.623–25. (Hebrew)
Cassuto, U.
1967. *A Commentary on the Book of Exodus.* Jerusalem.
Cazelles, H.
1962. "Sur les Origines du calendrier des Jubilés." *Biblica* 43: 202–16.
———.
1968. "Israel du Nord et arche d'aliance." *VT* 18: 147–58.
———.
1969. "Les Origines du Décalogue." *EI* 9: 14–19.
———.
1982. "Le Nom de Shear Yasuf, Fils D'Isaïe Concerne-t-l'l Tout Israël ou Seulement le Royaume du Nord?" *Proceedings of the Eighth World Congress of Jewish Studies,* Division A, pp. 47–50.
Childs, B. S.
1967. "Deuteronomic Formulae of the Exodus Traditions." In *Hebräische Wortforschung, Festschrift J. Baumgartner,* pp. 30–39. VTSup 16.
Cogan, M.
1985. "The Chronicler's Use of Chronology as Illuminated by Neo-Assyrian Royal Inscriptions." In *Empirical Models for Biblical Criticism,* ed. J. M. Tigay, pp. 197–209. Philadelphia.

——— and H. Tadmor.
1988. *2 Kings*, AB, New York.
Cogan, M. D.
1974. *Imperialism and Religion: Assyria, Judah and Israel in the Eighth and Seventh Centuries B.C.E.* Missoula, Mont.
Cohen, G.
1966. "The Song of Songs and the Jewish Religious Mentality." In *The S. Friedland Lectures, 1960–66*, pp. 1–21. New York.
Cohen, N. G.
1986. "Philo's Tefillin." In *Proceedings of the Ninth World Congress of Jewish Studies*, 1.199–206. Jerusalem.
Cohen, R.
1979. "The Iron Age Fortresses in the Central Negev." *BASOR* 236: 61–79.
———.
1981. "The Excavations at Kadesh Barnea, 1976–8." *BA* 44: 93–107.
Collon, D.
1975. *The Seal Impressions from Tell Atchana/Alalakh.* AOAT 27. Neukirchen.
Colson, F. H.
1929–53. *Philo,* Loeb Classical Library, London.
Couroyer, O. P. B.
1975. "Un Égyptianisme dans Ben Sira 4 11." *RB* 82: 206–17.
———.
1981. " 'Avoire de nuque raide': ne pas incliner l'oreille." *RB* 88: 216–25.
Coutler, C. C.
1940. "Further Notes on the Ritual of the Bithynian Christians." *Classical Philology* 35: 60–63.
Cowley, A. E.
1906. *Aramaic Papyri Discovered at Assuan 30:3.* London.
Crenshaw, J. L.
1975. *Hymnic Affirmation of Divine Justice.* Ph.D. diss. Missoula, Mont.
Cross, F. M.
1965. *Scrolls from the Wilderness of the Dead Sea.* London.
———.
1973. *Canaanite Myth and Hebrew Epic.* Boston.
———.
1977. "ʾEl." *TDOT* 1.242–61.
——— and D. N. Freedman.
1953. "Josiah's Revolt Against Assyria." *JNES* 12: 56–58.
Crüsemann, F.
1978. *Der Widerstand gegen das Königtum. Die antiköniglichen Texte des Alten Testaments und der Kampf am der frühen israelitischen Staat.* Neukirchen.

Dalley, S.
1986. "The God Ṣalmu and the Winged Disc." *Iraq* 48: 85–101.
Daube, D.
1947. *Studies in Biblical Law.* Cambridge.
———.
1963. *The Exodus Pattern in the Bible.* London.
Davies, G. I.
1979. "The Significance of Deuteronomy 1.2 for the Location of Mount Horeb." *PEQ* 111: 87–101.
Davies, N. de G.
1943. *The Tomb of Rekh-mi-Re at Thebes.* New York.
Day, J.
1986. "Ashera in the Hebrew Bible and Northwest Semitic." *JBL* 105, pp. 385–408.
Dearman, J. A.
1984. "The Location of Johaz." *ZDPV* 100: 122–26.
———.
"The Levitical Cities of Reuben and Moabite Toponymy," *BASOR* 276, pp. 55–57.
Degen, R., W. W. Müller, and W. Röllig.
1974. *Neue Ephemeris für semitische Epigraphie,* vol. 2.
Delcor, M.
1966. "Pentecôte." *Dictionnaire de la Bible, Supplément* 7.858–79. Paris.
Deller, K. and S. Parpola.
1968. "Ein Vertrag Assurbanipals mit dem arabischen Stamm Qedar." *Orientalia* n.s. 37: 464–66.
Dexinger, F.
1977. "Das Gerizimgebot im Dekalog der Samaritaner." In *Studien zum Pentateuch, W. Kornfeld zum 60 Geburtstag,* pp. 111–33. Vienna.
Dillmann, A.
1886. *Die Bücher Numeri, Deuteronomium und Josua.* Leipzig.
——— and V. Ryssell.
1897. *Die Bücher Exodus und Leviticus.* 3d ed. KEH. Leipzig.
Dohmen, C.
1984. "Massekah." *ThWAT* 4.1009–15.
Driver, S. R.
1902. *Deuteronomy.*[3] ICC. Edinburgh.
———.
1911. *Exodus.* CB. Cambridge.
———.
1913. *Notes on the Hebrew Text and the Topography of the Books of Samuel.* Oxford.

———.
1973. *Deuteronomy.* 3d ed. ICC. Edinburgh.
Duncan, J. A.
"A Critical Edition of Deuteronomy Manuscripts from Qumran, Cave IV: 4Q Dt^{b}, 4Q Dt^{e}, 4Q Dt^{h}, 4Q Dt^{j}, 4Q Dt^{k}, 4Q Dt^{l}." Ph.D. Thesis, Harvard University, 1989.
Ehrlich, A. B.
1900. *Miqra ki-Pheschuto.* Berlin. (Hebrew)
———.
1909. *Randglossen zur hebräischen Bibel,* Leipzig.
Eissfeldt, O.
1973. "ʾadon." *ThWAT* 1.62–78.
Elbogen, I.
1911. "Die Tefilla für die Festtage." *MGWJ* 55: 426–46 and 586–99.
———.
1931. *Der jüdische Gottesdienst in seiner geschichtlischen Entwicklung.* Frankfurt.
Ephal, I.
1977. "The Western Minorities in Babylonia in the 6th–5th Centuries B.C." *Orientalia* 46: 74–90.
Epstein, C.
1975. "The Dolmen Problem in Light of Recent Excavations in the Golan." *EI* 12 (N. Glück Volume): 1–8. (Hebrew)
Eslinger, L.
1987. "Watering Egypt (Deut. 11:10–11), *VT* 37, pp. 85–90.
Ewald, H.
1864. *Geschichte des Volkes Israel*^{3}, Göttingen.
Fabry, J.
1974–77. "huʾ", *ThWAT* II, pp. 364–68, Stuttgart, Berlin, Köln, Mainz.
Fahlgren, K. H.
1932. *Ṣedaqah, nahestehende und entgegengesetzte Begriffe in Alten Testament.* Uppsala.
Faulkner, R. O.
1955. "The Installation of the Vizier." *JEA* 41: 18–29.
Felix, J.
1968. *Plant World of the Bible.* 2d ed. Ramat Gan. (Hebrew)
Fensham, F. C.
1977. "The Numeral Seventy in the Old Testament and the Family of Jerubaal, Ahab, Pannamuwa and Athirat." *PEQ* 109: 113–15.
Fischer, G. and N. Lohfink.
1987. "Diese Worte sollst du summen." *Theologie und Philosophie* 62: 59–72.
Fitzmyer, J. A.
1966. *The Genesis Apocryphon of Qumran Cave 1.* Rome.

———.
1967. *The Aramaic Inscriptions of Sefire.* Rome.
Floss, J. P.
1975. *Jahwe Dienen—Göttern Dienen.* BBB 45. Cologne and Bonn.
Flusser, D.
1958. "The Dead Sea Sect and Pre-Pauline Christianity." *Scripta Hierosolymitana* 4: 215–66.
———.
1990. "The Ten Commandments and the 'New Testament.'" In *The Ten Commandments in History and Tradition,* ed. B. Z. Segal, pp. 219–46. Jerusalem.
Fohrer, G.
1965. "Das sogenannte apodiktisch formulierte Recht und der Dekalog." *Kerygma und Dogma* 11: 49–74.
———.
1979. *Einleitung in das Alte Testament.* 12th ed. Heidelberg.
Frankena, R.
1965. "The Vassal Treaties of Essarhaddon and the Dating of Deuteronomy." *OTS* 14, pp. 122–54.
Frankfort, H.
1948. *Kingship and the Gods.* Chicago.
Frey, J. B.
1952. *Corpus inscriptionum Iudaicarum,* vol. 2. Rome.
Friedrich, J.
1926. *Hethitische Texte in Umschrift.* MVAG 31.1. Leipzig.
Gaballa, G. A.
1969. "Minor War Scenes of Ramesses II at Karnak." *JEA* 55: 82–88.
Garcia Lopez, F.
1978a. *Analyse littéraire de Deutéronome 5–11.* Jerusalem.
———.
1978b. "Deut. 6 et la tradition—rédaction du Deutéronome." *RB* 85: 161–200.
———.
1979. "Deut. 6 et la tradition-redaction du Deutéronome (fin)." *RB* 96: 59–91.
Gardiner, J.
1947. *Ancient Egyptian Onomastica,* vol. 1. Oxford.
Geiger, A.
1857. *Urschrift und Übersetzungen der Bibel in ihrer Abhängigkeit von der innern Entwicklung des Judenthums.* Breslau. (2d ed. 1928.)
Gerstenberger, E.
1965. *Wesen und Herkunft des apodiktischen Rechts,* Neukirchen

Giesebrecht, F.
1930. *Jeremiah.* HKAT 2. Göttingen.
Ginsberg, H. L.
1950. "Judah and Transjordan States from 734 to 582 BCE." In *A. Marx Jubilee Volume,* pp. 347–68. New York.
———.
1961. "Hosea's Ephraim, More Fool than Knave." *JBL* 80, pp. 339–347
———.
1982. *The Israelian Heritage of Judaism.* New York.
Ginzberg, L.
1959. *The Legends of the Jews.* JPS. Philadelphia.
Gitin, S. and T. Dothan.
1985. "Tell Miqne, 1984." *IEJ* 35: 67–71.
———.
1986. "Tell Miqne, 1985." *IEJ* 36: 104–7.
Giveon, R.
1971. *Les Bédouins Shosou des documents égyptiens.* Leiden.
Glueck, N.
1951. *Explorations in Eastern Palestine,* vol. 4. AASOR 25–28 (for 1945–49), part 1.
———.
1954. *Transjordan.* Jerusalem. (Hebrew)
Görg, M.
1976. "Jahweh—ein Toponym?" *Biblische Notizen* 1: 7–14.
Goetze, A.
1925. *Haattaušiliš, MVÄG* 29, Leipzig.
———.
1977. "Etymologisch-semantische Perspectiven zu *brt.*" In *Bausteine biblischer Theologie, Festschrift G. J. Botterweck,* pp. 25–36. BBB 50. Cologne and Bonn.
———.
1979. "Ṭ(w)ṭpt—eine fast vergessene Deutung." *Biblische Notizen* 8: 11–13.
Gofnah, R.
1970. "Some Iron Age 2 Sites in Southern Philistia." *Atigot* 6: 25–30. (Hebrew)
Good, R. M.
1986. "The Carthaginian Mayumas." *Studi epigrafici e linguistici* 3: 99–114.
Goshen-Gottstein, M. H., ed.
1973. *The Bible in the Syropalestinian Version,* part 1: *Pentateuch and Prophets.* Jerusalem. (Hebrew)
Greenberg, M.
1951. "Hebrew *segulla:* Akkadian *sikiltu,*" *JAOS* 71: 172–74.

———.
1959. "The Biblical Concept of Asylum." *JBL* 67: 125–32.
———.
1960. "*nsh* in Exod. 20:20 and the Purpose of the Sinaitic Theophany." *JBL* 79: 273–76.
———.
1976. "On the Refinement of the Conception of Prayer in Hebrew Scriptures." *AJS Review* 1: 57–99.
———.
1983. *Ezekiel,* vol. 1. AB 22. New York.
———.
1985. "The Decalogue Tradition Critically Examined." In *The Ten Commandments as Reflected in Tradition and Literature Throughout the Ages,* ed. B. Z. Segal, pp. 67–94. Jerusalem. (Hebrew)

Greenfield, J. C.
1967. "Some Aspects of the Treaty Terminology of the Bible." In *Proceedings of the Fourth World Congress of Jewish Studies,* 1.117–19. Jerusalem.
———.
1971. "Scripture and Inscription: The Literary and Rhetorical Element in some Early Phoenician Inscriptions." In *Near Eastern Studies in Honor of W. F. Albright,* ed. H. Goedicke, pp. 253–68. Baltimore and London.
———.
1982. "Two Biblical Passages in the Light of Their Near Eastern Background —Ezek. 16:30 and Mal. 3:17." *EI* 16 (H. Orlinsky Volume): 56–61. (Hebrew)

Gressmann, H.
1924. "Josiah und das Deuteronomium." *ZAW* 42: 313–37.

Grimme, H.
1938. "Hebr. ṭṭpt und ṭet, zwei Lehnworter aus dem Ägyptischen." *OLZ* 41: 148–52.

Gruber, M. I.
1980. *Aspects of Nonverbal Communication in the Ancient Near East.* Studia Pohl. 12.1. Rome.
———.
1982. "The Change of the Name of the Decalogue." *Bet-Miqra* 27: 16–21. (Hebrew)

Güterbock, H. G.
1960. "Mursili's Accounts of Suppiluliuma's Dealings with Egypt." *RHA* 18/66–67: 57–63.
———.
1964. "Religion und Kultus der Hethiter." In *Neuere Hethiterforschung, Historia—Einzelschriften,* ed. G. Walser, 7.54–75. Wiesbaden.

Gulak, A.
1935. *Das Urkundenwesen im Talmud.* Jerusalem.
Gurney, O. R.
1977. *Some Aspects of Hittite Religion.* London.
Haberman, A. M.
1954. "The Phylacteries in Antiquity." *EI* 3: 174–77. (Hebrew)
Halbe, J.
1975. *Das Privilegrechts Jahwes, Exodus 34:10–26.* FRLANT 114. Göttingen.
Hallo, W. W.
1977. "New Moons and Sabbaths: A Case Study in the Conservative Approach." *HUCA* 48: 1–18.
———.
1985–86. "Biblical Abominations and Sumerian Taboos." *JQR* 86: 21–40.
Haran, M.
1958. "The Ark of the Covenant and the Cherubim." *EI* 5 (B. Mazar Volume): 83–90. (Hebrew)
———.
1959. "The Ark and the Cherubim: Their Symbolic Significance in Biblical Ritual." *IEJ* 9, pp. 30–38, 89–94.
———.
1963. "The Disappearance of the Ark." *IEJ* 13: 46–58.
———.
1968. "Mattanah." *EM* 5.674–75. (Hebrew)
———.
1970–71. "The Exodus Routes in the Pentateuchal Sources." *Tarbiz* 40: 113–43. (Hebrew)
———.
1972. *Ages and Institutions in the Bible.* Tel-Aviv.
———.
1978. *Temples and Temple Service in Ancient Israel.* Oxford.
———.
1988. "Temple and Community in Ancient Israel." In *Temple in Society,* ed. M. V. Fox, pp. 21–24. Winona Lake.
Hawkins, J. D.
1973. "Hatti." *RLA* 4.152–59.
Heinemann, J.
1966. *Prayer in the Period of the Tannaim and the Amoraim.* 2d ed. Jerusalem.
———.
1977. *Prayers in the Talmud: Forms and Patterns.* Berlin and New York.

Helck, W.
1955. "Das Dekret des Königs Haremheb." *Zeitschrift für ägyptische Sprache:* 109–36.
———.
1971. *Die Beziehungen Ägyptens zu Vorderasien in 3. und 2. Jahrtausend v. Chr.* 2d ed. Wiesbaden.
——— and E. Otto.
1972. "Akazie." *Lexikon der Ägyptiologie* 1.113. Wiesbaden.
Hermann, J.
1927. "Das zehnte Gebot." In *Festschrift E. Sellin,* pp. 69–82. Leipzig.
Hestrin, R.
1987. "The Calf Stand from Taᶜanach and Its Religious Background." In *Studia Phoenicia,* ed. E. Lipinski, 5.61–77. OLA 22. Louvain.
Hoffman, D. H.
1905. *Das Buch Leviticus.* Berlin.
———.
1908. *Midrash Tanaaim zum Deuteronomium.* Berlin.
1913. *Das Buch Deuteronomium.* Berlin.
Hoffman, H. D.
1980. *Reform und Reformen.* AThANT 66. Zurich.
Hoffman, Y.
1981–82. "Exigencies of Genre in Deuteronomy." *Shnaton* 5–6: 41–54. (Hebrew)
Hoffner, H.
1973. "The Hittites and Hurrians." In *Peoples of Old Testament Times,* ed. D. J. Wiseman, pp. 197–228. Oxford.
Holm-Nielsen, S.
1960. *Hodayot, Psalms from Qumran.* Acta theologica danica 2. Aarhus.
Holmes, S.
1914. *Joshua: The Hebrew and Greek Text.* Cambridge.
Horbury, W.
1985. "Extirpation and Excommunication." *VT* 35:13–38.
Horn, S. H.
1976. "Heshbon." *Interpreter's Dictionary of the Bible,* Supplementary Volume, pp. 410–11.
Hossfeld, F. L.
1982. *Der Dekalog.* Freiburg and Göttingen.
Hunger, H.
1968. *Babylonische und Assyrische Kolophone.* AOAT 2. Neukichen-Vluyn.
Ikeda, Y.
1978. "Hermon, Sirion, and Senir." *Annual of the Japanese Biblical Institute* 4:32–44.

Ishida, T.
1979. "The Structure and Historical Implications of the Lists of the Pre-Israelite Nations." *Biblica* 60:461–90.
Jackson, B. S.
1975a. "Liability for Mere Intention in Early Jewish Law." In *Essays in Jewish and Comparative Legal History,* pp. 202–34. Leiden.
———.
1975b. "Two or Three Witnesses." In *Essays in Jewish and Comparative Legal History,* pp. 153–71. Leiden.
Jacob, B.
1923–24. "The Decalogue." *JQR* n.s. 14:141–87.
Jacobsen, T.
1987. "The Graven Image." In *Ancient Israelite Religion: Essays in Honor of F. M. Cross,* ed. P. D. Miller, P. D. Hanson, and S. Dean McBride, pp. 15–32. Philadelphia.
Janssen, E.
1956. *Judah in der Exilzeit.* Göttingen.
Japhet, S.
1977. *The Ideology of the Book of Chronicles and Its Place in Biblical Thought.* Jerusalem. (Hebrew)
———.
1986. "The Relationship Between the Legal Corpora in the Pentateuch in Light of Manumission Laws." In *Studies in Bible,* ed. S. Japhet, pp. 63–89. Scripta Hierosolymitana 31. Jerusalem.
Jaubert, A.
1953. "Le Calendrier des Jubilés et de la secte de Qumran: *ses origines bibliques.*" *VT* 3: 250–64.
———.
1957. "Le Calendrier des Jubilés et les jours liturgiques de la semaine." *VT* 7: 35–61.
Jepsen, A.
1967. "Beiträge zur Auslegung und Geschichte das Dekalogs," *2AW* 79: 277–304
Josephus Flavius.
Antiquities of the Jews. Loeb Classical Library.
———.
The Jewish War. Loeb Classical Library.
Junker, H.
1953. "Die Entstehung des Ps. 78 und des Deuteronomium." *Biblica* 34: 487–500.
Kaddari, M. Z.
1977. "Mi Yitten in Biblical Hebrew." *Shnaton* 2: 189–95. (Hebrew)

Kallai, Z.
1960. *The Northern Boundaries of Judah from the Settlement of the Tribes Until the Beginning of the Hasmonaean Period.* Jerusalem. (Hebrew)
———.
1983. "Conquest and Settlement of Transjordan: A Historiographical Study." *ZDPV* 99: 110–18.
———.
1986. *Historical Geography of the Bible.* Jerusalem and Leiden.
Kasher, M. M.
1959. *Tora shĕlema,* vol. 19. Jerusalem. (Hebrew)
Katzenstein, H. Y.
1961. "Some Remarks on the Lists of the Chief Priests of the Temple of Solomon." *JBL* 81: 377–84.
Kaufman, S. A.
1978–79. "The Structure of the Deuteronomic Law." *Maarav* 1–2: 105–58. (Hebrew)
Kaufmann, Y.
1959. *Commentary on Joshua.* Jerusalem. (Hebrew)
———.
1960. *Tolĕdot haemunah hayisraelit.* 4 vols. Jerusalem and Tel-Aviv. (Hebrew)
———.
1966. *Mkibshonah shel hayetzyrah hamiqraʾyt.* Tel-Aviv. (Hebrew)
Keel, O.
1974. *Wirkmächtige Siegeszeichen im Alten Testament.* OBO 5. Freiburg and Göttingen.
———.
1977. *Yahwe-Visionen und Siegelkunst.* Stuttgarter Bibel Studien 84–85. Stuttgart.
———.
1978. *The Symbolism of the Biblical World: Ancient Near Eastern Iconography and the Book of Psalms.* New York.
———.
1981. "Zeichen der Verbundenheit. Zur Vorgeschichte und Bedeutung der Forderungen von Deuteronomium 6:8f. und Par." In *Mélanges Dominique Barthelemy.* OBO 38, pp. 159–240. Freiburg and Göttingen.
Kempinski, A., D. Zimchoni, E. Gilboa and N. Rösel.
1981. "Excavations at Tel-Masos: 1972, 1974, 1975, *EI* 15 (Y. Aharoni Memorial Volume), pp. 154–180.
Klein, H.
1976. "Verbot des Menschen—Diebstahls im Decologue?" *VT* 26: 161–69.
Klein, M. L.
1976. "Converse Translation: A Targumic Technique." *Biblica* 57: 515–37.

———.
1980. *The Fragment Targums of the Pentateuch According to Their Extant Sources.* Rome.
Knohl, I.
1983. "A Parasha Concerned with Accepting the Kingdom of Heaven." *Tarbiz* 53: 11–32. (Hebrew)
———.
1983–84. "The Sabbath and the Festivals in the Priestly Code and in the Laws of the Holiness School." *Shnaton* 7–8: 109–46.
———.
1987. "The Priestly Tora Versus the Holiness School: Sabbath and the Festivals." *HUCA* 58: 65–117.
Kogut, S.
1986. "On the Meaning and Syntactical Status of 'hinneh'." In *Studies in Bible,* ed. S. Japhet, pp. 133–54. Scripta Hierosolymitana 31. Jerusalem.
Kochavi, M., ed.
1972. *Judaea, Samaria, and the Golan: Archaeological Survey, 1967–68.* (Hebrew)
———.
1977. "Malḥata, Tel." *Encyclopedia of Archaeological Excavations in the Holy Land* 3.771–75.
Korošec, V.
1931. *Hethitische Staatsverträge.* Leipziger Rechtswissenschaftliche Studien 60. Leipzig.
Koschaker, P.
1951. "Zur Interpretation des art. 59 des Codex Bilalama." *JCS* 5: 104–22.
Kraemer, J.
1934. "Pliny and the Early Church Service: Fresh Light from an Old Source." *Classical Philology* 29: 293–300.
Kramer, S. N.
1963. *The Sumerians.* Chicago.
Krašovec, J.
1984. *Antithetic Structures in Biblical Hebrew Poetry.* VTSup 35. Leiden.
Kraus, H. J.
1951. "Gilgal, ein Beitrag zur Kultusgeschichte Israels." *VT* 1: 181–99.
Kristensen, A. L.
1977. "Ugaritic Epistolary Formulas: A Comparative Study of the Ugaritic Epistolary Formulas in the Context of the Contemporary Akkadian Formulas in the Letters from Ugarit and Amarna." *UF* 9: 143–58.
Kruchten, J. N.
1981. *Le décret d'Horemnele,* Brussels.
Kühne, C. and H. Otten.
1971. *Der Šaušgamuwa Vertrag, St. BoğT,* 16, Wiesbaden.

Labat, R.
1975. "Hemerologien." *Reallexikon der Assyriologie* 4.317–23. Berlin and Leipzig.
Laberge, L.
1985. "La Septante de Dt. 1–11." In *Das Deuteronomium, Enstehung, Gestalt und Botschaft,* ed. N. Lohfink, pp. 129–34. Bibliotheca ephemeridum theologicarum lovaniensium 68. Louvain.
Labuschagne, C. T.
1985a. "The Literary and Theological Function of Divine Speech in the Pentateuch." VTSup 36 (Congress Volume, Salamanca, 1983), pp. 154–73. Leiden.
———.
1985b. "Divine Speech in Deuteronomy." In *Das Deuteronomium, Entstehung, Gestalt und Botschaft,* ed. N. Lohfink, pp. 111–26. Bibliotheca ephemeridum theologicarum lovaniensium 68. Louvain.
Lafont, B.
1984. "Le Roi de Mari et les prophètes du Dieu Adad." *RA* 78: 7–18.
Lambert, W. G.
1975. "Himmel," *Reallexikon der Assyriologie* vol. 4, Berlin-New York.
Lambert, W. G. and A. R. Millard.
1969. *Atrahasis, the Babylonian Story of the Flood.* Oxford.
Lance, D. H.
1971. "The Royal Stamps and the Kingdom of Josiah." *HTR* 64: 315–32.
Lane, E. W.
1865–1877, *Arabic-English Lexicon,* 2 vols. London and Edinburgh.
Landsberger, B.
1953. "Studien zu den Urkunden aus der Zeit des Ninurta-tukul-Assur." *AfO* 10: 140–59.
Langdon, S.
1912. *Die Neuebabylonischen Königsinschriften. VAB* 4. Leipzig.
Langlamet, F.
1969. *Gilgal et les récits de la traversée du Jourdain (Jos. 3–4).* Cahiers de la Revue biblique 11. Paris.
Lapp, P. W.
1969. "The 1968 Excavations at Tell Taʿannek: The New Cultic Stand." *BASOR* 195: 2–49.
Lebrun, R.
1980. *Hymnes et prières hittites.* Louvain La Nueve.
Le Déaut, R.
1980. *Targum du Pentateuch,* vol. 4: *Deutéronome.* Paris.
———.
1981. "La Thème de la circoncision du coeur (Dt. 30:6; Jer. 4:4) dans les versions anciennes (LXX et Targum) et à Qumrân." VTSup 32 (Congress Volume, Vienna), pp. 178–205. Leiden.

Lemaire, A.
1977. "Les inscriptions de Khirbet el-Qom et L'Asherah de YHWH," *RB* 84, pp. 595–608.
Levenson, J. D.
1975. "Who Inserted the Book of the Torah?" *HTR* 68: 203–33.
———.
1981. "From Temple to Synagogue: 1 Kings 8." In *Traditions in Transformation: Turning Points in Biblical Faith, Festschrift F. M. Cross,* pp. 143–66. Winona Lake, Ind.
Levi, Y.
1969. *Studies in Jewish Hellenism.* 2d printing. Jerusalem. (Hebrew)
L'Hour, J.
1962. "L'Alliance de Sichem." *RB* 69: 5–36, 161–84, and 350–68.
Licht, J.
1973. *Testing in the Hebrew Scriptures and in Post-Biblical Judaism.* Jerusalem. (Hebrew)
———.
1978. "The Sinai Theophany." In *Studies in Bible and the Ancient Near East Presented to S. G. Loewenstamm,* pp. 251–68. Jerusalem. (Hebrew)
Lichtheim, M.
1973–76. *Ancient Egyptian Literature.* 2 vols. Berkeley, Los Angeles, and London.
Lieberman, S.
1952. "The Discipline of the So-Called Dead Sea Manual of Discipline." *JBL* 71: 199–206.
———.
1955–. *Tosephta kipheshuta,* New York.
Loewenstamm, S. A.
1954. "Gudgod." *EM* 2.431. (Hebrew)
———.
1958. "The Bearing of Psalm 81 upon the Problem of Exodus." *EI* 5: 80–82. (Hebrew)
———.
1968–69. "The Formula 'baʿet hahi' in Deuteronomy." *Tarbiz* 38: 99–104. (Hebrew)
———.
1972–73. "The Relation of the Settlement of Gad and Reuben in Num. 32:1–38, Its Background and Its Composition." *Tarbiz* 42: 12–26. (Hebrew)
———.
1980a. "Shopeṭ and shebeṭ." In *Comparative Studies in Biblical and Ancient Oriental Literatures,* pp. 270–72. AOAT 204. Neukirchen-Vluyu.

———.
1980b. "The Making and Destruction of the Golden Calf." In *Comparative Studies in Biblical and Ancient Oriental Literatures,* pp. 236–40. AOAT 204. Neukirchen-Vluyu.
———.
1983. "ʿam segulla." *Meḥqĕrey lashon: Festschrift Z. Ben Hayyim,* pp. 321–28. Jerusalem. (Hebrew)
Lohfink, N.
1962. "Der Bundesschluss im Land Moab—Redaktiongeschichtliches zu Deut. 28:69–32:47." *BZ* n.s. 6: 32–56.
———.
1963. *Das Hauptgebot.* Analecta biblica 20. Rome.
———.
1976. "Gott im Buch Deuteronomium." In *La Notion biblique de Dieu,* ed. J. Coppens, pp. 101–26. Bibliotheca ephemeridum theologicarum Lovaniensium 41. Louvain.
———.
1983. "Die Bedeutungen von hebr. jrš qal und hiph." *BZ* 27: 14–33.
———.
1986. "ḥrm." *TDOT* 5. 180–99.
———.
1987. "The Cult Reform of Josiah of Judah: 2 Kgs 22–23 as a Source for the History of Israelite Religion." In *Ancient Israelite Religion: Essays in Honor of F. M. Cross,* pp. 459–75. Philadelphia.
Loza, J.
1971. "Les Catéchèses étiologiques dans l'Ancien Testament." *RB* 78: 481–500.
McBride, S. Dean.
1973. "The Yoke of the Kingdom—An Exposition of Deuteronomy 6:4–5." *Interpretation* 27: 273–306.
McCarter, P. K.
1984. *Samuel.* AB 8–9. New York.
McKay, J. W.
1973. *Religion in Judah Under the Assyrians, 732–609 B.C.* London.
Malamat, A.
1955. "Doctrines of Causality in Hittite and Biblical Historiography: A Parallel." *VT* 5: 1–12.
———.
1963. "Hatzerim in the Bible and in Mari." *BJPES:* 180–84. (Hebrew)
———.
1970. "Northern Canaan and the Mari Texts." In *Near Eastern Archaeology in the Twentieth Century: Essays in Honor of N. Glueck,* ed. J. A. Sanders, pp. 164–77. New York.

———.
1971. "Syro-Palestinian Destination in a Mari Tin Inventory." *IEJ* 21: 31–38.

———.
1979. "The Last Years of the Kingdom of Judah." In *A World History of the Jewish People: The Age of the Monarchs; Political History,* ed. H. H. Ben Sasson, 1.228–34. Jerusalem.

———.
1980. "A Mari Prophecy and Nathan's Dynastic Oracle." In *Prophecy: Essays Presented to G. Fohrer on His 65th Birthday,* ed. J. A. Emerton, pp. 68–82. BZAW 150. Berlin and New York.

———.
1983. *Israel in Biblical Times.* Jerusalem. (Hebrew)

Mann, J.
1925. "Genizah Fragments of the Palestinian Order of Service." *HUCA* 2: 269–338.

Margaliot, M.
1980. "Jeremiah 10:1–16, A Re-examination." *VT* 30: 295–308.

Margalith, O.
1983–84. "The Girgashi." *Shnaton* 7–8: 259–63. (Hebrew)

Margulis, B.
1970. "A Ugaritic Psalm (RS 24.252)." *JBL* 89: 292–304.

Mayes, A. H. D.
1981. *Deuteronomy.* New Century Bible Commentary Grand Rapids, Mich. and London.

Mazar, A.
1982. "The 'Bull Site'—An Iron Age 1 Open Cult Place." *BASOR* 247: 27–42.

———.
1986. "The Early Israelite Settlement in the Hill Country." In *The Early Biblical Period: Historical Studies,* ed. S. Ahituv and B. A. Levine, pp. 259–63. Jerusalem.

Mazar (Maisler), B.
1938. "The Excavations at Sheik Ibreiq (Beth Sheʿarim), 1936–37." *JPOS* 18: 41–49.

———.
1945–46. "Lebo Hamath and the Northern Boundary of Canaan." *BJPES* 12: 91–102. (Hebrew)

———.
1959. *Views of the Biblical World* 1959–61. Chicago, NY/Jerusalem. 5 volumes.

———.
1961. "Geshur and Maacah." *JBL* 80: 16–28.

———.
1962. "Caphtor." *EM* 4. 236–38. (Hebrew)
———.
1965. "The Sanctuary of Arad and the Family of Hobab the Kenite." *JNES* 24: 297–303.
———.
1975a. *Cities and Districts in Eretz-Israel.* Jerusalem. (Hebrew)
———.
1975b. "Ezion Geber and Ebrona." *EI* 12 (N. Glueck Volume): 46–48. (Hebrew)
Meissner, B.
1918. "Die Beziehungen Ägyptens zum Hattireiche nach hattischen Quellen." *ZDMG* 72: 32–64. = KBO 1.24 Rs. 5ff.
Mendenhall, G. E.
1954. *Covenant Forms in Israelite Traditions.* Bibl. Arch. pp. 50–76.
———.
1973. *The Tenth Generation.* Baltimore.
Meshel, Z.
1975. "On the Problem of Tell el-Halifa, Eilat, and Ezion Geber." *EI* 12 (N. Glueck Volume): 49–56. (Hebrew)
———.
1978. *Kuntillet ʿAjrud: A Religious Center from the Time of the Judaean Monarchy on the Border of Sinai,* Catalogue No. 175, Jerusalem.
Milgrom, J.
1970. *Studies in Levitical Terminology.* Berkeley, Los Angeles, and London.
———.
1973. "The Alleged Demythologization and Secularization in Deuteronomy." *IEJ* 23: 156–61.
———.
1976. "Profane Slaughter and a Formulaic Key to the Composition of Deuteronomy." *HUCA* 47: 1–17.
Milik, J. T.
1959. *Ten Years of Discovery in the Wilderness of Judea.* London.
———.
1976. *The Books of Enoch.* Oxford.
Millard, A. R.
1988. "King Og's Bed and Other Ancient Ironmongery." In *Ascribe to the Lord: P. C. Craigie Memorial Volume,* ed. L. Eslinger and G. Taylor, pp. 481–92. *JSOT* Suppl. Series. Sheffield.
Miller, M.
1989. "The Israelite Journey Through Moab," *JBL* 108, pp 590–95.
Miller, P., Jr.
1984. "The Most Important Word: The Yoke of the Kingdom." *Illif Review:* 17–29.

Minette de Tellesse, G.
1962. "Sections 'tu' et sections 'vous' dans le Deutéronome." *VT* 12: 29–87.
Moberly, R. W. L.
1983. *At the Mountain of God: Story and Theology in Exodus 32–34. JSOT* Suppl. Series 22. Sheffield.
Mohler, S. L.
1935. "The Bithynian Christians Again." *Classical Philology* 30: 167–69.
Montgomery, J. A.
1934. "Archival Data in the Book of Kings." *JBL* 53: 46–52.
Moran, W. L.
1962. "A Kingdom of Priests." In *The Bible in Current Catholic Thought.* New York, ed. J. L. McKenzie, pp. 7–22.
———.
1963a. "A Note on the Treaty Terminology of the Sefire Stelas." *JNES* 22: 173–76.
———.
1963b. "The Ancient Near Eastern Background of the Love of God in Deuteronomy." *CBQ* 25: 77–87.
———.
1963c. "The End of the Unholy War and the Anti-Exodus." *Biblica* 44: 333–42.
———.
1966. "The Literary Connection Between Lv. 11:13–19 and Dt. 14:12–18." *CBQ* 28: 271–77.
———.
1967. "The Conclusion of the Decalogue (Ex. 20:17 = Dt. 5:21)." *CBQ* 29: 543–54.
Mowinckel, S.
1927. *Le Décalogue.* Paris.
Muffs, Y.
1969. *Studies in the Aramaic Legal Papyri from Elephantine.* Leiden.
———.
1975. "Joy and Love as Metaphorical Expressions of Willingness and Spontaneity in Cuneiform, Ancient Hebrew and Related Literatures." *Christianity, Judaism and Other Graeco-Roman Cults: Festschrift M. Smith,* ed. J. Neusner, 3.1–36. Leiden.
———.
1978. "Reflections of Prophetic Prayer in the Bible." *EI* 14 (H. L. Ginsberg Volume): 48–54. (Hebrew)
———.
1979. "Love and Joy as Metaphors of Volition in Hebrew and Related Literatures, Part 2: The Joy of Giving." *Journal of the Ancient Near Eastern Society of Columbia University* 11: 91–111.

Munn-Rankin, J. M.
1956. "Diplomacy in Western Asia in the Early Second Millennium B.C." *Iraq* 18: 68–110.
Muraoka, T.
1978. "On the So-Called 'Dativus Ethicus' in Hebrew." *JTS* 29: 495–98.
———.
1985. *Emphatic Words and Structures.* Jerusalem and Leiden.
Na'aman, N.
1974. "Sennacherib's 'Letter to God' on His Campaign to Judah." *BASOR* 214: 25–39.
Nauck, A.
1889. *Tragicorum graecorum fragmenta.* 2d ed. Leipzig.
Naveh, J.
1960. "A Hebrew Letter from the Seventh Century B.C." *IEJ* 10: 129–39.
———.
1962. "The Excavations of Meṣad Ḥašabyahu." *IEJ* 12: 27–32.
Nelson, H. H.
1932. *Medinet Habu,* vol. 2: *Earlier Historical Records of Ramesses 3.* OIP 9. Chicago.
Neufeld, E.
1980. "Insects as Warfare Agents in the Ancient Near East." *Orientalia* 49: 30–57.
Nicholson, E. W.
1977. "The Decalogue as the Direct Address of God." *VT* 27: 422–33.
———.
1986. *God and His People: Covenant and Theology in the Old Testament.* Oxford.
Nielsen, E.
1968. *The Ten Commandments in New Perspective.* Studies in Biblical Theology 2/7. London.
———.
1983. "Weil Jahwe unser Gott ein Jahwe ist." In *Law, History and Tradition: Selected Essays by E. Nielsen,* pp. 106–18. Copenhagen.
Nilsson, M. P.
1974. *Geschichte der Griechischen Religion,* vol. 2. 3d ed. Munich.
Nitzan, B.
1986. *Pesher Habbakuk.* Jerusalem. (Hebrew)
Nock, A. D.
1924. "The Christian Sacramentum in Pliny and a Pagan Counterpart." *Classical Review* 38: 58–59.
———.
1928. "Early Gentile Christianity and Its Hellenistic Background." In *Essays in the Trinity and the Incarnation,* ed. A. E. J. Rawlinson, 49–133. Lon-

don. = Nock 1972. *Essays on Religion and the Ancient World,* ed. Z. Stewart, 1.65ff. Oxford.

Noth, M.

1943. *Überlieferungsgeschichtliche Studien,* vol. 1. Halle.

———.

1966. *The Laws in the Pentateuch and Other Essays.* Philadelphia.

Oates, J.

1965. "Assyrian Chronology, 631–612 B.C." *Iraq* 27: 135–59.

Obbink, K. M.

1929. "Yahwebilder." *ZAW* 47: 164–74.

Oded, B.

1968. "Nebo, Mt. Nebo." *EM* 5.688–90. (Hebrew)

———.

1976. "Qenat." *EM* 7.203–5. (Hebrew)

———.

1979. *Mass Deportations and Deportees in the Neo-Assyrian Empire.* Wiesbaden.

Oesch, J. M.

1979. *Petucha und Setuma.* Freiburg and Göttingen.

Oppenheim, A. L.

1964. *Ancient Mesopotamia: Portrait of a Dead Civilization.* Chicago and London.

Otten, H.

1956. "Ein Text zum Neujahrfest aus Bogazkoy." *OLZ* 51: 101–5.

———.

1963. "Neue Quellen zum Ausklang des Hethitischen Reiches." *MDOG* 94: 1–23.

——— and C. Kühne.

1971. *Der Shaushgamuwa-Vertrag.* Studien zu den Boğazköy Texten 16. Wiesbaden.

Otto, E.

1975. *Das Mazzotfest in Gilgal.* BWANT 107. Stuttgart and Berlin.

Ottosson, M.

1969. *Gilead, Tradition and History.* Lund.

Parpola, S.

1970. *Neo-Assyrian Toponyms.* AOAT 6. Neukirchen.

Patrich, J.

1985. "Prohibition of Graven Image Among the Nabateans—The Non-Figurative Trend in Their Art." *Cathedra for the History of Eretz Israel* 38: 3–54. (Hebrew)

Paul, S. M.

1968. "The Image of the Oven and the Cake in Hosea 7:4–10." *VT* 18: 114–20.

———.

1970. *Studies in the Book of the Covenant in the Light of Cuneiform and Biblical Law.* VTSup 18. Leiden.

———.

1972. "Psalm 72:5, a Traditional Blessing for the Long Life of the King." *JNES* 31: 351–55.

———.

1978. "Adoption Formulae." *EI* 14 (H. L. Ginsberg Volume): 31–36. (Hebrew)

Pedersen, J.

1946–47. *Israel, Its Life and Culture.* 2d ed. London and Copenhagen.

Perlitt, L.

1969. *Bundestheologie im Alten Testament.* WMANT 36. Neukirchen.

———.

1977. "Sinai und Horeb." In *Beiträge zur Alttestamentlichen Theologie,* ed. H. Donner, R. Hanhart, and R. Smend, pp. 302–322. Göttingen.

———.

1981. "Wovon der Mensch lebt (Dt. 8:3b)." *Die Botschaft und die Boten. Festschrift H. W. Wolff,* 403–26. Neukirchen-Vluyn.

Peterson, E.

1926. *Heis Theos.* FRLANT n.s. 24.41. Göttingen.

Pettazzoni, R.

1937. "Confession of Sins and the Classics." *HTR* 30: 1–14.

Plöeger, J. G.

1967. *Literarkritische formgeschichtliche und stilkritische Untersuchungen zum Deuteronomium.* Bonn.

Pöbel, A.

1914. *Historical and Grammatical Texts.* Philadelphia.

———.

1932. *Das appositionell Bestimmte Pronomen der 1 Pers. Sing. in den Westsemitischen Inschriften und im Alten Testament.* AS 3. Chicago.

Pope, M. H. and J. H. Tigay.

1971. "A Description of Baal." *UF* 3: 117–30.

Porten, B.

1969. "The Religion of the Jews of Elephantine in Light of the Hermopolis Papyri," *JNES* 28: 116–21.

———.

1981. "The Identity of King Adon." *BA* 44: 36–52.

Postgate, J. N.

1969. *Neo-Assyrian Royal Grants and Decrees.* Studia Pohl. Series Maior 1. Rome.

Potin, J.

1971. *La Fête juive de la Pentecôte.* Études des textes liturgiques 2. Paris.

Qimron, E.
1986. "The Halakha of Damascus Covenant: An Interpretation of 'ʿAl yitʿarev'." In *Proceedings of the Ninth World Congress of Jewish Studies,* Division D, 1.9–16. Jerusalem. (Hebrew)
Quell, G.
1964. "The Concept of Law in the O.T." *ThDNT* 2.174–78.
Rabast, K.
1949. *Das apodiktische Recht im Deuteronomium und im Heiligkeitsgesetz.* Berlin.
Rabin, H.
1954. *The Zadokite Documents.* 2d ed. Oxford.
Rabinowitz, L. I.
1971. "Mezuzah." *EncJud* 11.1474–77.
Rad, G. von.
1963. *Studies in Deuteronomy.* Studies in Biblical Theology 9. London.
———.
1966. *The Problem of the Hexateuch and Other Essays.*
Reade, J. E.
1970. "The Accession of Sinsharishkun." *JCS* 23: 1–9.
Reid, P. V.
1975. "šbṭy in 2 Sam. 7:7." *CBQ* 37: 17–20.
Reider, J.
1966. *Index to Aquila.* VTSup 12. Leiden.
Reif, S. C.
1984. "Ibn Ezra on Psalm 1:1–2." *VT* 34: 232–36.
Reiner, E.
1958. *Shurpu: A Collection of Sumerian and Akkadian Incantations.* AfO 11. Graz.
———.
1982. "The Babylonian Fürstenspiegel in Practice." In *Societies and Languages of the Ancient Near East: Festschrift I. M. Diakonoff,* pp. 320–26.
Reitzenstein, R.
1927. *Die hellenistischen Mysterienreligionen nach ihren Grundgedanken und Wirkungen.* 3d ed. Leipzig and Berlin.
Riemschneider, K.
1958. "Die Hethitischen Landschenkungsurkunden." *Mitteilungen des Instituts für Orientforschung der Deutschen Akademie der Wissenschaften zu Berlin* 6.3: 321–81.
Riesener, I.
1979. *Der Stamm ʿbd im Alten Testament.* BZAW 149. Berlin.
Robinson, E.
1856. *Biblical Researches in Palestine and the Adjacent Regions,* vol. 2. Boston.

Rochberg-Halton, F.
1984. "Canonicity in Cuneiform Texts." *JCS* 36: 127–44.
Rofé, A.
1972. "The Strata of the Law About the Centralization of Worship in Deuteronomy and the History of the Deuteronomic Movement." *VTSup* 22 (Congress Volume, Uppsala), pp. 221–26. Leiden.
———.
1982. "Deuteronomy 5:28–6:1, Composition and Text in the Light of Deuteronomic Style and Three Tefillin from Qumran." *Tarbiz* 51: 177–84. (Hebrew)
———.
1983. "Historico-Literary Criticism Illustrated by Joshuah 20." In *I. L. Seeligmann Volume,* ed. A. Rofé and Y. Zakovitch, 1.137–50. Jerusalem. (Hebrew)
———.
1985. "The Monotheistic Argumentation in Deut. 4:32–40, Contents, Composition and Text." *VT* 35: 434–45.
Rothenberg, B.
1967. *Secrets of the Negev.* Ramat Gan. (Hebrew)
———.
1978. "Timna." *Encyclopedia of Archaeological Excavations in the Holy Land,* ed. M. Avi-Yonah and E. Stern, 4.1184–1203. Jerusalem.
Rudolph, W.
1958. *Jeremiah.* 2d ed. HAT 1.12, Tübingen.
Saeb, M.
1974. "Grenzbeschreibung und Landideal im Alten Testament mit besondere Berücksichtigung der 'min-ʿad' Formel." *ZDPV* 90: 14–37.
Ṣarfati, G. Ben Ami.
1990. "The Tablets of the Covenant as a Symbol of Judaism." In *The Ten Commandments in History and Tradition* (ed. B. Z. Segal, pp. 383–418, Jerusalem.
Sarna, N. M.
1979. "The Psalm Superscriptions and the Guilds." In *Studies in Jewish Religion and Intellectual History Presented to A. Altman,* pp. 281–300. University, Alabama.
Schachermeyer, F.
1982. *Die Levante im Zeitalter der Wanderungen vom 13. bis zum 11. Jahrhundert v. Chr.* Die Ägäische Frühzeit 5. Vienna.
Schäder, H. H.
1930. *Esra der Schreiber.* BHT 5. Tübingen.
Scharbert, J.
1957. "Formgeschichte und Exegese von Ex. 34:6f. und seiner Paralellen." *Biblica* 38: 130–50.

———.
1960. "Das Verbum pqd in der Theologie des Altes Testaments." *BZ* n.s. 4: 209–26.

Schiffman, L. H.
1975. *The Halakha at Qumran.* Studies in Judaism in Late Antiquity 16. Leiden.

Scholem, G.
1975. *Shabetay Tsevi, the Mystical Messiah, 1626–1676.* Bollingen Series 93. Princeton.

Schorr, M.
1913. *Urkunden des altbabylonischen Zivil- und Prozessrechts.* VAB 5. Leipzig.

Schottroff, W.
1964. *"Gedenken" im Alten Orient und im Alten Testament.* WMANT 15. Neukirchen.

Schuler, E. von
1957. *Hethitische Dienstanweisungen für höhere Hof- und Staatsbeamte. AfO* Beiheft 10. Graz.

Schwartz, B.
1979. "Psalm 50, Its Subject, Form and Place." *Shnaton* 3: 77–106. (Hebrew)

———.
1980. *Leviticus 19: A Literary Commentary to a Pentateuchal Legal Passage.* M.A. thesis. Hebrew University of Jerusalem. (Hebrew)

Seeligmann, I. L.
1961. "Aetiological Elements in Biblical Historiography." *Zion* 26: 141–69. (Hebrew)

———.
1963. "Menschliches Heldentum und Göttliche Hilfe." *Theologische Zeitschrift* 19: 385–411.

———.
1967. "Zur Terminologie für das Gerichtsverfahren im Wortschatz den biblischen Hebräisch." In *Festschrift W. Baumgartner,* pp. 251–78. VTSup 16. Leiden.

———.
1977. "Erkenntnis Gottes und historisches Bewusstsein im Alten Israel." In *Beiträge zur alttestamentlichen Theologie. Festschrift für W. Zimmerli,* ed. H. Donner, R. Hanhart, and R. Smend, pp. 414–45. Göttingen.

Segal, M. Z.
1947. "Papyrus Nash." *Leshonenu* 15: 27–36.

———.
1957. *Massoret uBiqqoret,* pp. 227–36. Jerusalem. (Hebrew)

Seidel, M.
1978. *Hiqrey Miqra.* Jerusalem. (Hebrew)

Seux, M. S.
1967. *Epithètes royales Akkadiennes et Sumeriennes.* Paris.
Seyring, F.
1891. "Der Alttestamentliche Sprachgebrauch im betreff des Namens der sogen. 'Bundeslade'." *ZAW* 11: 114–25.
Sherwin-White, A. N.
1966. *The Letters of Pliny.* Oxford.
Siewert, P.
1972. *Der Eid von Plataiai.* Munich.
Simons, J.
1937. *Handbook for the Study of Egyptian Topographical Lists Relating to Western Asia.* Leiden.
———.
1959. The Geographical and Topographical Texts of the Old Testament, Leiden.
Singer, S.
1915. *The Standard Prayer Book.* New York.
Skehan, P. W.
1955. "Exodus in the Samaritan Recension from Qumran." *JBL* 74: 182–87.
Skweres, D. E.
1979. *Die Rückverweise im Buch Deuteronomium.* Analecta biblica 79. Rome.
Slouschz, N.
1942. *Ancient Phoenician Inscriptions.* Tel Aviv. (Hebrew)
Smith, G. A.
1918. *The Book of Deuteronomy.* CB. Cambridge.
Soden, W. von
1967. "Assuretellilani, Sinsharishkun, Sinshum(u)lisher und die Ereignisse im Assyrerreich nach 635 v. Chr." *ZA* 58: 241–55.
Soggin, J. A.
1966. "Gilgal, Passa und Landnahme." *VTSup* 15, pp. 263–77. Leiden.
Sokolowski, F.
1955. *Lois sacrées de l'Asie mineure.* Paris.
Speiser, E. A.
1957–58. "Twtpt." *JQR* 48: 208–17.
———.
1958. "Census and Ritual Expiation in Mari and Israel." *BASOR* 149: 17–25.
———.
1960. " 'People' and 'Nation' of Israel." *JBL* 79: 157–63.
Spieckermann, H.
1982. *Judah unter Assur in der Sargonidenzeit.* FRLANT 129. Göttingen.

Spiegel, S.
1969. *The Last Trial.* New York.
Staerk, W.
1894. *Das Deuteronomium, sein Inhalt und seine literarische Form.* Leipzig.
Stamm, J. J.
1961. "Dreissig Jahre Dekalogforschung." *Theologische Rundschau* n.s. 27: 189–239 and 281–305.
——— and M. E. Andrew.
1967. *The Ten Commandments in Recent Research.* Studies in Biblical Theology. 2/2. London.
Stegemann, H.
1967–69. "40 mit Exzerpten aus Deuteronomium." *RevQ* 6: 193–227.
Steuernagel, C.
1894. *Der Rahmen des Deuteronomiums.* Halle.
———.
1923. *Das Deuteronomium.* 2d ed. HKAT. Göttingen.
Strange, J.
1980. *Caphtor/Keftiu: A New Investigation.* Leiden.
Streck, M.
1916. *Assurbanipal und die letzten Assyrischen Könige bis zum Untergang Ninvehs.* 2d ed. VAB 7.2. Leipzig.
Strugnell, J.
1967. "Quelques Inscriptions Samaritaines." *RB* 74: 555–80.
———.
1970. "Notes en marge du volume 5 des 'Discoveries in the Judean Desert of Jordan.' " *RevQ* 7.2: 163–276.
Sukenik, E. L.
1929. " 'Kathedra shel Moshe' in Ancient Synagogues." *Tarbiz* 1.1: 145–51. (Hebrew)
Tadmor, H.
1958. "The Campaigns of Sargon 2 of Aššur: A Chronological-Historical Study." *JCS* 12: 22–40 and 77–100.
———.
1973. "The Historical Inscriptions of Adad Nirari 3." *Iraq* 35: 141–50.
Talmon, S.
1961. "The Calendar Reckoning of the Sect from the Judean Desert." In *Essays on the Dead Sea Scrolls in Memory of E. L. Sukenik,* ed. H. Rabin and Y. Yadin, pp. 77–106. Jerusalem.
———.
1965–66. "Hebrew Apocryphal Psalms from Qumran." *Tarbiz* 35: 214–34. (Hebrew)
Thureau-Dangin, F.
1937. "Trois Contrats de Ras-Shamra." *Syria* 18: 245–55.

Tigay, J. H.
1982. "On the Meaning of 'ṭ(w)ṭpt'." *JBL* 101: 321–31.
———.
1983. "The Early Technique of Aggadic Exegesis." In *History, Historiography and Interpretation: Studies in Biblical and Cuneiform Literatures,* ed. H. Tadmor and M. Weinfeld, pp. 169–89. Jerusalem.
Toeg, A.
1977. *Lawgiving at Sinai.* Jerusalem. (Hebrew)
Tov, E.
1985. "The Nature and Background of Harmonizations in Biblical Manuscripts." *JSOT* 31: 3–29.
———.
1987. "Die Septuaginta in ihrem theologischen und traditionsgeschichtlichen Verhältnis zur hebräischen Bibel." *Die Mittel der Schrift? Ein Jüdisch-Christliche Gespräch, Texte der Berner Symposions von 6–12 Januar, 1985,* ed. M. Klopfenstein, V. Luz, S. Talmon, and E. Tov, pp. 237–68. Bern.
Trumbull, H. C.
1984. *Kadesh Barnea.* London.
Tscherikover, V. A.
1932–33. "Palestine in the Light of the Papyri of Zenon." *Tarbiz* 4: 226–47 and 354–65. (Hebrew)
———.
1959. *Hellenistic Civilization and the Jews.* Philadelphia.
Tsedaka, B.
1969. "Shabuoth and the Samaritans." *Ba-Maʿarakhah* 98 (June): 10–11.
Tur-Sinai (Torczyner), N. H.
1925. "Dunkele Bibelstellen." In *Vom Alten Testament. Festschrift K. Marti,* pp. 274–80. BZAW 41. Giesen.
———.
1957. *The Book of Job: A New Commentary,* Jerusalem.
Urbach, E. E.
1979. *The Sages.* Jerusalem.
———.
1978. *Sefer pitron Torah.* Jerusalem. (Hebrew)
Urman, D.
1972. "Jewish Inscriptions from Dabbura in the Golan." *IEJ* 22: 16–23.
van Selms, A.
1967. " 'Halo' in the Courtier's Language in Ancient Israel." In *Proceedings of the Fourth World Congress of Jewish Studies,* 1.137–40. Jerusalem.
van Zyl, A. H.
1960. *The Moabites.* Pretoria Oriental Series. Leiden.
Vaux, R. de
1968. "Le Pays de Canaan." *JAOS* 88 (In Memory of E. A. Speiser): 23–30.

Veijola, T.
1976. "Zu Ableitung und Bedeutung von heʿid I im Hebräischen." *UF* 8: 343–51.
Views of the Biblical World
1959–61. Chicago, New York/Tel Aviv, Ramat Gan, 5 vols.
Volkwein, B.
1969. "Massoretisches *ʿedut, ʿedwot, ʿedot*—'Zeugnis' oder 'Bundesbestimmungen'?" *BZ* n.s. 13: 18–40.
Waterman, L.
1930. *Royal Correspondence of the Assyrian Empire.* Ann Arbor, Mich.
Weidner, E.
1923. *Politische Documente aus Kleinasien.* Boghazköi Studien 8–9. Leipzig.
———.
1935. "Aus den Tagen eines assyrischen Schattenkönigs." *AfO* 10: 1–52.
———.
1951. "Assurbanipal in Assur." *AfO* 14: 204–18.
Weinfeld, M.
1964a. "Cult Centralization in Israel in the Light of a Neo-Babylonian Analogy." *JNES* 23: 202–12.
———.
1964. "The Awakening of National Consciousness in Israel in the 7th Century B.C." In *Oz LeDavid: D. Ben-Gurion Jubilee Volume,* pp. 396–420. Jerusalem. (Hebrew)
———.
1964b. "Universalism and Particularism in the Time of the Restoration." *Tarbiz* 34: 228–42. (Hebrew)
———.
1965. "Traces of Assyrian Treaty Formulae in Deuteronomy." *Biblica* 46: 417–27.
———.
1967–68. "God the Creator in Genesis 1 and in Deutero-Isaiah." *Tarbiz* 37: 105–32. (Hebrew)
———.
1968a. "Nekar, Nokri, Nokriya." *EM* 5.866–867. (Hebrew)
———.
1968b. "The Period of the Conquest and of the Judges as Seen by the Earlier and Later Sources." *VT* 17: 93–113.
———.
1969. "Theological Currents in Pentateuchal Literature." In *Proceedings of the American Academy for Jewish Research,* pp. 117–39. New York.
———.
1970–72. "The Covenant of Grant in the Old Testament and in the Ancient Near East." *JAOS* 90: 184–203; 92: 468–69.

———. 1971. "Tithe." *EncJud* 15.1156–62.

———. 1971–72a. "Habĕrith veHaḥesed—'Bond and Grace'—Covenantal Expressions in the Bible and in the Ancient World: A Common Heritage." *Leshonenu* 36: 85–105. (Hebrew)

———. 1971–72b. "King-People Relationship in the Light of 1 Kings 12:7." *Leshonenu* 36: 3–13. (Hebrew)

———. 1972a. *Deuteronomy and the Deuteronomistic School.* Oxford.

———. 1972b. "The Worship of Molech and the Queen of Heaven and Its Background." *UF* 4: 133–54.

———. 1973a. "Covenant Terminology in the Ancient Near East and Its Influence on the West." *JAOS* 93: 190–99.

———. 1973b. "On 'Demythologization and Secularization' in Deuteronomy." *IEJ* 23: 230–33.

———. 1973c. "The Origin of the Apodictic Law: An Overlooked Source." *VT* 23: 63–75.

———. 1974. "Concerning the Treaty Terms in Greek and in Latin." *Leshonenu* 38: 231–37. (Hebrew)

———. 1975a. *The Book of Genesis.* Tel Aviv. (Hebrew)

———. 1975b. "Bĕrith." *TDOT* 2.253–79 (or Weinfeld 1973d, *ThWAT* 1.781–808).

———. 1975–76. "Traces of 'Qedushat Yozer' and 'Pesuqey d'Zimrah' in the Qumran Literature and Ben Sira." *Tarbiz* 45: 15–26. (Hebrew)

———. 1976a. "Jeremiah and the Spiritual Metamorphosis of Israel." *ZAW* 88: 18–56.

———. 1976b. "The Loyalty Oath in the Ancient Near East." *UF* 8: 379–414.

———. 1976. "The Ten Commandments—Their Meaning and Place in Israelite Tradition," Reflections on the Bible (in Memory of Yishai Ron), Tel-Aviv, pp. 109–21.

———.
1977. "B. Mazar, Cities and Districts in Eretz Israel." *Shnaton* 2: 256–58.

———.
1977a. "Judge and Officer in Ancient Israel and in the Ancient Near East." *IOS* 7: 65–88.

———.
1977b. "The Genuine Jewish Attitude Toward Abortion." *Zion* 42: 129–42. (Hebrew)

———.
1978. "Pentecost as the Festival of the Giving of the Law." *Immanuel* 8: 7–18.

———.
1978–79a. " 'Temple Scroll' or 'King's Law.' " *Shnaton* 3: 214–37. (Hebrew)

———.
1978–79b. "The Prayers for Knowledge, Repentance and Forgiveness in the 'Eighteen Benedictions': Qumran Parallels, Biblical Antecedents and Basic Characteristics." *Tarbiz* 48: 186–200. (Hebrew)

———.
1980. "The Royal Guard According to the Temple Scroll." *RB* 87: 394–96.

———.
1981a. "F. Crüsemann, 1978, *Der Widerstand gegen das Königtum,* WMANT, 49, Neukirchen." *VT* 31: 99–106.

———.
1981b. "Sabbath, Temple and the Enthronement of the Lord." In *Festschrift H. Cazelles,* pp. 501–12. AOAT 212. Neukirchen-Vluyn.

———.
1982a. "Instructions for Temple Visitors in the Bible and in Ancient Egypt." In *Egyptological Studies,* ed. S. Israelit-Groll, pp. 224–50. Scripta Hierosolymitana 28. Jerusalem.

———.
1982b. "On the Primacy of Morality in Ancient Near Eastern Prophecy." *Shnaton* 5–6: 233–34. (Hebrew)

———.
1982c. "The Counsel of the 'Elders' to Rehoboam and Its Implications." *Maarav* 3.1: 27–53.

———.
1982d. "The King as the Servant of the People: The Sources of the Idea." *JJS* 33 *(Essays in Honor of Y. Yadin):* 189–94.

———.
1982e. " 'They Should Bring All of Their Mind, All of Their Strength and All of Their Wealth into the Community of God.' " In *Bible Studies: Y. M. Grinz in Memoriam,* ed. B. Uffenheimer, pp. 37–41. Teʿuda 2. Tel Aviv. (Hebrew)

———.
1982f. "The Tribal League at Sinai." In *Ancient Israelite Religion: Festschrift F. M. Cross,* ed. P. D. Hanson and S. D. McBride, pp. 303–14. Philadelphia.

———.
1983a. "Divine Intervention in War in Ancient Israel and in the Ancient Near East." In *History, Historiography and Interpretation: Studies in Biblical and Cuneiform Literatures,* ed. H. Tadmor and M. Weinfeld, pp. 121–47. Jerusalem.

———.
1983b. "Social and Cultic Institutions in the Priestly Source Against Their Ancient Near Eastern Background." In *Proceedings of the Eighth World Congress of Jewish Studies,* Panel Sessions, Bible Studies and Hebrew Language, pp. 95–129. Jerusalem.

———.
1983c. "The Extent of the Promised Land—The Status of Transjordan." In *Das Land Israel in biblischer Zeit,* ed. G. Strecker, pp. 59–75. Göttingen.

———.
1983d. "Zion and Jerusalem as Religious and Political Capital, Ideology and Utopia." In *The Poet and the Historian: Essays in Literary and Historical Biblical Criticism,* ed. R. E. Friedman, pp. 75–115. HSS 26. Chico, California.

———.
1984a. "Inheritance of the Land—Privilege Versus Obligation: The Concept of the 'Promise of the Land' in the Sources of the First and Second Temple Periods." *Zion* 49: 115–37. (Hebrew)

———.
1984b. "Kabod." *ThWAT* 4.23–39.

———.
1984c. "Kuntillet Ajrud Inscriptions and Their Significance." *Studi epigrafici e linguistici* 1: 121–30.

———.
1984d. "Minḥa." *ThWAT* 4.987–1000.

———.
1985a. "Freedom Proclamations in Egypt and in the Ancient Near East." In *Pharaonic Egypt: The Bible and Christianity,* ed. S. Israelit-Groll, pp. 317–27. Jerusalem.

———.
1985b. "The Aramaic Text from Egypt Concerning Morals and Cult and Its Relation to the Bible." *Shnaton* 9: 179–89. (Hebrew)

———.
1985c. "The Emergence of the Deuteronomic Movement: The Historical Antecedents." In *Das Deuteronomium, Entstehung, Gestalt und Botschaft,*

ed. N. Lohfink, pp. 76–98. Bibliotheca ephemeridum theologicarum Lovaniensium 68. Louvain.

———. 1985d. *Justice and Righteousness in Israel and the Nations.* Jerusalem. (Hebrew)

———. 1986a. "Contents and Different Layers of the Book of Numbers." In *Olam Hatanach.* pp. 10–12. Tel Aviv. (Hebrew)

———. 1986b. "The Day of the Lord: Aspirations for the Kingdom of God in the Bible and in Jewish Liturgy." In *Studies in Bible,* ed. S. Japhet, pp. 341–72. Scripta Hierosolymitana 31. Jerusalem.

———. 1986c. *The Organizational Pattern and the Penal Code of the Qumran Sect.* Freiburg and Göttingen.

———. 1987. "The Tribal League in Sinai." In *Ancient Israelite Religion: Festschrift F. M. Cross,* ed. P. D. Hanson and S. D. McBride, pp. 303–14. Philadelphia.

———. 1988. "The Pattern of the Israelite Settlement in Canaan." VTSup 40 (Jerusalem Congress Volume), pp. 270–83. Leiden.

Weinreich, O.
1919. *Stiftung und Kultsatzungen eines Privatheiligtums in Philadelphia in Lydien.* Sitzungsberichte der Heidelberger Akademie der Wissenschaften, phil.-histor. Klasse, Abhandlung 16. Heidelberg.

Weippert, M.
1972. "Assyrische Prophetien der Zeit Esarhaddons und Assurbanipals." In *Assyrian Royal Inscriptions: New Horizons,* ed. F. M. Fales, pp. 71–111. Rome.

———. 1982. "Die 'Bileam' Inschrift von Tell der Alla." *ZDPV* 98: 77–103.

Weiss, M.
1961–63. "Some Problems of the Biblical 'Doctrine of Retribution.' " *Tarbiz* 31: 236–63; 32: 1–18. (Hebrew)

———. 1984. *The Bible from Within: The Method of Total Interpretation.* Jerusalem.

Weiss, R.
1981. *Mehqĕrey Miqra.* Jerusalem. (Hebrew)

Wellhausen, J.
1905. *Prolegomena zur Geschichte Israels,* Berlin.

Werblowski, R. J. Z.
1962. *Joseph Karo.* London.

Wernberg-Møller, P.
1957. *The Manual of Discipline.* Studies on Texts of the Desert of Judah. Leiden.
Westermann, C.
1974. *Genesis,* vol. 1: *Gen. 1–11.* BK 1.1. Neukirchen.
Wette, W. M. L. de.
1805. *Dissertatio critico-exegetica, qua Deuteronomium a prioribus Pentateuchi libris diversum, alius cuiusdam auctoris opus esse monstratur.*
White, S. A.
"A Critical Edition of Seven Manuscripts of Deuteronomy: 4Q Dt (A, C, D, F, G, I, and N)," Ph.D. Thesis, Harvard University, 1990.
Wieder, N.
1976. "Leḥeqer nusaḥ haᶜamidah beminhag Babel haqadmon." *Sinai* 78: 97–122. (Hebrew)
———.
1981a. "Tza ᶜaqat 'hu'' bayamym hanoraʾym." *Sinai* 89: 6–41. (Hebrew)
———.
1981b. "The Controversy About the Liturgical Composition 'Yismah Moshe' —Opposition and Defence." In *Studies in Aqqadah, Targum, and Jewish Liturgy in Memory of J. Heineman,* ed. J. J. Petuchowsky and E. Fleischer, pp. 75–99. Jerusalem. (Hebrew)
Wijngaards, J.
1965. " 'Hotzi' and 'heᶜelah', a Twofold Approach to the Exodus." *VT* 15: 91–102.
Wilhelm, G.
1982. *Grundzüge der Geschichte und Kultur der Hurriter.* Darmstadt.
Wolff, H. W.
1964. "Das Kerygma des deuteronomistischen Geschichtswerk." *Gesammelte Studien zum Alten Testament Theolog. Bücherei* 22: 308–24 = *ZAW* 73 (1961): 171–86.
Wolfson, H. A.
1968. *Philo: Foundations of Religious Philosophy in Judaism, Christianity, and Islam,* vol. 2. 4th ed. Cambridge, Mass.
Wright, D. P.
1987. "Deuteronomy 21:1–9 as a Rite of Elimination." *CBQ* 49: 387–403.
Xella, P.
1981. *I Testi rituali di Ugarit,* vol. 1. Studi semitici 54. Rome.
Yadin, Y.
1955. *The Scroll of the War of the Sons of Light Against the Sons of Darkness.* Jerusalem. (Hebrew)
———.
1969. "Tefillin (Phylacteries) from Qumran (XQ Phyl. 1–4)." *EI* 9 (W. F. Albright Volume): 60–85. (Hebrew)

———.
1977. *The Temple Scroll.* 3 vols. Jerusalem. (Hebrew)
Yaron, R.
1959. "Redemption of Persons in the Ancient Near East." *RIDA* 6 (3d ed.): 155–76.
———.
1962. "Forms in the Laws of Eshnunna." *RIDA* 9: 137–53.
———.
1963. "Matrimonial Mishaps at Eshnunna." *JSS* 8: 1–16.
Young, G. D.
1972. "Utu and Justice: A New Sumerian Proverb." *JCS* 24.4: 132.
Zafrir, Y.
1968. "Nahal Zered." *EM* 5.811–12. (Hebrew)
Zakovitch, Y.
1985. *Every High Official Has a Higher One Set Over Him: A Literary Analysis of 2 Kings 5.* Tel Aviv. (Hebrew)
Zimmerli, W.
1953. *Geschichte und Altes Testament.* Beiträge zur Historischen Theologie 16. Albrecht Alt zum 70. Geburtstag durgebracht J. C. G. Mohr (P. Siebeck). Tübingen. (= W. Zimmerli, 1963, *Gottes Offenbarung, Gesammelte Aufsätze.* München.

DEUTERONOMY 1–11: TRANSLATION, NOTES, AND COMMENTS

THE SUPERSCRIPTION, PLACE, AND DATE OF THE ADDRESS (1:1–5)

1 [1]These are the words that Moses spoke to all Israel on the other side of the
Jordan. In the wilderness, in the ʿArabah near Suph, between Paran and Tophel,
Laban, Hazeroth, and Di-Zahab, [2]it is eleven days from Horeb to Kadesh-
Barnea by the Mount Seir route. [3]It was in the fortieth year, on the first day of
the eleventh month, that Moses spoke to the Israelites in accordance with all
that YHWH had commanded him concerning them, [4]after he had defeated
Sihon king of the Amorites who ruled in Heshbon, and Og king of Bashan who
ruled in Ashtaroth in Edrei. [5]On the other side of the Jordan, in the land of
Moab, Moses undertook to expound this teaching. He said:

TEXTUAL NOTES

1:1. *near Suph.* Hebrew: *mwl swp* literally, 'facing Suph'. *môl,* found only here, is a variant of the preposition *mûl* (see the NOTES). LXX: *plēsion,* 'hear'.

2. *It is eleven days from Horeb to Kadesh-Barnea by the Mount Seir route.* That is to say, a journey of eleven days. The word "journey" is missing in the Hebrew, and is supplied in the Targum. In Syriac the word "route" is transferred to the beginning of the verse, reading: "It is a route of eleven days from Horeb to Mount Seir, even unto Kadesh-Barnea."

3. *eleventh.* Hebrew: *ʿaštêy ʿaśar.* See *GKC* §97e n. 1. Contrast the use of *ʾaḥad ʿaśar* for 'eleven' at the beginning of the previous verse. The use of two different words for 'eleven' in such close proximity is unusual, hence v 3 should be considered the work of the priestly source, which characteristically uses *ʿaštêy ʿaśar* and is interested in precise dating. (J. Wellhausen viewed *ʿaštêy ʿaśar* as a post-Exilic term [1905, p. 389]; however, as the term is used in the Ugaritic texts [see lexicons], there are no grounds for this assertion.)

the Israelites. The LXX adds *pantas,* 'all (the Israelites)'.

4. *in Ashtaroth in Edrei.* According to Josh 12:4; 13:12; and 13:31 Og reigned in Ashtaroth *and* in Edrei. The LXX, Syriac, and Vg add the conjunction here as well: "in Ashtaroth and in Edrei" (see the NOTES).

5. *undertook.* Hebrew: *hwʾyl.* This verb can mean either 'agreed, willed' or 'began'. The second explanation is required by the context here and is found in all of the ancient versions. The verb, *hiphʿil* form of the root *yʾl,* in the sense 'to begin', is apparently connected with the root *ʾwl,* which means 'to precede, to be first'. The root *ʾwl* in this sense (cf. Arabic: *ʾwl)* has been preserved in Palestinian Jewish Aramaic *(ʾwlʾ* = 'beginning' in the Targumim), and according to Z. Ben-hayyim (1967, pp. 14–15), this word reflects an ancient Hebrew root, for it is unknown in non-Palestinian Aramaic. For *yʾl* instead of *ʾwl,* com-

pare the interchange of *ʿwṣ* and *yʿṣ* 'to counsel'; *ṭwb* and *yṭb* 'to be/do good'; *gwr* and *ygr* 'to be afraid'; *ʿwp* and *yʿp* 'to fly'.

to expound. Hebrew: *bēʾēr,* literally, 'he expounded', a finite verb instead of the expected infinitive *baʾēr.* See *GKC* §120g, h.

He said. Hebrew: *lʾmr,* literally, 'saying'. In the Vg: *et dicere* '(Moses undertook to expound) and he said'.

NOTES

1. *all Israel.* An expression characteristic of Deuteronomy and the writers influenced by it (cf. 5:1; 27:9; 29:1; 31:1; 32:45; Josh 23:2). The author of Deuteronomy describes Moses as speaking before a vast audience comprising tribal leaders, officers, elders, men, women, and children, and even resident aliens (cf. 29:1, 9 and 31:12). Such covenantal assemblies were convened regularly and on special occasions in Israel and in the ancient Near East; cf. Weinfeld 1976b, pp. 392–93. Deuteronomy itself is actually said to constitute the words of the covenant made in the land of Moab (28:69).

on the other side of the Jordan. In other words, on the eastern side, as is clear from v 5 and from the general context. The standpoint of the author on the West Bank showed to early critics (even Ibn Ezra) that Moses was not the author of these verses.

in the wilderness. This phrase may apply to the desert of Sinai, the desert of the south of Canaan, or the desert to the east of Moab (cf. 2:8, 4:43).

in the ʿArabah. "ʿArabah" generally denotes the depression extending from the Gulf of ʿAqaba northward to Lebanon, but sometimes refers to the depression between the Dead Sea and the Gulf of ʿAqaba (cf., e.g., "the Sea of the ʿArabah" for the Dead Sea in 4:49), which is also reflected in the Arabic name for this region: al-ʿAraba. In the present context and in 2:8 the word ʿArabah points to the depression between the Dead Sea and the Gulf of ʿAqaba.

near Suph. This may also be rendered "in front of" or "opposite" Suph *(môl Sûp* instead of *mûl Sûp* apparently for reasons of dissimilation, i.e., to avoid the clash of two similar vowels; cf. GKC §27w). *Sûp* has been identified with *Sûpah* in Num 21:14, somewhere in southern Moab. But this does not fit the itinerary, which seems to specify the way from Horeb to Kadesh (v 2). The versions (LXX, Targumim, etc.) take it as "the Sea of Suph," that is, the Sea of Reeds. It is possible that Suph was a place near the Sea of Reeds, and derives its name from its location.

between Paran and Tophel. Paran, like Sinai, is sometimes linked to the word *midbar* 'wilderness' (Gen 21:21; Num 10:12; 12:16; 13:3; 26:1; 1 Sam 25:1), and sometimes to "mountain" (Deut 33:2; Hab 3:3). From 1 Kgs 11:18 it is clear that Paran was situated between Midian and Egypt, and may be identical with modern Feiran near Jebel Serbāl in the southern part of the Sinai Peninsula. Like Sinai, Paran designates a very extensive area, reaching as far north as the

Negev (1 Sam 25:1), but generally it denotes the main desert of the eastern Sinai bordering on the wilderness of Zin and Kadesh (cf. Num 13:3, 26). Tophel has been identified with al-Ṭafila about twenty-four kilometers southeast of the Dead Sea, but this is dubious because of the different spelling of the name: al-Ṭafila is spelled with *ṭ* rather than the *t* of Tophel. See the article "Tophel" in *EM.*

Laban. This was located in the coastal area of the Mediterranean in the vicinity of Rafa and Al-ʿArīsh. It is attested in the Šišak inscriptions (cf. Simons 1937, p. 186) and in the Sargon annals *(nasīku ša* URU *Laban* VAS 8424:6–7; cf. Weidner 1951, pp. 204–18; Tadmor 1958, pp. 72–78). Compare also the *šʾsw* -land of Lābān *(rbn)* of the ʿAmara-West list of Ramesses II (see Giveon 1971, nl. 6a, 16a; and Görg 1976). In this list it appears next to *šʾsw yhwʾ* and *šʾsw sʿrr* (= Seir; see Weinfeld 1982f, pp. 304–5; also recently Aḥituv 1984, p. 129).

Hazeroth. These may be identical with Hazeroth (Num 33:17, 20) on the eastern coast of the Sinai Peninsula, somewhere between Mount Sinai and the Gulf of ʿAqaba.

Di-Zahab. This is commonly identified with Mina-al-Dhahab, one of the harbors between Raʾs Muḥammad and Eilat, along the eastern coast of Sinai.

2. *It is eleven days from Horeb to Kadesh-Barnea.* Horeb, the name for Sinai in Deuteronomy, is generally identified with one of the high mountains in southern Sinai: Jebel Musa (7,486 feet), Jebel Catherine (8,652 feet), or Jebel Serbāl (6,791 feet). The distance from Horeb to Kadesh, as specified here, agrees with the accounts of modern travelers in this area. In 1838 Edward Robinson traveled in eleven days from Jebel Musa to ʿAqaba and then across the desert to Ain Kadis (1856, pp. 565ff). J. Rowlands (apud Trumbull 1884, p. 215) also recounts that the trip by camel from Jebel Musa to Ain Kadis took eleven days. The French geographer and historian, F. M. Abel, made the same journey during eleven days (1933–38, 1.393). See the recent investigation of Davies 1979.

According to Perlitt 1977, the appellation "Horeb" was introduced in later times by the Elohist and the Deuteronomic school instead of "Sinai" because of the association of Sinai with Sin, the moon god of Assyria and Babylonia. Horeb, in his opinion, is a more general term denoting a desert and arid area, which indeed characterized the location of the holy site in question (cf. Exod 3:1; 4:27; 18:5; 1 Kgs 19:4ff.). Because the term "Sinai" occurs in the priestly code, which is usually dated in the Exilic and post-Exilic periods, Perlitt argues that the priestly code reintroduced the archaic appellation. In my opinion, the contrary is true. The usage of the term "Sinai" in the priestly code is another indication of its antiquity.

by the Mount Seir route. There are two possible interpretations: (1) by the route that crosses Mount Seir, or (2) by the road that is called "road of Mount Seir" because it leads to Mount Seir: compare "the way of the Sea of Reeds"

(Num 14:24; Deut 1:40), "the way of Egypt" (Isa 10:24; Jer 2:18), and the like. The region of Seir lies both to the east and to the west of the ʿArabah, and borders to the south of Palestine; see Josh 11:17; 12:7. Seir as a region in the south of Palestine is also known to us from the El-Amarna tablets (288:26), where it is clear that the lands of Seir *(matāti šerri)* are on the southern borders of the Jerusalemite kingdom.

Kadesh-Barnea. Tell al-Qudairat in northern Sinai has been identified with it. This mound is situated near the junction of two ancient routes: "the way to Shur" leading to Egypt, and a branch of the Via Maris running from the Mediterranean (from Al-ʿArīsh or Raphia) to the Gulf of ʿAqaba. It stands near ʿAin al-Qudairat, the richest spring in Sinai. The name Kadesh-Barnea may have referred to the entire oasis. This oasis was protected by several fortresses, the earliest of which dates to the tenth century B.C.E. (see R. Cohen 1979, pp. 72–80).

3. *It was in the fortieth year, on the first day of the eleventh month.* The exact dating by year, month, and day is characteristic of the priestly code, as is the use of *ʿšty ʿśr* instead of *ʾḥd ʿśr* (Exod 26:7, 8; Num 7:72; etc.). This verse seems to be part of the editorial framework of the priestly code, as is the use of "on that very day" (32:48), which is also of priestly character. With these two verses the editor creates a chronological envelope construction for the text.

4. *Sihon* and *Og.* See below, in the NOTE to 2:26–37.

who ruled. yšb in this context is to be rendered "who ruled," in other words, sat on the throne (cf. Amos 1:8; 2:3; and the Ugaritic text mentioned below).

in Ashtaroth in Edrei. In Josh 12:4 and 13:12: "who ruled in Ashtaroth and in Edrei," a reading adopted here by the LXX, Syriac, and Vg. It is possible, however, that "Edrei" is governed by the phrase "after he had defeated" and refers to the place in which the battle had taken place (cf. 3:1; Num 21:23). Both Ashtaroth and Edrei are mentioned in Egyptian documents (see Helck 1971, p. 55 no. 25; 127 no. 91) and have recently been found in a Ugaritic text, which reads that El sits *(yšb* 'is enthroned') in Ashtaroth and rules *(ṯ pṭ)* in Edrei (written: *hdrʿy;* see RS 24.252.2–3 and Margulis 1970). El's association there with Rafa is interesting in view of the fact that Og, king of Bashan, appears in 3:11 as the last of the Rephaim (see below).

5. *in the land of Moab.* In 3:29 and 4:46 (cf. also 29:6), the place is exactly specified: "in the valley opposite Beth-Peor." The priestly source uses instead of "the land of Moab," "the steppes of Moab" *(ʿarbôt Mōʾāb;* cf. Num 22:1; 26:3, 63; 31:12; 33:48–50; etc.).

Moses undertook to expound. hwʾyl is an auxiliary verb expressing a decision often connected with a new move, sometimes connecting initiative and boldness. See especially Gen 18:27; Josh 7:7; Judg 17:11; 19:7; 1 Sam 12:22 (see the TEXTUAL NOTE).

The verb *bʾr* originally meant 'to engrave or write down clearly' (cf. 27:8 and Hab 2:2: "Write down . . . inscribe it *(bʾr)* so that a man may read it easily").

In later Hebrew it developed the meaning of 'explain' or 'expound'. This meaning suits this verse because, in contrast to the previous books of the Pentateuch, the Torah in Deuteronomy is accompanied by all sorts of introductory remarks and elucidating comments.

this teaching. The expression *hattôrāh hazōt* does not appear in the other books of the Pentateuch, and in fact refers only to the book of Deuteronomy. In the Tetrateuch *tôrâ* means 'instruction' (cf. Exod 18:20) and defines specific cultic-religious regulations, as, for example, *tôrâ* of leprosy (Lev 13:59), of the burnt offering (Lev 7:1), of the Nazirite (Num 6:13), of the case of the jealous husband (Num 5:29), and more. Deuteronomy, however, expanded the concept of *tôrâ* by giving it the general sense of Mosaic law. Furthermore, the term applies not only to the law itself but also to the introductions and comments accompanying it. See also the NOTE to 4:44.

COMMENT

This long title, which specifies the place and the time at which Moses' address was delivered, is composite and reflects in a way the composite nature of the book. This may be seen by the repetition of the geographical data "on the other side of the Jordan" in v 5; by v 2, which looks like a gloss and can hardly be integrated within the given context; and by the exact dating formula of v 3, which is not otherwise of Deuteronomy, though it typifies priestly texts.

Various attempts have been made to explain the difficulties of this passage, but not with great success. According to some scholars "vv 1–2" are of retrospective nature and refer to Israel's wanderings in the desert as described in the book of Numbers. But Numbers itself also closes with a retrospective statement (36:13), and the places mentioned in v 1b do not occur there. Finally, one should ask why these verses were not appended to the book of Numbers if they belong there.

More plausible is Dillman's suggestion (1886, p. 232) that vv 1b–2 represent some sort of itinerary describing the way from Horeb to Kadesh. For some reason this short itinerary joined with v 1a.

According to the Rabbis *(Sipre),* the Targumim, and some medieval commentators, the words spoken by Moses (v 1) are really admonitions referring to sins committed by the Israelites during their wanderings at the different locations mentioned in v 1b. According to this view, v 2 alludes to the punishment for these sins as though to say: were it not for these sins the entire journey would have taken only eleven days rather than thirty-eight years of wandering from Sinai across Seir.

Ibn Ezra understands vv 1–4 in the following manner: these are the words that Moses spoke in the wilderness during the eleven days, on their journey from Horeb to Kadesh-Barnea, and in the fortieth year Moses again addressed, and so on. This understanding implies that Moses' addresses were given during the eleven days that they spent in the mentioned places, and that after the sin of the spies in Kadesh, Moses kept silent for thirty-eight years and renewed his speech only in the fortieth year.

A. Ehrlich (1909, pp. 244–75) also understands that the eleven days refer to the time of Moses' discourse, but according to him this does not mean that the journey lasted eleven days, only that during eleven days Moses recounted what had happened during the journey from Horeb to Kadesh-Barnea. The events of this long journey are to be found, according to Ehrlich, in chapters 1–11.

HISTORICAL SURVEY (1:6–3:29)

INTRODUCTORY REMARK

This section may be divided as follows:

1. the order to depart from Horeb (1:6–8);
2. the installation of judges by Moses (1:9–18);
3. the sin of the spies and the following punishment (1:19–46);
4. the circuit of Edom, Moab, and Ammon (2:1–23);
5. the conquest of the lands of Sihon and Og in Transjordan and their division among the two and a half tribes (2:24–3:17);
6. instructions to the Transjordanian tribes and to Joshua in connection with the conquest (3:18–22); and
7. Moses' prayer and the directions given to him in connection with his succession (3:23–29).

This historical survey, which is formulated as a speech by Moses, is mainly based on the historical traditions of Exodus and Numbers. In certain, not unimportant, respects, however, it deviates from those traditions and even supplies additional material. The main differences between the account in Deut 1:6–3:29 and the tradition in Exodus and Numbers will be discussed in the COMMENTS.

THE ORDER TO DEPART (1:6–8)

1 [6]YHWH our God spoke to us at Horeb, saying: You have stayed long
enough at this mountain. [7]Turn, set out and make your way to the hill country
of the Amorites and to all their neighbors in the ʿArabah, the hill country, the

Shephelah, the Negev, the seacoast, the land of the Canaanites, and the Lebanon, as far as the Great River, the river Euphrates. [8]See, I place the land at your disposal. Go, take possession of the land that YHWH swore to your fathers, Abraham, Isaac, and Jacob, to give to them and to their descendants after them.

TEXTUAL NOTES

7. *Turn . . . and make your way.* Hebrew: *sĕʿû lākem,* literally, 'journey for yourselves'. *lākem,* 'for yourselves', is the *dativus ethicus,* which is prefixed to the subject of the action. It is often attached to verbs of motion, emphasizing the absoluteness and finality of the journey. Cf. Gen 12:1, *lek lĕkā;* 27:43, *bĕraḥ-lĕkā;* Exod 18:27, *wayyēlek lô;* etc. See Muraoka 1978.

the Negev, 4Q Dt[h] fr 1 (Duncan 1989 Fig. 10), the Samaritan Pentateuch and Vg read: *wbngb,* with the conjunction.

8. *See!* Hebrew: *rĕʾēh,* imperative singular. Qumran (2Q10, DJD 3.60, pl. xii) and the Samaritan Pentateuch read: *rĕʾû,* imperative plural. So also in the LXX: *idete.* In Syriac and *Tg. Onq., ḥzw;* in *Tg. Ps.-J.* and *Tg. Neof., ḥwmn* (cf. v 20). All of these are hypercorrections (see the NOTES).

that YHWH swore. In the Samaritan Pentateuch and the LXX: "that I swore."

Isaac. 4Q Dt[h] fr 1 (Duncan 1989, Fig. 10) reads: *wlyṣḥg* 'and to Isaac'.

to them and. Omitted in the Samaritan text, here and in a similar context in 11:9. Apparently they were perplexed by the problem of giving the land to the fathers themselves (see the NOTES). The Rabbis also struggled with this difficulty and interpreted: *to give to them*—these are the returned exiles from Babylon; *and to their descendants*—these are their children *(Sipre,* pisqah 8). "To give to them" in Deut 11:9 was interpreted as the resurrection from the dead *(Sipre,* pisqah 47).

NOTES

6. *YHWH our God.* An expression that appears frequently in Deuteronomy (23 times). Much more common is the formula "YHWH thy/your God" (276 times). Both express the special covenantal relation between God and the people so characteristic of Deuteronomy, and it seems close to the credo: *"YHWH our God* is one YHWH [or YHWH alone]" in 6:4 (=Shemaʿ).

[YHWH our God] spoke to us at Horeb, saying. Every move of the Israelites comes in the wake of a divine command, and indeed Moses takes the trouble to inform each time that the move was executed according to God's command. In this case the command is given in v 7, "Turn, set out and make your way to the hill country of the Amorites," and its execution is found in v 19: "We set out . . . and traveled . . . to the hill country of the Amorites, as YHWH our God had commanded us." Compare also 1:40 with 2:1; 2:3 with 2:9; 2:13a with 13b.

Targum Pseudo-Jonathan adds here "and not myself *(wlʾ bʾnpy npšy),*" apparently influenced by the *Midr. Sipre* Deut sec. 5 (Finkelstein 1969, p. 13): "he said to them: it is not from myself which I tell you but from the mouth of the Holy One." Indeed, whenever we find the phrase "I said to you *(wʾmr lkm)*" referring to Moses, *Midr. Sipre* expounds, "it is not from myself." See secs. 9, 19, 25 (to vv 9, 20, 29); cf. John 12:49, "I am not speaking on my own," and 14:10.

The autobiographical style of the book of Deuteronomy could create the impression that the Torah of Deuteronomy emenates from Moses and not from the divinity itself, and therefore the statements are added that it is God who is speaking and commanding, not Moses. It is for this reason that the Temple Scroll from Qumran changed the style of God's address from the third person to the first person. Compare for example col. 43:8 ("before me," "I am YHWH") with Deut 12:25, 28 ("before YHWH your God"); col. 53:11 ("because I will require it from you") with Deut 23:22 ("because YHWH will require it from you"); and so on. For all of this see Yadin 1977, 1.61–62.

For the same reason *Tg. Neof.* adds the clause "and Moses said" whenever it is clear that Moses is the speaker and not God. Compare 2:3, 9, 31; 3:2; 5:28; all of this in order to indicate that the other things in the book are the words of God and not the words of Moses.

You have stayed long enough. Compare 2:3 and see also 3:26 and others.

7. *Turn . . . and make your way.* Compare 1:40; 2:1. *pnh* is an auxiliary verb of motion expressing the decision for a move, or a fresh start. Compare 16:7; Josh 22:4 (with *hlk);* Deut 1:24 (with *ʿlh*), and more.

the hill country of the Amorites. See vv 19, 20. The Hebrew *hr hʾmry* refers to the whole mountain range of Palestine or even to the whole land of Palestine. Compare, for example, 3:25: "the good land . . . that good hill country and the Lebanon" (see also Ps 78:54).

The term "Amorite," like "Canaanite," generally designates the inhabitants of Palestine before the conquest (cf., e.g., 1 Sam 7:14; 2 Sam 21:2; Amos 2:9, 10). Originally, however, the Amorites mainly occupied the hill country, while the Canaanites lived mostly along the seacoast and in the lowland areas (cf., e.g., Num 13:29; Deut 1:44; Josh 5:1; 10:5; 11:3). This division seems to be reflected also in the present verse, where the Amorite is associated with the "hill country" while "the land of the Canaanites" is coupled with the "seacoast."

In Akkadian documents of the third and second millennia, *Amurrû* (KUR MAR.TU = *māt Amurrî)* designates the "Westland," that is, Syria and Palestine. According to the Mari letters of the end of the eighteenth century B.C.E., *Amurrû* was a political unit between Qatna in the north and Hazor in the south. Both Qatna and Hazor were considered great and important city-states in that period. For Hazor, cf. Josh 11:10, "Hazor was formally the head of all those kingdoms" (see Malamat 1970, pp. 164–72, and 1971). During the New Kingdom in Egypt, the name *Amurrû* was known as a kingdom bounded by Ṣumur on the Phoenician coast to the Beqaʿ of Lebanon (cf. Gardiner 1947, 1.187–88). This designation seemed to be a remnant of the great *Amurrû* of the earlier period (see Aharoni and Rainey 1979, pp. 66, 149). The term *Amurrû* was never abandoned in Mesopotamian sources. In the neo-Assyrian inscriptions *Amurrû* is the common name for Palestine (cf. Altman 1981).

all their neighbors. This may also be translated "all its inhabitants." For *šāken* as 'inhabitant', cf. Isa 33:24; Jer 6:21; Hos 10:5. The word *šᵉkēnâw* seems therefore to refer to the whole population of the land. What follows is a listing of the various geographical regions of the country:

the ʿArabah. See the COMMENT on v 1, and for the extent of this region see Josh 12:3, "the Arabah as far as the Sea of Chinneroth . . . and (southward) as far as the Salt Sea" (cf. Deut 5:49).

the hill country. The central mountain range, which includes the hill country of Naphtali (cf. Josh 20:7) and the mountains of Ephraim, Benjamin, and Judah.

Shephelah. The lowland extending from the foothills of Judah to the coastal area.

the Negev. The southern part of Judah between the range and the deserts (cf. especially Num 13:17, 29).

the seacoast. The seashore extending from the northern end of the Shephelah up to Tyre or Sidon (cf. Gen 10:19; 49:13; 2 Sam 24:6).

the land of the Canaanites. To the west of the "hill country of the Amorites," which appears at the beginning (see above). It is also possible that it defines the preceding term, "the seacoast" (see Num 13:29; Josh 5:1). The name Canaan *(Kinaḫḫi)* appears frequently in the El Amarna letters from the first half of the fourteenth century, and the reference there is primarily to the Phoenician coastal area. The name also occurs with a wider connotation, however, as a general term for the whole region of Egyptian rule in Palestine (cf. Aharoni and Rainey 1979, pp. 67f.).

Lebanon. The mountain range running parallel to the Phoenician coast, famous for its wealth and beauty, and in particular for its cedar (see 3:25 and COMMENT there).

as far as the . . . river Euphrates. An ideal formulation of the limits of the promised land, cf. Gen 15:18: "from the river of Egypt to the great river, river Euphrates"; Exod 23:31: "from the sea of Reeds to the sea of the Philistines and from the wilderness to the river" (cf. Deut 11:24; Josh 1:4). Such ideal border limits, "from river to river," "from sea to sea," "from wilderness to river," are characteristic of the description of imperial rule. See, for example, Ps 72 (ascribed to Solomon): "let him rule from sea to sea and from river to the ends of the earth" (v 8; cf. Zech 9:10; Mic 7:12). Similar clichés are found in Mesopotamian inscriptions, for example, "from the upper sea to the lower sea" (Borger 1956, p. 77), or in the inscription of Adad-Nirari III (810–783 B.C.E.): "from the mountains to the great sea in the east," "from the Euphrates to the great sea where the sun sets" (*ANET*², p. 281), to which we may compare Josh 1:4, "from the Lebanon to the great river . . . Euphrates . . . to the great sea of the setting sun." Cf. Weinfeld 1983d, pp. 97ff.

8. *See! rᵉʾēh* here has the value of an interjection—"behold!"—and therefore appears in the singular even though it is in an address to many (cf. 4:5; 11:26). The LXX and the Samaritan Pentateuch misunderstood the form and corrected to the plural. Akkadian *amur* 'see!' has the same meaning (*CAD* A/2, 19 s.v. *amāru*), and it alternates with *anna*, which equals Hebrew *hinnēh* (cf. recently Kogut 1986). Declarations of gifts and appointments are usually preceded by *rᵉʾēh* (Gen 41:41; Exod 7:1; 31:2; Deut 1:8, 21; Josh 6:2; Jer 1:10, 40:4), as well as by *hinnēh* (Gen 1:29; 20:16; Num 18:8, 21; 25:12; Jer 1:18; 40:4). For *hinnēh* expressing volition of the donor, compare *Sipre* (Finkelstein 1969, p. 139) to Num 18:8, and see Muffs 1975, 3.26ff. For the gift of the land to the Patriarchs formulated as a royal grant, cf. Weinfeld 1970–72.

I place the land at your disposal. The land that was promised by pledge (see below) to the Patriarchs is now put by God at the disposal of the Israelites, their descendants. The past (= perfect) in this sentence, *nātatî*, is of declarative value and has to be understood as present: "I hereby give/place. . . ." Compare Gen 1:29 (with *hinnēh*); 15:18 (gift of land); 20:16; and so on.

Go, take possession of the land. An instructive parallel to this command is found in a Hittite text. The Hittite sovereign gives land to his vassal and says, "See, I gave you the Zipparla mountain land. Occupy it!" (cf. Weinfeld 1972a, p. 72).

that YHWH swore to your fathers. The promise to the Patriarchs was considered a covenant (*bᵉrît*), and covenant and oath are overlapping concepts (compare, e.g., Gen 26:28; and see Weinfeld 1975b).

to give to them and to their descendants after them. Compare Gen 17:8. This expression belongs to the legal phraseology known to us from donation texts of Mesopotamia, Ugarit, and Elephantine (see Weinfeld 1970–72, p. 199). Because the Patriarchs themselves were not living in their own land but were sojourners, the phrase "to give to them" is not strictly appropriate. Nevertheless, the use of the grant formula is determined by its fixed legal nature, and it usually consists of the statement "I give to you and to your descendants." Cf. Num 25:12–13: "I grant him my pact of peace . . . a pact of eternal priesthood for him and his descendants after him." For the Patriarchs as recipients of the promise on the one hand and as recipients of the land on the other, cf. Brettler 1982.

THE ORGANIZATION OF THE JUDICIARY (1:9–18)

1 ⁹At that time I said to you, "I cannot bear the burden of you by myself.

[10]YHWH your God has multiplied you until you are today as numerous as the
stars in the sky.—[11]May YHWH, the God of your fathers, increase your numbers a thousandfold, and bless you as he promised you.—[12]How can I bear
unaided the trouble of you, and the burden, and the bickering! [13]Pick for your
tribes men who are wise, discerning, and experienced, and I will appoint them as
your heads." [14]You answered me and said, "What you propose to do is good."
[15]So I took your tribal leaders, wise and experienced men, and appointed them
heads over you: chiefs of thousands, chiefs of hundreds, chiefs of fifties, and
chiefs of tens, and officials for your tribes. [16]At that time I charged your magistrates as follows: "Hear out you fellow men, and decide justly between any man
and a fellow Israelite or a stranger. [17]You shall not be partial in judgment; hear
out low and high alike. Fear no man, for judgment is God's. And any matter
that is too difficult for you, you shall bring to me and I will hear it." [18]Thus I
instructed you, at that time, about the various things that you should do.

TEXTUAL NOTES

9. *At that time.* kethib: *hwʾ;* kere: *hyʾ.* A common phenomenon in the Torah. For an explanation, see *GKC* §32i. A new section begins here in the Samaritan text, but not in the MT. A sign in 2QDeut 10 *(DJD* 3:60) before this verse may indicate the beginning of a new section. See Oesch 1979, pp. 268–69.

12. *How can I bear unaided.* Hebrew: *ʾykh ʾśʾ lbdy,* literally, 'how will I bear alone', as opposed to v 9, *lʾ ʾwkl lbdy śʾt,* 'I cannot bear alone'. The Vg translates here *non valeo solus sustinere* 'I am not strong enough to bear alone' (which is different from v 9: *non possum solus sustinere* 'I will not be able to bear alone'). Here perhaps the Hebrew *ʾēykâh* 'how' was interpreted midrashically, in the sense of *ʾē/ʾî kōaḥ* 'no strength' or 'where is strength'. Cf. *Midr. Lam. Rab.* to Lam 1:1, where the word *ʾēykâh* is likewise broken down into its component parts (Buber 1899, p. 41).

13. *Pick.* Hebrew: *hbw lkm,* literally, 'give for yourselves'. For the *dativus ethicus,* see the Textual Notes at v 7. Compare Exod 7:3; Josh 20:2; also *qḥw lkm śymw lkm,* etc. The normal Hebrew root for "give" is *ntn. yhb* is only used in the imperative of the *qal,* and this form is vocalized *hābû* rather than the expected *hăbû.* See *GKC* §69o.

experienced. Hebrew: *ydʿym,* not, as often translated, "well-known [to your tribes]" (as in *Sipre* 13 and Rashi ad loc.), but rather, "experienced, knowledgeable," as translated in the LXX: *sunetous; Tg. Onq.: mdʿn; Tg. Ps.-J.: mry mndʿ.* Compare Eccl 9:11, *ḥkmym . . . nbwnym . . . wydʿym,* where *ydʿym* is vocalized *yodʿîm,* which may be the correct vocalization here as well. According to the pointing, one should separate *wydʿym* from the word *lšbṭykm,* and indeed in v 15 *wydʿym* stands by itself.

for your tribes. In other words, one per tribe. Compare v 23, *ʾyš ʾḥd lšbṭ* 'one man per tribe'.

as your heads. Hebrew: *br'šykm,* literally, 'at your heads'. The *beth* here is the *beth essentiae* and does not have prepositional force, but is rather to be understood in the sense of "as/in the capacity of your heads" (see Driver 1902, ad loc.; and *GKC* §119i). Compare v 15: "and [I] appointed them heads over you," where no preposition precedes "heads." It is the same in all of the versions (except Syriac, which translates literally, *bryšykwn).* What facilitates this interpretation is the verb *w'śymm,* meaning 'I will appoint them'. On the verb *śwm* in the sense of 'to appoint', cf. Deut 17:14–15: "I will set *('śymh)* a king over me . . . you shall be free to set *(śwm tśym)* a king over yourself." The verb *ntn* also has the meaning of appointing. Compare 16:18: "you shall appoint *(ttn)* magistrates and clerks"; and also 1:15: "and [I] appointed *(w'tn)* them heads over you." Concerning the appointment of a prophet, the *hiphʿil* of the verb *qwm* is used (see Deut 18:15, 18; Jer 29:15; Amos 2:11; also for the appointment of judges in a charismatic sense; see Judg 2:16–18).

15. *So I took your tribal leaders.* This phrase is problematic, for those taken have not actually been appointed tribal leaders yet. LXX: *kai elabon ex humōn,* 'So I took from you' (cf. v 23); Vg: *tulique de tribubus vestris,* 'So I took from your tribes'. See the next paragraph.

and officials for your tribes. Hebrew: *wšṭrym lšbṭykm;* LXX: *kai grammatoeisagōgeis tois kritais humōn,* 'and officers to your judges'. The Hebrew for 'your judges' is *špṭykm,* similar in orthography to *šbṭykm* 'your tribes'. Similar substitutions are found in 2 Sam 7:7 (cf. 1 Chr 17:6; Deut 29:9; Josh 24:1). According to P. V. Reid (1975), *šobeṭ* is a denominative from *šebeṭ* and means 'tribal leader'. For the problem of *šbṭ* and *špṭ,* see also Loewenstamm 1980. The Vg translates *qui docerent vos singula* 'who will teach you each things'. *Singula* is apparently a corruption of *singulares* 'officers', and after *singulares* was corrupted to *singula, qui docerent vos* was added to make sense of the verse. The addition is apt, for *šôṭērîm* is elsewhere translated *doctores* 'scribes, teachers'.

The Greek word *grammatoeisagōgeis,* used to translate *šôṭēr,* is not found outside the LXX and is apparently meant to connote both "scribe *(grammateus)*" and "court bailiff *(eisagōgeis).*" These terms are taken from the realia of the period during which the LXX was translated (third and second centuries B.C.E.). See Weinfeld 1977a.

16. *Hear out.* Hebrew: *šamōaʿ,* the infinitive absolute of *šmʿ* 'to hear'. For the use of the infinitive absolute as an imperative, see *GKC* §113bb. The Samaritan text has *šmʿw,* the imperative.

Hear out your fellow men. The Hebrew is literally "hear between your fellow men," in other words, hear the arguments between them.

between any man, and a fellow Israelite or a stranger. The Hebrew is literally "between a man, and his brother, and his stranger," that is, both cases between a man and his fellow Israelite, and cases between a man and his neighbor who is an alien. Vg: *sive civis sit ille sive peregrinus* 'whether he be citizen or alien'.

17. *You shall not be partial . . . hear out.* These verbs are second-person plural in the MT, second-person singular in the LXX.

hear out. Hebrew: *tišmāʿûn.* For the ending, *-ûn,* in the imperfect third-person masculine plural, see *GKC* §47m; Driver 1902, ad loc. The *-ûn* ending is especially common in the book of Deuteronomy. Often the MT and the Samaritan text differ on this point; the MT has *-ûn* and the Samaritan text, *-û,* or vice versa. In this case, both read *tišmāʿûn.*

low and high alike. Hebrew: *kaqāṭōn kagādōl,* literally, 'as the small, as the great'. Similar constructions are used in Lev 7:7 and Hos 4:9.

NOTES

9. *At that time I said to you.* As will be indicated below, the phrase "at that time" usually comes before a digression. These digressions call attention to matters that might otherwise be overlooked. In this case the author wishes to remind us that the organization of the judiciary took place before the departure from Horeb. According to Exod 18 the event took place before the arrival at Sinai, which does not suit the time indication here. The time indication goes well with the tradition of Num 11, according to which Moses selected the seventy elders shortly before the departure from Sinai.

I cannot bear the burden of you by myself. The expression seems to be borrowed from Num 11:14, but see also Exod 18:18: "For the task is too heavy for you, you cannot do it alone" (cf. 1 Kgs 3:8).

10. *as numerous as the stars in the sky.* Compare 10:22; 28:62; and the promises to the Patriarchs in Gen 22:17; 26:4; Exod 32:13.

11. *May YHWH . . . increase your numbers.* This is stated in order to avoid the impression that Moses is dissatisfied with the multiplication of the people.

thousandfold. Compare 2 Sam 24:3: "may YHWH . . . increase the people a hundredfold." Compare, in letters from the neo-Assyrian period, "let them [the gods] increase these blessings a thousandfold" (Waterman 1930, no. 435:17–19); also in a letter from Elephantine, "may god . . . grant you favor . . . one thousand times more than now" (Cowley 1906, 30:3). Is "thousandfold" a later idiom than "hundredfold" (thus Ehrlich 1909)?

12. *the burden.* Compare Num 11:11: "You have laid the burden *(mśʾ)* of all this people upon me." For "the burden of rule" in Hebrew and classical sources see Weinfeld 1982d.

13. *wise, discerning. . . .* Compare the story of Solomon, who complains about the "heavy" people whom he is unable to judge and therefore asks for a "wise and discerning" heart (1 Kgs 3:8ff.). For wisdom as the principal requisite for the effective functioning of the judiciary, cf. Prov 8:15–16; Isa 11:2 (cf. Weinfeld 1972a, pp. 244ff.).

15. *chiefs of thousands. . . .* Compare Exod 18:21, 25. These titles are not

limited to the military. We find them in the ancient Near East also in connection with supervision of work crews. These officers were responsible for both administrative and judicial matters relating to their workers. A Hebrew ostracon found in Yabneh-Yam, from the seventh century B.C.E., provides an instructive case in this regard. In it we read that a worker who was fined by his supervisor then lodged a complaint with the officer *(śār)*, asking him to cancel the fine imposed on him (see Naveh 1960, pp. 129f.).

officials. Compare 16:18. The *šôṭēr* (derived from the Semitic verb *šṭr* 'to write') was an official who assisted the judge in secretarial work (see *ANEP*, no. 231 for an Egyptian illustration of scribes recording judicial evidence), as well as in other executive functions of the court (see Weinfeld 1977a, pp. 83–86). According to *Sipre* ad loc. the *šôṭērîm* here are "the Levites who strike with the strap" (for an Egyptian illustration, compare *Views of the Biblical World*, B. Mazar 1959, vol. 1.283). The term *šôṭēr*, designating a subordinate official, also occurs in connection with superintending forced labor (Exod 5:6ff.) and with maintaining military discipline (20:5, 8, 9; Josh 1:10; 3:2).

16. *At that time I charged your magistrates.* Compare 2 Chr 19:9. As will be indicated in the COMMENTS, judges in the ancient Near East received instructions at the time of their appointment by oath. Adjuration of judges is also well known in the Greek tradition. It seems indeed that *ṣwh* 'to command' here involves imposition of an oath or pledge (for *ṣwh* in the sense of pledging, cf. Judg 2:20; Ps 111:9 [coupled with *bĕrith]*). See Weinfeld 1975b, p. 256.

17. *You shall not be partial in judgment.* Literally, "do not recognize the face," an idiom found only in Deuteronomy (cf. also 16:19) and in the book of Proverbs (24:23; 28:21). Similar idioms are found in the Egyptian instructions the judges (cf. below in the EXCURSUS the instructions to Rekhmire by Thutmose III; also Weinfeld 1977a, p. 79).

for judgment is God's. Cf. 2 Chr 19:6; also Prov 16:33.

And any matter that is too difficult for you, you shall bring to me and I will hear it. Compare Exod 18:26: "the difficult matter they will bring to Moses." Similar provisions for the hearing by a higher authority are found in the Hittite instructions (cf. the COMMENTS). According to Exodus, any difficult matter has to be brought to Moses, who then lays it before God for a final decision (v 19), whereas here nothing is said about submitting the case to God. The Rabbis *(Sipre* Deut 17) considered Moses' words "you shall bring to me" as impudence for which he was punished: when the daughters of Zelophehad presented their case to him (Num 27:1ff.), he was unable to decide and was compelled "to bring their case before YHWH" (v 5). It seems, however, that the difference between Exodus and Deuteronomy is to be explained by Deuteronomy's reserved attitude regarding the sanctity of the judicial procedure (see Weinfeld 1972a, pp. 233ff.).

18. *I instructed you, at that time, about the various things that you should do.* Compare Exod 18:20: "and enjoin upon them the laws and the teachings, and

make known to them the way they are to go and what they must do *(wᵉʾet hammaʿśeh ʾăšer yaʿśûn).*" The reference there may be generally to the instructions given at Sinai (cf. Exod 24:3, 7, 8). The formula *bāʿēt hahîʾ* ties this verse to v 9 and closes the envelope around the story of the appointment of the judges. This last verse is a reminder that other things happened, and that they were connected with the main event. The implication is that some legislation was transmitted while they were still at Horeb.

COMMENT

Deuteronomy 1:9–18 is an independent unit: it is introduced by the formula *bāʿēt hahîʾ* 'at that time', which occurs quite often in the introduction to the book of Deuteronomy (chaps. 1–11) and usually serves as an opening formula for pericopes of intrusive nature (cf. Loewenstamm 1968–69). The passage we are dealing with indeed interrupts the story about the journey from Horeb. Thus in 1:8 we read about the command given by the Lord to move from Horeb, and in v 19 we hear that the command has been fulfilled, while the passage about the installation of judges in vv 9–18, which comes between, disturbs the continuity of the historical narrative. This intrusive passage itself consists of three separate units, each of which opens with the same formula *bāʿēt hahîʾ*: (1) vv 9–15, the appointment of the judges; (2) vv 16–17, the instructions to the judges; and (3) v 18, the instruction of the people.

The story told here about the installation of judges/officers, in order to assist Moses in administering the people, is dependent in many ways on the sources in Exod 18:13–23 and Num 11:11–17. There are phrases in our passage that even look like quotations from these sources (see the NOTES). But there are also significant differences among various accounts, which merit examination.

1. In Exodus the proposal to appoint judges is made by Jethro, in Numbers it is suggested by God, while in Deuteronomy it is Moses who initiates the idea.
2. In Exodus and Numbers Moses selects the candidates, while in Deuteronomy the people themselves are asked to make the selection (v 13). Furthermore, in Deuteronomy Moses proceeds to action only after the people express their agreement with his proposition (v 14).
3. In Exodus the choice of the candidates is to be determined by their moral qualities: fear of God, faithfulness, and hating unjust gain (Exod 18:21). In Deuteronomy the qualifications are of a more intellectual nature: wisdom, discernment, and knowledge. In Numbers it is divine inspiration that makes the candidates worthy of their position.
4. In Numbers and Deuteronomy those selected are provided with secretarial service *(šōṭᵉrîm)*, which is missing in Exodus.

5. In Deuteronomy the appointed judges are given instructions on impartial judgment (vv 16–17), about which nothing is said in Exodus and Numbers.

Although these differences can be explained as stemming from various independent traditions, it seems that the Deuteronomic tradition is not wholly independent and that the author of Deuteronomy adapted some elements in the old traditions available to him in order to make them conform to his own views. Thus the change in the qualities of the judges in Deuteronomy is to be explained by the author's predilection for wisdom (see the INTRODUCTION sec. 16); the omission of Jethro's role in the proposal may be motivated by the nationalistic attitude of the book of Deuteronomy (cf. Ehrlich 1909, at 1:9), while the democratic principle of the selection (no. 2) similarly reflects a characteristic feature of this book (cf., e.g., 1:22).

In trying to evaluate these traditions historically, we observe that Exodus and Deuteronomy deal with an institution altogether different from that described in Numbers. In contrast to Numbers, which is concerned with establishing a national body acting as a council (compare the elders in Exod 24:1, 9; and the seventy-one members of the Sanhedrin in the Second Temple period), Exodus and Deuteronomy deal with the appointment of executive officers (chiefs of thousands, hundreds, etc.). The different aims of these institutions explain the difference in the qualities of those selected. The seventy elders representing the whole nation have to be provided with divine prophetic qualities, while the judges/officers need capabilities of a more mundane nature.

In order to harmonize the conflicting traditions of Exodus and Deuteronomy, the Samaritan version inserted after Exod 18:24 the section of Deut 1:9–18.

EXCURSUS: THE JUDICIARY IN THE ANCIENT NEAR EAST

The function of the judiciary as described in Exodus and Deuteronomy is known to us from Near Eastern documents of the second millennium B.C.E., and especially from the Hittite instructions to officers and commanders of the time of Tudhalias IV (thirteenth century B.C.E.). Here we find military officers functioning as judges and, as in the biblical traditions, we find them classified according to ranks: "commanders of thousands," "major," and so on (cf. Alp 1947, pp. 405ff.). The instructions given by the Hittite king to these officers are similar to the instructions given by Moses in Deut 1:16–17. Thus we read in the king's instructions to the commanders of the border guards: "If anyone brings a lawsuit . . . the commander shall judge it properly . . . if the case is too big [= difficult] he shall send it to the king. He should not decide it in favor of a superior . . . nobody should take bribes. . . . Do whatever is right" (von Schuler 1957, pp. 36ff.).

Similar instructions are found in Egyptian documents, which describe the installation of judges. Thus we read in the stele of Horemheb (fourteenth century B.C.E.): "I toured the country. . . . I sought out persons of integrity, good in character, knowing how to judge. . . . I have instructed them saying: do not associate intimately with other people, do not take bribes" (Helck 1955, 107ff.).

Also similar are the instructions of Thutmose III to his newly appointed vizier Rekhmire: "He is the one who does not make himself a friend of anyone . . . it is an abomination of God to show face *(rdi ḥr* [=show partiality]). This is an instruction . . . regard him whom you know like him whom you do not know, him who is near you like him who is far from you" (Faulkner 1955).

As in Deuteronomy and Exodus we find in these documents selection of judges on the basis of their personal qualities (stele of Horemheb); instructions to, or rather adjuration of, the appointed to maintain impartial judgment; officers in the capacity of judges; and a high court (Moses in Deuteronomy and Exodus, the king in the Hittite documents). For similar procedures in Israel, compare Deut 16:18–20; 17:6–12; and 2 Chr 19 (Jehoshaphat). On the whole problem, see Weinfeld 1977a.

THE SIN OF THE SPIES (1:19–28)

1 [19]We set out from Horeb and traveled that great and terrible wilderness
which you saw, along the road to the hill country of the Amorites, as YHWH
our God had commanded us, and so we came to Kadesh-Barnea. [20]Then I said
to you, "You have come to the hill country of the Amorites which YHWH our
God is giving to us. [21]See, YHWH your God has placed the land at your
disposal. Go up, take possession, as YHWH, the God of your fathers, promised
you. Fear not and be not dismayed."

[22]Then all of you came to me and said, "Let us send men ahead of us, and
let them explore the land for us, and let them bring us back a word concerning
the route that we shall follow and the cities that we shall come to." [23]I approved
of the plan, so I selected twelve of your men, one from each tribe. [24]They set
out and made their way up into the hill country, and came to the Wadi Eshcol
and spied it out. [25]They took some of the fruit of the land with them and
brought it down to us. And they gave this report: "It is a good land that YHWH
our God is giving to us."

[26]Yet you refused to go up, and rebelled against the command of YHWH
your God. [27]You grumbled in your tents and said, "It is because YHWH hates
us that he brought us out of the land of Egypt, to hand us over to the Amorites,
in order to destroy us. [28]Where are we going? Our kinsmen have taken the

heart out of us, saying, 'We saw there a people stronger and taller than we, large cities with walls sky-high, and even Anakites.' "

TEXTUAL NOTES

19. *and traveled.* MT: *wnlk;* Samaritan text: *wnlkh.* The Samaritan Pentateuch often uses the lengthened ("cohortative") forms of the first-person singular and plural imperfect with *h,* where the MT uses the shorter form, *wnlk ʾt.* This verb means literally 'walked, went' and rarely takes a direct object, as it does here. Compare Num 13:17; Deut 2:7. See *GKC* §118d, h.

21. *your God.* Hebrew: *ʾlhyk . . .* etc. In the MT Israel is addressed in this verse in the second-person singular, in the LXX in the second-person plural.

22. *concerning the route.* Hebrew: *ʾt hdrk* 'the route' in the accusative case. It is either a second direct object of "bring back," in apposition to "word," or a second direct object of "explore," in addition to "the land" (see the Notes). In Syriac, the verb *ḥwy (wyḥwwkwn)* 'they will tell us' is added before "the route."

24. *came.* Syriac: "came up."

it. Vg: *terra* 'the land'; Syriac: *lʾrʿ* 'the land'. See the Textual Note to 1:25, below.

25. *They took some of the fruit of the land.* Vg: "They took some of its fruit [referring to the land, see the previous Textual Note] to show its fertility."

and they gave this report. Omitted in the LXX and the Vg.

26. *Your God.* LXX, Vg and Syriac: "our God."

28. *Our kinsmen . . . us.* The LXX puts these words in Moses' mouth and reads: "your kinsmen . . . you."

taller. MT: *wrm;* Samaritan text: *wrb* 'greater'; the LXX has both adjectives: *kai polu kai dunatōteron* 'more populous and mightier'. Compare Num 13:31; Deut 2:10, 21.

NOTES

19–21. These verses bring us back to vv 7–8, where the command for departure was given, and which were interrupted by the story about the appointment of the judges (vv 9–18). Verses 19–21 indeed recapitulate the theme of vv 7–8, namely, the journey to the hill country of the Amorites and the encouragement to take possession of the land promised to the Patriarchs. These verses also allude to the movement from Horeb to Kadesh-Barnea, mentioned in the outline given in v 2.

19. *We set out.* (Hebrew *wnsʿ*). This is in fulfillment of the commandment given in v 7 (Hebrew *wsʿw*). This verse, like the other verses in chaps. 1–3 that describe the itinerary of the Israelites in the desert (cf. 2:1, 9, 13b–14; 3:1, 29), is formulated in first-person plural. These verses mostly serve as connecting links

between the various episodes (see Ploeger 1967, pp. 1–59). But in contrast to Ploeger's opinion, it should not be seen representing a separate "source."

that great and terrible wilderness. Compare 8:15: "the great and terrible desert [with] . . . serpents and scorpions, a parched land with no water in it." Such vivid descriptions are characteristic of the author of Deuteronomy, who often employs rhetorical techniques in order to captivate his listeners (cf. Weinfeld 1972a, pp. 171ff.).

which you saw. Compare v 31. The sense here is of one who has *experienced.* Compare, e.g., 11:2: "who neither experienced nor witnessed the lesson of YHWH your God," literally, "who neither knew nor saw the lesson," etc. "Know" and "see" interchange when referring to experience (cf. Josh 24:31: "which knew the work of the Lord," with the parallel in Judg 2:7: "which saw the work of the Lord").

the hill country of the Amorites. See the NOTE to v 7.

Kadesh-Barnea. See the NOTE to v 2.

21. The substance of v 8 is repeated here, but the people are addressed collectively in the singular. Such variations are common in Deuteronomy (cf., e.g., 1:31; 2:24; etc.; see the INTRODUCTION sec. 7).

Fear not and be not dismayed. A characteristic phrase of Deuteronomy and the literature influenced by it (Deut 31:8; Josh 8:1; 10:25; cf. also Deut 1:29; 7:21; 20:3; 31:6). Similar formulas are attested in the oracles for kings confronted by enemies in the ancient Near East; cf. Weippert 1981. The corresponding phrase in Akkadian is *la tapallaḫ* and in Aramaic, *ʾal tizḥal (KAI* 202:12f.), both meaning "do not fear!"

22. *Then all of you came to me (wtqrbwn).* Compare 5:20: "you approached me *(wtqrbwn),* all your tribal heads and elders." *Sipre* (ad loc.) distinguishes between the two: in Deut 1:22 "they approached in disorder" (the phrase of *Sipre, bʿrbwbyh),* i.e., with mutinous intent, while in Deut 5:20 they came up in an orderly manner, and reported through their representatives.

let them explore [the land] for us. ḥpr, literally, 'to dig'. The same verb is used in Josh 2:2 in connection with the reconnoitering of Jericho.

and let them bring us back a word. Compare Num 13:26. The phrase *hšyb dbr* usually stands by itself, *dbr* being the object of *hšyb* (cf. Num 13:26; 1 Kgs 12:6, 9; Isa 41:28; etc.). It seems therefore that the ensuing words, "the route," etc., are to be attached to the verb "explore."

23. *twelve of your men.* This statement is attested only in the priestly stratum of Num 13, a fact that may point to the dependence of Deut on the priestly source.

24. *Wadi Eshcol.* This valley is near the city of Hebron. Compare Num 13:23, 24, where we find an etiological explanation for the name: "the place was named the Wadi Eshcol because of the cluster *(eškōl)* that the Israelites cut down there."

Brooks and valleys in the Bible are commonly named after the plant life in the area. Compare Nahal Zered ("green shoots") in Deut 2:8, 14; Nahal Qanah ("reed") in Josh 16:8; 17:9; Nahal Śorek ("vine tendril") in Judg 16:4; Wadi ʿArabah ("poplar") in Amos 6:14; Nahal Hashiṭim ("acacia") in Joel 4:18; Valley of Elah ("terebinth") in 1 Sam 17:2, 19; Valley of Baka ("pistacia") in Ps 84:7.

27. *You grumbled in your tents.* The verb *rgn,* translated 'to grumble', is close to Akkadian *rgm,* which has the meaning 'to complain'. In the parallel passage in Num 14:1–3 we indeed hear that the people wept and complained against Moses and Aaron. For complaints at the tents, compare Num 11:10: "Moses heard the people weeping, each person at the entrance of his tent."

to hand us over to the Amorites, in order to destroy us. Compare the parallel in Num 14:3: "to fall by the sword."

28. *a people stronger and taller than we.* Compare the parallel in Num 13:28: "men of great size."

large cities with walls sky-high. Literally, "fortified into heaven," this is a rhetorical phrase that reminds us of the description of the Judean fortresses in the Assyrian annals: "the city of Azekah . . . located on a mountain ridge . . . reaching high into heaven *(ana šamê šaqû)*" (Naaman 1974, pp. 26–27, lines 5–6). For the same phrase, cf. 9:1b, and cf. the parallel in Num 13:28.

Anakites. Compare the parallel passage in Num 13:28: *ylydy hʿnq.* These are named there as Sheshai, Aḥiman, and Talmai (v 22), who dwelled in Hebron. *ʿnqym* are associated with the Rephaim of the Transjordan, for which see the COMMENT to 2:11.

COMMENT

The original story of the mission of the spies is told in Num 13–14. The narrative here draws heavily on that tradition, but there are significant differences between the accounts. For one thing, in Num 13:1 it is Moses who is commanded by God to send out spies. In Deuteronomy it is the people who demand the sending of the spies. Several answers have been given to this problem: (1) Deuteronomy represents a tradition that is different from that of Num 13:1ff. (the priestly source); (2) the traditions complement each other; that is to say, the people asked for spies and their request was approved by God; and (3) the author of Deuteronomy changed the original tradition on purpose. In accordance with his view, the sinful act of the spies could not have been sponsored by God (cf. Ehrlich 1909).

The third argument is the most plausible, for Deuteronomy depicts the generation of the desert as unbelievers who do not trust God's promise (cf. v 32; 9:23–24), and the very request to send spies right after God's command to "go up, take possession," and not to fear (v 21) seems to be in the author's view an expression of disbelief. The same attitude seems to lie behind the statement in 9:23: "and when YHWH sent you on from Kadesh-Barnea, saying, 'Go up and occupy the land that I am giving you,' you flouted the command of YHWH your God; you did not put your trust in him."

Another difference is that, according to Num 13:18–20, the aim of the spying mission is twofold: to investigate the nature of the country and its qualities: "if it is good or bad" (v 19) and "if the soil is rich or poor" (v 20); and to collect information of a military nature: "if the people who dwell in it are strong or weak" (v 18); or "if the towns they live in are open or fortified" (v 19). Here the aim of the reconnaissance is merely strategic: to find the best route for approaching the country and attacking it (cf. Josh 2:1; 7:2; Num 21:33).

The divergence of Deuteronomy's tradition is motivated by the author's more profound theological reflections. The author of Deuteronomy could not ascribe to Moses a mission with the underlying aim of verifying the promise made by the Lord. The promised land is a *good* one (1:35; 3:25; etc.), it is a land flowing with milk and honey (6:3; 11:9; etc.), and there can be no doubt about it. The aim of the mission could only be strategic and military. According to Deuteronomy, it is indeed the military enterprise that disheartens the spies and frightens the people.

THE SPEECH OF MOSES CONCERNING THE SIN OF THE SPIES (1:29–46)

1 [29]I said to you, "Have no dread or fear of them. [30]YHWH your God, who
goes before you, will fight for you just as he did for you in Egypt before your
eyes, [31]and in the wilderness, where you saw how YHWH your God carried you
as a man carries his son, all the way that you traveled until you came to this
place. [32]Yet in spite of this you have no faith in YHWH your God, [33]who goes
before you on your journeys, to scout the place where you are to encamp, in fire
by night—to guide you on the route you are to follow—and in cloud by day."

[34]When YHWH heard your loud complaint, he was angry, and he vowed,
[35]"Not one of these men, this evil generation, shall see the good land that I
swore to give to your fathers—[36]none except Caleb the son of Jephunneh; he
shall see it, and to him and his descendants will I give the land on which he set
foot, because he was entirely loyal to YHWH."

[37]Because of you YHWH was angry with me too, and he said, "You shall
not enter it either. [38]Joshua son of Nun, who attends you, he shall enter it.
Imbue him with strength, for he shall allot it to Israel. [39]Moreover, your little
ones whom you said would become a prey, your children who do not yet know
good from bad, they shall enter it; to them will I give it and they shall possess it.
[40]As for you, turn about and march into the wilderness, toward the Sea of
Reeds."

[41]You replied to me, saying, "We have sinned against YHWH. We will go

up and fight, just as YHWH our God commanded us." And you all girded yourselves with your gear and dared to ascend the hill country. 42 But YHWH said to me, "Tell them: Do not go up and do not fight, for I am not in your midst; lest you be defeated by your enemies." 43 I spoke to you, but you would not listen. You flouted YHWH's command and willfully marched up into the hill country. 44 Then the Amorites who lived in those hills came out against you and chased you as bees do, and they crushed you at Hormah in Seir. 45 Then you sat weeping before YHWH; but YHWH would not heed your cry or listen to you. 46 Thus you stayed as many days as you remained at Kadesh.

TEXTUAL NOTES

30. *your God.* Many manuscripts of the LXX read "our God"; Vg: "God."

for you. Hebrew: *lākem;* LXX: *meta humōn* 'together with you'; Syriac: *ḥlpykwn* 'in your stead'.

in Egypt. LXX: "in the land of Egypt."

before your eyes. Omitted in the LXX; Vg: *cunctis videntibus,* "before the eyes of all," literally, 'in the seeing of everyone'. These versions are attempting to deal with the problem that the generation to which Moses was speaking did not themselves see the Exodus (see the NOTES).

31. *and in the wilderness.* In other words, "and according to all that he did for you in the wilderness."

you saw. MT: second-person singular; LXX: second-person plural.

33. *before you.* Some LXX manuscripts read "before us."

in fire by night—to guide you on the route you are to follow—and in cloud by day. "In cloud by day" is separated from "in fire by night" by the words "[in order] to guide you on route you are to follow," to signify that these words apply only to the latter and not to the former phrase. Thus, one does not need to interpret *lar'ōtkem badderek* as "to guide you on the route," but rather as "to enable them to see the route." Compare Exod 13:21, "to give them light" (and see the NOTES). Perhaps Driver (1902) is right in suggesting that the Hebrew word should be vocalized *lir'ōtkem,* "that you may see [the way]." Compare Deut 4:14, "for you to observe," a similar construction (and see the TEXTUAL NOTE there). For *lar'ōtkem* from *lĕhar 'ōtkem,* see *GKC* §53g. (Duncan 1989, Fig. 11) 4QDt^{h} fr 3 and Samaritan: *lhr'(w)tkm* LXX, Vg, Syriac: "to show you the way." *Tg. Onq., Tg. Ps.-J.,* and *Tg. Neof.* translate "to give you light on the way" (see the NOTES).

35. *this evil generation.* Omitted in the LXX. Dillman (1886) and Driver (1902) suggest that this may be an explanatory gloss.

to give. Omitted in the Samaritan text, LXX, and Vg, perhaps in order to mitigate the difficulty of giving the land to the fathers. See the TEXTUAL NOTES and the NOTES at v 8.

the good land. The LXX adds *tautēn* 'this'.

your fathers. In many manuscripts of the LXX, Syriac, and *Tg. Onq.*: "their fathers."

36. *because.* MT: *yʿn ʾšr;* Samaritan text: *yʿn ky.*

37. *it.* MT: *šām,* literally, 'there'; Samaritan text: *šāmâh.* Compare the next verse.

38. *he shall enter it.* Vg adds *pro te* 'in your stead'.

Imbue . . . with strength. MT: *ḥazzēq (piʿel);* Samaritan text: *ʾḥzq (ʾiphʿil,* variant of *hiphʿil).*

39. *your little ones whom you said would become a prey, your children.* LXX: "every little child." The phrase "your little ones," Hebrew *ṭappĕkem,* used in Num 14:14 as well, is omitted in the LXX. See the NOTES.

who do not yet know good from bad. Omitted in the Samaritan text. See the NOTES.

they. MT: *hm;* Samaritan text: *hmh.*

40. *turn about and march.* Hebrew: *pnw lkm wsʿw.* For *dativus ethicus,* here used with *pĕnû* 'turn'; see the TEXTUAL NOTES at v 7. Samaritan text: *pnw wsʿw lkm,* attaching the *dativus ethicus* to the verb *sʿw* 'march', literally, 'set out', as in v 7.

41. *YHWH.* The Samaritan text, LXX, Vg, and Syriac add "our God." This epithet is added in the versions in 4:3, 35, 39; 6:12, 18; 9:18; and 10:13. It is found in the MT but omitted in the LXX or the Samaritan text in 4:5; 9:3.

dared. Hebrew: *wthynw.* See the NOTES. LXX: *sunathroisthentes,* "when you assembled"; Vg: *instructi armis* 'armed'; Syriac: *wʾtgrgrtwn* 'you were incited'; *Tg. Onq.* and *Tg. Ps.-J.*: *wšrytwn* 'you began'; *Tg. Neof.*: *wʾwḥytwn* 'you hurried'. The Samaritan text has *wthyynw,* which the *Sam. Tg.* understands as *whwytwn* 'you were'.

43. *I spoke.* MT: *wʾdbr;* Samaritan text: *wʾdbrh.*

YHWH. The Samaritan text adds "your God."

44. *the Amorites.* The Samaritan text has "the Amalekite and Canaanite."

and they crushed. From the root *ktt* in the *hiphʿil.* See *GKC* §67g.

at Hormah. 4QDt[h] fr 4–5 (Duncan 1989, Fig. 12) reads: *hḥrmh,* cf. Num 14:45.

46. *as many days as you remained.* Literally, "many days, like the days that you remained." After the relative pronoun *ʾšr,* when the appositional clause is added to a word of time, the retrospective pronoun is omitted. See *GKC* §138c, and the NOTES at v 31.

NOTES

29–30. Compare the similar wording in Exodus in connection with the Egyptian enemy (14:13–14), and the end of the story there: "they had faith in the Lord and in his servant Moses" (14:31). In contrast to the situation in Exodus, here they "have no faith" (v 32).

29. *Have no dread.* The verb *ʿrṣ* is characteristic of Deuteronomy (cf. 7:21; 20:3; 31:6).

30. *who goes before you.* Compare Exod 13:21.

will fight for you just as he did for you in Egypt. The reference is to Exod 14:25: "The Egyptians said, 'let us flee from the Israelites, for YHWH is fighting for them against Egypt' " (compare Exod 14:14). The idea of God fighting for the Israelites is very common in Deuteronomy and the literature influenced by it: Deut 3:22; Josh 10:14, 42; 23:3, 10.

before your eyes. This phrase is dear to the author. It refers to the great experience of the generation of the Exodus (cf. 4:34; 6:22; 11:7; 29:1; 34:12; Josh 24:17). The new generation that is about to enter the promised land is considered here identical with the one that left Egypt.

The time of Moses and Joshua is conceived as the period in which God revealed himself and performed his marvelous deeds in the sight of his people (cf. especially 4:34; 10:21; 11:7; 29:1ff.; Josh 24:31; Judg 2:7). See Hoffman 1981–82.

31. *how YHWH . . . carried you as a man carries his son.* Like Hebrew *gdl* and *rwm/rwmm,* which literally mean 'to raise', 'to lift up', but actually imply 'to nurse' and 'to rear' (Isa 1:2; 23:4), so the verbs *nśʾ* and *sbl,* both literally 'to carry', similarly imply 'to sustain' and 'to provide for'. Compare Aramaic *sbl* and Akkadian *našû* (see Muffs 1969, pp. 39 n. 4, 198). For *nśʾ* and *sbl* in the sense of 'provide for, take care of, support' concerning Israel, cf. Isa 46:3–4: "carried *(haʿamūsîm)* from the belly, borne *(hannesūʾîm)* from the womb; and until your old age I am the one, and until hoary age I will take care [literally, "carry" = Hebrew *ʾesbōl]* of [you]; and I have created [you] and will bear [Hebrew *ʾeśśaʾ]* [you]; I will sustain [literally, "carry" = Hebrew *ʾesbōl]* [you] and keep [you] alive *[amallēṭ;* compare Akkadian *bulluṭu,* which means 'to provide with food']." For interpretation, cf. Greenfield 1971, pp. 262–63. See also Ps 28:9: *ureʿēm wenaśśʾem ʿad hāʿôlām* 'and shepherd them and sustain [literally, "carry"] them forever', and compare Isa 63:9: "And he raised them and sustained [literally, 'carried' = Hebrew *nśʾ]* them all the days of old."

In a context similar to that of Deut 1:31 we find the same idea in Num 11:12: "Did I conceive all this people, did I bear them, that you should say to me, 'carry them in your bosom as a nurse carries an infant'?" In this case also, "carrying" and "taking care" overlap. Compare also Hos 11:1, 3–4: "When Israel was a youth, I loved him. . . . I was a guide [see AB] for Ephraim . . . taking them in my arms [LXX]." Note that the motifs of carrying/loving a child and guiding it occur in both Deut 1 and Hos 11 (compare *trgl,* literally, 'to spy, reconnoiter' in Hos 11:3, with *ltwr* 'to scout, reconnoiter' in Deut 1:33). Compare also Jer 31:8, 19; and see Weinfeld 1972a, pp. 368–69. The idea of God's providential care of Israel in the wilderness is an oft-repeated theme in Deuteronomy (cf. 2:7; 8:3–4; 29:4). The idea of provision in the wilderness is expressed by the verb *klkl* 'to sustain, nourish' in Neh 9:21: "and you sustained them *(klkltm)* in the wilderness forty year long." Note also the idiom *wlklkl ʾt śybtk* 'to sustain your old age' in Ruth 4:15; and compare the quoted verse from Isa 46:4: "Until old age . . . I will take care."

until you came to this place. That is to say, the valley near Beth-Peor (3:29). For the phrase, compare 9:7; 11:5.

32. *Yet in spite of this you have no faith.* Compare Moses' address in Num 14:11: "How long will they have no faith in me despite all the signs that I have performed in their midst?" The *beth* in *bdbr* means 'in spite of', as also the *beth* in *bkl hʾtwt* in Num 14:11. See, however, Rashi, who interprets the *beth* with its normal meaning of 'in': "In this matter [of bringing you into the land] you have no faith."

33. *who goes before you.* The phrase is resumed from v 30, but developed differently: not in order to fight as in v 30, but in order to guide. Compare Exod 13:21; Num 14:14.

to scout the place. The statement is apparently dependent on Num 10:33–34: "the Ark traveled in front of them . . . to seek out [literally, 'to scout' = Hebrew *ltwr]* a resting place *(mᵉnûḥâ)* for them," except that here the Ark has been omitted (for the reason see the INTRODUCTION sec. 12).

to encamp. The LXX translates *hodēgōn* 'to guide you', as if it read *lanḥōtᵉkem.* This verb actually occurs in Exod 13:21, and it is probable that our Hebrew is an inadvertent inversion of an original *lnḥtkm* to *lḥntkm.*

in fire by night . . . and in cloud by day. Compare Exod 13:21 and Num 14:14. In those passages, however, the order of the terms is different: "a pillar of cloud and a pillar of fire."

to guide you on the route. Literally, "to show you." In the parallel verse of Exod 13:21: "to give them light *(lhʾyr lhm),*" which is reflected in *Tg. Ps.-J.* to this verse: *lʾnhrwtkwn.* Compare *Tg. Ps.-J.* to Exod 13:21. It seems that in this verse the author drew heavily on Exod 13:21, Num 10:33, and Num 14:14, but occasionally paraphrased the idioms of his sources.

34. *he was angry, and he vowed.* Compare the oath in Num 14:21–23.

35. *Not one of these men.* Literally, "if *(ʾim)* one of these men," a form that usually introduces a promise or threat confirmed by an oath. It means, "surely, not one of these men shall see," etc.

this evil generation. Compare Num 32:13: "the whole generation that has done evil in the eyes of the Lord," referring as here to the generation of the wilderness.

the good land. In the parallel verse in Num 14:23: "see the land." "The good land/soil" is a characteristic phrase of Deuteronomy (cf. 3:35; 4:21, 22; 6:18; 8:10; 9:6; 11:17). The author of Deuteronomy is unstinting in his glowing praise of the goodness and beauty of the promised land (compare, e.g., 8:7ff.).

36. *none except Caleb the son of Jephunneh:* Caleb is called in several places "the Kenizzite" (Num 32:12; Josh 14:6, 14; cf. also Josh 15:17 = Judg 1:13), a clan of foreign stock who lived in the region of Hebron and were gradually

absorbed into the tribe of Judah. According to Josh 14:12 and 15:14, it was Caleb who dispossessed the giants of Hebron. The story about Caleb the faithful spy, who came as far as Wadi Eshcol, near Hebron (v 24; compare Num 13:23), and the regard given to him for his faithful mission, actually explain Caleb's predominance in the Hebron area. In the ancient sources (cf. Num 14:24, JE), it was Caleb alone who reached Hebron during the spying mission. He proved faithful and therefore escaped punishment. The priestly source, however, added Joshua, the national hero of the conquest, and extended the range of the spying mission to bring it as far as Lebo-Hamath, which was the northernmost point of the border of the promised land. The provincial scope of the story has thus been eliminated: (1) Caleb was not the only one who remained loyal to God; Joshua the conqueror was faithful too; (2) Hebron was not the only target of the spying mission; the whole of the promised land was the objective. The author of the account in Deut 1:22–46 seems to be mainly dependent on the JE source.

the land on which he set foot. In Num 14:24: "the land which he entered." "Set foot on *(drk)*" is a characteristic phrase of Deuteronomy, and the literature influenced by it (cf. 11:24, 25; Josh 1:3; 14:9).

he was entirely loyal to YHWH. Literally, "filled up after *(mlʾ ʾḥr).*" This expression is especially characteristic of the Caleb traditions, Num 14:24; 32:11–12; Josh 14:8, 9, 14, and equals *hyh tmym/šlm* 'to be whole/perfect', 'with wholeheartedness', found in connection with gifts obtained by virtue of loyalty (cf. Gen 17:1; 1 Kgs 3:6; 9:4–5; etc., and Assyrian grants, for which see Weinfeld, 1972a, pp. 75ff.).

37–38. These two verses appear to be parenthetical, for they interrupt God's address directed to the people: v 37 is a monologue by Moses in which he complains about his own fate, while in v 38 God responds to Moses concerning the succession in leadership. Only v 39 resumes God's address. Both verses deal with the same topic: Moses' inclusion in the punishment of the desert generation, a fact that entailed the appointment of the new leader, Joshua. Moses' punishment and Joshua's exemption from the fate of the desert generation are extensively dealt with in the priestly tradition (Num 20:10–12; 14:6–10, 30, 38). In contrast to the priestly account in Num 20:10–12, however, there is no allusion here to Moses' own sin, and in contrast to the priestly account in Num 14:6–10, 30, 38, where Joshua appears like Caleb as the faithful spy, nothing is said about Joshua's role as a spy. He is simply presented as the successor of Moses. The bare facts given here about Moses' fate and Joshua's entering into the land were explained theologically by the priestly source. According to that source, Moses was punished because of his own sin (Num 20:7–13), and Joshua entered the land not only by virtue of being Moses' successor, but also because of his loyalty in fulfilling his mission as a spy (Num 14:30, 38).

37. *Because of you . . . you shall not enter it either.* This refers to the sin of the spies and its punishment. The priestly tradition linked Moses' sin and pun-

ishment to the "quarrel" at the waters of Meribah (Num 20:7–13), which took place in the thirty-ninth year of the Exodus.

38. *who attends you.* Literally, "stands before you," an idiom for serving (cf. 10:8; 1 Kgs 10:8; 12:8; etc.). Joshua is indeed described as the "servant of Moses" (Exod 24:13; 33:11; Num 11:28; Josh 1:1).

Imbue him with strength. Compare 3:28; 31:7. Strength is needed because of the difficult task of war and conquest, which he is to face, as is clear from the following phrase. In the priestly tradition the nomination of Joshua (Num 27:15–23) immediately follows the admonition to Moses to prepare for death following his sin at the waters of Meribah (27:12–14).

for he shall allot it to Israel. Literally, "he shall make Israel possess the land."

39. *your little ones whom you said would become a prey.* The phrase here is identical to the one in Num 14:31, and parallels the next phrase: "your children who do not yet know good from bad." Therefore, the first clause is considered by many to be an editorial addition from Num 14:31. The LXX omits the first clause, while the Samaritan version omits most of the second (i.e., "who do not . . . bad").

who do not yet know good from bad. Compare Isa 7:15: "by the time he learns to reject the bad and choose the good." Here it refers to the young men not yet of responsible age, which according to Num 14:31 is twenty years and over. Cf. Exod 30:14 and Num 1:3ff., where only males of twenty years and older should be taken into account. According to rabbinic tradition, man is not accountable before the age of twenty (*y. Bik.* 2:1; *y. Sanh.* 11:7; 30b; *b. Šabb.* 32b).

40. *turn about and march . . . toward the Sea of Reeds.* This phrase is identical with the conclusion of the condemning speech of God in Num 14:25. The next verse here corresponds to Num 14:40, which actually continues verse 25 there. Num 14:26–39 belong to a different source (priestly).

41. *We have sinned against YHWH. We will go up and fight. . . . And you all girded yourselves with your gear.* Compare Num 14:40, which is supplemented here by a military elaboration. To "the going up" (*ʿlh*) of Numbers, "the fighting and girding with gear" is added, which suits the military-nationalist attitude of Deuteronomy (cf. Weinfeld 1972a, pp. 45ff.).

and dared to ascend the hill country. "Dared (*wthynw*)" is taken as deriving from Arabic *hāna* 'to be light/easy'. Rashi and Rashbam, however, refer justifiably to Num 14:40, where the people say *hnnw wʿlynw* 'we are prepared to go up'. It is probable that the verb *hwn,* which does not occur elsewhere in the Bible, was constructed ad hoc out of the *hnnw* of Numbers. Aquila renders *homonoein* 'to agree' based on late Hebrew *hn* 'yes', and understood, "you said yes" or "you agreed" (compare Ibn Ezra and others).

42. Compare Num 14:42.

43. *You flouted YHWH's command.* Literally, "you defied the mouth of the

Lord" (compare v 26). The parallel phrase in Num 14:41 is "to bypass the mouth of the Lord *(ʿbr py).*"

and willfully marched up. The verb *zwd* implies "seething" or "overflowing" (compare Ps 124:5, *mym hzydnm).* The parallel verse in Num 14:44 expresses a similar concept *(wyʿplw lʿlt).* Compare the LXX to both verses: *parabiazesthai* in Deut 1:44 and *diabiazesthai* in Num 14:44, both of which mean 'to break through with force'. The construction *wtzydw wtʿlw* seems parallel to *wthynw lʿlt,* and both may be similar in meaning (D. N. Freedman). In Numbers the narrator adds that the Ark of the Covenant and Moses did not move from the camp, which apparently was considered to be the cause of the failure. In Deuteronomy the Ark is missing, because of Deuteronomy's reserved approach with respect to holy symbols. Compare also the omission of the Ark in v 33 (see there, and the INTRODUCTION sec. 12).

44. *Then the Amorites who lived.* Compare Num 14:45, but there we find the "Amalekite and the Canaanite." As indicated in the NOTE to v 7, Deuteronomy tends to use "Amorite" as the general designation for the people of the land before its conquest (cf. also vv 19, 20, 27).

[they] chased you as bees do. Compare the curse in the *VTE:* "Just as the honeycomb is pierced with holes, so may they pierce your flesh" (lines 594–98), and cf. also the simile in the *Iliad* 2.86ff.: "As the tribes of thronging bees come forth from some hollow rock," and Ps 118:12: "They surrounded me like bees." (Loeb Classical Library, Harvard).

at Hormah. A Canaanite city in the eastern Negev, which appears together with Arad (Num 21:1–3; Josh 12:14), originally called Zephath (Judg 1:17). The identification of the site is disputed, some identifying it with Tell Milḥ (Malḥata), and others identifying it with neighboring Khirbat al-Meshash, both located east of Beersheba. At both Tell Milḥ and Khirbat al-Meshash, which are located beside abundant wells, earthen remparts of the Hyksos period were discovered, the only ones in the area. No Late Bronze remains have been found. The big fortresses of Tell Milḥ and Khirbat al-Meshash prevented penetration by nomadic elements into the Negev region of Arad for a long period, and this seems to be reflected in the Israelite tribal traditions about their defeat at Hormah (on this region, cf. Mazar 1965, pp. 299ff.). The tribal occupation of this area (the occupation of the Negev of Arad by the Kenites [Judg 1:16], and that of Hormah by Simeon [Judg 1:17; Josh 19:4]) was later seen as a victory over the Canaanites, and the name Hormah was explained as a memorial to the banishment of the Canaanites by Israel (Num 21:3; cf. Aharoni, Fritz, and Kempinski 1975, pp. 114–24). For a recent survey and evaluation of the excavations at Tel-Masos, see Kempinski et al. 1981.

in Seir. The versions (LXX, Peshitta, Vg) translate, "from Seir to Hormah," which sounds more logical. The preposition *b* in Hebrew, as well as in Ugaritic and Phoenician, may indeed be rendered "from," and one can accept the translation of the versions without resorting to the correction of *b* to *m.*

45. *Then you sat weeping before YHWH.* In the MT: "You returned and wept," which may be understood that they returned to Kadesh after the defeat and wept. The LXX, however, reads, "You sat down *(kathisantes)* and wept" (compare also the LXX of Num 11:4), a reading *(watteš*ᵉ*bû* instead of *wat-tašūbû)* that may be supported by a parallel from Judg 20:26: "And they came to Bethel and wept and sat down before the Lord." "Sitting before the Lord" in such a context implies a ritual of lamentation (cf. Judg 21:1; see also Num 14:1).

46. *as many days as you remained at Kadesh.* Literally, "You sat at Kadesh many days, as the days you sat." This is "an example of the 'idem per idem' idiom often employed in the Semitic languages, when a writer is either unable or has no occasion to speak explicitly" (Driver 1902; compare 9:25; 1 Sam 23:13; 2 Sam 15:20; Zech 10:8). The expression "many days" *(ymym rbym)* is found in 2:1, and according to 2:14 this refers to the thirty-eight years during which the Israelites wandered between Kadesh and the Moabite border. If 1:46 belongs to the same tradition as 2:1ff., then *ymym rbym* in 1:46 can only mean a few months. In fact, the idioms "many days" *(ymym rbym)* in 1:46 and 2:1, as well as "long enough" *(rab lākem)* in 1:6 and 2:2, which occur in the first chapters of Deuteronomy (compare also 3:26), should not be taken in an absolute manner, as "years long," but should depend on the context for a precise meaning. The second part of the verse, "as long as you did," also points to an undefined period, short or long.

COMMENT

Moses' speech is inspired by the tradition in Num 14:7–19. Just as Caleb and Joshua urged the people not to fear the Canaanites because God was with them (Num 14:7–9), so here Moses similarly encourages them (vv 29–31). In the same way that God rebuked the people for their disbelief (Num 14:11), Moses now scolds them for their lack of faith (v 32). Moses in his prayer in Num 14:14 reminds the Lord of his past grace: "You go before them in a pillar of cloud by day and in a pillar of fire by night." The same acts of grace are mentioned by Moses in his address to the people in Deut 1:33: "who goes before you . . . in fire by night . . . and in cloud by day." The author develops his style by bringing in phrases from other Exodus traditions, such as Exod 13:21 and Num 10:33 (see the NOTES).

THE CIRCUIT OF EDOM, MOAB, AND AMMON (2:1–23)

2 [1]So, we turned and set out into the wilderness, toward the Sea of Reeds, as YHWH had spoken to me, and skirted the hill country of Seir a long time.

2And YHWH said to me, 3"You have been skirting this hill country long
enough; now turn north. 4Command the people as follows: 'You will be passing
through the territory of your kinsmen, the descendants of Esau, who live in Seir.
Although they will be afraid of you, be very careful 5not to start a fight with
them; for I will not give you of their land so much as a foot can tread on,
because I have given the hill country of Seir as a possession to Esau. 6You shall
acquire food from them for money, so that you may eat, and you shall procure
water from them so that you may drink.' " 7Indeed, YHWH your God has
blessed you in all your undertakings; he has watched over your wanderings
through this great wilderness. YHWH your God has been with you these forty
years; you have lacked nothing.

8We then moved on, away from our kinsmen, the descendants of Esau, who
lived in Seir, away from the road of ʿArabah, away from Elath and Ezion Geber,
and we marched on in the direction of the wilderness of Moab. 9And YHWH
said to me, "Do not harass the Moabites or engage them in war, for I will not
give you any of their land as a possession; I have given Ar as a possession to the
descendants of Lot."

10It was formerly inhabited by the Emim, a people great and numerous, and
tall like the Anakites. 11Like the Anakites, they are considered to be Rephaim,
but the Moabites call them Emim. 12Similarly, Seir was formerly inhabited by
the Horites, but the descendants of Esau dispossessed them, wiping them out
and settling in their place, just as Israel did in the land they were to possess,
which YHWH had given to them.

13Up now! Cross the Wadi Zered!

So, we crossed the Wadi Zered. 14The time that we spent in travel from
Kadesh-Barnea until we crossed the Wadi Zered was thirty-eight years, until
that whole generation of warriors had perished from the camp. 15Indeed, the
hand of YHWH struck them, to root them out from the camp to the last man.

16When all the warriors among the people had died off, 17YHWH spoke to
me, saying, 18"You are now passing through the territory of Moab, through Ar.
19You will then be close to the Ammonites. Do not harass them or start a fight
with them, for I will not give any part of the land of the Ammonites to you as a
possession; I have given it as a possession to the descendants of Lot.

20It was also reckoned as Rephaim country. It was formerly inhabited by the
Rephaim, whom the Ammonites call Zamzummim, 21a people great and numerous, and tall like the Anakites. YHWH destroyed them outright, so that
[the Ammonites] dispossessed them and settled in their place, 22as he did for
the descendants of Esau who live in Seir, when he wiped out the Horites before
them, so that they dispossessed them and settled in their place, as is still the
case. 23So too with the Avvim, who dwelled in villages as far as Gaza: the
Caphtorim, who came from Crete, destroyed them outright and settled in their
place.

TEXTUAL NOTES

2:1. *So, we turned and set out.* MT: *wnpn wnsʿ*; Samaritan text: *wnpnh wnsʿh.* See the TEXTUAL NOTES at 1:19.

2. *And YHWH said.* A new section begins here in the MT, on the same line as the previous section following a space *(setumah).*

3. *long enough.* See 1:6, 3:26. 4QDt[h] fr 4–5 (Duncan 1989, 68): *rb lk* like 3:26 but there the addressee is Moses while here it is the whole nation and therefore the plural is unjustified.

turn. See the TEXTUAL NOTES at 1:7.

4. *Command.* MT: *ṣw;* Samaritan text: *ṣwy,* an alternative spelling of the long form of the imperative *ṣwh (ṣaweh).*

You will be passing through. Hebrew: *ʾatem ʿōbĕrîm* 'you are passing through', i.e., "you are about to pass through."

be very careful. See the NOTES. LXX: *kai eulabēthēsontai sphodra* 'and they shall be cautious'. The Vg misunderstood the situation and therefore ascribed the cautiousness to the other party, transferring the phrase to the beginning of the next verse for the sake of clarity: *videte ergo diligenter.*

5. *not to start a fight.* Hebrew: *ʾal titgārû bām,* literally, 'do not stir yourselves up against them'. The same phrase is used in v 19. In vv 9 and 24 a similar expression is used with the addition of *milḥamâh* 'war' in the accusative of manner, i.e., "do not stir yourselves up against them in war." The LXX and *Tg. Neof.* have "in war" here as well, but this may reflect the exigencies of translation (cf. my translation, "start a fight"), and not a different *Vorlage.* But *Tg. Onq.* adds "in [order to make] war" in v 19, but this does not imply here that we are in fact dealing with different textual traditions.

of their land. The Samaritan version adds *yršh* 'as an inheritance', as does the MT in v 9.

6. *for money.* Many LXX manuscripts omit the first "for money."

procure. Hebrew: *tikrû,* from *krh,* an unusual verb for 'purchase', 'bargain', apparently unrelated to *krh* 'dig', which is much more common (cf. Hos 3:2; Job 6:27; 40:30; and see the NOTES). LXX: *metrō tēpsesthe* 'you shall receive by measure', perhaps understanding *krh* as derived from the ancient Hebrew measure *kor.* Vg: *haurietis* 'you shall draw', perhaps understanding *krh* in the usual sense of 'dig [a well]'. For the rendering of the phrase in *Tg. Neof.,* see the NOTES.

7. *your God.* In the MT the pronoun is in the second-person singular; in the LXX it is in the first-person plural.

undertakings. Hebrew: *maʿăśēh yādekā* 'the work of your *hands',* cf., Deut 16:15.

he has watched over. Hebrew: *yādaʿ,* literally, 'he has known'; LXX: *diagnōthi* 'know, consider' (in the imperative), reading *daʿ* (or, *yedaʿ*?) in the

Hebrew *Vorlage.* For the Aramaic Targumim, see the NOTES. Syriac translates *yādaʿ lektĕkā* as an idiom meaning "he knew how to lead you *(ydʿ lmdbrwtkwn).*"

great. The LXX adds *kai tēn phoberan* 'and terrible' (cf. 1:19; 8:15). Syriac omits "great."

these forty years. Hebrew: *zeh ʾarbāʿîm šānāh.* See *GKC* §136d. For the addition to this verse in Samaritan text, see the NOTES.

8. *We then moved on, away from our kinsmen . . . away from the road.* So Hebrew: *wannaʿabōr mēʾēt ʾaḥēynû midderek;* LXX: *parēlthomen tous adelphous hēmōn . . . para tēn hodon;* and Vg: *transissemus fratres nostros . . . per viam,* "and we passed through our (LXX, "your") kinsmen . . . via the road." It has been suggested (BHK, BHS) that the LXX and Vg reflect the original Hebrew, *wannaʿabōr ʾēt ʾaḥēynû . . . derek,* according to which Edom permitted Israel to pass through its territory, while the MT is an attempt to harmonize Deut 2:8 with Num 20:21 (see the COMMENT). But this reconstructed reading requires too many corrections of the MT. The Samaritan Pentateuch has the long cohortative form for the verbs in this verse.

and we marched on. A new section begins here in the MT in the middle of the verse, on the same line as the previous section, following the space *(setumah).*

9. *harass . . . engage.* These verbs are second-person singular in the MT, second-person plural in the LXX.

engage them in war. Hebrew: *titgār bām milḥāmâh,* literally, 'stir yourself up against them in war'. *milḥāmâh* is the accusative of manner or respect (see *GKC* §118m, q). The Samaritan text reads, *titgār bô* 'stir yourself up against *him* [Moab]', and omits "war." Compare vv 5, 19, where the MT and the Samaritan text omit *milḥāmâh,* but it is added in certain versions. See above, the TEXTUAL NOTE at v 5.

10. *a people great and numerous, and tall.* Compare v 21.

11. *Like the Anakites, they are considered to be Rephaim.* Omitted in the LXX. The Samaritan text, *Tg. Onq.,* and Syriac translate both Rephaim and Anakites in vv 10–11 *g(n)br(y)ʾ* 'mighty (men)', rendering (tautologically): "(10) . . . a people great and numerous, as tall as the mighty. (11) . . . Like the mighty, they are also thought of as the mighty. . . ." The tradition equating Anakites and Rephaim and identifying both as "mighty (men)" may have led the LXX to omit this passage as meaningless. *Tg. Ps.-J.* also identifies the Anakites and Rephaim as *g(n)bry* but translates midrashically, "the mighty who live in the plain of the mighty are thought of as the mighty who were wiped out in the Flood." *Targum Neofiti* renders Rephaim as *gwbryn/gybryn* 'mighty' and Anakites as *bnwy dʿnq gwbryyʾ,* apparently in an attempt to make sense of the original Targumic tradition equating the two.

12. *Ḥorites.* MT: *haḥōrîm;* Samaritan text: *haḥorî* 'the Ḥorite (nation)'.

dispossessed them. MT: *yiyrāšûm,* the imperfect, which is somewhat anomalous in this context (see Driver 1902, ad loc.).

wiping them out. MT: *wayyašmîdûm mippenêyhem,* literally, 'and they [the Edomites] wiped them [the Ḥorites] out from before their [the Edomites] face'. Samaritan text: *wyšmydm YHWH mpnyhm wyyršwm* 'and YHWH wiped them out from before their face and they dispossessed them' (cf. v 21), though *wyyršwm* 'and they dispossessed them' has already been stated immediately before this phrase.

13. *Up now!* MT: *ʾattâh qūmû,* literally, 'now arise!' The Samaritan Pentateuch adds *sʿw* 'and set out' (cf. v 24). This reading is followed by the LXX. The Vg renders the verse *surgentes ergo ut transiremus torrentem Zared venimus ad eum* 'thus rising up to cross the torrent Zared, we came to it'.

So, we crossed. MT: *wnʿbr;* Samaritan text: *wnʿbrh.*

14. *until . . . had perished.* Hebrew: *ʿad tōm,* literally, 'until the completion of [that whole generation]', in other words, until that whole generation was finished. It seems that *tōm* 'completion' is used here in the sense of "perishing." Compare Num 14:35, in the same context as this verse, also Jer 24:10; 27:8; 44:18. In v 16, however, the phrase *tām lāmût* 'finished dying' is used, implying that *tām* alone means not 'perish' but 'complete' (cf. Num 17:28). The LXX translates *tām* both here and in v 16 as *diepesen/an* 'fell', i.e., 'perished', and *tām lāmût* in v 16 is thus translated somewhat awkwardly, 'fell dying'. Some LXX manuscripts add *apothnēskontes* 'dying', here as well. Because this hinders instead of helping the translation, it probably reflects a *Vorlage* that had *lāmût* here as well. The Vg, Syriac, and the Targumim all translate 'perish' here. In vv 15–16 the Vg omits *tmm/tmmw,* and Syriac, *Tg. Onq.,* and *Tg. Ps.-J.* use various verbs meaning 'finish', varying their translation of *tmm* according to context. The superliteral *Sam. Tg.* has *šlm* 'complete' in all three verses.

15. *Indeed.* Hebrew: *wĕgam,* literally, 'also'. Omitted in the LXX and Vg.

the hand of YHWH. Vg: "whose hand" (dependent of "YHWH," at the end of the last verse). The Aramaic Targumim have *mḥʾ* 'plague' for the anthropomorphic "hand." See the NOTES.

to root them out from the camp. Hebrew: *lehummām miqqereb hammahănеh,* literally, 'to confuse them from the midst of the camp', that is, to throw them into a panic, until they die and are no longer in the camp. See the NOTES.

to the last man. Hebrew: *ʿad tummām* 'until they were completed (or perished)'. See the TEXTUAL NOTES at the previous verse. The phrase is omitted in the Vg. Compare *tammû ligwôaʿ* (Num 17:28), and, by contrast, *ûbaḥereb ûbārāʿāb tāmnû* (Jer 44:18), *ʾad tummām me ʿal hāʾadāmōh* (Jer 24:10), *ʿad-tummî ʾōtām bĕyādô* (Jer 27:8).

16. *among the people had died off.* Hebrew: *tammû . . . lāmût miqqereb hāʿām,* literally, 'finished dying from among [so that they were no longer among] the people'. Compare *lehummām miqqereb hammaḥănеh* in the previous verse (see the TEXTUAL NOTES). The Vg omits *tammû* and *miqqereb hāʿām,* translat-

ing simply *ceciderunt* 'had fallen dead'. For other versions, see the TEXTUAL NOTES at v 14.

17. *YHWH spoke to me, saying.* A new section begins here in the MT, on the same line as the previous section, following a space *(setumah).* The words "and YHWH spoke to me" are a harmonization with the rest of the *petucha* (a beginning of a new paragraph) vv 2, 9, 31; 3:2, 26.

19. *harass . . . start a fight.* The verbs are singular in the MT, plural in the LXX.

21. *tall.* Hebrew: *rām;* LXX: *dunatōteron* 'mightier', with some manuscripts adding *humōn* 'than you'. In 2:10 the word *ischuros* is used to translate it.

dispossessed them and. Omitted in the Vg.

in their place. MT: *taḥtām;* Samaritan text: *taḥtēyhem.*

22. *as he did for the descendants of Esau.* Syriac: "as the descendants of Esau did" (cf. v 12); LXX: "as they did *to* the descendants of Esau[!]."

so that they dispossessed them. The Vg has singular subject (God), translating: "giving over their land to them," perhaps reading *wayyorišum* for the MT's *wayyirāšum.*

23. *villages.* Many versions take Hebrew *ḥăṣērîm* as a place-name, for example, LXX: *Asēroth* (cf. 1:1); Vg: *Haserim;* Syriac, MT, *Tg. Onq.: Rapiah.* The *Sam. Tg.* has *dyryh* 'dwellings', but some manuscripts have *kpr(n)yh* 'villages'. The *Tg. Neof.* has *kwprnyyh* 'villages'. Rabbi Saadia Gaon in his commentary on the Torah interpreted the word here as both "their villages" and "Hazar-addar," which is on the southern border of Palestine (Num 34:4), as *Rapiah.* The *Tg. Ps.-J.* combines the two Targumic traditions with *kwprnyyʾ drpyʿ* 'the villages of Rapiah'.

NOTES

1. *we turned and set out into the wilderness . . . as YHWH had spoken.* This verse fulfills the commandment of 1:40; see the COMMENT on 1:19.

and skirted the hill country of Seir a long time. Compare Num 21:4. "Hill country of Seir," literally "Mount of Seir," stands for the whole land of Seir, that is, Edom; compare "mount of the Amorite" in 1:7 and the COMMENT there. The territory skirted is that of western Edom: the border ran from Kadesh to the Gulf of ʿAqaba on the Red Sea.

2. *And YHWH said to me.* Such opening formulas are characteristic of the first three chapters of Deuteronomy, and they add to the stories a prophetic dimension: each move follows a divine command; cf. 1:42; 2:2, 9, 17, 31; 3:2, 26. There seems to be significance in the fact that this formula occurs seven times in Deut 1–3 (1:42; 2:2, 9, 17, 31; 3:2, 26), using the phrase *wyʾmr Y. ʾly* six times and once *wydbr Y. ʾly* (2:17), the latter occurring in the middle; see the discussion of Langlamet 1969, pp. 79f.

3. *now turn north.* They have skirted the western and southern borders of

Edom, and now they are asked to turn northward, which would lead them along the eastern border of Edom.

4. *You will be passing through the territory.* Literally, "through the border," but the Hebrew word for border, *gĕbûl,* denotes territory (cf., e.g., Exod 13:7). In the parallel story of Numbers (20:14–21), the same phrase *ʿbr bgbl* occurs (v 21) and means undoubtedly "to cross the territory." Compare v 17 in the same passage: "Let us then pass through your country *(nʿbrh-nʾ bʾrṣk).*"

your kinsmen. Literally, "your brothers." Compare Num 20:14, "Thus says your brother Israel."

Although they will be afraid of you. This stands in contradiction to Num 20:18–20, where it says that "Edom went out against them" and that Israel had therefore to turn away from them; see the introductory remark to this section. In order to solve the difficulty, Rashbam distinguished between the Edomites in Num 20 and the people who live in Seir (Deut 2:4, 29). The former—according to this view—denied the passage of the Israelites, while the latter agreed to it. This view, however, can hardly be accepted because the people who live in Seir are always identical with the Edomites (cf. Gen 32:4; 36:9, 21). See the comment of Rashbam's student appended to the commentary (ed. Rosin 1882, p. 200, § b, notes).

be very careful (wmšmrtm mʾnd). The implication is, in order not to provoke them, as becomes clear from the continuation (cf. Rashi). The same psychology is attested in Isa 7:4, where Ahaz is asked by the prophet to refrain from any action that could provoke the enemy: "be careful *(hšmr)* and calm."

5. *for I will not give you of their land so much as a foot can tread on . . . I have given the hill country of Seir as a possession to Esau.* Compare vv 9, 19. God appears here as the sovereign who distributes the land to his vassals, and no vassal is allowed to trespass beyond the boundaries set by his overlord (cf. Deut 32:8). A similar situation is encountered in the Hittite treaties, wherein the Hittite overlord urges his vassal to take possession of the land given to him by his overlord (cf. above, in the Note to 1:8) but warns him not to contend with the other vassals because they too have received their lands from him (see Weinfeld 1972a, pp. 72ff.).

6. *You shall acquire food from them for money, so that you may eat, and you shall procure water from them so that you may drink.* Similar terms were offered according to Num 20:17, 19, but these were rejected by the Edomites, in contrast to the tradition presented here; compare also v 29.

The Samaritan version inserts between verses 7 and 8 the passage from Num 20:17–18 (plus 14a), which contains the offer by Moses and the rejection by the king of Edom, thus harmonizing the two sources. Palestinian *Tg. Neof.* 1 solves the difficulty by rendering the verse thus: "You need not purchase food from them for money because the manna comes down to you from the sky and you need not purchase water from them because the well of water comes up with you to the top of the mountains and to the deep valleys—because God has blessed you" (for the well accompanying the Israelites in the desert, cf. *t. Sukk.* 3:11–13, and see also the picture of the well in the desert in the paintings of Dura Europos). For contradictory renditions of the original Hebrew text in the Pentateuch in the various Targumim, cf. Klein 1976, at p. 527. According to the midrash, the Israelites were not in need of food. They only made the offer to purchase in order to placate the Edomites *(Num. Rab.* 19, 7).

procure. For the verb *krh* in this sense, cf. Hos 3:2.

7. *YHWH your God has blessed you.* This is a characteristic phrase of Deuteronomy, cf. 14:29; 15:10, 18; 16:15; 23:21; 24:19; 28:8, 12.

in all your undertakings. mʿśh ydk, literally, 'the work of your hands'. It sometimes interchanges with *mšlḥ yd,* 'all that you put your hand to'. The same idioms are attested in Akkadian: *epšet qat/šipir qat,* with identical meaning.

he has watched over your wanderings. Literally, "*knew* your wanderings," "has cared for" (compare Targumim: *sāpeq ṣōrkak* 'he supplied your needs', cf. Gen 39:6; Prov 27:23; etc.). See also Hos 13:5, "I knew you [i.e., looked after you] in the wilderness . . . in pasture." For an analogous semantic phenomenon, compare English "provide," which comes from Latin *providere* 'to foresee'.

has been with you these forty years; you have lacked nothing. Compare 8:2, 4; 29:4; Neh 9:21; and compare 1:31 with the NOTE there.

8. *away from the road of ʿArabah.* That is to say, away from the road that leads from the Dead Sea to the Gulf of ʿAqaba through the ʿArabah (on ʿArabah, see 1:1). The Israelites turn now in a northeasterly direction.

away from Elath and Ezion Geber. Two sites on the Gulf of ʿAqaba, which served as ports and shipyards during the time of Solomon and later, cf. 1 Kgs 9:26: "in Ezion Geber which is beside Elath on the shore of the Sea of Reeds in the land of Edom." (Cf. also 1 Kgs 22:49; 2 Kgs 14:22; and 2 Chr 8:17, 20, 36.) From the present text and especially from 1 Kgs 9:26 we may conclude that Eilat and Ezion Geber are two separate sites, and that Eilat was better known than Ezion Geber, as the text in 1 Kings locates the latter by noting its proximity to the former.

Ezion Geber was first identified by N. Glueck as Tell al-Ḥalifa, which is about six hundred meters from the Gulf of ʿAqaba (see Glueck 1954, pp. 86–122). B. Rothenberg (1967, pp. 212–17) later proposed that Ezion Geber should be identified with the island Jazirat Farʿun, eleven kilometers south of modern Eilat. This site has a harbor with a sheltered basin, and its entrance is guarded by two towers, a characteristic feature of Phoenician harbors of this type. One may thus assume that it was indeed built by Phoenicians (cf. ibid. and Aḥituv 1971). Although Glueck has retracted his suggested identification of Ezion Geber with Tell al-Ḥalifa, it was again proposed by Z. Meshel (1975). According to B. Mazar 1975, one should not identify Ezion Geber with Tell al-Halifa. He suggests that Ezion Geber was built adjacent to Eilat after David's victory over Edom, to serve as a terminus for caravan routes to Arabia and to protect the nearby port. The name "Geber" may, according to Mazar, be the name of the founder of the settlement, one of Solomon's officers, Geber ben Uri (1 Kgs 4:19).

Eilat (Elath, Elôt), by contrast, identified with al-Paran (Gen 14:6), is to be located in today's ʿAqaba, once a Nabataean port named Aila, the ruins of which are to be found just north of ʿAqaba.

In the Masoretic manuscripts of Deut 2:8, a blank space *(pisqāh bĕ ʾemṣaʿ pāsûq)* occurs between Ezion Geber and the words "and we marched in the direction . . . of Moab." According to some scholars (e.g., Talmon 1966, pp. 228–34), *pisqāh bĕ ʾemṣaʿ pāsûq* indicates that some complementary evidence is available in other books of the Bible. In the present case, the author or the scribe might have in mind the events referred to in Num 33:36–48, which took place between the stay in Ezion Geber and the arrival in Moab, including the death of Aaron and the encounter with the king of Arad.

9. *I have given Ar as a possession to the descendants of Lot.* It is not altogether clear whether *Ar* is the name of a place or an area, or an appellation for the whole of Moab. See e.g. Simons 1959, p 117, note 79. Ar appears also in three poetic texts: Num 21:14–15, 27b–30, Isa 15:1. In the latter, Ar-Moab parallels Qir-Moab, which might indicate a fortified important city (compare *Qerioth, Qiriathaim,* and *Qir-ḥereś* in connection with Moab, cf. e.g. Jer 48:1, 24, 31, 36, 41). Recently M. Miller (1989) suggested that Ar be identified with *Khirbet Bālu,* a major city ruin, located on another of the southeastern tributaries of the Arnon. It was occupied during the Bronze and Iron Ages, and was associated with Aroer, "the city which is in the middle of the valley" (Deut 2:36; 2 Sam 24:5). Indeed the LXX in Deut 2:9, 18, 29 reads *Aroer* instead of *Ar.* This is reflected as well in *Tg. Ps.-J.* and the *Tg. Neof.,* which use also *Aroer* instead of Ar.

For Ammon and Moab as descendants of Lot, cf. Gen 19:37; Ps 83:9.

10–12. These verses consist of archaeological notes relating to the previous populations of Moab and Edom; compare vv 20–23 about the previous population of Ammon and the Philistines. These intercalated notes occur between the direct commandments to Moses to avoid conflict with these neighboring peoples (9, 10) and the command to the Israelites to continue their journey to capture the land; thus they serve to connect God's instructions to Moses and to the people (cf. Labuschagne 1985b, pp. 113–14).

10. *the Emim.* Compare Gen 14:5, where the Emim are mentioned as dwelling in Shaveh-Qiriathaim in the plain of Moab, north of the Arnon; they were called *Emim* because they gave rise to *ʾymh* (fear/terror). Compare *Tg. Onq. (ʾymtny),* Saadiah, and Ibn Ezra.

11. *Like the Anakites, they are considered to be Rephaim.* Compare v 20 and the NOTE on 1:28 above. Rephaim is the name of a legendary race of giants originating in the Bashan (Deut 3:13, Gen 14:5), but found as well in other parts of Transjordan (Deut 2:10–11, 20–21; Gen 15:20; Josh 13:13). Their remnants, "children of the *rafah*" (cf. children of the *Anak,* Num 13:22; Josh 15:14)

are said to have lived in the Philistine cities and in the Hebron area (2 Sam 21:15–22; cf. Josh 11:22). They are described as being of great stature and "men of great measure" *(ʾnšy mdwt,* Num 13:32; cf. 2 Sam 21:20; 1 Chr 20:6). Rephaim/Anakim were considered to be the descendants of the ancient Nĕfilîm, the heroes of old, men of renown, descendants of the divine beings *(bĕnê hʾălhym),* mentioned in Gen 6:1–4. We read also in Num 13:33 that the "men of great measure" of Hebron are "sons of Anak of the Nĕfilîm." *Rephaim* was also the epithet for divine ancient heroes in Sheol (see Isa 14:9 and cf. Isa 26:14, 19). The same is apparent from Ezek 32:27. Spirits of the dead are also termed *Rephaim* in Phoenician inscriptions, *rpʾm* (Slouschz 1942, pp. 9, lines 7–8; and 10, lines 8–9). The term has been recently discovered in a Ugaritic inscription (RS 34.126), where we find the custom of memorial rites for the spirits of the dead termed *rpi arṣ* and *rpim qdmnym* (cf. Bordreuil and Pardee 1982, pp. 123–30). These would seem to parallel the gods of the underworld found in Hittite and Mesopotamian texts, particularly the *karuileš šiuneš,* "the ancient gods" who are identified as the *anunakkū* of Mesopotamia. We also find the use of the term *rpu* for divine heroes. Of great pertinence is the Ugaritic description of El, the chief god of the Ugaritic pantheon (RS 24.252). He is described as *rpu mlk ʿlm* 'dwelling in Ashtaroth and Edrei', ruling the cities of the Bashan as did Og (Deut 1:3; Josh 12:4; 13:12), who was king of the Bashan = *ereṣ rephaim* (3:13; see Margulis 1970, pp. 292–99, and NOTE to 1:4). In one instance *rpu* is associated with hero/warrior: *gzrm . . . rpu bʿl, mhr bʿl* 'the heroes . . . Baal the Raphu, the warrior of Baal' *(CTA* 22B, lines 7–9). This double usage of a term for both a legendary race of giants of the spirits of dead heroes dwelling in the netherworld *(sheol/hades)* is used by the ancient Greeks as well. *Heros* is the name of a legendary hero as well as the spirit of the dead for whom memorial rites were performed. It seems that the tradition of *ereṣ rephaim* being in the Bashan and on the eastern side of the Jordan River (2:20; 3:12) has its origin in the discovery of megaliths in these areas (cf. Epstein 1975). Basalt from which these burial monuments were prepared is found mainly in the Golan and Horon, making the construction of these structures possible. One may compare these legends to those about the Greek Cyclops, the race of giants to whom have been ascribed the erection of "Cyclopean" city walls and gates as seen in sites such as Mycenae.

The book of Jubilees describes the Rephaim as being nine to ten cubits high, in reference to which compare the note about the sarcophagus of Og, the king of Bashan in 3:11.

12. *Seir was formerly inhabited by the Ḥorites.* Compare Gen 14:6; 36:20–30. The Hurrians constituted an ethnic group that first appeared in the mountains east of the Tigris River in the third millennium B.C.E. They later spread to the Euphrates and southwest to Syria and Palestine. They reached the height of their power in the fifteenth and fourteenth centuries B.C.E. by forming a vigorous state (Mitanni) in the Khabur valley. Indicative of the spread of their cul-

ture into Palestine is the fact that the king of Jerusalem in the fourteenth century B.C.E. bears a Hurrian name: *Abdi-Hepa* 'the servant of [the Hurrian goddess] Hepat'. Similarly, the name of *Araunah* or *Avarnah* the Jebusite, who sold to David the threshing floor on Mount Moriah (2 Sam 24), is thought to be of Hurrian origin *(eweri* 'lord'); see Hoffner 1973, p. 225. It seems that a group of Hurrians managed to establish a colony in Mount Seir until it was conquered by the Edomites in the thirteenth century B.C.E. For a recent investigation of the history of Hurrian culture, see Wilhelm 1982.

wiping them out and settling in their place. This is not to be taken literally; according to Gen 36:20ff., some Ḥorite clans were absorbed by the Edomites.

just as Israel did in the land they were to possess. Written from the point of view of the Israelites after they had conquered their land.

13. *Wadi Zered.* Compare Num 21:12. Most probably Wadi al-Hesā, which flows in a deep rift for approximately forty-five kilometers from east to west as far as the Dead Sea. It creates a natural borderline between Edom and Moab; cf. van Zyl 1960, pp. 47–48, 56, 62; *EM,* s.v. "Nahal Zered," 5.811–12. The name *Zered* may be descriptive of the dense vegetation in the riverbed. In fact, *Nahal Zered* (Num 21:12) is rendered by *Tg. Ps.-J.* as *dmrby ḥlpy wgly wsygly,* a wadi in which grow a variety of flowers; the present name is rendered *ṭrwwyy*ʾ, an Aramaic transliteration of the Greek *tarfea,* which indicates a thicket of bushes and trees.

14. *thirty-eight years.* Compare above, at 1:46.

until that whole generation of warriors had perished. The 'warriors', *ʾnšy hmlḥmh,* here and in v 16, define in a military manner the adult males (compare 1:35). In the priestly tradition they are defined as "from the age of twenty years up" (Num 14:29, 32:11). The author of Deuteronomy and its school, in their description of the conquest of the land, emphasize its military character. We thus find (cf. above, 1:41) the marchers described in a military manner (girded with weapons of war), a description absent in the priestly tradition. The conquerors of the land are termed by the author of Deuteronomy as well as by the historiographer of the former Prophets as *ḥlwṣym gbwry ḥyl* 'heroes of valor' (Deut 3:18; Josh 1:14; 8:3; 10:7) as well as *ʾnšy mlḥmh* 'people of war' (Josh 6:3; 8:1, 3, 11; 10:7; cf. Weinfeld 1972a, pp. 41–49).

from the camp. This too belongs to the military manner of description, and cf. the NOTE above to 1:41.

15. *the hand of YHWH struck them.* Literally, "the hand of YHWH was against them." "Hand of God" is usually associated with pestilence, cf. Exod 9:3, 15; 1 Sam 5:6, 7, 9, 11; 6:3, 5, 9; compare too 2 Sam 24:16, 17. In Ugaritic as well as in Akkadian texts, the hand of the god (especially that of the god Nergal) also means pestilence. Compare, in a Ugaritic text, *wyd ilm p kmtm ʿz mid* 'the hand of the god is here, for the pestilence is very strong' *(UT* 54:13), and in Akkadian, *qāt Nergal ibašši ina mātiya* 'the hand of Nergal is in my country' (*EA* 35:37), in reference to death/pestilence. In the story of the spies

(Num 14), which Deuteronomy draws on, God actually threatens to destroy the people by pestilence (14:12, *dbr)* and about the spies it says there that they died by pestilence *(bmgph,* v 27).

to root them out from the camp. The verb *hmm* connotes panic and confusion and is frequently used in the descriptions of divine war (cf. Exod 14:24, where *hmm* occurs next to *mḥnh* 'camp' as here (Deut 7:23; Josh 10:10; Judg 4:15; 1 Sam 7:10). Compare *kudoimos* in the Homeric epic and see Weinfeld 1983a, p. 135. In the present passage, the rebellious generation of the wilderness is seen as the enemy of God, who accordingly treats them as such (cf. Moran 1963c).

16–17. *(When all the warriors . . . had died off) YHWH spoke to me.* Hebrew: *dibber;* the other opening formulas (compare 1:42; 2:1, 9, 31; 3:1, 26) employ *ʾamar* 'the Lord said to me'. It seems that the use of a more intensive verb, *dibber,* is to be explained by the turning point that comes to expression here: the rebellious generation has perished, and the words of God are now addressed to the generation that is about to enter the promised land (cf. Langlamet 1969, pp. 80f.).

18. *Ar.* See the NOTE to v 10.

19. *You will then be close to the Ammonites.* The Ammonites are usually called "Sons of Ammon *(bny ʿmwn).*" Compare also *bn ʿmy* in Gen 19:38 (KUR *Banammana* in the Assyrian inscriptions). They settled in the fourteenth century B.C.E. along the upper and central Jabbok River (cf. 3:16 and Num 21:24). The Arnon, which the Israelites are about to cross (cf. v 24), is some forty-eight kilometers from the Ammonite border. The warning not to attack them is therefore mainly intended to divert the Israelites from proceeding in a northeasterly direction.

20–23. Another archaeological note (cf. vv 10–12) concerning the former occupants of the land of the Ammonites.

20. *Rephaim country.* See v 11 and the NOTE there.

Zamzummim. The same as the *Zuzim* in Gen 14:5, who are mentioned there between the *Rephaim* and the *Emim,* as in the archaeological notes here. All three names seem to express terror: ghosts (Rephaim), Emim from *ʾymh* 'terror', and *zamzumim,* apparently from Arabic *zumzama* 'distant confused sound'.

23. *Avvim, who dwelled in villages as far as Gaza. Targumim Onqelos* and *Pseudo-Jonathan:* "from Raphia (south of Gaza) to Gaza," another instance of an autochthonous population expelled by immigrants. For the Avvim in the area of the Philistines, cf. Josh 13:3–4 and read there with the LXX: "and the Avvim from the south." The LXX seems to have identified them with Hivites (Evaioi).

The *ḥṣrym,* open, unwalled villages, are characteristic of nomadic or seminomadic settlements, especially in the Negev; cf. the place-names in the tribe of Simeon (Josh 15:25f.), and see also Gen 25:16 and Isa 42:11. For the term *ḥṣr,* see Malamat 1963.

the Caphtorim, who came from Crete. Caphtor (Egyptian *Kftyw)* was the home of the Philistines (Amos 9:7; Jer 47:4; Gen 10:11, where it should be read, "and the Caphtorim from whom the Philistines descended"); it is another designation for Crete, which is similarly mentioned as the home of the Philistines in Zeph 2:5 and Ezek 25:17. In 1 Sam 30:14, the Negev of the Cherethites (Hebrew *hakkĕrēti)* is the same as "the land of the Philistines." The ancient versions (LXX, Targum) have Cappadocia for Caphtor, which has been caused by misspelling *kptwk* for *kptwr. Kappatuk/Katpatuk* is Akkadian for Cappadocia, and cf. also *Kptwk* in the *Genesis Apocryphon* 21:23 (see Fitzmyer 1966, pp. 159–60). See "Caphtor," *EM* Mazar 1962 4.236–38, and Strange 1980. The conclusion of the latter that *Caphtor/Keftiu* is to be identified with Cyprus cannot be accepted.

COMMENT

After having reached Kadesh, which is at the edge of the promised land (cf. Num 34:4, Josh 15:3), the Israelites have to turn back into the wilderness "by the way of the Sea of the Reeds" as a punishment for the sin of the spies (see 1:40 and compare Num 14:25). In this tradition too, as in the traditions of the first chapter, the author is dependent on the sources of the book of Numbers and quotes from them. Compare Num 21:4 (see Haran 1972, pp. 37–76): *wysʿw . . . drk ym-swp lsbb ʾt-ʾrṣ ʾdwm* 'They set out by the road of the Sea of Reeds to skirt the land of Edom' with Deut 2:1: *wnpn wnsʿ . . . drk ym swp . . . wnsb ʾt-hr-śʿyr* 'We turned and set out . . . toward the Sea of Reeds . . . and skirted the hill country of Seir'. These statements correspond to the divine order given in Numbers and in Deuteronomy in identical wording: compare Num 14:25, "Turn and set out into the wilderness by the way of the Sea of Reeds *(pnw wsʿw lkm hmdbr drk ym-swp)*" with Deut 1:40, "turn about and march into the wilderness, toward the Sea of Reeds *(pnw lkm wsʿw hmdbrh drk ym-swp).*" There are, however, significant differences between the accounts of Numbers and those of Deuteronomy. According to Deut 2, the journey from Kadesh to Transjordan took thirty-eight years (2:14), but this is not so clear in Numbers. From the sources in Numbers (J and the priestly literature) one gets the impression that Kadesh was the main abode of the Israelites during their wanderings in the wilderness, and there they prepared themselves for the entrance into the promised land (20:14). According to Num 20:1, the people *stayed* at Kadesh, Moses' sister Miriam died there, and Aaron died at Mount Hor not far from Kadesh (20:22–29). It is true that, as in Deuteronomy so in Numbers (14:25, 21:4), the Israelites encircle the land of Edom/Seir but no hint is made in the latter that this trek lasted thirty-eight years. That Kadesh was the end and not the beginning of the wanderings is most explicit in the priestly traditions of Numbers. Unlike the other sources, according to the priestly source the Israelites do not surround Edom at all but march through it. That source presents the following route: after having reached Kadesh very close to the end of their journey (Num 33:36), the Israelites move to Mount Hor, where Aaron dies in the fortieth year (Num 33:38). From there they march straight through Edomite territory (Pûnōn in v 42 belongs to Edom, see Gen 36:41, and is identified with Fenan in Jubayl [Gebal], thirty-five kilometers south of the Dead Sea), into the plains of Moab. This account, according to which Kadesh is one of the last stations in the desert before crossing into the land, clearly contradicts —as indicated—the tradition in Deut 2, according to which the bulk of the time of wandering belongs to the thirty-eight years after Kadesh. According to Deuteronomy, the people start surrounding Mount Seir after leaving Kadesh, then they go down to Ezion Geber on the Sea of Reeds (2:8) and continue encircling Moab from the east (2:9). According to Num 33 (the priestly source), however, the main wanderings in the wilderness, including the stop at Ezion Geber (vv 35–36), took place before the arrival at Kadesh. In short, according to the Deuteronomic source, Kadesh marks the beginning of the journey whereas according to the priestly literature (and apparently J too) Kadesh belongs to the last stage of the journey (cf. Haran 1970–71).

The narrative about crossing at the border of Edom also draws on the tradition in Numbers: compare 2:6 with Num 20:19. There is, however, an important difference between the two sources. In Num 20 the Israelites ask permission to pass through Edom on their way to the land of Canaan. The Edomites refuse and even threaten the Israelites with war, following which Israel turns away from Edom (vv 20–21). In Deuteronomy, however, neither the request nor the refusal is mentioned. On the contrary, the Israelites are expected to purchase provisions as they pass through (v 6). Furthermore, they are commanded not to provoke the Edomites or start war with them because their land was allotted to them by God. In contrast to Num 20, where the Israelites are threatened by the Edomites, here in Deuteronomy the Edomites are afraid of the Israelites (v 4). It seems that a common episode underlies both accounts, but the presentation in Deuteronomy reflects a more patriotic attitude. Deuteronomy presents a picture of a proud and strong nation that is able to defeat its enemies but is not allowed to encroach on the rights of its neighbors. A similar approach is to be found in Deuteronomy's description of the circuit of Ammon and Moab. While describing the passing by the borders of Ammon and Moab, the author of Deuteronomy cites the divine warnings not to provoke the Ammonites and Moabites because their territories have been allotted to them by God (vv 9, 19). In Num 20–21, such warnings are not mentioned; on the contrary, the impression is conveyed that the Israelites were unable to capture Ammonite territory, not that they were not allowed to do so: "Israel took possession . . . from the Arnon to the Jabbok, as far as the Ammonites, for the boundary of the Ammonites was strong *(ʿaz)*" (Num 21:24), that is to say, the might and fortifications of the Ammonites prevented the Israelites from capturing portions of their territory.

The LXX reads there "as Yaazer is the border of the Ammonites," but this version does not fit the context, because the text is not describing the perimeters of a captured area. It tells us that they reached the Ammonite boundary (cf. Judg 11:22) and could not continue their conquest beyond the border as "the boundary of Ammonites was strong" = well fortified. For *ʿaz* with the meaning of "fortified," cf. Num 13:28, *ky ʿz hʿm hyšb bʾrṣ* "but if inhabitants are strong and the cities are very strongly fortified" = the people's strength lies in its fortifications. Compare Amos 5:9, where *ʿaz* is equivalent to a fortress, and Judg 9:51, Ps 61:4, and Prov 18:10, where *ʿz* and *mgdl* appear together. Compare also association of *mśgb, mbtḥ, mḥsh* with *ʿz: (mśgb)* Ps 59:10, 18; *(mḥsh)* Ps 46:2, Prov 14:26, Ps 62:8; as well as with *ḥwmwt/ḥl,* (Isa 26:1) and *ḥwmh nśgbh* (Prov 18:11). In Akkadian as well, the words *dannu/dannātu,* meaning 'strength' and 'courage', also have the meaning of fortified places, in particular *āl dannūti,* which means a fortified city.

In the priestly tradition no difficulties or obstacles exist in connection with the passage through Edom or Moab. The Israelites travel from Kadesh into the heart of Edom, Pûnōn, and ʾObôt, reaching the border of Moab at ʿJyeî Haʿabarîm and then proceeding to Dibon Gad, ʿAlmon, and Diblatayîm (Num 33:44–46). This tradition does not record any difficulties in connection with the Israelites' journey from Sinai. There is no war with the Canaanites in the south (cf. Num 14:25; 21:1–3; Deut 1:41), and no requests for passage are made of Edom or Sihon, king of the Amorites. Everything is accomplished miraculously (cf. Weinfeld 1986a, p. 12). The Samaritan tradition recognizes the contradiction between Num 20:14–21 and Deut 2:2–8 and harmonizes it by intercalating a portion of Num 20:17–18 after Deut 2:7.

THE CONQUEST OF TRANSJORDAN (2:24–3:17)

A. THE DEFEAT OF SIHON (2:24–37)

2 [24]Up! Set out across the Wadi Arnon! See, I give into your power Sihon the Amorite, king of Heshbon, and his land. Begin the occupation; engage him in battle! [25]This day I begin to put the dread and fear of you upon the peoples everywhere under heaven, so that they shall tremble and quake because of you whenever they hear you mentioned.

[26]Then I sent messengers from the wilderness of Kedemoth to Sihon, king of Heshbon, with an offer of peace, as follows: [27]"Let me pass through your country on the highway; on the highway I will proceed, turning off neither to the right nor to the left. [28]Food for money you will supply me, so that I may eat, and water for money you will supply me, so that I may drink. Just let me pass

with my feet, [29]as the descendants of Esau who dwell in Seir did for me and the Moabites who dwell in Ar, that I may cross the Jordan into the land that YHWH our God is giving us."

[30]But Sihon, king of Heshbon, would not let us pass through, because YHWH your God had stiffened his will and hardened his heart, in order to deliver him into your power, as is now the case. [31]And YHWH said to me, "See, I begin by placing Sihon and his land at your disposal. Begin the occupation; take possession of his land!"

[32]Sihon, with all his men, took the field against us at Jahaz. [33]YHWH our God delivered him to us, and we defeated him and his sons and all his men. [34]At that time we captured all his towns, and we banned every town—men, women, and children—leaving no survivor. [35]We retained as booty only the cattle and the spoil of the cities that we captured. [36]From Aroer on the edge of the Arnon valley, including the town in the valley itself, to Gilead, not a city was too mighty for us. [37]But you did not encroach upon the land of the Ammonites, all along the Wadi Jabbok and the towns of the hill country, just as YHWH our God had commanded.

TEXTUAL NOTES

24. *Set out.* Hebrew: *sĕʿû,* spelled *ssĕʿû* with dagesh forte in the samekh. Compare *qûmû ṣṣĕʾû* (Gen 19:14); Exod 12:31; etc. See *GKC* §20g.

Begin the occupation. Hebrew: *hāḥēl rāš,* literally, 'Begin! Take possession!' See *GKC* §110h; 120g, h. All versions translate "begin to take possession" except *Sam. Tg.,* which translates literally as usual (cf. v 31 and the Textual Notes ad loc.).

25. *I begin.* MT: *ʾāḥēl.* LXX: *enarchou* 'begin' (imperative), reading *hoḥel,* as in the previous verse; and so the *Sam. Tg.,* the margin of *Tg. Neof.,* and VL: *inchoare.* It is possible that the reading of the LXX is correct and that the Masoretic rendering is a theological correction, in order to ascribe the cause of fear to the Deity (cf. Laberge 1985, p. 133).

upon the peoples everywhere under heaven. Hebrew: *ʿl hʿmym tḥt kl hšmym.* LXX: "upon *all* the peoples [reading *kl hʿmym]* under heaven" (omitting *kl* 'all' = 'everywhere'). The *Tg. Ps.-J.* has a conflated reading: "upon all the peoples under all the heaven." Compare 4:19: *lkl hʿmym tḥt kl hšmym.*

so that. Hebrew: *ʾăšer,* the relative pronoun, which can mean either 'who' or 'so that' (see *GKC* §165b), among other uses. Both meanings make sense in this context. LXX: *hoitines* 'whoever'; Vg: *ut* 'so that'. The Aramaic version has *d(y),* which has the same ambiguity as the Hebrew.

whenever they hear you mentioned. Hebrew: *ʾšr yšmʿwn šmʿk.* LXX: *akousantes to onoma sou* 'who hear your *name',* reading *šmk* instead of *šmʿk;* compare Vg: *audito nomine tuo.* The confusion of *šmʿ* with *šm* occurs in other instances: Gen 29:13; Num 14:15; Josh 6:26; 1 Kgs 10:1; Esth 9:4.

26. *I sent.* MT: *wʾšlḥ;* Samaritan text: *wʾšlḥh.*

with an offer of peace. Literally, "words of peace," either a second direct object of "I sent," in apposition to "messengers" (though hardly parallel), or the accusative of manner (see *GKC* §118q). The LXX has the dative of manner: *logois eirēnikois;* Vg has the ablative of manner: *verbis pacificus.* Syriac adds *bĕ* 'with [words of peace]'. The Aramaic Targumim translate literally, without a preposition.

27. *on the highway; on the highway I will proceed.* Hebrew: *badderek badderek ʾēlēk.* See *GKC* §123c, 133k. The LXX has only one *badderek.* Vg: *publica gradiemur via* 'we will go on the public road'. Compare Num 21:22: "the king's highway." *Tg. Ps.-J.: bʾwrḥʾ dhyʾ ʾwrḥ kbyšʾ ʾyzl* 'on the road that is a paved road I shall go'. Verses 27–29 have first-person plural verbs in the Vg and Syriac, as opposed to the MT's first-person singular. In *Tg. Ps.-J.* and *Tg. Neof.* this verse is in the singular, but vv 28–29 are in the plural.

30. *let us pass through.* Hebrew: *ʾābâh . . . haʿăbirēnû bô* '[was not] willing to let pass us through him [= his territory]'.

your God. LXX and margin of *Tg. Neof.: "our* God."

as is still the case. See the Textual Notes at 6:24.

31. *And YHWH said to me.* A new section begins here in the MT on the same line as the previous section following a space *(setumah).*

Sihon. The Samaritan Pentateuch and the LXX add "King of Heshbon, the Amorite." Compare v 14.

Begin the occupation; take possession of his land. Hebrew: *hāḥēl rāš lārešet et ʾarṣô,* literally, 'Begin! Take possession! To take possession of his land!', apparently a conflation of two readings, *hāḥēl rāš* 'Begin! Take possession!' as in v 24, and *hōḥēl lārešet ʾet ʾarṣô* 'Begin to take possession of his land!', which is the reading of the LXX here. Syriac and *Tg. Onq.:* "Begin to dispossess him and take possession of his land!", understanding *rāš* in the sense of *hiphʿil horiš* and changing it from imperative to infinitive. The *Tg. Neof.* also changes the imperative *rāš* to infinitive, rendering, "Begin to inherit and take possession of his land!", which, like the MT, is redundant.

33. *his sons.* MT: *bnw* (vocalized *bānāw).* Samaritan text: *bānāyw,* as is expected.

34. *and we banned every town—men, women, and children.* Hebrew: *wannaḥărēm et kol ʿîr* [Samaritan text: *ʿarayw] mĕtim wehannâšîm* [Samaritan text: *hannâšîm] wĕhaṭṭâp.* The MT means, literally, 'we banned every city of men [i.e., the male population of every city], and the women, and the children'. The Samaritan version means 'we banned all of his cities: men, the women, and the children'. But cf. 3:6, where a similar construction is used; also MT's and Samaritan text's *mĕtim,* which is a rare poetic word for "men" (see the Notes). The LXX, *Sam. Tg.,* Syriac, and probably also *Tg. Neof.* vocalize *mĕtim* as *mĕtōm* 'soundly, completely', as it is in fact misvocalized in Judg 20:48.

36. *for us.* MT: *lĕpânênû.* The Samaritan Pentateuch, followed by the LXX: *bĕyadênû* 'into our hand(s)'.

37. *you did not encroach.* LXX, Vg, and *Tg. Neof.*: "we did not."

just as YHWH . . . commanded. MT: *wĕkōl ʾăšer ṣiwwâh YHWH,* literally, 'and all that YHWH . . . commanded [not to encroach]' or 'and all that YHWH . . . forbade.' Compare 4:23, and the TEXTUAL NOTES ad loc. The LXX and *Tg. Ps.-J.* translate "according to all," etc. for *kĕkōl,* and this reading is followed in my translation.

NOTES

24. *Set out across the Wadi Arnon.* The valley of Arnon (Wadi al-Mawjib) with the river flowing through it, second in length to the Jordan, formed the frontier between Moab in the south and the Israelite territory of the plateau *(mishor,* cf. 3:10) in the north. The *mishor* was once part of the Moabite territory but was later captured by Sihon, the Amorite (Num 21:26).

I give into your power Sihon the Amorite. . . . Begin the occupation. Compare 1:21, "See, YHWH your God has placed the land at your disposal. Go up, take possession." According to Deuteronomy, the crossing of the Arnon marks the beginning of the occupation of the promised land (cf. the next verse).

25. *This day I begin to put the dread and fear of you upon the peoples.* A similar opening, "This day I begin," is found in Josh 3:7 on the eve of the crossing of the Jordan. By the same token, the infinitive *tēt* (from the verb *nātan)* is found both here and in Josh 10:12. These similarities led the sages to suggest *(b. Taʿan.* 20a; *ʿAbod. Zar.* 25a) that the conquest of Transjordan by Moses was accompanied by miracles as in the time of Joshua: the sun stood still for Moses as it stood still for Joshua (Josh 10:13). See also *Tg. Ps.-J.* on Deut 2:25; cf. Le Déaut 1980, p. 35.

everywhere under heaven. For *all* (see TEXTUAL NOTE) of the nations standing in fear of the people of Israel, compare 28:10; see also Josh 4:24.

they shall tremble and quake because of you whenever they hear you mentioned. This is very close in content and phrasing to Exod 15:14, "the peoples hear *(šmʿ*), they tremble *(yrgzw),* quaking *(ḥyl)* grips the Philistines," which is also said in connection with the entrance of Israel into the holy land (cf. Moran 1963c, pp. 333–42). It also reminds us of Josh 4:24 and 5:1, where the nations are astonished by the wonders done by the Lord for the Israelites while crossing the Jordan into the promised land.

Because the author considers Transjordan an integral part of the holy land (see the COMMENT), it is quite understandable that he describes the entrance into Transjordan by crossing the Arnon in terms similar to those used of the crossing of the Jordan. The crossing of the Arnon River is perceived as the beginning of the conquest and the fulfillment of the promises to the Patriarchs (see the COMMENT).

26. *I sent messengers . . . with an offer of peace.* This stands in contradiction to v 24, where Moses is commanded to start war with Sihon. The Rabbis indeed saw in Moses' offer of peace an act that was not commissioned by God *(Midr. Num. Rab.* 5, 13). Naḥmanides takes the initial verb as a pluperfect: "After I had sent away messengers," in other words, God commanded Moses to start war with Sihon after the latter rejected the terms of peace. As will be indicated below, the request to pass through Sihon's territory was a mere pretext aimed at provoking war, for God knew in advance that Sihon would not let the Israelites pass through his territory.

from the wilderness of Kedemoth. Kedemoth is mentioned as a city belonging to the tribe of Reuben (Josh 13:18; compare 21:37 in the framework of the Levitical cities); it seems to have been situated east of the Moabite territory in the wilderness *(midbar;* cf. Num 21:23, Judg 11:18) where the tribes are encamped and from which they advance to meet Sihon in the battle of Jahaz (v 32) (cf. Dearman 1989, pp. 55–57). According to Dearman, Kedamoth can be identified with *Saliya,* the southeastern-most Iron Age site on the plateau; cf. also Boling 1985, pp. 23–32.

Sihon, king of Heshbon. Heshbon was located close to the present town of Ḥesbān in the southern Beika (eighty kilometers east of Jerusalem). Excavations at Tel Ḥesbān from 1968 to 1974 have revealed remains of the Iron Age period but not anything antedating Iron Age I. The late Bronze Age city, that is, the city of King Sihon, must have been located somewhere in the vicinity (perhaps Jahul, which contains late Bronze Age pottery).

Heshbon was a fertile area (Isa 16:8–9; Jer 48:32f., 49:4) and was renowned for its pools (Cant 7:5), one of which was apparently discovered in the excavations (cf. Horn 1976, pp. 410–11).

an offer of peace. Literally, "words of peace *(dbr šlwm)";* for *dbr* in the sense of offering a settlement or bargain, see Weinfeld 1982c, pp. 27–53. Peace gifts were normally dispatched by messengers (Hebrew *mlʾk,* Akkadian *mār šipri).*

27. *on the highway; on the highway I will proceed.* Repetition expresses absoluteness: on the highway only; cf., e.g., 16:20 *(ṣdq ṣdq);* 1 Sam 2:3 *(gbhh gbhh);* Zeph 3:5 *(bbqr bbqr).* In the parallel verse in Num 21:22 we read, "We will follow the king's highway" *(drk hmlk).*

28. Compare v 6.

with my feet. With the sole purpose of passing physically, excluding any broader interpretation of "passing."

29. *as the descendants of Esau who dwell in Seir did for me and the Moabites who dwell in Ar.* For the Edomites, cf. v 6. We have not heard elsewhere about Moabites selling food to the Israelites; on the contrary, in 23:4–5 Ammonites and Moabites are denounced for not having met the Israelites "with bread or water on the way." Nevertheless, this must not be seen as a contradiction because the passage there contains two denunciations: one for not having met the Israelites with food (v 5a), and the other for having hired Balaam to curse

Israel (v 56). The first denunciation may refer to the Ammonites, while the second refers to the Moabites, as may be inferred from Num 22–24. It is also possible that the facts mentioned here have no historical basis and are just diplomatic devices in an address that in itself is not sincerely meant.

that I may cross the Jordan into the land. This phrase follows (unconsciously) the old traditional notion that the promised land includes only the territory of the Jordan River.

30. *would not let us pass.* Literally, "did not consent *(wlʾ ʾbh),*" in contradistinction to the phrase in the parallel verse in Num 21:23, "did not let pass *(wlʾ ntn . . . ʿbr),*" which sounds more aggressive toward and contemptuous of Israel (see above).

because YHWH your God had stiffened his will and hardened his heart. Compare Exod 4:21; 7:3; 9:12; 10:20; and especially 10:27, where "the stiffening of the heart" goes together with *wlʾ ʾbh* 'did not consent', as here. Compare also 1 Kgs 12:15.

to deliver him into your power, as is now the case. Literally, "as at this day *(kywm hzh).*" The phrase is very common in Deuteronomy and in Deuteronomic literature (Deut 4:20, 38; 6:24; 8:18; 10:15; 29:27; 1 Kgs 3:6; 8:24), and is used for the purpose of stressing the significance of the event for the contemporary scene, the "this day" of the author (cf. Seeligmann 1961, p. 146).

31. *See, I begin by placing Sihon and his land at your disposal.* The "beginning" refers to the conquest of the promised land. According to the author's view, the promised land extends to both banks of the Jordan (cf. the COMMENT).

Begin the occupation. Compare v 24.

32. *Jahaz.* Jahaz seems to be located on the eastern outskirts of the plateau. It occurs together with Kedemoth (Josh 13:18; 21:37; 1 Chr 6:63), a city placed at the edge of the desert (see the NOTE to v 26). It is mentioned in the Mesha inscription and cf. also Isa 15:4; Jer 48:21, 34). It has been recently identified with *Khirbet Medeiniyeh* located on a bend of the *Wadi al Themed* (J. A. Dearman 1984, 122–126) cf. also Dearman 1989, pp. 55–57.

33. *and we defeated him and his sons.* In the parallel in Num 21, the defeat of "sons" is found in the pericope about Og, king of Bashan (v 35) but not in that about Sihon (v 24).

34–37. This passage has no parallel in the account in Num 21, and the phrase *bāʿēt hahîʾ* 'at that time', attached to it (v 34), reveals its intrusive nature (see above).

34. *and we banned every town—men, women, and children.* In accordance with the law of *ḥērem* in 20:16–18. As already indicated, Transjordan is considered here part of the promised land, wherein the inhabitants are subject to *ḥērem.*

men. Hebrew: *mtm;* compare *mūtu* in Akkadian, which means grown-up man, husband, and warrior.

leaving no survivor. This phrase is used especially by Deuteronomy (cf. 3:3) and Deuteronomic writers in connection with the war with the Canaanites (Josh 8:22; 10:28ff.; 11:8).

35. The *ḥērem* was not applied to cattle and spoils, as may be learned from the Deuteronomic war descriptions in the book of Joshua: 8:2, 27; 11:14.

36. *From Aroer on the edge of the Arnon valley.* Identified with Khirbat ʿAra ʿir on the northern rim of the Wadi al-Mawjib, about five kilometers southeast of Dhiban (= Dibon), see also note to v 9.

including the town in the valley itself. Compare Josh 13:9, 16.

to Gilead. A vague description. Gilead in its broad meaning encompassed central Transjordan, on both sides of the Jabbok (cf. the division of Gilead into two halves in vv 12–13). The parallel tradition in Num 21 defines the conquered area of Sihon more exactly: "from the Arnon to the Jabbok" (v 24). This, however, is the ancient view of Sihon's (limited) territory, which might well reflect the genuine situation. The later, Deuteronomic view is different in this respect. According to the description of Deuteronomy here (chaps. 2–3) and the Deuteronomic historiography in Joshua (12:2–5; 13:9ff.), the conquered land of Sihon, which was given to the Reubenites and Gadites (Deut 3:16–17), goes far beyond the Jabbok in the north. It encompasses Gilead north of the Jabbok and the ʿArabah up to the Sea of Chinnereth (3:16–17). As will be shown later, a similar change in view is encountered with respect to the extent of the territory of Og, king of Bashan. For the two different outlooks about the conquest of Transjordan, see Kallai 1986, pp. 214–59.

37. *But you did not encroach upon the land of the Ammonites.* For *qrb* in the sense of "encroach", see Milgrom 1970, 1.33ff.

all along the Wadi Jabbok and the towns of the hill country. The land of Ammon lay on the upper course of the Jabbok (Wadi Zarqa), which runs from southwest to northeast before turning to the west (cf. Num 21:24). The Ammonite territory that lay to the east is hilly in contrast with the plateau to the west of the Jabbok.

just as YHWH our God had commanded. Read perhaps with *Tg. Ps-J.* and the LXX: *kkl* 'according to all'. "Commanded" is to be understood here in the sense of "forbidden" (cf. v 19).

COMMENT

According to the ancient sources, the land that the Israelites were to conquer did not include Transjordan. Thus, in the border description of "the land of Canaan" in Num 34:1–12 we find that in the north, the land given to Israel includes Lebanon as well as Damascus in the northeast. From there the boundary descends in a southwesterly direction to the shores of the Sea of Galilee and the Jordan River so that the Gilead and all of the southern Transjordan are excluded from the borders of the land of Canaan (compare Ezek 47:17–18). In

Josh 22, we read that Transjordan was considered unclean *(tĕmeʾâʾereṣ*, v 19) as any land outside Israel was considered to be (compare Amos 7:17; Hos 9:3–5). In fact, according to Num 21, Transjordan was taken by accident. Sihon did not let the Israelites pass through his country on their way to Canaan, so they engaged in a battle and defeated him (Num 21:21ff.). The Gadites and Reubenites, who especially desired the land of Gilead because of its pasturage (Num 32), asked to settle in Transjordan, but their request was a surprise to Moses. Their desire for land in Transjordan was considered sinful by Moses, who compared it to the sin of the spies (vv 7–15).

In fact, the whole tradition about the settlement in Transjordan in Num 32 has an apologetic character. It tries to justify the settlement of the tribes on the eastern side of the Jordan by showing that the Gadites and Reubenites actually fought with the other tribes on the western side of the Jordan and therefore were permitted to settle in Transjordan. For a thorough analysis of this chapter, see Loewenstamm 1972–73.

The exclusion of Transjordan from the original boundaries of the promised land actually lies behind the traditions of conquest and settlement in the Pentateuch and the book of Joshua. Thus, the pre-Deuteronomic sources in the Hexateuch take it for granted that the crossing of the Jordan marks the entrance into the promised land. The realization of the promise to the Patriarchs comes with the crossing of the Jordan, hence the dramatization of this event at the beginning of the narrative cycle of the conquest in Josh 3–4. The manna eaten by the Israelites in the desert stopped immediately after crossing the Jordan (Josh 5:12; cf. Exod 16:35). The circumcision of the Israelites and the celebration of the Passover by Joshua and the people could be performed only after arriving at Gilgal on the west bank of the Jordan River (Josh 5:2–11). Furthermore, the angel, which, according to Exod 23:20 and 33:2, was sent to guard the children of Israel and help them to expel the Canaanites, appears on the scene only after Joshua reaches Gilgal. He reveals himself to Joshua there, saying, *ʿattâ bāʾtî* 'Now I have come' (Josh 5:14), which means that with the coming of the angel the mission of the conquest begins. Transjordan, then, is not part of the promised land according to ancient biblical sources.

How do we explain this? It is strange that Gilead, which was settled hundreds of years by Israelites, was not included within the borders of the promised land, while Lebanon and Damascus, which were never settled by Israelites, are considered to be part of it. The best solution to this problem was offered by B. Maisler (= Mazar) 1945–46 (English 1986, pp. 189–202) and later by de Vaux 1968; see Weinfeld 1977c, pp. 257–58. Analyzing the border list of Canaan in Num 34, Mazar reached the conclusion that the northern line of the land of Canaan, in the center of which Lebo-Hamath stands, was the same as the border of the Egyptian province of Canaan, which was fixed in the peace treaty between Egypt and the Hittites at the beginning of the thirteenth century B.C.E. Furthermore, the whole extent of Canaan, or "the land of Canaan with its boundaries" as formulated in Num 34:2, overlies the Egyptian province of Canaan as it crystallized after the battle of Kadesh on the Orontes. The borders of this province are the same as the border delineation in Num 34. The Egyptian province, like Canaan in Num 34, includes the territory east of Lake Chinneret and the region of Damascus (Egyptian *Upe),* but excludes Transjordan south of the Chinneret. The land of Canaan, as fixed in the Egyptian empire, that is, without Transjordan, was taken over by the Israelites in the period of the conquest. It is possible that an oracle in this matter was current before YHWH in Šiloh (Josh 18:8), and this could not be changed (cf. Aharoni and Rainey 1979, p. 254). Even after the colonization of the eastern side of the Jordan, nobody would dare change the borders of the promised land as sanctioned by the Word of God. The Israelites took over the Egyptian province of Canaan given to them by God after he redeemed them from Egypt (cf. Lev 25:38, "I am YHWH your God who brought you forth out of the land of Egypt to give you the land of Canaan"). The extreme border points of Canaan as presented in Num 34 are Lebo-Hamath in the north and *naḥal Miṣrayim* 'the brook of Egypt' in the south. These were known in Israel over a long period. They are attested in the various geographical lists in Joshua and in Judges (Josh 13:4; Judg 3:3), in the historical accounts in the books of Kings (1 Kgs 8:65; 2 Kgs 14:25), and in the book of Amos (6:14), and were adopted by Ezekiel for his blueprint of the division of the holy land (47:16–20). This delineation of borders must then reflect a very old tradition in ancient Israel, which is based on actual historical conditions and is not merely the fantasy of a priestly author.

In contrast to this old tradition, which excludes Transjordan from the borders of the promised land, the author of Deuteronomy considers Transjordan to be an integral part of the promised land and presents here its ideology and full legitimization. Let us adduce the evidence:

1. When describing the promised land shown to Moses before his death, Deut 34 enumerates: "Gilead, Dan, Naphtali, Ephraim, Manasseh, Judah, Negev, and the valley of Jericho" (vv 1–3). This is said to be the land that God swore to the Patriarchs to give to their children (v 4). The promised land then includes, explicitly, the eastern side of the Jordan, in contrast to the ancient sources discussed above.

2. According to Deut 1–3, the beginning of the conquest is not the crossing of the Jordan by Joshua but the crossing of the river Arnon by Moses, as we read in Deut 2:24–25: "Up! Set out across the Wadi Arnon! See, I give into your power Sihon the Amorite, king of Heshbon, and his land. *Begin the occupation (hāḥēl rāš);* engage him in battle! This day I begin to put the dread and fear of you upon the peoples everywhere under heaven, so that they shall tremble and quake because of you." These verses are reminiscent of Josh 4:24 and 5:1, where the nations are awed by the wonders performed by YHWH for the Israelites when they crossed the Jordan into the promised land (cf. Exod 15:16). In Deut 2 these wonders refer to the crossing of the river Arnon.

The idea of beginning the occupation of the land by conquering Sihon occurs also in v 31 (cf. 1:4): "See, I begin by placing Sihon and his land at your disposal. Begin the occupation; take possession of his land." From these verses it becomes clear that the inheritance of the land started with the battle with Sihon. In contradistinction to Num 21, according to which the Israelites were caught in battle perforce because Sihon did not let them pass in his territory, in Deuteronomy the request for passage was a pretext aimed at provoking war: the Israelites knew that Sihon would not let them pass through his land because God had hardened his heart. As a result, there would be a victory in battle and the occupation of Sihon's territory by Israel.

3. Because Transjordan is, according to Deuteronomy, an integral part of the promised land, one must apply to this conquest the rules of war as they apply to the Canaanites (Deut 20:15f.). The inhabitants of the Mishor and the Bashan, men, women, and children, must be put under ban *(ḥerem,* 2:34–35; 3:6–7). Only the animals and spoils might be taken. Nothing is said about *ḥerem* in the parallel account of this battle in Num 21.

4. Furthermore, not only is Transjordan regarded here as an integral part of the promised land, in contrast to the traditions in Numbers, but its territory is far more extensive than that described in Numbers. In Num 21 the conquered area of Sihon extends "from Arnon to Jabbok" (v 24), while according to Deuteronomy (cf. also Josh 12:2–5; 13:9ff.), the conquered land of Sihon goes far beyond the Jabbok in the north. It encompasses Gilead north of the Jabbok and the ʿArabah as far as the sea of Chinneret (3:16–17). A similar extension is attested in connection with the villages of Yair, Havvôth Yāîr. According to Num 32:41, the villages conquered by Yair, son of Manasseh, are said to have been in Gilead (cf. v 40 there), which is supported by Judg 10:4: "*Havvôth Yāîr* in the land of Gilead." In Deuteronomy, these villages are said to be located in the Bashan, that is, north of Gilead. Furthermore, by situating Havvôth Yāîr in the district of Argob in the Bashan, the author seems to have identified villages with large cities: "fortified with high walls, gates and bars" (3:4), which is artificial. Indeed, in the list of the Solomonic districts in 1 Kgs 4, a clear distinction is made between *Havvôth Yāîr* in Gilead and the Argob district, with its sixty cities with walls and bronze bars (v 13). By expanding the area of the conquest of Transjordan, Deuteronomy widened the meaning of *Havvôth Yāîr,* linking it to the territory of Bashan. This expansion was followed by the Deuteronomic historian in Josh 13:10: "and all the Havvôth Yāîr in Bashan—sixty cities" (cf. Kallai 1986, pp. 247–59). One has to admit that indications of an expansion toward Bashan by Manasseh are already found in Num 32:42, where Nobah conquers Kenath (southern Bashan; see Oded 1976, 7.203–4). Even so, this is still quite different from the description in Deuteronomy, which contains such large cities and areas as Ashtaroth, Edrei, Salcah, Argob, "the sixty cities" of the kingdom of Og in Bashan, which find no mention in Num 32. It should be noted that Bashan is included within the boundaries of the promised land

according to the outline of Num 34, but this does not deter Deuteronomy from putting it on the same level with the territory of Sihon, which was outside the legitimate borders of Canaan (cf. Kallai 1983).

5. Another instructive point in this respect is the delivery of Transjordan to the Gadites and Reubenites (half of the Manasseh tribe has been interpolated in Numbers). In Num 32:16ff., the land is given to these tribes on the condition that they cross the Jordan to fight with their brothers before YHWH. In Deuteronomy, the land is given to them without any condition because, according to the author, it is part of the land that is to be inherited by these tribes. Moses says to them, "YHWH . . . has given you this country to possess. Therefore go as shock troops, warriors all, at the head of your Israelite kinsmen . . . until YHWH has granted your kinsmen a resting place such as you have, and they too have taken possession of the land that YHWH . . . is giving them, beyond the Jordan" (3:18–20). In other words, in Numbers the Transjordanian tribes gain rights over their land by virtue of their participation in the war *before YHWH* for the conquest of the holy land. In Deuteronomy, they gain their land as their tribal rights in the framework of the division of the promised land. Because they have attained their allotted rest *(mĕnuḥa wĕnaḥalah),* they are asked to help their brethren who still have to fight for it.

What was in Numbers a marginal settlement outside the borders of the promised land becomes in Deuteronomy a legitimate inheritance of land with vast territories. The same applies to the description of the allotment of the Transjordanian tribes in Josh 13 by the Deuteronomic author.

When was this tradition fixed? It seems that the final crystallization of this tradition can easily be put in the Hezekianic or Josianic period, the period of expansion. I refer to the literary-ideological formation of the tradition and not to its historical antecedents. The real periods of expansion in the Transjordanian area started in the Davidic and Solomonic period, as the list of the Solomonic provinces attests. But it was the ideologist of the Hezekianic–Josianic period, the so-called Deuteronomic author or school, who fixed an ideology about the extent of the promised land. Until his days, as we tried to show, the sources cling to the old idea that Transjordan is not an integral part of the promised land. During the awakening of national consciousness in Israel in the Hezekianic–Josianic period (cf. Weinfeld 1964), the new idea about the extent of the promised land was propagated. Such ideology could not have been created at the time of the great expansion in the time of David and Solomon or of Jeroboam II. In those days, no scribe would confuse the Havvôth Yāîr of Gilead with the sixty fortified cities in the Bashan. Only a late scribe writing when Bashan and even Gilead were no longer in Israelite hands could make an error of this kind.

The problem is, to which stage of the Deuteronomic school could one ascribe the theology under discussion? I based my evidence mainly on Deut 2–3 and 34, which seem to be part of a later edition of the book and may even be the work of the Deuteronomist who edited the historiography of the Former

Prophets (see above). One must mention, however, that a reference to the imperial borders, including Transjordan in the framework of the promised land, is found in Deut 11 (v 24), which is considered an original part of the book of Deuteronomy. Here we read, "your territory shall be from the wilderness and the Lebanon, from the river—the Euphrates—to the western sea" (cf. above).

Be that as it may, this ideology is anchored in the Deuteronomic school and should be seen as the expression of the national self-consciousness that characterizes this school.

B. THE DEFEAT OF OG (3:1–7)

3 [1]We then turned and went up the road toward Bashan, and Og, king of Bashan, with all his men took the field against us at Edrei. [2]But YHWH said to me, "Do not fear him, for I am delivering him and all his men and his country into your power, and you will do to him as you did to Sihon, king of the Amorites, who lived in Heshbon."

[3]So YHWH our God also delivered into our power Og, king of Bashan, with all his men, and we dealt them such a blow that no survivor was left. [4]At that time we captured all his towns; there was not a town that we did not take from them: sixty towns, the whole district of Argob, the kingdom of Og in Bashan. [5]All of them were fortified towns with high walls, gates, and bars, apart from a great number of unwalled towns. [6]We banned them as we had done in the case of Sihon, king of Heshbon; banning every town—men, women, and children— [7]and retained as booty all the cattle and the spoil of the towns.

TEXTUAL NOTES

3:1. *We then turned and went up.* MT: *wnpn wnʿl.* Samaritan text: *wnpnh wnʿlh.*

took the field against us at Edrei. Hebrew: *wayyēṣēʾ . . . liqrāʾtēnû . . . lammilḥāmâh ʾedreʿî,* literally, 'came out toward us for the war [at] Edrei'. Compare 2:32, where the locale of Sihon's war is described as *yāhṣâh,* Yahaz plus *he* locative. The *he* locative is apparently omitted here because the final *yod* in Edrei would make it phonologically awkward. Driver (1902, ad loc.) insists that *ʾedreʿi* here means not 'at Edrei' but 'to Edrei' and is the predicate of *wayyēṣēʾ* 'came out'. He refers to his note (1913) to *wayyēlkû kol habbitrôn* (2 Sam 2:29). There he aptly suggests that *kol habbitrôn* is the direct object of *halak.* The present verse, however, is in no way analogous. A direct object of *yaṣaʾ* 'come out' would refer to the place whence a person departed, which is clearly not the intention here. It seems that the sense of the locative both here and in 2:32 is the *place in which* the war took place (*GKC* §90d), not the *place toward which*

Sihon or Og moved. The word *lammilḥāmâh* 'for *the* war', with the definite article, requires some nearer definition of the war referred to *(the* war *at* Edrei). Furthermore, if Driver were correct, the word order would rather be *wayyēṣēʾ . . . ʾedreʿi lammilḥāmâh.* LXX: *eis polemon eis Edreïn* 'to battle at Edrei'; Vg: *ad bellandum in Edrai* 'to wage war in Edrei'; Targumim: *lʾgḥʾ qrbʾ lʾdrʿy* 'to wage war, to Edrei'.

2. *his country.* LXX: "all his country."

power. Literally, "hand." LXX, Syriac: "hands."

3. *power.* Literally, "hand." LXX, Vg, *Tg. Onq.*: "hands."

and we dealt them such a blow. Hebrew: *wnkhw.* Samaritan text: *wnknw,* literally, 'and he smote him.'

that no survivor was left. Hebrew: *ʿad bilti hišʾîr lô śārîd,* literally, 'until not to leave him a survivor'. According to Ibn Ezra, the subject, "the Israelite people," is missing, but *hišʾîr* is more likely a (misvocalized?) variant of *hašʾîr,* the infinitive absolute of the verb *hišʾîr* (see *GKC* §164d). LXX: *eōs tou mē katalipein autou sperma* 'until not to leave him seed'; Vg: *usque ad internicionem* 'until extermination'; Syriac: *wlʾ šbqn lh śrydʾ* 'and we did not leave him a survivor' (cf. 2:34); Targumim: *ʿd dlʾ ʾštyyr lyh mšyzyb lšyzbw* 'until no survivor was left to him'.

4. *At that time.* Vg: *uno tempore* 'at one time', unlike 2:34, where the phrase is translated as expected, *in tempore illo.*

Argob. MT: *ʾrgb;* Samaritan text: *hʾrgb.*

5. *All of them were fortified towns with high walls, gates, and bars.* Heb.: *kol ʾēlleh ʿārîm bĕṣurôt ḥômâh gĕbōhâh dĕlâtayim ûbĕrîah.* According to Driver (1973), ad loc., and *GKC* §128c, this is rendered literally: "all of them were fortified cities, high wall, gates, and bar," with "high wall, gates, and bar" in loose apposition to "fortified cities." This interpretation is based on a similar construction in 1 Kgs 4:13, which has *ʿārîm gĕdōlôt* 'great cities' instead of *ʿārîm bĕṣurôt* 'fortified cities'. In these verses this syntax can only be explained as loose apposition. In 3:5, however, there is every reason to translate, less awkwardly, "cities fortified of [i.e., with] high wall, etc." This common syntactic construction is known as the construct of "improper annexation" (see *GKC* §128x). The verses in Kings and Chronicles may in fact be based on a misunderstanding of Deuteronomy's verse; the LXX has "high wall," etc., in apposition to "cities." The Vg uses the ablative case, "[with] high walls," etc.; Syriac: "cities whose walls were strong and whose gates and bars were high"; Targumim: "cities surrounded by high walls," etc.

unwalled towns. Hebrew: *ʿărēy happĕrāzi,* literally, 'the cities of the open country dwellers' (cf. 1 Sam 6:18; Ezek 38:11; Jer 49:21; Esth 9:19); LXX: *ton poleon ton Pherazaion* 'the cities of the Perizzites' (cf. Gen 15:20); *Tg. Neof.*: *qwry mldrth* 'scattered towns', taking *perazzi* as a metathesis of *pzr* 'to scatter' (cf. LXX Esth 9:19).

6. *every town—men, women, and children.* Literally, "every town of men,

the women and the children." See the TEXTUAL NOTES at 2:34. The LXX reads *mĕtōm* for *mĕtim* here as well.

7. *retained as booty.* MT: *bazzônû lānû;* Samaritan text, LXX: *bzznw lnw* (cf. 2:34). See *GKC* §67aa.

NOTES

1. *Bashan.* The region north and northeast of the Yarmuk, it is to be divided into four parts: the Golan heights, east of the Sea of Galilee, continuing upward to Mount Hermon; the al-Nuqra plain, which stretches from northwest to southeast, bordering on Mount Hauran; the basaltic highland north of al-Nuqra known as Laja; and Mount Hauran (Jebel Druze) east of the Bashan. In spite of the volcanic-basaltic enclaves of the Bashan, especially in the Laja and Hauran, the Bashan is very fertile and was even considered to be the chief granary for Syria and Palestine. It was renowned for its rich pastures and fat animals (Deut 32:14; Amos 4:1; Ps 22:13; etc.). The western slopes of the Hauran were covered with oak forests of extraordinary quality (cf. Isa 2:13; Ezek 27:6; Zech 11:2). No wonder that the Bashan was densely populated and cities, walled and unwalled (cf. vv 4–5), were distributed throughout the area. King Shalmaneser III of Assyria (858–834 B.C.E.) recounts that on his expedition to Hauran (841 B.C.E.) he destroyed innumerable *(ana lā mani)* cities (cf. *ARAB* 1.243).

Edrei. On the southern border of Bashan, it is identified with the modern town of Darʿa in Syria near the Jordanian border.

2. *Do not fear him.* Compare 1:21.

3. *no survivor was left.* Compare 2:34.

4. *At that time.* The phrase indicates the independent nature of the passage; compare 2:34.

there was not a town that we did not take from them. Compare 2:36, "not a city was too mighty for us." The language is hyperbolic, expressing the intense patriotism of the Deuteronomic author. Compare the phrase, "no survivor was left" (v 3) and see above, NOTE to 2:34.

the whole district of Argob. Identified in the Targumim with Trachon or Trachonitis, the basaltic highland desert known as Laja. This identification cannot be upheld. The remains of the ancient cities mentioned here cannot be confined to the Laja. It seems therefore that the Argob lay east of the Golan and extended over the whole area from the river al-Ruqd as far as the desert.

5. *All of them were fortified towns with high walls,* etc. Compare 1 Kgs 4:13. The sixty fortified cities seem to represent an ancient traditional motif bearing witness to the greatness and importance of the Bashan region.

gates, and bars. Compare 1 Sam 23:7; 2 Chr 8:5; 14:6.

6. *We banned them.* Compare the NOTES to 2:34–35.

COMMENT

A parallel tradition is found in Num 21:33–35. Because of the verbal overlapping of the latter with Deut 3:1–3 and the Deuteronomic phrases found in it (within a tradition that is otherwise free from Deuteronomic phraseology), it has been argued (especially by Dillmann 1886) that Num 21:33–35 is an addition based on Deut 3:1–3. According to this opinion, it was added there by a scribe who was troubled by the omission of the conquest of Bashan. There is no justification, however, for completely dismissing the tradition about the conquest of Bashan from the ancient sources. According to Num 32:42, Qenat in Bashan was conquered by the Israelite tribes. It should be admitted that, like Gilead, Bashan has been vastly expanded in the Deuteronomic tradition. Bashan in Deut 3:4, 13 and Josh 13:30 encompasses a huge area: the al-Nuqra plain, the Laja, and Mount Hauran (cf. above, in the NOTE on v 1). It seems that this large area was conquered at the time of the united monarchy (cf. 1 Kgs 4:12), and the Deuteronomic tradition used it for the reconstruction of the conquest of Transjordan.

C. SUMMARY OF CONQUESTS AND THEIR ALLOTMENT (3:8–17)

3 [8]Thus we seized at that time, from the two Amorite kings, the country
beyond the Jordan, from the Wadi Arnon to Mount Hermon [9](the Sidonians
call Hermon Sirion, and the Amorites call it Senir), [10]all the towns of the
plateau, and the whole of Gilead and Bashan as far as Salcah and Edrei, the
towns of Og's kingdom in Bashan. [11](Only Og, king of Bashan, was left of the
remaining Rephaim. His bedstead, an iron bedstead, is now in Rabbah of the
Ammonites; it is nine cubits long and four cubits wide, by the standard cubit.)
[12]And this is the land that we occupied at that time: the part from Aroer
along the Wadi Arnon, with part of the hill country of Gilead and its towns, I
assigned to the Reubenites and the Gadites. [13]The rest of Gilead, and all of
Bashan under Og's rule—the whole Argob district, all that part of Bashan which
is called the Rephaim district—I assigned to the half-tribe of Manasseh. [14]Jair,
son of Manasseh, received the whole Argob district, that is, Bashan, as far as the
boundary of the Geshurites and the Maacathites, and named it after himself,
Havvoth-Jair, as it still is. [15]To Machir I assigned Gilead. [16]And to the
Reubenites and the Gadites I assigned the part from Gilead down to the Wadi
Arnon, the middle of the wadi being the boundary, and up to the wadi of
Jabbok, the boundary of the Ammonites.
[17]We also seized the ʿArabah, from the foot of the slopes of the Pisgah on

the east, to the edge of the Jordan, and from Chinnereth down to the Sea of the ʿArabah, the Dead Sea.

TEXTUAL NOTES

8. *to.* MT: *ʿd;* Samaritan text: *wʾd.*

9. *Sirion.* Hebrew: *śiryon;* LXX: *Saniōr* (cf. *Śenir* at the end of the verse); *Tg. Ps.-J.* and *Tg. Neof.: ṭwrʾ dmsry pyrwy* 'the mountain whose fruits are rotted', taking *siryon* as if from the Aramaic *srh/sry* 'to rot'.

Senir. Tg. Onq. and *Tg. Ps.-J.: ṭwr hgʾ* 'mountain of snow'. Compare Rashi's commentary ad loc.: "Senir = snow in German *[Schnee]* and Canaanite [= Slavic *snêg]*". In *Tg. Neof.* Hermon is translated *ṭwrʾ dtlgʾ,* while Senir is simply *snyr,* as in Hebrew. *Sam. Tg.* has *mšʿbdh* 'enslaved' for Senir, deriving the word from *še-nîr* 'of the yoke'. The Samaritan Pentateuch translates *nîr ʿol* 'yoke' (cf. Num 19:2).

11. *is now.* Literally, "is it not," mispelled in the MT (see *GKC* §100i, 150e); LXX: *idou hautē* 'behold it' (cf. *hinnēh* 'behold' in the first part of the verse, also translated *idou);* Vg and Syriac omit *hlh.*

13. *the whole Argob district, all that part of Bashan which is called the Rephaim district.* Hebrew: *kol ḥebel hāʾargōb lĕkol habbāšān hahûʾ yiqqārē ʾereṣ repāʾîm,* which according to the Masoretic punctuation is to be rendered literally: "the whole Argob district to all Bashan. That is called Rephaim country." "To all Bashan" is meaningless in this context (cf. my paraphrase "all that part of Bashan"). If the Masoretic punctuation is ignored, however, the entire verse can be rendered, "The rest of Gilead and all of Bashan under Og's rule, the whole Argob district, I assigned to the half-tribe of Manasseh. That whole country. That whole Bashan is called Rephaim country" (see BHK, BHS).

of Manasseh. Hebrew: *hammĕnašeh.* See *GKC* §125d n. 1.

14. *Jair.* Samaritan text: *wyʾyr* 'and Jair'.

Argob. MT: *ʾrgb;* Samaritan text: *hʾrgb.*

that is, Bashan. In the Hebrew, this parenthetical statement follows "and named it [literally, 'them'] after himself."

16. *being the boundary.* Hebrew: *ûgĕbūl.* See the NOTES.

down to. MT, Samaritan text, Syriac, Targumim, Vg: *wʿd.* 4Q Dt^{d} col 2:2, (White 1990 ibid p. 145) LXX: *ʿd.*

up to. MT: *wʿd;* Samaritan text: *ʿd.*

17. In my translation the word order of the verse has been rearranged for clarity. It is literally rendered, "and the ʿArabah and the Jordan being the boundary [see the NOTES], from Chinnereth down to the Sea of the ʿArabah, the Dead Sea, beneath the slopes of Pisgah on the east." LXX mistakenly juxtaposes *ûgĕbūl mikkineret* 'being the boundary, from Chinnereth', and translates "are the boundary of Manachareth."

NOTES

8–11. This passage summarizes the conquest of the whole Transjordanian area, from the Arnon in the south to Mount Hermon in the north.

8. *Hermon.* A mountain range on the northwest of the Transjordan, called by the Arabs Jebel al-Sheikh 'the mountain of the chieftain', its highest peak reaching 2,814 meters above sea level. In the Targumim and in talmudic literature it is also called 'the snowy mountain' *(ṭwr tlgʾ).* The name "Hermon" is derived from the root *ḥrm* 'sacred' and was indeed considered to be a holy place; compare *baʿal ḥermôn* (Judg 3:3). The place Baal Gad "in the plain of Lebanon beneath Mount Hermon" (Josh 11:17; 12:7) marks the extreme northern point reached by the Israelites at the time of the conquest. The territory extending from Baal Gad to Lebo-Hamath was counted among "the remains," that is to say, the residual territories that, while belonging to the ideal promised land, were not conquered by Joshua (cf. Josh 13:5; Judg 3:3). Hermon was thus considered the northern border of the *real* land of Israel on both sides of the Jordan. "Dan," as the northern frontier in the geographical designation "from Dan to Beer Sheba," actually lies below Mount Hermon.

9. *Sidonians call Hermon Sirion, and the Amorites call it Senir.* A parenthetic note like 2:11, 20. Sirion is identical with the Anti-Lebanon and is mentioned, for example, in Ps 29:6 alongside Lebanon, and likewise in the Ugaritic literature *(CTA* 4.6:18–21: *llbnn wʿṣh lšryn mḥmd ʾarzh* 'to Lebanon and its trees, to Sirion and its choicest cedars') and in the Hittite treaties (Weidner 1923, pp. 68:36, 24:3–4).

Saniru is the name for the Anti-Lebanon in the annals of the Assyrian kings. In the Song of Songs it also occurs next to Hermon and Lebanon (4:8); cf. also Ezek 27:5 and 1 Chr 5:23. It seems that Hermon was considered part of the Anti-Lebanon, hence the identification of it with *Sirion* and *Senir;* cf. Ikeda 1978.

10. *all the towns of the plateau.* This phrase refers to v 8, which was interrupted by the note of v 9, and enumerates in detail the regions of the conquered area of Transjordan: the plateau, Gilead, and Bashan. The plateau, that is, the Mishor (cf. 4:43; Josh 13:9, 16, 17, 21; Jer 48:8, 21), constitutes an elevated plateau between the river Arnon in the south and Wadi Heshbon in the north. It was a place of rich pasture; cf. Num 32:1–4.

the whole of Gilead. The mountainous area north of the plateau up to the Yarmuk, which was divided in half by the Jabbok; cf. above, 2:36.

Salcah and Edrei. These two places mark the southern border of Bashan, Salcah in the east, Edrei in the west. Salcah, the present Ṣalhad, is situated on the southwestern slope of Mount Hauran. For Edrei, cf. v 1.

11. An archaeological note similar in nature to 2:10–12, 20–23.

Only Og . . . was left of the remaining Rephaim. After defeating him, no resistance by this giant race would be possible again. Og as a representative or even patron of the heroes of the underworld (compare *rp'i 'arṣ* in an invocation of the ancestral spirits in a recently discovered cultic text from Ugarit RS 34.126, and see Isa 14:9; cf. above, in the NOTE on 2:11) is mentioned in a Phoenician coffin inscription (sixth or fifth century B.C.E.). The deceased declares that "the mighty Og will take revenge" upon the one who violates his tomb *(wlrgz ʿṣmy hʿg utbqšn h'dr);* cf. Degen, Müller, and Röllig 1974, 2.1ff., which shows that Og was considered a legendary-mythological hero. According to Jewish legends, Og survived the flood and was identified with the "fugitive" who brought to Abram the news of the capture of Lot in Transjordan during the attack of the four kings (Gen 14; cf. Ginzberg 1959, 1.160, 3.340, and the corresponding notes, pp. 667–68). In the pseudoepigraphical writings, Og along with Sihon was associated with the giants from before the flood; cf. the reference in *b. Nid.* 61a and see the recent discussion in Milik 1976, pp. 320–21, 324, 329: Aramaic fragments of Qumran Cave 4. The kingdom of Og reached as far as Mount Hermon, a mountain that was cursed according to a pseudoepigraphical literature, because the fallen angels conspired there against God; cf. Milik 1976, pp. 150 (4Q En^{a} 1 III:4–5), 318ff., 336ff.

His bedstead, an iron bedstead, is now in Rabbah of the Ammonites. This clause seems to refer to his sarcophagus, where he was buried. The word *ʿrś* 'couch' is used figuratively for bier or tomb, as is *mškb* in 2 Chr 16:4 and in the Phoenician inscriptions. Ammon, along with Bashan, was considered to be the land of the Rephaim (2:20, 3:13), which explains why the bedstead of the last survivor of the Rephaim was placed in the capital of Ammon.

iron bedstead. brzl may indicate here basalt, which is common in Bashan; sarcophagi of black basalt were found in great numbers in the Golan area. As Millard has recently shown, however, the terms "iron chariot" (Josh 17:16, 18; Judg 1:19; 4:3, 13) and "iron bedstead" reflect an earlier period, when iron was of special value. In the Iron Age, that is, the first millennium B.C.E., one did not mention that chariots were made of iron, as this was understood. One should note that these items were in fact made of wood and only sheathed with iron for strengthening (cf. Millard 1988).

Rabbah of the Ammonites. The capital city of the Ammonites, now Amman. The LXX translates "in the citadel *(akra)* of the Ammonites" (reading perhaps *bîrah* instead of *rabbah),* while *Tg. Ps.-J.* renders "in the treasure house or governors' house *(byt 'rkywn)* of Rabbat of the Ammonites."

the standard cubit. Literally, "by a man's cubit (forearm)," in contradistinction to the royal cubit, which was different from the standard measure (cf. 2 Chr 3:3). The units of weight were also of different types: the royal weight (2 Sam 14:26), the merchant weight (Gen 23:16), and the sacred weight (Exod 30:13). The *Tgs. Onq.* and *Neof.* 1 translate "by the king's cubit," while *Tg. Ps.-J.* has "by his own [= Og's] cubit," stressing the extraordinary measurements of the sarcophagus. There are similar legends about the ancient Greek heroes. Herodotus (2.68) tells of a blacksmith who found the sarcophagus of Orestes, son of Agamemnon, saying that it was seven cubits long and was later sent to Sparta.

12–13. A description of the allotment of the conquered territories.

12. *from Aroer along the Wadi Arnon.* The LXX and Samaritan versions have, as in 2:36: "from Aroer on the edge of Wadi Arnon."

with part of the hill country of Gilead. Literally, with *half* of the hill country, etc., in other words, the half of Gilead that is south of Jabbok.

I assigned to the Reubenites and the Gadites. Compare Num 32.

13. *all that part of Bashan which is called the Rephaim district.* Compare 2:11, 20.

14. *Jair, son of Manasseh, received the whole Argob district . . . and named it after himself, Havvoth-Jair.* As has been indicated above, the Deuteronomic tradition assigns to Manasseh a much larger area than the previous sources. The Argob district, which is given to Manasseh, includes here sixty fortified cities of which there is no mention in the tradition of Numbers. According to Num 32:41, the "villages" conquered by Jair, son of Manasseh, are said to have been in Gilead (cf. v 40 there), which is supported by Judg 10:4: "Havvoth-Jair . . . in the land of Gilead." In Deut 3:14 these "villages" are said to be located in the Bashan, that is to say, north of Gilead. Furthermore, by situating the "Havvoth-Jair" in the district of Argob, the author identifies, as it were, "villages" with fortified cities (v 4), which is artificial. Indeed, in the list of Solomonic districts in 1 Kgs 4, there is a clear distinction between the "Havvoth-Jair" in Gilead and the Argob district with its sixty cities in the Bashan (v 13; cf. Kallai 1986, chap. 10, pp. 247–59). It seems that by expanding the area of Manasseh to the north, the author of Deuteronomy extended the meaning of Havvoth-Jair by linking it to the territory of Bashan. This was followed up by the Deuteronomic historian in Josh 13:30, "and all the Havvoth-Jair in Bashan, sixty cities."

Havvoth-Jair. Ḥawwah is apparently a cognate of Arabic *ḥiwā* 'circle of tents'.

as far as the boundary of the Geshurites and the Maacathites. The Geshur and the Maacah, two ethnic groups to the west of the Bashan between the Hermon and Gilead in the north, that is, in the present Golan (cf. 2 Sam 3:3; 10:6; 13:37–38; etc.). According to tradition, they were not subjugated by the Israelites during the conquest (see Josh 13:13 and compare 12:5). Geshur and Maacah existed as independent kingdoms during the time of David. Geshur established friendly relations with David (2 Sam 3:3) while Maacah fought against him (2 Sam 10:6). After the rise of the Aramaic kingdom of Damascus, both states were apparently incorporated into that state. According to 1 Chr 2:23, the Havvoth of Jair, along with the sixty cities of the Bashan, were conquered by Geshur and Aram, which seems to have happened during the expedition of Ben-Hadad I, king of Aram (circa 886 B.C.E.; see B. Mazar 1961).

15. *To Machir I assigned Gilead.* Compare Num 32:30–40, which seems to

be the original source for this verse, as Num 32:11 is for v 14. "Gilead" here signifies the northern half (see the NOTE on 2:36). Machir is called in Josh 17:1 "the firstborn of Manasseh and ancestor of Gilead." In the song of Deborah (Judg 5), however, the Machir is counted among the tribes of the western part of the Jordan, together with the Benjamin and the Ephraim, who fought with the Canaanites (v 17). It seems therefore that the settlement of Machir in Gilead belongs to a later period (see Weinfeld 1983c, p. 60).

16. *the middle of the wadi being the boundary.* Literally, "the middle of the wadi and border." The *waw* is explicative and has to be understood as "at the same time." This peculiar use of *wgbwl* is characteristic of borderlines demarcated by river and sea (v 17; Num 24:6; Josh 13:23, 27; 15:12, 47), and it seems to indicate that neither the bank of the river nor the shore of the sea constituted the border, rather a line in the center of the river or other body of water.

and up to the wadi of Jabbok. That is, to the upper course of the Jabbok, which runs from south to north (before turning west) and forms the western border of Ammon (see the NOTE on 2:37).

17. *the ʿArabah . . . to the edge of the Jordan.* Literally, "and the ʿArabah and the Jordan and border," that is, the ʿArabah (on which see 1:1) with the Jordan as a boundary.

the slopes of the Pisgah on the east. "The slopes of the Pisgah" (cf. 4:49) are the opposite of "the summit of Pisgah" (3:27; 34:1; compare Num 21:20; 23:14). *ʾšd* as slope was suggested by Dillmann 1886 in his commentary on Num 21:15 and may now be corroborated by *Tg. Neof.* on this verse, which translates *ʾšdt hpsgh* by *špwʿ byt rmt* 'the slope of the highland'. *išdu* in Akkadian means 'bottom' (or 'foundation', cf. Hebrew *ysd)* and seems to be the etymological root of Hebrew *ʾšd,* which means 'slope' or 'foothill'. *Pisgah* denotes the range of hills: compare *mrmt* or *byt rmt* in the Targumim and the Peshitta, which slopes down to the Moabite plain and to the northeastern part of the Dead Sea. Mount Nebo is situated on the summit of the Pisgah, which Moses ascended in order to see the promised land before his death (3:27; 34:1; compare 32:49; Num 27:12). Eusebius *(Onomast.* 16, lines 24–26) testifies that in his time, the district of Nebo was called *Fasgō.*

from Chinnereth. The name of the lake into which the Jordan enters and flows out of in the south, as well as the name of a town on the northwest of the lake (Josh 19:35). The lake is also called "the sea of Chinnereth" or Chinneroth (Num 34:22; Josh 12:3; 13:27) and is known from the Second Temple period as the "lake of Gennesareth" (Josephus, *Wars* 3:506) or the water of Gennesar (1 Macc 11:67). In talmudic sources, it is usually called "the sea of Tiberias."

down to the sea of the ʿArabah, the Dead Sea. Literally, the salt sea. The appellation "Dead Sea" is known to us from the classical writers; in the Bible it is named "sea of ʿArabah" (cf. 4:49; 2 Kgs 14:25), "Salt Sea" (Gen 14:3; Num 34:3, 12; etc.), or both names, as here and in Josh 3:16; 12:3.

COMMENT

Verses 14–17 repeat in chiastic order what has been said in vv 12–13 (proceeding from north to south instead of from south to north), but add information, taken from ancient tradition, about the families of Manasseh who occupied the Gilead area and provide supplementary details about the western borders of the Reubenites and the Gadites.

INSTRUCTIONS TO THE TRANSJORDANIAN TRIBES CONCERNING THE CONQUEST (3:18–22)

3 18At that time I charged you, saying, "YHWH your God has given you this
country to possess. You must go as shock troops, warriors all, at the head of your
Israelite kinsmen. 19Only your wives, children, and livestock—I know that you
have much livestock—shall be left in the towns I have assigned to you, 20until
YHWH has granted your kinsmen a resting place such as you have, and they too
have taken possession of the land that YHWH your God is giving them, beyond
the Jordan. Then you may return each to the homestead that I have assigned to
him."

21I also charged Joshua at this time, saying, "You have seen with your own
eyes all that YHWH your God has done to these two kings. So shall YHWH do
to all the kingdoms into which you shall cross over. 22Do not fear them, for it is
YHWH your God who will do battle for you."

TEXTUAL NOTES

19. *your wives, children, and livestock.* The Samaritan text has "your children, wives, and livestock."

20. *until YHWH has granted . . . a resting place.* The LXX adds "your [some manuscripts, our] God"). Compare the end of the verse:

YHWH your God. Omitted in the Vg. Some manuscripts of the LXX have "YHWH our God."

21. *You have seen with your own eyes.* Literally, "your eyes are those that have seen." See the NOTES for the Septuagintal reading.

all. Omitted in the Samaritan text.

your God. Omitted in the Samaritan text. LXX: "our God."

shall YHWH. Some manuscripts of the LXX add "our God"; others, "your God."

NOTES

18. *I charged you.* "You" refers to the two-and-a-half tribes.

shock troops. Literally, girded troops *(ḥlwṣ,* derived from *ḥlṣym* 'loins'); compare 1:41 and Judg 18:11, 16f. In the parallel passage in Josh 1:14, *ḥmšym* is used instead of *ḥlṣym. ḥmšym* derives from *ḥmš,* which, like *ḥlṣym,* connotes loins.

warriors all. This expression does not occur in the tradition of Numbers; for a similar military elaboration, see 1:41 and my NOTE there. In the parallel Deuteronomic passage of Josh 1:14, the military sense is even more developed: instead of *bny ḥyl,* we find there *gbwry hḥyl.* In Numbers, the divine nature of the enterprise is stressed: the fighters cross "at the instance of YHWH," literally, "before YHWH," an expression repeated there seven times (vv 20, 21, 22bis, 27, 29, 32).

19. *your wives, children, and livestock.* In the parallel tradition of Num 32, we find children *(ṭp)* and livestock (vv 16, 17b, 24) without wives, but *ṭp* (outside the Deuteronomic traditions) generally means 'household', that is, women, old men, and children who belong to the family headed by a man. See, for example, Gen 43:8; 47:12, 24; 50:8, 21; etc.; compare *ṭplʾ* in Aramaic (from *ṭpl* 'to join'), which connotes family or household. Compare also LXX *aposkeue* and Syriac *yqrtʾ* for *ṭp,* both of which refer to household stuff, baggage, and the like.

I know that you have much livestock. This parenthetic sentence seems to presuppose the knowledge of what is told in Num 32:1ff. (see Loewenstamm 1972–73, pp. 15–16).

in the towns I have assigned to you. Compare Num 32:16ff., though there they built the towns before leaving with the rest of the people (vv 32ff.). Here, the towns were given to them by Moses. This is in line with the Deuteronomic outlook that the land with all the appurtenances of civilization and affluence was transferred as it was by God to Israel (cf. 6:10ff.). In Josh 1:14, there is no longer mention of towns but simply "*the land* that Moses assigned."

20. *until YHWH has granted . . . a resting place.* A characteristic phrase of the Deuteronomic writers: cf. Deut 12:10; 25:19; Josh 1:13, 15; 21:42; 22:4; 23:1.

21. *I also charged Joshua at this time.* The verb *ṣwh,* here translated 'charge', is used twice in the parallel tradition (see below, in the COMMENT) in Num 27:19, 23 with the meaning of "commissioning" by means of instructions. Compare 2 Kgs 20:1: *ṣw lbytk* 'give your last directions [= will] to your family', and cf. 2 Sam 17:23; hence late Hebrew *ṣwʾh.* The Deuteronomic author adopted this verb (cf. v 28) from the tradition in Numbers (cf. Num 27:19, "commissioned him *in their sight,*" with Deut 31:7, "called Joshua . . . *in the sight of all Israel*"), though he replaced the sacred rite in connection with the commis-

sioning—*putting his hand* upon Joshua (Num 27:18, 23)—by an encouraging speech (see the COMMENT).

You have seen with your own eyes. A characteristic phrase of the Deuteronomic writer (see 4:3; 11:7; and compare 4:9; 7:19; 10:21; 29:2), it belongs to the rhetorical technique of Deuteronomy (see Weinfeld 1972a, p. 173). The LXX reads the plural here, as in the Masoretic text of 4:3 and 11:7 *(ʿynykm hrʾt),* which may be correct in the light of v 22 and in the light of the fact that the commissioning is done in the sight of all Israel (31:7; cf. Num 27:19; see the previous NOTE).

to all the kingdoms into which you shall cross over. Canaan on the western side of the Jordan consisted of petty kingdoms, and the ruling system on the eve of the conquest was one of city-states (cf. Josh 12).

22. *Do not fear them, for it is YHWH . . . who will do battle for you.* Compare 3:2; 31:6, 8. Similar encouragement formulas are known to us from ancient Near Eastern oracles imparted to kings confronted by enemies (see the NOTE to 1:21).

COMMENT

This section consists of two passages (vv 18–20 and 21–22), each one marked by the opening formula *bāʿet hahîʾ* 'at that time' (vv 18, 21), which is characteristic of an independent unit (see above). The first passage describes Moses' instructions to the two-and-a-half tribes in connection with their participation in the conquest of Canaan on the western side of the Jordan. This draws on the tradition in Num 32 about the settlement of the Reubenites and Gadites in Transjordan. The second passage describes the commissioning of Joshua as leader of the conquest. This has its antecedent in Num 27:15–23, though there, because of the priestly nature of the tradition, the commissioning bears a sacred character: Joshua has to follow the decision of the Urim as presented by Eleazar the priest, while in the Deuteronomic tradition, the commissioning of Joshua involves encouragement for the battle with the Canaanites.

THE PRAYER OF MOSES (3:23–29)

3 [23]I pleaded with YHWH at that time, saying, [24]"O Lord YHWH, you who
let your servant see the first works of your greatness and your mighty hand, you
whose powerful deeds no god in heaven or on earth can equal, [25]let me, I pray,
cross over and see the good land on the other side of the Jordan, that good hill
country and the Lebanon." [26]But YHWH was wrathful with me on your account and would not listen to me. YHWH said to me, "Enough! Never speak to
me of this matter again! [27]Go up to the summit of Pisgah and gaze about to the

west, the north, the south, and the east. Look at it well, for you shall not go across yonder Jordan. [28]Give Joshua his instructions, and imbue him with strength and courage, for he shall go across at the head of this people and he shall allot to them the land that you may only see."

[29]And we camped in the valley, opposite Beth-Peor.

TEXTUAL NOTES

23. *I pleaded.* MT: *wʾtḥnn.* Samaritan text: *wʾtḥnnh.* A new section begins here in the MT, on the same line as the previous section following a space *(setumah).*

24. *your mighty hand.* The LXX and Syriac add "and outstretched arm," which together with "mighty hand" forms a Deuteronomic stereotype (see NOTES below at 4:34).

you whose powerful deeds no god in heaven or on earth can equal. Literally, *(ʾăšer)* "who is the god in heaven and on earth who can do the like of your deeds and power." *ʾăšer,* the relative particle introducing the clause, is either "for, because" (so LXX, Vg, Syriac), or "who," i.e., "[O Lord God . . .] who [= of whom it can be said] who is the god . . . who can do the like of your deeds and power" (cf. my translation: "whose").

25. *let me . . . cross.* MT: *ʾʿbrh.* Samaritan text: *ʾʿbr.*

the good land. LXX and Vg: "this good land."

26. *was wrathful.* Hebrew: *wayyitʿabber,* a rare word, to be associated with the noun *ʿebrâh* 'wrath' (cf. 1:37 [there *htʾnp]*; also Pss 78:21, 59, 62; 89:39; Prov 14:16). LXX: *hupereiden* 'overlooked', i.e., 'ignored', taking *hitʿabber* literally as 'passed over'.

27. *to the summit of Pisgah.* MT: *rʾš hpsgh,* without preposition. Samaritan text: *ʾl rʾš hpsgh;* 4Q Dt[d], col 2:17 (White 1990, 145): *ʿl rʾs hpsgh*

to the west. MT and Samaritan text: *ymh* with the locative *he.* 4Q Dt[d] col 2:17 (White 1990, 145): *ym* without the locative *he.*

28. *Give . . . instructions.* MT: *ṣw.* Samaritan text: *ṣwy.* See the TEXTUAL NOTES at 2:4.

NOTES

23. *I pleaded with YHWH at that time, saying.* Note the similar opening formulas of the two preceding sections: "I . . . charged Joshua *at this time, saying*" (v 21), "*At that time* I charged you, *saying*" (v 18), which points to the independent nature of each one of them (see above, note to 1:9 *bāʿet hahî).* Verses 21–22 do indeed tell about the execution of the commandment, which occurs in the following section only (v 28). This caused Ibn Ezra to interpret "I pleaded" in 3:23 in the sense of the pluperfect: "I had already pleaded before."

24. *O Lord YHWH.* This form of address expresses a personal relationship

with God, hence it is characteristic of prayers; see 9:26; cf. Gen 15:2, 8; Josh 7:7 (compare note to v 28 below); Judg 6:22; 16:28; 2 Sam 7:18f. (passim); and especially frequent occurrences in Amos and Ezekiel. The original reading of *ʾdny* may have been *adonī* or *adonai* (plural. majest.) 'my Lord, Monsieur' (compare late Hebrew "Rabbi"), but the vocalization has been changed into *adonāi* with *qamaṣ* in order to distinguish between the profane usage of the address and the sacred one (cf. Eissfeldt 1973, 1.66–78). The relationship of Moses and God is like the relationship of a master and his servant, as may be seen from the designation "your servant" in the prayer (v 24; cf. 2 Sam 7:19), a relationship also recognizable in the secular royal sphere. Compare Gen 44:18, "my Lord . . . let your servant" (but note *bī adonī* there and *bī adonāi* in the prayer to God, Josh 7:8).

who let your servant see the first works. Literally, "you began to show your servant," compare 2:25, 31 and Rashi's reading of this verse: "You began to show your servant the battle with Sihon and Og as it is written 'See I begin by placing Sihon,' show me also the battle with the thirty-one kings." Indeed, in the address to Joshua in v 21, there is a reference to the kingdoms on the western side of the Jordan, to which Joshua will cross over (but not Moses).

you whose powerful deeds no god in heaven or on earth can equal. Compare *b. Ber.* 32a: "One should always offer praise to the Lord first, and then pray (for what he needs), whence it is proven, from Moses as it is written: 'I pleaded . . . you began.' " Opening a prayer with the proclamation of the uniqueness of God, as here, is a characteristic feature of Deuteronomy and the Deuteronomic literature; compare 2 Sam 7:22–24; 1 Kgs 8:23; 2 Kgs 19:15–19; Jer 32:17–23; and see Weinfeld 1972a, pp. 37–45. The "mighty deeds" of God praised here are often referred to in Deuteronomy in connection with the Exodus, see, e.g., 10:21–11:2: "He is your glory and he is your God, who wrought for you those marvelous *(hgdlt)* awesome deeds that you saw with your own eyes . . . his majesty *(gdlw),* his mighty hand *(ydw hḥzqh),* his outstretched arm . . . the deeds *(mʿśyw)* that he performed in Egypt." The LXX has in 3:24: "Your greatness, your mighty hand, and your outstretched arm," as in 11:2.

25. *that good hill country and the Lebanon.* Lebanon was famous for its luxuriant vegetation (Ezek 31:3; Hos 14:6–8; Ps 72:16; etc.) and natural beauty (Cant 5:15; 7:5) and thus symbolizes the beautiful land that Moses longs to see. *Targumim Onqelas* and *Pseudo-Jonathan* translate Lebanon as the Temple and the "good hill" as the mount of the Temple, a midrashic view based on Jer 22:6; compare *Sipre Deut.* to this verse. Lebanon symbolizes the Temple in the Qumran scrolls too (cf. Nitzan 1986, pp. 93–94). The LXX translates "Lebanon" as *Antilibanos,* which is identical with Hermon and Sirion, mentioned previously as the northern limits of the land (vv 8–9).

26. *YHWH was wrathful with me on your account.* Compare 1:37 and 4:21, where a different verb is used *(ʾnp).*

27. *the summit of Pisgah.* Pisgah is the top of Mount Nebo (34:1), which is

situated on the heights of the Abarim (cf. 32:49). Mount Nebo is identified with Jebel Nebo (802 meters) above Wadi ʿAyn Musa, which is considered the valley *(gyʾ)* near Beth-Peor (v 29). Jebel Nebo is located seven kilometers southwest of Heshbon, and from its peak there is a very wide vista of the surrounding areas. Others identify Mount Nebo with the ridge of Jebel Nebo known today as Rugum el-heri, which has a similar view. For Pisgah, see the COMMENT on v 17.

gaze about. Literally, "raise your eyes." Compare Gen 13:14 (to Abram): "Raise your eyes and look out to the north and south."

28. *Give Joshua his instructions.* Compare the NOTE to v 21.

imbue him with strength and courage. Compare 31:7, 23 and Josh 1:6, 7, 9, 18; 10:25; the expression is characteristic of the Deuteronomic literature.

29. *And we camped in the valley, opposite Beth-Peor.* This verse refers back to "in Transjordan in the land of Moab did Moses expound his Torah" (Deut 1:5), but with a more detailed description of the place (cf. 4:46 as well as 34:6). The valley *(gyʾ)* is probably Wadi ʿAyn Musa at the foot of Jebel Nebo (cf. Oded, 1968). Eusebius in his *Onomastikon* places Beth-Peor opposite Jericho about 10 kilometers from Levias on the road from Levias to Heshbon. Beth-Peor is Beth Baal-Peor (the house of Baal-Peor), the site of the Israelites' first encounter with cultic prostitution, part of the Baal worship (cf. Num 25:1–9; Hos 9:10). On the Madeba Map (sixth century B.C.E.) Baal-Peor is named *bētomarssa he kai maioumas* which is a drinking place and a Mayumas temple as well, where water-drawing festivals associated with sexual licentiousness were held. Rabbinic sources also associate Baal-Peor with drinking and Mayumas festivals (cf. *Lev. Rab.* 13 [Margaliot], p. 108, *Sipre Num.* [Horowitz], pp. 170–71; cf. also Good 1986).

COMMENT

Moses prays to YHWH to let him enter Canaan but is refused because of the sin of the people; he is then commanded to go up to the summit of Mount Pisgah in order to see the promised land, and finally is directed to appoint Joshua as his successor. All of these themes are principally reflected in Num 27:12–23: (1) the sin of Kadesh, following which Moses is denied entrance into Canaan (v 14); (2) the ascension of Moses to Mount Abarim (= Nebo, Deut 32:49) to see the land (vv 12–13); (3) a prayer from Moses and the nomination of Joshua as Moses' successor (vv 15–23). In Deuteronomy, however, these themes have undergone a thorough change. It is not the sin of Moses himself that caused his exclusion but the sin of the people (v 26; compare 1:37). The prayer in Numbers, which is concerned with appointing a leader for Israel, is turned here into a personal prayer from Moses to be permitted to enter the land (vv 23–25). The appointment of Joshua is carried out not in a sacred ceremony (see above), but by a speech of encouragement for the military expedition (v 28).

HORTATORY ADDRESS (4:1–40)

4 1And now, oh Israel, listen to the laws and rules that I am teaching you to
observe, so that you may live to enter and occupy the land that YHWH, the
God of your fathers, is giving you. 2You shall not add anything to what I
command you or take anything away from it, in order to keep the commandments of YHWH your God that I command you. 3You saw with your own eyes
what YHWH did at Baal-Peor, that YHWH destroyed from among you every
person who followed Baal-Peor. 4But you who held fast to YHWH your God are
all alive today.

5See, I am teaching you laws and rules, as YHWH my God has commanded
me, for you to observe within the land that you are about to invade and occupy.
6Observe them carefully, for that will be proof of your wisdom and discernment
to other peoples, who upon hearing of all these laws will say, "Surely, that great
nation is a wise and descerning people." 7For what great nation is there that has
a god so close at hand as is YHWH our God whenever we call on him? 8Or
what great nation has laws and rules as just as all of this teaching that I set
before you this day?

9But take utmost care and watch yourselves scrupulously so that you do not
forget the things that you saw with your own eyes, and so that they do not fade
from your mind as long as you live. And make them known to your children and
to your children's children; 10when you stood before YHWH your God at
Horeb, when YHWH said to me, "Gather the people to me that I may let them
hear my words, so that they may learn to revere me as long as they live on earth,
and may so teach their children." 11You came near and stood at the foot of the
mountain. The mountain was ablaze with fire up to the very skies; there was
darkness, cloud, and thick mist. 12YHWH spoke to you out of the fire; you
heard the sound of words but perceived no shape, nothing but a voice. 13He
declared to you his covenant, which he commanded you to observe: the Ten
Commandments; and he inscribed them on two tablets of stone. 14At the same
time YHWH commanded me to teach you the laws and rules for you to observe
in the land that you are about to cross into and occupy.

15Therefore, for your own sake be most careful, for you saw no shape on the
day that YHWH spoke to you at Horeb out of the fire, 16not to act destructively
and make for yourselves a sculpted image in any likeness whatever: the form of a
man or a woman, 17the form of any beast on earth, the form of any winged bird
that flies in the sky, 18the form of anything that creeps on the ground, the form
of any fish that is in the waters below the earth. 19And when you look up into
the sky and behold the sun and the moon and the stars, the whole heavenly
host, you must not be lured into bowing down to them or serving them. These

YHWH your God allotted to the other peoples everywhere under heaven. [20]But you did YHWH take and bring out of Egypt, the iron blast furnace, to be his very own people, as it is today.

[21]Now, YHWH was angry with me on your account and swore that I should neither cross the Jordan nor enter the good land that YHWH your God is giving you as an inheritance: [22]for I must die in this land; I shall not cross the Jordan. But, you will cross and take possession of that good land. [23]Take care, then, not to forget the covenant that YHWH your God has concluded with you, not to make for yourselves a sculpted image in any likeness, against which YHWH your God has enjoined you, [24]for YHWH your God is a consuming fire, an impassioned God.

[25]Should you, when you have begotten children and children's children and are long established in the land, act destructively and make for yourselves a sculpted image in any likeness, causing YHWH your God displeasure and vexation, [26]I call heaven and earth this day to witness against you that you shall soon perish from the land that you are crossing the Jordan to occupy; you shall not long endure in it, but shall be utterly destroyed. [27]YHWH will scatter you among the nations, and only a scant few of you shall be left among the nations to which YHWH will drive you. [28]There you will serve manmade gods of wood and stone, that cannot see or hear or eat or smell.

[29]But if you search there for YHWH your God, you will find him if only you seek him with all your heart and soul. [30]When you are in distress and all these things shall befall you, then in the end you will return to YHWH your God and obey him. [31]For YHWH your God is a compassionate God: he will not fail you, nor will he destroy you; he will not forget the covenant that he made by oath with your fathers.

[32]You have but to inquire about bygone ages that were before you, from the day that God created man on earth, from one end of heaven to the other. Has anything as grand as this ever happened, or has its like ever been known? [33]Has any people heard the voice of God speaking from the midst of a fire, as indeed you have, and survived? [34]Or has any god attempted to go and take for himself one nation from the midst of another by prodigious acts, by signs and portents, by war, by a mighty hand and an outstretched arm, by great terrors, as YHWH your God did for you in Egypt before your very eyes? [35]You have been shown to know that YHWH alone is God; there is none beside him. [36]From heaven he let you hear his voice, to instruct you; on earth he let you see his great fire; and from the midst of that fire you heard his words. [37]Because he loved your fathers, he chose their offspring after them; he by his own presence, with his great might, led you out of Egypt, [38]to drive out before you nations greater and more populous than you, to bring you to their land and give it to you as an inheritance, as it is today. [39]Know therefore this day and keep in mind that YHWH alone is God in heaven above and on earth below; there is none beside him. [40]Observe his laws and commandments, which I enjoin upon you this day, that

it may go well with you and your children after you, and that you may prolong your days in the land that YHWH your God is giving you all the time.

TEXTUAL NOTES

4:1. *that I am teaching you to observe.* The LXX and Peshitta add "today."

live to enter. Hebrew: *tiḥyu uba'tem,* an imperfect followed by perfect consecutive. See *GKC* §112p. The Samaritan Pentateuch has *tiḥyun* instead of *tiḥyu.* See the NOTE to 1:17.

2. *to what I command you.* The Samaritan text adds "today"; *Tg. Neof.* adds "now *(kʿn).*"

in order to keep. The LXX and Vg translate the infinitive *lišmor* 'to keep' as an imperative, 'keep' (LXX: *phylassasthe;* Vg: *custodite),* and the Peshitta has *'l' ṭrw* 'but keep'. *Targum Pseudo-Jonathan: min la leᵉmintur* 'from not keeping'.

that I command you. Most LXX manuscripts add "today" here as well.

3. *You saw with your own eyes.* Hebrew: *ʿeyneykem haro'ôt,* literally, 'your eyes are those that see/saw'. See *GKC* §116q.

at Baal-Peor. Others translate "in the matter of" or "because of" Baal-Peor, a rather unconventional understanding of the preposition *bᵉ.* This is unnecessary, because it is clear from Hos 9:10 that Baal-Peor was the name of a place as well as of a deity. The LXX's *tō(i) Beelphegor* preserves the ambiguity of the Hebrew. The Vg has *contra Beelphegor* 'against Baal-Peor'. *Targumim Onqelos, Pseudo-Jonathan,* and *Neofiti* all retain the *bᵉ* of the Hebrew but translate *bplḥy bʿl (Neof.: ṭʿwwth) pʿwr* '[that which the Lord did] *with* the worshipers of Baal-Peor'. Peshitta: *lbʿl pʿwr* (cf. *Tg. Neof.* margin *lplḥy bʿl pʿwr* 'to Baal-peor').

5. *See.* See the NOTE to 1:8.

for you to observe. Hebrew: *laʿaśot ken,* literally, 'to do thus'. The force of the adverb *ken* 'thus' is not altogether apparent. Ehrlich suggests amending to *laʿaśotkem* 'for you to observe', as in v 14 (see the NOTE). Peshitta renders *dtʿbdwn 'nwn* 'that you may do *them*'.

6. *Observe them carefully.* Literally, "observe and do" (cf. 7:12; 16:12; 26:16; 28:13) but, more commonly, "observe to do *(šmr lʿśwt)*" (cf. 5:1, 29; 6:3, 25; etc.). The priestly source uses "to remember and do *(zkr wʿśh),*" cf. Num 15:39, 40. The object must be understood from the preceding verse. It is supplied in the Peshitta *('nwn* 'them') and in *Tg. Ps.-J. (yt 'wryyt'* 'the Torah').

Surely. Hebrew: *raq,* literally, "only." LXX: *idou* 'behold'. The particle *raq* here has an affirmative, assertive force, and the phrase is to be understood as "this nation is nothing but a wise and discerning people." Compare Ehrlich 1909, ad loc. See also Muraoka 1985, p. 131.

7. *a god so close at hand.* Hebrew: *'elohîm qᵉrobîm,* perhaps 'gods so close at hand'. Compare *GKC* §124 e.g., §132h, §142.

8. *just.* The adjective *ṣaddiq* is, except here, used only for persons; cf. the cy below.

9. *But.* Hebrew *raq* has affirmative, assertive force; cf. Muraoka 1985, p. 131.

10. *when.* Hebrew: *yom ʾăšer,* literally, 'the day that'; cf. Akkadian *ūm(u) ša* (neo-Babylonian), which simply means 'when' *(AHW* s.v. *ūmu* 6/C). The entire verse is in apposition to "the things that you saw" of v 9.

at Horeb. The LXX adds "on the day of the assembly"; cf. 9:10; 10:4; 18:16.

so that. Hebrew: *ʾăšer,* the relative pronoun. This meaning of *ʾăšer* is especially common in Deuteronomy.

11. *the very skies.* Hebrew: *ʿad leb haššamayim,* literally, 'to the heart of the heavens'. The LXX does not translate "heart," while *Tgs. Onq., Ps.-J.,* and *Neof.* render *ʿad ṣeyt šemaya* 'to the direction of (toward) the heavens'.

there was darkness, cloud, and thick mist. Hebrew: *ḥošek ʿanan weʿarapel,* three nouns in a row, syntactically unconnected to the body of the verse. They must be understood as accusatives of manner *(NJPS:* "dark with densest clouds"); see *GKC* §118q. Some LXX manuscripts add "and a great voice"; cf. 5:19.

12. *nothing but a voice.* Hebrew: *zulatī qôl,* literally, 'except a voice'. Compare 1 Kgs 3:18.

13. *He declared his covenant . . . to observe. bᵉrit* 'covenant' must here be understood in light of its appositive, "the ten words," therefore it is governed by such verbs as *higgid* 'declare' and *ʿaśah* 'observe'.

14. *for you to observe.* Hebrew: *laʿaśotkem ʾotam.* The suffix *-kem* 'you' is the subject of the infinitive construct *ʿaśot.* The preposition *-la* is not the usual prefix of the infinitive construct, but rather has the meaning 'for', 'in order that'. See Bergsträsser 1926–29, vol. 2, §11k.

to cross. YQDtᶜ tr 2–3 White 1990 ibid, 27 reads: "to cross the Jordan by influence of" v 26.

15. *for your own sake be most careful.* Hebrew: *wenišmar-tem mĕʾod lenap-šoteykem,* a fusion of the two expressions used in v 9: *hiššamer lĕka ušĕmor nap-šĕka mĕʾod.* Compare the same phrase in Josh 23:11, which is Deuteronomic. For variations, see 2:4 above and Mal 2:16.

on the day that YHWH spoke to you. Hebrew: *bĕyom dibber,* the relative pronoun, is missing, and the noun *yôm* in the construct state governs a sentence beginning with a finite verb. See *GKC* §130d; Driver 1902, ad loc., for various opinions regarding this syntax.

16. *likeness.* Hebrew: *sml,* a rare word in the Bible (Ezek 8:3, 5; 2 Chr 33:7), is found in a number of Phoenician inscriptions (see *KAI,* glossary). In the bilingual Phoenician–Greek inscription from Cyprus, *sml* is rendered by *andrias* 'an image of a man' *(KAI* 41:1).

19. *These YHWH your God allotted.* Hebrew: *ʾăšer ḥalaq YHWH ʾeloheyka ʾotam,* literally, 'which YHWH your god allotted—them'. Because the relative clause is not adjacent to its antecedent, the pronoun *ʾotam* is added. The legitimacy this verse grants—as it were—to the worship of celestial bodies on the part of the gentiles posed a problem for the rabbis (cf. *sipre* to Deut 17:3). This is

also reflected in *Tg. Ps.-J.*: *dplyg Y. ʾlhkwn bhwn dʿthwn dkl ʿmmyʾ* 'regarding which Y. your God caused differences of opinion among all nations'. Hebrew: *ḥlq* is here understood not as 'allotted' but as 'divided', 'caused differences of opinion among'. According to a rabbinic tradition *(Mek. Exod* 12:40, *b. Meg.* 9a), the translators of the LXX rendered here, "these the Lord your God allotted to *give light to* all nations." There is no hint of such a translation in early Greek manuscripts, however. See Geiger 1857, pp. 444ff. Only later Greek translators like Symmachus render *ḥlq* with *diakosmein* 'to divide', like the Targum.

20. *YHWH.* LXX: *ho theos* 'God'.

21. *on your account.* Hebrew: *ʿal dibreykem,* literally, 'on your words'. The LXX and Vg translate literally "because of words said by you."

the Jordan. Most LXX manuscripts and Peshitta translate here and in the following verse *"this* Jordan." Compare 3:27.

nor enter. On the syntax of the Hebrew, cf. 17:20.

good. This word is omitted in most LXX manuscripts and in *Tg. Ps.-J.* In *Tg. Neof.*, it is added in the margin.

23. *against which YHWH your God has enjoined you.* "Against" is missing in the Hebrew and must be understood from the context. Compare 2:37. *Tg. Ps.-J.* adds *dlʾ lmʿbd* '[which the Lord your God has enjoined you] not to make'.

24. *consuming fire. Tg. Ps.-J.*: fire devouring fire *(ʾšʾ ʾklh ʾšʾ);* cf. *Tg. Ps.-J.* to Exod 24:17 and Gen 38:25; and see the TEXTUAL NOTE for 9:3.

26. *soon.* This is omitted in the LXX here, as in 9:3 and 9:16.

28. *gods.* LXX, Peshitta, and *Tg. Neof.* margin: "other gods."

29. *But if you search.* The MT has *ubiqqaštem,* the plural, though the rest of the verse is in the singular. The Samaritan Pentateuch and many versions read the singular here as well. The MT can be accounted for by viewing the *mem* at the end of *ubiqqaštem* as a dittography of the following *miššām.*

30. *When you are in distress . . . shall befall you.* Hebrew: *baṣṣar lĕka umĕṣaʾuka.* According to Driver 1902, ad loc., *baṣṣar* is the infinitive construct of *ṣrr,* to be pointed *bᵉṣar.* But the phrase *baṣṣar lᵉka* occurs a number of times, and the noun *ṣar* 'distress' is quite common. Hence *baṣṣar lᵉ* is apparently an idiomatic expression meaning 'when disaster strikes'. For the prepositive adverbial phrase separated from the rest of the sentence with *waw*- consecutive, see Blau 1977–82, §2:1:3. The Samaritan Pentateuch, followed by the LXX, divides the verses differently, reading, "[29]. . . if you seek him with all your heart and all your soul when you are in distress. [30]All these things will befall you in the end, and you will return."

in the end. According to the Masoretic punctuation and in accordance with the Hebrew syntax, this can be connected with the following phrase: *beʾaḥarit hayyamim wešabta* 'in the end you will return' (cf. Driver 1902, p. 74 n.; 6). Deuteronomy 31:29, however, which contains identical ideas (apostasy in the future, invoking heaven and earth as witnesses, distress in the end; cf. the

COMMENT), speaks explicitly about "the evil that will befall you in the end *(wqrʾt ʾtkm hrʿh bʾ ḥryt hymym),*" which proves that "in the end," in such a context, goes with the impending evil and not with the return.

32. *from* [Hebrew *lmn] the day . . . from one end of heaven* [Hebrew *lmqṣh hšmym].* The Hebrew preposition in both cases is the pleonastic *lĕmin(n),* a variant of *mi(n),* signifying terminus a quo, whether of time (cf. 9:7; 2 Sam 7:6, 11; Judg 19:30) or of space (cf. Judg 20:1; Mic 7:12; etc.).

33. *the voice of God.* The Samaritan Pentateuch, LXX, *Tg. Ps.-J.*, and *Tg. Neof.* all add "living" God; Hebrew: *ʾelohim ḥayyim,* as in 5:26.

and survived. Hebrew: *wayyeḥi;* the LXX, Vg, and Peshitta translate "and you survived," implying a Hebrew reading of *wateḥi.*

34. *has any god attempted.* Hebrew: *ʾô hanissah ʾelohim.* The Targumim, understanding "Did ever God attempt," were troubled by the use of the verb *nsy* 'attempt' with reference to the omnipotent God, and translated *ʾw nsyn (dy) ʿbd Y* 'or the miracles that YHWH performed' changing the verb *hanissah* into a late Hebrew noun *nsyn* 'miracles'. The Peshitta deals with the same problem by making God the object, rather than the subject, of *hanissah: ʾw nsyh lʾlhh* 'or did (anyone ever) tempt God'.

prodigious acts. Hebrew: *massôt,* from *nsy* 'to test'.

outstretched arm. The LXX's *en brachisni hypsēlā* 'with an uplifted arm' seems to be influenced by the Palestinian translators; cf. the Targumim: *ʾdrʿʾ mrmmʾ* (compare Peshitta: *drʿʾ ʾrmʾ).*

great terrors. Hebrew: *mwrʾym gdlym* was taken by the Samaritan Pentateuch, LXX, Peshitta and the Targumim as *mrʾym gdlm* 'great visions', LXX: *en horasmasin megalois,* Targumim: *hzwnyn rbrbyn.* All of this goes well with the midrashic Palestinian exegesis, which expounds Deut 26:8, *wbmrʾ gdl,* as "this is the revelation of the Shekhinah" *(Midr. Tanaaim,* ed. Hoffmann 1908, p. 173).

before your very eyes. MT: *leʿeyneyka* 'before your [sing.] eyes'. This is inconsistent with the rest of the verse, which is in the second-person *plural.* The LXX, which often deviates from the MT in the choice of pronouns, omits or changes the other pronouns in the verse, while the Samaritan text reads here the plural, *leʿ eyneykem,* followed by *Tgs. Onq.* and *Ps.-J.* and by the Peshitta.

35. *YHWH.* The LXX adds "your God."

37. *their offspring after them.* The MT has the singular, *bezarʿo aḥarayw* 'his offspring after him', but the Samaritan Pentateuch has *bezarʿam aḥareyhem* in the plural (cf. MT 10:15), and all versions translate thus, because of the exigencies of the sense. LXX: "he chose *you* their offspring after them."

by his own presence. Hebrew: *bepanayw,* literally, 'with his face/presence'. LXX: *autos* 'he himself'. *Targum Onqelos:* "with his word *(memreh).*" *Targum Pseudo-Jonathan:* "with his will *(reʿuteh).*"

38. *to bring you to their land and give it to you.* The Hebrew is, literally, "to bring you and give you their land."

NOTES

4:1–4. This section inculcates the obligation to observe the commandments of God. Scrupulous observance of the law, without the slightest deviation (v 2), will ensure life and inheritance of the land, in contrast to the ones who sinned with Baal-Peor just on the threshold of the promised land (cf. Num 25:1–5; Hos 9:10). In this way a link with 3:29 is created.

The motif of "life" serves as an *inclusio* for the unit of vv 1–4. "Life" embodied in observance of the law stands here in contrast to "death" symbolized by Baal-Peor and its worship; compare the choice offered in 30:15ff. between "life" involved in following God and "death" coming as a result of worshiping idols.

This verse that opens the sermon of chap. 4 overlaps its conclusion:

4:1	*4:40*
Now . . . listen to the laws and rules that I am teaching you to observe, so that you may live to enter and occupy the land that YHWH, the God of your fathers, is giving you.	Observe his laws and commandments, which I enjoin upon you this day, that it may go well with you . . . and that you may prolong your days in the land that YHWH your God is giving you.

1. *And now.* This word *(wʿth)* occurs frequently at the beginning of discourse and marks the transition from a story to the moral-religious lesson that is to be drawn from it. Compare "and now" in 10:12, which comes after the historical survey of 9:7–10:11, and see also Judg 9:16; 10:23, 25; 1 Sam 12:13; etc. This is also the term used to commence the body of a letter; cf. Weinfeld 1972a, p. 175.

o Israel, listen [or hear]. The phrase *Shemʿa Israel,* "Hear, o Israel" (here *Israel Shemaʿ,* because of the preceding "and now") is characteristic of the beginning of a didactic address (cf. 5:1; 6:4; 9:1; 20:3; 27:9); compare "Hear, o my son" in the teacher's address to his pupil in the book of Proverbs (1:8; 4:10; 23:19; compare 8:33). In the psalm referring to the Sinai revelation we find similarly, "Hear, o my People" (50:7; 81:9). A slight distinction, however, should be made between *Shemaʿ* with a vocative as an opening address without an object, like Deut 6:4; 9:1; 20:3; 27:9, and *Shemaʿ* with an object (the commandments), like Deut 4:1 (with *ʾel)* and 5:1 (with *ʾet).* The same applies to the book of Proverbs, where a distinction should be made between 8:33; 23:20 (compare Ps 34:12) and 1:8; 4:10; etc.

that I am teaching you to observe. The verb *lmd* 'to teach' occurs here for the first time in the Pentateuch and is very characteristic of the book of Deuteronomy, which possesses a strong didactic tone; cf. vv 9–10; 6:2, 7, 20ff.; 11:19; 31:12–13, 19, 22. According to the book of Deuteronomy, Moses was commanded *to teach* Israel the laws that were imparted to him by God after the Sinai revelation (see vv 13–14; compare 5:19, 28). Only after forty years of wanderings did he do this to the generation that was about to enter the land of Canaan. Moses is thus considered the first great teacher of Israel. In the synagogues of the Second Temple period we indeed find "the chair of Moses" (Matt 23:2; compare *Pesiq. Rab Kah.* 1:7 [Mandelbaum, p. 12], and cf. also the "chair of Moses *(qtdr' dMšh)*" discovered in various ancient synagogues (see Sukenik 1929, pp. 145f.) designating the place of the teacher and preacher.

and occupy the land. The motif of possessing land as reward for proper behavior is also found in wisdom literature (cf., e.g., Ps 37:11, 22, 29, 34; Prov 2:21–22; 10:30), but there it is individualistic while in Deuteronomy it has assumed a national cast (see Weinfeld 1972a, pp. 313–16).

2. *You shall not add anything . . . or take anything away from it.* Compare 13:1. This kind of warning has its proper place either at the beginning of a divine work, as here, where it opens Moses' exhortation about the observance of the law, or at the end of a work, as in Rev 22:18–19; compare also the warning at the beginning of the prophecy of Jeremiah in Jer 26:2. In 13:1 the warning does not apply to all of the commandments but to the specific injunction about imitating pagan worship; cf. 12:29–31 (see the NOTES there).

Identical warnings are found in wisdom literature concerning the completeness of God's work (Eccl 3:14; Prov 30:5–6; these may have some affinities to Deut 4:2; see Weinfeld 1972, pp. 260–65) and are also attested in treaty literature of the ancient Near East (cf., e.g., Güterbock 1960, pp. 59–60:7ff., "To this tablet I did not add a word nor did I take one out"), as well as in ancient Greek treaties (cf. Bengtson 1962–69, see indexes); compare 1 Macc 8:30 (the treaty of Judas Maccabeus with the Romans). Similarly, we find this formula in Mesopotamian literature concerning prophecy: "He [the deity] revealed to him in the night, and when he spoke in the morning, he did not leave out a single line, nor did he add one to it" (Cagni 1969, 5:43–44), which reminds us of the warning to Jeremiah before the reciting of the prophecy: "Do not leave out a word" (Jer 26:2).

in order to keep the commandments. Literally, "to keep the commandments" *(lišemor* = infinitive construction); compare v 5, *laʿăśôt* 'that you should do'. This sort of asyndetic syntax has caused difficulties for translators ancient and modern; see the TEXTUAL NOTE.

3. *You saw with your own eyes.* See 3:21 and the NOTE there.

what YHWH did at Baal-Peor. Compare Num 25:1–5. Baal-Peor here seems to be a locality; compare Hos 9:10, "they came to Baal-Peor." For various places named after the Baal located in them, compare the places Baal Gad, Baal

Zephon, Baal Meon, and Baal Tamar. The people before whom Moses delivers his farewell address were standing in front of Beth-Peor (3:29), the place in which the tribes of Israel, for the first time, came into contact with the local pagan worship (cf. Hos 9:10). This was then an ideal opportunity to juxtapose the true worship of God with the false worship of Peor.

from among you [sing.]. LXX, Syriac: from among *you* in plural, harmonization with next verse; but this diminishes the strength of the contrast, cf. the COMMENT below and INTRODUCTION above concerning singular and plural.

4. *But you who held fast to YHWH your God.* Rejecting the temptation of pagan worship. The danger of imitating pagan worship is clearly expressed in 12:30–31 and is followed there, as in our passage, by the command not to add anything to the law and not to subtract from it (13:1). It is possible that the proximity of the exhortation about Baal-Peor to the injunction about not adding and not subtracting (v 2) was also motivated by the temptation to imitate foreign worship.

"Holding *(dbq)* fast to YHWH" creates a contrast with *following (hlk ʾḥr)* Baal-Peor (v 3); compare 13:15, "You will *follow* YHWH your God . . . and *hold fast (dbq)* to him."

5–8. This passage starts with "See" in parallel to "listen" of the preceding one. It has the inclusive framework starting with "laws and rules" and concluding with them *(ḥqym wmšpṭym).* The beginning of v 5 corresponds to the beginning of the former passage (v 1): "listen to the laws and rules that I am teaching you to observe, so that you may live to enter and occupy the land" (v 1); "See, I am teaching you laws and rules . . . for you to observe within the land that you are about to invade and occupy" (v 5). This pericope serves as a kind of motivation for observing the law by showing the superiority of the law of Israel. The unique laws are intertwined with the uniqueness of the God of Israel and the uniqueness of Israel: a great nation that has an extraordinary God (close to his nation) and extraordinary laws. Compare the parallel statements—in the form of questions, as here—in the epilogue of the sermon (vv 32–34).

5. *See, I am teaching you laws and rules.* The tense here is past, which has raised serious questions among the commentators, and especially so because in this very context Moses says that he is teaching the people now (v 1) and not in the past. Steuernagel in his commentary (1923) even suggested that this verse actually belongs to the concluding section of Deuteronomy. Nevertheless, the truth is that in the Semitic languages, when one makes a formal declaration, one uses the finite verb, though the declaration pertains to the present or future and not to the past. Thus 1:8 reads, literally, "See, I *placed* the land at your disposal," but it actually means, "I *hereby place* the land at your disposal"; cf. the NOTE there. Such formal declarations styled in the perfect tense are mostly accompanied by "see *(rʾh)*" or "behold *(hnh)*"; cf. Gen 1:29; 41:41; 47:23; Deut 2:31; 30:15; etc.

According to Deuteronomy, Moses received the law at Sinai (5:28) but delivered it to the people only in the plains of Moab before their entrance into the promised land (4:1; 6:1; 12:1ff.).

6. *Observe them carefully.* Literally, "observe and do *(šmr wʿśh)"*; see also 7:12; 16:12; 26:16; 28:13; compare "observe to do *(šmr lʿśwt)*" in 5:1, 29; 6:3, 25; etc. The priestly code uses the pair *"remember* and do *(zkr wʿśh)"*; see Num 15:39, 40 and compare Esth 9:28 *(nzkrym wnʿśym). šmr* interchanges with *zkr,* as for example in the Decalogue, Exod 20:8, *zkr* versus Deut 5:12, *šmr* (see the NOTES to Deut 5). Compare especially Gen 37:11, "and his father kept *(šmr)* the matter" (in mind), which means, "held in memory" *(zkr).*"

for that will be proof of your wisdom . . . to other peoples. Observance of such laws shows Israel's wisdom, which will be admired by the nations. This verse brings to expression the connection between Torah and wisdom, which is so characteristic of Deuteronomy (cf. the INTRODUCTION, §16). In the Second Temple period, Torah was even identified with wisdom; see Ben Sira 24. For the unique phenomenon in the revelation of the law to Israel, see Ps 147:19–20, "He issued his commands to Jacob, his laws and rules to Israel. He did not do so for any other nation, of such rules they knew nothing."

Surely, that great nation is a wise and discerning people. "Great nation" here is intended in the spiritual sense, in contrast to the old concept of "great nation," which signifies the political greatness of Israel, as, e.g., Gen 12:2; 17:5–6, 16; 18:18; 28:14; 35:1; 46:3 (Deut 26:5 draws on the old tradition of Exod 1). According to Deut 7:7, politically speaking, Israel is the smallest of all the peoples.

7. *that has a god so close at hand as is YHWH our God whenever we call on him.* Compare 1 Kgs 8:52, Ps 145:18. By way of association the author adds two more arguments for the uniqueness of Israel: the proximity to its God, and the righteousness of the laws.

8. *laws and rules as just as all of this teaching.* The Mesopotamian kings boasted that by their profound wisdom they established "just laws *(dīnāt mīšarim)"*; cf. the Code of Hammurabi 4:9–10; 24:1–5, 26–31. It is not impossible that by using the exceptional expression "just laws *(mišpaṭim ṣaddiqim)*" the author of Deuteronomy employs a polemical note against the Hammurabi Code. This code was well known and copied in the schools of the ancient Near East for a thousand years. Thus, in opposition to "the wise" Babylonian king who established, as it were, "just laws," Deuteronomy takes pride in the "just laws" observed by "the wise" and discerning people of Israel.

9–14. *The revelation of Sinai and its implications.* The people are warned not to forget the Sinaitic covenant and not to be lured into idolatry by shaping images and worshiping them because they saw no form at the revelation. They should always remember the revelation and the covenant engraved on the two tablets.

9. *take utmost care and watch yourselves* [literally, *your soul] scrupulously so*

that you do not forget the things that you saw. Forgetting the revelation at Sinai is like renunciation of the soul, that is, denial of the very existence of the nation.

that you saw with your own eyes. The nation and all of its generations are conceived here as one personality. Moses is here addressing the people as if all of them would have been present at Mount Sinai, though most of them were born after the event there (see 1:35f.; 2:16; and compare the midrashim in L. Ginsberg 1959, XI, 222).

make them known to your children and to your children's children. Because the memory of the revelation is crucial for national existence, it is most important that it should be perpetuated throughout generations. Compare 6:7, 20f.; 11:19; 31:13; 32:46.

10. *when you stood* (literally, *the day you stood*) *before YHWH.* This phrase explains the situation implied in "the things that you saw" of the previous sentence. "*Standing* before the Lord" at Sinai is the origin of the existentialistic concept in Judaism: *maʿmād har Sīnaî* 'the scene of Mount Sinai', which was understood as a collective experience of Israel bequeathed to all coming generations. Every Israelite is committed to God's rules because he was sworn to them from Mount Sinai (cf. *m. Šebu.* 3:6), and just as the Israelites were cleansed before the revelation at Sinai (Exod 19:10, 15), so are they to be clean when they read the words of Torah. Compare *Tg. Ps.-J.* to this verse: "You will clean yourself when you are engaged in it [in the Torah] as on the day that you stood before God . . . at Horeb." This corresponds to the dictum of Rabbi Yehoshua, the son of Levi (third century C.E.), that a man with pollution *(baʿl Qerī)* is not allowed to read Torah, just as those of the Sinai generation were not admitted to the Assembly when unclean (*b. Qidd.* 21b). The term *maʿamād har Sīnaî* occurs in the midrashic literature (*Midr. ha-gadol* to Deuteronomy ad loc. [Fish 1972, p. 79, line 15]) and became prevalent in the medieval literature. On the connection between Deut 4:1–40 and the Sinai description in chap. 5, as well as on the centrality of Sinaitic experience in Deut 4, see Toeg 1977, pp. 131–36.

Gather the people to me that I may let them hear my words. Deuteronomy describes the revelation at Sinai as a covenant gathering in which all segments of population participate (cf. 29:9ff.). Compare the covenant assemblies in the ancient Near East (see Introd. sec. 4). The day of the revelation is therefore named "the day of the Assembly" (cf. the LXX here and MT in 9:10; 10:4; 18:16). In the Second Temple period, the Pentecost Festival, which commemorated the Sinai revelation, was indeed called *ʿaṣeret* (cf. Josephus Antiquities 3:252), which means 'assembly' or 'solemn gathering'.

so that they may learn to revere me. Literally, "to fear me." This sounds like an echo of Exod 20:20(17): "God has come to test you [or, let you experience], so that the fear of him may be ever with you." The experience of the dramatic encounter with God at Sinai will implant, in the people of Israel, fear of God forever. The interchange of the verbs *nsh* 'test' found in Exod 20:20 with *lmd* 'learn' or 'experience' found in Deut 4:10 is clearly attested in Judg 3:1–2, "These are the nations that YHWH left in order to test/experience *(nsh)* the Israelites who had not known the battles of Canaan so that succeeding generations of the Israelites might learn/experience *(lmd)* war"; cf. Greenberg 1960.

they live on earth. Compare Weinfeld 1972a, p. 358.

and may so teach their children. Compare the end of v 9: "make them known to your children and to your children's children." The perpetuation of the covenant by teaching the future generations, which is also expressed in 6:2–3, 7; 11:19; 31:12–13; and 32:46, is a characteristic feature of covenant formulations in the ancient Near East. Thus we read, for example, in the treaty of Esarhaddon, king of Assyria, with his vassals (672 B.C.E.), "[you swear] that you inform and give orders to your sons, grandsons . . . saying: 'Keep this treaty . . . lest you lose your lives and deliver your land to destruction and your people to be deported' " *(VTE* 11.288ff.)

This quotation is especially close to Deut 4:9, which contains, besides the injunction to teach the children and the children's children, the warning to take utmost care in this matter and to guard one's soul not to neglect the words of the covenant (compare also v 23). The punishment of exile and loss of the land appears later in chap. 4 in a manner similar to the quoted passage from the Esarhaddon treaty: "Take care, then, not to forget the covenant . . . not to make for yourselves a sculpted image. . . . you shall soon perish from the land. . . . YHWH will scatter you among the nations" (vv 23ff.).

11. *You came near and stood at the foot of the mountain.* Compare Exod 19:17.

The mountain was ablaze with fire . . . there was darkness, cloud, and thick mist. Compare Exod 19:18; 20:18; 21:61; but lightning and the sound of the trumpet are not mentioned here.

12. *you heard the sound of words but perceived no shape.* In contrast to Exod 19:21, where the people are warned not to break through *to gaze* (compare Exod 24:10), according to Deuteronomy there was nothing to see: God revealed himself by sound of words only. This served for the author as the basis of the prohibition of physical representation of the Deity (vv 15ff.). The development of this notion seems to be based on Exod 20:22–23 (19–20), where we find the juxtaposition of speaking from heaven (v 22) and the prohibition of idols (v 23). The juxtaposition of the two ideas in Exod 20:22–23 may have given rise to the view that they belong together and that there was a genuine connection between them: because God spoke from heaven and no image of him was seen, there is no legitimacy for making any image of him (cf. Toeg 1977, pp. 89–90).

13. *his covenant, which he commanded you to observe.* The covenant here is a commitment by oath; compare the hendiadys *bĕrīt wĕʾālh* (Gen 26:23; Deut 29:11, 13, 20; Ezek 16:59; 17:18), which equals Akkadian *riksu u māmītu* 'bond

and oath'. Therefore, one can command an oath/covenant that means to impose; see also Judg 2:20; Ps 111:9; and cf. Weinfeld 1973d, 1.784.

the Ten Commandments. Here in 10:4 it is for the first time explicitly stated that the tablets of the covenant contained the Ten Commandments given at the Sinai revelation and enumerated in chap. 5. In Exod 34:28, it is not altogether clear that the "ten words" refer to the Decalogue and not to the preceding rules in 34:17–26. At the same time, it is made clear that the covenant at Sinai consisted only of the Ten Commandments. This is in harmony with the Deuteronomic view that only the Decalogue was proclaimed at Sinai, while the other laws were not given to Israel until they had come to the plains of Moab, and that a covenant based on them was established there supplemental to the covenant at Horeb (28:69).

two tablets of stone. Compare 9:10; 10:4.

14. *At the same time YHWH commanded me to teach you the laws.* These are the laws he is now about to impart; see v 5 and compare 5:28 with 6:1.

15–22. This passage constitutes a warning against idolatry and looks like an elaboration of the second commandment of the Decalogue. The prohibition of idolatry is motivated by the fact that the revelation at Sinai was achieved without the appearance of the divine person or the use of any image; astral worship was assigned to the nations while Israel's sole object of worship was YHWH himself.

15. *be most careful, for you saw no shape.* This resumes v 12 after the digression of vv 13–14, which described the contents of the revelation.

16. *a sculpted image in any likeness whatever.* Literally, "of any figure of a statue." To strengthen the prohibition, the author accumulates a whole series of terms associated with iconolatry—*psl, tmwnh, sml, tbnyt*—and forms out of them a chain of synonyms in the construct state. Thus, whereas the Decalogue in Exodus has image *(psl)* next to the figure *(tmwnh)* in 20:4, the Decalogue in Deuteronomy forms out of them two expressions of construct state: "a carved image of any figure" (5:8; compare 4:23, 25); in the present verse a third word, *sml* 'statue', is added and a triple construct is formed: literally, "a sculpted image of a figure of any statue." This is further explicated by what follows: "the form of a man or a woman . . . beast . . . bird," and so on. This exhaustive listing of iconography expresses undoubtedly the rigoristic approach of the Deuteronomic school toward idolatrous practices of any sort. The Deuteronomic prohibition of stone pillars and wooden poles in the worship of God (16:21–22) expresses the same rigoristic attitude to pagan symbols; compare the expression *psl kl tmwnh* 'a carved image *of any figure*' (5:8; 4:23, 25) with *ʾšrh kl ʿṣ* 'a sacred post *of any kind of wood*' in 16:21.

17–18. *the form of any beast on earth . . . winged bird . . . in the sky . . . any fish . . . in the waters below the earth.* The tripartite cosmic division —sky, earth, the subterranean waters—in connection with pagan iconography, is taken from the second commandment, "you shall not make for yourself a carved image, any likeness of what is *in the heavens above,* or *on the earth below,* or *in the waters below the earth*" (5:8 = Exod 20:4). The species of these spheres are here elaborated in detail. Mark the rhetoric here: repetition of the word "form" five times. The vocabulary in vv 16–18 is characteristic of the priestly literature in the Pentateuch: *zkr nqbh, ṣpwr knp,* and *rmś.*

19. *when you look up into the sky . . . you must not be lured.* The temptation to worship the sun and moon in the ancient world was great. The beauty of the heavenly bodies appealed very much to ancient man, hence the expressions, "to look up . . . and be lured." Compare Job 31:26–27, "if ever I saw the light shining the moon on its course in full glory . . . and my heart was secretly enticed and my hand kissed the mouth." Astral worship was very common in the Assyrian and Babylonian culture and was widespread in Judah during the eighth and seventh centuries B.C.E. (2 Kgs 21:3, 5; 23:4, 5, 12; etc.). The worship took place mostly on the roofs of the houses (Jer 19:13; Zeph 1:5; 2 Kgs 23:12); cf. Weinfeld 1972b, pp. 149–54.

YHWH your God allotted to the other peoples. The heavenly bodies as objects of worship were assigned to the nations by God himself. The stars were considered divine beings *(bny ʾlhym/ʾlym,* literally, 'the sons of God'). See, e.g., Job 38:7, where the morning stars parallel the divine beings *(bny ʾlhym),* and compare in Ugarit: "the sons of El / the assembly of the stars" *(bn ʾil / pḫr kkbm) (CTA* 10.1.3–4). These were put in charge of the nations; only Israel remained under the direct aegis of YHWH. The same notion is clearly expressed in Deut 32:8–9, where Elyon is said to have set divisions and boundaries of nations according to the number of the *bny ʾl* 'divine beings' (read with the LXX and the Qumran version), leaving Israel as the "portion *(ḥlq)*" and "allotment *(nḥlh)*" of YHWH; compare Jer 10:16 = 51:19. Israel's allotment, in contrast to that of the other nations, is expressed in the next verse (v 20), where Israel is the people of YHWH's "inheritance" *(ʿm nḥlh).* We find then here the terms *ḥlq* and *nḥlh,* as in Deut 32:9 and in Jer 10:16; 51:19.

This view about the "sons of God" being in charge of the nations has been criticized in the OT itself. Thus we read in Ps 82 about God standing in the assembly of gods *(ʿdt ʾl = pḫr ʾlm* in Ugarit) and judging the "sons of God" and "the sons of Elyon" who are in charge of the nations. God is disappointed by the judgment of the "sons of God" on earth and decides to dismiss them from their positions: "I thought you are gods, sons of Elyon, yet you shall die as men and like the [fallen] princes *[nplym;* cf. Gen 6:1–4] you shall fall. Arise, O God, and judge the earth for you will inherit all the nations" (vv 6–8). The view that the nations are subject to the divine beings (in other words, angels) was very common in the Second Temple period. Thus we read in the book of Jubilees: "he has many peoples . . . and he made them ruled by spirits . . . and Israel was not ruled by any spirit or angel, he himself rules them" (15:31–32). The spirits and the angels were later called princes *(śrym),* as we read in Ben Sira: "for every nation he raised a prince but the portion of YHWH is Israel (alone)"

(17:17); compare in Daniel "the prince of the Kingdom of Persia" (10:13) and "the prince of Greece" (10:20).

20. *But you did YHWH take and bring out of Egypt.* In contrast to the pagan nations, Israel was taken (that is, elected) and redeemed by God himself and chosen as his peculiar possession.

the iron blast furnace. Compare 1 Kgs 8:51 and Jer 11:4, figuratively of the very hard work in Egypt, "the house of bondage" (5:6; 6:12; 8:14; 13:11). Compare the Egyptian description of the smith: "I have seen the smith at work at the opening of his furnace, with fingers like claws of a crocodile" (Lichtheim 1973–76, 1.186). See also Ben Sira 38:28, "So it is with the smith, sitting by his anvil, intent on his iron-work, the smoke of the fire shrivels his flesh, *as he wrestles in the heat of the furnace,*" and compare Isa 48:10, "furnace of affliction." For another description of the hard labor in Egypt, see Ps 81:7, "I relieved his shoulder of the *burden* his hands were freed from the basket."

to be his very own people. Literally, "to be for him a people of inheritance," which is tantamount to "treasured people *(ʿm sglh)*" in 7:6; 14:2; and 26:18.

21–22. These two verses serve as a connecting link with the next section. The death of Moses in Transjordan is inevitable, and there exists the danger that after his death the Israelites will forget the covenant with God and will worship idols, a fear expressed explicitly in Deut 31:16–22 (see the COMMENT below). The worship of foreign gods will of course bring punishment, namely, exile, which is described in vv 25–31.

21. *Now, YHWH was angry with me on your account.* See 1:37; 3:26.

23–31. *Exile and return.* This passage, which may be seen as the pivot of the sermon (see the COMMENT below), reflects the situation of the addressed audience. The people experienced the punishment of exile, following which they confessed their sins and therefore were given hope for the renewal of the patriarchal covenant, which means return to the land (compare 30:1–10).

The passage reveals an interesting antithetical structure. It opens with the idea of the people *forgetting their covenant* with God (v 23) but concludes with the idea that God will *not forget his covenant* with the Patriarchs (v 31). The God who is impassionate *(qannāʾ)* because of the sin of the people (v 24) turns into a compassionate God *(ʾēl raḥûm)* after Israeli repentance (v 31). The people act in a *destructive* manner *(hšḥt,* v 25) but God will *not destroy* them (v 31). The punishment of Israel is also described in an antithetical manner. In contrast to the multiplication of the Israelites in the past (v 25), few will be left in the future among the nations (v 27); unlike the past, when they took roots in the land and were well established in it (v 25), they will be eradicated from the land in the future and perish quickly *(mhr)* from it (v 26).

There is also a clear contrast in the presentation of the foreign gods as opposed to the God of Israel. The foreign gods are impotent, "they cannot see or hear," etc. (v 28). On the contrary, the God of Israel is omnipotent; he is also compassionate and cares for the people by fulfilling his commitment (v 31; cf.

Braulik 1978, pp. 59–60). For antithetical structure in biblical poetry, see Krašovec 1984.

23. *which YHWH your God has enjoined you.* About which you were commanded; compare 2:37.

24. *For YHWH . . . is a consuming fire, an impassioned* (literally, *jealous) God.* The root *qnʾ* denotes not only jealousy but also zeal ("jealousy" in English is derived from Latin *zelus)* and means intolerance of rivalry or unfaithfulness; cf. Exod 34:14; Deut 6:14–15; etc. For the fire of passion/jealousy, cf. Ezek 36:5; Zeph 1:8; 3:8; Ps 79:5; and note Deut 32:21–22, where the fire of God flares after being moved to jealousy *(qnʾh).*

The juxtaposition of idol worship in v 23 with the notion of the impassioned God *(ʾēl qannāʾ)* seems to indicate that the author was influenced by the Decalogue, where the prohibition of idol worship is reasoned by the statement that YHWH is an impassioned God *(ʾēl qannāʾ).*

The "consuming fire" also seems to refer us to the "fire" that represents God at the Sinai revelation (vv 11, 36); compare 9:3 and Exod 24:17, "as a consuming fire on the top of the mountain."

25. *when you have begotten children . . . and are long established in the land, act destructively.* The possession of the land for a long time creates a sense of self-confidence that causes the forgetting of the Lord. Compare 6:10–12; 8:11ff.; 32:13ff.

are long established. Literally, "are grown old *(wnwšntm).*"

a sculpted image in any likeness. See the NOTE to v 16.

causing . . . displeasure and vexation. hkʿs, literally, 'provoking', an expression frequently used in Deuteronomic literature in the context of apostasy.

26. *I call heaven and earth . . . to witness.* Heaven and earth, which endure forever, will testify in the future that God warned the people about the consequence of disobedience. Compare 30:19; 31:28; see also 32:1; Isa 1:2. For the use of the perfect tense of the verb *hʿyd* 'testify' here, see the NOTE to v 5 above. The LXX indeed translates the verb in the present.

this day. A legal formula that accompanies a declaration of judicial nature; see note to 26:17f.

27. *among the nations to which YHWH will drive you.* The author of Deuteronomy avoids the use of the verb *glh* 'exile', which is expected here and is widely used in the historical and prophetic literature since Amos (1:6, 9; 5:27). He uses instead less specific terms such as *nhg* 'lead away', compare 28:37, Gen 31:26; or *ndḥ* 'banish'. Mass deportation was introduced by the neo-Assyrian Empire in the ninth century B.C.E. (cf. Oded 1979). The Israelites experienced it for the first time in 734 B.C.E., when Tiglath Pileser deported the inhabitants of Transjordan and Galilee to Assyria (2 Kgs 15:29). Since then the territories of Israel and Judah were often threatened by exile. It seems that the usage of the

term *glh/glwt* 'exile' in a speech by Moses would sound anachronistic and therefore was circumvented by the author.

28. *There you will serve manmade gods.* See also 28:36, 64. Banishment from God's land meant cessation of his worship and serving of foreign gods; see 1 Sam 26:19, "for they have driven me out today so that I cannot have a share in YHWH's inheritance but am told: 'Go and worship other gods!' " and Hos 9:3–5, "they shall not dwell in YHWH's land, they shall pour out no wine to YHWH, they shall not bring their sacrifice to him . . . what will you do about feast days, about the festivals of YHWH?" Subjugation to a foreign power in juxtaposition with idol worship is also found in Jeremiah: "Because you forsook me and served alien gods on your own land, you will have to serve foreigners in a land not your own" (5:16; compare 16:13; 30:8–9). This was actually the basis of the zealot's resistance to serving the Roman Empire at the end of the Second Temple period, the so-called "fourth philosophy" described by Josephus (Antiquities 18:21–25; Wars 2:118).

The Targumim *(Tg. Onq.* and *Tg. Ps.-J.)* indeed translate this verse, "you will serve there the worshipers of the idols," and in 28:36, 64, *Tg. Ps.-J.* even specifies more: "you will raise taxes to the worshipers of idols." Compare, for this idea, *Midr. Lev Rab.* ed Margaliot, 1953–60, pp. 768–69 33:6, "Nebuchadnezzar told them [to Shadrach, Meishach, and Abed Neg, Dan 3:1–12]: 'Hasn't Moses written about you in the Torah, and you will serve their manmade gods' [Deut 4:28], they said to him: 'my Lord king, not to bow down but to serve with taxes.' "

gods of wood and stone, that cannot see or hear or eat or smell. Sarcasm about manmade idols is found in the Pentateuch only in Deuteronomy (27:15; 28:36, 64; 29:16; 31:29) but is very common in the prophetic literature (Hos 4:12; 8:6; 13:2; 14:4; Isa 2:8; Mic 5:12) and especially in Deutero-Isaiah (40:19f.; 41:7; 44:9–20; 46:6f.). For the senselessness of the idols, compare Pss 115:5–7; 135:16–17.

29–31. The conversion of the people in exile occurs again at the conclusion of the book, at 30:1–10 (see the COMMENT below), and appears likewise in the concluding chapter of the holiness code in Lev 26:40ff. The latter, however, does not speak about "return" but about the people's confession of their sins (in the land of their enemies). In Leviticus, as in our passage, the covenant, with the fathers as a token of God's favor (see below), is mentioned. For the idea of conversion in exile, see especially 1 Kgs 8:47ff.; Jer 29:12ff. The latter passages are phrased in a language identical with that of Deut 4:29f. and Deut 30:1ff. (see the COMMENT below).

It is commonly believed that all of these passages were written under the impact of the exile of Judah, which seems plausible. One must admit, however, that the idea of conversion in exile started to crystallize in northern Israel and is reflected in Hosea (see the COMMENT below).

29. *if you search there.* Literally, "from there." The prayers pass to God, as it

were, through his land; compare 1 Kgs 8:48, "and they turn back to you with all their heart and soul . . . and they pray to you *in the direction of their land.*" Compare also Jer 29:13.

you will find him. Compare Isa 55:6; 65:1; Jer 29:13; 1 Chr 28:9; 2 Chr 15:2, 4.

if only you seek him with all your heart and soul. Deuteronomy demands utmost devotion to God (see 6:5; 11:13; etc.), hence only sincere and wholehearted "return" will be accepted by God. Compare 1 Kgs 8:48, quoted above, and Jer 29:13.

30. *When you are in distress . . . return to YHWH.* Compare Hos 5:15–6:1, "when they are in distress they will seek me . . . come let us return!" The idea of "return" appears, as indicated above, in the epilogue of the book (30:2) and was a common motif in the prophetic literature (Hos 6:1; 14:2–3; Amos 4:6ff.; etc.). "Return" or "repentance" *(tĕšûbāh)* became one of the pillars of Rabbinic theology, and the concept continues to play a central role in Judaism (cf. Urbach 1975).

in the end. Literally, "in the coming days *(bʾḥryt hymym)*" *(ʾḥr* means 'next, latter;' see, e.g., Gen 33:2; and compare *ywm ʾḥrwn* in Ps 48:14 and *dwr ʾḥrwn* in Ps 78:4, which mean 'future day' and 'future generation', respectively). The "coming days" or "latter days" denote then the future period, the distance of which varies with the context. In Gen 49:1 it refers to Israel's settlement in Canaan; in Num 24:14 it refers to the future conquest of Moab and Edom; while in Deut 31:29 it denotes the period of rebellion after Moses' death.

31. *For YHWH your God is a compassionate God.* Accepting the repentant without punishing him for his sins is a matter of divine grace.

he will not forget the covenant . . . with your fathers. God shows his grace to the sinners of Israel by virtue of his promise to the Patriarchs of Israel. Compare Moses' prayer after the sin of the golden calf: "Give thought to your servants Abraham, Isaac, and Jacob, and pay no heed to the stubbornness of this people" (9:27; cf. Exod 32:13; Lev 26:42, 45). In rabbinic literature, this turned into the doctrine of "Merit of the Fathers *(zĕkhût Ābôt),*" which implies the benefit granted to Israel by virtue of the righteousness of its ancestors and the ensuing promise to them. For the righteousness of the Patriarchs, which motivated God's promise, see Gen 15:6–7; 22:16, 18; 26:5.

that he made by oath with your fathers. The oath of God with the Patriarchs of Israel was an unconditional promise, a covenant of grace *(hbryt whḥsd;* see 7:9, 12) and therefore could be invoked even in the time of sin (for the nature of the covenant with the Patriarchs, see Weinfeld 1970–72).

32–40. Verse 32 resumes the topic of Israel's uniqueness, dealt with in vv 5–20, and elaborates the notion of uniqueness stressing the extraordinary phenomenon of a God choosing a people by means of redemption and revelation. This serves the purpose of deepening the monotheistic belief (v 39) and encouraging of the observance of God's laws (v 40). The passage bears the character of a faith declaration, which is indeed reflected in the Jewish liturgy, as shown in the COMMENT below.

The religious motifs embodied here and in two other passages of similar nature in the prologue of Deuteronomy, namely, 7:6–11 and 10:12–11:19, are

1. God's love of Israel and its election (v 37; compare 7:7–8; 10:15),
2. the redemption from Egypt (v 34; compare 7:8, 15; 11:2–4),
3. the revelation at Sinai (vv 33, 35–36),
4. God's unity (vv 35, 39; compare 7:9; 10:14, 17), and
5. observance of the Law (v 40; compare 7:11–12; 10:13; 11:1, 8).

These motifs lie, in fact, at the basis of the Jewish liturgy. Thus the Shemaᶜ prayer (Deut 6:4f.), which was recited together with the Decalogue (Deut 5:6–18; cf. *M. Tamid* 5:1), is preceded by the benediction of *ʾAhabāh,* which centers around the idea of love of Israel by God and its election (cf. the conclusion of this benediction: "who has chosen his people Israel with love"). God's love and grace are being expressed by the fact that God gave Israel righteous laws, a concept reflected in Deut 4:8, as well as in Neh 9:13–14 and Ps 147:19 (see the COMMENT below); and note the blessing before the recital of the Torah, which combines election with giving the Torah (cf. Elbogen 1931, pp. 171–72). The benediction that follows *Shemaᶜ (Gĕʾûlāh, b. Ber.* 9b; *y.* 1.1, 2d) is dedicated to the redemption from Egypt. We find then in the Shemaᶜ liturgy all of the motifs found in the homiletic passages of Deuteronomy discussed here: love and election in connection with the law in the *ʾAhabāh* benediction, revelation and unity of God in the Decalogue and Shemaᶜ, and redemption in the *Gĕʾûlāh* benediction.

This pattern of election, revelation, law, unity of God, and redemption is clearly reflected in the prayer of Nehemiah (chap. 9), as shown in the COMMENT below. The liturgical pattern reflected in Deut 4 serves thus as a proper introduction to the Decalogue and the Shemaᶜ that follow in chaps. 5 and 6.

32. *to inquire about bygone ages.* Compare Job 8:8, "for inquire the past generation"; and see 32:7, "remember the days of old, consider the years of generations, ask your father and he will tell you, your elders, and they will say to you."

Has anything as grand as this ever happened. Israel felt its uniqueness not only by the possession of a particular and extraordinary series of just laws (vv 7–8) but also by the way these laws were revealed to the nation.

33. *Has any people heard the voice of God . . . and survived.* In other biblical sources we hear that no man can "see God and survive" (Gen 16:13; 32:31; Exod 33:20; Judg 6:22f.; 13:22). In Deuteronomy a shift is made from

seeing to *hearing* the voice of God. Compare 5:21–23, and see also the COMMENT to v 12.

34. *has any god attempted to go and take for himself one nation from the midst of another . . . by great terrors.* Compare 2 Sam 7:22–23, "What other nation is there on earth whom a god led to ransom as a people of his own . . . doing great and fearful deeds?" (see the COMMENT below).

After the description of the revelation comes the description of the redemption. The two events are inseparable. The redemption of the Israelites from Egypt coincides with the receiving of the law of God by revelation (27:9–10), and just as revelation was a unique phenomenon in history, so was the redemption from Egypt.

by prodigious acts, by signs and portents. This refers to the acts (plagues) performed by God in Egypt in order to move Pharaoh to free the people of Israel; compare 6:22.

by war. The divine war with the Egyptians at the Red Sea; see Exod 14:14; 15:3; and compare Deut 11:4 (cf. Childs 1967).

by a mighty hand and an outstretched arm. These two expressions, "mighty hand" and "outstretched arm," which appear separately in various sources, appear as a combination first in Deuteronomy (4:34; 5:15; 7:19; 11:2; 26:8) and then in the literature influenced by it (1 Kgs 8:42; Jer 32:21; Ezek 20:33, 34; Ps 136:12; cf. Weinfeld 1972, p. 329). The two expressions belong to Egyptian royal typology; see especially the references to the Egyptian king in the Amarna letters, as, for example, the letters of the king of Jerusalem, Abdi-Hepa, in which we find the "strong arm" *(zuruḥ dannu)* of the king (EA 286:12; 287:27; 288:14, 34). Similarly, we find in the Egyptian royal hymns the idiom "outstretched arm" *(pḏ ḏr.t;* cf. Gaballa 1969, p. 87, fig. 5A; Nelson 1932, vol. 2, pls. 18, 2 *(pdʿ)* and 28, 62 *(pd imn.t).* For the gesture of outstretched arm in Egyptian iconography concerning kings and gods, see Keel, 1974, pp. 158–60.

great terrors. Compare 26:8; 34:12. Compare also 10:21, where the two expressions appear as two separate adjectives: "those great and awesome [deeds] *(gdlt wnwrʾt).*" The LXX and the Targumim took *mwrʾ* here and in 26:8 and 34:12 as *mrʾh* from *rʾh* 'to see', and translated "visions" as related to the theophany at Sinai. See the TEXTUAL NOTE above.

35. *You have been shown.* This phrase refers to the following, that is to say, the revelation at Sinai.

to know. See the NOTE to v 39.

YHWH alone is God; there is none beside him. Affirmation of absolute monotheism is characteristic of Deuteronomy (v 39; 7:9; 10:17; cf. also 6:4) and 2 Isaiah (45:5, 6, 14, 18, 21, 22; 46:9). The phrase *ʾyn ʿwd* 'none else' is found only in chap. 4 (vv 35, 39) and in 2 Isaiah (cf. also the late passages in 1 Kgs 8:60; Joel 2:27), and it seems to be of late (Exilic) origin.

36. In contrast to the account about God's descent upon Mount Sinai in Exod 19 (vv 11, 20), according to the account here (see the NOTE to v 12), God

did not descend and did not show himself on the mount: only his fire was shown there, and out of it came his words, which were proclaimed from the heavens. The very two ideas—(1) God speaking from heaven and (2) the fire on the mountain, which was shown to the people—are already embedded in the heavy composite and variegated narrative cycle of the Sinai theophany in Exodus. (On the complexity of this cycle, see, e.g., Licht 1978.) The former is expressed in Exod 20:22(19): "You saw that I spoke to you from heaven," and Deut 4:36 is dependent on it and not vice versa, as argued by Nicholson (1977). For the dependence of Deut 4:36 on Exod 20:22(19), see Toeg 1977, pp. 134–35. The latter is found in Exod 24:17: "The glory of YHWH appeared in the sight of the Israelites as a consuming fire on the top of the mountain." The particular contribution of the author of Deut 4:1–40 is the synthesis of the various traditions and the explicit manner in which this outlook is presented, which is not found yet in Exodus. He combines the speaking from heaven with the fire on the mountain in order to advance his abstract notion of the revelation: neither did God descend upon the mountain nor did the Israelites see any image during the revelation, they only heard God's words from the fire (see Weinfeld 1972a, 206–8). The same kind of synthesis has been elaborated by the author in reference to the ideas of speaking from heaven and the prohibition of making images in Exod 20:22–23, as was indicated above. What appeared there as two separate statements has been combined by the author of Deut 4:1–40 (v 15): the prohibition of idols was motivated by the fact that God spoke from heaven, and thus no image of him was seen. By the same token, the darkness at revelation (v 11), which prevented the vision of the astral bodies, adds presumably a cause to the illegitimacy of astral worship (v 19).

Deuteronomy 4:36 helped the Rabbis to solve the contradiction between the tradition that grants God's descent upon Mount Sinai and the one that has God speaking out of heaven. Thus in *Mek. R. Ishmael,* Jethro §9 (Horowitz 1928, pp. 238–39), we read, "One passage says: 'I spoke with you from heaven' [Exod 20:22] and another passage says: 'YHWH descended upon Mount Sinai' [Exod 19:20], how can both passages be maintained? The matter is decided by the third scripture: 'Out of heaven he made you to hear his voice . . . and upon the earth he made you to see his great fire' [Deut 4:36]" (translation Lauterbach 1933, *Mek.* 2, pp. 275–76).

to instruct you. Compare Exod 20:20(17): "for God has come to test you in order that the fear of Him may be ever with you" and its parallel in Deut 4:10: "so that they may learn to revere me"; cf. the NOTE to v 10, above.

37. *Because he loved . . . he chose.* Compare 7:7–8, "YHWH . . . chose you . . . because of YHWH's love for you"; see also Jer 31:2, "I have loved you with eternal love, therefore I will extend my grace to you." Some commentators see vv 37–38 as a long protasis and vv 39–40 as apodosis: "because he loved your fathers *and* chose, etc. . . . know this day . . . and observe his laws."

he by his own presence (led you out of Egypt). Literally, "by his face." Compare Exod 33:14, *pny ylkw* 'I will go in person' and 2 Sam 17:11, *wpnyk hlkym* 'you shall go in person'. Especially instructive for the present purpose is Isa 63:9, "No messenger or angel but his own presence delivered them," reading with the LXX; and cf. *NEB* and *JPS* translations (note). The statement that God redeemed Israel in person comes to exclude the notion of a mediator, namely, an angel active, as it were, in the redemption of Israel, such as is found in Num 20:16, "he sent a messenger [angel] who freed us from Egypt" (cf. also Exod 23:20, 23; 33:2; and the COMMENT to chap. 7). The conception that there was no mediator in the act of liberating the Israelites from Egypt is most clearly expressed in the midrash on Deut 26:8, "And the Lord freed us from Egypt, not through an angel . . . and not through a messenger, but the Holy one . . . by himself" *(Midr. Tanaaim,* Hoffmann 1908, p. 173).

38. *to drive out before you nations greater and more populous than you.* Compare 7:1; 9:1; 11:23.

as it is today. Compare 2:30 and the NOTE there.

39. *Know therefore this day and keep in mind that YHWH alone is God.* "Know" and "keep in mind/heart" *(hšb ʿl lb)* are characteristic expressions in the Deuteronomic orations; they are directed toward deepening the religious conscience of the listeners; cf. 7:9; 8:5 ("know in your heart"); 9:3, 6; 11:12; 30:1 *(hšb ʿl lb);* compare 1 Kgs 8:47; Isa 44:19; 46:1; Lam 3:21.

in heaven above and on earth below. This expression is associated with the exclusiveness of the one God; compare Josh 2:11; 1 Kgs 8:23; and compare, in the Decalogue (in connection with the prohibition of idols), Exod 20:4; Deut 5:8.

there is none beside him. See the NOTE to v 35.

40. *that it may go well with you.* A characteristic phrase of Deuteronomy, which serves as a material incentive, employed to encourage the observance of the law; cf. 5:16, 26; 6:3, 18; etc. This kind of material motivation is very prominent in wisdom literature, which apparently influenced the author of Deuteronomy; see also the NOTE to v 1, in reference to "that you may live."

that you may prolong your days in the land. Compare 5:30; 11:9; 32:47; for the opposite, in case of sin, see v 26 and 30:18.

all the time. Literally, "all the days." This seems to refer to the gift of the land. According to D. H. Hoffmann (1913), it refers to the keeping of the law mentioned in the opening, immediately preceding this clause. Compare 5:26; 11:1; 12:1; 19:9; etc. It cannot belong to the phrase "that you may live long," because this would be tautology.

COMMENT

Unlike Deut 1–3, which uses past events and historical facts in order to educate the people, this chapter uses, for the same purpose, religious ideology on the one hand and rhetorical media on the other. It actually constitutes an elaborate sermon, the first one in the chain of sermons so characteristic of the Deuteronomic literature (see the INTRODUCTION sec. 2). If there are allusions in this chapter to history, they refer not to details—expeditions and itineraries, as those in chaps. 1–3—but to the glorious acts of salvation such as the Exodus (vv 20, 34, 37) and the theophany at Sinai (vv 10–13, 36). These serve the basic motivation for the staying away from idolatry, which might endanger not only Israel's election and superiority (see below) but even its very existence (vv 25–28). The sermon actually starts the long farewell speech of Moses, which will continue throughout Deuteronomy to the end of chap. 30. Indeed, one may see chap. 30 as a speech of conclusion corresponding to chap. 4, thus forming a kind of *inclusio* for the main contents of the book.

The sermon in chap. 4 comes, as indicated, to warn Israel against idol worship, especially after the death of Moses (vv 21–22), by predicting its dire consequence, namely, exile (vv 25–28). At the same time, it foresees the redemption from exile, should Israel return to God (vv 29–31).

The same tendency is to be seen in chap. 30, which forms the conclusion of Moses' long oration. Chapter 30 contains a warning against idolatry and describes its consequence, exile (vv 15ff.) but foresees, as well, redemption in case of Israel's repentance (vv 1–10), though in chap. 30 the topics are put in inverted order, that is, chiastically, first repentance and return, then the warning. There is also a possibility that the passage between, and see 30:11–14, about the accessibility of the word of God to the Israelites, corresponds to 4:7, which stresses the closeness of God to Israel (cf. Lohfink 1962, p. 42 n. 43).

The overlap between chap. 4 and chap. 30 exists not only in contents but also in verbiage. Whole phrases and clauses in the two are identical. Compare:

4:25–26	*30:17–18*
Should you . . . act destructively and make for yourselves a sculpted image in any likeness, causing YHWH your God displeasure . . . *I call heaven and earth this day to witness against you that you shall soon perish from the land . . . you shall not long endure in it.*	but if your heart turns away . . . and you will be lured to bow down to foreign gods . . . *you shall certainly perish. You shall not long endure on the soil. I summon heaven and earth to witness against you this day.*

The two overlapping motifs, the warning about perishing and the summoning of witnesses, appear in both passages with verbal congruity, but in chiastic order: in chap. 4 the witnesses come first and then the warning about perishing, while in chap. 30 we find the opposite.

The same congruity occurs in the theme of repentance and restoration:

4:27–31	*30:1–10*
YHWH will *scatter you among the nations. . . .* But if you search there for YHWH your God, you will find him if only you seek him *with all your heart and soul.* When you are in distress *and all these shall befall you, then in the end you will return to YHWH your God and obey him.* For YHWH your God is a *compassionate* God: he will not . . . destroy you; he will not forget the covenant *that he made . . . with your fathers.*	*When all these things befall you* . . . and you take them to heart *amid the various nations to which YHWH your God has banished you, and you return to YHWH your God and obey him with all your heart and soul . . .* then YHWH your God will restore your fortunes and *have compassion on you:* he will gather you again from all the peoples *to which he has scattered you.* YHWH your God will bring you into the land *which your fathers inherited.*

Exile, repentance, and renewal of divine grace are formulated here in almost identical terms, which points to a connection between the two pericopes. The passage about exile and repentance in chap. 4 stands in the center of the sermon and actually constitutes the main object of the speech. After exhorting the people to keep the law (vv 1–8) and to stay away from idols (9–20), Moses states that if his fate was decreed, he would die before the entrance into the land (vv 21–22), and therefore he comes to warn the people not to engage in idolatry after crossing the Jordan and settling in the land (vv 23–24). He then calls heaven and earth as witnesses for the fact that the consequences of Israel's apostasy have been foretold (vv 25–26) but also predicts that the punishment will not last forever (vv 29–31). The same pattern obtains in chap. 30, which is likewise a prediction by Moses made before witnesses: heaven and earth (v 19).

In fact the whole book of Deuteronomy is considered a witness against Israel in case of disobedience (31:26), as is the song of Moses (32:1–43 concerning 31:21, cf. the Comment to ch. 31). Chapters 4 and 30 as well as 31:16–29 may then be seen as a kind of envelope for Deuteronomy, which conveys the basic message for the audience to which the book addresses itself. It appears as if the addressed people experienced exile and as if the book of Deuteronomy comes to remind them that there is hope for restoration if the nation returns to its God with sincerity. The message is that just as Moses predicted exile, which became true, so he predicted restoration, which will be realized once the people repent. Indeed, the pericope of Deut 4:25ff. is recited, according to Jewish tradition, in the synagogue on the ninth of the month Ab, the day of the destruction of the Temple.

The Theology of Repentance

The idea of repentance and redemption, which has been ascribed in Deuteronomy to Moses, was later also attributed, by the editor of the Books of Kings, to Solomon in his liturgical oration (1 Kgs 8:44–53) while dedicating the temple, which is considered there to be the house of prayer (cf. Weinfeld 1972a, pp. 36–37). Like Deut 4:1–40 and 30:1–10, the editor of this liturgy elaborates the theme of repentance through which Israel could be brought back to its land from exile (cf. Wolff 1964; Levenson 1975 and 1981). Thus we find in 1 Kgs 8 the exiles "turning to God with all their hearts and souls" (v 48) and God having compassion on them (v 50), as in Deut 4:27–31 and 30:1–10. As will be shown below, there are many verbal connections between 1 Kgs 8:44–53 and Deut 4:1–40.

The theology of repentance, which actually dominated the life of the exiles who once and for all abandoned idolatry (cf. Kaufmann 1960 4.18), is reflected not only in 1 Kgs 8:44–53, as indicated, but comes clearly to expression in Jeremiah's address to the exiles (29:12–14). This address contains formulas identical to those found in Deut 4:27–31 and 30:1–10 and in 1 Kgs 8:44–45.

> You will call me . . . and I will listen to you. You will search me and find me *(wbqštm ʾty wmṣʾtm),* seeking me with all your heart *(ky tdršny bkl lbbkm,* cf. Deut 4:29) . . . and I will restore your fortune *(wšbty ʾt šbwtkm)* and I will gather you from all the nations . . . to which I banished you *(wqbṣty ʾtkm mkl hgwym . . . ʾšr hdḥty ʾtkm)* and I will bring you back. (Cf. Deut 30:2, 3)

The problem of whether these verses are authentic to Jeremiah is irrelevant, because for the purpose here it does not matter whether Jeremiah himself said it or whether it was formulated by editors or scribes of the Jeremianic school.

The same theology is attested in the prayer of Nehemiah (Neh 1:5–11), which has affinities to Deuteronomy and the Deuteronomic prayer in 1 Kgs 8 as well as to the priestly code (on the latter, see below):

> O, YHWH, God of heaven . . . who keeps the covenant *(šmr hbryt,* cf. Deut 7:9, 12) . . . let your ear be attentive and your eyes open to hear the prayer (cf. 1 Kgs 8:29, 52; 2 Chr 6:40; 7:15) . . . I confess the sins *(wmtwdh ʿl ḥṭʾwt)* of the Israelites . . . and I and my father's house sinned (cf. Lev 26:40). . . . Remember what you commanded. . . . If

> you trespass *(tmʿlw,* cf. Lev 26:40) I will scatter you among the peoples (cf. Deut 4:27; 30:3), but if you return to me . . . even if you are banished to the end of the heavens I will gather you from there, and will bring into the place (cf. Deut 30:4). . . . they are your servants and your people whom you have redeemed (cf. Deut 9:29; 1 Kgs 8:51) . . . grant your servant success . . . and dispose that man to be compassionate *(wtnhw lrḥmym,* cf. 1 Kgs 8:50).

Although the examples from Jer 29 and Neh 1 refer to the repentance of the Babylonian exiles, it should not be inferred that the repentance pattern originated in the Babylonian exile (pace Levenson 1975 and 1981). The repentance pattern is to be clearly recognized in Hosea, the prophet who predicted the fall of Samaria. In Hos 5:15–6:3 we find a passage that contains reflections about national repentance and prayer structured similarly to the passages from Deuteronomy that were discussed earlier, and it is even possible that Deuteronomy was influenced by Hosea (cf. the INTRODUCTION). As in Deut 4:29–30 we find in Hos 5:15 seeking God out of distress and returning to God expressed in identical terms:

Hos 5:15–6:1	*Deut 4:29–30*
they will seek my face *(wbqšw ny),* when they are in distress *(bṣr lhm)* they will seek me *(yšḥrnny)* [saying]: Let us return to YHWH *(lkw wnšwbh ʾl YHWH).*	if you search there for YHWH *(wbqštm mšm ʾt YHWH).* . . . When you are in distress *(bṣr lk)* . . . you will return to YHWH your God *(wšbt ʿd YHWH ʾlhyk).*

Compare this with Deut 30:1–10, "when all these things befall you . . . and you return to YHWH your God . . . YHWH will restore your fortunes *(wšb YHWH . . . ʾt šbwtk).*" The expression *šb šbwt* 'restore fortune' is actually found in the continuation of Hos 6 (v 11, *bšwby šbwt ʿmy).* The idea of return to YHWH is also found in Hos 14:1–2: "Samaria will realize her guilt. . . . Return Israel to YHWH your God"; compare also Amos 4:6–13, where the prophet denounces Israel for not returning to YHWH (vv 6, 9, 10, 11) in spite of the afflictions sent upon them. The topos of return to God and seeking him following distress prevails in other parts of the Bible; cf., e.g., Prov 1:27–28: "When trouble and distress come upon you *(bbʾ ʿlykm ṣrh wṣwqh)* then they shall call me but I will not answer; they shall seek me but not find me *(yšḥrnny wlʾ ymṣʾnny).*" Most outstanding in this respect is the old prosaic introduction to the Song of Moses (Deut 31:16–22), which heavily influenced the Deuteronomic theology of repentance (Deut 31:14–22 is non-Deuteronomic, it refers to the song and not to the book of Torah, as does the Deuteronomic passage [vv 24–29] that follows it; see Weinfeld 1972a, p. 10 n. 2). The main idea of this introduction is that the Song of Moses should serve as a witness for the Israelites: when after Moses' death distress and great evil will befall the people *(mṣ'hw rʿwt rbwt wṣrwt,* vv 17, 21) the Song will testify before the people that what happened was foretold by Moses: "When many evils and troubles shall befall the people then this song will testify as a witness before it" (v 21). The people then shall confess, "It is because our God is not in our midst that all of these evils have befallen us" (v 17). This notion was revised by the Deuteronomic editor (vv 24–29), who put the Torah as witness instead of the Song (v 26) and added the cosmic witnesses, heaven and earth (v 28), just as in Deut 4:26 and 30:19. (The idea itself might have been inspired by the opening of the Song in 32:1.) Likewise, he phrased the warning in the typical Deuteronomic manner. Instead of the phrases, "go astray *(znh)* after foreign gods" (v 16), "turn to *(pnh 'l)* other gods" (vv 18, 20), "violate my covenant *(hpr bryt)*" (vv 16, 20) found in the old introduction, the Deuteronomic author uses the stereotypical formulas used for apostasy in the Deuteronomic literature:

hšḥt tšḥtwn 'act wickedly' 31:29; cf. 4:16, 25

swr mn hdrk 'turn from the way' 31:29; cf. 9:12, 16; 11:28

ʿśh hrʿ bʿyny YHWH lhkʿysw 'to do evil in the sight of YHWH to vex him' 31:29; cf. 4:25

Instead of the phrase *mṣ'hw rʿwt rbwt wṣrwt* 'many evils and troubles shall befall him' (31:17, 21) the Deuteronomic author uses the phrase *qr't 'tkm hrʿh b'ḥryt hymym* 'the evil shall befall you in the end' (31:29), which is close to the phrase *mṣ'wk kl hdbrym h'lh b'ḥryt hymym* 'all these things shall befall you . . . in the end' in 4:30.

Indeed, a whole range of expressions has been developed to render the idea of distress that will motivate repentance:

1. *mṣ'hw rʿwt rbwt wṣrwt* 'many evils and troubles shall befall him' (Deut 31:17, 21; cf. Ps 71:20; 1 Sam 10:19)
2. *qr' 'tkm hrʿh b'ḥryt hymym* 'evil will befall you at the end' (Deut 31:29; cf. Gen 49:1; Dan 10:14).
3. *mṣ'k kl hdbrym h'lh b'ḥryt hymym* 'all these things shall befall you . . . in the end' (Deut 4:30)
4. *b'w kl hdbrym h'lh ʿlyk* 'all these things will come upon you' (Deut 30:1; cf. Josh 23:15)
5. *bb' ʿlykm ṣrh wṣwqh* 'when trouble and distress come upon you' (Prov 1:27)
6. *wtqr' 'tm 't kl hr ʿh'hz't* 'all the evil will befall them' (Jer 32:23)

The main idea of distress bringing about repentance is, then, attested in old sources and, as has been shown, is most prominent in Hosea; therefore, it cannot be seen as originating in Exilic or post-Exilic times.

Furthermore, the theology of repentance is found in various literary genres, especially in prayers and penitential liturgies, similar to those found in Hosea. Thus we find in Jer 14:19–23 the people's lament over their affliction followed by a confession of their sins and of their fathers' sins. They then ask God to remember his covenant with them. At the beginning of the prayer, a question is posed: "Have you rejected *(mʾst)* Judah, have you spurned *(gʿlh npšk)* Zion?" This structure corresponds to Lev 26:38–45, the conclusion of the holiness code. There we find the same motifs: the distress of the nation (in exile); confession of the sin of the people and of their ancestors (vv 39, 40); remembrance of the covenant (vv 42, 45); and the promise not to reject *(mʾs)* and spurn *(gʿl)* Israel (v 44). An identical pattern is encountered in the people's prayer in chap. 5 of the book of Lamentations. Here the people mention their and their fathers' sin (vv 7, 16) following the distress of the destruction; afterward they ask God not to forget them (v 20), to bring them back to him so that they return (v 21) lest they be "rejected *(mʾs)*." A similar pattern is encountered in chap. 3 of Lamentations. First comes the description of the nation's afflictions (vv 1–21), then God's grace and mercy are mentioned (vv 22–39), which is then followed by a cry of repentance and confession of sins (vv 40–92).

The same typology is reflected in Ps 85:1–8. Here the people pray over the restoration of the fortune of Jacob (northern Israel?) and the forgiveness of the people's sin (v 3), then they ask God to return to them and to reverse his anger with them (v 4) and express the hope that he will revive them again *(tšwb tḥyynw;* v 7) and show them his grace (v 8). The plea "to revive" them reminds us of the penitential prayer in Hos 6:2, "after two days he will revive us," which also comes after the "return of God" (v 1). "Revival" after distress is also found in Ps 71:20: *ʾšr hrʾytnw ṣrwt rbwt wrʿwt, tšwb tḥyynw.* The term *ṣrwt rbwt wrʿwt* appears, as has been shown, in Deut 31:17, 21.

Psalm 106:40–46 brings the theology of repentance to its full expression: "YHWH was angry with his people . . . he handed them over to the nations . . . and they pined away *(ymqw)* under their iniquities [compare Lev 26:39]. When he saw them in distress . . . he remembered in their favor his covenant . . . he granted them mercy in the sight of all their captors." The theology of repentance has then its Sitz im Leben in ancient penitential prayers, as reflected in the popular prayers and in quotes by Hosea and Jeremiah, as well as in the Psalter and the book of Lamentations. These prayers in distress are anticipated in the description of the Exile in Lev 26 and Deut 4 and 30. In the later post-Exilic prayers, we are indeed able to recognize influences of both the priestly and the Deuteronomic descriptions of the people's reaction to the Exile. Thus in Ps 106:43–46 we find traces of Deut 4 and 30 as well as of Lev 26. *wymqw bʿwnm* in v 43 is influenced by Lev 26:39, while *wyzkwr lhm brytw* reminds us of

Lev 26:42, 45. *Bṣr lhm* in v 44 is under the influence of Deut 4:30, while *wytn . . . lrḥmym lpny kl šwbyhm* in v 46 is influenced by Deut 30:3 and 13:18 and by 1 Kgs 8:50 (see above). By the same token, the prayer in Neh 1:5–11 has elements from Deuteronomy and Leviticus as well as from the Deuteronomic prayer in 1 Kgs 8.

All of this may indicate that the theology of repentance in chaps. 4 and 30 is anchored in liturgy and prayer as practiced in times of national disaster, beginning with the fall of Samaria in the eighth century and down to the destruction of Jerusalem in the sixth. As will be seen in the next paragraph, the whole sermon of Deut 4:1–40 has a liturgical vein and reflects the principal ideas of the synagogal liturgy as crystallized in the Second Temple period (see also Janssen 1956, pp. 105–15).

Structure and Composition

The chapter opens with an exhortation to observe the laws of God (vv 1–8) and concludes with an identical exhortation (v 40), but the central concern of the chapter is the preservation of Israel's uniqueness by its abstention from idolatry. Israel is asked always to remember the revelation at Sinai, which should turn the people away from the worship of idols, and the whole pericope of 9–20 is actually a homily on the first and most important commandments of the Decalogue, to which chap. 4 serves as a kind of a foreword. The following verses (21–29) introduce—as indicated above—the main point of the speech: the anxiety about what will happen to the people after the death of Moses. This is naturally followed by the passages about exile and repentance, which reflect the state of mind of the exiles (cf. above) and represent a liturgical pattern that had been developing since the exile of the northern tribes (see above). The last paragraph (vv 32–39) brings up the topic of the election of Israel and its particularity (vv 32–38) as well as the uniqueness of the God of Israel (v 39), both of which turned into a cornerstone of Jewish Sabbath and festival liturgy (see the INTRODUCTION and below).

The unity of the composition of Deut 4:1–40 comes mainly to expression through the recurring motifs and phrases, which often correspond to one another. Thus the central section of the sermon (vv 9–24) is tied up by a common phrase: "beware"—*hšmr/w, wnšmrtm lnpštykm,* and *šmr npšk*—which appears at the beginning of the section (v 9), in the middle (v 15), and at its end (v 23). This section, which warns intensively against idolatry, is tied with the following section, which speaks about the sin of idolatry and the punishment for it (exile), by the characteristic phrases: *hšḥt wʿśh psl* 'act destructively and make a sculpted image' (cf. v 16 with v 25) and *škḥ bryt* 'forget the covenant' (cf. v 23 and v 31); these correspond to each other in an interesting manner: Israel may "forget the covenant with God" (v 23) but God will not "forget his covenant with the Patriarchs" (v 31). Similarly, *hšḥt* appears in the two sections with two different meanings: Israel will act "destructively" (vv 16, 25), but God will not "destroy" Israel (v 31).

Another feature that runs through Deut 4:1–40 is the use of the experience of the audience in order to stir emotion: "*You saw with your own eyes* what God did at Baal-Peor" (v 3); "the things *that you saw with your own eyes*" (at Sinai, v 9); "as YHWH your God did for you *in Egypt before your very eyes*" (v 34).

Another unifying stylistic feature in the oration is the group of rhetorical questions that occur at the beginning and at the end of the chapter:

> For what great nation . . . has a god so close at hand? (v 7)
>
> What great nation has laws and rules as just as all of this teaching? (v 8)
>
> Has any people heard the voice of God speaking from the midst of a fire? (v 33)
>
> Has any god attempted to go and take for himself one nation from the midst of another? (v 34)

The two questions at the beginning come to express and intensify the uniqueness of the people of Israel, while the two questions at the end express the uniqueness of the God of Israel. In such a manner the author connected the prologue (vv 1–8) with the epilogue (vv 32–40), putting in the center (vv 9–31) the main topic: the warning against worship of idols and the consequences of such worship.

Another phenomenon that points to the unity of composition of Deut 4:1–40 is the way the author connects the separate sections of the sermon. The various sections are linked by means of imperative addresses preceded by emphatic particles: "And now . . . listen" *(wʿth . . . šmʿ,* v 1), "But take utmost care" *(rq hšmr,* v 9), "You have but to inquire" *(ky šʾl,* v 32).

Attempts to divide the chapter into sources according to singular or plural addresses have not succeeded. The shifts from singular to plural or vice versa serve to bring out the contrast or to heighten the tension. Thus, after the direct "singular" exhortation to refrain from astral worship, which has been allocated to other peoples (v 19b), the author shifts to the "plural" in order to create a contrast and to bring out the difference between the nations and Israel: "These YHWH *your* (sing.) God allotted to the other peoples. . . . But *you* (pl.) *(wʾtkm)* did YHWH take and bring out of Egypt . . . to be his very own people" (vv 19–20). Verse 20 is a natural continuation of 19b: worship of heavenly bodies has been assigned to the pagan nations, while Israel's share is worship of YHWH alone; compare Jer 10:2–3, with v 16 there: "Not like these is the share *(ḥlq)* of Jacob . . . Israel is the tribe of inheritance." Therefore v 20 cannot be dissociated from 19b, and the plural address of v 20 has to be seen as intentional.

The same applies to the change of address in vv 34–35. When the author wants to dramatize the experience of the Israelites in the Sinai revelation he changes his manner of address from "plural" to "singular": "As YHWH *your* (pl.) God did for *you* (pl.) in Egypt before *your* (sing.) very eyes *You* (sing.) have been shown." The same effect was created by the shift from "singular" to "plural"; compare vv 10–11: "when *you* (sing.) stood before YHWH *your* (sing.) God at Horeb, when YHWH said to me . . . so that *they* may learn. . . . *You* (sing.) came near and stood." In some instances the verse would lose its sense completely if one isolated sources in it; compare, for example, v 25: "when *you* (sing.) have begotten children and children's children and *[you* (pl.)] are long established . . . in the land, *[you* (pl.) shall] act destructively." The singular without the continuing plural does not make any sense.

The vacillation between second-person singular and plural occurs very often in ancient Near Eastern literature (see the INTRODUCTION, sec. 7), therefore it is to be considered a stylistic device, not an indication of divergent layers. For a comprehensive analysis of the structure of this chapter and its integrity, see Braulik 1978. One should add here that this sermon contains the Tetragrammaton twenty-six times, a number that represents the numerical values of the four letters of YHWH (10 + 5 + 6 + 5). The use of letters as numerals is attested in West Semitic inscriptions (see most recently Tigay 1983, p. 179 n. 30). For the importance of counting, the numbers of divine features and attributes in biblical texts, see recently Labuschagne 1985a.

The Nature of the Sermon and Its Sitz im Leben

We have seen that the passage in vv 25–31 about Exile and restoration, which has a central place in the chapter, has its roots in liturgy. The same may be said about other elements of the oration.

Basic theological principles embodied in the oration, such as Exodus, Election, and the giving of the law at Sinai (vv 20, 32–34, 37, 9–10); the monotheistic belief versus idol worship (vv 15–19); and the uniqueness of the God of Israel (vv 32–39) and of the people of Israel (vv 6–8) are cornerstones of Jewish liturgy as known to us from Exilic and post-Exilic literature. Thus the prayer ascribed to Solomon in 1 Kgs 8, which is of Deuteronomic origin (see Weinfeld 1972a, pp. 35ff.), opens with a declaration of God's exclusiveness (*ʾyn kmwk bšmym mmʿl wʿl hʾrṣ mtḥt,* v 23; cf. Deut 4:39) and the keeping of his covenantal promise *šmr hbryt whḥsd,* v 23), which occurs as a liturgical formula in the post-Exilic literature (Dan 9:4; Neh 1:5; 9:32).

After the enumeration of the various situations that call for prayer comes, in the prayer ascribed to Solomon, the section about repentance, forgiveness, and divine grace (vv 47–50), which contains many phrases found in Deut 4 and 30: compare v 47, *whšybw ʾl lbm* 'they will take it to heart' with *whšbt ʾl lbbk* in Deut 4:39; v 48, *wšbw ʾlyk bkl lbbm wbkl npšm* 'and they turn to you with all their heart and soul' with Deut 4:29; 30:2, 10; v 50, *wnttm lrḥmym* . . .

wrḥmwm 'grant them mercy' with Deut 30:3, and *wrḥmk* (compare 13:18); v 51, *hwṣ't . . . mtwk kwr hbrzl* 'you took them out from the iron furnace' with Deut 4:20; and v 52, *lšmʿ ʾlyhm bkl qrʾm ʾlyk* 'to listen to them whenever they call you' with Deut 4:7; compare also 1 Kgs 8:59.

The "Solomonic" prayer continues with the idea of the people of Israel as God's inheritance: "For you have set them apart for you as an inheritance from all the peoples of the earth" *(ky ʾth hbdltm lk lnḥlh mkl ʿmy hʾrṣt,* v 53), an idea that is clearly expressed in Deut 4:20: "But you did YHWH take and bring out of Egypt, the iron blast furnace [cf. v 51], to be his very own people" *(lhywt lw lʿm nḥlh).* (For the phrase "setting apart *(hbdl)*" from the peoples, cf. Lev 20:26.) It is significant that the two motifs occurring in Deut 4:20, bringing out Israel from the iron furnace and Israel as God's inheritance, appear next to each other in 1 Kgs 8:51–53.

After a technical interruption (v 54) we hear Solomon praying again, asking for divine grace especially for inclining the heart of the people "to walk in all the ways of YHWH *(llkt bkl drkyw)*" and to keep his commandments *(mṣwt, ḥqym,* and *mšpṭym,* v 58; compare Deut 5:28–61; 7:11; 11:22), a topic that opens and closes the oration of Deut 4. Afterward, he expresses the wish that his words of prayer be close to YHWH *(qrbym ʾl YHWH ʾlhynw,* v 59), which finds its resonance in Deut 4:7, *ʾlhym qrbym ʾlyw kYHWH ʾlhynw bkl qrʾnw ʾlyw.* This motif is actually very dominant in the "Solomonic" prayer, which speaks so much about the acceptance of prayer by God; cf. vv 29–30, 36, 39, 43, 52.

The prayer concludes with the proclamation of YHWH's uniqueness and exclusiveness: "that all the peoples of the earth may know that YHWH alone is God, there is no other *(lmʿn dʿt kl ʿmy hʾrṣ ky YHWH hwʾhʾlhym ʾyn ʿwd)*" (v 60). This corresponds to Deut 4:35, "YHWH alone is God; there is none beside him *(YHWH hwʾ hʾlhym ʾyn ʿwd mlbdw),*" and 4:39, "Know therefore this day and keep in mind that YHWH alone is God . . . there is none beside him *(wydʿt hywm whšbt ʾl lbbk ky YHWH hwʾ hʾlhym . . . ʾyn ʿwd).*"

One should, however, be aware of the difference between Deut 4 and 1 Kgs 8. In Deut 4, the proclamation of monotheism is addressed to Israel, while in 1 Kgs 8:60 it refers to all peoples of the earth, as in Deutero-Isaiah (Isa 45:5–6, 18, 21–22; 46:9, *hšybw ʿl lb . . . wʾyn ʿwd ʾlhym).* For the affinities with Deutero-Isaiah, see Weinfeld 1972a, p. 42 n. 2). After the proclamation of God's exclusiveness comes the exhortation to keep God's laws and commandments *(ḥqyw wmṣwtyw,* v 61), which looks out of place in a prayer. Surprisingly enough, both motifs—the exclusiveness of YHWH and the exhortation to keep the laws and the commandments—also conclude the sermon of Deut 4:1–40 (vv 39–40). It appears therefore that both motifs were important parts of the homilies in the Exilic period. Monotheism and the Torah were rightly seen as the pillars of Jewish worship.

Another less elaborate prayer that has affinities to Deut 4:1–40 is that of David in 2 Sam 7:22–24 (also of Deuteronomic nature; see Weinfeld 1972a, pp.

37f. etc.). It opens with the uniqueness of the God of Israel and passes to the Exodus and the uniqueness of Israel (vv 22–24). The formulation of the latter is identical with Deut 4:34. Compare 2 Sam 7:22–23, "There is none like you . . . according to everything *we have heard (kkl ʾšr šmʿnw) with our own ears, what other nation* [read: *gwy ʾḥr* instead of *gwy ʾḥd* with LXX; cf. McCarter 1984, ad loc.] is there on earth, a nation whom . . . a god led to ransom as a people of his own making a name for himself and *doing great and fearful deeds (hgdwlh wnrʾwt),*" with Deut 4:33–34, "Has any people heard the voice of God speaking . . . as indeed you have *(kʾšr šmʿt).* . . . Or has any god attempted to go and take for himself one nation *(gwy)* . . . by great terrors *(wbmwrʾym gdlym)?*"

As in Deut 4, so in the prayer of 2 Sam 7, there is this juxtaposition of uniqueness of a nation and its god, a nation hearing the voice of its unique god and a god choosing for himself a nation by great and fearful deeds (cf. Weinfeld 1972a, pp. 38, 207–8).

Another prayer of Deuteronomic origin (cf. Weinfeld 1972a, pp. 39–40) that contains motifs identical with those of Deut 4:1–40 is Jer 32:17–23. It opens with a declaration of divine sovereignty by creation, "You made heaven and earth" (v 17), which is attested in Hezekiah's prayer (2 Kgs 19:15) and in the prayer of Nehemiah (9:6), then passes to the idea of divine retribution (v 18; cf. Deut 7:9–10) and an enumeration of divine titles, "the great and the mighty *(hgdwl hgbwr),*" found in Deut 10:17; Dan 9:4; Neh 1:5; 9:32 Afterward we find a description of God's uniqueness in the Exodus and the election of Israel, which recalls Deut 4:34 and 2 Sam 7:22–23. The phrase "God making a name for himself *(wtʿś lk šm)*" in v 20 appears in the prayers (cf. 2 Sam 7:23 and Neh 9:10), while v 21 is a typical liturgical formula, characteristic of Deuteronomic literature: "You brought out your people Israel from the land of Egypt with signs and marvels, with a strong hand and an outstretched arm and with great fearful-deeds *(mst ʾtt wbmwptym, yd ḥzqh wzrʿ nṭyh, mrʾym gdlym).*" This description of the wondrous deeds of the Exodus is identical with that of Deut 4:34 and 6:21–22 and with that of the prayer in Deut 26:8 (cf. Childs 1967, pp. 30–39).

Subsequently comes a description of the sin of disobedience and the distress following it found in Deut 4:25–31. The verse (23) reads, "But they did not listen to you and did not follow your Torah, they did nothing of what you commanded them to do. Therefore you have caused all this evil to befall them *(wtqrʾ ʾtm ʾt kl hrʿh hzʾt).*" As has been indicated above, the "evil/distress befalling Israel," which should bring the return to YHWH, is a kind of topos in the Deuteronomic literature rooted in prayer.

Most instructive for the present purpose is the prayer in Neh 9. In this prayer, which may be seen as a predecessor of the Amidah prayer of Sabbath and festival in Judaism (see the INTRODUCTION, §17), we similarly find the basic elements of Deut 4: the omnipotence and sovereignty of God (v 6), the election of Israel by taking them out of Egypt by great wonders *(ʾtt wmptym),* and the making of a name for himself (v 10, *wtʿś lk šm;* cf. 2 Sam 7:23; Jer 32:20). Afterward comes a description of the revelation at Sinai (v 13), which reflects the particular understanding of the event in Deut 4:36 (the harmonization of Exod 19:20 with Exod 20:19(22); see the NOTE above to 4:36). Then there follows a passage about the sin of apostasy (vv 26–30) and God's mercy (v 31), which is formulated as in Deut 4:31, "For YHWH your God is a compassionate god *(ʾl rḥwm):* he will not fail you, nor will he destroy you; he will not forget the covenant that he made by oath with your fathers." Neh 9:31–32 says, "Yet in your great compassion you did not destroy them or abandon them, for you are a gracious and compassionate god *(ʾl ḥnwn wrḥwm).* And now, our God, who keeps the gracious covenant. . . ." The only element in Neh 9 that is not found in Deuteronomy 4 is the giving of the Sabbath (v 14). This gives us a clue for understanding the Sitz im Leben of Nehemiah's prayer: Sabbath liturgy of the synagogue worship (see the INTRODUCTION in §17), a liturgy that apparently crystallized in that period.

Another liturgy, close in its nature to Deut 4, especially by its stress on the superiority of Israel because of separating itself from idolatrous worship, is found in Jer 10:6–16 (on the date and authorship of this chapter, see recently Margaliot 1980). The prophet apparently incorporates a liturgy into his prophecy, as occurs in other instances: compare chap. 14. Here we read in the framework of an address to the exiles (cf. Margaliot 1980),

O YHWH, there is none like you!
You are great and Your name is great in power . . .
Who would not fear you, O King of the nations . . .
for among all the wise of the nations
and in all their kingdoms there is none like you.
But they are both dull and foolish.
It is teaching vanity, a piece of wood . . .
But YHWH is a true God, a living God . . .
When he is angry, the earth trembles . . .
He made the earth by his power . . .
By his understanding he stretched out the heavens.
Every man is proved dull . . .
Every goldsmith is put to shame because of the idol . . .
There is no breath in them . . .
Not like this is the *portion (ḥlq)* of Jacob, for it is he who created all things,
Israel is the tribe of his inheritance *(nḥlh).*

The pericope of Jer 10:1–16 actually starts with a warning not to fear the signs of the heavens—it is the nations who fear them (v 2)—and concludes with the statement that idol worship is not the portion of Jacob because Israel is the tribe of God's inheritance (v 16). This is in line with Deut 4:19–20, which expresses an identical idea: the (worship of) heavenly bodies is assigned to the nations, while Israel is YHWH's inheritance and thus is subject to his worship alone.

As in Deut 4:6, we find here the juxtaposition of the "wisdom of the nations" with the wisdom that comes from the God of Israel, and, as in Deut 4:33 where the living God *(ʾlhym ḥyym;* cf. the TEXTUAL NOTE) proves his greatness by revelation accompanied by cosmic transformations, so in Jer 10:10 the living God makes the earth tremble *(trʿš hʾrṣ;* cf. this idiom in connection with Sinai in Judg 5:4; Ps 68:9).

The idols that are made by men do not talk and do not walk and have no breath according to Jer 10:5, 14; this passage resembles Deut 4:28, which states that the idols are the works of *men,* made of wood and stone, and do not eat and drink and cannot smell.

The main idea of the Jeremiah homily is expressed in the conclusion (v 16), where it says that idols are not the portion of Jacob and that Israel is God's inheritance, which overlaps Deut 4:19–20, where we read that astral worship (cf. Jer 10:2) was *apportioned* to all of the nations and that God chose Israel to be the nation of *his inheritance.* That the Jeremianic passage is of liturgical nature is to be learned from the fact that v 13 occurs in Ps 135:7 and that vv 12ff. are incorporated into a Qumran hymn (11Q Psa 26:1–15, *DJD* 4, 1965).

A most important prayer used in the synagogue to this day, which reflects the ideology of Deut 4 and Jer 10, is the Aleinu prayer originated in the Temple service (cf. Heinemann 1966, pp. 173–75). Like Deut 4 and Jer 10:1–16, this prayer is based on the idea that the particularity of Israel and its distinction is expressed by the fact that the Israelites worship not vanity but the real God, the true king:

> It is our duty to praise the Lord of all, to ascribe greatness to the creator of all from the beginning *(yôṣer bĕrēʾšît),* since he had not made us like the nations of other lands . . . he had not assigned to us a portion *(ḥeleq)* as to them . . . for they prostrate before vanity *(hebel)* and pray to a god that saves not, but we kneel and prostrate before the supreme King of Kings. . . . he is our king, there is none else, he is our king in truth *(ʾemet),* there is none besides him, as it is written in his Torah: "and you shall know this day and keep it in mind that YHWH alone is God in heaven above and on earth below, there is none else [Deut 4:39]."

The idea that the "creator of all" did not "assign to us a portion" as to other nations is verbally overlapping Jer 10:16 and clearly implied in Deut 4:19, while the idea that YHWH is the true king occurs in Jer 10:10. The conclusion that the true God is YHWH alone and none else is quoted from Deut 4:39. The latter serves indeed as the climax of the whole pericope of Deut 4:1–40, and may be seen as the testimony of the believers in the Exilic period, because such monotheistic proclamations are found only in Deutero-Isaianic passages (cf. above).

The affinities of Deut 4:1–40 with various national prayers of the pre-Exilic, Exilic, and post-Exilic periods show that this creation constitutes a sermon apparently preached to the exiles within a liturgical setting. What we have here is an epitome of Jewish liturgy formulated as a sermon. Let us isolate the liturgical elements of Deut 4 one by one.

1. The notion of the distinctiveness of Israel's laws and commandments, brought to expression in vv 1–8, is one of the pillars of Jewish liturgy. The Sabbath and festival prayers open with the idea of God's election of Israel by giving them the commandments, as is found already in Neh 9:13–14. As in Deut 4:8, where the laws are praised as just laws and judgments *(ḥqym wmšpṭym ṣdyqm),* so in Neh 9:13 the laws are named righteous rules, true teachings, good laws and commandments *(mšpṭym yšrym wtwrwt ʾmt, ḥqym wmṣwt ʾmt),*" attributes that occur in the so-called precious (jewel, *mrgnytʾ)* prayer quoted in *b. Ber.* 33b: "You made known to us your righteous judgments; you have taught us to perform the laws of your will . . . true teachings, good laws and commandments." This notion is fully expressed in Ps 147:19–20:

> He revealed his words to Jacob,
> his laws and judgments to Israel.
> He did not do so for any other nation;
> of such rules they know nothing, Hallelujah.

2. Connected with the above is the revelation at Sinai, which indeed comes in Deut 4 right after the passage about the superiority of the law: "take utmost care and watch . . . that you do not forget the things that you saw . . . when you stood *(ʿmdt)* before YHWH your God at Horeb. . . . You came near and stood *(wtqrbwn wtʿmdwn)*" (vv 9–11). The idea of "standing before YHWH" at Sinai implied here turned into one of the central doctrines in Judaism, *mʿmd hr syny* 'the scene of Mount Sinai', and is actually appended in the liturgy to the idea of election and giving of the law. Thus in the prayer of Neh 9 the motif of the Sinai revelation precedes the one of lawgiving: "You came down on Mount Sinai and spoke to them from heaven; you gave righteous judgments and true instructions" (v 13). Both motifs were later intertwined in Jewish liturgy; see, for example, the festival prayer according to the Cairo Genizah documents: "You have chosen Israel . . . and made us approach *(wtgyšm)* Horeb and brought us near with love *(wtqrbm bʾhbh)* around Mount Sinai, and gave them righteous rules" (Elbogen 1911, pp. 433–34; 586). Compare also the New Year Mūsaph liturgy: "You revealed yourself in a cloud of glory . . . out of heaven you did make them hear your voice . . . when you revealed yourself . . .

upon Mount Sinai to teach your people law and commandments" (Singer 1915, pp. 364–70).

3. The idea of election, which is so boldly pronounced in Deut 4:19–22, evolves from the scene of revelation to Israel at Sinai (vv 9–15); as shown above, this idea is reflected in liturgical hymns (Jer 10:1–16 and the Aleinu prayer) and is motivated by the fact that Israel inherited the true divine worship, as stated in Deut 4:19–20. The motif of election opens the prayer of Neh 9 (cf. v 7) and serves as the opening clause of the Sabbath and festival prayers in later Jewish liturgy (cf. above).

4. The passage about sin, confession, and return (vv 25–31) has, as shown above, its antecedents in national prayers embedded in prophetic literature (Hosea and Jeremiah) and is clearly reflected in the Deuteronomic prayer of 1 Kgs 8 and in the prayer of Neh 9. This liturgical genre continued to exist in Jewish prayer throughout history; see, for example, the benedictions of return and forgiveness of the Eighteen Benedictions (see Weinfeld 1978–79b).

5. The motif of the wonders and miracles of the Exodus (v 34) has its clear prototype in the prayer of Deut 26:5–9 and is typical of the liturgical oration of Deuteronomic literature; compare Deut 6:21–22; 7:19; 9:26; 11:2–3; 29:2; 2 Sam 7:23; Jer 32:21; and in the prayer of Nehemiah (9:10).

6. The motif of God's love for Israel coupled with election (v 37), which is also characteristic of other Deuteronomic orations (Deut 7:7–8; 10:15), constitutes an introductory liturgy of the Shemaᶜ proclamation (the Benediction of ʾAhabah), which closes with the formula "who chooses his people Israel with love *(hbwḥr bᶜmw yśrʾl bʾhbh)"* (cf. Singer 1915, pp. 48–49 and see Elbogen 1931, pp. 20–21). As will be shown in the COMMENT to Deut 6:5, God's love for Israel corresponds to Israel's love for God; the love of God was expressed by the election and giving of the law, while the love of Israel implies the keeping of the law. It is for this reason that the Benediction of Ahabah precedes the Shemaᶜ proclamation, with its injunction to love God (Deut 6:5).

7. The promise of land in Deut 4:38 (cf. vv 1, 5, 21–22) also belongs to the liturgical pattern; compare Deut 26:9; Jer 32:22; Ps 105:44; Neh 9:15.

8. Finally, the proclamation of exclusive monotheism in Deut 4:35 and 39, which corresponds ideologically to the Shemaᶜ proclamation in Deut 6:4, is found in the various Deuteronomic prayers at the beginning (2 Sam 7:22; 1 Kgs 8:23; 2 Kgs 19:15) and at the end (1 Kgs 8:60; 2 Kgs 19:19), and, as has been shown above, has turned into the conclusion of the Jewish prayer throughout generations (the Aleinu prayer).

One cannot say that the oration of Deut 4:1–40 has influenced late prayers, for most of the motifs in this oration—especially those of confession and repentance, the wondrous deeds of the Exodus and the revelation at Sinai, the promise of land, and Israel as God's inheritance—existed in a liturgical setting before the crystallization of this chapter. We must therefore admit that this chapter is based on prevalent liturgical patterns; but they have been used by the author for the composition of a sermon preached to a generation that experienced exile (cf. vv 25–31). The fact that the monotheistic exclamation "none else *(ʾyn ʿwd)*" is found in the Pentateuch only in this chapter (vv 35, 39) and that elsewhere it is attested in the literature of the Exilic period (Isa 45:5, 6, 18, 21, 22; 46:9; Joel 2:27; 1 Kgs 8:60) supports my supposition about the background of this chapter.

THE ASSIGNMENT BY MOSES OF THE CITIES OF REFUGE IN TRANSJORDAN (4:41–43)

4 [41]Then Moses set apart three cities on the east side of the Jordan, [42]to which a manslayer could flee; one who unwittingly slays his fellow man without having been hostile to him in the past; he could flee to one of these cities and live.

[43]Bezer in the wilderness in the tableland, belonging to the Reubenites; Ramoth, in Gilead, belonging to the Gadites, and Golan, in Bashan, belonging to the Manassites.

TEXTUAL NOTES

41. *Then Moses set apart.* Hebrew: *ʾaz yabdil Mošeh.* (See *GKC* §107c).

the east. MT: *mizrĕḥah šameš,* literally, 'toward the rising of the sun'. Samaritan text: *mizraḥ hašameš,* without specification of the directive nature of the adverbial phrase. Compare below v 47, where the MT has *mizraḥ šemeš,* the Samaritan text *mizraḥ hašemeš,* as here.

42. *in the past.* Hebrew *mitmol šilšom,* literally, 'since yesterday or the day before'.

these. MT: *haʾel,* a rare variant of *haʾelleh.* The Samaritan text reads here and elsewhere *haʾelleh* instead of the MT's *haʾel.*

NOTES

41. *Then.* Hebrew *ʾaz* is tantamount to *baʿet hahiʾ* 'at that time', prevalent in the prologue of Deuteronomy and in the work of the Deuteronomic historian (cf. above, at 1:9). For such formulas compare *ina tarṣi* 'in the course of time' and *ina ūmišuma* 'at that time' in Assyrian historiography (cf. Montgomery 1934, p. 49). These formulas usually open quotations from epic or historical sources in Israel and Mesopotamia as well (Exod 15:1; Num 21:17; Josh 8:30; 10:12, 33; 1 Kgs 8:12; 11:7; etc.).

42. *to which a manslayer could flee.* This phrase completes the previous verse

about the appointment of the cities of refuge by defining the purpose of the appointment. The following phrase, "one who unwittingly slays his fellow man without having been hostile . . . he could flee . . . and live," begins a new sentence, which defines the case of the manslayer who has the right of refuge. The *w^{e}nas* 'he could flee' at the end is not a corrective resumption of *lanus* 'to flee' at the beginning of the verse, as S. R. Driver argues (1902, note ad loc.), because it forms a part of a new sentence and a new definition. The same construction is found in 19:3–4, which deals with the same topic and also has two separate sentences. The first states the function of the refuge: "that any manslayer may flee there *(lnws šmh kl-rṣḥ)*" (v 3; cf. the beginning of 4:42); the second defines the circumstances under which the manslayer may benefit from refuge: "one who unwittingly slays his fellow man without having been hostile to him in the past *(ʾšr ykh ʾt-rʿhw bbly-dʿt whwʾ lʾ-śnʾ lw mtml šlšm)*" (v 4; cf. 4:42).

Sentences structured in this fashion are characteristic of legal proclamations in Deuteronomy, as for example 15:2, "every creditor shall remit his claim; whoever claims from his fellow man *(ʾšr yšh brʿhw)* shall not sue his fellow man." First comes the general acknowledgment of the remission; then comes the specification of the case under remittance. In all of these cases the word *ʾašer,* which opens the second phrase, is not a relative particle depending on a governing substantive, as usual, but expresses a substantive in itself, like *awēlum ša* in Akkadian, 'the one who' or 'whoever'; cf. Yaron 1962, pp. 150–53.

43. *Bezer in the wilderness in the tableland.* Compare Josh 20:8 and 21:36. Apparently Bezer is present-day Umm al-ʿAmad, fourteen kilometers northeast of Medeba (cf. Abel 1933–38, 2.264). Dearman 1989, p. 61, suggests, however, that Bezer is located at Tell Jabul, a large and impressive site which has Iron Age pottery. Jabul is 5 kilometers east of Medeba and 6 kilometers south of Umm-al-ʿAmad. Bezer is mentioned in the inscription of Mesha, king of Moab, alongside other cities that he built on the Moabite plateau: Medeba, Beth-diblathen (biblical Almon-diblathaim, Num 33:46–47), and Beth-Baal-meon *(KAI* 181.27ff.). *Tg. Ps. Jon.* has *Kewathirin* (may be read *Bwtyryn* with D. Rieder, 1974 *Tg. Ps. Jon.* Add. 27031), which is unidentified.

Ramoth, in Gilead. According to Eusebius *(Onomasticon* 144:4), Ramoth Gilead is located in the Peraea district on the Jabbok River, twenty-four kilometers west of Amman. The *Tg. Neof.* has here *Geram,* which stands for Geras(a) (thirty-six kilometers north of Amman). This is confirmed by various midrashim, which render Gilead (the city) as Geras *(Midr. Shemuel* 30 [Buber 1893, p. 136]; cf. *Gen. Rab.* 94:9 [Theodor-Albeck 1965, p. 1182]), which is sometimes miswritten, as in the *Tg. Neof.*, *Geram* (see Theodor-Albeck p. 1182n.).

According to biblical evidence, however, it should be located in northern Transjordan. Thus in the list of the Solomonic districts in 1 Kgs 4, Ramoth Gilead was the capital of the sixth district, which contained the village of Jair and the region of Argob in Bashan (v 13; cf. above). Ramoth Gilead was a bone of contention between the Israelites and the Aramaeans (1 Kgs 22; 2 Kgs 9) and must have been close to the borders of Aram. Modern scholars locate it at Tel-Ramith, south of Edrei near the village of Al-Ramta (Glueck 1951, pp. 98ff.). This site had a strategic position—it controlled the main road that connected Rabat-Ammon with Damascus. Its ascription to the tribe of Gad reflects the extension of this tribe toward northern Transjordan (cf. 1 Chr 5:11, 16; cf. recently Ottosson 1969, pp. 32–34; Weippert 1972, pp. 154–58).

Golan, in Bashan. Identified with Sahm al-Jawlān, seven kilometers southeast of Ashtaroth. This city, which became the capital of Geshur (see above, NOTE to 3:14), gave its name to the whole region of Geshur and the western part of northern Transjordan (Gaulonitis) and was in use during the Second Temple period (see Mazar 1961).

Tg. Ps.-J. has *Dabura* in Bashan (= Matnan), a place that was flourishing during the Hellenistic-Roman period (see Urman 1972). A Hebrew inscription was discovered there, which reads, "Eliezer ha-Qappar, this is the school of the Rabbi *(ʾlyʿzr hqpr, zh byt mdršw šl hrby)*" (third century C.E.).

COMMENT

This passage looks like an intrusion because it deviates from the autobiographical style of Moses so dominant in Deuteronomy; it actually constitutes a historical note that pertains to the allotment of Transjordan to the two-and-a-half tribes as described in 3:12–20. The note comes to inform us that after the allotment, Moses provided for the Transjordanian tribes three cities of refuge in accordance with the law in Num 35. That law, which commands the setting apart of cities of refuge, comes indeed after chap. 34 there, which deals with the borders of the promised land and its division to the tribes. Similarly, we find in the book of Joshua the chapter about the cities of refuge right after chaps. 13–19, which treat the division of the land.

One would expect to find Deut 4:41–43 after 3:20, but because it seems to be a source for itself (cf. above in the NOTE to v 41), styled in the third-person singular, the author did not want to interrupt Moses' speech and inserted it only after the speech was terminated. Some scholars suppose that a later author, who missed in the Deuteronomic code a law about the cities of refuge in Transjordan, inserted this passage here in order to supply the omission (see Driver 1902, p. 78). This view was already expressed by the Rashbam, (ed. Rosin, 1881) who explains the appearance of this command here with the same reason: "Why was Moses' speech interrupted with this episode? Because he is about to expound the laws in which comes the law of refuge (chap. 19) which does not mention the cities of refuge in Transjordan; therefore, he writes here that Moses set apart these cities. Hence no command about them was necessary." The act of Moses here complies with the priestly law of Num 35, according to which six cities are to be set apart for refuge: three to the east of the Jordan and three to the west of it, in the land of Canaan (v 14). According to Numbers, however, the law of cities of refuge is to be implemented only after the crossing of the Jordan (v 10; cf. *m. Mak.* 2:4). Indeed, according to Josh 20, which is basically of priestly nature (except vv 4–5), the Israelites set apart the cities of refuge in the west, as well as in the east of Jordan, only after the division of the whole land of Canaan (vv 7–8), and nothing is said there about Moses' having already handled the matter. On the contrary, the separation of the cities of refuge is attributed there to the Israelites (cf. vv 7–8: they consecrated *[wyqdyšw,* v 7], they assigned *[ntnw,* v 8], unlike the LXX^B, who read it as singular *[edoken . . . diesteilen];* cf. Rofé 1983, p. 139) and not even to Joshua. The matter becomes more complicated when we compare the present passage with the law of refuge in Deut 19. There the Israelites are commanded to set apart three cities of refuge after the conquest and occupation of the whole land (vv 1–2), and nothing is said about cities of refuge in Transjordan. One may argue that the cities of refuge in Transjordan were not mentioned in Deut 19 because these were already dealt with in 4:41–43, but it is still hard to explain the avoidance of any allusion to them in a general law about cities of refuge.

Deuteronomy 4:41–43 uses the language of Deuteronomy and not that of Numbers (the priestly code), and unless it is a late post-Deuteronomic addition —an assertion for which there is no proof—we may assume (with Dillman, Hoffmann, and others) that Deut 19 presupposes the setting apart of the cities in Transjordan by Moses, as described in 4:41–43.

4:44–11:32

INTRODUCTION

This is the second prologue for the Deuteronomic code, which parallels the first prologue 1:1–4:43 (see the INTRODUCTION). Like the first prologue, which includes lessons from history (chaps. 1–3) as well as sermonizing about loyalty to the Sinaitic covenant (chap. 4), so the second prologue contains inculcation of the Sinaitic covenant (Decalogue—chap. 5) and the demand of exclusive loyalty (chaps. 6–7) on the one hand, and lessons from history (8:1–11:12) on the other. The only difference between the two prologues is that the first opens with history and ends with a sermon, while the second opens with sermons and then proceeds to history.

There is also a difference in the aim of the historical lesson in both prologues. The historical section of the first prologue is mainly concerned with rebelliousness in connection with the conquest of the land (not trusting God and his promise [1:22–46]), whereas the historical section of the second prologue concentrates on the disloyalty in connection with worshiping the golden calf (9:7–29). The first three chapters of Deuteronomy are concerned with the beginning of the occupation of the promised land. It is no wonder, therefore, that the sin described in these chapters pertains to the theme of the conquest of that land.

INTRODUCTION TO THE EXPOSITION OF THE LAW IN CHAPTERS 5–26 (4:44–49)

4 [44]This is the teaching that Moses set before the Israelites.
[45]These are the precepts, laws, and rules that Moses proclaimed to the
Israelites after they left Egypt. [46]In Transjordan, in the valley opposite Beth-
Peor, in the land of Sihon, king of the Amorites who dwelled in Heshbon,
whom Moses and the Israelites defeated after they had left Egypt. [47]They had
taken possession of his country and that of Og, king of Bashan—the two kings
of the Amorites who were on the east side of the Jordan—[48]from Aroer, on the
bank of Wadi Arnon, as far as Mount Śion, that is, Hermon. [49]Also the whole
ʿArabah on the east side of the Jordan, as far as the Sea of the ʿArabah at the
foot of the slopes of the Pisgah.

TEXTUAL NOTES

45. *Egypt.* LXX: "the land of Egypt," here and in the following verse.

47. *east.* See the NOTE to v 41 above.

48. *Śion.* This name of Mount Hermon is otherwise unattested. The Peshitta renders "Śirion," which is the Sidonian name for the mountain according to 3:9.

49. *the Sea of the ʿArabah.* The Samaritan text adds "the Dead Sea" (cf. 3:17). The LXX omits the entire phrase "as far as the Sea of the ʿArabah."

NOTES

44. *This is the teaching that Moses set before the Israelites.* Compare Ps 78:5, "and he set teaching *(wtwrh śm)* in Israel," but here it is "set before *(śm lpny),*" as in Exod 21:1: "the rules *(hmšpṭym)* that you will *set before* them *(tśym lpnyhm).*" This verse is actually duplicated by the succeeding one (v 45)—"These are the precepts, laws," etc.—but it is stylized in a way that aims to recapture the beginning of the first introduction to Deuteronomy. There it is stated that "Moses *undertook to expound this teaching*" (1:5). Here "this teaching" is being presented: "This is the teaching," etc. The final editor of the book,

who wanted to integrate the two introductions, made clear by this verse that the teaching alluded to in Deuteronomy 1:5 actually starts now with the Decalogue. This technique of a general statement followed by specification ("this is *[wzʾt],*" "these are *[wʾlh]")* is characteristic of Deuteronomic style. Compare 5:28, "I may set before you all *the instruction and the laws,*" and the continuation in 6:1, *"And this is (wzʾt) the instruction, the laws,"* etc.; similarly Deuteronomy 11:32, "take care to observe all *the laws and rules*" and its succeeding passage in 12:1, *"These are the laws* and rules" (cf. also Judg 2:23 and 3:1). Sometimes the recapture of the transition *formula* occurs after a long interruption (cf. Josh 11:16–20 with 12:7–8a there. See recently Rofé 1982.

45. *precepts.* Hebrew: *ʿēdōt.* The term, which is common in Deuteronomy (4:45; 6:17, 20) and Deuteronomic literature (1 Kgs 2:3; 2 Kgs 17:15; 23:3; Jer 44:23), occurs as well in psalmodic literature (25:10; 78:56; 93:5; 99:7; 119 [passim]; 132:12 [sing.]; Neh 9:34; and in 1 Chr 29:19). The same consonants are occasionally punctuated by the Masoretes *ʿēdwot,* but there seems to be no real difference between the two forms. Both are plurals of *ʿēdūt,* but *ʿēdwôt* is a later form, apparently influenced by Aramaic *sahadwātā* ('testimonies' in plural), as suggested by the late E. Y. Kutscher.

The term *ʿēdūt* is common in priestly literature but occurs elsewhere in the Bible (cf. 2 Kgs 11:12; Pss 60:1; 80:1) with a royal coloration (ornamental inscription; cf. the parallel *šūšan* 'rosette' in Pss 60:1; 80:1).

Although *ʿēdūt* is usually translated 'testimony' *(ʿed* 'witness' + abstract noun suffix *-ut),* for example, the LXX, Targumim, etc., in the Bible it is never used literally in this sense. This has led some scholars (e.g., Volkwein 1969, pp. 19–20) to deny this derivation of *ʿēdūt,* though no satisfactory alternative has been posited. In the priestly source *ʿēdūt* constitutes the symbol of divinity (the winged disk of the cherubim); see Note to 9:9.

that Moses proclaimed. Alternatively, promulgated, fixed the rules; for *dibber* in this sense see Weinfeld 1982c, pp. 43–45.

Verses 44 and 45 actually form a parallel: *Tôrāh//ʿēdot* are proclaimed for Israel. Compare Ps 78: "he established *ʿēdût* in Jacob and set *Tôrāh* in Israel."

after they left Egypt. The whole period of wanderings is considered the period of the Exodus; compare in 23:5 the encounter with the Ammonites and Moabites: "on the way after you left Egypt"; see also 24:9; 25:17. The *Tg. Neof.* always translates the phrase *yṣʾ mmṣrym* by "leave free *(yṣʾ pryqyn),*" which is close to the original meaning of this phrase; compare 5:6, "who freed you *(hwṣʾtyk)* from the land of Egypt, from the house of bondage." See the Note ad loc.

46. *in the valley opposite Beth-Peor.* Compare 3:29.

in the land of Sihon, king of the Amorites, who dwelled in Heshbon. Compare 1:4; Josh 12:2.

whom Moses . . . defeated. Compare 1:4; Josh 12:6.

47. Compare 3:12a; Josh 12:1a.

48. Compare 2:36; 3:8–9.

Śion. Another name for Hermon (cf. 3:9) from the word *śy*ʾ, which denotes a lofty peak (from the root *nś*ʾ*).* Compare Job 20:6, "though his peak *(śy*ʾ*)* reaches heaven and his head touches the clouds."

Mount Śion (= Hermon) stands in juxtaposition to *psgh* (v 49), the peak of the Moabite mountains (cf. Num 21:20), thus these verses are a delineation of the land between two peaks. Compare the extent of the conquest in Josh 11:17: "from Mount Halak that ascends to Seir till Baal Gad . . . at the foot of Mount Hermon."

49. Compare 3:17; see the NOTE there.

THE PROLOGUE TO THE DECALOGUE (5:1–5)

5 [1]Moses summoned all the Israelites and said to them: hear, O Israel, the laws and rules that I proclaim to you this day! Study them and observe them carefully. [2]YHWH our God made a covenant with us at Horeb. [3]It was not with our fathers that YHWH made this covenant, but with us, the living, all of us here today. [4]Face to face YHWH spoke to you on the mountain out of the fire —[5]I was standing between YHWH and you, at that time, to convey to you the word of YHWH, for you were afraid of the fire and did not go up on the mountain—saying:

TEXTUAL NOTES

5:1. *that I proclaim (dober) to you.* Literally, "which I proclaim in your ears." Compare Jer 28:7. *dbr* in *qal* exists only in the participial form. It is possible that there were also other forms in the *qal,* but they were assimilated to *piʿel; 4Q Dt*^{j} *fr 1* (Duncan 1989 Fig. 17). *this day* MT and others have *hywm hywm hzh;* LXX: *bywm hzh.*

study them. The root *lmd* ('study' in *qal,* 'teach' in *piʿel)* appears in the Pentateuch only in Deuteronomy (cf. the NOTE to 4:1).

2–3. The LXX has second-person plural forms instead of the first-person plural forms of the MT. This seems to be "harmonization" with the style of vv 1, 4–5.

but with us. Hebrew *ʾtnw ʾnḥnw,* 'with us, even us', an independent pronoun added to give strong emphasis. Cf. Hag 1:4: *lkmʾtm* 'for you yourselves'; cf. *GKC* §135g.

the living, all of us here today. MT: literally, "here today all of us living" *(ph hywm klnw ḥyym).* LXX and 4Q Dt^{n} col. 2:7 *[ibid.]:* 'here today all of us living today' (twice *hywm)* (cf. 4Q Phyl. A. *DJD* 6).

4–5. *Face to face YHWH spoke to you on the mountain out of the fire—I was standing between . . . for you were afraid of the fire and did not go up to the mountain—saying.* The last word of v 5, *le(ʾ)mor* 'saying' is the continuation of v 4. The bulk of v 5 is either a parenthetical statement or a circumstantial clause, "I standing between," in other words, "while I was standing between." Peshitta and Vg translate the last word *le(ʾ)mor* as a finite verb, 'and he said' (Peshitta: *wʾmr;* Vg: *et ait),* prefacing the Ten Commandments.

5. *I was standing.* LXX, Samaritan text, Syriac, and 4Q Dt^n col. 2:9 (White 1990, 272): *wʾnky* with *waw* conjunctive.

word of YHWH. The LXX, Samaritan, Pentateuch, Peshitta, Vg, and 4Q Dt^n col. 2:10: *words* of YHWH. Peshitta and 4Q Dt^n, col. 2:10 (White 1990, 272) add to YHWH: *ʾlhyhm,* 'your God'.

NOTES

5:1. *Moses summoned all the Israelites.* The verb *qrʾ* here does not mean 'to call' but 'to summon' and 'to convene'; cf. Num 10:3: *lĕmiqrāʾ haʿedah* 'to summon the community'. It appears again in connection with the summoning of the people for the covenantal assembly at the plains of Moab (29:1) and in connection with the convening of the people before the death of Joshua (Josh 23:2). In the context of these assemblies we always find leaders of the tribes, elders, judges, and the like; compare Deut 5:20 (see the NOTE ad loc. and Josh 23:2; 29:9 [cf. Perlitt 1969, p. 78]). Compare also the covenantal assembly at Shechem (Josh 24:1), where we have two verbs for convening the tribes of Israel and its leaders: *ʾsp* 'assemble' and *qrʾ* 'summon': "Joshua *assembled* all the tribes of Israel at Shechem. He *summoned* Israel's elders and its heads, judges, and officers." As remarked in the NOTE to 1:1, such gatherings were held at covenantal assemblies in Israel and in the ancient Near East.

all the Israelites. Compare 1:1 and the NOTE ad loc.

hear, O Israel. This is the only verb in the passage formulated in the singular because, like *rĕʾēh* 'see' (cf. 1:8), it bears the character of an interjection. Compare the NOTE on 4:1, and see also 20:3.

observe them carefully. See the NOTE on 4:6.

2–3. These two verses formulated in the first-person (plural) disrupt the address of Moses, styled in the second-person (plural). They constitute, in fact, an explanatory gloss, which comes to solve a major problem in the theology of Deuteronomy. According to Deuteronomy, the people addressed by Moses on the plains of Moab and sworn there to keep the covenant (26:16–19; 29:9–14) must also keep loyalty to the Sinaitic covenant (the Decalogue, chap. 5), in spite of the fact that the new generation addressed by Moses on the plains of Moab was not present at Horeb. According to the traditions in Numbers and Deuteronomy, the Exodus generation, which stood at Sinai, died out during the forty years of wanderings in the desert (cf. Num 14:23, 30; Deut 1:35; 2:14–16). In order to make the Sinaitic covenant binding for the new generation, the author had to make the Israelites declare that the Sinaitic covenant was actually directed to them and not just to their fathers: "not with our fathers . . . YHWH made this covenant, but with us, the living, all of us here today." The generation that stands on the plains of Moab is then conceived as standing at Sinai. Compare 4:10, "when you stood before YHWH your God at Horeb" (and see the NOTE there).

A similar explanatory digression is found in Deut 11:2–9. There the author stresses the fact that the signs and miracles done by God at the Exodus were experienced, not by the sons of the listeners (who are the ones actually being spoken to), but by the listeners themselves (11:7; cf. 29:1). The blurring of generations concerning the covenantal commitment is clearly expressed in 29:13–14: "I make this covenant not with you alone, but with those who are standing here with us this day . . . and with those who are not with us here this day." The notion of the eternal validity of the covenant is found in Assyrian treaties. Compare the beginning of the vassal treaties of Esarhaddon: "This is the treaty of Esarhaddon, king of the world . . . with Ramataya . . . with his sons, grandsons . . . with all those *who will live in the future*" (*ANET* ³, p. 534, lines 1–12), and the beginning of the Aramaic treaty from Sefire: "A treaty of Bargaʾya, king of Ktk, with Maltreʿl, the son of Attarsamak, king of Arpad; a treaty of the sons of the sons [and the offspring] of Bargaʾya with the offspring of Mattiʿel . . . and with his sons who will come up after him" (1. A:1–5; see Fitzmyer 1967 and see Weinfeld 1976b, pp. 391–92).

Israel throughout its generations is thus presented in Deuteronomy as one body, a corporate personality. In passages addressed to the new generation, we find phrases that suit only the Exodus generation: "you refused to go up" (1:26); "in Egypt before your eyes" (1:30); "you have seen all that YHWH did before your very eyes in the land of Egypt" (29:1). Especially striking is 29:15, where the experience of the Exodus generation intermingles with the experience of the generation of the conquest: "You know that we dwelled in the land of Egypt and that we passed through the midst of various other nations [bordering on Canaan]."

In order to remove the gap between the two generations, the author resorts to polemical notes, using an adversative tone, *loʾ . . . ky* 'not . . . but': "*not* with our fathers . . . *but* with us" (5:3); "*not* your children . . . *but* it was with your own eyes" (11:2, 7); "*not* with you alone . . . *but* . . . with those who are . . . here and those who are not here" (29:13–14). For such usage in the polemics of Jeremiah, see Weinfeld 1976a.

This perception of a continuous covenant was born at the time of Josiah, when the people gathered in Jerusalem to make a covenant with YHWH concerning the "book of the covenant" (= the book of Deuteronomy, cf. 2 Kgs 23:1–31; see the INTRODUCTION §4). The people then identified themselves with those who stood at Sinai and on the plains of Moab, and, like their ancestors, pledged to keep the law of Moses. Although the book of Deuteronomy is addressed to the generation entering the land of Canaan, the actual audience of the book belongs to the Josianic period. On the literary fiction in Deuteronomy, the people in the period of Josiah spoken to as the Israelites of the Mosaic period, see Hoffmann 1982–83.

This cyclic concept of all generations being present at the Exodus and the Sinai revelation has been perpetuated in Jewish tradition to the present. On the Passover night the following proclamation is to be recited: "In every generation each one has to see himself as if he was freed from Egypt. . . . Not only our ancestors had he, the Holy one blessed be his name, released from Egypt, but he also released us with them, as it is written: 'and *us* he freed from there', etc. (Deut 6:23). (Cf. *m. Pesaḥ.* 10:5, supplemented by a statement common in all Passover Haggadah versions.) The sentence "Not only our ancestors," etc., resembles the phrase of Deut 5:3 discussed above. On the perpetuity of the Sinai covenant in Jewish tradition, see the NOTE to 4:10.

2. *made a covenant.* Literally, "cut a covenant"; cf. the NOTE on 4:6.

3. *It was not with our fathers that YHWH made this covenant.* In accordance with the discussion in the introductory NOTE to vv 2–3, this is meant to say that God's real intention was to conclude the covenant with the new generation and not with the old, sinful one; cf. the commentary of Don Isaac Abravanel: It was known to him (God) that they (= the first generation) would not enter the land and would not fulfill the commandments, so he established the covenant for the next generations and therefore it says: "with us here today."

Ibn Ezra expounds: "Not *only* with our ancestors but also with us." Compare the Passover liturgy quoted above. Others understand it as meaning, not with the Patriarchs, Abraham, Isaac, and Jacob (1:8; 4:31, 37; 7:8, 12; 8:18; 9:5; etc.), with whom God also concluded a covenant, which, however, is entirely different from the Sinaitic one. The covenant with the Patriarchs is a covenant of grace, a divine promise to give them the land (cf. Weinfeld 1970–72), while the Sinaitic covenant is an obligation imposed on Israel to observe the law.

the living, all of us here today. Compare 4:4: "all alive today." In 29:14 even "those who are not with us here today" are included in the covenant. Here, with the Sinaitic covenant, the author is more scrupulous and adds *ʾēlleh* 'those (here)', the whole phrase, literally, "with us, we, those, the living, all of us here today."

4. *face to face YHWH spoke to you.* Hebrew: *pānīm bĕpānīm,* literally, "face in face." The phrase is to be compared with the more common one (Gen 32:31; Exod 33:11; Deut 34:10) *pānīm ʾel pānīm* 'face to face'. See Exod 33:11: "YHWH spoke to Moses face to face." But the concept of face-to-face encounter of the people with God is foreign to Deuteronomy (see 4:15 and the NOTE ad loc.). Besides, it was only with Moses that God spoke face to face (Num 12:8, "mouth to mouth," and cf. Deut 34:10). It is therefore possible that the author deliberately obscures the more common phrase *pānīm ʾel pānīm* by substituting

panim bepanim. Compare *ʿayin beʿayin,* literally, 'eye in eye', used in the context of divine revelation in Num 14:14 and Isa 52:8, meaning "directly."

on the mountain out of the fire. This is an important theologoumenon in the description of the revelation in Deuteronomy (4:12, 15, 33, 36; 5:19, 21, 23; cf. also 9:10; 10:4).

5. *I standing between YHWH and you, at that time, to convey to you the word of YHWH.* This parenthetical statement (see the TEXTUAL NOTE) is an intrusion, as might also be deduced from the phrase "at that time," *bāʿēt hahîʾ* (see the NOTE on 1:9). It seems to contradict the previous statement in v 4 about God speaking to the people face to face and other instances in Deuteronomy, which say that God spoke directly to the people (5:19; 4:12, 15, 32–33, 36; 10:4). Some scholars would, therefore, ascribe this verse to a late editor who reacts critically to v 4, noting that there was no direct contact at all between YHWH and the people and that even the Decalogue was transmitted by Moses, the mediator. As Dillmann, Driver, and others have noted, however, the glossator does not deny the fact that the people heard "the voice" of God; he only argues that the people needed an interpreter in order to understand the words of YHWH, which were indistinct and unclear. This tradition about Moses as the mediator between God and the people at the Sinai revelation is actually preserved in the Elohistic (?) source of the Tetrateuch. Thus we read in Exod 19:9, "I come unto you in a thick cloud so that the people may hear when I speak with you." See also Exod 19:19: "Moses speaks and God answers him in a thunder-voice *[qôl].*" According to A. Toeg (1977, pp. 48–59), Deuteronomy 5:5 is rooted in the basic tradition of Exod 19–24, which does not yet posit a revelation to the whole nation but ascribes the Sinai revelation solely to Moses. This view has been adopted, in Toeg's opinion, by the glossator of Deut 5:5, who inserted the harmonizing parenthesis, which recalls the old idea about the exclusive revelation to Moses.

The tension between the two approaches, reflected in vv 4 and 5, has been resolved by the sages, who stated that the first two of the Ten Commandments were heard by the people from the mouth of God (note that in the first two commandments God speaks in the first person, whereas from the third commandment onward God is referred to in the third person), while the rest was heard by Moses alone (b. *Mak.* 24a; *Hor.* 8a). The rabbis understood Moses' position here as mediator and deduced from this verse that a mediator/translator should be present at the recital of the Torah: "Just as the Torah was given through a middleman *(srswr)* so we ought to handle it through a middleman"; and in connection with this, Deut 5:5 is mentioned there (y. *Meg.* 4:1, 74d). Rashi, in his comment to v 4, used the simile of the middleman in a different manner, thus solving the contradiction with v 4. He quotes Rabbi Berekiah, saying, "Thus said Moses: 'I do not mislead you as the middleman does between the seller and the buyer, because the seller himself speaks with you' " (paraphrase of the saying in *Pesiq. R.* 21 [Ish-Shalom 1880, p. 102]). In this way

Rashi reconciles the contradiction between v 4, which states that God spoke with the people face to face, and v 5, which says that Moses was standing between God and the people. Rashi tries to show that both facts are true: God spoke to the people in the presence of Moses the mediator.

for you were afraid of the fire and did not go up on the mountain. This is the second part of the gloss, which, like the first one, aims to rectify a statement in the previous verse. In v 4 it was said that God spoke *on the mountain* out of the fire. The glossator comes to harmonize this with the old tradition. In agreement with Exod 20:15 that "the people fell back and stood at a distance" (cf. Exod 20:21, and see the NOTE to v 24), the glossator adds here that the people did not ascend the mountain out of fear. According to another tradition (J?), the people were prohibited from ascending the mountain (Exod 19:12, 21, 24; cf. 34:3) in order to prevent their "seeing" the Deity, but this is not in line with Deuteronomy, which never speaks of "seeing" God but only of "hearing" him (cf. the NOTE on 4:12).

COMMENT

The main topic of this unit, which opens the second prologue of Deuteronomy, is the covenant at Horeb in its relation to the covenant at the plains of Moab. The author presents the people of Israel as participating in both covenants. In the first covenant they listened to God himself proclaiming the Decalogue (vv 6–19[22]), but as they were afraid to hear God's voice after the first shocking experience (vv 20[23]–23[26]), God made an agreement with the people that only Moses would continue to listen to him and would later deliver his law to the people. This law, contained in chapters 12–26, was proclaimed by Moses at the plains of Moab, where the people pledged obedience (26:16–19).

Such a presentation of events stands in contradiction to the Exodus traditions, according to which not only the Decalogue but also the other laws were given to Israel at Sinai (Exod 24:3–8). A middle position was taken by the priestly author of the Pentateuch, who ascribed to Moses at Sinai the laws of the Tabernacle and the sacrifices (Exod 25–29; Lev 1–7), as well as other laws, such as the laws of *shemiṭṭa* and Jubilee (Lev 25); but at the same time, he also ascribed to Moses the lawgiving at the plains of Moab, especially laws connected with the conquest of the land and its allotment (Num 33:50–56; 35:1–8; 36).

Deuteronomy, however, left for Horeb only the great experience of revelation and the Decalogue. The rest of the law was given, according to Deuteronomy, to the people at the plains of Moab on the verge of their entering the land and was thus linked to the Shechemite covenantal tradition (chap. 27).

In the description of the revelation, the author is dependent on the Exodus tradition. Following Exod 20:18–21, the author describes how the people feared the direct contact with God and asked Moses to be their mediator (5:24–25). In a manner similar to Exod 24:12, where Moses is given the two tablets (with the

Decalogue), on the one hand, and the written Torah and *Miṣwah* to instruct the people, on the other, so in Deuteronomy Moses receives from God the two tablets (5:19) but is also asked to accept the rest of the law from YHWH and to teach the people the *Miṣwah* and the *laws* before they enter the land. The cosmic phenomena that accompanied the revelation at Sinai—fire, cloud, and thunder (Exod 19:9, 16; 20:18)—are also found here (5:19, 22). What is missing are the lightning (Exod 19:16; 20:18) and the sound of the horn (Exod 19:16; 20:18), apparently because of the more abstract nature of the revelation in Deuteronomy (see below).

In the description of the great experience of the revelation at Sinai, chap. 5 has much in common with chap. 4. In chap. 4 the terrible spectacle of revelation is described: "The mountain was ablaze with fire . . . darkness, cloud, and thick mist" (v 11). The same description is found in 5:19–20. By the same token the uniqueness of Israel in its hearing the voice of God out of fire is expressed in chaps. 4 and 5 with similar wording: "Has any people heard the voice of God speaking from the midst of a fire, as indeed you have, and survived?" (4:33). "For what mortal ever heard the voice of the living God speak out of the fire, as we have, and lived?" (5:23).

In the center of chap. 5 stands the Decalogue, the creed of ancient Israel, connected with the Sinaitic covenant, which precedes the Shemaᶜ pericope (6:4–9), which in turn constitutes the creed of the plains of Moab. Both creeds were recited in the Temple every day during the period of the Second Commonwealth (*m. Tamid* 5:1) and were recited daily in the Jewish liturgy; cf. also the Nash papyrus (second century B.C.E.), which contains the Deuteronomic text of the Decalogue, followed by the Shemaᶜ passage; also the Qumran phylacteries (see the "Introduction to the Decalogue" below).

THE DECALOGUE (5:6–18)

INTRODUCTION

As will be indicated in what follows, one should distinguish between the original, short form of the Decalogue and the expanded form developed in later times. Concerning its date, one should admit that although we do not have any concrete evidence about the date of the original Decalogue, it is nevertheless clear that during the times of Hosea the prophet (eighth century B.C.E.) it was already existent (Hos 4:2; cf. Jer 7:9). The quotations of the Decalogue in Pss 50:7, 18–19; 81:10–11 also point to an early existence of the Decalogue in northern Israel (see especially Ps 81:5: "he laid testimony/creed in Joseph").

The basic injunctions have affinities with ancient Israelite literature, such as Exod 23:12, 34; 34:7, 14, 17, 21; Lev 19:3–4, 11–12, 30, 36, and are especially imbued with ancient, cultic, priestly terminology. Thus the phrase "I am YHWH . . . you shall have no other gods" *(ʾny YHWH . . . ʾl yhyh lk ʾlhym ʾḥrym,* literally, 'there will be no other gods to you') is a characteristic coinage of priestly theology, as for example, "I am YHWH . . . who brought you out from Egypt to be a God to you" (Num 15:41; cf. Exod 6:6–7 etc.). Similarly, the phrases about the "sanctification *(qdš)*" of the Sabbath and the prohibition of doing any work *(ʿśh kl mlʾkh)* on the Sabbath are rooted in the priestly cultic instruction (see NOTE to v 12), and the same applies to respect for parents (cf. Lev 19:3; 20:9), theft, false oath, and more (Lev 19:11–12). The priestly vocabulary here does not point to late post-Exilic style, as is usually maintained, but on the contrary to conservative priestly usage.

Expansions of the Decalogue by motive clauses (see below) occur in both versions of the Decalogue, but in general the expansions in Exod 20 seem to be older than those of Deut 5. As shown in the NOTES to Deut 5:6–18, there is no clear proof that the Exodus version was influenced by Deuteronomy. If we find in Exodus phrases that look Deuteronomic, such as *byt ʿbdym* 'the house of bondage', *psl, tmwnh* 'carved image and likeness', *lśnʾy* 'those who hate me', *lʾhby* 'those who love me', *wgrk ʾšr bšʿryk* 'the alien (resident) in your gate', and *lmʿn yʾrkwn ymyk* 'that your days may be prolonged', we have to consider the possibility that these are genuine phrases of the *northern* Decalogue, which greatly influenced the Deuteronomic literature. By contrast, phrases and clauses introduced in the Deuteronomic Decalogue, such as *šmwr* 'observe' instead of *zkwr* 'remember', the motivation clause of the Sabbath commandment (Deut 5:14–15), the additional phrase in Deut 5:16, *lmʿn yyṭb lk* 'so that it may go well with you', as well as the change of *lʾ tḥmd* into *lʾ ttʾwh* of the tenth commandment, can all be explained on the basis of Deuteronomic ideology or phraseology (see the NOTES).

The thesis of F. L. Hossfeld (1982) that the Deuteronomic version of the Decalogue is original and that the Exodus version is a reworked edition of it is hardly convincing, in spite of the industrious, scholarly labor put into his work. See detailed arguments in the NOTES.

1. The Ten Words

Although in Exod 34:28 there is clear mention of "ten words," it is not clear there to what they refer. It is possible that reference is made to the ritual Decalogue (Exod 34:17–26). In Deuteronomy, however, the "ten words" clearly refer to the Ten Commandments written on the two tablets and given to Moses after the revelation at Sinai (4:13; 10:4). The problem is how to count the ten. There are three systems of division:

A. According to Philo *(On the Decalogue* 50–51) and Josephus *(Antiquities of the Jews* 3.91–92) the division of the Ten Commandments is as follows: (1) the unity of God; (2) prohibition of the worship of images; (3) false oath; (4)

Sabbath observance; (5) honoring parents; (6) murder; (7) adultery; (8) theft; (9) false witness; (10) covetousness. This division is followed by the Church Fathers (see Dillmann and Ryssell 1897, p. 222; Jacob 1923–24).

B. According to Augustine, the Roman Catholic church, and the Lutherans, the injunctions concerning the oneness of God and the worship of images are considered to be one commandment, while the last "word" (covetousness) is counted as two: coveting another's house and coveting another's wife (cf. Dillmann and Ryssell 1897; Jacob 1923–24).

C. The conventional Jewish division (alluded to in Jerome on Hos 10:10) takes the first verse of the Decalogue, "I am YHWH your God who freed you from the land of Egypt, from the house of bondage," as a commandment by itself (see the NOTE), while vv 7–10 are seen as the second commandment, and the verses *lʾ tḥmd* and *lʾ ttʾwh* as one (cf. *Mek. R. Ishmael,* Bahodesh, §8 [Horowitz 1928, 233–234]; *Tg. Ps.-J.* and Jewish medieval commentators). One must admit, however, that this view is not the exclusive one in rabbinic literature. Thus we read in *Sipre* on Numbers (§112 [Horowitz 1928, p. 121]):

> R. Ishmael says . . . "Because he has spurned the word of the Lord" (Num. 15:31)—means who spurned the *first commandment* as said to Moses by the Great One: "I am YHWH your God; you shall have no other gods beside me." Similarly the Rabbinic saying that *ʾnky* and *lʾ yhyh lk* were heard from the mouth of the Great One" may also indicate that we are dealing with one commandment, and to be sure, this tradition is brought in TB Horayot 8a in the name of a Tanna of R. Ishmael's school. (And cf. *b. Mak.* 24a.)

The various Masoretic divisions of the text actually reflect all three of the systems mentioned before:

A. According to the *superior accentuation (hṭʿm hʿlywn),* which divides the text according to "words," in contrast to the *lower accentuation (hṭʿm hthtwn),* which divides the text according to verses *(pĕsūqīm),* the first "word" contains the verse "I am . . . from the house of bondage," whereas the second encompasses the verses "You shall have no other gods" until "those who keep my commandments." This represents the conventional Jewish division, but—as will presently be shown—Jewish tradition knew other divisions too.

B. The *lower accentuation (hṭʿm hthtwn),* which divides the text according to verses *(pĕsūqīm),* sees vv 6–7 as one verse *(pāsūq),* which overlaps the division of Philo, Josephus, and the Church Fathers.

C. According to the Masoretic division of the text into sections, *parashoth (pĕtuḥah* or *sĕtumah),* the first *parasha* starts with "I am YHWH," the second with "you shall not take the name of YHWH," while the last commandment (covetousness) has two *parashoth.* This fits the Roman Catholic and the Lutheran enumerations.

It seems, therefore, that in the early Jewish tradition there was no fixed system of division of the Decalogue (cf. most recently Breuer 1990).

The Masoretic division into sections has in fact its coherence because vv 6–10 represent from a formal point of view a complete unit for itself (unity of God and prohibition of idolatry), whereas v 18 was treated by Deuteronomy as two separate commandments: coveting one's wife *(lʾ ttʾwh)* and coveting one's property *(lʾ tḥmd)*. See the NOTE.

From the point of view of contents, however, it seems that one should divide the Decalogue into two parts. The first part consists of five injunctions pertaining to the divine and thus constituting particular Israelite commandments: monotheism, the prohibition of foreign worship, prohibition of using the divine name for a false oath, observing the Sabbath, and honoring parents (on the nature of the latter, see the NOTE). Each of these injunctions contains the phrase "YHWH your God"; the first occurs right at the beginning, the second in the motive clause for the prohibition of foreign worship, the third in the main clause of commandment three, the fourth in the expansion of the fourth commandment, and the fifth in the reward formula attached to the fifth commandment. In contrast to the second pentad, which has no motive clauses or expansions, the first pentad abounds with motive clauses and literary expansions. This can easily be explained. In contrast to the second pentad, which reflects social morality based on natural reason guided by the principle of reciprocity, which is common to mankind (cf. the Philadelphia inscription mentioned below, §5), the first pentad reflects particular religious-spiritual duties that need explanation and inculcation. The first pentad forms, then, a list of duties relating to the divine sphere, while the second contains rules pertaining to the human-social sphere. Both pentads together express love of God and love of man, respectively. Indeed, in the New Testament (Matt 19:18–19 etc.) and other early Christian writings, as well as in the Apocrypha and rabbinic literature (cf. Urbach 1978, pp. 79–80), the second pentad appears as the embodiment of the command "You shall love your neighbor as yourself" (Lev 19:18), while the first pentad represents, as it were, the command "You shall love YHWH your God with all your heart" (Deut 6:5). See Flusser 1990. If the two tablets each contained five commandments (as tradition has it), then this dual nature of the Decalogue is even more salient; for the two tablets of the covenant in history and art tradition, see Ṣarfati 1990.

2. *The Decalogue: Its Nature and Its History*

The peculiarity of the Decalogue does not express itself in its contents, for almost all of the commandments are found in a similar form elsewhere in the Pentateuch. Thus the prohibition of idolatry, swearing falsely, the observance of the Sabbath, respecting parents, prohibition of murder, adultery, theft, and false witness all appear again and again in the various laws of the Pentateuch. For example, the ancient collection of laws called "the book of the covenant," which is adjoined to the Decalogue in the book of Exodus, already opens with the laws concerning idolatry: "With me, therefore, you shall not make any gods of silver, nor shall you make for yourselves any gods of gold" (Exod 20:23 [Hebrew, 20:20]). In this same collection of laws almost all of the other commandments given in the Decalogue are found in the following passages: observance of the Sabbath (23:12); respecting parents—which, however, is formulated in the negative (21:15–16)—see below; murder (21:12); kidnapping and theft of property (21:16, 27; 22:1–3); and false witness (23:1). What makes this collection of commandments peculiar is its specific nature: it is a creed, a basic formal affirmation in the religion of Israel.

Let us, then, state the particular and most characteristic features of the Decalogue.

A. In contrast to the ordinary laws, the enactment of which depends on particular personal or social conditions, such as sacrifices conditioned by certain circumstances of the individual (vows, sin offerings, etc.) and of the community (the Temple service), or other ordinances dependent on specific circumstances, such as the laws of purity, release of land, and liberation of slaves (Shemiṭṭah and Jubilee, the civil code and laws of matrimony, the priestly dues, etc.—in contrast to these, the ordinances of the Decalogue apply to every individual in Israelite society. Every Israelite commits himself not to practice idolatry, not to swear falsely, to observe the Sabbath, to honor parents, not to murder, not to commit adultery, not to steal, not to give false witness, and not to covet. Everyone is apt to commit such things, regardless of personal status or environment or period of life; therefore everyone is warned to abstain from them.

Indeed, according to Deuteronomy, the Decalogue was given for people in the desert without land and state, whereas the rest of the law was given for the people due to enter the land.

B. The Decalogue is for the most part formulated in the negative, and even the "positive" commandments (observance of the Sabbath and honoring parents) are in fact prohibitives.[1] The observance of the Sabbath is clarified explicitly by way of prohibition: "Six days you shall work . . . but the seventh day is a Sabbath . . . you shall not do any work" (Exod 20:9–10), whereas the main object of the commandment to honor parents is to prevent offense or insult, as implied by the various and related laws in other collections of laws: beating (Exod 21:15), cursing and disgraceful conduct (Exod 21:17; Lev 20:9; Deut 27:16), rebellion and disobedience (Deut 21:18–21). In Lev 19, which refers to the Decalogue (see below), the command is indeed formulated in the negative by the opposite of "honor": "You shall each fear his mother and his father" (v 3; see Note to v 16.)

[1] Accordingly, some have incorrectly tried to change the formulation of these two commandments; see, e.g., Rabast 1949, pp. 35ff.; Nielsen 1968, pp. 84ff.

The inclination toward a negative formulation is due to the overall character of this group of commandments, which sets forth the basic conditions for inclusion in the community of Israel, conditions that were transmitted to the people through the prophet who first conveyed to them God's word and God's will. These conditions determine what a member of this special, divine community is to refrain from doing.

A similar state of affairs can be found in the set of commands that Jonadab, son of Rechab, father of the house of the Rechabites, passed on to his sons: "You shall not drink wine . . . and a house you shall not build and a seed you shall not sow and a vineyard you shall not plant . . . so that you may live many days on the land you inhabit (Jer 35:6–7).[2] I will present below a parallel from the Hellenistic world, where we find a set of prohibitions given by the god to the founder of the temple, a set of prohibitions to which the worshipers commit themselves with an oath.

C. The commandments of the Decalogue are precisely and concisely formulated and contain a typological number (ten) of commands. As has been indicated, the text of the Decalogue has, with time, undergone expansion and revision. This process is most conspicuous with respect to the commandment of the Sabbath: the explanation for the observance of the Sabbath in the book of Deuteronomy is completely different from that found in the book of Exodus (see the NOTE to vv 12–15). Besides this instance, expansions and revisions can be discerned in the present form of the Decalogue as a whole (see the NOTES). The original Decalogue can be reconstructed as follows:

1. I, the lord, am your God; you shall have no other gods besides me.
2. You shall not make for yourself a sculpture and image.
3. You shall not swear falsely by the name of YHWH your God.
4. Remember to keep the Sabbath day.
5. Honor your father and mother.
6. You shall not murder.
7. You shall not commit adultery.
8. You shall not steal.
9. You shall not bear false witness against your neighbor.
10. You shall not covet the house of your neighbor.

It is true, there is no uniformity of rhythm here, and the commandments can be divided into three groups according to their length (cf. Fohrer 1965 and 1979,

[2] The Rechabites also observe their laws because they are "the commandments of their father" (vv 14, 16, 18); cf. Gerstenberger 1965, no. 17.

pp. 73–74): (1) commandments with four stresses or more (the first, the second, the third, the ninth, and the tenth); (2) commandments with three stresses (the fourth and the fifth); (3) commandments with two beats (the sixth, the seventh, and the eighth). But there is no reason to view the whole, on this basis, as secondarily and artificially contrived. The length of the sentence and its rhythm depends on its content, and some topics cannot be fully expressed in only two words. Moreover, formal heterogeneity by itself is no indication of an eclectic and secondary compilation, as certain scholars assume; original collections of sayings of varying length are found in the Bible and in the literature of the ancient Near East (cf. Cazelles 1969, p. 16 n. 27). Accordingly, there is also no justification to reformulate the two affirmative commandments in the negative in order to attain a unity of form.[3] At the same time, the structure of the Decalogue does reveal some unifying features: their short form, the typological number ten, the arrangement into two groups (commandments concerning man and God and commandments concerning man and his neighbor; see above). These features testify to the integrity of the unit. A form and structure of this kind permit the engraving of the commandments on stone tablets and their memorization, which implies that these commandments comprise a set of fundamental conditions that every Israelite was obliged to know and learn.

D. The commandments are essentially "categorical imperatives" of universal validity, above time and independent of circumstances (see Alt 1934, 1.321–22). No punishment is prescribed and no details or definitions are given. Accordingly, it is doubtful whether these commandments would satisfy the needs of the legislator or the citizen or the courthouse itself. One might ask what kind of theft is treated in the eighth commandment and what would be a thief's punishment; does murder apply to one's fellow only or to any human being; what kind of work is prohibited on Sabbath (contrast Exod 34:21; 35:3; Num 15:32–36); and more. But such questions are irrelevant, because these commandments are not intended to be concrete legislation, rather a formulation of conditions for membership in the community. Anyone who does not observe these commandments excludes himself from the community of the faithful. This is the function of the Decalogue. The definition of laws and punishments is given in various legal codes, but this is not the concern of the Decalogue, which simply sets forth God's demands of his people. Most instructive in this respect is the last commandment: "Do not covet." As B. Jackson has shown (1975a), there is no justification for challenging the traditional interpretation of *lʾ tḥmd* as mere coveting (see Greenberg 1990, p. 108). This is a command that cannot be enforced, hence violators cannot be punished by men. This command consti-

[3] Compare Cazelles' attempt in 1969. According to p. 16, the Sabbath commandment originally read, "You shall do no work on the Sabbath day *(lʾ tʿśh mlʾkh bywm hšbt),*" whereas the commandment "you shall honor *your father and your mother*" was added later under the influence of wisdom literature.

tutes a violation of ethics, which can be punished by God alone. In other words, this is not law in the plain sense of the word but the revelation of God's postulate, as are the other commands of the Decalogue.

Indeed, the commandments are called *debarim* 'words' and not *ḥuqqim* 'laws' (cf. Exod 20:1; Deut 4:13; 5:19; 10:4; see Ehrlich 1909, p. 340). Furthermore, in rabbinic literature the Ten Commandments are named *ʿAśeret hadibbĕrôt. Dibbĕrôt* is the plural formation of *dibbēr,* a noun that has the meaning of divine prophetic revelation (Gruber 1982), as may be learned from Jer 5:13: "the prophets shall prove mere wind, and the *dibbēr* [divine *word]* is not in them." The "words" of the Decalogue were therefore conceived not as the other "laws" of the Pentateuch but as divine commands given by revelation, which are different altogether from the "laws" that could be enforced by an earthly court.

E. The commandments are formulated in the second-person singular, as if they were directed personally to each and every member of the community. Philo astutely indicated that an individual might evade a command given to a whole group, "because he takes the multitude as a cover for disobedience" *(On the Decalogue* 30), which is not the case with a command addressed to the individual. Philo thus stresses the I–Thou relationship, the importance of which is expressed in the writings of Martin Buber.[4] Buber did, in fact, apply the idea to the Decalogue (1964, pp. 100–2), but he did not use the literary-critical criterion with respect to the character and origin of the apodictic style of biblical law. A. Alt's distinction between the casuistic and apodictic forms of biblical legislation has deepened our understanding of the style of biblical law (see Alt 1934). He pointed out the uniqueness of the apodictic style and, more precisely, the peculiarity of the prohibitive and prescriptive commandments in the legislation of the Bible.[5] Unlike the casuistic style typical of both ancient Near Eastern and modern law, the apodictic formulation, either negative or affirmative, is alien to the legal sphere. It seems now that it originated in a covenantal ritual in which the king stood before his subjects and imposed their duties upon them (Weinfeld 1973c, pp. 70–71). The Decalogue is indeed considered to consist of obligations that the king, who appears personally before his subjects, imposes upon them his commandments.

F. It should be indicated that the Decalogue is not a set of abstract moral

[4] *I and Thou,* trans. R. G. Smith (Edinburgh, 1937). For the development of the work, see R. Horowitz, "The Development of Buber's *I and Thou,*" *Proceedings of the Israel Academy of Sciences* 5.8 (1975).

[5] Alt included in the apodictic category both commandments formulated in the third person and declarations in the participial form (Exod 21:12, 15–17). Later studies further sharpened distinctions, showing that the commandments in the second person cannot be placed on the same plane with the above-mentioned commandments; cf. Weinfeld 1973c.

rules like those found in other bodies of law, such as "love your neighbor as yourself" (Lev 19:18), "You shall love the stranger" (Deut 10:19), "justice, justice shall you pursue" (Deut 16:20); accordingly, there is no justification for the claim that the Decalogue constitutes the epitome of Israelite morality. The Decalogue is, rather, a fundamental list of concrete commands applicable to every Israelite, comprising the essence of God's demands from his confederates. To the first part of the list is assigned those particular commandments which express the people of Israel's special connection with their God. This relationship requires exclusive loyalty (as opposed to the multiple loyalty of idolators), the prohibition of sculpted images and of the false swearing by God's name, the obligation to observe the Sabbath and to honor parents. The second part of the list has a socio-moral character and includes the prohibition of murder, adultery, theft, false witness, and coveting another's wife and property.

Honoring parents is quite suited to serve as a connecting link between the two sets of commandments, those dealing with man–God relations and those dealing with man–man relations, because father and mother belong to an authority higher than man, and they constitute an authority to be respected similarly to God. The medieval commentator Ibn Ezra discerned a gradation in the order of the second set of commandments: first, murder, which entails destruction of body; second, adultery, which is violating another's body; (?) third, taking by force another's property; fourth, crime against another's property, not by physical force but by mouth; and finally, coveting, which is neither by force nor by mouth, but through mere intention.

3. Other Law Collections that Resemble the Decalogue

Another place in the Pentateuch in which a set of commandments similar to the Decalogue is found is Lev 19 (for an analysis of this chapter, see, recently, Schwartz 1980). This, to be sure, is the only chapter of the holiness code (Lev 17–26) that contains a combination of religious and moral laws such as those of the Decalogue. The other chapters of this code are not so heterogeneous; each chapter treats a specific law.

It must be admitted that the common denominator of all of the laws in this chapter is the idea of holiness (Schwartz 1980); but it is clear, nevertheless, that the chapter as a whole is based on the Decalogue. The Rabbis, in fact, learned from Lev 19:1 ("Speak to the *whole* Israelite congregation")[6] that this chapter was proclaimed in full assembly *(behiqqahel).* Indeed, the revelation on Mount Sinai is called *yom haqqahal* 'the day of the Assembly' (Deut 9:10, 14; 18:16;

[6] *Sipra, Qidd.* §1 and *Wayyiqra Rab.* 24.5 (Margaliot 1953–60, p. 647) in the name of Rabbi Hiyya. The homily is influenced by Exod 35:1: "Moses then convoked the whole Israelite community." See also Schwartz 1980, p. 26.

and see below). Later on, in the midrashic discussions,[7] we find indications about the connection of this chapter to the Decalogue: "Why was this proclaimed in full assembly? Because the essential parts of the Torah hang on it." Rabbi Levi said, "Because the ten commandments are included in it" *(Wayyiqra Rab.* 24.5). Compare the similar phrasing in Matt 22:40 (concerning the commandments "Love the Lord" and "Love your neighbor as yourself"): "On these two commandments hang all the law and the prophets" (cf. recently Flusser 1985, pp. 172–73).

Indeed, Lev 19 opens with a reference to the fifth, fourth, and first commandments of the Decalogue (honoring parents, observing the Sabbath, and prohibition of idolatry): "You shall each fear his mother and his father,[8] and keep my Sabbaths: I am YHWH your God. Do not turn to idols or make molten gods for yourselves: I am YHWH your God" (vv 3–4).

The reference is chiastic (in reverse order), as is common with quotations from (and reference to) other texts (see Seidel 1978, pp. 1–97). The author opens with the fifth commandment (honoring parents), continues with the fourth (Sabbath), and concludes with the second (idolatry). Even within the sentence he changes the order of the components: the object precedes the predicate (not "you shall [each] fear his father and his mother" but "[each] his father and mother shall you fear," and similarly concerning the Sabbath), and even the order of the objects themselves is interchanged: not "his father and mother" but "his mother and father."

These three topics recur, with slight variations, toward the end of this section, in vv 30–32: observance of Sabbath, appealing to ghosts and to soothsayers, and respecting the elderly.[9] Two of these topics (Sabbath and idolatry) conclude the holiness code in Lev 26:1–2, which testifies to their central importance in the author's world view.[10]

In the continuation of Lev 19, we find commandments concerning theft and false witness and oaths (vv 11–12). The Rabbis found in this chapter *(Wayyiqra Rab.* 24.5) allusions to murder, "Do not stand against the blood of your neighbor" (v 16).[11] and adultery, "Do not degrade your daughter and make her a

[7] *Sipra Qidd.* §1; *Wayyiqra Rab.* 24.5 (Margaliot 1953–60.

[8] On the relation between "fear" and "honor," see Note to v. 16.

[9] On the structural-stylistic similarity of vv 30–32 to vv 3–4, see Schwartz 1980, pp. 92–94. Honoring parents and honoring the elderly are also combined by Philo *(On the Decalogue* 165–67) in the fifth commandment.

[10] Note that Ezekiel constructs his admonition in chap. 20 around these two sins: idolatry and desecration of the Sabbath (vv 16, 18–20, 24). For the priestly origin of the Sabbath commandment in the Decalogue, see the Note to the Sabbath commandment.

[11] This law follows an injunction against slander *(hlk rkyl),* and it seems, then, that "standing against someone's blood" here means being involved in a plot against somebody by endangering his life; cf. Ezek 22:9: "slanderers *[ʾnšy rkyl]* were amidst you to shed blood."

harlot" (v 29). It is possible that "You shall not commit adultery" is also the basis for the laws of mixing kinds *(kilʾayīm)*, of having intercourse with a slave girl, and of *ʿōrlāh* 'uncircumcised fruits' (= firstfruits of the tree) contained in this chapter (vv 25–29). In Deuteronomy 22:9ff. we find laws forbidding mixture of kinds next to laws on adultery,[12] which might explain the proximity of the laws on mixture of kinds and on intercourse with a slave girl in Lev 19:19–22. It seems probable that the law on "uncircumcised fruits" was attached to these laws by way of concatenation, a common way of arranging laws in the ancient Near East (on this phenomenon, see Paul 1970, pp. 106f. and Kaufman 1978–79, p. 115). If the assumption of S. A. Kaufman regarding the connection between the falsification of measures and weights in Deut 25:13–16 and "You shall not covet" is correct (see Kaufman 1978–79, pp. 143–44), then Lev 19 concludes in a way similar to the Decalogue (cf. vv 35–36).

It should be added that like the Decalogue, which opens with the self-presentation of God, thus conferring authority on the laws that follow, the commandments of Lev 19 similarly open with "I am YHWH your God" (v 2), and this formula is repeatedly affixed to the various laws in the chapter.

In view of all of this, it seems clear that Lev 19 comes to fill a gap in the priestly literature of the Pentateuch. In contrast to the Deuteronomic legislation that repeats the Decalogue as it appears in the book of Exodus, we do not find the Decalogue in the priestly legislation, even though it explicitly declares that it transmits the laws and rules that were given by YHWH "through Moses on Mount Sinai between himself and the Israelite people" (Lev 26:46; cf. 27:34). The absence of any reference to the Decalogue in the priestly legislation gives the impression that the main point is lacking. Accordingly, Lev 19 comes to fill this lack by giving us a "Decalogue" in a reworked and expanded form of its own.[13]

Yet it should be emphasized that although this chapter is essentially a *variation of the Decalogue,* it does not come to replace it. Substantially, it is completely different from the Decalogue itself. As I have said, the main characteris-

[12] According to Kaufman (1978–79, pp. 138–39), the whole legal section in Deut 22:9–23:19 relates to "you shall not commit adultery." The laws of this group are the mixing of sorts, forbidden sexual relations, the exclusion of groups from religious communion with Israel (23:1–9), purity of the camp (23:10–15), and cultic prostitution (23:18–19), all of which relate to sexual matters.

[13] See Abrvaanel's comments on Lev 19: "What is correct is that God ordered Moses to convoke the whole Israelite community that he warn them concerning these commandments and remind them of the Ten Commandments and the principal laws, because all of this was preparation for the making of a covenant, which is written at the end of this book in the section *ʾim beḥuqotai'* [Lev 26:3]. The Ten Commandments are not mentioned as they were mentioned and given to Israel, because they do not come nor are they mentioned here in order to announce them, as they were given to Israel, but . . . only to be explained here."

tic of the Decalogue is its applicability to each individual, regardless of circumstances. But this is not the case in Lev 19. Except for the laconic laws (vv 3–4, 11, 13) that are paralleled in the Decalogue, all others in this chapter are contingent on the special circumstances in which they were given. The law of *piggûl* 'unclear sacrificial objects' (vv 5–8) relates to one who sacrifices a well-being offering, the law of gifts for the poor (vv 9–10) obligates the landowner only, the warning against perverting justice (vv 15–16) concerns only the judge, the laws against mixed kinds (v 19) concern a field or vineyard owner, and so on; and the same holds true for the law of the ravished slave girl (vv 20–22) and the law of forbidden fruits (vv 23–25). The remaining commandments concerning idolatrous practices and the like (vv 26–29) are also accompanied by a detailing of the circumstantial background, and accordingly deviate from the "categorical imperative" characteristic of the Decalogue, as we have seen in paragraph D above. The sections on hatred in one's heart and love of one's neighbor (vv 17–18) are essentially paraenetic and constitute an appeal to the conscience; as I have emphasized, there is no place for such in the Decalogue, which contains realistic rules void of any abstraction. Finally, unlike the Decalogue, which does not include ritual laws at all (see below), Lev 19 does contain such laws (vv 5–8, 21–22, 24–25). Accordingly, this chapter cannot be placed on the same plane with the Decalogue.

In the framework of their investigations of the Decalogue, scholars have often compared it to other collections of laws and instructions in the Bible,[14] but it is apparent that none of these collections possesses the same uniqueness that characterizes the Decalogue. I will investigate here the most prominent of these collections.

1. Deuteronomy 27:14–26 comprises a collection of "curses" containing warnings of which the content (idolatry, incest, murder, dishonor of parents) somewhat coincides with the provisions of the Decalogue, but differs from the Decalogue in its orientation, form, and character.

These warnings are not obligations imposed on the whole community but are aimed rather at those who commit their crimes in secret. This is the common denominator of chap. 27, as Ibn Ezra and others have observed. It treats transgressions that are generally committed in secret, in a way that is difficult to discover, such as adultery (vv 20–23), trespassing, and misleading a blind person (vv 17–18), dishonor and contempt of parents,[15] perverting justice and taking bribes (vv 19, 25). As for the two offenses that are usually not committed in private (idolatry in v 15 and murder in v 24), only those committing these crimes in secret are explicitly warned here. What is dealt with here is a cultic ceremony that purges the community of criminals over whom it has no control,

[14] See the preface of Stamm and Andrew 1967, pp. 22–75, and the references there.

[15] *mqlh ʾbyw wʾmw.* On the difference between *mqll* 'curse' and *mqlh* 'dishonoring', see the NOTE to v 16.

and accordingly the punishment is transferred to the authority of God. By casting a curse on the offender, they would excommunicate him from the community, thereby avoiding the collective punishment of the entire community.[16]

There are no categorical commandments here as in the Decalogue, which lacks circumstances and details of punishment. On the contrary, the character of the offense is described in detail with the accompanying punishment being simply "cursed be." Similarly, warnings are directed at landowners (v 17) and those standing trial (vv 19, 25), unlike the Decalogue, where the commandments apply to each and every individual of the community (see section A, above). Needless to say, from the aspect of form and style, Deut 27:14–26 greatly differs from the Decalogue. Unlike its apodictic commandments "You shall" and "You shall not," we find here the present participle form along with the prefixed "cursed be." This form is similar to the commands of Exod 21:12–17 ("He who strikes . . . shall be put to death," etc.), which are also formed with the present participle plus punishment.[17]

2. In Ezek 18:5–8 we find a set of basic moral-religious obligations that reminds us of the Decalogue. The passage deals with a righteous man who does what is just and right: "he does not eat on the mountains [pagan practice], he does not raise his eyes to the idols, he does not commit adultery, he does not lie with a menstruous woman, he returns the debtor's pledge, he does not steal and does not cheat, he does not lend at interest, abstains from evil and executes true justice between man and man, and moreover, he even gives bread to the hungry and clothing to the naked."

Even though certain details here correspond to the Decalogue (idolatry, adultery, and theft), it should be noted that we find here moral virtues (the giving of bread and clothing to the needy) as well, which do not appear in the laws of the Pentateuch but only in wisdom literature and the prophets (cf., e.g., Isa 58:7). Also, this passage mentions lending money at interest and adjudication, matters intended for property owners and judges and not for everyone, unlike the Decalogue, where the commandments are intended for everyone. It should be added that murder is not mentioned here at all, which also indicates that this passage does not deal with fundamental human obligations like the ones in the Decalogue.

Alongside moral issues we find here cultic matters, such as "eating on the mountain" and lying with a menstruous woman (v 6), which are not found in the Decalogue. The list is characterized by a beginning and an end that define,

[16] From the religious aspect the ceremony fits the ancient, premonarchic period, when the community felt a collective religious responsibility, and the existence of one wrongdoer in their midst could have endangered the whole community (cf. the story of Achan in Josh 7; cf. 1 Sam 13:36ff.). On the premonarchic society and the place of curses and oaths as sacral sanctions in it, see Weinfeld 1983d, pp. 81–85).

[17] See treatment of this issue in Weinfeld 1973c, pp. 63–65.

in effect, the man who avoids these transgressions: "If a man is righteous and does what is just and right" (v 5), "he is righteous; such a man shall live" (v 9). What are dealt with here are the qualities of a righteous man, who not only refrains from evil deeds but is also benevolent to the poor. In this respect this list is similar to lists of moral-religious virtues in Pss 15 and 24, which will be discussed below, and which were intended for those who wish to approach the Temple precincts and the sphere of the Divine (see Weinfeld 1982a). From the aspect of form as well, this list is different from the Decalogue in that, in contrast to the latter's categorical formulation with no elaboration, in Ezek 18 the matters are defined and detailed.

A similar list is found in Ezek 22:6–12. Here we find even more items corresponding to the Decalogue than found in Ezek 18, such as observing the Sabbath and honoring parents (vv 7–8), and bloodshed and incest (vv 10, 9, 10–11). But alongside these we also find bribery and fraud (vv 7, 12), interest (v 12), as well as matters of sancta and cult (vv 8, 9) and of purity (v 10). In fact, there is a considerable correspondence here to Lev 19. In the opening of the list here, we find the matter of honoring parents (v 7), similar to the opening in Lev 19:3. After the exhortation against exploiting a stranger and defrauding an orphan or widow (cf. Lev 19:33–34), we read, "You have despised my holy things and profaned my sabbaths" (v 8), which is essentially identical to the commandment of Lev 19:30, "You shall keep my Sabbath and venerate my sanctuary."[18] The next sentence (v 9), "informers in your midst were intent on shedding blood," is but an allusion to Lev 19:16, "Do not spread calumny about your fellows. Do not stand against the blood of your neighbor," which refers to slander and bloodshed (cf. NOTE 11 above).

Like Lev 19, however, this list also does not represent a compilation like that of the Decalogue.[19] We find here matters of cult and purity that are wholly absent from the Decalogue. Moreover, here are found, as in chap. 18, prohibitions against lending at interest and bribery, which are directed at property owners and people of standing and not at each person, as in the Decalogue. In fact, the prophet explicitly states that the list of sins is aimed at the princes of Israel (v 6). And here also the formulation of the items is not absolute and categorical, as in the Decalogue, but includes details and definitions. It may be that, as for Lev 19, the Decalogue stands in the background of this list in Ezek 22, but the prophet developed his exhortation far beyond the scope of the Decalogue and adapted it to the particular reality that applied to the princes of Israel.[20]

[18] *mqdš* is not necessarily the Temple; it often indicates holy objects in general. See Lev 21:23; Num 18:29; etc.

[19] Cf. Greenberg 1983, 1.342ff. Greenberg rightly stresses the Ezekielian priestly character of the lists of virtues in Ezek 18 and 22.

[20] Bloodshed here is not actual murder but actions of rulers that lead to murder. Most instructive is the sentence "Slanderous men in your midst were intent on shedding

3. Mowinckel found a relation between the Decalogue and Pss 15, 24 and Isa 33:14–15, which he terms "entry liturgies" (1927, pp. 141ff.). In these psalms the entry and dwelling in the House of the Lord are conditional on the fulfillment of moral commandments, such as innocence and purity of heart, avoiding slander, false oaths and contempt of friends and relatives, honoring the God-fearing, and not accepting bribes or taking interest. These lists open with a question: "Who may ascend the mountain of the Lord" (Ps 24), "who may stay in your tent" (Ps 15), "Who of us can dwell with the devouring fire" (Isa 33:14). Accordingly, Mowinckel sees in these psalms a reflex of the entry ceremony into the Temple. At a later period, in his view, these moral demands—under the influence of prophecy—were removed from the sphere of the cult, and thus the way was paved for the collection of the Decalogue as we know it.

But there is, in fact, no justification for the comparison of these psalms with the Decalogue. These psalms mention only refined moral demands; gross sins such as murder, theft, and adultery, found in the Decalogue, are not referred to at all. Unlike the Decalogue, which contains national-religious laws, these psalms are on a universalistic level. As I have shown elsewhere (Weinfeld 1982a), these psalms come to define the "righteous," who is entitled to dwell in God's tent, and not the average man. Identical demands are found on the doorposts of the gates of Egyptian temples, (ibid.), which explains the questions at the opening of the lists in the Bible: "Who will dwell," "Who will ascend," etc. These psalms, then, treat of general moral demands and not of a set of obligations imposed on every Israelite, like those of the Decalogue or the similar ones of Lev 19 and Ezek 18 and 22. The stylistic features, as well, are completely different from those of the Decalogue as well as from those of Lev 19 and Ezek 18 and 22.

4. The commandments of the Decalogue used to be compared to the "negative confession" contained in chap. 125 of the Egyptian *Book of the Dead* (see recently Lichtheim 1973–76, 2.124–32) and to the Mesopotamian *Šurpu* incantations (Reiner 1958, tablet II, pp. 13ff.). But these compositions as well differ significantly from the Decalogue in both form and content. As to form, the Egyptian *Book of the Dead* is a sort of confession of the deceased prior to his entrance into the next world, whereas the *Šurpu* are a set of incantations meant to free the sick from every possible sin and thus bring about his recovery.

As to the difference in content, the sins of the *Book of the Dead* include murder, adultery, and theft, on the one hand; and lesser transgressions, such as the falsifying of weights and measures, slander, and insulting one's neighbor, on the other. Alongside these we also find cultic sins, such as cursing the god,

---

blood," which is parallel to Lev 19:16 (see NOTE 11). In Lev 19 the sentence is incorporated into a set of laws dealing with judges (vv 15–16), and it refers to judges whose reliance on slander might lead to blood guilt. On the relations between judge and officer see Weinfeld 1977a.

negligence in the divine service, desecration, and sacrilege. Similarly, the sins of the *Šurpu* incantations include murder, adultery, theft, false oath, gossip, hypocrisy, oppression, falsifying weights and measures, trespassing, and not clothing the naked. Here, too, we find cultic sins, such as eating forbidden foods, desecration of sancta, contact with the banned, and the like. What we have here, then, is clearly a literary encompassing of every possible sin, and there is thus no similarity with the collection of commandments of the Decalogue.

The collection of the Decalogue is thus different from all other collections of commandments. It is distinguished in that it incorporates a set of brief and concise, basic obligations directed at a member of the Israelite community, which is connected with a special covenant with God. This set is a sort of Israelite creed. In this respect it is similar to the Shemaᶜ (Deut 6:4), a declaration also comprised of an easily remembered verse that contains an epitome of the monotheistic idea and serves as an external sign of identification for the monotheistic believers; and it is no accident that both the Decalogue and the Shemaᶜ occur close to one another in Deuteronomy and were read together in the Temple *(m. Tamid* 5.1).

Just as the monotheistic principle expressed in the Shemaᶜ is realized in many legal particulars (such as the destruction of idols, the ban of inciters to worship foreign gods, the excommunicated city, etc.) that are detailed in the various legal corpora, so also the religious and moral principles of the Decalogue take form in various laws of the Pentateuch. As we have seen, attempts to construct units and sections of laws around the Decalogue, which become essentially its commentary, are also found in biblical literature (cf. especially Lev 19). Jewish philosophers, such as Philo (Amir 1990) and later Saadia Gaon, have indeed tried to base all of the Pentateuch's commandments on the Decalogue (cf. Urbach 1979 pp. 359ff.).

As the God of Israel's fundamental demand from the community of Israel, the Decalogue was borne on the lips of every Israelite true to his heritage and became the pinnacle of Israel's religious and moral heritage. It is thus no wonder that of all the laws of the Pentateuch, the list of commands contained in the Decalogue was taken as fundamental and primary in establishing the relationship of God and Israel. The people of Israel attained the merit of hearing the Decalogue alone directly from God, and accordingly it is the testimony *par excellence* of the relation between Israel and its God.

4. The Decalogue in Worship: The Renewal of the Obligation

In the past fifty years the view has become increasingly accepted that the event at which God pronounced his words at Sinai was not regarded as a once-and-for-all event but as an occurrence that repeated itself whenever the people assembled and swore allegiance to their God. The reason for this view was given by Mowinckel in his book of 1927, *Le Décalogue.* In the course of an investigation of Pss 50 and 81, he concluded that in Israel assemblies were held at which the revelation at Sinai was reenacted and celebrated. These psalms, which allude to covenant rites and a festival day, quote the opening of the Decalogue, "I am YHWH your God and you shall have no other gods," etc. (50:7; 81:10–11), and in Ps 50 we find references to the last commandments, theft, adultery, and false witness (vv 18–20). Psalm 50 is composed against the background of God's revelation in Zion (v 2), appearing in a storm and while proclaiming justice for the pious,[21] making a covenant with a sacrifice (vv 5–6), which reminds us of the giving of the law at Mount Sinai by means of a sacrificial covenant (Exod 24:1–8). Psalm 81 is composed against the background of a festival accompanied by the trumpeting of the shofar, while proclaiming that God set up the law and justice and testimonies for Israel (vv 4–5). If we can combine the evidence of both psalms, including quotations from the Decalogue and the revelation at the festival with the giving of law and justice, the assumption that these psalms relate to a festival in which the event of the giving of the law is celebrated, as Mowinckel assumed, is indeed reinforced. Still, one must be aware of the fact that these psalms were not meant to mark the event of covenant renewal but to admonish the people. Psalm 50 comes to admonish a people concerning their making sacrifices while disregarding God's commandments (vv 8–13), and likewise admonishes the wicked hypocrite who indeed bears the words of the covenant on his lips but does not uphold it (vv 16–21; cf. Greenberg 1976, pp. 76–77; Schwartz 1979). Similarly, Ps 81 mentions the giving of the law and the Decalogue in order to admonish the people who do not hear God's voice and do not walk in his ways (vv 12–16). Reproofs of this type, based on the Decalogue, are found in the prophecies of Hosea and Jeremiah (cf. Andersen and Freedman 1980, pp. 336–37). Both of these prophets complain about the breaking of the Decalogue's basic commandments, and this in proximity to polemics against the priests and sacrifices. Hosea complains about the absence of "knowledge of God" in the land (4:1), which is expressed in the verse, "[False] swearing, lying, murdering, stealing, and committing adultery" (4:2). The prophet then proceeds to condemn the priests who reject the knowledge of God and forget his law while eating the sin offering (vv 6–8). Similarly, Jeremiah admonishes the people when they come to the Temple gates to worship the Lord (7:2) while referring to five of the Ten Commandments, "Will you steal and murder and commit adultery and swear falsely, and sacrifice to Baal, and follow other gods?" (7:9).[22] Later on the prophet turns to polemics against the sacrifices: "Thus said YHWH, the Lord of Hosts, the God of Israel: Add your burnt offerings to your

[21] "The heavens proclaimed His righteousness, for He is a God who judges" (v 6). Justice and righteousness in this context of a covenant refers to the giving of the law; cf. Ps 99:4: "You who worked judgment and righteousness in Jacob," which appears there alongside *testimony and law* given to Moses and Aaron (vv 6–7). See Weinfeld 1985d, pp. 109–12.
[22] On the chiastic correspondence of the Jeremianic verse to the Decalogue, see Weiss 1984, pp. 256–59 and Note 14 above.

other sacrifices and eat the meat! For when I freed your fathers from the land of Egypt, I did not speak with them or command them concerning burnt offerings or sacrifice. But this is what I commanded them: Listen to My voice, that I may be your God and you may be My people; walk only in the way that I enjoin upon you, that it may go well with you" (7:21–23).

I have shown elsewhere (1976a, pp. 52–55) that this statement by Jeremiah that the people of Israel were not ordered to make sacrifices when they left Egypt can be understood only on the assumption that Jeremiah was referring here to the Decalogue, which, to be sure, does not mention sacrifices at all. According to Deut 5:19ff., God spoke only the Decalogue to the people of Israel at Mount Sinai, whereas the other laws were spoken then to Moses only, and he made them known to the people close to his death in the desert of Moab (see above). We have seen, then, that Pss 50 and 81, which relate to the event of the lawgiving at Sinai, are, in the main, psalms of admonitions and thus similar to the admonitions of Jeremiah and Hosea, which appear against the background of the Decalogue. It seems that the combination of revelatory event and reproof in these psalms can be explained in that the exhorters chose to voice their reprimands precisely at the festival that celebrates the giving of the law and during which the Decalogue was publicly read as part of the festivities. In relation to the reading of the Decalogue in an assembly, the prophets and poets protest against the hypocrisy of the people who do not practice what they preach (cf. Ps 50:16–21). Likewise, they also reject the abundant sacrifices, which are not mentioned at all in the Decalogue.[23] The difference between the prophets and the poets of the psalms is that the former, whose main interest is admonition, have no need to describe the ceremony at which the admonition is voiced, whereas the Temple poets, whose main interest is liturgy, describe and exalt the ceremony of covenant renewal and mention alongside it words of reproof concerning those who do not observe the conditions of the covenant. Thus we find that Ps 50 opens with the revelation at Zion, in language similar to that of the revelation at Mount Sinai,[24] which demonstrates that the event of revelation was transferred from Sinai to Zion.

The fire and the storm that appear here in these psalms are signs of theophany (50:3; 81:8), and the pious followers who make a covenant with sacrifice (50:5) remind us, as I have already said, of the revelation at Mount Sinai (Exod 24). Psalm 81 clarifies another side of the picture. The text refers to the historical background of the festival that celebrates the giving of the "law and rule" in Jacob (81:5) and "testimonies" to Joseph (81:1; cf. Loewenstamm 1958). It describes the Exodus from Egypt, the history of the people on their way up to

[23] Cf. Amos 5:25: "Did you bring me sacrifices and oblation to forty years in the desert?" In connection with festivals 5:21 reads, "I detest, I loathe your festivals."

[24] Compare Deut 33:2, "The Lord came from Sinai. . . . He appeared *[hwpyʿ]* from Mount Paran" with Ps 50:2, "From Zion . . . God appeared *[hwpyʿ]*."

Massah[25] and Meribah,[26] after which comes the quotation from the Decalogue. The sounding of the shofar mentioned in connection with the giving of law and rule in Jacob (vv 4–5) refers apparently to the shofar that was heard at the giving of the law at Mount Sinai (Exod 19:16, 19) and that was sounded at the ceremonies of covenant renewal in Israel, as can be learned from 2 Chr 15:14 (cf. below).[27]

The order of events in Ps 81 coincides with that of the book of Exodus, where the giving of the Torah comes after Massah and Meribah (Exod 19, after Exod 17). If so, the festival reflected here might be Shabuoth, the festival of the giving of the law (see below).

The linguistic usages found in these psalms in relation to the recital of the Decalogue by God are of great importance:

Ps 50:8	*Ps 81:9–10*
Hear, My people *(šmʿh ʿmy),* and I will speak, O Israel, and I will instruct you *(wʾʿydh bk).* I am God your God.	Hear, My people *(šmʿ ʿmy)* and I will instruct you *(wʾʿydh bk);* Israel, if you would but listen to Me! You shall have no foreign god, you shall not bow to an alien god. I am YHWH your God who brought you out of the land of Egypt.

The expressions "hear my people" and "Israel" preceding "I am YHWH your God" recall the declaration "Hear, O Israel! YHWH our God is one YHWH" in Deut 6:4 and may shed light on the joining of the Shemaʿ to the Decalogue as it appears in Deut 5 and 6.

[25] "I shall answer you hidden in a thunder" *(ʾʿnk bstr rʿm)* means answer in the cloud accompanied by God's thunder and lightning; cf. Ps 18:12–14, "He made darkness His hiding . . . then the Lord thundered from heaven." The answer in the cloud can be interpreted as God's speaking to Moses out of the cloud (see Exod 19:18–19, "Now Mount Sinai was all in smoke . . . and the whole mountain trembled. . . . As Moses spoke, God *answered* him in thunder"; cf. also Ps 99:6–7, "Moses and Aaron . . . when they called to the Lord *He answered them.* He spoke to them in a pillar of cloud—they obeyed His decrees, the law He gave them").

[26] On the ambiguity of the testing at the waters of Meribah: on the one hand God tests Israel, and on the other hand Israel tests God. See Loewenstamm 1958.

[27] In late Jewish tradition, which knows only the sounding of the shofar on Rosh Hashanah, this psalm was, to be sure, related to this festival *(b. Roš. Haš.* 8a–b; 34a; etc.), but this is midrash. In accordance with the midrash, the sounding of the shofar at the revelation at Mount Sinai (Exod 19:16, 19) is mentioned at the Rosh Hashanah liturgy; see below, NOTE 55.

The combination of Shemaᶜ with the beginning of the Decalogue is actually reflected in a Jewish liturgical tradition of fourth century C.E. Thus we read in *Midr. Deut. Rab.* (§2.31), "From where did Israel get the recital of Shemaᶜ? Rabbi Phinehas the son of Hama said: from the giving of the law at Sinai did Israel get the recital of Shemaᶜ. You find that the Holy One, blessed be he, opened like this, he said to them: 'Hear, O, Israel, I am YHWH your God.' Then all responded and said: 'YHWH [is] our God, YHWH is one,' and Moses said: Blessed be the name of his glorious kingdom forever and ever." A. Kimmelman of Brandeis University, who kindly informed me of this source, suggested that this tradition demonstrates the way Shemaᶜ was recited in the synagogue at that time. The cantor recited the words ascribed to God, "Hear, O Israel, I am YHWH," etc., while the congregation responded, "YHWH [is] our God, YHWH is one."

Most instructive in the quoted passages from Pss 50 and 81 is the verb *haᶜed,* literally, 'testify'.[28] When it takes the preposition *b,* the verb usually has the meaning of "warn" (by testimony), but in certain contexts this verb receives the connotation of "instruct." Thus in 2 Kgs 17:15 this verb combined with the noun in plural *ᶜedwot* has undoubtedly the meaning 'to teach/impart', as may be learned from its parallel there, "the commands *[ḥq]* and the covenant *[bryt]* imposed upon their fathers." The same applies to Neh 9:34, where we read, "they did not listen to Your commandments *[mṣwh]* and to your *ᶜedwot* which you imparted *[hᶜydt]* to them." To be sure, recent studies make it likely that in addition to the usual meaning of the verb *hᶜyd b* 'warn,' this verb indicates the imposition of laws on one hand (Veijola 1976), and teaching on the other hand (Couroyer 1975).

Thus we have found a connection between lawgiving and admonition, a situation reflected in Pss 50 and 81. It should be added that the verb *hzhyr* reflects this double meaning: *lawgiving* ("and enjoin *[whzhrt]* upon them the laws and the teachings," Exod 18:20) and *warning* as well (2 Kgs 6:10, etc.).[29] The connection between lawgiving and warning is reasonable, for the essence of a law is in fact a warning against transgressions. It is thus not surprising that in Pss 50 and 81 we find admonition bound up with lawgiving. This integration is reflected in Jer 11 when the prophet, who is ordered to spread the words of the covenant in Jerusalem (v 6), formulates his words as a threat, "Cursed be the man who will not obey this covenant" (v 3). In this context we read, to be sure, "for I repeatedly and persistently warned your fathers *(hᶜd hᶜdty hškm whᶜd)* from the time I brought them out of Egypt to this day, saying, Obey My

[28] The "Shemaᶜ Israel" prayer was taken as a *testimony* by the Rabbis (see *b. Ber.* 14b).
[29] The LXX translates *whzhrth* 'enjoin' in Exod 18:20, with the same verb as *hᶜd* in Ps: *marturomai.* It is interesting to note that the medieval liturgy surrounding the Decalogue was called *azharot* 'enjoinments' (see Elbogen 1931, p. 217), a term that apparently has a long tradition behind it.

commands" (v 7), and in the light of the above we can certainly understand the verb *hʿyd* here not only as "warn" but as an admonitory command. This speech may be compared with that of Moses in Deut 32:46: "take to heart all the words with which I have warned you *(mʿyd bkm)* this day. Enjoin them upon your children, that they may observe faithfully all the terms of this Teaching." These verses together may show that the giving of the law and admonition are in fact two sides of the same issue, which accounts for the connection of the two in Pss 50 and 81.

As we shall see below, the festival of Shabuoth served in Second Temple times as an occasion for an 'assembly' *(ʿaṣeret)* to renew and reconfirm the Sinai covenant. We may then assume that this festival was the background of these psalms. Mowinckel sensed that the festival rite was the background of these psalms, but because of his insistence on finding everywhere a reflection of the New Year holiday, he found it here too, though without any basis. The festival to be envisaged here could well be Pentecost. The Pentateuch does not give a date for the festival of Pentecost, but according to the book of Jubilees and the writings of the Qumran sect, the festival was celebrated on the fifteenth day of the month (see below). Accordingly, the *ksh*[30] of Ps 81:4 would conform also to the festival of Shabuoth, a festival on which the people annually renew their covenant with their God. The yearly renewal of a covenant is known from the ancient Near East, from the beginning of the second millennium B.C.E. up to the Hellenistic and Roman era (see Weinfeld 1973a, p. 72n.1, and 1976b, pp. 393–94), and is explicitly found in the Qumran "Rule of the Community" in regards to the annual entering of sect members into the covenant (col. 2, line 19; see below).

5. The Tradition of the Decalogue and Its Evolution

In endeavoring to reconstruct the development of the tradition of the Decalogue, it is possible to assume the following process:

1. At the dawn of Israelite history the Decalogue was promulgated in its original short form as the foundation scroll of the Israelite community, written on two stone tablets, which were later called "the tablets of the covenant" or "tablets of the testimony."[31] The tablets, to be sure, functioned as a testimony

[30] *ksʾ* or *ksh* is the day of the full moon, as we learn from Phoenician and Akkadian, where *kusiu* means the aureola of the moon, apparently originating from *kasû* III 'to tie (the crown)'; cf. recently KB, vol. 2 s.v. Scholars maintain that the calendar of the Bible and especially the calendar of the priestly source is identical to that of the book of Jubilees and that of the sect of the Judean desert (cf., e.g., Jaubert 1953 and 1957). Cazelles 1962, p. 206 even proposed to see *ksʾ* and ḥdš in Ps 81 as parallel concepts, both indicating the day of the full moon.

[31] 'Covenant' *(bĕrît)* and 'testimony' *(ʿdwt)* are parallel; cf. "ark of the covenant"/"ark of the testimony." On *ʿēdût* see below, NOTE to 9:9.

to Israel's commitment to observe the commandments inscribed upon them. These tablets were placed in the Ark of the Covenant, which, together with the cherubim, symbolized God's abode. The cherubim were considered the throne, and the Ark was conceived of as God's footstool (cf. Haran 1958, pp. 87–88). We know today from Hittite documents, contemporary with Moses' time, that nations used to place the covenant documents at their gods' feet, that is, at the feet of their divine images.[32]

This analogy to covenant practices in those days explains Moses' breaking of the tablets when he saw the children of Israel worshiping the golden calf. From the nations of the ancient Near East and mainly from Mesopotamia, we learn that the breaking of the tablet meant the cancellation of the commitment. The classic Mesopotamian expression of this matter is *ṭuppam hepû* 'break the tablet'[33] (cf. the Roman *tabulae novae,* which were written after prior obligations were canceled). It is thus likely that Moses did not act out of weakness or anger, but with forethought.[34] The breaching of the first condition of the Decalogue (the making of sculpted images) necessarily entailed the breaking of the tablets on which the condition was inscribed. Ibn Ezra correctly perceived this matter in his comment to Exod 32:19: "and from overwhelming zeal Moses broke the tablets which were in his hands like a *document of testimony (šṭr ʿdwt),* and thus he tore up the certificate of conditions *(šṭr htnʾym)* and this was in view of all of

[32] So, e.g., in Ramses II's letter to the king of Mirah in the north: "See, the writ of covenant which I have made for the great king of Heth has been laid at the (storm) god's feet; the great gods will be witnesses to it. . . . And behold, the writ of covenant which the great king of Heth made for me has been laid at the god Ra's feet; the great gods will be witnesses to it" (Meissner 1918, p. 58-KBO 1, 24 Rs. 5ff.). For additional references, see Korošec, 1931, pp. 100ff.

[33] See *CAD* 6, H, pp. 171–72. It seems to me that this is the origin of the rabbinical expression *šwbr,* the annulment of the validity of a marriage contract or debt. In certain places we can still interpret "breaking" as used by the Rabbis in its plain meaning of voiding, such as, "If she said, 'I am unclean,' she breaks the Ketubah [= the ostracon on which the Ketubah was written]." In the course of time, when the custom of writing receipts (of debt repayment) developed, this receipt annulling the validity of the commitment was called *šobar,* and there is a derived denominative verb, "break," which means "to write a receipt"; cf. the phrase *šwbrt ʿl ktwbth* in *t. Ketub.* 4:11; 9:1. As known, the Mishnaic terms for documents, such as *geṭ* 'bill of divorce' and *šeṭar* 'bill, note', are taken from Akkadian. After noting the origin of the term *šobar* (see Weinfeld 1976c, p. 116 n. 17), I found that A. Gulak (1935, p. 148 n. 1) came to the same conclusion, even though he did not adduce any supporting data from Akkadian literature.

[34] Cf. the rabbinic tradition, "Moses preached *a minori ad majus:* If about Passover, a single commandment, it says 'No uncircumcised person may eat of it,' how much more the Torah which contains all the commandments" *(y Taʿan.* 4.7 68c and parallels) and ibid., "R. Yishmael taught, the Holy One, Blessed be he, told him to break them."

Israel, for thus it is written" (i.e., Deut 9:17, "and I broke them before your eyes").

2. It should be assumed that the Decalogue was read in the sanctuaries[35] at ceremonies of covenant renewal, and that the people would commit themselves each time anew, as may be learned from the usual ancient Near Eastern custom of renewing covenants annually (see Weinfeld 1973a and 1976b). Psalms 50 and 81 do indeed testify to such rituals, as I have already endeavored to show, and, in my view, these rituals took place on the festival of Shabuoth, the festival of the giving of the law.

3. In Second Temple times, the Decalogue was read daily in the Temple together with the Shemaᶜ prayer, close to the time of the Daily Offering *(m. Tamid,* 5.1). In the Nash papyrus, discovered in Egypt, we also find the Decalogue preceding the Shemaᶜ passage, a text that reflects a liturgical form (see below; and cf. Segal 1947, pp. 227–36). In phylacteries found at Qumran (cf. Yadin 1969, pp. 60–85), we also find the Decalogue next to the Shemaᶜ and, according to the testimony of Jerome, this was the custom in Babylonia up to a late period (cf. Haberman 1954).

4. Rituals of the ancient world may illuminate the process of the evolution of the religious custom under discussion. In a private sanctuary of the first century B.C.E. in Philadelphia, Asia Minor, the sanctuary's foundation inscription was discovered (Weinreich 1919), which details the commandments of the goddess Agdistis, to whom the sanctuary was dedicated. The man who initiated the inscription, Dionysius, received a revelation in a dream in which Zeus gave him the commandments written in the inscription. The commandments oblige all of this sanctuary's visitors, or whoever belongs to this house *(oikos),* and the sanctuary's visitors swear to observe them. The commandments are as follows:[36]

> Not to destroy an embryo and not to use means to abort a fetus (on this issue, see Weinfeld 1977b).
>
> Not to rob.[37]
>
> Not to murder.

[35] Psalm 50 was read in Jerusalem, as v 2 shows. Psalm 81 belongs to a northern tradition (cf. "a testimony to Joseph," v 6) and apparently originated in one of the sanctuaries in the north; on northern psalms, including Ps 81, which were transferred to Jerusalem after the destruction of Samaria, see Sarna 1979, pp. 288ff.

[36] On a parallel to these instructions in the teaching of the twelve apostles (Didache), see Weinfeld 1977b.

[37] Based on the reconstruction *m[ē harpagmon mē]phonon;* however, in Sokolowski's edition, it is *m[ē allo ti paido]phonon* (1950, no. 20, lines 20ff.), and, if so, the sentence relates to infanticide. But the reading of Keil and Paremerstein, on which Weinreich based his extensive study (1919), has been generally accepted. See also Nock 1928, pp. 72ff. (= Nock 1972).

Not to steal anything.

To be loyal *(eunoein)*[38] to the sanctuary.

If somebody commits (a transgression) or plans (to commit one), he shall not be allowed to, and it will not be kept silent, but they will make it known[39] and punish him.

A man shall not lie with a strange woman except for his wife . . . not with a boy and not with a virgin.

In the continuation we hear that

> A man or a woman who has committed one of these transgressions shall not enter this sanctuary, for here great gods sit (on their seats) who keep watch against these transgressions and will not tolerate transgressors.[40] . . . The gods shall pardon the obedient and grant them blessings, and they will hate those who transgress (against the commandments) and impose upon them great punishments.[41] . . . The men and women who are certain of their uprightness shall touch the inscribed pillar[42] every month and year at the time of offering sacrifices.

Without relating to the Decalogue, Nock (1924, pp. 58f.)[43] compared this inscription to Pliny's epistle to Trajan[44] concerning the Christians who get up at dawn *(ante lucem)* in order to sing canons *(invicem,* a sort of precentor and choir),[45] and afterward they commit themselves with an oath

[38] For the understanding of this verb as loyalty, see Weinfeld 1976b, pp. 383–84.

[39] For references on the extradition of violators of the covenant and agitators in covenant documents (cf. Deut 13), see Weinfeld 1976b, pp. 389–90.

[40] Compare in the Decalogue, "a jealous God visiting guilt," "for the Lord will not clear," and, in Josh 24:19, "Because he is a holy God, a jealous God, he will not forgive your transgressions and your sins."

[41] This recalls the motive clause in the Decalogue (Deut 5:9–10 = Exod 20:5–6) about the jealous God on the one hand, and the gracious God on the other; cf. the NOTES.

[42] This is a sort of "swearing on the Bible" or other holy object, which was customary in the Ancient Near East and Greece. See my comments in *Lešonenu* (38 [1977] 232) and note 5 there.

[43] In his article "Early Gentile Christianity" (1928), Nock indicates that O. Casel had already seen the parallel in Pliny's epistles.

[44] *Epistola ad Traianus* 10.96.7. The epistle dates from the year 112 B.C.E.; see Sherwin-White 1966, pp. 327ff.

[45] In my opinion, this is akin to the psalms *(Pesuke de Zimrah)* recited before the Shema^c and the benedictions belonging to Shemaᶜ in the daily liturgy. See Weinfeld 1975–76, pp. 23ff. A good example of the worshiper's response in morning psalms is Ps 145 from

(sacramentum)[46] not to steal, not to commit adultery, not to betray confidence, and not to deny any deposit.[47] After Nock, the assumption was made that Pliny's epistle referred to the Decalogue,[48] and to be sure, as known, the reading of the Decalogue and the Shemaᶜ prayer every morning were considered to constitute acceptance of the yoke of the heavenly kingdom, a kind of commitment by oath (see the discussion in Weinfeld 1976b).

Even though the sanctuary of Philadelphia in Asia Minor dates from the first century B.C.E., there is no doubt that the custom discovered there has roots in an ancient Near Eastern religious tradition.[49] This ancient custom can serve as a sort of background for understanding the evolution of the Decalogue tradition in Israel. We may rightly assume that the beginning of the Decalogue tradition is grounded in a reality similar to that which was found in Philadelphia in Asia Minor. The old community was unified around the Ark, which contained the tablets of the covenant. The believers were sworn to observe the Decalogue written on the tablets, which were given by revelation to Moses, the founder of the community and its cult. Dionysius of the Philadelphia sanctuary appears to have fulfilled a role parallel to that of Moses in Israel.

The tablets containing the Decalogue thus constituted a kind of binding foundation-scroll of the Israelite community (perhaps similar to a constitution). With the disappearance of the Ark and the tablets of the covenant, the Decalogue was freed from its connection to the concrete symbols to which it was previously attached. At festive assemblies, and every morning in the sanctuary, the Decalogue was customarily read, and all present would commit themselves over it by oath to the covenant.[50]

Qumran, where we find after every verse the response "Blessed be YHWH and blessed be his name for ever and ever" (see ibid., pp. 24–25).

[46] For *sacramentum* meaning an oath of allegiance in a religious context, see Weinfeld 1976b, pp. 406–7.

[47] "Ne furta, ne latrocinia, ne adulteria commiterent, ne fidem fallerent, ne depositum apellati abnegarent."

[48] Kraemer 1934; Mohler 1935; Coutler 1940. The last two items are apparently parallel to the two last commandments: "You shall not bear false witness against your neighbor" and "You shall not covet." In Mark 10:19, to be sure, we find instead of "you shall not covet," *mē apostereses,* meaning "you shall not defraud," which was found in Lev 19:13 in a unit based on the Decalogue; cf. also Lev 5:21, which deals with abnegation of a deposit or about a pledge, and, according to my interpretation, all of these items are included in "you shall not covet"; see above, §2e. Cf. Coulter 1940, pp. 60ff.

[49] Cf. Nock 1928, pp. 74ff. On the consciousness of sin bound up with confession in Near Eastern and Asian peoples, see Pettazzoni 1937, and on the confession in Egypt, see Weinfeld 1978–79b, pp. 196–97 n. 56, along with Weinfeld 1982a.

[50] *ʾemeth we-yaṣṣib,* which was said in the Temple after the Decalogue and the Shemaᶜ prayer *(m. Tamid* 5.1), is a kind of obligation by oath to fulfill the demands included in the Decalogue and the Shemaᶜ. See Weinfeld 1976b.

On the importance of the tablets inscribed with the traditions under discussion, it is worth recalling here Pausanias's story about a holy place in Greece (Arcadia) where two stones stood with the sacred books placed between them (cf. the book of the Torah that was placed "beside the Ark of the Covenant" in which the tablets of the law were set, Deut 31:26), and the worshipers would take oaths by these stones (8.15.2).

Despite the similarity in background between the Decalogue tradition and the oaths of the worshipers at the temple in Philadelphia, the decisive difference between the place of the Decalogue in Israel and the place of the ordinances among the worshipers at Philadelphia should be pointed out. In contrast to the Israelite conception of the Decalogue as a set of obligations placed upon all Israelites wherever they might be, in the pagan tradition what is dealt with are obligations upon a group of *temple visitors* who are required strictly to observe ritual purity in order to prevent the desecration of the holy site. In this respect, the Philadelphian oath is similar to the conditions of entrance for temple visitors in Israel and in the ancient Near East, mentioned above. Needless to say, the basic religious demands particular to Israel, which are included in the first half of the Decalogue, are not found and are not expected to be found in the Philadelphian oath.

The Rabbis indeed felt that, in contrast to the first five commandments, which are of specifically Israelite nature, with the name YHWH mentioned in each of them, the last five commandments are of universal nature, and thus do not mention the Tetragrammaton at all (cf. *Pesiq. R.* 21 [Ish Shalom 1880, 99a]).

6. The Revelation at Sinai and the Festival of the Giving of the Law

The festival at which it was customary to dramatize the revelatory event at Sinai and to make a renewed oath on reception of the law, was the Feast of Weeks, and, in my view, this rite is reflected in Pss 50 and 81. In Second Temple times this festival was called *ʿaṣeret* 'Assembly',[51] and it is so called by Josephus *(Antiquities* 3.252). This term can be explained by realizing that the Feast of Shabuoth was a day of assembling together or, in biblical language, *yom haqqahal* 'the day of the Assembly', which indicates the day on which the people assembled together in order to receive the Word of God, as expressed in the Decalogue (Deut 9:10; 10:4; 18:16).[52] On this festival day the wondrous

[51] See *Tgs. Onq.* and *Ps.-J.* to Num 28:26 *(bšbʿwtykm* 'your Feast of Weeks' = *bʿṣrtykwn* 'in your assemblies'); cf. *Tg. Neof.* to Deut 16:10, *ḥgh dšbwʿyh hyʾ ʿṣrth* 'the Feast of Weeks, which is *ʿṣrth*'.

[52] See D. H. Hoffmann's thorough discussion of this problem in his commentary on *Leviticus* (1905) 2.158ff. Note that *Tg. Ps.-J.* and *Tg. Neof.* both translate *bywm hqhl* as

event was apparently dramatized in a ritual, and the people took the Decalogue upon themselves by covenant and oath.

Exodus 19:1 indicates that the Israelites reached the wilderness of Sinai in the third month, and the account of the preparation for the revelation at Sinai follows immediately. Following Mowinckel, some scholars have correctly assumed that the rites of sanctification and shofar blowing, described in this chapter, reflect the course of a ritual customarily performed during covenant-renewal ceremonies. The preparations for the revelation at Sinai are in fact preparations for a divine encounter that comes about at every assembly held at the Temple. Like the sanctification, washing of clothes, and abstention from women as preparation for revelation, which are described in Exod 19 (vv 10, 15), we find in Gen 35:1–3 that Jacob commands his household to purify themselves and to change clothes (v 2)[53] before going up to Beth-El. The setting of bounds around the mountain and the distancing of the people from the most holy site found in Exod 19 (vv 11–13, 21–24) are also characteristic of the restriction of access to a holy site.[54] The blowing of the shofar indicated an occasion of oath and commitment,[55] and indeed in the covenant of Asa in the third month (2 Chr 15:14), which I will mention below, the shofar was blown on making the oath. Ehrlich already concluded from this (1900, p. 455, on 2 Chr 15:14) that the Jewish custom practiced in accompanying an oath with the sound of the shofar (see NOTE 55) is based on the Bible.

It thus appears that, just as the Feast of Passover and the Feast of Unleavened Bread come to dramatize the event of the Exodus, and the Feast of Tabernacles, involving sitting in "booths," comes to dramatize the "booths" in which the Israelites lived in the wilderness (Lev 23:42–43), so also the Feast of Shabuoth commemorates the revelatory event at Mount Sinai.

That the Feast of Shabuoth was a day on which the people assembled at the

---

"on the day of the assembling of the community" and Deut 18:16 as "on the day of assembly of the tribes to receive the Torah."

[53] Similar restrictions for visitors to a sanctuary were found in ancient Greece. See Nilsson 1974, 2.74. The inscription in the Temple of Zeus Kynthios is instructive. It requires that all temple visitors be pure, be clad in white clothes, and be barefoot. They must also have abstained from sexual relations and not be unclean by reason of contact with the dead.

[54] Naḥmanides already pointed out the similarity between the bounding of Mount Sinai in Exod 19 and the warnings concerning approaching the tent of meeting (see his preface to the book of Numbers and his preface to Exod 25); cf. recently Milgrom 1970, 1.44ff.

[55] Thus, for example, at the inauguration of a king, when all of the people obligate themselves to be loyal to the new king (see 2 Sam 15:10; 1 Kgs 1:49; 2 Kgs 9:13; 11:14, "blowing of the trumpets"). On the sounding of the shofar to accompany an oath, see *hst* in *Aruch Completum sive Lexicon, vocabula et res, quae in libris Targumicis, Talmudicis et Midraschicis, continentur, explicaus auctore Nathane filio Jechielis,* ed. A. Kohut (1878–92), 3.229: "And they blow the shofar with the oath."

Temple can be learned from Josephus and from the book of Acts in the New Testament. Josephus tells us twice about assemblies in Jerusalem during the Feast of Weeks—once in connection with the invasion of the Parthians in 40 B.C.E.: "When the feast called Pentecost came round, the whole neighborhood of the temple and the entire city were crowded with the country folk" *(Wars* 2.43; cf. *Antiquities* 17.254). The assembly, to be sure, served as a cover for the rebels but was itself motivated by the tradition of observing a day of popular, mass assembly at this time of year (and see *Wars* 2.73). Similarly, we read in the book of Acts, chap. 2, that the crowd that told of the great (sights) *(ta megaleia)*[56] that took place on the Feast of Weeks contained Parthians, Medes, Elamites, inhabitants of Mesopotamia, of Judea and Cappodocia, of Pontus and Asia, of Phrygia and Pamphylia, of Egypt and the districts of Libya around Cyrene (Acts 2:9–11). Acts 20:16 reveals that the Feast of Weeks was an especially important pilgrim festival. There it is said that Paul made an effort to arrive in Jerusalem for the Feast of Weeks, which reminds us of what is said concerning Judah the Maccabee (2 Macc 12:31–32), that he returned from Scythopolis in time for the Feast of Weeks.

Philo calls the Feast of Weeks a festival observed in the most national-popular way *(demotelestatē heortē; Special Laws* 1.183), and when he describes the celebration of the Feast of Weeks by the *therapeutae,* he calls this festival the "greatest festival" *(megistē heortē; De vita contemplativa* 65).

The following sources testify concerning the observance of covenant-renewal ceremonies and of the day of the giving of the law at the Feast of Weeks:

1. In 2 Chr 15:8–15 we read that in the third month[57] of the fifteenth year of Asa's reign, men from Judah and Benjamin, as well as from Ephraim, Manasseh, and Simeon, assembled together in Jerusalem in connection with the rededication of the altar. They offered sacrifices, entered a covenant to seek the Lord with all their heart and soul, and made oaths in a loud voice, to the accompaniment of blasts from trumpets and shofars. The oath is an oath of covenant,[58] which reminds us of the covenant at Sinai, also made with the offering of sacrifices (Exod 24:3f.). The oath is made rejoicingly, *with all the heart and*

[56] *ta megaleia* = 'the great works' (v 11) or 'the great visions'; cf. *mwrʾym gdwlym* (Deut 4:37) and *mrʾ gdwl* (Deut 26:8), which in the LXX are translated *en horamasin megalois;* in the Aramaic translations, *ḥzwnyn rbrbyn;* in the Samaritan Pentateuch and in the rabbinic homilies, *wbmrʾ gdwl:* "this is the revelation of the Divine Presence" *(Midr. Tanaaim: Deuteronomium* [D. H. Hoffmann 1908, on Deut 26:5, p. 173]) is interpreted as a vision and revelation.

[57] The *Targum* adds here in v 11, *bḥgʾ dšbwʿy* 'on the Feast of the Weeks'; cf. Sperber 1959, 1.45.

[58] On *bryt* and *ʾlh* and their congruency with the *bryt* and *šbwʿh,* see Weinfeld 1971–72a, pp. 85–87.

willingness, which comes to give more validity to the obligation.[59] The joy, however, may also refer to a festival on which a rite of covenant renewal was observed.[60] The root *šbʿ*, which appears in this section three times (vv 14–15), undoubtedly comes to connect the subject with the Feast of Weeks *(šbwʿt),* and it thereby receives a double meaning: the weeks *(šbwʿwt)* of wheat harvest and the oaths *(šbwʿwt)* of the covenant.[61] This ambiguity of *šbwʿwt* is found also in the book of Jubilees 6:21, "this feast is twofold and of a double nature"[62] and is reflected in the Temple Scroll, which refers to this festival, "It is the Feast of Weeks and the Feast of Firstfruits for an eternal memorial" (col. 19, line 9).[63] It seems that the scroll's addition of *lzkrwn ʿwlm* 'for an eternal memorial' testifies to the special importance of this festival. As I have already mentioned, the sounding of the shofar in the rite of 2 Chr 15 accompanies the oath, and according to my view (see above), the sounding of the shofar mentioned in Ps 81:3 is also connected with the Feast of Weeks.[64]

[59] Joy and love will come to express full readiness in those who enter the covenant and indicate that the commitment was not made out of pressure or coercion; such clarifications are to be found in legal documents in the ancient world; cf. Muffs 1975. Concerning the Sinai covenant, cf. *Mek. Bahodesh* §2 (Horowitz 1928, p. 209): "they all agreed single-heartedly to accept the yoke of the kingdom of heaven with joy *(bešimḥah)";* see also Muffs 1979, p. 110. Compare also in the Benediction after Shemaʿ, which is acceptance of the yoke of the kingdom of heaven (cf. above and Weinfeld 1976b): "And his kingdom they took upon themselves willingly *(brṣwn).*"

[60] On the joy at the Pentecost festival, see Deut 16:11. Compare also the relation between this festival and the covenant of Sinai, in the Aramaic Targumim of Exod 24:11: "and they were joyous with their sacrifices."

[61] For the tendentiousness of the double name-derivation in the Books of Chronicles, see Y. Zakovitch, *Kpl mdršy hšm,* M.A. thesis, Hebrew University of Jerusalem, 1971, pp. 166ff.

[62] See Charles 1913, vol. 2 on this passage. Charles wondered about the meaning of "double nature" in this sentence (2.53 n. 21). In my opinion, the double nature originated from the ambiguity of *šebuʿwt* here. It should be added that the Festival of Shabuoth in the book of Jubilees is bound up with the covenants that God made with the Patriarchs (see below), and thus the doubleness is also expressed by God's making an oath on this day to the Patriarchs on the one hand, and the children of Israel's making an oath to God on the other hand.

[63] See Yadin's comments in 1977, 2.82.

[64] According to Philo *(On the Laws* 2.188), the sounding of the shofar on Rosh Hashanah appears to recall the giving of the Torah. The same idea is reflected in the liturgy that opens the order of *Shofaroth* in the prayers of Rosh Hashanah: "You did reveal yourself in a cloud of glory to the holy people in order to speak to them. Out of heaven you made them hear your voice . . . amidst thunders and lightnings you did manifest yourself to them and while the shofar sounded you did appear to them." But the sounding of the shofar indicates, rather, the enthronement of God (see NOTE 55 above), as Mowinckel already pointed out (1927); cf. Ps 47:6ff., a psalm that indeed is

2. The Feast of the Giving of the Law is most clearly portrayed in the book of Jubilees. There we read that it was determined in the heavenly tablets that "the Feast of Weeks be observed in the month of Sivan, in order to renew the Covenant each year" (6:17). The Covenant with Noah was established in the month of Sivan, and Noah was the first to observe the Feast of Weeks. The "Covenant Between the Pieces" was also made in the middle of the month of Sivan, of which we read: "And on that day we made a covenant with Abram, according as we have covenanted with Noah . . . and Abram renewed the festival . . . forever" (Jub 14:20). On the fifteenth of the month of Sivan, which is the Feast of Weeks according to the book of Jubilees (see Charles 1913, p. 52) and the calendar of the Qumran sect (see Talmon 1961), God reveals himself to Abram and makes a covenantal promise to give him offspring, whereupon he is given the ordinance of circumcision, which he immediately performs (chap. 15). Isaac was born on the Feast of Weeks (in the middle of the third month) and was circumcised eight days later (16:13). God reveals himself to Jacob also in the middle of the third month (chap. 44). The covenants with Noah and with Abraham were made with a sacrifice (6:3; 14:19), as was the Sinai covenant (Exod 24:3f.; and cf. Ps 50:5), as well as the covenant in the days of Asa mentioned above (2 Chr 15:11).

3. The Qumran sect renewed the covenant every year *(Manual of Discipline,* col. 1, 16f.), and, according to an unpublished text from cave 4, this rite also took place on the Feast of Weeks (see Milik 1959, pp. 113ff. and Delcor 1966, 858–79).

4. The *therapeutae* in Egypt described by Philo in *De vita contemplativa,* especially close in character to those of the Qumran sect, considered the Feast of Weeks the "greatest festival" *(megistē heorte);* [65] they observed a vigil on the eve of this festival during which hymns of thanksgiving were sung. As we shall see below, this tradition exists in later Judaism. It is not said what was done on the festival day itself, but it would not be too much to assume that they observed a covenant-renewal ceremony, as did the members of the Qumran sect.

5. The Feast of Weeks, as the Feast of the Giving of the Law, is the background of the account in Acts 2 concerning the establishment of the first Christian community. We read here that when the Festival of Weeks came, everyone was assembled together with one accord, and there was suddenly a

---

read today at Rosh Hashanah before the sounding of the shofar. The mention of the shofar-blowing at the revelation at Mount Sinai in the liturgy of Rosh Hashanah is no different from other references to shofar-blowing in this liturgy that are not necessarily related to Rosh Hashanah.

[65] Although it is not said that "the fiftieth day" is the fiftieth day from the beginning of the waving of the Omer, the expression "after seven weeks" *(dia hepta hebdomadon),* along with the expression "the greatest Festival," support the assumption that the festival of Shabuoth is meant.

great rushing sound from heaven, as of a stormy wind, which filled the house; whereupon tongues of fire materialized, which separated and alighted on the heads of each one. After this, everyone was filled with the Holy Spirit and began to speak in diverse languages, as the Spirit so led them (vv 1–4). The basic elements of this account are taken from the tradition of the lawgiving at Sinai:

A. The rushing sound from heaven and tongues of fire are rooted in the descriptions of the revelation at Sinai as reflected in legends from Second Temple times. Midrashic literature, the Aramaic Targumim, and Philo as well describe the words that came from the mouth of God as flames of fire, a notion based on the verse "all the people witnessed the thunder and lightning" (Exod 20:15). On the words "all the people witnessed," and so on, Rabbi Akiva comments, "A Word of fire was seen coming out from the mouth of the Almighty and engraved itself into the tablets, as it is written: 'the voice of the Lord kindles flame of fire' (Ps 29:7)" *(Mek. R. Ishmael, Baḥodeš* §9 [Horowitz 1928, p. 235]).

Philo speaks similarly of a flame that became "an articulate speech in the language familiar to the audience" *(On the Decalogue* 46). Similar descriptions are found in *Tg. Ps.-J.*, in Targum fragments from the Cairo Genizah, and in *Tg. Neof.*: "A Word . . . as if going out from the mouth of the Holy One, blessed be His name, like sparks and flashes and flames and fiery torches, a torch from the right and a torch that came out of the left, flew in the air and went forth and showed itself on the camps of Israel and came back and returned and engraved itself on the tablets of the Covenant."[66] This description derives from Deut 33:2, "lightning flashing at them from his right," concerning which we read in *Sipre Deut.* §343 (Finkelstein 1969, p. 399): "When a Word went out from the mouth of the Holy One blessed be He, it went out from his right side . . . to Israel's left side and encompasses the camp of Israel . . . and the Holy One retrieves it . . . and engraves it on the tablet . . . as it is written: 'the voice of the Lord kindles flames of fire.' "

B. A fire that divides into tongues of flame, whereupon everyone begins to speak in various languages, has its source in a midrash according to which the Word was divided into seventy tongues, that is, the tongues or languages of all nations.[67] Thus Rabbi Yohanan says, "Every word that came out of the mouth of the Holy One, blessed be his name, was divided into seventy tongues" *(b. Šabb.* 88b),[68] and in the continuation we read, "A student of R. Ishmael taught, 'like a hammer that shatters rock' (Jer 23:29), just as the sledgehammer (when shattered by the harder rock) is divided into many slivers, so every word which was uttered by the Holy One was divided into seventy tongues." Most impor-

[66] On the various versions in translations, see Potin 1971, pp. 37ff.

[67] On the seventy nations of the world, see Gen 10 and my short commentary (Weinfeld 1975a); and on the rabbinic legends about this matter, see Ginzberg 1959, no. 4, n. 72.

[68] See *Midr. Tehillim* 92:3 (Buber 1891, p. 22); and for other sources see Ginzberg 1959, no. 11, n. 214.

Kadesh-Barnea, excavations *(Y. Schiff, Revivim, Hamavdil, Ramat Gan, Israel)*

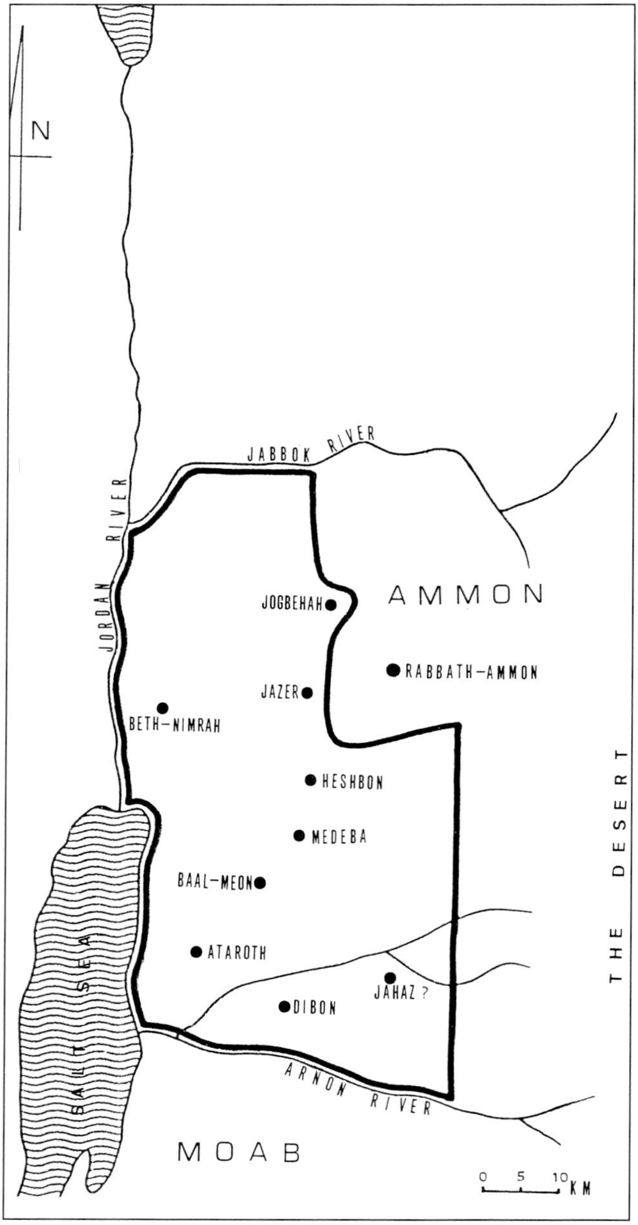

Map of the Kingdom of Sihon, the King of Heshbon

The arc of the Covenant, Justus van Grand, ca. 1475 *(G.B.A. Zarphati)*

Giving the Law; Venice, Italy *(G.B.A. Zarphati)*

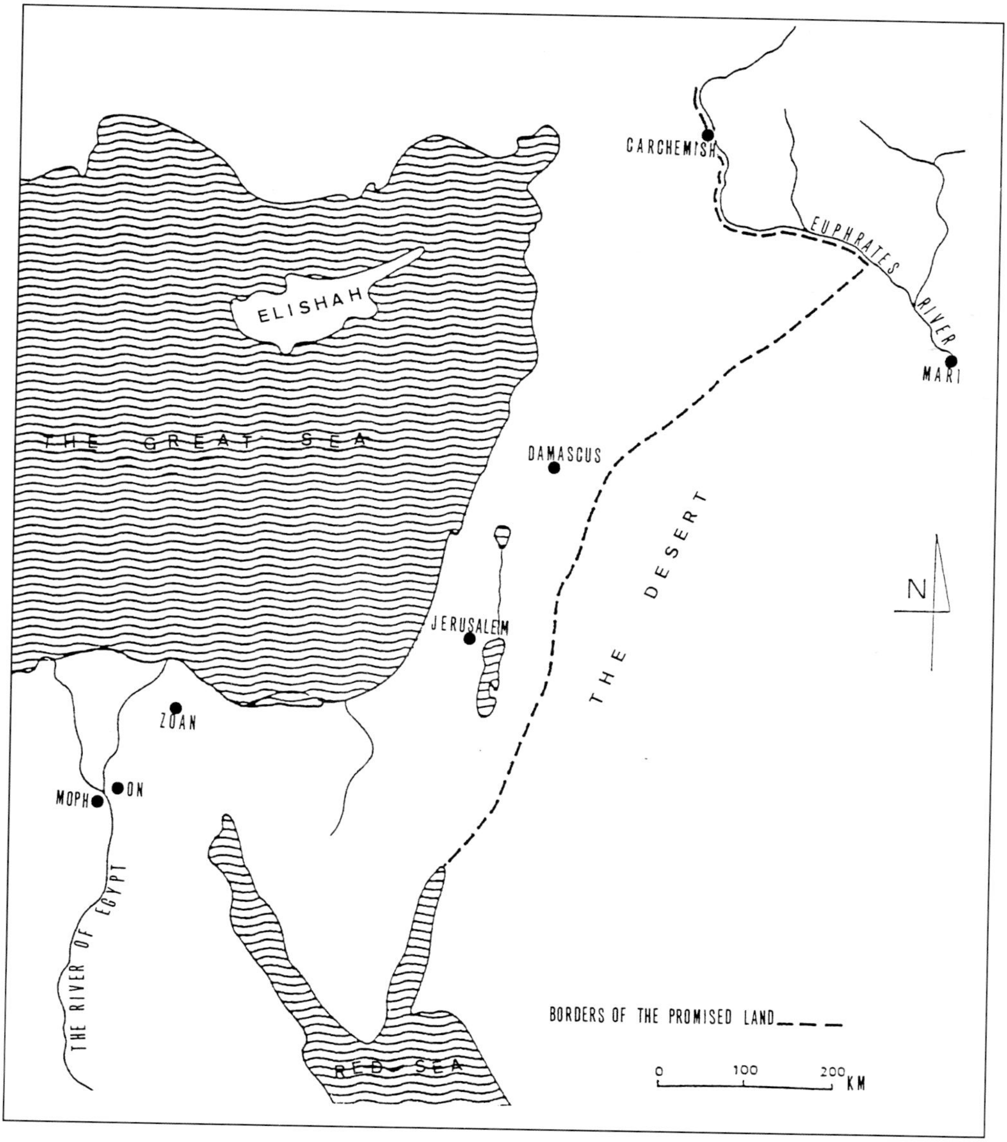

Map of the Promised Land

Mountains of Edom *(Y. Schiff)*

Plaster cast of the interior capsula of Phylacteries from Qumran
(Israel exploration Society)

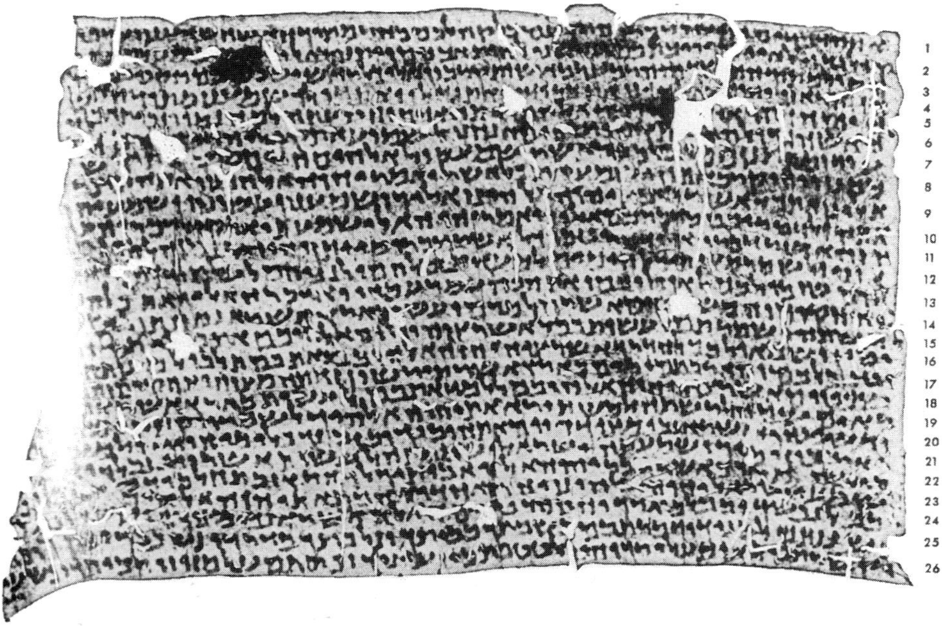

A text from Phylacteries of Qumrun containing Deut 5:22-6:9
(Israel Exploration Society)

tant to the present discussion is the congruence between the language of the midrash—a word (as fire) *divided* into seventy tongues—and the language of Acts 2—"tongues *divided* like flames of fire" (v 3).

In rabbinic tradition, the Word is divided into seventy in order to allow its diffusion among the nations, and in *m. Soṭa* 7.5 we read that all of the Words of the Law were written on the stones of the altar on Mount Ebal in seventy languages.[69] The Christian tradition similarly speaks of tongues of fire that divided and alighted upon the people present at the revelatory event and bestowed on the participants the ability to spread the new word in all the world's languages, as described in the continuation of the account (see also Potin 1971, pp. 310ff.).

It should be added that *Sipre Deut.* on Deuteronomy 33:2, in which §343, p. 399) *a Word likened to fire* is mentioned as an interpretation of *mymynw ʾš dt lmw,* also deals with a word given in various languages: "When the Holy One revealed himself to give the Law to Israel, he did not speak in one language but in four, as it is written: 'from Sinai'—this is Hebrew; 'from Seir'—this is Latin; 'from Mount Paran'—this is Arabic; *mrbbt qdš*—this is Aramaic" (§343, p. 395).

C. The tongues of fire that rested[70] upon each one of the participants remind us of the crowns that the Israelites received at the revelation at Sinai;[71] the "crowns" *(ʿṭrwt)* are none other than a radiance of the divine presence around their heads.[72] In another place I have pointed out (Weinfeld 1978, pp. 15ff.) that the tradition discussed here of men[73] upon which tongues of fire alighted, and who were thus filled with the Holy Spirit, derives from Num 11, which speaks of the elders upon whom the Spirit fell and made them the leaders of the congregation. The institution of the seventy elders corresponds to the

[69] See also *t. Soṭa* 8.6–7 and the *Mek.* on Deuteronomy discovered by Schechter (p. 189). An extensive discussion of the subject was made by Lieberman 1955–, 8.699–701.

[70] *ekatisen.* The verb *katizo* translates in the LXX "came to rest" in Gen 8:4.

[71] See *Pesiq. Rab Kah.* (Mandelbaum 1987, p. 266) and the parallels mentioned there and also *b. Sabb.* 88a. See also the discussion by Urbach 1979, pp. 147ff.

[72] Compare "and you adorned him with glory and majesty" in Ps 8:7, meaning the divine radiance around his head (compare *melammu* in Akkadian, and see also Job 19:9, "He has stripped me of my glory, removed the crown from my head"). The *klyl tpʾrt* 'diadem of glory' bestowed on Moses according to Ben Sira 45:8, which is paralleled there with glory and might, is the radiance around his face (Exod 34:29ff.) and in the scrolls of the Judean desert is called *klyl kbwd* 'diadem of glory' in 1QS 4, line 8; Thanksgiving scroll 9, line 25. In Hellenistic literature this aureole is called *diadema tēs doxēs;* see Reitzenstein 1927, pp. 359–60); and it is this aureole that is put on the pious ones in the world to come "who enjoy the radiance of the divine presence" *(b. Ber.* 17a). For glory as an aureole in the Bible and in the ancient Near East, see Weinfeld 1984b.

[73] It is not clear whether Acts 2:4 refers to the 120 men mentioned in 1:15 or to the twelve apostles.

seventy members of the Sanhedrin, who had to know seventy languages (see *t. Sanh.* 8:1; *y. Seqal.* 5.1, 48d; *b. Sarh.* 17a; *b. Menaḥ.* 65a). This tradition was now transferred to the founding meeting of the Christian community. According to Christian tradition, the Holy Spirit fell upon the leaders of the Christian community as well, and, like the Sanhedrin, they also were able to speak in diverse languages by virtue of the tongues of fire that alighted upon them.

The first revelation to the people of Israel served, then, as a point of origin for the crystallization of various traditions concerning prophetic-mystical experiences, which took place on the Feast of Weeks. Josephus relates *(Antiquities* 6.299) that on the eve of the Feast of Weeks before the war, the priests heard a voice of declaration, "We are leaving" (cf. Tacitus, *Historia* 5.13).

The mystical experience of Rabbi Joseph Caro (1488–1575) is also connected with the festival of Shabuoth. On the eve of the Feast of Shabuoth, during the all-night vigil, a voice came out from his mouth, and the men about him heard the voice, fell on their faces, and fainted.[74]

The second experience is related to Shabbetai Tsevi's messianic declaration. On the eve of the Feast of Shabuoth, the Holy Spirit came upon Nathan from Gaza, he fainted, and out of his faint he was heard to utter various voices, which were afterward interpreted to mean that Shabbetai Tsevi was worthy to be king over Israel.[75]

A relic of the ancient celebration of Feast of Weeks has been preserved up to our day in the different customs attached to the observance of this festival in Jewish worship. Thus the all-night vigil on the eve of the festival *(tiqûn lêl Šabuʿôt)* recalls a kind of vigil on the eve of the giving of the law. Indeed, the Samaritans preserved a tradition of reading the Torah on the eve of the revelation at Mount Sinai, from the middle of the night until the following evening, while ascending Mount Gerizim and praying (cf. Boys 1961; Tsedaka 1969, pp. 10–11).

The recital of the Decalogue during Pentecost is accompanied in the Jewish tradition by festive liturgies of ancient origin. Various introductory poems *(rešuyot)* in the Aramaic language were composed for reciting before the reading of the Ten Commandments on the day of Shabuoth. These were preserved in the Aramaic Targumim to the Pentateuch (cf. Klein 1980, 1.117–25). Similarly,

[74] For this evidence see Werblowsky 1962, pp. 19–21.

[75] G. Shalom, *Shabetai Tsevi and His Movement* (Tel Aviv, 1975), 1.178 [Heb.]. In my opinion, the swooning on the night of Shabuoth originated from the revelation at the giving of the Torah, when, according to tradition, all those present there fainted or fell down in a swoon. Cf. *b. Šabb.* 88b: "with every word coming out of the Holy One . . . the souls of the Israelites fled as it says: 'My soul departs when he spoke' (Cant 5:6)." Compare the Rosh Hashanah liturgy in the Geniza version (Order of *Shofaroth)* concerning the Sinai revelation: "they all fainted and fell on their faces and their souls departed because of the voice of the words (of God)" (Mann 1925, p. 330).

we find a category of liturgical poems for the Feast of Weeks, so-called *ʾazharot,* in which all of the 613 Torah commandments are enumerated and classified according to the Ten Commandments (cf. Elbogen 1931, pp. 217–18). All of this seems to indicate that the revelation and giving of the law were dramatized in Israel from ancient times.

THE DECALOGUE (5:6–18)

5 6I am YHWH your God who freed you from the land of Egypt, from the
house of bondage. 7You shall have no other gods in my presence.
8You shall not make for yourself a carved image, any likeness of what is in
the heavens above, or on the earth below, or in the waters below the earth. 9You
shall not bow down to them or serve them, for I am YHWH your God, an
impassioned God, visiting the iniquities of the fathers upon the children, and
upon the third and fourth generation for those who hate me, 10but showing
kindness to the thousandth generation to those who love me and keep my
commandments.
11You shall not take up the name of YHWH your God in vain, for YHWH
will not acquit one who takes up his name in vain.
12Observe the Sabbath day to keep it holy, as YHWH your God commanded you. 13Six days you shall labor and do all your work. 14But the seventh
day is a Sabbath to YHWH your God. You shall not do any work, you and your
son and your daughter and your male servant and your female servant and your
ox and your ass and any of your animals and the alien [resident] in your gates, so
that your male and female slave may rest as you do. 15Remember that you were
a slave in the land of Egypt and YHWH your God freed you from there with a
strong hand and outstretched arm; therefore, YHWH your God commanded
you to observe the Sabbath day.
16Honor your father and your mother, as YHWH commanded you, that
your days may long endure and that you may fare well upon the land that
YHWH your God is giving you.

17You shall not murder
and you shall not commit adultery
and you shall not steal
and you shall not bear false witness against your neighbor.

18And you shall not covet your neighbor's wife, and you shall not crave your
neighbor's house, his field, his male and female slave, his ox and his ass and
anything that is your neighbor's.

TEXTUAL NOTES

5:6. *I am YHWH your God who.* "I *(ʾnky)*" is the subject and "YHWH who," etc. is the predicate, that is to say, I am YHWH (cf. Masoretic accents); otherwise the verb *hwṣyʾ* in the relative clause should be in the third person, *hwṣyʾk* and not *hwṣʾtyk* (see Luzzatto, ed. Schlesinger, 1965, p. 318 [orig. 1871]).

7. *in my presence.* Hebrew: *ʿal panay,* literally, 'upon my face'. The exact meaning of the phrase has been the subject of much scholarly debate. KB[3] offers six possible meanings: "beside me," in the spatial sense ("next to me"); "beside me," in the figurative sense ("except for me"); "in addition to me," "to my disadvantage"; "before me," "in front of me"; "in my presence"; and "to spite me," "in defiance of me." There is little difference between the first, fourth, and fifth definitions. *ʿal peney* is well attested in the sense of "before," "in front of" (fourth definition): Gen 32:22; Exod 33:19; Lev 10:3; 1 Kgs 6:3; Ps 18:43. This is the most common definition of the similar prepositional phrases *lipney* and *ʾel pĕney.*

"In my presence" is simply another way of saying "in front of me," though the semantic range may be greater, in that one can stand in another's presence without being directly in front of him. This definition is more faithful to the Hebrew in that it is a phrase that contains a preposition plus the noun "presence," equivalent to *panim* 'face'. Indeed, the LXX to Deut 5:7 has *pro prosopou mou* 'before my face'.

The meaning "next to," "near" (first definition) is used only of place-names, though according to some scholars the meaning in this context is "east of." This definition is clearly a development from the preceding meanings, and it hardly seems preferable to them in this case.

The definition "except for me" is also a semantic development of the preceding meanings. It is found in the LXX *(plen emou),* Peshitta, and Aramaic Targumim *(br mny)* to Exod 20:3. Such a meaning of *ʿal peney* is nowhere else attested in the Bible, though it may be the meaning of a Phoenician cognate (see below). It seems that the use of this definition in the ancient versions is based on theological considerations. The preceding definitions suggest, as it were, a physical deity, in whose presence no other deities are allowed. The existence of other deities, and the physical nature of God, both proved an anathema to later Israelite religion and later Judaism; hence the understanding of *ʿal panay* in the sense of "except me," similar to the semantic development of the English "besides me."

The two phrases cited by KB[3] in juxtaposition as the third definition must certainly puzzle the English reader. This definition is taken by KB[3] from Stamm 1961, p. 238. Stamm cites these as alternative definitions based on the Phoenician cognate *ʿlt pn,* which Albright 1940, p. 258, translates as "in addition to" or "except." The German word for "disadvantage" is *Nachteil,* literally, 'additional part', and therefore Stamm allowed himself the liberty of extending the semantic range of the Phoenician and Hebrew to the extent of the German, though this does not seem justified. If we disregard "to my disadvantage," the definition "in addition to me" is virtually identical to the second definition, "besides me, except me." If Albright's definition of Phoenician *ʿlt pn* is correct, we have philological evidence for what otherwise seems to be an apologetic theological interpretation (see above). But *KAI* (69:5, 7, 10) defined the Phoenician *ʿlt pn* as simply "gegenuber, vor" ("in front of").

The most interesting definition is the last one, "to spite me, in defiance of me." Edward König, in his commentary on Deuteronomy, is the first to suggest this definition. He cites Isa 65:3; Job 1:11; and Job 21:31 as further evidence for this use of *ʿal pĕney.* In Job, however, the issue of God's immanence is of paramount importance, and it seems most likely that *ʿal pĕney* in the two Job verses means quite literally 'to [God's] face' or 'in his presence'. The use of *ʿal panay* in Isa 65:3 is similar to its use in the Decalogue and is equally ambiguous: "The people who provoke my anger continually, *ʿal panay,*" that is, "to my face" or "in my presence."

Stamm (1961) cites as further evidence for this "hostile nuance" of *ʿal pĕney* the following verses: Gen 16:12; 25:18 (Ishmael dwells, or falls, *ʿal pĕney* his brethren); Deut 21:16 (preference of younger son *ʿal pĕney* the elder); Nah 2:2 ("A shatterer shall come *ʿal paneyka"*); and Ps 21:13 ("with your bows you will aim *ʿal pĕneyhem").* All of these, however, can be understood in the neutral senses of "in the presence of," "near," or "in the face of." There is no evidence that *ʿal pĕney* alone carries a hostile connotation. It should be noted that only this definition is offered in the previous edition of KB; hence it has achieved undue popularity in recent years.

8. *any (likeness).* MT: *kl;* MT Exod 20:4, LXX, Samaritan, Peshitta, 4Q Dt^n (White 1990, p. 275), 4Q Phyl. G, J *(DJD* 6.59, 65), XQ Phyl. 3 (Yadin *EI* 9 [1969] P.82, P1.27): *wkl.* See NOTE.

9. *serve them.* The MT and 1Q 13 (DJD 1.74: *tʿwbdm)* read *toʿobdem* instead of the expected *taʿabdem.* Compare Exod 20:5; 23:24; and Deut 13:3. It seems that the Masoretic vocalization in the *hophʿal* is tendentious. It is meant to imply compulsory idolatry, as though the meaning were "you shall not allow yourself to be brought to worship them" (cf. *GKC* §60b), an idea alluded to in Deut 4:28; 28:36, 64; see the NOTE to 4:28.

visiting the iniquities. Hebrew: *poqed.* The verb *pqd* has a very wide semantic range in biblical Hebrew. Some of the meanings are entrust *(hiphʿil),* appoint, attend to, visit, seek, muster, miss *(niphʿal),* and test. This multitude of apparently unrelated meanings has led to much scholarly debate as to which meaning is original and how the other usages derive from it. KB^3 cites three suggestions for the original meaning: to miss; to attend to with care (Speiser

1958, p. 21); and to seek out, to visit (Fahlgren 1932, p. 66). To these we must add two more definitions: to examine, to test, to investigate, and to act in accordance with the results of the investigation (Scharbert 1960); and to set in order, organize (M. Buber, in the introduction to Buber and Rosenzweig trans. of the Bible [1954–62], p. 25).

The most difficult question is how to encompass the meanings "to miss" and "to attend to, to care for" within the same verb, because they are, in fact, opposites. If we accept "to miss" as the original meaning, we are at a loss to explain the vast majority of the usages of *pqd,* which involve attention bestowed on someone in his presence. The other definitions may satisfactorily explain most meanings but fail to explain *pqd* in the sense of "to miss."

It seems therefore that a polarity exists in the various meanings of *pqd.* In the context of Deut 5:9 (cf. Exod 34:7; Lev 18:25; Num 14:18; Isa 13:11; 26:21; Jer 25:12; 36:31; Amos 3:2; Ps 89:33), that of retribution, *pqd ʿwn ʾbwt* is derived from the second and third meanings. If we accept Scharbert's definition, God examines the actions of the fathers (and children) and requites the children accordingly. According to Buber, God *zuordnet* (coordinates, associates) the sins of the fathers with the children.

and upon the third. MT, Samaritan, 4Q Phyl. G, J *(DJD* 6.59, 65): *wʿl* with conjunctive *waw;* MT Exod 20:5, LXX, Peshitta, Nash Papyrus, Vg and 4Q Dt^{n} (White, *ibid.),* XQ Phyl. 3 (Yadin, *ibid.),* without *waw: ʿl.* See Note for discussion.

10. *But showing kindness.* MT, Samaritan, 4Q Phyl. G *(DJD* 6.59), XQ Phyl. 3 (Yadin, *ibid.),* LXX, Peshitta, Vg: *wʿwśh;* 4Q Dt^{n} (White, *ibid.),* 4Q Phyl. J *(DJD* 6.65: *ʿwśy),* 8Q Phyl. 3 *(DJD* 3.154): *ʿwśh* without *waw* conjunctive.

my commandments. MT, Samaritan: *mṣwtw* (his commandment) but *qĕrē* (= to be read): *mṣwty* "my commandments." 4Q Dt^{n} (White, *ibid.): mṣwwty.* All the other versions and MT Exod: "my commandments."

11. The exact semantic significance of "taking up" the name of YHWH is unclear. Psalms 16:4 and 50:16 refer to "taking up" words upon one's lips or mouth (see the NOTE). *nśʾ* also means "to recite" poetry or prophecy (e.g., Num 23:7; 2 Kgs 9:25; Isa 37:4; Amos 5:1; and Ps 81:3), and the passage recited is termed a *maśśaʾ* 'burden'. In the present context, however, the metaphor of "taking up" words upon one's lips is not explicit, nor are we dealing with a lengthy poetic passage that might be termed a *maśśaʾ,* as in the second group of examples. The following may be compared to this verse: Exod 23:1, "You must not take up false rumors *(lʾ tśʾ šmʿ šwʾ)";* Ps 15:3, "and has not taken up reproach against his neighbor"; and Ps 139:20, "taken up falsely." In these verses "take up" means "take upon one's lips." Deuteronomy 5:11 must be seen as an elliptical rendering of "You shall not take up the name of YHWH your God *upon your lips* falsely," which, like "mention the name of the Lord" in 2

Sam 14:11, is an idiom for "swear in God's name," as suggested by Jepsen (1967, p. 291).

in vain. Hebrew: *lašawʾ*, literally, 'for falsehood'. Hebrew *šwʾ* also has the meaning 'emptiness, vanity.' Peshitta translates "falsely"; the LXX and *Tg. Ps.-J.* have "in vain." The Vg translates the first *lšwʾ* in the verse *frustra* 'in deception', and the second *super re vana* 'over a vain matter'. Below, in v 17, *šwʾ* is used clearly in the sense of "falsehood," and the Exodus Decalogue has *šqr* instead.

12–18. Exod 20:8–17 presents a significantly different version of the latter part of the Decalogue. Furthermore, a number of non-Masoretic textual witnesses exist that present significant variants: the Samaritan text, the Nash papyrus (the Qumran text 4Q Deut^{n}). In addition, it is apparent that the LXX *Vorlage* differed in a number of places with the MT, often agreeing with one or another of these texts. The following is a comparison of the Exodus and Deuteronomy versions of these commandments (in translation). It should be noted that the non-Masoretic witnesses show a tendency to harmonize between the Exodus and Deuteronomy versions.

Exod 20:8–17	*Deut 5:12–18*
8. Remember [Sam. text, "Observe"] the Sabbath day and keep it holy.	12. Observe the Sabbath day to keep it holy, as YHWH your God has commanded you.
9. Six days shall you labor and do all your work.	13. Six days you shall labor and do all your work.
10. But [some add "on"; see textual note] the seventh day is a Sabbath to YHWH your God. You shall not do any work [some add "on it"; see textual note]—you, your son, your daughter, your male or female slave, or your [some add "ox, your ass, or any of your"; see textual note] cattle, or the alien in your gates.	14. But [some add "on"; see textual note] the seventh day is a Sabbath to YHWH your God. You shall not do any work [some add "on it"; see textual note], you and your son and your daughter, your male servant and your female servant, your ox and your ass and any of your animals and the alien in your gates.
11. For in six days YHWH made heaven and earth and sea, and on the seventh day he rested.	15. Remember that you were a slave in the land of Egypt and YHWH your God freed you from there with a strong hand and outstretched arm;

Therefore YHWH blessed the Sabbath and hallowed it.	therefore, YHWH your God commanded you to observe the Sabbath day [LXX and 4Q Dt^{n} add "and keep it holy"].
12. Honor your father and your mother [papyrus Nash and LXX, "that you may fare well and"] that you may long endure upon the [LXX "good"] land which YHWH your God is giving you.	16. Honor your father and your mother, as YHWH commanded you, that your days may long endure and that you may fare well [LXX, "fare well and . . . long endure"] upon the land that YHWH your God is giving you.
13. You shall not murder. You shall not commit adultery.	17. You shall not murder and you shall not commit adultery and you shall not steal
You shall not steal. [See Textual Note at v 13 below for order of these clauses.]	
You shall not bear false witness against your neighbor.	and you shall not bear false witness against your neighbor.
14. You shall not covet your neighbor's house [LXX "wife"].	18. And you shall not covet your neighbor's wife [Samaritan Pentateuch, "house"],
You shall not covet [papyrus Nash, "crave"] your neighbor's wife [LXX "house"] [some add "his field"; see textual note] [or] his male or female slave [or] his ox, or his ass [LXX "or any of his cattle"] or anything that is your neighbor's.	and you shall not crave [some read "covet"; see textual note] your neighbor's house [Samaritan Pentateuch, "wife"], [or] his field, [or] his male and female slave, [or] his ox and his ass [LXX "or any of his cattle"] and anything that is your neighbor's.

12. *Observe . . . to keep it holy.* Literally, "Observe . . . to sanctify" *(šmr . . . lqdšw). šmr* with *lamed* infinitive has an adverbial meaning: "sanctify the day carefully." Compare *šmr lʿśwt* (5:1, 29; etc.) with *šmr wʿśh* (4:6); see the Textual Note on 4:6.

13. *do all your work.* MT: *wʿśyt kl mlʾktk;* 4Q Dt^{n} (White, *ibid.);* 4Q Phyl. J *(DJD* 6.65); and 4Q Mez A *(DJD* 6.80) add direct object marker: *ʾt: wʿśyth ʾt kl mlʾkt̂kh.*

14. *but the seventh day.* MT, Samaritan, Peshitta, Tg. Onq., MT Exod, Samaritan Exod, Vg: *wywm;* 4Q Dt^{n} (White, *ibid.),* 4Q Phyl. G *(DJD* 6.60:

wb[ywm], 4Q Phyl. J (DJD 6.65: *w{IbI}ywm),* 8Q Phyl. 3 *(DJD* 3.154), Nash Papyrus, LXX, LXX Exod, read: *wbywm,* "on the seventh day."

you shall not do any work. MT, MT Exod, Samaritan Exod, Tg. Onq.: *lʾ tʿśh;* Samaritan, 4Q Dt^n (White, *ibid.),* 4Q Phyl. J *(DJD* 6.65: *bwh),* Nash Papyrus, LXX, Peshitta, Vg: *lʾ tʿśh bw,* "on that day."

you and your son and your daughter and your male servant and your female servant and your ox and your ass and any of your animals and the alien [resident].

MT Deut:	*ʾth wbnk wbtk*	*wʿbdk wʾmtk*	*wšwrk wḥmrk*	*wkl bhmtk wgrk*
4Q Dt^n:	*ʾth bnk btk*	*ʿbdk wʾmtk*	*šwrk wḥmwrk*	*wbhmtk gryk*
LXX (ACLO), Samaritan Deut:	*ʾth wbnk wbtk*	*ʿbdk wʾmtk*	*šwrk wḥmrk*	*wkl bhmtk wgrk*
MT Exod:	*ʾth wbnk wbtk*	*ʿbdk wʾmtk*		*wbhmtk wgrk*
Nash Papyrus, LXX Exod:	*ʾth wbnk wbtk*	*ʿbdk wʾmtk*	*šwrk wḥmrk*	*wkl bhmtk wgrk*
Samaritan Exod:	*ʾth wbnk wbtk*	*ʿbdk wʾmtk*		*bhmtk wgrk*
4Q Phyl. G *(DJD* 6.60):	*ʾt]h wbnk wbtk*	*ʿbd btk [wʾm]tk*	*wšwrk wḥmrk*	*wkwl bh[mtk wgrk*
4Q Phyl. J *(DJD* 6.65):	*ʾth wbnkh wbtkh*	*ʿbdkh w[ʾm]tkh*	*šwrkh wḥmwrkh*	*wk[wl bhmtk]h wgrykh*

On the difference between MT Exod and MT Deut concerning *ox* and *ass* see the Note. The 4Q Dt^n (White, 1990 pp. 275, 280) is unique for its paucity of the *waw* conjunctive, while MT shows the greatest use of the *waw* conjunctive. Objects which can be grouped into sets of two—e.g. son–daughter, male servant–female servant, and ox–ass—are usually connected with the *waw* conjunctive; *bnk btk* in 4Q Dt^n (White 1990, p. 275) is an exception.

15. *to observe the Sabbath day.* Literally: to make/institute (*śh*); see the Note. MT, Samaritan, XQ Phyl. 3 (Yadin, *ibid.),* Targumim: *lʿśwt;* 4Q Dt^n (White 1990, p. 280), LXX, Peshitta: *lšmwr.* 4Q Dt^n and LXX add *lqdšw* (4Q Phyl. G: *w[y]qdšhw),* "to keep it holy," and thus form an inclusion with the opening of the commandment in v 12: *šmwr . . . lqdšw,* "observe . . . to keep it holy." See Note to vv 12, 15.

16. *that you may fare well.* Nash Papyrus, LXX: *lmʿn yyṭb lk* before *lmʿn*

yʾrykwn ymyk, for the reversed order: "that you may fare well" before "that you may long endure."

that your days may long endure. Hebrew: *lĕmaʿan yaʾarikun yame(y)ka.* In 4:40 a similar expression, *lĕmaʿan taʾarik yamim,* literally, 'that you may lengthen days', is used. In both verses the verb *ʾrk* is used in the *hiphʿil* form.

The verb *ʾrk* in the *qal* form is a stative verb meaning 'to be long'. The *hiphʿil* has two meanings: stative (= *qal),* as in this verse; and causative ('to lengthen'), as in 4:40. The *hiphʿil* with the stative meaning is attested only in the imperfect, the consonantal text of which is nearly identical to the *qal.* This has led Ehrlich (1909, at Exod 20:12) to suggest that these forms are misvocalized and should be read *yeʾerkun* or *yaʾarkun,* as *qal.*

In both the stative and causative uses of *ʾrk ymym,* the idiom is that one lengthens one's own days, hence these days are lengthened. But in 1 Kgs 3:14 *God* promises to lengthen *(wehaʾarakti)* Solomon's days. The same expression is used in a number of Phoenician and Aramaic inscriptions, in which a god or goddess is asked to lengthen the days *(y/tʾrk ymt; yʾrk ywmy)* of the supplicant (see the NOTE).

17–18. *you shall not murder and you shall not commit adultery and you shall not steal.* This order is found in LXX (ACO), Samaritan Deut and Exod, Peshitta Deut and Exod, MT Deut and Exod, 4Q Dt^n (White, *ibid.,* p. 280), 4Q Phyl. B *(DJD* 6.52) XQ Phyl. 3 (Yadin, *ibid.),* 1Q Phyl. *(DJD* 1.73), Matt 5:21, 19:18, Mark 10:19; and compare Josephus, *Antiquities,* 3:92. According to the system of F. Cross, this order reflects the Old Palestinian group; see White *ibid.,* p. 283.

In LXX Vaticanus, LXX Exod (LC), Nash Papyrus, Luke 18:20, Rom 13:9, and Jas 2:11, the order is: adultery, murder, and theft. Cf. also Philo, *On the Decalogue,* 21; *Special Laws* 3:8; *"Who Is the Heir?",* p. 173. According to F. Cross this reflects the Egyptian text group (White, *ibid.,* p. 284).

The *waw* conjunctive before the commandments in vv 17–18—*and you shall not (wlʾ)*—appears in MT, Targumim, 4Q Phyl. B *(DJD* 6.52), and Vg; 4Q Phyl. G *(DJD* 6.60), XQ Phyl. 3 (Yadin, *ibid.)* Peshitta: *lʾ,* without the *waw* conjunctive. For an explanation see the Note to vv 17–18.

17. M. Weiss (1984, pp. 256–59) maintains that Hos 4:2 (which has murder, theft, and adultery) was familiar with the order in the LXX's Exodus and quotes it chiastically, while Jer 7:9 (which has theft, murder, adultery) was familiar with the order of the LXX's Deuteronomy, the Nash papyrus, and Philo, and also quotes it chiastically (see Note).

In some editions of the Bible, each of the four clauses in this verse is considered a separate verse. The rest of the verses in this chapter are enumerated as follows:

my enumeration	*alternate enumeration*
18	21
19	22
20	23
21	24
22	25
23	26
24	27
25	28
26	29
27	30
28	31
29	32

false witness. MT, 4Q Dt^{n} (White, *ibid.*, p. 280), Samaritan, Tg. Onq., Peshitta, Nash Papyrus have: *ʿd šwʾ.* MT Exod, Samaritan Exod, XQ Phyl. 3 (Yadin, *ibid.)* have: *ʿd šqr.* The English word "witness" is used here in the Old English sense of "testimony." The Hebrew, however, is literally *ʿd šqr/šwʾ* 'false witness (testifier)', instead of the expected *ʿdwt šqr* 'false testimony'. The Hebrew phrase is therefore most likely an accusative of manner, and the verse is to be understood "you shall not testify against your neighbor as a false witness." Still other explanations of the syntax have also been advanced. Luzzatto (ed. Schlesinger, 1965, p. 333) maintains that the phrase is elliptical, the noun "testimony" having been left out, hence "you shall not testify against your neighbor *the testimony of* a false witness." Luzzatto quotes Kimḥi as saying that the noun *ʿd* can mean 'testimony' as well as 'witness'. In a number of cases inanimate objects are termed *ʿd* (e.g., Exod 22:12), and in these verses the rendering "testimony, evidence" is likewise appropriate.

The LXX, Vg, Tg. Onq., and Peshitta render "false testimony"; the other Aramaic Targumim have a lengthy paraphrase. For *ʿnh b* in the sense of 'bear witness', cf. Num 35:30; Deut 19:18; 1 Sam 12:3; 2 Sam 1:16; Jer 14:7.

false. šwʾ; in Exodus *šqr;* for the interchange of *šwʾ* and *šqr* see the NOTE to v 11.

18. *And you shall not covet your neighbor's wife and you shall not crave your neighbor's house.*

MT, Tg. Onq.:	*wlʾ tḥmd*	*ʾšt rʿk*	*wlʾ ttʾwh*	*byt rʿk*
4Q Dt^{n}, LXX, LXX Exod:	*lwʾ tḥmwd*	*ʾšt rʿyk*	*lwʾ tḥmwd*	*byt rʿyk*

Samaritan, Samaritan Exod:	*lʾ tḥmd*	*byt rʿk*	*wlʾ tḥmd*	*ʾšt rʿk*
Peshitta, Peshitta Exod:	*lʾ tḥmd*	*ʾšt rʿk*	*wlʾ tḥmd*	*byt rʿk*
MT Exod	*lʾ tḥmd*	*byt rʿk*	*lʾ tḥmd*	*ʾšt rʿk*
Nash Papyrus:	*lwʾ tḥmd*	*ʾt ʾšt rʿk*	*lwʾ tḥmd ʾt*	*byt rʿk*

The Masoretic text of Deuteronomy differs from the others in two major points: (1) The verb related to the house is *ttʾwh,* while the one related to the wife is *hmd.* (2) The order of the objects in Deuteronomy is: wife, house, while the order in Exodus is: house, wife. These differences can be explained by the way of development from Exodus to Deuteronomy (see NOTE).

his field, his male and female slave, his ox and his ass and anything that is your neighbor's.

MT, 4Q Phyl. G, Targumim:	*śdhw*	*wʿbdw wʾmtw šwrw*	*wḥmrw wkl*	*ʾšr lrʿk*
4Q Dt^{n}:	*śdhw*	*ʿbdw ʾmtw šwrw*	*ḥmwrw wkwl*	*ʾšr lrʿyk*
LXX, LXX Exod:	*wśdhw*	*wʿbdw wʾmtw wšwrw*	*wḥmrw wkwl bhmtw wkl*	*ʾšr lrʿk*
Samaritan, Samaritan Exod:	*śdhw*	*ʿbdw wʾmtw wšwrw*	*wḥmrw wkl*	*ʾšr lrʿk*
Peshitta:	*wśdhw wkrmw (wlʾ ḥqlh wlʾ krmh)*	*ʿbdw ʾmtw wšwrw*	*wḥmrw wkl*	*ʾšr lrʿk*
MT Exod:		*wʿbdw wʾmtw wšwrw*	*wḥmrw wkl*	*ʾšr lrʿk*

In two of the lists a certain amount of expansion occurred: (1) LXX and LXX Exod have added *wkl bhmtw* ("and all his animals"), due to the influence of 5:14. (2) The Peshitta expansion: *krm* ("wineyard") may be due to the fact that *krm* and *śdh* appear together many times in the Hebrew Bible: Exod 22:4; 1 Sam 22:7; Jer 32:15; Neh 5:3, 4, 5. The 4Q Dt^{n} dropped out the conjunctive *waws;* compare 4QDt^{n} to 5:14. On the lack of *śdhw* in MT Exod, see the NOTE.

NOTES

First Commandment

6. *I am YHWH your God.* The phrase constitutes a self-presentation formula that adds authority to the proclamation that follows; compare the phrases *ʾani YHWH* 'I am YHWH' (without the accompanying "your God") at the beginning as well as at the end of divine proclamations, especially in the priestly source (Exod 6:2, 6, 8, 29; 12:12; Lev 18:5; 19:12, 14, 16, 18, 32, 37; etc.), on which see Zimmerli 1953.

Self-presentations, in the form of a nominal sentence with the personal pronoun as subject, are very common in the openings of royal inscriptions in the ancient Near East, a form that fits well the beginning of a proclamation of God, the King of Kings (cf. Deut 10:17). Indeed, self-presentation of this kind is found in various royal inscriptions. Thus *Yḥwmlk*, king of Byblos (tenth century B.C.E.), opens his royal inscription by saying, "I am *(ʾnk) Yḥwmlk* king of Byblos . . . whom *(ʾš)* the princess, lady of Byblos, made king over Byblos" *(KAI* 10:1–2). Similarly, we find King Azitawwada saying, "I am *(ʾnk)* Azitawwada, the blessed of Baal, whom *(ʾš) ʾwrk* strengthened" *(KAI* 26 A 1:1–2) and Mesha, the king of Moab, "I am *(ʾnk)* Mesha the son of . . . the king of Moab . . . my father reigned over Moab" *(KAI* 181:1–2). Yet all of these opening formulas cannot be seen merely as self-presentations because, as A. Poebel has shown (1932, pp. 12ff.), these formulas often repeat themselves in the inscriptions (cf. *KAI* 10:1–2), and it would be illogical to assume that a person introduces himself several times at the same scene. Poebel proposed, therefore, to understand the phrases opening with "I PN (= Personal Name)," not as a nominal clause, "I am PN," but as "I PN . . . declare," that is, PN stands in apposition to the pronoun. In the case of the Decalogue's opening, Poebel translates, "Besides me YHWH your God, who freed you . . . you shall have no other gods." Although his suggestion is in general correct because of the contrast implied in vv 6–7, "YHWH *your God*" in v 6 in contradistinction to *other gods* in v 7 (and see also below), one cannot go along with Poebel in excluding the understanding of *ʾanoki YHWH* as self-presentation. Poebel himself admits that, side by side with the appositional pronoun, one also finds in the inscriptions the nominal clause of self-presentation. Indeed, this phenomenon is also attested in Scripture. In Lev 19:36–37 we find both types of clauses: (1) the sentence with the relative particle that is subordinate to the command, "I am YHWH your God who freed you from the land of Egypt. You shall observe all my laws" (36b–37a); and (2) the self-presentation, "I am YHWH" (v 37b), without any following relative clause (cf. also Num 15:41).

Indeed, the beginning of Lev 19, which is related to the Decalogue (see the INTRODUCTION to the Decalogue), has a stylistic feature identical with that of the first commandment. Verse 4 there reads, "Do not turn to idols and do not make molten gods for yourselves; I am YHWH your God." Here the self-presentation formula serves as a motivation for the prohibition of idolatry, and it is even possible that this verse constitutes a chiastic quotation from the Decalogue, as the two commands that precede it seem to be: "You shall each fear his mother and his father and observe my Sabbath; I am YHWH your God" (v 3).

In light of these observations, one should consider v 6, "I am YHWH your God," as a motive clause for the command "You shall have no other gods." This can actually be substantiated by the quotation of the Decalogue (see the INTRODUCTION to the Decalogue) in Ps 81:10–11:

You shall have no foreign god;
You shall not bow down to an alien god;
I am YHWH your God
who brought you out of the land of Egypt.

Here the command comes first, and then the titulary gives authority to it.

The same phenomenon is found in the mouth of the prophet-messenger who quotes YHWH, saying, "I brought you out of Egypt and freed you from the house of bondage . . . and I said to you, I am YHWH your God; you shall not revere the gods of the Amorites" (Judg 6:8–10). Here also the clause "I YHWH your God" serves as a motivation for not worshiping foreign gods.

In fact, the phrase "I am YHWH your God" appears in the Decalogue itself as a motive clause. Thus the command not to bow down and not to worship idols in v 9 is explicitly motivated, *"for I am YHWH your God,* an impassioned God."

The same is attested in Deuteronomy 6:12–15. This passage, which comes after the proclamation of the unity of God and his love (6:4–9; see the NOTE there), recaptures the beginning of the Decalogue by warning not to forget "YHWH who freed you from the land of Egypt, the house of slaves" and not to "follow other gods . . . for YHWH . . . is an impassioned God *(ʾl qnʾ)."* That the phrase "I (am) YHWH your God" is to be taken as the basis for the demand to recognize him alone as sovereign may be clearly deduced from Hos 13:4 (cf. 12:10): "But I YHWH am your God *(wʾnky YHWH ʾlhyk)* ever since the land of Egypt. You have never known any God besides me." This cannot be seen as a self-presentation formula because it occurs in the adversative manner, "But," in contrast to the idols mentioned before. Therefore the translation should be, *"I YHWH am your God"* and not *"I am YHWH your God,"* as in the opening of the Decalogue and in other instances. (As indicated above, I tend to consider the phrase *anoki YHWH ʾeloheyka* as self-presentation because of the phrases *ani YHWH* [without "your God"], which cannot be translated otherwise than *"I am YHWH.")*

My discussion has made clear that there is no justification for taking v 6 as a separate commandment that comes to proclaim the Kingdom of God *(Mek. Bahodesh* §8 [Horowitz 1928, p. 233]) or to present an article of faith (Maimonides, *Sefer ha-Mitswot,* Commandment 1 [Heller 1946]). Indeed, the medieval commentator Abravanel observed in his commentary on the Decalogue (in Exodus) that the first sentence of the Decalogue cannot be considered a *commandment* by itself, as it states a fact only.

Ibn Ezra, on Deut 5:16, also excludes the first sentence from the Decalogue because "it concerns God the commander and is not a commandment." One should recognize, however, that in spite of its integration with the commandment against foreign gods, it also may be conceived as an appropriate foreword for the entire Decalogue. As indicated above, in the priestly code the formula "I am YHWH your God" regularly accompanies the laws, either at their opening or at their conclusion (cf. especially Lev 18–26). The priestly self-introductions have rightly been recognized by Zimmerli (1953) as a theophanic formula that points toward a connection between the appearance of God and the promulgation of law, a connection that is boldly dramatized in the Sinai traditions of Exod 19–24 and in Deut 4–5.

Because the Decalogue contains "words" *(dĕbarim = logoi)* and not *commands* (see the INTRODUCTION to the Decalogue), it was not hard for the Jewish sages to see the first sentence as a "word" *(dibber)* by itself.

who freed you from the land of Egypt. Literally, "took you out" *(hwṣ'tyk).* The verb *yṣ'* 'go out' in the context of slavery (cf. the following phrase, "the house of bondage") has the meaning of "go free" or "be released"; see especially the law of slaves in Exod 21:2–11, where *yṣ'* 'go out' denotes "release," as in "he shall serve six years; in the seventh year he shall *go out (yṣ')* free." (Note that in vv 3, 4, 7, 11 of this legal pericope, *yṣ'* occurs as "release" without the adverb *ḥpšy* 'free'.) By the same token the causative of *yṣ', hwṣy',* has the meaning of 'to release'; cf. Deut 13:6, *hmwṣy' 'tkm m'rṣ mṣrym,* which parallels *hpdk mbyt ʿbdym,* "who redeemed you from the house of bondage." (Cf. also 5:15 in the Sabbath commandment, "Remember that you were a slave in the land of Egypt and YHWH your God freed you *[wywṣ'k]* from there," and Exod 6:6, "I will free you *[whwṣ'ty]* from the burdens [= *corvée]* of the Egyptians and deliver you from their bondage.") The same connotation is attested in the Akkadian verb *waṣû/šuṣu* 'go out'. For the legal aspects of these verbs see Yaron 1959 and Daube 1963.

Indeed, *Tg. Ps.-J.* and *Tg. Neof.* usually translate *YHWH hwṣy'k mmṣrym* as "YHWH took you out *liberated (pryqyn)* from Egypt." The translation of the self-introductory phrase *'ny YHWH . . . 'šr hwṣ' tyk m'rṣ mṣrym,* or *hwṣ'ty 'tkm/'wtm m'rṣ mṣrym,* is even more explicit there: "I am YHWH . . . who released *(prqyt)* and took you out *(w'pyqyt)* liberated *(pryqyn)* from the land of Egypt." A variant of "freed *(hwṣy')* from Egypt" is *"brought up (hʿlh)* from Egypt," which implies the entrance into the promised land. In contrast to *hwṣy',* which is guided by the aspect of liberation, *hʿlh* is oriented toward settlement in the new land; compare, for example, Gen 50:24, "God will surely remember you and bring you up *(whʿlh)* from this land to the land which he promised," and Exod 3:8, 17; 32:1; 33:1; Deut 20:1; Amos 2:10; 9:7. On the difference between *hwṣy'* and *hʿlh,* see Wijngaards 1965. (In Mic 6:4 *hʿltyk* is used [though one would expect *hwṣ'tyk* as parallel to *pdytyk]* because of the play on words with *hl'tyk* in v 3; see Anderson 1951, p. 192.)

Deuteronomy, which stresses the humanistic aspect of freedom from Egypt (cf. 5:15; 15:15; 16:12; 24:18), prefers the *hwṣy'* formula over the other one. Some scholars suggest that *hʿlh* was used in the Northern Kingdom, while *hwṣy'* was prevalent in the south (see Wijngaards 1965).

from the house of bondage. Literally, "house of slaves." Slavery was widespread in Egypt, and various sources of the New Kingdom period bear evidence of groups of slaves working in the region of the Delta. The tombs of Rekhmire at Thebes (fifteenth century B.C.E.) are especially rich in illustrations of slaves of Semitic stock working as brickmakers and bricklayers (cf. Exod 1:14; 5:4ff.). An inscription over the scene of bricklayers reads, "The taskmaster says to the builders: 'the rod is in my hand; be not idle.' " In one of these inscriptions, the term "house of slaves" is attested (Davies 1943, p. 123). Liberation from human slavery was usually connected with the passing of the liberated to the service of God (cf. Weinfeld 1985d, pp. 133–44), and this is indeed explicitly expressed in Lev 25:42: "for they are my slaves whom I freed *(hwṣʾty)* from the land of Egypt; they may not be sold as [human] slaves"; cf. v 55 there.

The phrase *byt ʿbdym* 'house of bondage' is very common in Deuteronomic literature (Deut 6:12; 7:8; 8:14; 13:6, 11; Jer 34:13); it seems, however, that its roots are to be sought in older, perhaps northern, literature; cf. Exod 13:3, 14; 20:2; Josh 24:17; Mic 6:4 (see Lohfink 1963, pp. 100ff.).

7. *You shall have no other gods.* "Other gods *(ʾlhym ʾḥrym),*" or older "another god *(ʾl ʾḥr)*" (Exod 34:14), sometimes interchanges with *ʾl zr* 'foreign god/gods' (Pss 44:12; 81:10; cf. Deut 32:16), *ʾl/ʾlhy nkr* (Gen 35:2, 4; Deut 31:16; Josh 24:20, 23; Judg 10:16; 1 Sam 7:3). Compare especially Ps 81:10, which is related to the first commandment of the Decalogue (see above in the INTRODUCTION to the Decalogue): *lʾ yhyh bk ʾl zr wlʾ tštḥwh lʾl nkr ʾnky YHWH ʾlhyk* 'You shall have no foreign god; you shall not bow down to an alien god; I am YHWH your God'. In Judaism, pagan worship is named *ʿabodah zarah* 'foreign worship', and it generally refers to idolatry. Indeed, there is no distinction in the Bible and in the ancient Near East between "gods" and their representatives, the "idols." Having gods means having idols (see Kaufmann 1966, pp. 149–51); and, according to the Israelite monotheistic concepts, just as fetishes made of stone, wood, silver, or gold have no "life," neither do the gods who are represented by them (Jer 10:2–10). The pagans themselves could not conceive a deity without an image, and the deity was considered present in its image (see Oppenheim 1964, pp. 183–84).

Therefore "having no other gods" actually means "having no images," and the second commandment, in fact, continues the idea or concretizes the first one. For "gods," compare, for example, Exod 23:20, "gods of silver" and "gods of gold"; 32:21, "golden gods"; Lev 19:4, "molten gods"; Josh 24:14, "remove the gods"; 2 Kgs 17:29; 19:18; etc. By the same token, the word *ʾlhy nkr* 'foreign gods' implies "gods" as well as "idols"; cf. the phrase, "remove foreign gods" in Gen 35:4; Josh 24:23; Judg 10:16; 1 Sam 7:3; 2 Chr 33:15.

According to one rabbinic interpretation *(Mek. R. Simeon bar Yochai* [Epstein and Melamed 1955, p. 146], and so Rashi), the prohibition refers to keeping idols in one's house. Naḥmanides, however, interprets "having" in the sense of accepting them for worship, clearly referring to deities and not to idols. He compares it to phrases like Gen 28:21, "YHWH shall be my God *(whyh*

YHWH ly l'lhym)," or "to be God to you *(lhywt lk l'lhym)"* (Gen 17:7 etc.) and includes in the term "other gods" celestial divinities (angels, etc.).

in my presence. Literally, "on or against my face," that is to say, in my presence, as long as I exist, which is tantamount to Exod 20:23, "You shall not make *with me ('ty)* gods of silver," etc. For the language compare Gen 11:28, "Haran died in the presence/in the lifetime *('l pny)* of Terah his father"; Num 3:4, "Eleazar and Ithamar served as priests in the presence/lifetime *('l pny)* of Aaron their father"; Deut 21:16, "he shall not prefer the son of the beloved in front/in the presence *('l pny)* of the son of the unloved"; see the TEXTUAL NOTE.

Second Commandment

8. *You shall not make for yourself a carved image, any likeness of what is in the heavens above* [etc.]. The construction of the sentence is heavy and complex: for one thing, the relation of "the carved image *(psl)"* to "any likeness/form *(kl tmwnh)"* is unclear. According to the Exodus version (20:4), "any likeness/form" is *added* to the first object "the carved image" *(psl wkl tmwnh),* while according to the Deuteronomic version "any likeness/form" appears in apposition to "carved image" *(psl, kl tmwnh):* "a carved image, [that is] any likeness," etc.

For another, the relative clause "of what is in the heavens above," etc., which relates to "any likeness/form *(kl tmwnh),"* may be subordinated to *tmwnh,* "any likeness of what is in heaven," or to *kl* 'any', which is the *nomen regens* of "likeness": "likeness of anything in heaven," etc. The latter sense occurs in the elaborations of this commandment in Deut 4, where we find, "a likeness/form of anything" *(tmwnt kl,* 4:16, 23, 25); see below.

Finally, the noun *tmwnh* 'likeness/form' occurs as a direct object of "You shall not make," which is problematic because by making an image, one shapes it in accordance with a form, but does not create the form. Hence we find commentators (Ewald 1864, 2.160) who connected the phrase "any likeness/form" with the following sentence: "any form that is in heaven above . . . you shall not bow down to them." As will be seen below, however, there is an identity in the Semitic language between the word for "model" and the word that expresses the real physical imitation of the model, so that this difficulty is not insurmountable.

It seems that the difficulties of this verse are to be explained as the result of its composite growth. The way of the division of the Decalogue into ten "words" is unclear for us, and it is possible that verses 6–10 (= Exod 20:2–6) constitute one commandment, as we have it in some Masoretic traditions and in the Catholic/Lutheran circles (see the INTRODUCTION to the Decalogue), so that the first original commandment contained only "You shall have no other gods beside me," and the continuance is an accretion that may itself have undergone expansions and elaborations. Although some expansions bear a Deuteronomic imprint, they are not necessarily of Deuteronomic origin. Thus, for example, it is true that the pairing of *psl* and *tmwnh* is not found outside the Decalogue and Deuteronomy (4:16, 23, 25). In other sources we find *psl* and *mskh* 'molten image' (Deut 27:15; Judg 17:3, 4; 18:14; Nah 1:14), but it is possible that the origin of the phrase is to be sought in the expanded pre-Deuteronomic Decalogue, which in turn influenced Deuteronomy and especially Deut 4, which focuses on the Sinai revelation. The same applies to the relative clause "what is in the heavens above, or on the earth below," etc. This phrasing, found in Deut 4:39 and in later Deuteronomic literature (Josh 2:11; 1 Kgs 8:23), may have its origin in the expanded pre-Deuteronomic Decalogue (see the INTRODUCTION to the Decalogue). But the changes in the Deuteronomic version of the Decalogue vis à vis the Exodus version could be explained by virtue of Deuteronomic character and ideology. Thus, for example, even the small change in v 8, the omission of *and* in "any likeness/form," can easily be explained.

The Deuteronomic version takes *kl tmwnh* as apposition, a feature characteristic of Deuteronomy, which tends to add explanatory appositions in order to make sure that the entire category involved is meant and not just the specified objects mentioned; compare, for example, 4:19, "and behold the sun and the moon and the stars, *the whole heavenly host (kl ṣbʾ hšmym)*"; 16:21, "You shall not set up an *ʾašerah, any kind of wooden pole (kl ʿṣ)*"; see also 15:21 *(kl mwm)*; 17:1 *(kl dbr rʿ)*; 23:20 *(kl dbr)*; and compare below v 14, *wkl bhmtk,* and the NOTE there. In all of these instances the Hebrew *kl* means 'any' or 'any kind'. This Deuteronomic interpretation of the second commandment is made more explicit in the sermon of chap. 4, where one finds, in connection with idolatrous imagery, "a sculpted image in any likeness *(psl tmwnt kl)*" (vv 16, 23, 25). Here the words *kl tmwnh* 'any likeness' are inverted and turned into a construct state, *tmwnt kl,* literally, 'the likeness of anything'. It seems that a development should be discerned here: from Exod 20:4 through Deut 5:9 to Deut 4:16, 23, 25. In Exodus the prohibition applies to "You shall not make an image *and* any form"; in Deuteronomy this becomes, according to the Deuteronomic usage, "You shall not make an image, [that is,] any form," while in Deut 4:16, 23, 25 it turns into "an image *of* any form." Indeed, the latter phrasing actually contains in itself the definition of the Decalogue: "what is in the heavens, on earth," etc.

F. L. Hossfeld (1982, pp. 21–26), who dates the Exodus version of the Decalogue in the post-Exilic period and therefore later than the Deuteronomic one (see the INTRODUCTION to the Decalogue), explains the syndetic form in Exodus ("a carved image *and* any form") as a later development, which is intended to make v 4 independent of v 3 and to link it with the following: "You shall not bow down *to them,*" etc. In this manner, he argues, "to them" relates to *psl* and *tmwnh* and not to the "other gods" of v 3, and the command about *not bowing down and serving* applies to the idols, not to foreign gods. Thus the second commandment in the version of Exodus becomes close to the Deutero-Isaianic polemic against idols. In contrast, the Deuteronomic version combines the second commandment (about the idols) with the first (foreign gods) and thus makes the command about *not bowing down* in v 9 refer to the gods and not to the idols.

As it turns out, neither Hossfeld's thesis about the priority of the Deuteronomic version of the Decalogue nor his reasoning about the development of the formulation of the two discussed commandments can be sustained. As has been shown above, the change of the syndetic form *(psl wkl tmwnh)* into an asyndetic form in Deuteronomy was motivated by Deuteronomic ideology (cf. Deut 4:16, 23, 25) and style (appositional glosses), and what concerns the object to which bowing down and worshiping (Exod 20:5; Deut 5:9) is related; there is no justification for the distinction between the *gods* and their representatives, the idols. Both the Exodus version and the Deuteronomic version, then, when speaking about *bowing down and worshiping,* refer to "other gods," which is to "images." W. Zimmerli's suggestion that the prohibition of worshiping idols in Exod 20:4/Deut 5:8 is an interpolation because it disrupts the connection between "other gods" and the "bowing down" to them, therefore, cannot be accepted (Zimmerli 1950). *hšt̲ḥwh* 'bow down' refers then to gods, that is, to idols (objects representing the gods); compare Exod 32:8 (to the calf); Isa 2:8, 20 (to hand work); 44:15, 17 (to carven image); and elsewhere.

The prohibition of making images and statues for YHWH is attested in other law codes of the Pentateuch, but there the prohibited object of worship is concretely defined as, for example, the mention of the material out of which the image is made, "gold or silver"; the way of production, "molten image"; the form, "(stone) pillar." Compare "You shall not make with me gods of silver, nor shall you make for yourselves gods of gold" (Exod 20:23; "gods" here means "idols"; cf. above); "You shall not make molten gods *(ʾlhy mskh)* for yourself" (Exod 34:17; cf. Lev 19:4); "You shall not erect for yourselves a carved image *(psl)* or pillar *(mṣbh)*" (Lev 26:1; cf. Mic 5:12); and "Cursed be the man who makes a carved or molten image *(psl wmskh)* . . . a craftsman's handiwork" (Deut 27:15).

In the Decalogue, however, the prohibition is more general: "a carved image [and] any likeness/form." By such phrasing the second commandment becomes the most comprehensive form of idolatry prohibition and indeed perfectly suits the categorical nature of the commandments of the Decalogue (see the INTRODUCTION to the Decalogue). The Deuteronomic version of the Decalogue makes the commandment even more radical, as shown above.

The prohibition of images in Israelite worship is attested in all of the legal codes of ancient Israel (Exod 34:17 [= J]; Lev 19:4; 26:1 [= priestly version or holiness code]; Deut 4:15; 27:15) and seems to have roots in the Israelite tradition from its beginning. It apparently originated among the Hebrew tribes during their stay in Sinai. Indeed, the aniconic tendency is also characteristic of other nomadic tribes in the desert of Sinai and southern Palestine. Excavations at Timna, some thirty kilometers north of the Gulf of ʿAquaba, have shown that the Midianites, who built a shrine on top of an Egyptian sanctuary, mutilated the statue of the Egyptian goddess Hathor and reused many objects from the original structure (cf. Rothenberg 1978). This may explain the friendly relationship of Moses and the Israelites with Jethro, the Midianite, and the recognition of YHWH by Jethro (Exod 2:16–22; 4:18–20; 18:1–27; Num 10:29–32; see Weinfeld 1987). The aniconic tendency of the tribes in the desert area of Palestine seems to have persisted down to the period of the Nabataeans in the third and second centuries B.C.E.; cf. Patrich 1985.

It should be stressed that, in spite of its seemingly abstract nature, the prohibition of making any image in any form should not be taken in the philosophical sense of rejecting any sensuality in connection with the divine being and conceiving of the deity as a sublime spirit. The prohibition of making any image is a practical one, and its significance is existential: the feeling that the majestic power cannot be degraded by any earthly representation. The commandment as such does not profess to present a philosophical doctrine about the nature of deity (cf. also Zimmerli 1950).

By the same token, the prohibition undoubtedly enhanced the transcendental nature of Israelite monotheism. In Deut 4:15 the objection to the representation of God by image is explained by the fact that at the Sinai revelation the Israelites did not see any image. This could be understood philosophically: that God is beyond nature and therefore cannot be represented by anything earthly and natural. This is, of course, close to Aristotle's philosophy, which tries to prove that God is not corporeal *(Physica* 8.6.259a, 8ff.). H. A. Wolfson (1968, 2.96) rightly observed the great philosophical potentialities contained in the second commandment and in Deut 4:15: "All that was necessary for its transformation into the philosophic principle of the incorporeality of God was an acquaintance with philosophical speculations about the world and its constituent parts."

Although erection of images is prohibited in the legitimate Israelite cult, as attested in the various legal codes of the Pentateuch, the practice of setting up images was not unheard of in ancient Israel. Gideon, the great judge of Israel, made an *ephod,* some sort of image (cf. Hos 3:4), and the people went astray after it (Judg 8:27). Similarly, Micah's mother consecrated silver to make a carved image *(pesel)* and a molten image *(massekah)* to YHWH (Judg 17:3). It seems, however, that these events should be seen as deviations from the purely legitimate, as were other incidents in the history of Israel (cf. the worship of the Baal during the period of Ahab) caused by Canaanite influence. By contrast, the worship of the golden calf cannot be considered pure idol worship. The iconic art of the ancient Near East shows that the calf or bull usually represented the pedestal of a god and not the deity itself. The latter was usually carved in human form (see below, in the COMMENT to chap. 9).

any likeness. The word *tmwnh,* like its synonyms *dĕmūt* and *tabnit,* usually denotes the form for shaping the object but can be identified with the physical object prepared according to it. Thus *dĕmūt* 'likeness/similitude' parallels the word *ṣelem* 'statue' (cf. Gen 1:26, 27; 5:1), and furthermore, the word *ṣelem* itself connotes both "statue" and "image." (*ṣalmu* in Akkadian also has both meanings; cf. *AHW,* s.v. *ṣalmu* II.6.) In a recently discovered bilingual inscription from Tel Fakhariya in Syria, the Aramaic terms *dmwtʾ* 'likeness' and *ṣlmʾ* 'statue' both denote the statue of the governor of Gozan (cf. Abou-Assaf, Bordreuil, and Millard 1982, p. 23, lines 1, 12, 15). Indeed, these two Aramaic terms translate *psl* and *tmwnh* in the Aramaic versions of the Decalogue. Similarly, the word *marʾah,* which means 'vision/appearance', connotes also "mirror," the physical object by which the vision is made to appear (Exod 38:8; cf. 10:4; 5:5). The phrase "You shall not make" may then refer to *psl* as well as to *tmwnh* (cf. above).

of what is in the heavens above, or on the earth below, or in the waters below the earth. This prohibition is made explicit in Deut 4:17–19, where the people are warned against astral worship (sun, moon and stars), as well as worship of sky birds; the worship of any earthly creature (male and female); and worship of any creature in the water beneath the earth.

9. *You shall not bow down to them or serve them.* Compare Exod 23:24: "You shall not bow down to their gods and not serve them (*lʾ tštḥwh lʾlhyhm wlʾ tʿbdm* [spelled *toʿobdem* as in the Decalogue; see TEXTUAL NOTE])." This kind of imagery is also common in the political sphere; cf. Gen 27:29, "peoples will serve you (*yʿbdwk*) and nations will bow down (*wyštḥww*) to you," and in an inverted order, "bow down" before "serve" in Ps 72:11, "and all the kings shall bow down to him [the king]; all the nations shall serve him." Prostration/falling down before monarchs, as well as before the deity, is well attested in the iconography of the ancient Near East (see Keel 1978, pp. 308–10), but it has usually gained the meaning of "obeisance/worship" in general; see recently Gruber 1980, pp. 102–3, 120–23.

The idiom "serve and bow down" was adopted by the Deuteronomic school in connection with foreign worship (cf. Weinfeld 1972a, pp. 320–21) but did not originate there. It is found in Exod 23:24 (Elohistic source), as indicated above, and in the Exodus Decalogue. The latter may have influenced the Deuteronomic literature. J. P. Floss (1975, p. 170) and F. L. Hossfeld (1982, p. 25) try to distinguish between an older form that puts *ʿbd* 'serve' before *hštḥwh* 'bow down', and a later form that has *hštḥwh* 'bow down' before *ʿbd* 'serve', but this has no justification. The change in the order of verbs is just for literary variation. Thus in the two poetic passages quoted above, which refer to royal obeisance, we find once *ʿbd* before *hštḥwh* (Gen 27:29) and once *hštḥwh* before *ʿbd* (Ps 72:11). There is no proof that the order of one text is older than that of the other.

for I am YHWH your God, an impassioned God, visiting the iniquities of the fathers upon the children . . . but showing kindness. Just as "I am YHWH your God" in the first commandment serves as motivation for the next statement, "You shall have no other gods" (see above in the NOTE), so also in the second commandment, "I am YHWH your God," etc., serves as a motivation for the preceding clause, "You shall not bow down," etc. In Ps 81:10–11 both prohibitions are combined and motivated by "I am YHWH your God. *You shall have* no foreign god, *you shall not bow down* to a strange god; *I am YHWH your God* who brought you out of the land of Egypt."

In 5:9 a definition of God is added that dwells on his double nature: being zealous or impassioned *(qannaʾ)* on the one hand, and showing love and kindness *(ʿośeh ḥsd)* on the other. These ambiguous attributes of the deity seem to belong to old Israelite hymnic liturgical tradition. Thus we find in the hymnic liturgy of Exod 34:6–7, "a God, compassionate/merciful and gracious *(ʾel raḥum weḥanun),* slow to anger, abounding in kindness and faithfulness, *keeping kindness to the thousandth generation,*" and next to it "who does not remit punishment *(wnqh lʾ ynqh)* [cf. Deut 5:11] *but visits the iniquity of the fathers . . . upon the third and fourth generation.*" Similarly, in Num 14:18, we read, "YHWH, slow to anger, abounding in kindness, yet not clearing punishment *(lʾ ynqh)* but *visiting the iniquity of fathers upon children, upon the third and fourth generations*"; and, in Nah 1:2–3, "A God impassioned *(qannowʾ)* and avenging . . . YHWH, slow to anger . . . but does not clear punishment *(wnqh lʾ ynqh).*" Compare also the passage in Deut 7:9–10, influenced by the Decalogue (see the NOTE to these verses), "the steadfast God who keeps his gracious covenant *(šmr hbryt whḥsd)* for those who love him . . . to the thousandth generation, but who repays them who hate him . . . to destroy them"; and Jer 32:18, "You show kindness to the thousandth generation but requite the sin of the fathers to their children after them."

One must recognize, however, a certain discrepancy in formulation between the gracious part of these hymns and the part of jealousy and anger. The measure of punishment is smaller than the measure of grace. God's anger lasts for four generations, while his grace extends for a thousand generations. This has been observed by the sages, "the dimension of grace is bigger than the dimension of punishment" *(t. Soṭa* 4:1), although, as will be seen below, in the general sense there is no difference between the punitive clause and the beneficial one—both wish to express the endurance of divine retribution. The difference, however, in formulation of the duration of retribution undoubtedly has significance. There is a desire to stress the positive attributes of God much more than the negative ones.

In spite of the preponderance of grace in the discussed liturgical declaration, it should be noted that the declarations do not always open with grace. The nature of the opening epithet depends on the context. In Exod 34:6–7 and Num 14:18, which are woven into a frame of supplication, the opening epithet is "compassionate and gracious" (Exod 34:6) or "abounding in kindness" (Num

14:18); whereas in the Decalogue, as well as in Nahum, where emphasis is laid on the punitive character of the deity, the opening epithet is "the impassioned God *(ʾel qannāʾ).*"

The gracious part of the declaration is broadly used in prayers and supplications, and in late texts the negative part of the declaration is omitted altogether; cf. Joel 2:13; Jonah 4:2; Pss 86:15; 103:8; Neh 9:17, 31.

The double nature of God, compassionate/merciful *(raḥum)* on the one hand, and impassioned *(qannāʾ)* on the other, has been taken up and developed in the sermon of Deut 4. Speaking about forgetting the covenant of YHWH and making idols, the author warns that "YHWH your God is a consuming fire, an impassioned God *(ʾel qannāʾ)*" (v 24, and see the NOTE there), but when referring to the repentance of Israel after its punishment, he recalls that "YHWH your God is a merciful/compassionate God; he will not fail you, nor will he destroy you; he will not forget the covenant . . . with your fathers" (v 31), thus alluding to the attributes of God in the liturgical declarations discussed here, "keeping kindness to the thousandth generation."

For the antiquity of the divine attribute "compassionate and gracious," compare the Ugaritic epithet of El: *lṭpn il dpid* 'the gracious, El the merciful' (cf., e.g., *CTA* 6 1:49, 3:10). Note that in the Hebrew epithets discussed, the word "El" precedes the attributes *qannaʾ* and *raḥūm* (see Cross 1977, 1.263), which seems to point to a frozen old formula.

an impassioned God (ʾel qannāʾ). The root *qnʾ*, which connotes both jealousy and zealousness (see TEXTUAL NOTE) and is typical of a lover (cf. Num 5:14, 30), occurs often in the context of Israel's loyalty to its God, especially when there is the danger of "whoring *(znh)* after other gods." Thus in Exod 34:14, which has affinities to the second commandment, we read, "You shall not bow down to another god because YHWH's name is impassioned *(qnʾ)* [he is an impassioned God], lest you make a covenant with the inhabitants of the land, for they will *whore* after their gods . . . and invite you . . . to eat of their sacrifices." Here, as in the Decalogue, the motivation for prohibiting idol worship is the "impassioned" God, and, furthermore, the practice of idolatry is depicted as "whoring." By the same token, when Joshua warns the people in Shechem not to worship the gods of trans-Euphrates or the gods of the Amorites (24:15), he turns to them, saying, "You will not be able to worship YHWH, for he is a holy God, he is an impassioned God *(ʾel qnwʾ),* he will not forgive your transgressions *(lʾ yśʾ lpšʿkm)* [cf. the opposite, *nśʾ ʿwn wpšʿ*, in the attributes of the merciful God in Exod 34:7 and Num 14:18] when you forsake YHWH and worship foreign gods" (24:19–20). Similarly, we read in Deut 6:14–15, "Do not follow *(hlk ʾḥr)* other gods . . . for YHWH your God in your midst is an impassioned God *(ʾel qannaʾ)* . . . he [will] wipe you off the face of the earth." One has to be cognizant of the fact that the verb "follow after" has conjugal connotations (cf. Jer 2:2, 25; Hos 2:7, 15; compare the Akkadian idiom *alāku arki,* for which cf. Koschaker 1951, pp. 107–8; Yaron 1963, pp. 9–16), and that fits well the epithet *ʾel qannaʾ.* The love imagery in the sphere of relations between God and Israel indicates that the metaphor of God as the husband of Israel, so strongly developed in the prophecies of Hosea (chaps. 1–3), Jeremiah (chap. 3), and Ezekiel (chaps. 16, 23), may have its origins in the Pentateuchal literature; see G. Cohen 1966 and Weinfeld 1972a, pp. 81–82 n. 6. That the epithet *ʾel qannaʾ* is directed against pagan worship and that it is based on the love metaphor have already been observed by Naḥmanides in his commentary on the Decalogue: "For I am . . . *ʾel qannaʾ*—that I will be jealous of anyone who *yields my glory to another and my renown to idols* [cf. Isa 42:8]; this language of jealousy referring to the Holy Name is found only with respect to idol worship . . . and the reason for jealousy being that Israel is God's own property and if his people, his servants, turn to other gods, God will be jealous of them as a husband is jealous of his wife when she turns to other men."

Although *ʾel qannaʾ,* in the context of idolatry, has a negative meaning ("avenging and punishing"), one must admit that the basic meaning of *qnʾ,* which is 'jealousy', applies also to passionate love. Love causes jealousy, and jealousy brings anger that burns like fire (Deut 4:22; 32:21–22). There is, then, a possibility that the term *ʾel qannaʾ* refers not only to the clause of punishment, but also to the clause of divine grace (see Weiss 1961–63, 32.42–43).

visiting the iniquities of the fathers upon the children, and upon the third and fourth generation . . . but showing kindness to the thousandth generation. M. Weiss (1963, 32.29–46) has correctly seen that the two parts of the declaration used as two motive clauses in verses 9b–10 are not concerned with the *doctrine* of collective retribution as such; rather they come to teach us about divine reward and punishment in the most absolute sense. God's punishment lasts for generations, just as his grace endures for generations. The phrase "upon children and upon the third and fourth generations" is, then, not to be taken literally (meaning only four generations will suffer because of the sins of the fathers). It refers, in general, to a very large number of descendants and actually parallels the corresponding clause, "[showing grace] to the thousandth generation," which also designates an unspecified number of future generations and not exactly a thousand generations. As Weiss has shown, the same idea is to be found in Jer 2:9, "Therefore I will quarrel with you, said YHWH, and with your children's children," which also is not to be understood literally ("I will quarrel only with three generations") but "I will quarrel with you severely" (see Weiss 1984, pp. 108–13).

The mention of four generations marks the common span of human life: we usually live to see our descendants until the fourth generation; see Job 42:16 "[Job] saw four generations of son and grandsons," for which compare the Nerab inscription *(KAI* 226.5), "and with my eyes what do I see? Children of the fourth generation *(wbʿyny mḥzh ʾnh bny rbʿ),"* and the inscription of Nabonidus's mother (ANET[3], p. 661), "I saw my descendants to the fourth generation, all in full health *(adi 4 lipiya balṭussunu amurma).*" See also 2 Kgs

10:30; 15:12, "Your sons to the fourth generation shall sit upon the throne of Israel *(bny rbʿym yšbw lk ʿl ksʾ yśrʾl),*" and Gen 50:23, "Joseph lived to see children of the third generation of Ephraim; the children of Machir, son of Manasseh, were likewise born upon Joseph's knees," as well as Gen 15:16.

The question, however, is whether the four generations include the father. In Exod 34:7 it is clear that the father is not counted, "upon the children, and the children's children, upon the third and fourth generations" (see TEXTUAL NOTE), and the situation is the same in 2 Kgs 10:30; 15:12, where Jehu is promised four generations, which do not include Jehu himself, for the four generations constitute Jehoahaz, Joash, Jeroboam II, and Zechariah.

It seems, as indicated, that the author in the Decalogue does not intend to be precise here, and that what he means is "to the third *or* fourth generation," that is, X or $(X + 1)$, a pattern common in biblical language; see Jackson 1975b. Nevertheless, there is also a tendency here to extend the limits as far as the family unit might go, all being alive at one time. In any given family it might not extend that far, but the formula is intended to be inclusive (according to D. N. Freedman).

Hossfeld (1982, pp. 26–32), following his thesis that the Deuteronomic version of the Decalogue is earlier than the Exodus version, argues that in the older sources, including Deuteronomy, the father is counted among the four generations, while in the later sources, which include the Exodus Decalogue, the father is not counted. The lack of *waw* 'and' before the *šillešim* in Exodus signifies, in his opinion, that the *šillēsim* and *ribbēʿim* stand in apposition to the *banim* 'descendants' and actually mean "great-grandchildren" and "great-great-grandchildren." His supposition that the earlier sources count the father among the four generations might be refuted by the evidence of Exod 34:7, an old text in which four generations are listed without the father: sons, grandsons (the third generation, *šillēšim),* and the fourth generation *(ribbēʿim).* In order to overcome this difficulty, he argues that the *šillēšim* after *bĕnei-banim* 'grandsons' in Exod 34:7 do not indicate the next generation, "great-grandsons," but stand in apposition to *bĕnêy-banim.* This is highly hypothetical.

In fact, there is no justification for ascribing to the Deuteronomic clause a different interpretation from that of the Exodus clause, in spite of the additional *waw* in Deuteronomy. One should mention that the *waw* does not occur in the Qumran texts and is not reflected in several other versions (see the TEXTUAL NOTES) and therefore cannot serve as a sound basis for chronological reconstructions.

The persistence of God's anger, which results in collective punishment of family and society, implied in the verse discussed here, is clearly expressed in the literature of the Hittite empire of the fourteenth and thirteenth centuries B.C.E. The religious literature of this period is an amalgam of Hittite–Hurrian elements that pervaded the Syro-Palestinian world (Ugarit; Alalah) and seem also to have influenced the cult of pre-Israelite Jerusalem (see Weinfeld 1983b).

Thus we read in the Hittite instructions for priests and temple officials, "The temper of the gods is strong; it does not quickly take hold but when it takes hold it will not let go" (KUB 13.4, 2:27f.; cf. *ANET*², p. 208, and see the translation of Hoffner 1973, p. 220), which reminds us of Exod 34:6–7: "YHWH . . . slow to anger . . . who does not remit punishment but visits the iniquity of the fathers . . . upon the third and fourth generation." The notion of the sins of the fathers falling upon their descendants occurs in the same Hittite text in a most explicit manner: "If anyone arouses the anger of a god, does the god take revenge on him alone? Does he not take revenge on his wife, his children, his descendants, his kin . . . and will utterly destroy him?" (*ANET*², p. 208).

The idea of collective, familial punishment also appears in the plague prayer of Mursilis, where the Hittite king complains that he suffers because of his father's sins: "My father sinned and transgressed against the word of the Hattian god . . . but I have not sinned in any respect. It is only too true, however, that the father's sin falls upon the son. So my father's sin has fallen upon me" (*ANET*², p. 395; cf. Lebrun 1980, 4.192–239; for biblical parallels see Malamat 1955).

The idea of familial solidarity pervaded ancient Greek literature. Thus we find, in the fragments of Solon's poems: "because of them [the sinful parents] the children and those who come after them will bear punishment" (13:31; compare *Theognis* 731–42). Similarly, we read in Aeschylus: "Swift is its retribution [of the transgression]; yet unto the third generation it abides" *(Seven Against Thebes,* 743–44) and in the fragments of Euripides' tragedies: "the sins of the parents on the children the gods do visit" (cf. Plutarch, *de sera numinis vindicta,* 556F; 562F; see Nauck 1889, Euripides 980). Cicero ascribes to Stoic philosophy the following: "the divine power is such that even if a person has escaped punishment by dying, the punishment is turned on his children and grandchildren and their descendants," to which he reacts, "What a remarkable instance of divine justice! Would any state tolerate a lawgiver who should enact that a son or grandson was to be sentenced for the transgressions of a father or grandfather?" (*De natura Deorum* 3.38).

The theology of communal punishment was quite popular in ancient Israel; see, for example, Lev 26:39–40 and Lam 5:7: "Our fathers have sinned and are gone; we have suffered for their iniquity." The notion was so common that in the days before the destruction of Jerusalem a proverb was circulating in Jerusalem, "Fathers ate unripe grapes and their sons' teeth are set on edge" (Jer 31:28; Ezek 18:2), and the prophets Jeremiah and Ezekiel fought against this view. Jeremiah foresees a time in which this principle will be abandoned: "everyone shall die for his own sins; he who eats unripe grapes, his teeth shall be set on edge" (31:29). Similarly, Ezekiel states that this proverb shall not be used any more in Israel: "it is the person who sins that shall die" (18:2–3). By the same token, the Deuteronomic author who refers to the principle of solidarity in 7:9–

10 reinterprets the principle of visiting the father's sins on his descendants by stating that he "repays them who hate him *to their face;* . . . he is never late with the one who hates him—he repays him *to his face*" (for the phrase "to his face," meaning "personally," cf. Job 19:15; 21:9: "Is God reserving his punishment for his sons? Let him pay back to him that he may feel it?").

This individualistic principle suits the Deuteronomic law in Deut 24:16, "Fathers shall not be put to death for children, nor children be put to death for fathers; a person shall be put to death only for his own crime," which nicely answers Cicero's questioning of the divine justice of familial solidarity (see above): would any state tolerate a son's being sentenced for the transgressions of his father?

The Deuteronomic author (Deut 7:9–10) in fact revises the old principle of familial solidarity by altogether denying communal punishment. He quotes the old hymnic credo of Exod 34:6–7 and Num 14:18 and retains the beneficial part of it, "keeping kindness to the thousandth generation," but omits altogether the clause about visiting the fathers' sins on their descendants and argues just the contrary: God repays the sinner personally. Although there is no evidence for a development in the concept of retribution (from collective to individual) in ancient Israel (see Weiss 1961–63), one must admit that Deut 7:9–10 opposes collective retribution and thus is in line with the prophecies of Jeremiah and Ezekiel quoted above. This may explain the additional phrases in the Decalogue, "to those who hate me" or "to those who love me and keep my commandments," which are missing in the parallels of Exod 34:6–7 and Num 14:18. These phrases look like explanatory glosses, which come to stress that God punishes only those of the sons who propagate the evil ways of their fathers (cf. *b. Ber.* 7a; *Sanh.* 27b; Targumim; and medieval commentators) and keeps his kindness for those of the descendants who love God and keep his commandments.

These explanatory glosses seem to be of Deuteronomic origin (cf. J. Scharbert 1957). True, the syntax of the verse seems strange; one would expect to read, "he visits the iniquities of the fathers upon the sons . . . *who hate me* [without the *lamed]*" etc. But for an addition one cannot demand from the author perfect compliance with the rules of grammar.

10. *but showing kindness to the thousandth generation to those who love me and keep my commandments.* In the parallel hymnic declarations we find the verbs *nṣr* and *šmr* 'guard/keep' (Exod 34:7; Deut 7:9), which render the same notion: rewarding the loyal servants with kindness. The phrases "guarding/doing kindness" *(nṣr* or *šmr/ʿśh ḥsd)* in a master–servant relationship are very common in the various political documents of the ancient Near East. There we find the phrases *ṭābtu naṣāru* 'to keep kindness', as well as *ṭābtu epēšu* 'to do kindness', in the sense of a reward given by the king to his loyal servant (cf. Weinfeld 1973a, pp. 193–96).

those who love me. Alternatively, "who are faithful to me." "Love" to God is a concept characteristic of Deuteronomy and means covenantal loyalty (cf. the COMMENT below to 6:5). One should not exclude, however, its usage from pre-Deuteronomic sources; cf. Judg 5:30; see Moran 1963b, pp. 85–87.

Third Commandment

11. *You shall not take up the name of YHWH your God in vain.* In contrast to the first two commandments, in which God speaks in the first-person singular, from the third commandment onward God is addressed in the third person. This is the basis for the rabbinic view that the first two "words" were proclaimed directly from God to the people, whereas the rest was transmitted by Moses *(b. Mak.* 24a).

The phrase *nś*ʾ*šm* 'bear the name' actually means "to take/bring up (on the lips/mouth)"; cf. the Greek and Vg translations and cf. Ps 16:4, *wbl ʾśʾ ʾt šmwtm ʿl śpty* 'I will not take/bring up their names on my lips', along with Ps 50:16, *wtśʾ bryty ʿly pyk* 'and bear/take my covenant on your mouth'. See also the Aramaic inscriptions of Sefire, "if the idea should come up to your mind *(ysq ʿl lbb)*" and "you should bring up on your lips *(wtśʾ ʿl śptyk)*" (Fitzmyer 1967, 3.14–15). Indeed, *Tg. Neof.* translates *tśʾ* 'take' (= *tsb).*

The question is, what is meant by "take [up] the name"? The rabbis distinguish between "swear by name falsely *(tšbʿw bšmy lšqr)*" (Lev 19:12) and "take the name in vain." The former involves, in their opinion, false oath, while the latter implies taking an oath in order to refute the commonly known: "he declared about a pillar of stone that it is of gold and about a man being a woman . . . that is an oath taken in vain" *(m. Šebu.* 3:8). According to another, more radical view, even if he takes an oath in truth for something commonly known (he swears about a pillar of stone that it is of stone), this is also an oath taken in vain *(Jer. Šebu.* 3:8, 34d). Josephus also understands the third commandment in a similar manner, "not to swear by God on any frivolous matter" *(Antiquities* 3.91). Philo also, speaking about the third commandment, says, "There are some who without even any gain in prospect have an evil habit of swearing incessantly and thoughtlessly about ordinary matters where there is nothing at all in dispute . . . for from much swearing springs false swearing and impiety" (*On the Decalogue* 92). In fact, the word *lšwʾ* 'in vain' means both "groundless/unreal" (Jer 2:30; 4:30; 6:29; 46:11; Mal 3:14; Ps 127:1) and "false" (Isa 59:4; Prov 30:8; Pss 12:3; 41:6; 144:8, 11; Job 31:5; Hos 10:4); cf. also Exod 20:16, *ʿed šeqer* 'false witness' with Deut 5:17, which has for the same, *ʿed šawʾ*. It is therefore hard to decide what exactly is prohibited by this injunction "false oath" or an "oath of vanity." *Targum Onqelos* translates both ways: the first *lšwʾ* is translated by *lmgnʾ* 'in vain' while the second *lšwʾ* he translates by *lšqrʾ* 'falsely'.

It seems that the plain meaning of the verse is swearing falsely. Jeremiah, who refers to the Decalogue in his Temple address in 7:9, understood it this way *(hšbʿ lšqr),* and the same may be deduced from Hosea's reference to the Decalogue in 4:2, *ʾlh wkḥš* 'swearing in dishonesty'. Compare also Zech 5:4 (see the INTRODUCTION to the Decalogue).

for YHWH will not acquit one who takes up his name in vain. Compare the same phrase in connection with the zealous God in Exod 34:7 *(wnqh lʾ ynqh),* which has affinities to the previous commandment (see above). Acquitting *(nqh,* literally, 'clearing'), in connection with an oath or any judicial imposition, is widely attested in the Bible; cf. Gen 24:8, 41; Num 5:19 (in connection with an "oath" [*ʾālāh*], vv 19, 21); Josh 2:17, 20; Zech 5:3; and is very common in rabbinic literature (*zakhâi/zikkāh*).

False oath was considered one of the gravest crimes in antiquity. Thus Diodorus Siculus (quoting Hecataeus of Abdera), when speaking about legislation of the Egyptians, brings up first the crime of false oath and says that it involves the two greatest transgressions, impiety toward the gods and violation of the mightiest pledge among men (1.77.2). Hesiod, in *Opera et dies* 283–85, states that whoever swears falsely will never be forgiven and his descendants will perish. Similarly, we hear from Herodotus (6.86) that the perjurer's house and race will be utterly destroyed. This idea is also expressed in rabbinic literature, "For all transgressions in the Torah the man alone is punished but for a false oath he and his family" *(b. Šebu.* 39a), and this is deduced from the phrase *lʾ ynqh* 'he will not acquit' in the verse under discussion.

The grave offense of perjury comes boldly to expression in the loyalty oath of the vassal kingdoms in the neo-Assyrian period; cf. Weinfeld 1976b, pp. 397–99.

Fourth Commandment (The Sabbath)

Days in which work should not be performed have been observed from earliest times. In Mesopotamia there was a long tradition of hemerologies (cf. Labat 1975), and especially important for our subject are the so-called "bad days *(ūmē lemnūti),*" the seventh, fourteenth, nineteenth, twenty-first, and twenty-eighth of the month, in which the king should not ride in his chariot or give a verdict, the physician should not heal, and so on. Similarly, we read in Hesiod's *Works and Days* that the "days of Zeus" should be observed: on the thirteenth when the moon grows one should not sow; on the sixteenth one should not plant; and so on (lines 765ff.). In Rome we also find *dies nefasti,* when certain business, especially legal business, might not be done. But all of these are unlucky days associated with certain phases of the moon, whereas the Sabbath in ancient Israel has nothing to do with luck or lack of luck and is not associated at all with the moon. It is observed every seventh day without any connection to the month or the year (cf. Hallo 1977). It is considered a day of joy and pleasure (Hos 2:13; Isa 58:13) and not a day of abstinence and asceticism. By the same token, we find in Mesopotamia the so-called *šapattu* on the fifteenth of the month, the day of the full moon, which is a day of appeasing God's heart and serves for festivity and sacrifice. Alongside the *šapattu,* the first and the seventh of the month were also celebrated. Thus we read in an old Babylonian letter in connection with a ritual, "do it thoroughly, as you have been shown, on the first, the seventh, and the fifteenth day of the month" (TCL 1.50:23). Similarly, we hear in the Atrahasis epic that on the first, the seventh, and the fifteenth days of the month a cleansing and a bathing will be carried out (Lambert and Millard 1969, pp. 56, 59, 206, 221). Herodotus tells us that the Spartan kings used to sacrifice on the first and the seventh of each month (6.57). That these days were popular holy days may be learned from a Nuzi text, where it says, "the female slave will accompany her mistress to the house of God and carry her chair on the fifteenth day *(šappatu)* and on the day of the new month (ITU *eššši)*" (HSS 14, p. 106); cf. Deller 1972, p. 206. But these days are not associated with cessation of work.

The Israelite Sabbath combined elements of both mentioned types of hemerology: abstention from work on the one hand, and days of celebration on the other. The day of Sabbath, however, remained unique, not only because of this combination, but because of its dissociation from lunar phases. The only connection with the moon is the association of the Sabbath with the new-moon day *(ḥdš wšbt);* cf. 2 Kgs 4:28; Isa 1:13; 66:23; Ezek 46:1; Hos 2:13; Amos 8:5; etc.

More significant are the spiritual-symbolic values attached to the Sabbath. Sabbath is a day of identification with the creator who rested from his work in order to contemplate (cf. Philo, see below) on the one hand (Exodus version), and a day of identification with the slave and servant who need to rest, on the other (Deuteronomic version). Thus on the Sabbath man resembles God in two ways: by creating and contemplating on the created work, and by giving freedom to those dependent on him. For the concept of rest after creation in Mesopotamia and in Israel, see Weinfeld 1981b.

12. *Observe (šamor) the Sabbath day to keep it holy.* The Sabbath commandment, like the commandment about respecting parents, is formulated in the positive, unlike the others, which are formulated in the negative because of the broad nature of these injunctions. The day of the Sabbath is marked not only by cessation of work but by its sacred character: "to keep the Sabbath holy" means to preserve its distinctive features by positive action, such as visiting holy places (Ezek 46:3; Isa 66:23), consulting the prophet (2 Kgs 4:23), and performing special sacrificial and ceremonial rites (Lev 24:8–9; Num 28:9–10; 2 Kgs 11:9). Similarly, respecting parents involves a broad range of duties (see the NOTE to Deut 5:16).

In the Exodus version the verb for observing is *zkr: "Remember* the Sabbath day to keep it holy." In fact, there is no significant difference between the two, for both verbs, *zkr* and *šmr,* connote "keep" as well as "remember." Thus we find in Gen 37:11 that Jacob "kept *(šmr)* the matter" (i.e., Joseph's dream), which means *remembered* it or *kept it in mind. šmr* and *zkr* parallel each other in

Ps 103:18: *lšmry brytw wlzkry pqwdyw* 'of those who *observe* his covenant and *remember/keep* his precepts'. Similarly, the idiom *šmr wʿśh* 'observe and do', which is so characteristic of Deuteronomy (see Weinfeld 1972a, pp. 336, 17a), has its counterpart in Num 15:39, 40: *zkr wʿśh* 'to remember/keep in mind and do' (cf. Esth 9:28, *nzkrym wnʿśym* 'these days are kept and observed'.

That *zkr* means not only to "recall" but also to "keep in mind" may be learned from those verses in the Bible which speak about the future and use *zkr,* as, for example, Lam 1:9, *lʾ zkrh ʾḥryth,* which cannot mean "she did not remember her future," but rather "she did not keep in mind her future"; cf. also Isa 47:7 and Ps 104:16 *(lʾ zkr ʿśwt ḥsd).* Similarly in Akkadian, the observance of the oath (of loyalty) is expressed by both verbs, *naṣāru* 'to guard/keep' and *ḫasāsu* 'to remember/think about': *adê naṣāru* 'keep the oaths' on the one hand, and *adê ḫasāsu* 'remember/think about' on the other (see Weinfeld 1973a, pp. 193–94). For *ḫasāsu* as equivalent to *zkr* in Hebrew, cf. the El-Amarna letter, where *zkr* glosses Akkadian *ḫasāsu* (Knudtzon 1908–15, 228:18–19: *liḫsusmi* glossed by *yazkurmi).*

It should be noted, however, that *zkr* connotes commemoration, a concept so central to the priestly theology (cf. the term *zkrwn,* characteristic of priestly literature). Indeed, the idea of commemoration comes up clearly in the motivation clause of the Sabbath commandment: the Israelites ought to rest because God rested on this day (Exod 20:11). Deuteronomy, however, which provides a different motivation for the Sabbath, distinguishes between *šmr* 'observe' and *zkr* 'remember'. The former is used for observance of the law, while the latter is reserved for historical remembrance; thus for the observance of the Sabbath he uses *šmr,* whereas for its motivation he uses *wzkrt: "Remember (zkr)* that you were a slave in the land of Egypt . . . therefore YHWH . . . has commanded you to *observe* the Sabbath day" (v 15; for the shift in the meaning of *zkr,* see Schottroff 1964, pp. 117–25).

It seems that the author of Deuteronomy was cognizant of the formulation *zkwr* in the fourth commandment but changed it on purpose in order to avoid the allusion to sacred commemoration. In contrast, he made use of the old *zkwr* in order to further his motivation about the historical remembrance of Exodus. The usage of *zkr* by Deuteronomy looks, then, like a twist of the original.

to keep it holy. God consecrated the day (see Exod 20:11b; cf. Gen 2:3), and therefore Israel must keep it holy (cf. Exod 31:14; Jer 17:22, 24; Ezek 20:20; 44:24; Neh 13:22) and not to profane it *(ḥll);* cf. especially Isa 56:2, "who keeps the Sabbath, not to profane it *(šmr šbt mḥllw),*" and see Exod 31:14; Ezek 20:13, 16, 21, 24; Neh 13:18. God's consecration of the day and Israel's obligation to keep it holy are both expressed by the same verb, *qiddeš.* The same applies to the priesthood and to the firstborn: God consecrates them (Lev 21:23; 22:9, 16; Num 3:13; 18:17), and Israel should keep them holy (Lev 21:23; Exod 13:2); and similarly regarding the people of Israel: God consecrates them (Exod

31:13; Lev 22:32), and they should keep themselves holy (Lev 11:44–45; 19:2; etc.).

Thus there is a correspondence between the opening of the fourth commandment, "to keep it holy," and its original conclusion as we have it in Exod 20:11b, "Therefore YHWH blessed the day of Sabbath and made it holy." In the Deuteronomic version of the Decalogue, this correspondence has been blurred by the humanistic reason introduced there. One should mention, however, that the LXX's version of Deuteronomy and the Qumran texts preserved this correspondence by reading in v 15: "Therefore God commanded you to keep the Sabbath and consecrate it" (see TEXTUAL NOTE). That the "consecration" of the day is genuine in the fourth commandment may be learned from the proclamation (in both versions) that "the Sabbath is for YHWH your God," that is, the Sabbath belongs to the divine sphere and is not originally a social-humanistic institution, the way the Deuteronomic version of the Decalogue seems to present it (v 15).

As indicated above, the sanctity of the day is expressed in the Bible by specific rules of behavior characteristic of the day, as visiting the Temple (Isa 66:2; Ezek 46:3) and "the man of God" (2 Kgs 4:23). Similar rules were observed by the Babylonians on the days of *šappatu,* as seen above. According to the book of Jubilees, cohabitation of husband with wife was also considered desecration of the day (50:8). According to E. Qimron (1986) this prohibition is attested in the Damascus Covenant 11.4: *ʾl ytʿrb ʾyš mrṣwnw bywm hšbt* 'let no one cohabit out of his desire on the day of Sabbath'. The rabbis understood the command of "keeping it holy" as the duty of sanctification of the day by a hymnic prayer over a cup of wine at the evening meal (cf. *Mek. Bahodeš* §7 [Horowitz 1928, p. 229]). This constitutes the so-called *Qidduš* reflected in the Christian Eucharist (cf. the prayers of the early Christian writings: Didache, Ignatius, and Justin).

as YHWH your God commanded you. This is a typical formula of Deuteronomy, which is dependent on older literary sources and quotes them; cf. Milgrom 1976; Skweres 1979. In this case the reference is to the priestly injunctions about the Sabbath; these are the proofs: First of all, the phrases "keep the Sabbath *(šmr šbt)*" and the "holiness *(qdš)*" of the day are found elsewhere in the Pentateuch only in the priestly legislation; thus we read in Exod 31:14, "You shall keep the Sabbath *(wšmrtm ʾt hšbt),* for it is holy *(qdš)* for you" (cf. v 13 there; Exod 35:2; Lev 19:3, 30; 26:2, where the Sabbath is connected with *mqdš;* Lev 23:3, *mqrʾ qdš* 'holy convocation'; cf. also Gen 2:3; Isa 1:23; Jer 17:22, 24; Ezek 20:20; 44:24; etc.).

Second, the idiom *lʾ tʿśh kl mlʾkh* 'You shall not do all/any work', used in connection with the Sabbath in the Decalogue, is typical of the priestly prohibitions of working on the Sabbath and holidays; cf. Exod 12:16; 31:14–15; 35:1–3; Lev 16:29; 23:3, 8, 28; cf. also Gen 2:2–3.

Third, the idea of the *holiness* of the Sabbath seems to be rooted in the priestly circles of ancient Israel, hence its prevalence in priestly literature. As I have shown in Weinfeld 1981b, the Sabbath rest was connected with God's rest in his sanctuary and was therefore especially emphasized by the priestly circles. The Sabbath, in fact, represented the conclusion of a cultic cycle, for on the Sabbath the shewbread was changed (Lev 24:5–9) and the changing of the Temple guards took place (2 Kgs 11:5–9); cf. Weinfeld 1967–68, pp. 109–10.

The priestly legislation of the Sabbath influenced the Sabbath commandment in the Decalogue, and the reference in the Deuteronomic version of the Decalogue to a previous Sabbath command can only be to the priestly laws that preserved identical formulations of the Sabbath's observance, as shown above. Such references in Deuteronomy to priestly regulations are to be discerned in the following verses: (1) 4:31 (see the NOTE there); 8:18 *(hqym bryt;* dependent on Exod 2:24; 6:4; Lev 26:2; Gen 17:7, 21; and Exod 6:4); (2) Deut 29:12, "to be a people to him and he will be your God," is a priestly formula (cf. Exod 6:7; Lev 26:12; and see Weinfeld 1972a, pp. 80–81); (3) Deut 10:9 and 18:2 are dependent on Num 18:20; and (4) Deut 24:8 refers to the priestly regulations of leprosy (Lev 13–14).

As will be shown below, the fifth commandment, which also contains a citation formula, corresponds similarly to priestly injunctions about respecting parents.

All of this does not necessarily mean that the author of Deuteronomy quoted from the priestly literature as preserved in the Pentateuch today, but he seems rather to have drawn from the priestly lore, which grew and developed over hundreds of years. See most recently Y. Knohl (1987), who traces the development of the priestly laws in the various sources of the priestly law from old, dry legislative to the more pragmatic and homiletic law, as presented in the holiness code.

Hossfeld (1982, pp. 53–57) argues that the citation formula in Deut 5:12 refers to Exod 23:12 and 34:21a, but this claim can hardly be accepted. The commands in 5:12–13 are formulated in a manner quite different from the Exodus laws above (no "keeping holy" and no "doing *ml'kh*" is found there), and these laws cannot therefore be seen as the origin of the commandment. It is only the enumeration of the dependent persons who are to be given rest, and the motivation for rest in v 14, which have affinities to Exod 23:12 (see below).

13–14. *Six days you shall labor and do all your work. But the seventh day is a Sabbath.* Compare Exod 23:12, "Six days you shall do your labors *(tʿśh mʿśyk)* and on the seventh day you shall cease from work *(tšbt).*" "Labors *(mʿśyk)*" denote here agricultural work, as in v 16 there, *mʿśyk . . . bśdh/mn hśdh,* whereas *ʿśh ml'kh,* which occurs in the Decalogue, means performance of any kind of labor, skilled and unskilled alike. Similarly, in Exod 34:21 the work prohibited on Sabbath is connected with work of the field: "Six days you shall work *(tʿbd)* and on the seventh day you shall cease [from work = *tšbt],* you shall cease [from work] in plowing and harvest."

In the fourth commandment here, as in the priestly laws (see above), any kind of work *(kl mlʾkh)* is prohibited. *mlʾkh* is derived from *lʾk* 'to send' and mainly connotes "sending" or "stretching out" one's hand for work; cf. *mšlḥ yd* 'sending one's hand' (Deut 12:7, 18; 15:10; 23:21; 28:8, 20), which means any undertaking (cf. Ben-Hayyim 1974, pp. 46–49). Compare Akkadian *šipru* (derived from *šapāru* 'to send'), 'work', which is also associated with hand: *šipir idu/qātu* 'hand work' *(AHW,* s.v. *šipru* 10, p. 1246).

In accordance with this broader focus, the priestly laws of the Sabbath are formulated as follows: "Six days work *(mlʾkh)* will be done, but on the seventh there shall be a Sabbath . . . holy to YHWH" (Exod 31:15; 35:2); "Six days work *(mlʾkh)* may be done, but on the seventh day there shall be a Sabbath . . . a sacred convocation—you shall not do any work *(kl mlʾkh lʾ tʿśw)"* (Lev 23:3), which resembles the Sabbath formulation of the Decalogue: "Six days you shall . . . do all your work *(kl mlʾktk).* But the seventh day is a Sabbath to YHWH your God. You shall not do any work *(lʾ tʿśh kl mlʾkh)."* For the term *mlʾkh* in the priestly literature, see Milgrom 1970, pp. 76–82, and cf. its review by Weinfeld in *IEJ* 23 (1973):61.

Sabbath to YHWH your God. The Sabbath has a divine purpose and thus is of theocentric nature. On the seventh day man and beasts return, as it were, to their creator, God, and are freed of subjugation to man or nature. A similar idea occurs in connection with the seventh-year rest of the earth: "every seventh year *the land shall rest, a Sabbath to YHWH"* (Lev 25:4). The divine nature of the Sabbath explains its inclusion in the first pentad of the Decalogue. The social motivation of the Sabbath is secondary, and cannot be considered the genuine reason for its observance. As indicated above, the day of the Sabbath was indeed dedicated to sacred duties (visiting holy places and holy men).

In the Judaism of the Second Temple period, the Sabbath was conceived as a day of contemplating God and of studying the Torah. Thus we hear Josephus saying that Moses enjoined "that every week men should desert their occupations and assemble to listen to the Law" *(Against Apion* 2.175; see also Josephus' *Antiquities* 16.43). The reading of the Torah on the Sabbath is also mentioned in Acts 15:21: "For generations Moses has been preached in every town and has been recited on every Sabbath." Not only the law has been recited, but also the prophets, as may be learned from Luke 4:16–19 and Acts 13:15 and from Jewish synagogal practice to the present.

According to Philo, the Sabbath should be devoted to contemplation, just as God, the creator, contemplated on his work after creation: "We are told that the world was made in six days and that on the seventh God ceased from his works and began to contemplate what had been so well created, and therefore he asked [the people of the nation] . . . to follow God . . . and commanded that they should work for six days but rest on the seventh and turn to the study of wisdom" *(On the Decalogue* 97–99). In his book on Moses he says that "the Jews occupy themselves every seventh day with the philosophy of their fathers, dedicating that time to the acquiring of knowledge and the study of truth of nature" *(Moses* 2.216).

The rabbinic sources likewise learned from the phrase "Sabbath to YHWH" that the Sabbath should be dedicated to the study of Torah *(Midr. Hagadol* to Exodus; cf. y. *Šabb.* 15:3, 15a, *Pesiq. Rab.* 23 [Ish-Shalom 1880, p. 121]). The distinctive feature of the Sabbath made it a day of special significance for Israel: "a sign of the covenant" between YHWH and Israel (Exod 31:16–17). The Sabbath testifies to the sanctification of Israel: "You must keep my Sabbaths, for this is a sign between me and you throughout the ages, that you may know that I YHWH have sanctified you" (Exod 31:13; cf. Ezek 20:12, 20).

During the Second Temple period the Sabbath, being a sign of distinction, was linked to the idea of the election of Israel: "And the Creator of all things blessed it [the Sabbath], but he did not sanctify all people and nations to keep Sabbath thereon, but Israel alone: them alone he permitted to eat and drink and to keep Sabbath thereon on earth" (Jubilees 2:31–32; cf. Charles 1913, 2.15). This idea turned out to be the central motif in the Jewish liturgy of Sabbath. The kiddush prayer over a cup of wine, which opens the Sabbath evening meal (see above), reads as follows: "Blessed are you, O Lord our God, King of the universe, who has sanctified us by his commandments . . . for you have chosen us and sanctified us from all nations" (Singer 1915, p. 181). Similarly, in the Sabbath morning prayer, "And you did not give it, O Lord our God, to the nations of the lands, nor did you give it as an inheritance to worshippers of idols" (Singer 1915, p. 201).

You shall not do any work. The work prohibited on Sabbath is not defined in the Bible. An explicit prohibition is found in Exod 35:3, "You shall kindle no fire throughout your settlements on the Sabbath day," and associated with it is the story about the "wood gatherer [to kindle fire]" in Num 15:32–36, who was executed because of breaking the law of the Sabbath. Exodus 34:21 prohibits the work of plowing and harvest on the seventh day, and from Amos 8:5 we learn that people abstained from business on the Sabbath. Warnings against hauling burdens and leading commercial activity on the Sabbath are explicitly mentioned in Jer 17:19–27 and Neh 10:32. Identical activities are condemned in Isa 58:13 (see Weinfeld 1982c, pp. 43–45).

The lack of a clear definition of "work," however, caused arguments about the kind of work prohibited on the Sabbath amongst the various Jewish sects of the Second Temple period. In the book of Jubilees we find that one is forbidden to draw water on the Sabbath (50:8), which was not forbidden by the Pharisees. (For the sectarian laws of the Sabbath, see Schiffman 1975.) The Pharisees did set definite rules for forbidden labor: thirty-nine main classes of work *(aboth melaʾkhoth),* which encompass activities of agriculture and basic labors of mankind, such as building, weaving, baking, sewing, writing, and the like *(m. Šabb.* 7:2–4).

you and your son and your daughter. The wife is not mentioned because the word "you" refers equally to the husband and to the wife; cf. 12:12, 18; 16:11, 14, where all members of the household are mentioned as participating in the festal pilgrimage—sons, daughters, slaves, and maidservants—but only the wife is absent. It certainly did not mean that the wife alone was to remain at home and not participate in the celebration (cf. 1 Sam 1 for a pilgrimage of the whole family with the two wives of Elkanah).

your male servant and your female servant. Compare Exod 23:12.

your ox and your ass and any of your animals. The Exodus version does not enumerate ox and ass because it is influenced by the priestly terminology (see above), which uses the word *bhmh* as a generalization for domestic animals and is the opposite of *ḥayah* 'wild animal'; cf. Gen 1:24–26; Lev 1:2; 25:7; 27:26. This priestly usage comes out clearly in the comparison of Lev 19:19, "You shall not let *your animal (bhmtk)* mate with a different kind," with Deut 22:10, "You shall not plow with an *ox* and *ass* together." Both laws have an identical context, namely, mixing species (seeds, animals, and fabrics in a garment), but the priestly author uses *bhmtk,* while the Deuteronomic author has *šor* and *ḥamor.* In the present case the Deuteronomic author, who used the priestly Exodus term *bhmh* as a general term for "animal," added—perhaps under the influence of Exod 23:12—the "ox" and "ass" (cf. also Exod 21:33; 22:3, 8, 9; 23:4–5, 12; Josh 6:21; Judg 6:4; 1 Sam 12:3; 22:19; and cf. Deut 22:4, 10; 28:31), at the same time turning "any of your animals *(wkl bhmtk)*" into an explanatory gloss, a generalization for which he has a special fondness (cf. above, the NOTE to v 7). A similar structure is to be found in Exod 22:9: "if a man gives to another an ass, an ox, a sheep *and any animal (wkl bhmh)* to guard."

and the alien [resident] in your gates (wgrk ʾšr bšʿryk). This expression, which is common in the book of Deuteronomy (14:21, 29; 24:14), was not coined by the Deuteronomic author. It is found in Ugaritic literature in a text that speaks about an expiation ritual for the people of Ugarit, as well as for the "alien at the walls of Ugarit *(gr ḥmyt ugrt)*" *(KTU* 1.40:18, 35–36; see Xella 1981, pp. 256–57, 266). Another text in the Akkadian language speaks "about the people of Ugarit together with the men living within their gates *(amēli ša bābišunu)*" (RS 18.115, *PRU* 4.158–59). See also the texts from Nuzi about a category of people, *ša bābi* 'those of the gate', which means those not belonging to the citizens (HSS 19, p. 79). The expression is common in Deuteronomy because of the clear urban background of this book (cf., e.g., 28:62 and see the INTRODUCTION, sec. 16.)

so that your male and female slave may rest as you do. This is influenced in contents and wording by Exod 23:12: "Six days you shall do your work but on the seventh day you shall cease [from work], so that your ox and your ass may rest and that your slave *(bn ʾmtk)* and the alien *(hgr)* may be refreshed *(ynpš).*" Deuteronomy, however, does not put the animal and the man on the same level, as Exodus does, and applies the idea of equality to man alone. In this respect it resembles Job 31:13–15: "Did I ever neglect the case of my male and female slave when they made a complaint against me? . . . did not one form us both in the same womb?"

15. *Remember that you were a slave in the land of Egypt and YHWH your God freed you from there with a strong hand and outstretched arm.* The recollection of the deliverance from Egypt as a motive for generosity to slaves, the poor, and the needy is also found in other places in Deuteronomy: 15:15; 16:12; 24:18, 22. For the humanistic tendency of the book of Deuteronomy, see Weinfeld 1972a, pp. 282–97.

therefore, YHWH your God commanded you to observe [literally, 'to do or make', lʿśwt] the Sabbath day. This is not to be understood as suggesting that the Sabbath day was instituted because of the Exodus; rather, because of the deliverance from Egypt, Israel *is urged to observe* the Sabbath, which means letting the slaves and other dependents rest on this day. To *"do/make* the Sabbath," meaning to "establish," is a phrase found only in priestly literature; cf. Exod 31:16: "The Israelites shall observe the Sabbath *to do/make* [= establish] *the Sabbath* throughout the ages." This verb is also used by the priestly author in connection with the Passover (Exod 12:47, 48; Num 9:2–6, 13; cf. Deut 16:1; 2 Kgs 23:21 [= Dtr]).

The LXX has, instead of *"to do/make* the day of the Sabbath," "to observe the day . . . and to keep it holy *(fulassestai kai hagiazein),"* which forms a kind of *inclusio* with the beginning of the commandment: "observe . . . to keep it holy"; see above, in the NOTE on v 12.

Fifth Commandment

16. *Honor your father and your mother.* The verb for "honor" *(kibbed)* is derived from the root *kbd* 'heavy/weighty', just as *qillel* 'dishonor/disgrace' derives from *qll* 'light/scanty'. For the antinomy *kbd–qll,* cf. 1 Sam 2:30: "I honor those who honor me *(mkbdy ʾkbd),* but those who spurn me *(wbzy)* shall be dishonored *(yqlw)";* see also 2 Sam 6:22 *(nqlty* versus *ʾkbdh);* Isa 23:9 *(lhql . . . nkbdy);* Hos 4:7; Hab 2:16; Prov 3:35 *(kbd* versus *qlwn).* Indeed, the opposite of "honoring *(kbd)"* one's parents is expressed by the root *qll,* "one who insults or curses *(mqll)* his father and mother" (Exod 21:12; Lev 20:9 cf. Deut 27:16 *[mqlh];* Ezek 22:7; Prov 20:20; 30:11). These two opposites are clearly juxtaposed in a document from Ugarit that speaks of a son who dishonors *(uqallil)* his mother, as against the one who honors *(ukabbit)* her (Thureau-Dangin 1937, p. 249). Compare also Matt 15:4, "For God said: 'Honor your father and your mother' " and "the one who reviles his father and his mother shall be put to death."

One must recognize that the *piʿel* form of *qll* mainly signifies cursing, in contrast to the *niphʿal* and *hiphʿil* forms, which express contempt (see, e.g., 1 Sam 2:30; 2 Sam 6:22; and Deut 27:16). It should be admitted, however, that the basic meaning of *qll* is like Akkadian *qullulu/gullulu* 'to discredit/dishonor', and this connotation is also attested in the Bible, especially in the instances dealing with discrediting God and king, as in 1 Kgs 21:10, 13 *(brk* as euphemism for *qll); cf.* also Deut 21:22–23 *(qllt ʾlhym),* for which see Weinfeld 1972a, p. 51 n. 4. Compare now the Temple Scroll of Qumran, *wyqll ʾt ʿmw wʾt bny yśrʾl* (64:7–13), which means 'he will dishonor the people and the children of Israel'. For the "curse" in the Bible, see Brichto 1963.

Leviticus 19:3, in a passage that is related to the Ten Commandments (see the INTRODUCTION to the Decalogue), has instead of the verb *kbd* the verb *yrʾ*, literally 'fear' (out of respect); cf. Prov 24:21, "My son, fear YHWH and the king," which actually means "respect" and thus parallels *kbd.* (Mark the distinction between the usual *yrʾ mn* = fear of X, and *yrʾ ʾt,* as in Lev 19:3 and Prov 24:21, which means "respect"; cf. also *yrʾ ʾt YHWH* 'to serve YHWH'.) "Fear," or rather "awe," is conceptually related to "honor"; cf. Deut 28:58, "honored and awesome/feared *(hnkbd whnwrʾ)* name of YHWH," and in the Akkadian documents dealing with the treatment of parents we find next to *kabātu* 'honor', *palāḫu* 'fear' in the sense of "serve respectfully"; see, for example, in an old Babylonian document related to parents: *ipallaḫ ukabassi* 'he will serve and respect her' *(CT* 2.35:8; Schorr 1913, 13a, p. 28). The duties involved in *palāḫu* are "to support *(našû/wabālu),*" "to provide cloth *(lubuššu)* and grain *(šèu),*" "to bury the parent when he dies *(qebēru),*" and "to wail over him *(bākû)*" (cf. Cassin 1938, pp. 278ff.). Identical duties of sons regarding their parents, by virtue of the fulfillment of the fifth commandment, are enumerated in the rabbinic sources *(b. Qidd.* 31b; m. *Peʾa* 1:1, 15c; *t. Qidd.* 1:11; etc.). For the significance of the fifth commandment in comparison with the duty of the son *vis à vis* his parents in the ancient Near East (especially in Mesopotamia), cf. Albertz 1978.

A list of filial responsibilities is also found in Ugaritic literature. Danel, the pious judge, is blessed with a son whose duties to his father are described as follows: "he erects a pillar for his father . . . he chases away any of his oppressors . . . he holds his hand when he is drunken . . . feeds him . . . plasters his roof and washes his clothes" *(CTA* 17.1:27–34). See also Ben Sira 3:8–16:

> honor your father by word and deed . . .
> look after your father in his old age . . .
> even if his mind fails him, help him.

The rabbis distinguish in the field of filial responsibility between these two terms: *kibbud,* according to their view, implies feeding, clothing, and taking care of, while *moraʾ* (from the root *yrʾ)* implies reverence, in other words, not to sit in his place nor contradict his words, and so on *(b. Qidd.* 31b and the various parallels); for a thorough discussion of the problem, see Blidstein 1975, pp. 37–59.

In the Bible the service of the parents appears in Mal 3:17, where it is said that God will reward Israel "like a man who rewards his son who serves him *(bnw hʿbd ʾtw)*"; cf. Greenfield 1982, pp. 57–59.

The filial duties are mainly twofold: *reverence,* which means obedience and is widely attested in the didactic sources of the Bible (Prov 1:8; 23:22; Ben Sira 3:1–16); and *care,* which is not specified in the Bible but is attested in external sources (see the Ugaritic passage above) and in the rabbinic literature, as shown above. The fifth commandment is formulated in a positive and abstract manner so that it might encompass all the possible filial duties. "Honor your father and your mother" refers to reverence as well as to physical care.

Filial piety, which is embodied in the fifth commandment, stands, rightly, in the middle between the commandments concerned with duties to God and those concerned with duties to men. This idea was nicely elaborated by Philo in his discussion of the Decalogue: "This commandment he [God] placed on the borderline between the two groups of five; it is the last of the first set in which the most sacred injunctions are given, and it adjoins the second set, which contains the duties of man to man. The reason I consider is this: we see that parents by nature stand on the borderline between the mortal and the immortal" *(On the Decalogue* 106–7). Compare also "For parents are midway between the natures of God and man and partake of both. . . . Parents, in my opinion, are to their children what God is to the world, for just as he achieved existence for the nonexistent, so they in imitation of his power . . . immortalize the race" *(The Special Laws* 2.225). In another place he cites an opinion, according to which father and mother are in fact gods, the difference being that God created the world, while parents created individual beings only *(On the Decalogue* 120).

These ideas have roots in Greek philosophy, where the point is made that ancestors are like gods (Plato, *Laws* 11.931a–d) and that honor should be given to the parents such as is given to the gods (Aristotle, *Nicomachean Ethics* 9.2.8). Such ideas are alien to genuine Jewish thought. Jewish sages express the idea that parents *share* with God the creation of the human being *(b. Qidd.* 30b); in other words, they are partners with God in creating man (cf. Gen 4:1), but they are not like him.

Josephus, likewise, expresses the idea that parents rank second to God *(Against Apion* 2.206) but are not like God. In fact, after divine authority comes paternal and regal authority. Cursing parents, the king, or God are capital crimes, punishable with death (Exod 21:17; Lev 20:9; 24:15; Deut 21:17; 27:18). For cursing/dishonoring the king as capital crime, cf. 1 Kgs 21:13.

as YHWH commanded you. As indicated above, the fifth commandment relates clearly to Lev 19:3, which, like the Decalogue, links fear of parents with observing the Sabbath. The verb *yrʾ* parallels *kbd,* connoting both fear and respect. It stands to reason, therefore, that, just as the citation formula in the fourth commandment in Deuteronomy refers to the priestly laws (see above), so the citation in the fifth commandment also refers to the priestly injunction about revering parents (cf. also Lev 20:9).

that your days may long endure [be prolonged] *and that you may fare well.* Longevity is the reward for the care for (old) parents, a kind of measure for measure: those who care for parents will themselves grow old and be well taken care of (see the commentary of Abravanel, ad loc.). It is possible that this promise refers not only to this specific commandment but intends to form a conclusion to the first pentad of commandments, so the national aspect of the reward is stressed here: longevity upon the land that YHWH is giving to Israel.

Indeed, this is the only commandment that is accompanied by a promise of reward (cf. Eph 6:2) and is in fact considered by the sages to be foremost among the commandments for which man is rewarded in this world *(m. Peʾa* 1:1). It is therefore reckoned as the weightiest commandment *(mṣwh ḥmwrh),* even more important than reverence for God. Rabbi Simeon ben Yohai says, "Great is the commandment of *honoring father and mother* because God preferred it over the honoring of himself" *(y. Peʾa* 1:5, 15d; see the discussion in Urbach 1979, pp. 345–46).

Although the promise of "prolonging the days" is typical of Deuteronomy, it is also found elsewhere in the Bible (Isa 53:10; Prov 28:16; Eccl 8:13) and in the Phoenician and Aramaic inscriptions (cf. *KAI* 4:3; 6:2; 7:4; 10:9; 226:3). What makes the phrase specifically Deuteronomic is the combination of "long life" with "faring well *(yyṭb),*" which is attested only in Deuteronomy (cf. 4:40; 5:30; 6:2, 24; 22:7). (The order of the Decalogue, *long life* and *good,* appears only in 6:2–3; in other instances "good" comes before "life." See 4:40; 5:30; 6:24; 22:7. The LXX also has "good" before "life" in the Decalogue.) Nonetheless, one must be aware of the fact that in the Nerab inscription *(KAI* 226) we find before "lengthening the days *(hʾrk ywmy),*" giving a "good name *(šm ṭwb),*" which may indicate that the combination of "life" and "good" was prevalent in the ancient Near East, though "good name" there is not the same as "fare well *(hyṭyb)*" in Deuteronomy.

Hossfeld (1982, pp. 66–68), who argues for the priority of the Decalogue in Deuteronomy over that of Exodus, has difficulty with the omission of the phrase "that you may fare well" in Exodus. His explanation for the omission is that the conditioning of the well-going in the land by observing the law would contradict the priestly doctrine about the unconditional gift of the land and the unshaken belief in its goodness, which is expressed especially in the story about the spies in Num 13–14. In Hossfeld's view, because the Decalogue in Exodus was edited by a priestly author, that author could not incorporate the phrase *lmʿn yyṭb lk* into his version of the Decalogue. One must say that this explanation is highly speculative.

upon the land that YHWH your God is giving you. Although this phrase appears frequently in Deuteronomy, it is also attested outside the Deuteronomic sources (cf., e.g., Lev 23:10; 25:2; Num 13:2). What makes such phrases

Deuteronomic is the completion *lnḥlh* or *lršth* 'for an inheritance', and this does not occur in the Decalogue. We cannot be sure, therefore, that the phrase as it appears in the Exodus Decalogue is originally Deuteronomic.

The ending of the first pentad forms an inclusion with the opening statement about YHWH bringing the people out of slavery in Egypt; at the end of the pentad comes the gift of land, which thus rounds it out: Exodus aiming to the possession of the promised land (courtesy of D. N. Freedman).

The Second Pentad

vv 17–18. In contradistinction to the first pentad, where "YHWH (your God)" appears in each commandment, the second pentad does not contain the Tetragrammaton at all. In the second pentad one finds commandments of a moral nature that appeal to the human being as such (see the INTRODUCTION to the Decalogue) and not just to the Israelite people. The Deuteronomic version of the Decalogue enhances the uniformity of the second pentad by making it, as it were, one sentence: "You shall not murder *and* not commit adultery *and* not steal *and* not bear false witness . . . *and* not covet."

Indeed, the commandments of the second pentad have been seen by Jewish and Christian writers as the embodiment of the command to love one's neighbor (Lev 19:18; see the INTRODUCTION to the Decalogue), and the addition of "and" before each commandment has been understood as alluding to a chain reaction: "if he broke one law he would break the other" *(Mek. R. Simeon ben Yohai* to Exod 20:14 [Epstein-Melamed 1955, p. 154]) and cf. Jas 2:10–11: "If you observe the sovereign law as written: 'Love your neighbor as yourself,' you do well. But if you show partiality you are sinners and you stand convicted by the Law as transgressors. For if a man keeps the whole law apart from one, he is guilty of breaking all of it. For the one who said, 'You shall not commit adultery,' said, *'and [kai]* you shall not commit murder'; you may not be an adulterer, but if you commit murder you are a law-breaker all the same." For an analysis of the preceding sources, see Flusser 1990, pp. 224–25.

Ibn Ezra discerned a gradation in this set of injunctions: first comes murder, which entails destruction of body; second, adultery, which is violating another's body; then comes taking by force another's property; afterward, crime against another's property not by physical force, but by mouth; and finally comes coveting, which is neither by force nor by mouth but through mere intention.

The LXX, Exod, the Nash papyrus, and Luke 18:20, Rom 13:9, Jas 2:11 have a different order: adultery, murder, and theft (see the TEXTUAL NOTE). It seems, however, that the order in the Masoretic text is the genuine one. From Deut 22:26 we learn that murder is a more outrageous crime than adultery. Violation of a woman pledged in marriage is *compared* there to murder, which means that murder is the only crime to which adultery can be compared; cf. also the gradation of crimes as presented by Ibn Ezra (above).

Sixth Commandment

17. *You shall not murder.* It is significant that, unlike the ninth and the tenth commandments, which note the object, "neighbor/fellow man *(rʿk),*" this commandment and the next two are formulated in the most absolute manner, without specifying the object of the crime, in order to include any possible object, any human being (including suicide). (For the casuistry concerning murder, cf. Gen 9:6; Exod 21:12; Lev 17:21; 24:17; Num 35:30–34; Deut 19:11–13; 27:16.)

Seventh Commandment

and you shall not commit adultery. The verb *nʾp* refers to relations with married or engaged women (cf. Lev 20:10; Jer 29:23; Ezek 16:32; Hos 3:1; 4:13; Prov 6:32; etc. (For the casuistry, cf. Lev 18:20; 20:10; Deut 22:22; Num 5:11–30.)

Eighth Commandment

and you shall not steal. Cf. Lev 19:11, "You shall not steal *(lʾ tgnbw),*" which precedes the injunction against false imputation *(wlʾ tšqrw ʾyš bʿmytw),* similar to the present commandment, which comes before the injunction not to give false witness. Theft has its developed casuistry in Exod 21:37–22:12.

The rabbis understood the commandment as referring to kidnapping (cf. Exod 21:15; Deut 24:7) by way of judicial interpretations. Because stealing is put on the same level with murder and adultery, which are capital crimes, it occurred to them that stealing here involves capital punishment, which can be applied only to kidnapping (cf. *b.* Sanh. 86a; see also *Mek.* ad loc.).

The same interpretation was proposed by A. Alt (1963), who was unaware of the old rabbinic interpretation. Alt's proposal is based mainly on three arguments: (A) The separation of the eighth commandment from the tenth, which deals with property, by the commandment about false witness, seems to indicate, in his view, that the eighth and tenth commandments are concerned with different subjects. The former has to do with man's freedom (deprived by kidnapping), while the latter is concerned with house and property. (B) Because according to Alt the last commandment involves not just coveting but machinations toward appropriation (see below), which is almost identical with theft, the traditional interpretation of "You shall not steal" would mean that the eighth commandment overlaps the tenth. (C) Because most of the commandments have an object after the verb, the three short commandments must have had objects, and the eighth commandment should be reconstructed as, "You shall not steal a man or woman" or "You shall not steal any soul from Israel" (cf. Deut 24:7).

This reasoning, however, cannot be sustained: for one thing, as suggested by Ibn Ezra, there is gradual progress in the order of the last commandments: taking away property by force, causing the taking away of another's property by mouth (bearing witness), and mere coveting of another's property. Therefore the ninth commandment is not to be seen as a disruption. Besides, the second pentad has a consistent structure: three short injunctions with two strokes each, and two longer injunctions with four strokes each *(lʾ tʿnh brʿk ʿd-šwʾ, lʾ tḥmd byt rʿk)* having identical objects: your neighbor *(rʿk)*. Also, as will be seen below, there is no overlap between *ḥmd* and *gnb,* as Alt suggests, and the conventional understanding of the eighth commandment does not, therefore, create any difficulties. Finally, as I show in the INTRODUCTION to the Decalogue, there is no justification for reconstructing the three short commandments; they should be left as they are.

The absolute-categorical nature of the commandments of the Decalogue should, therefore, be applied to this commandment too: "You shall not steal" includes all possible objects, people as well as goods (for refutation of Alt's thesis, see H. Klein 1976, pp. 167–69). The fact that "You shall not steal" is attached to two injunctions that deal with capital crimes (murder and adultery) does not mean that all three transgressions are to be punished similarly. Besides, punishment is irrelevant in the Decalogue (see the INTRODUCTION to the Decalogue).

Ninth Commandment

and you shall not bear false witness against your neighbor. The ninth commandment, false witness, has its parallels in Exod 23:1: "You must not carry false rumors *(šmʿ šwʾ),* you shall not join hands with the guilty to act as a malicious witness *(ʿd ḥms)* . . . keep far from a false charge *(dbr šqr)";* and, in a casuistic setting, Deut 19:16–19: "When a malicious witness *(ʿd ḥms)* comes forward to give false testimony *(ʿnwt srh)* against a man . . . the judges shall make a thorough examination; if the man who testified is a false witness *(ʿd šqr)* giving false evidence against his fellow man *(šqr ʿnh bʾḥyw)* . . . you shall do to him as he schemed to do to his fellow."

The common expressions in all of these commands are *ʿd šqr/šwʾ, ʿd ḥms,* and *ʿnh brʿ/bʾḥ.* It seems that the Deuteronomic version of the Decalogue used the unusual combination *ʿd šwʾ* in order to prohibit not only false witness but also testimony by way of circumvention that comes to evade true evidence. Hossfeld (1982, pp. 72–75; see also n. 3), who considers the Deuteronomic version to be original, argues that the Exodus version changed *šwʾ* into *šqr* in order to make a more profound distinction between the third prohibition, false oath, and the ninth prohibition, false witness. This explanation is, of course, in line with his thesis, but it is not convincing.

your neighbor. *rʿk* Connotes anyone else, here "adversary"; cf. 1 Sam 15:28; 2 Sam 12:11; see Weinfeld 1972a, p. 131 nn. 1, 3.

Tenth Commandment

18. *And you shall not covet.* Like the other commandments of the Decalogue so especially this commandment is addressed to the believer and not to the lawyer (see the INTRODUCTION to the Decalogue). Therefore the question of how covetousness can be controlled and punished is irrelevant. Because of this misunderstanding, various forced interpretations of this commandment have been proposed. Thus it has been suggested (since Hermann 1927) that the Hebrew verb *ḥmd* means more than "covet"; it actually implies appropriation (cf. Alt 1963). This suggestion is based on the observation that *ḥmd* often appears together with *lqḥ* (Deut 7:25; Josh 7:21 [cf. LXX Josh 6:18]; Mic 2:2), and in the Phoenician building inscription of Azitawwadda *(KAI* 26A.3:14–16 = C.4:16–17) this verb joins *nsʿ* 'to remove' "he will covet this city and remove this gate *(yḥmdʾyt hqrt z wysʿ hšʿr).*" But the fact that *ḥmd* joins verbs like *lqḥ* 'take' (Deut 7:25; Josh 6:18 [LXX]; 7:21), or *gzl* 'rob', or *nśʾ* 'carry' (Mic 2:2) only shows that the verb *ḥmd* by itself cannot mean "taking" or "appropriating." The verb *ʾwh* in Deut 5:20, which stands in parallel to *ḥmd,* is even more difficult to interpret as "to appropriate," as has already been noted by Ibn Ezra in his commentary on Deut 5:16.

One must admit, however, that in Hebrew and in other Semitic languages, the distinction between cause and effect is sometimes blurred (cf. *pĕʿulāh* 'work', as "wages" in Lev 19:13 and *ḥaṭaʾt* 'sin', in the sense of product of sin = [golden calf in Deut 9:21), and therefore *ḥmd* might sometimes connote more than just intention. Thus, for example, in Exod 34:24, "no one will covet *(yḥmd)* your land" does not imply that the land will not be desirable, but that no one will make plans to invade the land when the Israelites go up for pilgrimage. As J. Pedersen has observed (1946–47, 2.128), Israelites, like other ancient peoples, saw desire and action as bound together in a deep unity, so that the first by a kind of inner necessity implied the second (and see Moran 1967, pp. 545–48).

What is meant, therefore, by *lʾ tḥmd* is "You shall not plan to appropriate the other's wife and the other's property." In this way the last two prohibitions in the Decalogue correspond to the two commandments of *lʾ tnʾp* and *lʾ tgnb,* but, whereas there the culprit commits the crime stealthily, without intention to get hold of the object in a legal manner, here his intention is legally to appropriate the other's wife or the other's household (by means of improper maneuvers and machinations). But all of this does not imply active misappropriation. As W. L. Moran puts it: "The mere fact that a verb like *ḥamad* occasionally implies some act of seizure or the like, is not to be understood in the sense that such an act belongs to its proper *denotation*" (1967, p. 348).

An interpretation of the tenth commandment similar to that of Hermann and Alt was presented by the rabbis. The rabbis who wanted to conform this law to halakhic rules also interpreted this commandment as actual appropriation: "Perhaps even the mere expressing of one's desire for the neighbor's things . . . is also meant? But it says: 'thou shall not covet the silver or the gold that is on them so that thou take it unto thee' (Deut 7:25). Just as there *carrying out* of one's desire into practice is forbidden, so here it is forbidden only to carry out the desire into practice" *(Mek.* to Exod 20:17 [Lauterbach 1933, 2.266; cf. *Midr. Tanaaim* to Deuteronomy [Hoffmann 1908] to Deut 5:21). As indicated, however, this is not the plain sense of the commandment. Translators and commentators understood it correctly as covetousness. The LXX translated it by *epitymeo* 'to lust', and Philo also took it as lust and passion *(epitymia)* for women, money, and the like. In his opinion, it is this trait that causes wars and brings disaster to the human race *(On the Decalogue* 151–53). Similarly, we read in the *Tgs. Ps.-J.* and *Neof.* to the tenth commandment, "Do not covet because through the guilt of covetousness the empires break in upon the possession of men . . . and exile comes upon the world." For a recent discussion of the whole problem, see Jackson 1975a.

and you shall not covet your neighbor's wife, and you shall not crave your neighbor's house. In contradistinction to the sixth through eighth commandments, which could be epitomized in one verb—murder *(rṣḥ),* commit adultery *(nʾp),* steal *(gnb)*—the verb *ḥmd* alone would not suffice to render the proper meaning of the injunction. *lʾ tḥmd* by itself means "You shall not desire" (Hebrew has no special word for "covet"), which is not the intention of the legislator; because desire as such is not illegitimate, it is only the desire of somebody else's object (covetousness) that makes it illegitimate.

The mention of the object "wife/house of your neighbor" cannot therefore be avoided and actually constitutes a part of the genuine commandments. It seems that these two commandments, which, as indicated above, correspond to the commandments of "You shall not commit adultery" and "You shall not steal," originally formed two separate commandments, while the first commandment—according to this enumeration—encompassed the passage from "I am YHWH" to "my commandments" (Deut 5:6–10 = Exod 20:2–6); see the INTRODUCTION to this section on the division of the Decalogue. The main objects of the covetousness are, then, *house* and *wife,* in other words, property and family, which form the kernel of a man's existence. Compare, for example, Prov 19:14, *"House* and property are bequeathed by ancestors but a successful *wife* comes from YHWH"; for the order of house, wife, as in Exod 20:14 (10), cf. Ugaritic letters and Deut 20:5–7 (an old law); Jer 6:11–12; 29:5–6. The other objects in this commandment—field, slave, ox, and so on—are expansions, like the other expansions in the Decalogue.

The Deuteronomic version inverted the order of these two commandments. Unlike the Exodus version, which has "house" before "wife," Deuteronomy puts first "wife" then "house" and devotes to the "wife" a separate command, which suits the general tendencies of this book. Deuteronomy gives special attention to women's rights (cf. Deut 15:12–18 with Exod 21:2–11; Deut 22:28–29 with Exod 22:15–16; see Weinfeld 1972a, pp. 282–92), and therefore he gives preference to the wife and reserves for her a separate injunction. By the same token she does not join the slave, the animal, and so on, contrary to the arrangement in the Exodus version. Furthermore, the verbs for coveting were also differentiated in Deuteronomy: *ḥmd* for the wife and *ʾwh* for the house, which mars the original intention of the commandment. As has been shown above, *ḥmd,* which usually goes with *lqḥ,* signifies the wish to appropriate, and this is what is prohibited in the two discussed commandments. By substituting *ʾwh* 'desire' for *ḥmd* 'covet', the Deuteronomic author takes away the edge of the original prohibition and brings in, by contrast, a more intensive meaning to this commandment. True, the verbs *ʾwh* and *ḥmd* are usually synonyms, as Moran has shown (1967, pp. 545–48), but Moran himself admits (p. 548 n. 18) that *ʾwh* is to be distinguished from *ḥmd:* "*ʾwh* denotes a desire rising from an inner need while *ḥmd* refers to a desire stimulated by sight"; for *ʾwh,* cf. especially Num 11:4; Amos 5:8; Prov 21:25–26; and note especially the connection of *ʾwh/tʾwh* with *npš* 'soul'; and for *ḥmd,* cf. Gen 2:9, *nḥmd lmrʾh* ('pleasing to sight').

The last commandment, according to Deuteronomy, connotes, then, not only a wish for appropriation of somebody's property, but also lust and inner desire for wealth. Philo elaborates this commandment much more and explains it as directed against the hardest of all passions: the very desire, "the insidious enemy" *(On the Decalogue* 142). As an adherent of Stoic philosophy, he sees in this commandment not just a prohibition of covetousness of what is another's but a prohibition of lust in general (for affinities with Stoic phraseology, see Colson 1937, 7.612).

Hossfeld (1982, pp. 87–144), who posits the priority of the Deuteronomic version over the Exodus version, argues that *lʾ ttʾwh* is the original prohibition and that the author of Exodus changed *lʾ ttʾwh* to *lʾ tḥmd* because he wanted to unify the two commandments and to have one commandment instead of the two of the Deuteronomic version. But again, this opinion is conditioned by the prejudice of his own making, according to which the Exodus version created two commandments out of one in 20:2–6 (cf. the discussion above in the NOTE to v 8) and therefore, in his view, had to eliminate from the enumeration one of the last two commandments. Furthermore, if the Deuteronomic version is original, why did the Exodus version change the order from *wife, house* to *house, wife?* One can explain, as shown above, why Deuteronomy inverted the order *house, wife,* but one is unable to explain the opposite.

his field. "Field" forms a pair with "house" and is a typical formulaic expression for immovable property in the legal documents of the ancient Near East and especially in the documents from Ugarit; see Moran 1967, p. 549 and the references there for *bītu* and *eqlu.* Compare in the Bible Gen 39:5; 2 Kgs 8:3, 5;

Isa 5:8; Mic 2:2. "Field" does not occur in the Exodus version because the "house" appears there as a separate item preceding the "wife," and "field" would not pair well with "wife." Hossfeld's explanation (1982, p. 125) that "field" is missing in Exodus because the Exodus version reflects the Exilic period, when there were no fields available for the Judahites, is highly speculative.

his male and female slave, his ox and his ass and anything that is your neighbor's. A similar enumeration of property is found in a royal grant from Ugarit (RS 16.148+, *PRU* 3.115–16). Here we find an identical list of property: "houses *(bītātu),*" "fields *(eqlētu),*" "slaves *(ardūtu),*" "female slaves *(amātu),*" "oxen *(alpū),*" "asses *(imērū),*" and "everything belonging to him *(gabbu mimmušu)*"; see the discussion of Moran 1967, pp. 550–52; and for the formula "everything belonging to him," cf. Kristensen 1977. It seems that property was listed in the same typical manner in ancient Syria, Ugarit, and Canaan for centuries. Enumerations of immovable property in connection with the resources of a whole country are found in various royal grants of the Hittite, Ugaritic, and Assyrian kings (cities, houses, vineyards, etc.). These are paralleled in Deut 6:10–11 (cf. Josh 24:13); cf. Weinfeld 1972a, p. 71.

EPILOGUE TO THE DECALOGUE (5:19–6:3)

5 [19]These words YHWH proclaimed to all your assembly at the mountain
from the midst of the fire and the cloud and thick mist with a mighty voice, and
he said no more, and he wrote them on two tablets of stone, which he gave to
me. [20]When you heard the voice out of the darkness while the mountain was
ablaze with fire, you approached me, all your tribal heads and elders. [21]And said:
YHWH our God has shown us his glory and his greatness, and we have heard
his voice out of the fire; we have seen this day that man may live though God
has spoken to him. [22]Now, why should we die, for this great fire will consume
us; if we hear the voice of YHWH our God any longer, we shall die. [23]For what
mortal ever heard the voice of the living God speak out of the fire, as we have,
and lived? [24]You approach and hear all that YHWH our God says and then you
will tell us everything that YHWH our God tells you, and we will obey and do
it.

[25]YHWH heard the words that you were speaking to me and YHWH said
to me: I have heard the voice of the people who were speaking to you; they have
well spoken. [26]Oh, that this their heart was such that they would fear me and
observe all my commandments all the days, that they may fare well and their
children forever. [27]Go say to them: Return to your tents. [28]But you remain here
with me, so that I may set before you all the instruction and the laws and rules
that you shall teach them to do in the land that I am giving them to possess.

[29]You shall observe to do as YHWH your God has commanded you; do not
turn aside to the right or to the left. [30]In all the way that YHWH your God has
commanded you, you shall go so that you may live and that it may go well with
you and that you may prolong your days in the land that you are to occupy.
6 [1]And this is the instruction, the laws, and the rules that YHWH your God
has commanded to teach you to do in the land that you are about to cross into
and occupy, [2]so that you may fear YHWH your God and observe all his laws
and commandments that I command you, you and your son and your son's son,
all the days of your life, so that your days may be prolonged. [3]You shall obey, O
Israel, and will observe to do that it may go well with you and may increase
greatly [in] a land flowing with milk and honey, as YHWH your God of your
fathers promised to you.

TEXTUAL NOTES

5:19. *to.* MT: *ʾel.* XQ Phyl. 13: (Yadin 1969) *ʿm* 'with'.

19. *cloud and thick mist.* 4Q Dt^{n} (White, *ibid.*, p. 288), 4Q Phyl. B *(DJD* 6.52), LXX, and Samaritan: *hʾš ḥšk ʿnn wʿrpl.* The reading "darkness" is due to v 20 and also to 4:11: *ḥšk ʿnn ʿrpl.* The omission of the article *(he)* in the three words occurs because of the influence of 4:11. In both cases the words should be understood as expressing manner or circumstances. See *GKC* 118m.

he said no more. Hebrew: *wlʾ ysp;* XQ Phyl.: *lʾ ywsp;* literally, "he did not add." The verb is the *qal* form of *ysp. Tasgumim Onqelos* and *Pseudo-Jonathan* translate, "he did not cease [Rashi: did not pause, as for breath]," deriving *ysp* from *swp* 'to end.' This is based on the rabbinic view that the Torah has eternal validity; cf. *y. Meg.* 1:7, 7d, and see Urbach 1979, p. 309.

21. *YHWH our God has shown us his glory.* MT, Samaritan: *hn hrʾnw.* 4Q Dt^{3} (Duncan, *ibid.*, Fig. 19): *hnh hrʾn[w].*

this day. MT, Samaritan, 4Q Phyl. J *(DJD* 6.66), Peshitta, Targumim: *hywm hzh* "today," 4Q Dt^{n} (White, *ibid.*, p. 288): *bywm hzh (bet* is written over *he),* also the same in the LXX: *ēn tê hēmera taute:* "on this day."

though God has spoken. MT, Samaritan, LXX, Peshitta: *ky ydbr ʾlhym.* 4Q Dt^{n} (White, *ibid.*, p. 288), 4Q Phyl. J *(DJD* 6.66): *ky ydbr YHWH.*

22. *if we hear the voice of YHWH any longer.* MT, Samaritan: *ywspym;* 4Q D^{t} (Duncan, *ibid.*, Fig. 19) *[mw]sʿpym.* About the substitution of the *Hiphil* for the *kal* form at Qumran see Qimron, "The Hebrew of the Dead Sea Scrolls," *Harvard Semitic Studies,* 1986, pp. 34–79.

we shall die. wmtnw is an apodosis: then we shall die; cf. *GKC* §112.5a.

23. *living God.* MT, Samaritan, 4Q Phyl. J *(DJD* 6.66): *ʾlhym ḥyym;* 4Q Dt^{n} (White, *ibid.*, p. 288): *ʾlhym hy. ʾlhym ḥyym* is used in 1 Sam 17:26, 36; Jer 10:10; 23:36. The noun *ʾelohim* 'god,' which is plural, takes a plural adjective. In 2 Kgs 19:4, 6 (= Isa 37:4, 17) the singular adjective *ḥay* is used with the plural

ʾelohim. In Josh 3:10; Hos 2:1; Pss 42:3; 84:3 and Dan 6:21, 27, *ʾel ḥay* is used with both noun and adjective in the singular, see Note.

24. *that YHWH says.* MT, Samaritan: *yʾmr,* 4Q DTⁿ (White, *ibid.,* p. 288): *ydbr (yod* is written above the line).

That YHWH our God says. 4Q Dtᵗ (White, *ibid.,* p. 288) 4Q Phyl. J (*DJD* 6.66), LXX MSS, Peshitta, Vg: add *ʾlyk[h]* "to you," as in the latter part of the verse.

you . . . tell. MT: *wʾt;* Samaritan, XQ Phyl. 2 (Yadin, *ibid.,* p. 80): *wʾth.* The Hebrew for "you" in MT is *ʾat,* as opposed to normal form *ʾattah.* So also in Num 11:15 and Ezek 28:14. In other cases the consonantal text reads *ʾt,* but the vocalization is *ʾatta* (Sam 24:18; Ps 6:4; Job 1:10; Eccl 7:22; Neh 9:6); cf. *GKC* §32g. The Samaritan text and XQ Phyl. 13 read *ʾth.*

26–28. The Samaritan Pentateuch adds portions of Deut 5:26–28 and Deut 18:17–22 after Exod 20:21, in order to harmonize the Exodus account of the Sinai theophany with that of Deuteronomy. Fragments of this passage were found in Qumran Scroll 4Q158, and this scroll therefore contains variants of the verses in Deuteronomy. For further details about this text, see Strugnell, 1970, pp. 171ff.

26. *that this their heart was such.* MT: *whyh lbbm zh lhm.* 4Q 158: *whyh hlbb hzh lhmh.*

all my commandments. MT, LXX (OL), Peshitta, Targumim: *ʾt kl;* Samaritan, 4Q DTⁿ (White, *ibid.,* p. 288), 4Q Dtᵏˡ (Duncan, *ibid.,* Fig. 27): *wlšmwr mṣwt[y].*

27. *Return.* Hebrew: *šûbu lākem* with *dativus ethicus.* See *GKC* §119s.

28. *and rules.* MT: *whmšpṭym.* 4Q 158: *wʾt hmšpṭym.* 4Q 158 adds after this verse the words *wyšwbw hʿm ʾyš lʾhlyw wyʿmd mšh lpny [ ],* "and the people returned each to his tent, and Moses stood before. . . ."

29. *as.* MT, Samaritan: *kʾšr.* XQ Phyl. 13: *kkl ʾšr* 'all that'.

30. *so that you may live.* Hebrew: *lʿmaʿan tiḥywn.* LXX: *hopōs katapausē(i) se* 'so that he may give you rest', is apparently based on a misreading, perhaps *tnḥw* instead of *tḥwn/tḥywn* (metathesis).

it may go well. Hebrew: *wĕṭob,* third-person masculine singular perfect of the verb *ṭwb,* not the adjective.

5:28–6:1. Alexander Rofé (1982) argues on stylistic and epigraphic grounds that 5:29–30 is a late addition. He notes that 5:28 and 6:1, when juxtaposed, form a transitional formula characteristic of the Deuteronomic style (cf. 11:32–12:1; 19:3–4; Josh 11:16–20; 12:7–8a; Judg 2:23–3:1), in which a subject is introduced and the introduction is repeated before it is expanded upon in detail (see above, in the Note to 4:44). Furthermore, he points out that J. T. Milik's reading of Qumran phylactery 4Q128 1.17 (DJD 6.49) is mistaken, and he reads instead, *]l[h]mh lršth wzʾt[,* that is, the end of 5:28 juxtaposed with the beginning of 6:1. He posits this reading in two other phylactery texts as well, in which the line containing the end of chap. 5 and the beginning of chap. 6 is missing, but letter counts would indicate that the texts did not contain 5:29–30. Nevertheless, vv 29–30 are preserved in 4Q Dt[j], 4Q Phyl. 140 (DJD 6.72) and XQ Phyl. 1–4.

6:1. *And this.* 'and' *(waw)* is omitted in 4Q Phyl. M *(DJD* 6.72) and XQ Phyl. 2 (Yadin, *ibid.*, p. 80).

the laws. XQ Phyl. 13: "and the laws."

to do. LXX and 4Q Phyl. M *(DJD* 6.72) add *houtos,* 'thus' (= *kn).* Compare 4:5 *(l'śwt kn)* and the Note *ad loc.*

cross into. MT, Samaritan: *'brym;* 4Q Phyl. B, M *(DJD* 6.52, 72); 8Q Phyl. 2 (Yadin, *ibid.*, p. 80); and LXX *(eisporeu este): b' ym,* 'enter into.'

2. *all.* MT: *'t kl,* omitted in XQ Phyl. 13. Compare the TEXTUAL NOTE to 5:26 above.

his laws. MT: *ḥqtyw;* Samaritan: *ḥuqyw;* XQ Phyl. 2 (Yadin, *ibid.*, p. 80): adds *wmšptyw,* 'and rules.'

command you. Samaritan tt, Qumran 8Q 3, fragment 15 *(DJD* 3.150, 152), and 4Q 140 *(DJD* 6.72) add 'today', cf. LXX *sēmeron.*

your son and your son's son. LXX and Vg: "your sons and your sons' sons."

days . . . prolonged. MT: *y'rykwn ymyk.* See the TEXTUAL NOTE to 5:16. 4Q 129 Phyl. B *(DJD* 6.52) and XQ Phyl. 13 have *y'rkwn,* a consonant cluster that can be vocalized *ye'erkūn* or *ya'arkūn,* in accordance with Ehrlich's suggestion cited above (TEXTUAL NOTE to 5:16).

3. *increase.* MT: *trbwn,* second-person plural, and so XQ Phyl. 13, XQ Phyl. 1–6, 4Q 140 *(DJD* 6.72), though the rest of the verse is in the singular. The Samaritan text has singular: *trbh.*

[in] a land flowing with milk and honey, as YHWH your God of your fathers promised to you. Hebrew: *k'šr dbr YHWH 'lhy 'btyk lk 'rṣ zbt ḥlb wdbš.* The syntax is difficult. The LXX and Peshitta render "as the Lord God of your fathers promised *to give you* a land flowing with milk and honey." The Vg says, "as the Lord . . . promised you a land flowing with milk and honey." But *ka'ăšer* 'as' is meaningless in this context. According to Ibn Ezra, either the phrase "a land flowing with milk and honey" connects with the end of v 1 and the intervening verses are parenthetical, or one must mentally supply the preposition *bĕ,* in order to read, *"increase . . . in* a land flowing with milk and honey." Both proposals have taken the form of textual emendations by modern critics. Dillman (1886) proposed transposing the phrase to the end of v 1, while Driver (1902) and others suggest that a preposition or prepositional phrase such as "in the land that the Lord your God is giving you" (cf. 27:3) be added. *GKC* §118g, however, cites many examples of the *accusativus loci* without preposition. While Gesenius prefers the LXX reading in this verse, he implies that the MT can be understood as *accusativus loci,* pace Driver, who calls such an interpretation "illegitimate." Driver's objection should be understood as the basis of his comment on 1 Sam 2:29 (1913, p. 37 n. 2): "by custom the use of the accusative to express rest in a place is restricted to a case in which a noun in the

genitive follows, as *byt ʾbyk.*" Because the locus in our verse is not a construct phrase, but a noun + adjective phrase, Driver rules out the *accusativus loci* here. Even so, Driver himself cites exceptions to this "custom," one of which is Isa 16:2, where the locus is a noun + adjective.

NOTES

5:19. *These words.* This refers to the ten words; cf. Exod 20:1, *hdbrym hʾlh.* In the rabbinic literature: *dibber/dibbĕrot* 'revealed word(s)'; cf. the INTRODUCTION to the Decalogue.

to all your assembly. qahal 'assembly' is especially applied in Deuteronomy to the covenant gathering at Horeb. "The day of the assembly" is the day on which the Decalogue was given by solemn revelation (9:10; 10:4; 18:16).

with a mighty voice. This is the accusative of manner (cf. 2 Sam 19:5; 1 Kgs 8:55). The voice might be "thunder"; cf. Exod 19:16 ("thunder and lightnings"); 20:18; in Exod 19:19 we also encounter *qwl hšpr* 'voice of the horn', but the "horn" is not mentioned here at all.

and he said no more. Compare Num 11:25 in a prophetic context; see the NOTE above to 4:2. This appears to exclude the possibility of other laws revealed to Israel at Sinai besides the Decalogue.

and he wrote them on two tablets of stone. This clause anticipates the account in 9:9–11 and is noted here in order to complete the information about the Decalogue revealed to Israel.

20. *you approached me, all your tribal heads and elders.* A delegation of the people approaches *(qrb)* Moses in order to propose him as mediator between God and Israel. A similar verb *(qrb)* is employed in 1:22 when Moses is asked to confirm the sending of spies. In both cases approval is given for the proposition by Moses (1:23) and by God (5:25), and the approval is expressed by the idiom *ṭwb hdbr* 'the matter is good' (in other words, it is approved; cf. also 1:14 and 1 Kgs 18:24). *qrb ʾl* 'approach' has a formal-juridic connotation (cf. Exod 16:9; 22:7; Josh 7:14; Isa 41:21) and therefore is to be done by the leaders, the formal representatives of the people. The word *klkm* 'all of you' in 1:22 is not to be taken literally, because in 29:9, after *klkm,* comes "the heads of the tribes and elders," as in the verse here.

elders. Compare 27:1; 29:9; 31:9, 28.

21. *YHWH . . . has shown us his glory (kbdw) and his greatness.* The *glory* and the *greatness* here are to be understood figuratively, "his majestic presence" *(NJPS),* because the people have not seen anything corporeal (cf. 4:15); they have only heard his voice, in contrast to the priestly sources, in which *kabod* has a corporeal nature; cf. Weinfeld 1984b, 4.32–34.

we have seen this day that man may live though God has spoken to him. Compare 4:33, with the NOTE there.

22. *if we hear the voice of YHWH our God any longer, we shall die.* This

does not contradict the previous verse (21b), which states that man can survive though God has spoken to him, as A. Rofé argues (1985). The people just say that if they hear the voice *any longer,* they may die (cf. 18:16). The truth is that they managed until now to hear the voice of YHWH and survived.

23. *For what mortal.* Literally, flesh *(bśr);* cf. Gen 6:17, 19; Num 16:22; 27:16; Isa 40:5, 6; etc. In later Hebrew, a mortal is named *bśr wdm* 'flesh and blood'; cf. Ben Sira 14:18 and rabbinic literature; cf. Akkadian *šīru and damu* (Atrahasis 1.210 in connection with the creation of man). A similar rhetorical question is posed in 4:33, but there, instead of "what mortal," we read "any people *(ʿm).*"

the living God. This God stands in opposition to the ineffective pagan gods; cf. 1 Sam 17:26, 30 (an uncircumcised Philistine defies the ranks of the living God); 2 Kgs 19:4, 16 = Isa 37:4, 17 (a pagan king taunts a living God); Jer 10:10 (a living, true God in contrast to the fetishes of the pagan peoples) and Dan 6:21, 27. Daniel 6:27 reads, "a living and ever-enduring God *(ʾlhʾ ḥyʾ wqym lʿlmyn),*" which turned into a liturgical formula in Judaism; see, for example, the end of the first benediction of the evening prayer: "God living and ever-enduring *(ʾel ḥay weqayyam),* reign over us" (Singer 1915, pp. 130–31). In the present verse, however, there is also a contrast between the "mortal *(bśr)*" and the "ever-living" God: the *bśr wdm* versus *ʾel ḥy wqym.*

24. *You approach and hear.* As indicated above, in the NOTE to v 20, *qrb* 'approach' has an official touch, connoting the privilege of approaching the sovereign; cf. Jer 30:21: "I will bring him close *(whqrbtyw),* that he may approach me *(wngš ʾly)* . . . for who would otherwise dare approach me?"

This verse is dependent on the (Elohistic?) source in Exod 20:21, where it is explicitly stated that only Moses was privileged to approach YHWH: "The people remained at a distance, while Moses *approached (ngš)* the thick cloud where God was." Instead of *ngš,* Deuteronomy uses *qrb;* but, as seen above, Jer 30:21 uses both *qrb* and *ngš* in the context of the privilege of admission. Both verbs are used in Jewish liturgy for describing the Israelites who were privileged to approach Sinai at the revelation of God: "You have chosen Israel . . . made them approach *(wtgyšm)* to Horeb and brought them close *(wtqrbm)* with love round Mount Sinai" (Palestinian Festival Prayers; see Elbogen 1911, pp. 436–46, 586–87).

and then you will tell us everything that YHWH our God tells you, and we will obey and do it. Compare Exod 24:7, "we shall do and obey" but in an inverted order, first *obey* and then *do,* which is illogical. The advancing of "do" before "hear" was considered a great merit for the Israelites (cf. rabbinic references in Kasher 1959, pp. 261–65).

25. *YHWH heard the words that you were speaking.* The same phrasing is used in 1:34.

they have well spoken. Compare 18:17; 1:14, 23. This is an approval of their proposal; cf. the NOTE to v 20 above.

26. *Oh, that this their heart was such that they would fear me.* For the construction of sentences with the interrogative *mi yitten,* see Kaddari 1977. God expresses the wish that the fear of the people, caused by the theophany, should be transformed into fear of God in their heart, which will produce observance of God's commandments. The idea is taken from Exod 20:20, where Moses says that the theophany was aimed to "put God's fear upon their faces so that they do not sin." But there is a significant difference between the two sources. In Exodus the "fear *(yrʾh)*" is the divine terror (= Akkadian *pulḫu;* cf. Ezek 1:18 and see Weinfeld 1984b, 4.32), which will be spread *over the faces* of the Israelites, which will deter them from sin (see Dillman and Ryssell 1897, p. 246), and for "fear/terror *(pḥd yrʾh)*" spread over the face, cf. Deut 2:25, "the dread and fear *(pḥdk wyrʾtk)* of you upon the peoples." The divine terror was enhanced by the shocking experience of the theophany (see Greenberg 1960). In Deuteronomy, however, the fear of God is given in their heart. The "fear" here is not terror but inner religious feeling, which suits the spiritualization of religious values in Deuteronomic and Jeremianic prose. For the fear of God in the heart formulated in language overlapping Deut 5:26, see Jer 32:39–40:

Jer 32:39–40	*Deut 5:26*
I will give them one heart . . . *to fear me all the days so that it shall be well with them and their children after them . . . and I will put my fear into their hearts (wʾt yrʾty ʾtn blbbm).*	Oh, that this their heart was such that they *would fear me . . . (my ytn whyh lbbm zh lhm lyrʾh ʾty) all the days, that they may fare well and their children forever.*

Compare also Ps 86:11, "Let my heart be one in fearing your name," and for the general notion of having a *heart* to observe God's commands, cf. 1 Kgs 8:58, 61; 1 Chr 28:9; 29:19. Compare also the prayer in 2 Macc 1:3–4, "May he give you a heart to worship him . . . let him open your heart to his law and precepts" and the parallel Jewish prayer in *Qeduššah de Sidra,* "May he open our heart unto his law and place his love and fear within our hearts" (Singer 1915, pp. 91–92). For similar ideas in Qumran literature, see Weinfeld 1978–79b.

The idea of putting fear of the gods into the heart of men *(puluḫtu ili ina libbi)* is found in neo-Babylonian royal inscriptions (see, for example, Langdon 1912, 122I:37; 124I:70–71, II:7; 136VIII:31–32; 242I:21–22; 252II:12; 262I:3), and is also attested in Ptolemaic Egypt; see Weinfeld 1982a, p. 246.

that they may fare well and their children forever. Compare 4:40.

27. *Return to your tents.* During Moses' stay with God on the mountain, the

people should be away in their camp; cf. Exod 20:21; 24:14; and see the NOTE above to v 24.

According to *Tg. Ps.-J.*, this implies that the Israelites are now permitted to cohabit with their wives, which was prohibited during the period of revelation; cf. Exod 19:15 (and see *b. Šabb.* 87a).

28. *so that I may set before you* [literally, *"speak to you"*] *all the instruction and the laws and rules that you shall teach them.* In Exod 24:12 (Elohistic source?), on which Deuteronomy seems to be dependent, we read, "Go up to me on the mountain and stay there . . . and I will give you the stone tablets and the law [Torah] and the instruction *(whmṣwh)* which I write to instruct them *(lhwrtm).*" Instead of Torah there, we have here *ḥqym wmšpṭym* 'the laws and the rules', and instead of *lhwrtm* 'to instruct', we have in Deuteronomy the verb *lmd* 'to teach', which is found in the Pentateuchal literature only in Deuteronomy (see above, in the NOTE to 4:1).

As has already been shown by A. Dillmann (1886, pp. 268, 384), *hamiṣwah* here and in 6:1, 25; 7:11; 8:1; 11:8, 22; 30:11 refers to the basic demand for loyalty, to which chaps. 5–11 are devoted. Indeed, the *miṣwah* is attached to the demand for love of God, following his ways, serving him, and holding fast to him (11:22; 19:9; 30:11, 16). The *miṣwah* seems to correspond to the basic stipulation of allegiance known to us from the treaties, or rather loyalty oaths, in the ancient Near East (see Weinfeld 1972a, pp. 65–91). This understanding of *hamiṣwah* could be corroborated by Jer 32:11, which refers to the two basic parts of the purchase deed: *hamiṣwah wehaḥuqqim* 'the basic stipulation and the specified terms of the deed'.

29–30 (32–33). These two verses turn abruptly from the divine address (vv 25–28) to the address of Moses. Another difficulty involved in the two verses is the mention of "what God has commanded" before Moses sets the commandments (chap. 6 onward). But these anomalies are not enough to treat the verses as a later addition (so Rofé 1982); see Smith 1918, p. 94: "It was surely quite logical for the writer of the rest of the chapter to put the phrase in Moses' mouth in Moab, because God had already at Horeb charged him with these laws; the phrase does not imply their previous publication." Exhortation to obey the commandments before they are set up in detail is characteristic of the paraenetic chapters in Deuteronomy, such as 4:2, 6, 40; 5:1. For the alleged omission of these verses in the Qumran text, cf. the TEXTUAL NOTE.

Structurally these verses form an *inclusio* with the beginning of the chapter, v 1. In 5:1 Moses urges the Israelites "to observe [the laws] to do them *(šmr lʿśwt)"*; the same occurs in v 29, *wšmrtm lʿśwt.*

29. *do not turn aside to the right or to the left.* This is a characteristic phrase in the Deuteronomic literature; cf. Deut 17:11, 20; 28:14; Josh 1:7; 23:6; 2 Kgs 22:2. Compare Prov 4:27, with *nṭh* instead of *sr.* In the literal sense it is also found in Num 22:26; Deut 2:27; 1 Sam 6:12.

30. *In all the way that YHWH your God has commanded you, you shall go.*

"The way" as a metaphor for right behavior is very common in biblical (e.g., Gen 18:19) and Mesopotamian literature (see Weinfeld 1985d, pp. 15–17) and is especially common in Deuteronomistic literature (cf. Weinfeld 1972a, p. 332). For the phrase "to follow *all* the way/ways," see Deut 10:12; 11:22; Josh 22:5; 1 Kgs 8:58; 2 Kgs 21:21; 22:2; Jer 7:23.

so that you may live and that it may go well with you and that you may prolong your days. These rewards are characteristic of Deuteronomy (cf. the NOTE to v 16); see Weinfeld 1972a, p. 345. What is peculiar here is the accumulation of benefits: life, goodness, and longevity.

6:1–3. This passage continues the discourse of chap. 5 (see the NOTE below) but serves, at the same time, as a preparation for the sermon that starts with the essential creed Shemaᶜ in v 4. As indicated above, the word *hamiṣwah* 'instruction', which opens the passage, refers to the basic demand for loyalty that is actually expounded in 6:4–11:30. In 12:1, where the laws proper begin, the term *miṣwah* does not appear.

1. *And this is the instruction, the laws, and the rules.* This brings us back to 5:28, where God asks Moses to stay with him in order to impart to him "the instruction and the laws and rules." For this stylistic feature of "recapturing" in the Deuteronomic composition, cf. 11:32–12:1. It was especially necessary here after the digression of 5:29–30; and see above, in the NOTE to 4:44 (which recaptures 1:5). The conjunction "and" before "the laws" is dropped because of "this *(wzʾt),*" which refers grammatically to *hamiṣwah.*

As indicated already, chaps. 6–11 actually constitute the *hamiṣwah;* "the laws and the rules" will come late, beginning with chap. 12.

2. *that you may fear YHWH your God.* For fear of God that accompanies obedience to the law, see 4:10; 5:26; 6:13, 24; 8:6; 10:12, 20; 13:5; 14:23; 17:19; 28:58; 31:12, 13. See also the NOTE to 5:26, and Weinfeld 1972a, pp. 332–33. The transition to the singular might be motivated by the wish to address the individual and might not necessarily point toward a different layer, as some suggest. In fact, the singular in vv 2–3 is not consistently preserved; see "ye may increase *(trbwn)*" in v 3.

his laws and commandments. ḥqyw wmšpṭyw; cf. 10:13; 28:15, 45; 30:10; and see Weinfeld 1972a, pp. 337, 21b.

3. *You shall obey, O Israel.* Compare v 24b: "we will *obey* and do."

and may increase greatly. Compare 7:13; 8:1; 13:18; 28:63; 30:16.

a land flowing with milk and honey. See the TEXTUAL NOTE.

as YHWH your God of your fathers promised to you. Compare 1:11, 21.

EXCLUSIVE ALLEGIANCE TO YHWH (6:4–25)

INTRODUCTION

This section, which follows the Decalogue, centers on exclusive allegiance to YHWH, which means scrupulous observance of his commandments. The section is part of the *miṣwah* 'command' (see the NOTE to 5:28), which precedes "the laws and the judgments" *(haḥuqqîm wĕhhamišpāṭîm)*" (cf. 5:28; 6:1) included in chaps. 12–26. The *miṣwah* 'command' opens with the basic demand for loyalty to the one God (Shemaᶜ), which actually constitutes a theoretical restatement of the first two commandments of the Decalogue: the unity of God corresponds to the first commandment, while the denial of all other divinities corresponds to the second (cf. Miller 1984). The sermons that come after 6:4–25 follow the same line and elaborate the demand for loyalty to God. Chapters 5–11 were correctly defined by N. Lohfink (1963) as *Hauptgebot,* in other words, the principal command on which all of the other specific commandments in chaps. 12–26 depend.

The present section, which opens the great homily in 6:4–11:32, is marked by its credal-catechistic nature. It starts with a declaration of faith (6:4–5) and continues with a didactic passage—the injunction to educate the children through the monotheistic creed (6:7)—and with the demand to memorize the words of YHWH by phylacteries and door inscriptions (6:8–9). The section ends with the command to teach successive generations the great deeds of the Exodus, thus motivating the observance of the laws (6:20–25).

These two edifying pericopes, 6:7–9 and 6:20–25, serve in fact as a frame for the homily in Deut 6:10–19, which contains references to the Decalogue (6:12–15, see the NOTES below) and is dedicated to the topic of complete devotion to God (cf. v 5). Affluence should not divert the people of Israel from their true God, especially when they are exposed to the gods of the nations into whose country they are about to enter (vv 10–15). Full devotion to God should prevent the people from testing God, putting him to the proof, as they did in the desert, to see whether he will really act as he is supposed to do. The people must trust him completely without any scruples (vv. 16–19; see NOTES and COMMENT).

The structure of 6:4–25 is patterned after Exod 13:1–16, which consists of two catechisms (vv 8, 14–16) connected with the entrance into Canaan. For the relations between Exod 13 and Deut 6 see Caloz 1968, pp. 5–21. The two catechistic passages there (vv 8, 14–16) are introduced by the phrase *whyh ky ybyʾk YHWH ʾl ʾrṣ* 'when YHWH brings you into the land' (vv 5, 11), a phrase found also in Deut 6:10 (compare 7:1), which also contains two catechistic passages (6:7–9, 20–25). The linking of the instruction of the children to the entrance into the land of Canaan is clearly reflected in the Gilgal traditions of the Israelites' entrance into Canaan in Josh 4:6–7, 21–24. Especially instructive for this point is the comparison of Exod 13:14 with Josh 4:6 and 21 and Deut 6:20. Exodus 13:14 opens with *whyh ky yšʾ lk bnk mḥr lʾmr* 'when, in time to come, your son asks you'. The same opening occurs in Josh 4:6, *ky yšʾ lwn bnykm mḥr lʾmr* 'when, in time to come, your sons ask you' (cf. 4:21) and in Deut 6:20, *ky yšʾ lk bnk mḥr lʾmr* 'when in time to come, your son asks you'.

The Gilgal tradition, which seems to lie behind Exod 12–13, in turn influenced Deut 6:4–25 (cf. Lohfink 1963, pp. 121ff.; Loza 1971). Three elements are interwoven in the Gilgal traditions and in Exod 12–13: entrance into the land, Passover celebration, and the instruction of children. Thus Josh 4, which treats the wondrous deeds of the crossing of the Jordan followed by the erection of monuments, commands the education of the children by means of the monuments (vv 6–7, 21–24) and then passes on to the description of the celebrations of Passover (Josh 5). Exodus 12–13 touches the same topics but starts with the Passover (chap. 12) and connects it with the education of the children (12:25–27; 13:8), all of this being linked to the entrance into the land (12:25; 13:5; cf. 13:11).

As several scholars have already noted (Kraus 1951; Soggin 1966; Langlamet 1969, pp. 123–37), the catechisms attached to Passover and the crossing of the Jordan are rooted in a liturgical tradition that came to actualize the soteriological events of the Exodus and the conquest. This liturgical tradition apparently originated in the sanctuary at Gilgal, situated close to the Jordan. The fact that the command to celebrate Passover in Exod 12:25 and 13:5 is conditioned by the entry into the land of Canaan points to the Gilgal tradition according to which Passover is celebrated in Gilgal after crossing the Jordan. Similarly, the fact that the education of children is connected with the Passover traditions on the one hand (Exod 12–13) and with the tradition of the entrance into the land on the other (Josh 4) seems to indicate that both events are related. Because this relationship is so clearly reflected in the stories about the crossing of the Jordan at Gilgal (Josh 3–5), it stands to reason that Gilgal was the birthplace of religious education and dramatization of salvation history in ancient Israel. On another occasion I have shown (Weinfeld 1988) that foundation ceremonies like that of Gilgal (erecting memorial stelae) are known from Greek colonization, and, as in Israel, these ceremonies included lawgiving and especially ritual apotropaic prescriptions intended for the settlers in the new land. Gilgal on the Jordan is, then, the right place for combining foundation ceremonies with the Passover ritual.

Deuteronomy 6:4–7:26 also follows the old Gilgal tradition by placing the catechism (6:20–25) next to the pericope about entrance into the land of Canaan (chap 7), but with one exception: the Passover ritual is missing here. In contrast to the three catechistic passages in the Tetrateuch, which serve to explain the Passover, Mazzoth, and firstborn rituals (12:25–27; 13:7–9, 14–16), the fourth catechism[1] in Deuteronomy is freed from any connection to a ritual. In Exodus the "signs" on both the head and the arm (13:9, 16), as well as the instruction of children (13:8, 14–15; cf. 12:26–27), are linked to the ritual of Passover and the sacrifice of the firstborn animal. This is different in Deuteronomy. In Deuteronomy the "signs" (6:8) and the instruction of children (6:7, 20–25) were retained (cf. 11:18–19). But the ritual that served as the motivation for "signs" and the child's question is absent altogether in Deuteronomy. Unlike Exod 12:26 and 13:14, where the child's question refers to the peculiar ritual of Passover and the firstborn, the question of the son in Deut 6:20 refers to the laws in general without any indication of a specific ritual. Education in Deuteronomy does not depend on ritual ceremonial media (cf. Weinfeld 1972a, pp. 190ff.), but is formal and abstract. Similarly, the answer of the father in Deut 6:21–25 corresponds to the question by giving an elaborate answer that contains references not only to the redemption from slavery, as in the other instances, but also to the plagues of the Egyptians, the giving of the law, and the entrance into the promised land.

EXCLUSIVE ALLEGIANCE TO YHWH (6:4–25)

6 [4]Hear, O Israel! YHWH our God is one YHWH. [5]You shall love YHWH
your God with all your heart and with all your soul and with all your might.
[6]These words which I command you this day shall be on your heart. [7]You shall
inculcate them to your children and you shall recite them when you stay at
home, when you are away, when you lie down, and when you get up. [8]And you
shall bind them as a sign on your hand and as a frontlet on your forehead. [9]You
shall inscribe them on the doorposts of your house and on your city gates.

[10]When YHWH your God brings you into the land that he swore to your
fathers, Abraham, Isaac, and Jacob, to give you—great and flourishing cities that
you did not build, [11]houses full of all good things that you did not fill, hewn
cisterns that you did not hew, vineyards and olive groves that you did not plant
—and you eat your fill, [12]beware that you do not forget YHWH who freed you

[1] The four catechistic passages are the basis of the rabbinic midrash about the four types of sons represented in Scripture: the wise son (Deut 6:20), the wicked son (Exod 12:26), the simple son (Exod 13:14), and the one who has not the wit to ask (Exod 13:8) *(Mek. Bo'* 18, p. 73; Jer. *Pesaḥ.* 10, 4, 37a). The wise son is reflected in the Deuteronomic tradition, which is more abstract than the other and is formulated in an intelligent manner.

from the land of Egypt, the house of slaves. [13]Fear [only] YHWH your God and worship him [alone], and swear [only] by his name. [14]Do not follow other gods, any gods of the peoples who are around you [15]—for YHWH your God in your midst is an impassioned God—lest the anger of YHWH your God blaze forth against you and he wipe you off the face of the earth.

[16]Do not try YHWH your God as you did at Massah. [17]Be sure to keep the commandments, precepts, and laws of YHWH your God as he commanded you. [18]Do what is right and good in the eyes of YHWH, that it may go well with you and that you may be able to occupy the good land that YHWH your God promised on oath to your fathers, [19]to drive out all your enemies before you, as YHWH has spoken.

[20][When] in time to come, your son asks you, "What mean the precepts, laws, and rules that YHWH our God has commanded you?" [21]you shall say to your son, "We were slaves to Pharaoh in Egypt and YHWH freed us from Egypt with a mighty hand. [22]YHWH wrought before our eyes great and grave signs and portents in Egypt, against Pharaoh and all his household; [23]and us he freed from there, to bring us to the land and give it to us, that he had promised on oath to our fathers, [24]and YHWH commanded us to observe all these laws, to fear YHWH our God, for our own good all the days and for our life, as is now the case. [25]It will be to our merit to observe faithfully this whole commandment before YHWH our God, as he commanded us."

TEXTUAL NOTES

4. The LXX and the Nash papyrus preface this verse with "These are the laws and rules that YHWH (other manuscripts: Moses) commanded the Israelites in the desert (some manuscripts lack 'in the desert') as they left Egypt" (see the NOTE below). The preface in the Nash papyrus reads as follows: *ʾlh hḥqlym whmšpṭym ʾšr ṣwh Mšh ʾt* [. . .] *bmdbr bṣʾtm mʾrṣ mṣrym.* See Segal 1947, p. 230.

Hear, O Israel. Rabbinic tradition *(Sipre Deut.* §31 [Finkelstein 1969, pp. 49–53] and parallels) and the Targumim understand Israel as a personal appellation, namely, Jacob, the patriarch. Jacob questions his children to see whether they will keep loyalty to the one God and they respond, "Hear, O Israel [= Jacob], our God is YHWH." Jacob responded and said, "Blessed be his glorious name forever" (for this response see the COMMENT below).

YHWH our God. According to some scholars these words are an addition. It is the only phrase in the passage styled in the plural and causes difficulties for understanding the verse (see the NOTE). See Garcia Lopez 1978b, pp. 163–66. It seems, however, that "YHWH our God" belongs to the credal-liturgical part of the sentence, the confirmation of faith by the believers; hence it is styled in the first-person plural; see the NOTE.

is one YHWH. MT: *Y. ʾeḥad,* a noun clause, without a verb or a resumptive pronoun. The Nash papyrus has *Y. ʾeḥad hu[ʾ]* 'YHWH, he (is) one'. LXX (quoted in Mark 12:29): *kyrios eis estin* 'the Lord is one'. The use of the verb *estin* in the Greek has led many scholars to conclude that the Hebrew reading of the Nash papyrus was the *Vorlage* of the LXX. But Hebrew noun clauses are often translated with the verb *einaî* 'to be', whether or not they contain a resumptive pronoun. Compare Gen 42:13 (also with numeral as predicate), *šnêim ʿaśar ʿabadêka* 'your servants [are] twelve', which is translated in the LXX *dōdeka esmen hoi paīdes sou* 'your servants *[we] are* twelve'. Be that as it may, with the LXX version, the word *huʾ* in the Nash papyrus has its justification. *huʾ* played an important part in the credal exclamations; cf. Deut 32:39, *ʾani ʾani huʾ*, Isa 43:10, *ʾani huʾ*; compare *ʾani waho* in *m. Sukk.* 4:5. In Qumran *hwʾ (h)* sometimes occurs as a substitute for YHWH (see Fabry 1977, p. 368). In the Jewish liturgy we find *ʾḥd hwʾ ʾlhynw* as a response to *shemaʿ YHWH ʾḥd.* Compare the Kedusha in the Musaf service for Sabbath (Singer 1915, p. 228, and see Wieder 1976, pp. 110–11). *ʾani huʾ* by itself became an important exclamation in prayers and litanies; cf. Wieder 1981a.

5. *with all your heart (bkl lbbk). lb* and *lbb* are interchangeable; cf. 1 Sam 6:6a versus 6b; Gen 31:20 versus 31:26; Judg 19:6 versus 19:9; but there is a predilection for *lbb* in Deuteronomy and the Deuteronomic literature. *Targum Pseudo-Jonathan* has *btry yṣry lbkwn* 'with the two geniuses of your heart'; see the NOTE.

with all your soul. Targum Pseudo-Jonathan has *wʾpylw nṭyl yt npškwn* 'even if he takes your soul'; cf. the NOTE.

with all your might. mʾd is translated by the LXX with strength *(dynamis)* and force *(ischys;* Vg. *et ex tota fortitudine tua* in 2 Kgs 23:25; cf. Mark 12:33; Luke 10:27). The Aramaic versions have *bkl nksk* 'with all your property' *(Tg. Onq.),* "with all your money *(mmwnk)" (Tg. Ps.-J.* and *Neof.),* as does the rabbinic tradition *(Sipre Deut.* 32; *m. Ber.* 9:5). Syriac has "wealth *(qnyn)"* and "strength *(ḥyl)"* (2 Kgs 23:25). In fact, "strength" and "force" *(dynamis, ischys)* in Greek imply wealth too, like *kḥ* and *ḥyl* in Hebrew. Thus in Ezek 27 the word *hwn* 'wealth' is translated by the LXX once as *ischys* (v 12) and twice as *dynamis* (vv 18, 27).

6. *on your heart.* The LXX adds *kai en tē psychē sou* 'and in your soul'. Compare the Masoretic text in the parallel passage, 11:18–20, "you shall put . . . on your heart *and on your soul*" (v 18).

7. *inculcate them.* Hebrew: *wešinnantam.* The *piʿel* form of the verb *šnn* occurs only here. The *qal* means "to sharpen" (cf. Deut 32:41; Isa 5:28), and here perhaps the meaning is "to teach sharply, diligently; to impress upon." (Cf. German *erschärfen.)* Ehrlich (1909, ad loc.) rejects this derivation, comparing instead Arabic *sunnah* 'way of life, rule of conduct'. But the Arabic *sunnah* itself derives from the root *snn,* cognate with Hebrew *šnn,* the semantic range of which includes "sharpen" as well as "institute, establish, prescribe (a custom)." See Lane 1863, p. 1436. *Targum im Onqelos* and *Neofiti* and the Peshitta

translate with *tnʾ* (= *šnh* in Hebrew: *mtnytʾ* = *mšnh*), that is, 'to rehearse, teach', which influences the translation of Aquila, *deuterōseis.* It is not confusion of roots by Aquila, as J. Reider argues (1966, p. 52), but adherence to Jewish tradition.

and you shall recite them. Dibber b-, like *qrʾ b-* (Deut 17:19), *hgh-b* (Josh 1:8; Ps 1:2) involves recitation and reading or murmuring. Compare in a similar context Exod 13:9, where the sign and reminder (compare v 8 here) should serve the purpose, "that the teaching of YHWH shall be in your mouth."

at home . . . away . . . lie down . . . get up. Compare Prov 6:22; Ps 139:2. See Weinfeld 1972a, pp. 299–300. The meaning is obviously "always." "Coming" and "going" are a merismus used in the same sense in Deut 28:6, 19 and Ps 121:8. Isaiah 37:28 (Qumran: *qwmkh), wšbtk wṣʾtk wbʾk,* combines elements from both phrases.

at home. MT: *bebêteka.* Samaritan Pentateuch: *babayit* 'at home', followed by the LXX.

8. *your hand.* MT: *yadeka.* Some manuscripts and the Samaritan text: *yadêka* 'your hands'.

frontlet. Hebrew: *ṭṭpt,* vocalized as a plural noun, *ṭoṭapot.* The same word is used in a similar context in Exod 13:16 and Deut 11:18, but is otherwise unattested. The LXX's versions translate in each case as follows:

Exod 13:16: *asáleuton* 'immovable' (sing. adj.)
Deut 6:8: *asáleuta* 'immovable' (pl. adj.)
Deut 11:18: *asáleuta* 'immovable' (pl. adj.)

Some LXX manuscripts have *saleutón* 'moving', which is reflected in the Old Latin version *mobilia* and in Philo (see below). Compare the discussion of Tigay 1982, pp. 330–31, who points out that, although "moving" and "immovable" are opposite interpretations, "their shared theme of motion suggests that they did not develop independently of each other but have a common basis. . . . The antithetic reflections . . . could be a case of converse translations" (and Tigay refers to Klein 1976).

Vg:	Exod 13:16: *ad pensum quid ob recordationem* 'something hung as a remembrance'
	Deut 6:8: *movebuntur* 'move to and fro'
	Deut 11:18: (no equivalent)
Peshitta:	Exod 13:16: *dwkrnʾ* 'remembrance' (cf. Exod 13:9)
	Deut 6:8: *rwšmʾ* 'sign/mark'
	Deut 11:18: *rwšmʾ* 'sign/mark'

Tgs. Onq., Ps.-J.:	Exod 13:16: *tp(y)lyn* 'phylacteries'
	Deut 6:8: *tp(y)lyn* 'phylacteries'
	Deut 11:18: *tp(y)lyn* 'phylacteries'
Tg. Neof.:	Exod 13:16: *dwkrn ṭb* 'good remembrance' (cf. Exod 13:9)
	Deut 6:8: *tpylyn* 'phylacteries'
	Deut 11:18: *tpylyn* 'phylacteries'
Sam. Tg.:	Exod 13:16: *ṭpyn* 'drops' (see Ben-Hayyim 1957, 2.477)
	Deut 6:8: *ṭpyn* 'drops'
	Deut 11:18: *ṭpyn* 'drops'

Other *Sam. Tg.* manuscripts have *tplyn* 'phylacteries', as in the other Targumim.

The orthography and context of *ṭ(w)ṭpt* suggest that perhaps the singular *ṭoṭepet* was originally intended, and indeed Peshitta, along with Vg to Exodus, seem to support this vocalization. (On the singular in the LXX's Exodus, see below.) It should be noted, however, that the *Sam. Tg.* of Deut 11:18 reads *ṭṭpwt,* which is certainly plural.

It is commonly held that *ṭōṭapot* reflects an underlying *ṭapṭapot* (a situation analogous to that of *kōkab* 'star', which reflects an underlying *kabkab;* see *GKC* §19o). The etymology of the reduplicated root *ṭpṭp* is unclear, however. Speiser (1957–58) connects the stem *ṭapṭap-* with Akkadian *tappû* 'companion' and posits an unattested Akkadian word *taptapu* in the sense of 'double (-headed) companion (-figurine)'. The word is of Sumerian origin, hence the confusion of *ṭ* and *t.* But this etymology and interpretation of *ṭoṭapot* seem farfetched. KB suggests a connection with Arabic *ṭafṭāf* (from *ṭpp),* 'extremity and seam of garment' (see, however, Lane 1863, s.v., where *ṭafṭāf* is defined 'extremities of trees', though *ṭaffa* and *ṭafṭafah* are defined 'bank' and 'flank', respectively). It is unclear, however, exactly how this sense is relevant. Others have compared the Arabic verb *ṭāfa* (from *ṭwp)* 'walk around, make a circuit' (see Driver 1902, ad loc.). Finally, the word has been compared with the rabbinic Hebrew verb *ṭpṭp* 'to drip' and noun *ṭippah* 'drop', which are based on *ṭpp,* a variant of the biblical root *nṭp* 'to drip'. *Ṭoṭapot* would thus be 'pendants', which drop down; cf. *neṭipot,* an article of women's jewelry (earrings?) in Isa 3:19. This etymology of *ṭoṭapot* seems to be supposed by the *Sam. Tg.* and the Vg to Exod 13:16.

The word *ṭoṭepet* is used in the mishna *(Šabb.* 6:1) as an article of women's jewelry, and in Mandaic in the sense of 'amulet'. Compare also the Targum to 2 Sam 1:10 where *ʾṣʿdh* "armlet" is rendered by *ṭwṭpt*.

The Aramaic Targumim usually render *ṭoṭapot* as *tepillin,* the usual rabbinic term for the phylacteries, boxes strapped to the forehead and arm in fulfillment of the biblical verses. Originally the word *tepillin* itself seems to have denoted an amulet. Compare *tplh zy ksp* 'amulet/phylactery of silver' in Aramaic documents from Egypt (see the NOTE for v 8).

The LXX terms *asaleuton, asaleuta* 'immovable' reflect the metaphorical interpretation of these verses (see the NOTE), according to which the ritual of Exod 13:15 and the "words" of Deut 6:6 and 11:18 are not to be moved from one's mind. Hence the Greek words are adjectives, not abstract nouns; therefore, in the Exodus passage, where a single ritual is referred to, the singular is used, while in the Deuteronomy passages, where "words" are referred to, the plural is used (though some manuscripts incorrectly read *asaleuton* in the Deuteronomy passages as well).

The Vg to Deut 6:8 has "and they shall be and move to and fro between your eyes." Philo *(On Special Laws* 4.137, 139) writes that the head phylactery must "shake before the eyes" and "have movement and vibration." Some Philo scholars have assumed that Philo never saw phylacteries, hence he gives this inapt description based on a misreading of LXX *asaleuton* 'immovable', which he read as "movable." But N. G. Cohen (1986) argues that Philo reflects an independent tradition. According to Cohen, Philo's description of the phylactery may very well be "an accurate description of *tefillin shel rosh* as he knew them," for early phylacteries found at Qumran were tiny, and rabbinic polemics suggest that the rabbis knew of a custom to suspend the phylactery below the hairline, though they themselves rejected such a practice. The Vg to this verse offers independent confirmation of this thesis (cf. Vg to Exod 13:10 *adpensum* 'hung', and the *Sam. Tg.* translation *ṭpyn* 'drops'). If *ṭoṭapot* is connected with the root *ṭpp/nṭp* (see above), Philo's tradition may reflect the original intention of the verse.

on your forehead. Literally, "between your eyes *(byn ʿynyk).*" *Bn ʿn* parallels *rʾš* 'head' in Ugaritic (see Avishur 1984, pp. 715–17), and therefore should not be taken literally. In Ugaritic the pair *riš/bn ʿn* is found in connection with *tply (rišh tply tly b ʿnh, Ugaritica* 5.3:5–7) and, according to J. H. Tigay, this refers to phylacteries *(tpylyn).* See Pope and Tigay 1971, p. 118.

9. *doorposts.* Hebrew: *mĕzuzôt.* Compare Deut 11:19. As vocalized, the word seems to reflect a root *zwz,* but no satisfactory etymology has been found on the basis of this root or its cognates. Most likely, the word harks back to Akkadian *manzāzu/mazzāzu* 'stand, position', which is attested also with the meaning 'door socket' *(CAD* M1, p. 235). The Hebrew, however, should have been vocalized *mazzuzot.*

your house. MT: *bêteka.* Samaritan text: *batêka* 'your houses'.

and on your city gates. The Samaritan text omits the preposition *be* 'on'.

10. *great and flourishing cities that you did not build.* This phrase and the following verse stand in apposition to "the land" (contra Ehrlich 1909, ad loc.).

11. *good things. ṭûb* is here *status absolutus* (see also Isa 13:7 and Neh 9:25)

and not *status constructus* (contra Ehrlich 1909); cf. Akkadian *ṭābu* alongside *ṭūbu.* The same applies to *rôm* vis-à-vis *rûm* (cf. Hab 3:10 *[rôm]* with Isa 2:11 *[rûm]).*

12. *YHWH.* The Samaritan text and Peshitta add *ʾlhyk* 'your God' and the LXX follows suit, both here and in v 18, which might be original. Compare the parallel passages in 5:6, *YHWH ʾlhyk ʾšr hwṣʾtyk mʾrṣ mṣrym,* and 12:18b, *hṭwb whyšr bʿyny YHWH ʾlhyk.*

13. *Fear [only] YHWH your God.* Although the adverb alone *(lbdw,* cf. next note) is missing, it is implied here, as it stands in opposition to the next statement in v 14, "do not follow other gods."

worship him [alone]. See the previous Textual Note. The LXX and Matt 4:10, Luke 4:8 add *monō* 'alone'. Compare 1 Sam 7:3, 4, *ʿbd lbdw* 'worship him alone'. Such a formulation is reflected in the sixteenth benediction of the Amidah prayer, the Palestinian form of which is *šʾwtk lbdk byrʾh nʿbd* 'whom alone we shall serve with fear' (Singer 1915, p. 348). For the form of this benediction and its rabbinic references see Elbogen 1931, p. 56. The LXX also adds here *kai pros auton kollethese(i)* 'and to him you shall cleave'. Compare 10:20.

14. Here we have plural style in a singular context, but this does not justify our regarding it as an editorial addition (pace Smith 1918). It is linked to the motivation of the next verse, and both verses (14–15) represent the second commandment of the Decalogue, while vv 12–13 reflect the first (see above).

15. The *Tg. Ps.-J.* adds *whšmydk* 'destroy you', *bsrhbyʾ* 'soon'. Compare 7:4 (end).

16–17. The plural (LXX has singular) is used with the exception of 17b, which is singular. Compare also the mixed style in vv 14–15 (see the previous Textual Note).

18. *YHWH.* The LXX, Samaritan, and Peshitta add "your God." See the Note to v 12.

19. *drive out.* MT: *lahădop* (from *hdp*). Samaritan text, *lĕhaddip (hiphʿil* of *ndp*).

20. *[When].* MT: *ki.* The Samaritan text has *wĕhayah ki* and the LXX, *kai estai,* as in Exod 13:14.

in time to come. Literally, "tomorrow."

our God has commanded you. Some LXX manuscripts and the Vg read *ʾwtnw* 'us' (cf. *Mek. Exod.* 13:14; *y. Pesaḥ.* 10:4, 37d), others, "you." A third group deletes the pronoun "you/us" altogether.

23. *to bring us to the land and give it to us.* See the Note at 4:38.

24. *for our own good.* Hebrew: *lĕṭôb lānu,* literally, 'that it may be well for us'. *lĕṭob* is the infinitive construct of the verb *ṭwb.*

as is now the case. MT: *kĕhayyôm hazzeh,* literally, 'as this day'. The article in *kĕhayyôm* is not elided. *GKC* §35n distinguishes between *kayyôm* 'first of all' and *kĕhayyôm* 'about this time'. In the phrase *k(ĕh)ayyôm hazzeh, k(ĕh)ayyôm* has neither of these meanings, hence either form is used.

25. *before YHWH our God, as he commanded us.* The verse is best understood if "before YHWH our God" is transposed to follow "it will be to our merit"; cf. 24:13. According to Ehrlich (1909, ad loc.), the text need not be emended. He compares Exod 29:27, which is literally rendered, "You shall consecrate the breast and the thigh which were waved and lifted," but actually means, "You shall consecrate the breast that was waved and the thigh that was lifted." The problem in Deut 6:25 is clearly more difficult, however.

NOTES

6:4. This is preceded in the LXX and in the Nash papyrus by a title: "And these are the laws and the rules that Moses [YHWH in the LXX] commanded [the Israelites] in the desert when they left Egypt" (see the TEXTUAL NOTE). It seems to be a liturgical addition serving as an introduction to the Shemaᶜ proclamation (compare the benediction of ʾAhabah before the Shemaᶜ dedicated to God's laws and commandments (see Singer 1915, pp. 47, 130). This preface is patterned after Deut 4:45 and 6:1 and looks redundant especially because 6:1–3 constitutes an introduction by itself, and therefore this preface cannot be considered genuine.

Hear, O Israel. Compare the NOTES to 4:1 and 5:1, and in the context of the proclamation of faith see Pss 50:7 and 81:9, "Hear my people *(šmᶜ ᶜmy).*"

YHWH our God is one YHWH. There are four possibilities of translation:

1. YHWH is our God, YHWH is one *(RSV* footnote reading);
2. YHWH is our God, YHWH alone (Ibn Ezra, *NJPS, RSV* footnote reading);
3. YHWH our God is one YHWH (cf. Driver 1902); and
4. YHWH our God, YHWH is one *(RSV* footnote reading).

The first two translations, which take YHWH as subject and *ʾlhynw* as predicate, cannot be substantiated because in Deuteronomy the phrase *YHWH ʾlhynw* never occurs as subject and predicate but *ʾlhynw* always stands in apposition to *YHWH* (cf. 1:6; 5:2; 6:20, 24, 25; etc.; see Lohfink 1976, 108–9). The fourth translation looks awkward because the first subject is discontinued. The third translation is therefore adopted here, with a clarification, however: the connotation of "one" here is not solely unity but also aloneness. The word "one *(ʾeḥad)*" implies exclusiveness, as may be learned from 1 Chr 29:1, "God has chosen my son Solomon alone *(bny ʾḥd bḥr bw ʾlhym).*" An objection often made to this last translation is that "alone" in Hebrew is *lĕbaddo*, not *ʾeḥad.* But

Ehrlich (1909, ad loc.) justifiably argues that *lĕbaddo* is an adverb, and thus inappropriate in a nominal sentence, hence *ʾeḥad* is correct.

That oneness in reference to a god involves aloneness may be learned from a proclamation about the god Enlil in a Sumerian dedication inscription: "Enlil is the Lord of heaven and earth, he is king alone [literally, his oneness] *(dEnlil an-ki-šu lugal-ám, aš-ni lugal-ám)"* (Poebel 1914, no. 66, 1.1–3). Similarly, we read about the god Baal or Mot in Ugaritic literature, "I am one [= alone] *who* rules over the gods *(aḥdy dymlk ʿl ilm),* who rules over gods and men *(dymrʾu ilm wnšm)" (CTA* 4.7:49–50). Compare the proclamations of the Mysteries, *Isis quae es omnia; Hermes omnia solus et unus; heîs Zeus Sarapis* (cf. Peterson 1926, pp. 227ff.). All of these pagan proclamations cannot of course be seen as monotheistic, yet they are of hymnic-liturgical nature. By the same token, Deut 6:4 is a kind of liturgical confessional proclamation and by itself cannot be seen as monotheistic; it is its association with the first two commandments of the Decalogue and its connection with other proclamations in the sermons of Deuteronomy, such as Deut 10:17, that make it monotheistic (see the COMMENT).

In the Torah Scrolls the final letters *(ʿayin* and *dalet)* of the first and last words of this verse *(šĕmaʿ . . . ʾeḥad)* are exaggerated *(littera majuscula)* so as to form the word *ʿed* 'witness', thus referring to the testimony of faith contained in the Shemaʿ (Abudarham, fourteenth-century liturgical commentator [Wertheimer 1963]). For *šĕmaʿ* associated with testifying *(haʿed)* to God's unity, cf. Ps 81:9, *šĕmaʿ ʿami wĕʾaʿidah bak* 'hear my people and I will instruct you [literally, give testimony] . . . you shall have no foreign god'. Compare Ps 50:7 and see in the Introduction to the Decalogue. The rabbis indeed conceived it as a testimony, "whoever recites the Shemaʿ without putting on phylacteries is like one who gives false testimony" *(b. Ber.* 14b).

5. *You shall love YHWH.* Love of God is most characteristic of Deuteronomy (7:9; 10:12; 11:1, 13, 22; 13:4; 19:9; 30:6, 16, 20) and the Deuteronomic literature (Josh 22:5; 23:11; 1 Kgs 3:3) but is also attested in the Decalogue 5:10 (= Exod 20:6), in the Song of Deborah (Judg 5:31), and in the Psalms (31:24; 97:10; 145:20). In Deuteronomy the term *love* has a special meaning of loyalty, as in the vassal loyalty oaths; see the COMMENT.

with all your heart. The phrase is predominant in Deuteronomy and the Deuteronomic literature (cf. Weinfeld 1972a, p. 334 no. 9a), though attested already in proto-Deuteronomic texts such as 1 Sam 7:3; 12:20, 24. "Heart" connotes mind, and indeed LXX has *dianoia* 'mind' instead of *kardia* 'heart'.

In the NT the element of "mind" and "understanding" is even more explicit in the discussed context. There we find both the "heart" and the "mind": "you shall love with all the heart *(kardia)* and with all the mind *(synesis)"* (Mark 12:30), and similarly in Matt 22:37: "with all your heart *(kardia)* . . . with all your mind/understanding *(dianoia)";* and compare Luke 10:27. "Heart" as "mind" and "understanding" was prevalent in late Hebrew literature. As will be seen presently, *daʿat* 'mind' occurs instead of "heart" in Qumran literature; but this is also a feature of Mishnaic literature, see Ben-David 1967, 1.92, and cf. Ibn Ezra to Deut 6:5, "the heart *(hlb)* is the mind *(hdʿt)* and is the designation of the spirit of understanding."

According to rabbinic interpretation, *bkl lbbk* here implies the personal genii/spirits of the man; one has to serve God with both the good genius/spirit *(yeṣer ṭwb)* and the evil one *(yeṣer raʿ)*. Compare *Tg. Ps.-J.* to this verse and *Sipre Deut.* 32 (Finkelstein 1969, p. 55) with its parallels. *Dianoia* in the LXX to Deut 6:5 and in the NT instances cited above also alludes to this interpretation because *dianoia* translates the *yeṣer* of Hebrew scripture (LXX Gen 8:21; 1 Chr 29:18; and in the addition to Prov 9:10: *dianoia agathē,* which corresponds to Hebrew *yeṣer ṭwb).*

In the literature of the Qumran sect we find that every member of the sect must bring his mind *(dʿt)* and his might *(kḥ)* and property *(hwn)* into God's community. This corresponds to the command of Deut 6:5 to love God with all one's mind and force *(lbb* and *mʾd).* Compare Weinfeld 1982e.

with all your soul. The full phrase "with all the heart and all the soul" is attested only in Deuteronomy and in the Deuteronomic literature; cf. Deut 4:29; 10:12; 11:13; 13:4; 26:16; 30:2, 6, 10; Josh 22:55; 23:14; 1 Kgs 2:4; 8:48; 2 Kgs 23:3, 25; Jer 32:41 (Deuteronomic editorial strand). This has been understood by the rabbis and the Targum as readiness to sacrifice life for God, which might reflect the original intention (see the COMMENT). Nonetheless, one must take into account that the idiom itself expresses full devotion, like the idiom "with all your heart," so that the interpretation of readiness to sacrifice one's life does not exclude the more general meaning of the idiom, namely, full devotion. This is clear in Jer 32:41, where God is speaking. Compare also 1 Sam 18:3, "Jonathan and David made a pact that one would love the other like himself *(bʾhbtw ʾtw knpšw)*" and 1 Sam 20:17, *ky ʾhbt npšw ʾhbw.*

your might. Hebrew: *mĕʾodeka. meʾod* is used only here and in the deuteronomistic passage 2 Kgs 23:25 in this sense; otherwise it is an adverb meaning "very." The implication of "might" is twofold: ability (i.e., power, strength), and means (i.e., wealth). The semantic range is similar to that of the nouns *koăḥ* and *ḥayil,* which mean primarily 'strength' but are also used in the sense of 'wealth' (see Weinfeld 1971–72a, p. 89).

mʾd in the sense of wealth occurs in Ben Sira and in Qumran literature. Thus in Ben Sira 7:30–31, "Love your maker with all your might *(mʾdk)* and do not leave his ministers without support. Fear God and honor the priest and give him his dues." According to the context it is clear that "might" *(mʾd)* here connotes wealth, which enables one to give gifts to the priests. Compare Prov 3:9, where we find *hwn* instead of *mʾd* in an identical context. In the passage of Qumran cited above (1QS 1:12) about the need for full devotion on the part of the members of the sect we read that the members should bring into the community of God, besides their mind *(daʿat),* which corresponds to "heart *(lb),*" their strength and wealth *(kwḥm whwnm),* which corresponds to *mʾd.*

Similarly, in the Covenant of Damascus (14:11) the new member of the sect is asked about his mind *(śwkl)* and his strength, force and wealth *(kwḥw gbwrtw whwnw).* In the Qumran sect this demand for loving God with all one's wealth receives a practical meaning: one has to surrender all private property for the common use of the sect (compare Acts 5:1–11 in connection with the early Christian community, and Weinfeld 1986c, pp. 30–31).

6–9. These verses have their parallel in 11:18–20, where we find the same motifs: "putting these words upon the heart" (compare 6:6 with 11:18a), "the teaching of these words to the children" (compare 6:7a with 11:19a), "the recitation in house, on the way and when one lies down and gets up" (compare 6:7b with 11:19b), "the binding of the words upon the arm and the forehead" (compare 6:8 with 11:18b), and "the inscribing on the doorposts" (compare 6:9 with 11:20). A difference in order occurs, however: in 11:18–20 the binding of the words comes before the teaching of the children, reversing the order to 6:6–9. It seems that the order of 6:6–9 is genuine because the symbolic signs, binding and inscribing, belong together. Besides, 11:18–20 is styled in the plural (except 11:19b, which, like the other singular passages in the plural sections, are quotations from 6:7b: see Begg, 1987, pp. 1179–1219), which seems to be a later strand in the book. Furthermore, in Exod 13:8–9, 14–16, which are related to Deut 6:5 (see the COMMENT), the education of the children appears before the signs and the symbols, as in Deut 6:6–9 and unlike Deut 11:18–19.

6. *These words which I command you this day.* Commentators usually understand the subject as referring to vv 4–5: the proclamation of the unity of God and the command to love him. In the parallel passage, 11:18–20, however, "these words" refers to the general paraenetic discourse of Deuteronomy. According to some commentators, it refers to the Decalogue, which is indeed defined as "these words *(hdbrym h'lh)*" in Exod 20:1 and Deut 5:19. Compare also Deut 4:9–10, which urges Israel to remember "the words *(hdbrym)*" so that they will not be removed from the heart and that they may be transmitted to the children, as in the present passage. In chap. 4 the reference is clearly to the Sinai theophany, that is to say, the Decalogue (cf. Deut 4:10). See, however, Ibn Ezra ad loc., "the liars [= the Karaites] said it refers to the Ten Commandments and concerning them it says [in v 5] 'You shall write them on the doorpost', the truth is that it refers to all the commandments."

shall be on your heart. The idea of placing words upon the heart and soul (compare 11:18) occurs in the political loyalty oaths, as, for example, in the Hittite treaty of Muršili II with Kupanta-KAL: "and the following word let it into the heart (ŠÀ-ta *tarna),* . . . Let it into the soul (ZI-ni *tarna)*" (Friedrich 1926, 22:23, p. 138) and in the vassals' oath to Esarhaddon: "an evil word you shall not put on your heart" *(VTE,* lines 183–85).

7. *You shall inculcate them to your children.* Compare 11:19: "and [you shall] teach *(limed)* them to your children." Pupils are often named "sons *(banim)*" especially in wisdom literature (cf., e.g., Prov 2:1; 3:1; 4:1; 5:7; 8:33; etc.); and so

in Mesopotamia the teacher was called "father" and the pupil "son" (cf. Kramer 1963, p. 232). The Rabbis indeed interpreted "sons" here as pupils (see *Sipre* 34 [Finkelstein 1969, p. 61]).

you shall recite them (. . . at home . . . when you lie down . . . when you get up). Constant reading of the law is mentioned in the king's law in 17:19, "he shall read in it all his life," which is paraphrased in God's command to Joshua, the leader, "the book of the law shall *not cease from your lips* and you shall recite it *(hgh b)* day and night" (Josh 1:8). The same idea is expressed in Ps 1:2, "and his law he murmurs *(hgh b)* day and night." Compare recently the discussion of Fischer and Lohfink 1987, and on the affinities of Ps 1 to Deut 6:7, cf. André 1982, p. 327 and Reif 1984.

when you stay at home, when you are away, when you lie down, and when you get up. And you shall bind them as a sign. Compare Prov 6:20–22, "My son keep your father's commandments . . . bind them *(qšrm)* on your heart always; tie them about your neck. When you walk *(bhthlkk)* it will guide you, when you lie down *(bškbk)* it will watch you, when you wake up it will talk to you."

As in Proverbs so in Deuteronomy constant awareness of the divine message is demanded. It should be tied to the body like an amulet and should accompany the person all the time. The similes, expressing constant awareness, are found in political loyalty declarations. Compare in a Hittite covenantal text, "as you wear a dress so shall you carry with you these oaths" (KUB 35.25:6ff.; Otten 1963, p. 4), and a declaration of loyalty of Abdimilki the king of Tyre to the Egyptian sovereign, "I carry upon my belly and upon my back the words of the King" *(ana muḫḫi gabītija muḫḫi ṣurīja ubbal amātu šarri* (El Amarna letter no. 147:39). According to rabbinic tradition, the book of the Torah, which the king is commanded to read day and night (Deut 17:19, and see above in the previous NOTE), had to be tied as an amulet to the king's arm *(b. Sanh.* 22a).

8. *you shall bind them as a sign on your hand and as a frontlet (ṭṭpt) on your forehead.* Compare Exod 13:9, 16; but there it refers to the Passover ritual or to the ritual of the firstborn, while in Deut 6:8 it refers to the words of God. The question is whether the author speaks of these objects ("sign and frontlet") literally or figuratively. There is no doubt that in Prov 6:21, quoted above (compare Prov 3:3 and 7:3), the "binding" is meant figuratively. This can be deduced from Prov 4:9, where it is said of Wisdom: "she will give to your head a chaplet of grace, a crown of glory will she bestow on you," meaning that Wisdom will add honor to you. The LXX also took Deut 6:8 metaphorically because it translates *ṭṭpt* as *asaleuton* 'immovable' (see the TEXTUAL NOTE), implying that the words of God shall be immovable and firm. Compare Philo's *Life of Moses* 2.14: "his [Moses'] laws are firm, unshaken *(asaleuta),* immovable," etc. The Samaritans also make a distinction between the command to write on the doorposts (v 9), which is taken literally (see below), and the verses about the sign and *ṭṭpt,* which are interpreted metaphorically. Some of the medieval commentators also understand the verse figuratively, such as Samuel ben Meir (Rashbam) of the

twelfth century. In his comment on Exod 13:9 he says, " 'a sign on your hand/arm'—according to its plain meaning: it will be always remembered by you as if written on your hand . . . 'on your forehead'—as a jewel and golden ornament which one puts on his forehead for beauty" (Rosin 1881, ad loc.). This was also the opinion of the Karaites, against whom Ibn Ezra rightly argues,

> there are some who disagree with our ancestors (who understood the binding literally) and who say that "for a sign and reminder" (Exod 13:9) has the same meaning as Prov 1:9, "for they are a graceful wreath upon your head, a necklace about your throat," and that "You shall bind them for a sign on your arm" (Deut 6:9) is like Prov 3:3, "Tie them over your head always" . . . but this analogy is not correct because at the beginning of the book is written "The Proverbs of Solomon." Thus, everything is styled as proverb (whereas) what is written in the Pentateuch is not a proverb, God forbid, but is meant as said.

In fact, as S. R. Driver (1902, ad loc.) and A. Dillmann (KEH Deut ad loc.) have seen, v 9 clearly refers to real writing (Dillmann also compares Deut 27:3, 8) and therefore v 8 is intended, in their opinion, to be carried out literally. From various literary and iconographical sources we indeed learn that people used to carry on their arms inscribed and uninscribed objects that marked their affiliation to a deity as their protector (cf. Keel 1981, pp. 212–15), and similarly there was a widespread custom to carry on the forehead frontlets with sacred signs, which served as a kind of memorial sign before the deity *(ibid.,* pp. 193–212). Such symbolic headwear was carried by the Israelite high priest. The latter is commanded to make a frontlet of gold on which will be engraved an inscription "Holy to YHWH." This should be suspended on a cord and should hang on his forehead all the time as a sign of conciliation before YHWH (Exod 28:36–38).

This custom of carrying amulets has now been brought to light by archaeological discoveries. Two silver plaques with Hebrew inscriptions recently discovered in Jerusalem testify to the custom among the ancient Israelites of wearing written amulets (cf. Barkai 1986, pp. 29–31). These plaques of the seventh or sixth century B.C.E. bear written texts in ancient Hebrew script, including the priestly benediction found in Num 6:24–26. The plaques have holes in the middle through which a string could be threaded, so that they could be tied to the body. They are apotropaic in nature (offering protection from evil) and seem to be identical with the amulet of silver *(tplh zy ksf)* from Egypt mentioned in the TEXTUAL NOTE. It appears that originally Deut 6:8 prescribed the writing of the Shemaᶜ (and/or the Decalogue) on bracelets and frontlets indicating the religious affiliation of its bearer. Only later, toward the end of the Second Temple period, did the custom of phylacteries *(tefillin)* develop; these were cubical boxes of leather containing passages from Exod 13:1–10, 11–16; Deut 6:4–9;

11:13–21 written on parchment (passages in which the binding of symbols is prescribed). In the phylacteries found in Qumran the scriptural passages also contain the Decalogue, which precedes the Shema' (Deut 5). Compare the references in Keel 1981, pp. 169–71. The boxes are bound by leather strips on the left hand and on the head. In Qumran the phylacteries were about two centimeters broad, but later they were enlarged. Compare Matt 23:5, which criticizes the Pharisees for making phylacteries wide.

frontlet. The etymology of the word *ṭṭpt* is unclear. H. Grimme has suggested (1938) that it is derived from Egyptian *ḏdf.t,* which denotes the symbol of the Uraeus snake that was put on the forehead of the Egyptian kings as a sign of protection. Recently M. Görg (1979) strengthened this supposition by comparing it with *nzr,* the frontlet of the high priest (see above), which is derived from Egyptian *nzr.t* (the protective snake/flame of the forehead). Alternatively, the word is associated with *ṭpp/nṭp* 'to drip' or 'drop', in other words, to be suspended (see the TEXTUAL NOTE). At any rate, the meaning of *ṭ(w)ṭpt* as headwear and frontlet is the most plausible one; cf. Tigay 1982.

9. *You shall inscribe them on the doorposts of your house and on your city gates.* The ancient Egyptians used to write on doorposts words of a sacred nature (cf. Keel 1981, pp. 183–92). More than a dozen stone plaques of Samaritan origin have been preserved on which the Decalogue is inscribed and which were put near entranceways (cf. Ben-Zevi 1953–54; Dexinger 1977, pp. 122f.; Strugnell 1967, pp. 558f.). As with the phylacteries so with the *mĕzuzah* (the name of the inscribed object put on the doorpost) a development took place. At the end of the Second Temple period the "words" were inscribed not on stone but on parchment (cf. DJD 3.158, 161 and cf. *m. Ber.* 3:3, *Meg.* 1:8, etc.), which was encased in a box and affixed to the upper part of the right-hand doorpost in every house (see Rabinowitz 1971).

10. *When YHWH your God brings you into the land that he swore to your fathers, Abraham, Isaac, and Jacob, to give you.* Compare Exod 13, "when YHWH brings you into the land of the Canaanite . . . which he swore to your fathers to give you" (cf. v 11 there). The differences are significant: first of all, YHWH is supplemented here by "your God," a term characteristic of Deuteronomy, which wants to stress the close relation between Israel and its God (see the NOTE to 1:6). Second, "Canaanite" as a definition of the land is omitted here because this old term applies to the western part of Palestine only, which would limit the extent of the promised land as understood by the author of Deuteronomy (see above). Finally, "the fathers" in Deuteronomy are specified: Abraham, Isaac, and Jacob. In the previous sources we find either the promise to the ancestors (Gen 48:21; Exod 13:8, 11; Num 14:23; Judg 2:1) or the promise to Abraham, Isaac, and Jacob (Gen 26:3; 28:4; 35:12; 50:24; Exod 6:8; 32:13; 33:1; Num 32:11). In Deuteronomy "the ancestors" are mentioned along with their individual names (1:8; 6:10; 9:5; 29:12; 30:20). (Deut 31:20, which does

not have the individual names, belongs to the old stratum incorporated by Deuteronomy [Elohistic Source].)

great and flourishing cities that you did not build. The background depicted here is the wealth of an urban society given to temptations, in particular, forgetting YHWH. Compare Neh 9:26, which is an elaboration of the verse here, "they captured fortified cities and rich lands; they took possession of houses filled with every good thing, of hewn cisterns . . . they ate, they were filled, they grew fat . . . and they rebelled." And compare Josh 24:13, "I gave you a land for which you did not labor and towns which you did not build, and you have settled in them, you are enjoying vineyards and olive groves which you did not plant."

11. *hewn cisterns that you did not hew.* Rock-cut cisterns for storing rainwater were very common, especially in the Iron Age, when lime plaster was used for lining them. Private cisterns were a common feature in every household (cf. 2 Kgs 19:31 = Isa 36:16; Mesha inscription, lines 24–25, "and there was no cistern in the *girḫu* (acropolis?) and I said to all people, 'make you each a cistern *(bôr)* in his own house' " *[KAI* 2.169–78]; cf. also 2 Chr 26:10).

and you eat your fill. Compare 8:10, 12; 11:15; 14:29; 26:12; 31:20, sometimes in the positive sense (8:10; 14:29; 26:12) and sometimes, as here, in the negative sense, causing haughtiness (8:12; 11:15; 31:20).

12–15. These verses are a clear reflection of the first two commandments of the Decalogue. Verses 12 and 13 render the contents of the first commandment, which implies the sole authority of the God who freed the people from Egypt, thus precluding the service of other gods. A similar formulation, namely, authority plus "fear *(yrʾ),*" is found in Judg 6:8–10, "Thus said YHWH . . . I freed you from the house of slaves . . . and said to you, 'I am YHWH your God, you shall not fear [= worship] the gods of the Amorites.' " Compare also the chiasm in 2 Kgs 17:35–36, "You shall not fear other gods, you shall not bow down to them nor worship them, nor sacrifice to them. Only YHWH your God, who brought you out of the land of Egypt, him [alone] shall you fear, to him [alone] shall you bow down and to him alone shall you sacrifice."

Verses 14 and 15 render the contents of the second commandment, which warns against worshiping other gods with the reason that YHWH is an impassioned God *(ʾel qannaʾ)* who will punish Israel severely for following other gods.

12. *beware that you do not forget YHWH.* See the COMMENT below and cf. Weinfeld 1972a, pp. 367–68.

YHWH who freed you from the land of Egypt, the house of slaves. This clause is a quotation from 5:6.

13. *Fear [only] YHWH your God.* This expression is dominant in Deuteronomy and Deuteronomic literature for performing religious duties. Compare 4:10; 5:26; 6:2, 24; 8:6; 10:12, 20, etc.; 13:5; 14:23; 17:19; 28:58; 31:12, 13. See Weinfeld 1972a, p. 332. (The verb "fear" is also used in Akkadian literature for loyally serving God and king *[palāḫu];* cf. Weinfeld 1972a. "Fear" goes together

with *ʿbd* 'serve', *hlk ʾḥr* 'follow/go after', *ʾhb* 'love', *šmʿ bqwl* 'to hearken to (YHWH's) voice', etc., therefore it is to be taken as following God and observing his commandments. Indeed, the epithet *yrʾ ʾlhym/YHWH* 'who fears God/YHWH' denotes the pious man who reveres God and honors him (cf., e.g., Gen 22:12; Mal 3:16; Pss 25:12; 128:1, 4; Job 1:1, 8; 2:3; etc.), and the same can be said about the epithet *ʾhb YHWH ʾlhym* 'who loves God/YHWH' (Exod 20:6 = Deut 5:10; Judg 5:31; Pss 97:10; 145:20). Ben Sira refers to these terms as synonyms (2:16, 17; cf. 7:29–30). Philo made a distinction between the one who serves God out of love and the one who serves out of fear (*On the Unchangeableness of God* 60–64). The sages at first combined the ideal of love (i.e., serving God without receiving reward) with reverence *(mwrʾ šmym, m. ʾAbot* 1:3; cf. Urbach 1979, pp. 402–4). Only in late times did they sharpen the distinction between one who serves God out of love, as Abraham did, and one who, like Job, serves him out of fear *(m. Soṭa* 5:5).

worship him [alone]. The verb *ʿbd* here connotes fulfilling religious duties in the broad sense of the word, for it goes with revering, prostrating, and expressing loyalty by swearing an oath. Elsewhere it is coupled with following YHWH *(hlk ʾḥr Y.),* loving him, cleaving to him, keeping his commandments, and listening to his voice (10:12–13, 20; 13:5). Most significant is the expression "to worship *(lʿbd)* him with all the heart and soul" (10:12; 11:13), which parallels the expression "to love him with all the heart and soul" (6:5; 30:6; etc.; see Riesener 1979, p. 205). In the Second Temple period the noun *ʿabodah* signified cultic worship. *ʿAbodah* then turned into a term for temple service, and *ʿabodah zarah* defined pagan cult. In the priestly literature of the Pentateuch the term *ʿabodah* denotes physical work in connection with the tabernacle; see Milgrom 1970, p. 60; Floss 1975, p. 19.

and swear [only] by his name. Loyalty to YHWH means to recognize him alone as the arbitrating power in all man's dealings with his fellows and especially in one's oaths in which the name of one's God is invoked. The invocation of other gods' names means betraying YHWH (Jer 12:16–17). "He who swears by YHWH" (Ps 63:12) is a true worshiper of YHWH (cf. Isa 48:1; Jer 4:2; 5:2; 12:16). An oath is also involved in the confession of faith (cf. above on the pledge of loyalty to YHWH), and this seems to be reflected in Isa 45:23, "to me every knee shall bend, every tongue swear [loyalty]."

14. *Do not follow other gods.* Literally, "go after *(hlk ʾḥry),*" which is a characteristic idiom of Deuteronomy and Deuteronomic literature and means to follow loyally (cf. 4:3; 8:19; 11:28; 13:3; 28:14). It equals Akkadian *alāku arki,* which occurs in treaty contexts (see Weinfeld 1972a, p. 320). In the sense "following YHWH" it is found in 13:5 in a context similar to the present one, "to follow . . . to fear, and to serve."

any gods of the peoples who are around you. Compare 13:8; Judg 2:12. This expression is used by Deuteronomy and the Deuteronomic school based on the supposition that the former inhabitants of the land were all destroyed (cf. 7:2;

20:17), therefore idolatry only exists among the surrounding nations (cf. Weinfeld 1968b). In the older sources one speaks about the danger of idolatry coming from the inhabitants of the land *itself (yšby hʾrṣ);* see Exod 34:12, 15; Deut 31:16 (Elohistic Source); Josh 24:15, 23; Judg 2:2.

15. *in your midst.* Compare Exod 33:3, 5; Deut 1:42; 7:21; 23:15; Josh 3:10; Hos 11:9; Jer 14:9.

impassioned God. Compare 4:24; 5:9 (= Exod 20:5); Josh 24:19; and above, in the NOTE to 5:9.

lest the anger . . . blaze forth . . . and he wipe you off. Compare 7:4. Similar expressions about God in the midst of his people getting angry and deciding to destroy them are attested in the story of the golden calf in Exod 32–33; cf. Exod 32:10, "my anger may blaze forth against them that I may destroy them"; Exod 33:5, "If I were to go in your midst . . . I would destroy you" (cf. v 3).

wipe you (whšmydk) off the face of the earth. Compare, in connection with the sin of the golden calf in Exod 32:12, "to destroy them *(wlkltm)* off the face of the earth," and in 1 Kgs 13:34 in connection with the sin of Jeroboam (with the golden calves), "a sin . . . to destroy *(lhšmyd)* off the face of the earth." See also Amos 9:8.

16. *Do not try YHWH your God as you did at Massah.* Compare Exod 17:1–7, where it says that the people tried YHWH there in order to see "if YHWH is present among us or not" (v 7). In times of distress the people try their God to see whether he can help them. This theme comes to the fore during the wanderings in the desert, and especially at Massah or Meribah, when the people were thirsty and had no water. They tested God to see whether he would be able to provide them with water (Exod 17:1–7; Num 20:7–13; Ps 95:8–9). The same thing happened when they lusted for meat, and so on (Num 11; Deut 9:22; Pss 78:18–20; 106:14). The period of the wandering in the desert actually became the classical period of testing God (cf. Num 14:22; Ps 78:41). Sometimes it is God who tries the people in distress in order to see whether they remain faithful to him in spite of their suffering (cf. Exod 15:25; 16:4; Judg 2:22; 3:4). For tests of individuals see Gen 22:1; Job 1:9–12; 2:4–6; Ps 26:2). In fact, the same event of distress may serve as a test by God as well as a test by man: God tests the man to see whether he remains faithful in spite of suffering, while man tests God to see whether he will prove himself as God and release him from suffering. This actually happened in the case of Massah. According to Exod 17:1–7, Num 20:7–13, and Deut 6:16, the people at Massah tested God to see whether he would provide them with water, whereas according to Ps 81:8 it was God who tested the people there. Compare Deut 8:2, 16, where God is said to have tried the people, first subjecting them to hunger, then feeding them with manna, which is seen there as the people's merit: they have endured the test (cf. 8:5; cf. also Deut 33:8). On this ambiguous view of testing see Licht 1973, pp. 43–47; and on the tension between the two different approaches to

the manna narrative as represented in the midrash, see Boyarim 1986. As indicated in the COMMENT below, the testing here stands in opposition to keeping the law (v 17) and, like Ps 78:56, the intention is to try the patience of God by not keeping his commandments.

17–18. Keeping the commandments and doing what is right and good in order that things may go well appears also in Deut 12:28, therefore v 17 cannot be disconnected from v 18 (pace Smith 1918) in spite of the change from plural to singular. Note that the end of v 17 *(ʾšr ṣwk)* is styled in the singular, a change attested in 8:1; see the NOTE there.

17. *as he commanded you.* Compare 5:31–33; 6:1. See Skweres 1979, pp. 59–60.

18. *Do what is right and good (hyšr whṭwb) in the eyes of YHWH.* The usual phrase in Deuteronomy and the Deuteronomic literature for approval of one's behavior is "to do what is right *(hyšr)* in the eyes of YHWH" (cf. Deut 12:25; 13:19; 21:9; 1 Kgs 11:36, 38; etc.) and the opposite phrase is "to do what is evil *(hrʿ)* in the eyes of YHWH" (Deut 4:25; 9:18; 17:2; Judg 2:11; etc.). Only in Deut 6:18; 12:28 (13:19 in the LXX and the Samaritan version) and 2 Chr 14:1; 31:20 do we find the double phrase "right and good *(hyšr whṭwb).*" It seems that in Deut 6:18 and 12:28 "good" has been added for stylistic reasons, in order to create measure for measure: do good *(ṭwb)* in order that it may go well *(yyṭb)* with you. In the Second Temple period there was a tendency for pleonasms in these expressions. For example, 2 Chr 14:1 has "right and good" where the parallel in 1 Kgs 15:11 has only "right *(hyšr)*"; 2 Chr 31:20—the author's own words—has three attributes for Hezekiah: good, right, and truth *(hṭwb, hyšr, whʾmt).* For the pair "right and good" compare also Qumran literature: 1QS 1:3, Temple Scroll 55:14; 59:17. The Rabbis made a distinction between that which is *good* in the sight of heaven and that which is *right* in the sight of man (Rabbi Aqiba, *Sipre* 79 § [Finkelstein 1969, p. 145]; *t. Sheqalim* 2:2). Others (sages of Nehardea) understood "right and good" as things beyond the requirement of the Law *(lpnym mšwrt hdyn; b. B. Meṣ.* 35a).

19. *to drive out all your enemies before you.* The verb *hdp min* in the context of removing the Canaanites appears also in 9:4 and Josh 23:5 (=Dtr.), avoiding intentionally the more common verb *grš* (see below).

as YHWH has spoken. Compare Exod 23:27, and see recently Skweres 1979, p. 192.

20. *[When] in time to come.* Literally, "tomorrow *(mḥr).*" Compare Exod 13:14 and Josh 4:6, 21 in an identical context (the child's question). Hebrew *mḥr* along with *ywm ʾḥrwn* 'next day' also have a future meaning. Compare Gen 30:33; Josh 22:24, 27; Isa 30:8 *(ywm ʾḥrwn),* Aramaic *mḥr ʾw ywm ʾḥrwn* (Cowley 1906, 7.18–19); and Akkadian *urram šēram,* see Weinfeld 1970–72, p. 189 n. 43.

What mean the precepts, laws, and rules. For this triple combination cf. 4:45. These expressions pertain to the laws proper and not to the *miṣwah,* the basic command to keep loyalty, as in 5:5 (see the INTRODUCTION to 6:4–25). Unlike the questions in Exod 12:26 *(mh hʿbdh hzʾt lkm),* 13:14 *(mh zʾt),* and Josh 4:6 *(mh hʾbnym hʾlh lkm)* and 4:21 *(mh hʾbnym hʾlh),* which refer to the particular ceremonies of the Passover and sacrifice of the firstborn animal or the erecting of stones at Gilgal, the question here refers to the laws in general (see the INTRODUCTION to 6:4–25 and the COMMENT to 6:20–25).

21. *YHWH freed us from Egypt with a mighty hand.* An established liturgical formula existed in variants. Compare Exod 13:9 *(byd ḥzqh),* 13:14 *(bḥzq yd),* Deut 26:8, and "with a mighty hand and outstretched arm *(byd ḥzqh wbzrʿ nṭwyh).*" Compare the NOTE to 4:34.

22. *great and grave (gdlym wrʿym).* These adjectives define the disastrous afflictions of Pharaoh. Compare Gen 12:17 in connection with the affliction of Pharaoh and his house, "YHWH afflicted Pharaoh and his household with great plagues *(ngʿym gdlym).*" The LXX has there, as in the verse here, "great and evil *(megálois kai ponēroîs).*" The act of affliction is rendered by *ētasen etasmois* 'proved by tests', which is identical with the "trials *(massôt)*" used in connection with the Egyptians in Deut 4:34; 7:19; and 29:2. The LXX's rendering of Gen 12:17 seems to be a resonance of the plagues of Egypt in Exodus.

grave. Literally, "bad." *Raʿ* 'bad' (sore) often serves as an adjective for diseases and characterizes the Egyptian afflictions. Compare Deut 7:15, "all the evil diseases of Egypt *(wkl mdwy mṣrym hrʿym),* about which you know." See also Deut 28:59; Job 2:7; Eccl 6:2; 2 Chr 21:19.

signs and portents. The phrase *ʾotôt umôpĕtim* belongs to the tradition of the plagues in Egypt (cf. 4:34; 7:19; 26:8; 29:2; 34:11), but in Exodus these expressions usually do not appear as a pair: "signs *(ʾtwt)*" in Exod 10:1, 2; Num 14:11, 22, "portents *(mwptym)*" in Exod 4:21; 11:9, 10. Only in Exod 7:3 do we find the pair *ʾtwt wmwptym.* Compare also Pss 78:43; 105:27, where "signs and portents" serve as a title for the plagues of Egypt; see also Jer 32:20, 21; Ps 135:9; Neh 9:10.

against Pharaoh and all his household. Compare Gen 12:17, "Pharaoh and his household."

23–24. *and us he freed . . . and . . . commanded us to observe all these laws.* The liberation took place in order to enable the Israelites to serve God, the real master (cf. Lev 25:42, 55). Compare Lev 19:36–37, "I am YHWH your God who freed you . . . you shall keep all my laws and my rules" (for the structure of the sentence, see above in the NOTE to 5:6). The author of Deuteronomy, however, adds to keeping the law the motif of the fear of God, so characteristic of him (see the NOTE to 6:13).

24. *for our own good all the days and for our life.* Compare 5:30, but there the form used *(tiḥyūn)* is *al* of the root *ḥyh* while here the form used is *piʿel,* which has the meaning: "let somebody live"; cf. Deut 20:16; 32:39 (restore to life), Exod 1:22; Num 31:15; Josh 9:15; 1 Sam 27:9; 1 Kgs 18:5; Pss 33:19; 41:3. God redeemed Israel from the Egyptians and let them live under his patronage,

now as slaves of YHWH, which reflects the juridical concept of *paramone,* i.e. change of master. In our case instead of Pharaoh comes the overlord YHWH, see Lev. 25:42, 45 and cf. Weinfeld 1985, 133–42. In Akkadian the D stem of *balāṭu* 'to live' *(bulluṭu)* has indeed the meaning of to let live, or to maintain somebody even in the status of a slave (compare Lev 25:35: let him live by our side, *wḥy ʿmk).* For this understanding of the *lĕḥayōtam* in our verse see N. Lohfink "Deut 6:24 'to maintain us' ". . .", *Festschrift S. Talmon* (forthcoming); I thank Professor Lohfink for letting me see the manuscript before its publication.

25. *It will be to our merit.* Hebrew: *uṣĕdāqāh tihyeh lānû* 'and it will be *ṣedaqah* to us'. The root *ṣdq* has a number of meanings in biblical Hebrew. It refers both to moral righteousness and to legal innocence, with the extended meaning of acquittal, justification, privilege, or rather "credit" or "merit" (= *zĕkût* in late Hebrew; see Quell, 1964, 2.177 n. 11). The Targumim indeed translate *ṣedaqah* here *zĕkū/zĕkūta. Ṣĕdāqāh* in this sense occurs in Gen 15:6 and Deut 24:13. The same phrase with the same meaning is invoked in the petition of the Jews of Elephantine to the governor of Judea asking his help in rebuilding the Jewish temple in Elephantine. He is told that a positive response will be a "credit to you before Y *(wṣdqh yhwh lk qdm Y)"* (Cowley 1906, 30.27). Similarly, we read in the Aramaic Nerab inscription, "on the account of my merit *(bṣdqty)* he established for me a good name and he lengthened my days" *(KAI* 226.2–3). As in the verses here, we find in the Nerab inscription the three motifs together: good, life, and merit before God.

COMMENT

6:4–9

These verses constitute a solemn proclamation of the unity of God. No explicit notion of exclusiveness is attested here, such as we find in Deut 4:35, "YHWH alone is God; there is none beside him" *(YHWH hwʾ hʾlhym ʾyn ʿwd mlbdw;* cf. 4:39), or Deutero-Isaiah 44:6, "there is no God but me *(wmblʿdy ʾyn ʾlhym),"* 44:5, "I am YHWH, there is none else *(ʾny YHWH wʾyn ʿwd),"* 45:6, 14, 18, 22; 46:9, "there is no other god at all *(ʾps ʾlhym),"* and in later deuteronomistic literature (1 Kgs 8:60, "YHWH is the God, there is none else *[YHWH hwʾ hʾlhym ʾyn ʿwd],"* 2 Kgs 19:15, 19, "you alone are the God *[ʾth hwʾ hʾlhym lbdk]").* Still, it seems that the statement of unity here implies monotheism. It is true that during the Exile the monotheistic consciousness sharpened and came to full expression (see Lohfink 1976; Braulik 1985; and see the Note on 6:4), but this does not mean that the concept of monotheism was created then. Declarations about YHWH being the only God are found in the Elijah stories —*YHWH hwʾ hʾlhym* 'YHWH [alone] is God' (1 Kgs 18:39)—and in the Elisha stories as well—"Now I know that there is no God in the whole world except in Israel" (2 Kgs 5:15; cf. v 17 and see Zakovitch 1985, p. 75). Such declarations often occur in the older parts of Deuteronomy (e.g., 7:9; 10:17), and no justification can be given for interpreting these phrases in a henotheistic manner (contra Lohfink and Braulik). The mention of "other gods" (Deut 6:14; 13:8; etc.) does not presuppose the existence of polytheism, as Lohfink contends (1976, p. 106), for *ʾelohim ʾaḥerim* 'other gods' implies also idols (see NOTE to 5:7) and actually connotes foreign worship in general. Besides, it is a conventional expression for deviation and apostasy, hence nothing can be learned from it about Israelite belief in the existence of other deities. The depiction of "other gods" as man-made, which begins with Hosea (8:6; 13:2; 14:4; cf. Isa 2:8; Mic 5:12) may also indicate that in eighth-century Israel other gods were considered futile and without any real power.

The phrase "YHWH is one *(ʾḥd)*" constitutes a proclamation of a liturgical nature (see below) that connotes exclusiveness and uniqueness; though similar proclamations are found in pagan religions (see the NOTE), its occurrence in the special context of Deuteronomy gives it a monotheistic flavor. Whether the unity of YHWH in Deut 6:4 is intended to exclude the existence of local manifestations of YHWH's, as, for example, the ones discovered at Kuntillet Ajrud *(YHWH šmrn, YHWH tmn*—see Weinfeld 1984c, p. 125) is a moot question. The phenomenon of local features of YHWH might have been reflected in the statements of Jer 2:28 and 11:13, "for your gods have become . . . as many as your towns." One must admit, however, that this phenomenon is never brought up as an argument in the issue of unification of worship, and the fragmentation of YHWH into numerous deities is never explicitly recognized as a problem (see McBride 1973, p. 295). It is clear that the uniqueness of God here has been understood as sole and exclusive. This is to be deduced from the sequence: to love God with one's whole entity, to the exclusion of any rival to that love, is compared to the love of a woman for her husband and of a father for his son (see Nielsen 1983 and below).

This understanding of God's sole sovereignty and kingship comes clearly to expression in the definition of the Shemaʿ in the Jewish tradition as "the acceptance of the yoke of kingship" (see below), a conception anticipated in Zech 14:9, "YHWH shall become King over all the earth. On that day YHWH shall be one and his name one *(YHWH ʾḥd wšmw ʾḥd).*" Admittedly, Deuteronomy is not concerned with the eschatological kingdom of YHWH as is Zech 14. It depicts him, however, as the sole sovereign who is owner of the cosmos and Lord of the world, in other words, the king (cf. Deut 10:14, and especially v 17, "God of gods and the Lord of lords *(ʾlhy hʾlhym wʾdny hʾdnym),*" paraphrased in Dan 2:47, "God of gods and Lord of kings *(ʾlh ʾlhyn wmrʾ mlkyn),*" and the Targumim to Deut 10:17).

That uniqueness (of the god) is associated with kingship may be deduced from a Ugaritic text (see the NOTE to 6:4) wherein the god declares, "I am one

[= alone] who rules over the gods *(dymlk ʿl ilm).*" One would expect to find in Deuteronomy the term "king" in reference to the one God, but Deuteronomy avoids the use of "king" for God apparently on purpose; see Weinfeld 1972a, p. 84 n. 4.

Love of God

The allegiance to YHWH alone is expressed by the command that follows the Shemaʿ declaration: "you shall love YHWH your God with all your heart, with all your soul, and with all your might." Syntactically the verb *weʾāhabta* joins the imperative *šĕmaʿ* and is conceived as a corollary of the declaration of unity. Compare 5:1, "hear . . . and study *(šĕmaʿ . . . ûlmadtem).*" Verses 4 and 5 form, then, a unit: YHWH is our God alone, he is "one" and (therefore) you shall love; etc. Indeed "the one" is usually the beloved one, as may be learned from Cant 6:9, "[only] one *(ʾḥt)* is my love, my perfect one." Compare also Gen 22:2, "take your son, your only one *(yḥydk)* whom you love *(ʾšr ʾhbt).*" As indicated above, love with all the heart means sole recognition of the beloved to the exclusion of any rival. Indeed, "love" in the ancient Near East connotes loyalty. Thus, when the suzerain demands loyalty from his vassal, he adjures him that he shall love *(raʾāmu)* the king as he loves himself *(VTE,* lines 266–68). Similarly, in the treaties and loyalty oaths of the Greek, Hellenistic, and Roman periods, terms for love and affection *(phileîn* or *eunoieîn)* serve to express loyalty (see Weinfeld 1976b, pp. 383–85).

Although love between God and Israel involves also affection and emotion (compare God's love for Israel in Deut 7:8, 13; 23:6), the practical meaning of the command of love is loyalty and obedience, as is clear from the continuation in 6:6, "These words which I command you this day shall be on your heart," and from other passages in which love is paired with reverence, obedience, and service, such as, "to fear . . . to love him, . . . to serve . . . to observe YHWH's commandments," etc. (10:12; cf. 11:13; 30:16, 20).

Furthermore, the way love is described here ("with all your heart and with all your soul and with all your might *[mʾdk]*"; see the Note) corresponds to the way loyalty is depicted in the vassal treaties. The commands of love there are accompanied by demands of exclusive devotion, as in Deut 6:5, "[love me] with all the heart *(ina kul libbi),* with all the soul *(ina kul napšati).*" Often we find in addition that the vassal should come to the aid of his suzerain with all his force, that is to say, with his army and chariots (see Weinfeld 1976b, pp. 384–85). Thus we read in a Hittite vassal treaty, "If you do not come to aid with full heart . . . with your army and your chariots and will not be prepared to die . . ." (Kühne and Otten 1971, 2.32ff.). Indeed, Deut 6:5 contains all of the elements found in the treaties: devotion with all the heart, with all the soul (i.e., readiness to give one's life), and provision of might and force when necessary. The Targumim and the sages explain the verse exactly in that manner: " 'with all the heart'; 'with all the mind'; 'with all the soul' = 'to be ready to sacrifice one's life' (see the NOTE) and 'with all might' = *(m'd)* with all one's physical capacity and resources (see the NOTE).

"With all the soul" in Deut 6:5 corresponds, then, to the demand in the vassal treaties to be prepared to die for the suzerain, and "with all your might *(bkl m'dk)*" corresponds to the demand to come with all one's military forces to help the suzerain. It is remarkable indeed that Josiah, the only king who is said to have served the Lord "with all his heart, with all his soul and with all his might" (2 Kgs 23:25), sacrificed his life when he came with his army to fight the Egyptian king.

The command in Shemaᶜ to love God "with all the soul" triggered a martyrological tradition in Judaism. Jewish martyrs died with the words of Shemaᶜ on their lips (see, e.g., Spiegel 1969, pp. 17–27). This tradition is classically exemplified by Rabbi ᶜAqiba, who was tortured to death by the Romans bearing on his lips the Shemaᶜ and welcoming his martyrdom as an opportunity to fulfill the command, "you shall love YHWH . . . with all your soul," even if it means that he takes your life *(y. Ber.* 9:7, 14b; *b. Ber.* 61b).

The Yoke of the Kingdom of Heaven

In the rabbinic tradition the Shemaᶜ testimony was defined as the "acceptance of the yoke of the kingdom of heaven *(qbwl/qblt ᶜwl mlkwt šmym)*" (cf. *m. Ber.* 2:2), which perfectly fits the imagery of loyally serving the sovereign on earth. Thus, for example, Nabonidus, the king of Babylon, says that "by mentioning his honorable name let all his enemies bear his yoke forever *(ana zikir šumiya kabtu kullat nākiri . . . ana ūmē ṣâti lišdudu nīri)*" (Langdon 1912, p. 260, 2:44–45). It is interesting that after the recital of Shemaᶜ, which constitutes acceptance of the yoke of the kingdom, the audience proclaims a response used in the Second Temple, "Blessed be the name of his glorious Kingdom forever *(brwk šm kbwd mlkwtw lᶜwlm wᶜd)*" (see *t. Pesaḥ.* 3(2):19; *y. Pesaḥ.* 4:9, 31b; *b. Pesaḥ.* 56a; and cf. Urbach 1979, pp. 400–2). This is similar to Nabonidus's statement that the people bear his yoke forever following the mention of his honorable name *(zikir šumu kabtu = šm kbwd).* Furthermore, the term *kbwd mlkwt* 'glorious kingdom' of the response corresponds literally to Akkadian *melam šarrūti* 'glory of the kingdom', which is used in connection with earthly kings and deities as well (cf. Cassin 1968, pp. 50, 70, 72f.).

In fact, "bearing the yoke" refers to the deity even in Mesopotamia. Thus, the same Nabonidus, who demands that people bear his yoke, declares that he "keeps the words of the gods," that he prays to them "with all his heart," and that "his neck is bowed to draw their yoke" (Langdon 1912, p. 262, 1:7–14). Compare also in the annals of Ashurbanipal, "be gracious toward me, your loyal servant, and let me carry your yoke *(yāti arad pāliḫka kurbannima lašūṭa ab-*

šanka)" (Streck 1916, 2.22, 2:125). It should be added here that the idiom "yoke of the kingdom" is the conventional expression in Akkadian for fulfilling one's duties to the king *(nīr bēlūti/šarrūti).*

"The acceptance of the yoke" means in fact taking a pledge of loyalty, and this turned into the most important liturgy. In the Second Temple period, Shemaᶜ appears to be an established liturgical custom. Every morning in the Temple, the Decalogue and the Shemaᶜ were recited along with the prayer of *ʾEmet wĕyaṣṣib,* on which see below (cf. *m. Tamid* 5:1). The Nash papyrus, which contains the Decalogue and the Shemaᶜ passage, along with the phylacteries of Qumran, which also include the Decalogue with the Shemaᶜ, testify to the fact that the Shemaᶜ liturgy was a prevalent custom during the Second Temple period (see above). As I have shown above, there is evidence that Christians at the time of Trajan observed this morning liturgy. The Shemaᶜ was recited antiphonally: the cantor apparently recited the words, "Hear O Israel, YHWH is our God," while the congregation responded, "YHWH is one." This recital before the public explains the phrase "to read out Shemaᶜ *(prs Šĕmaᶜ)*" in connection with the performance of the Shemaᶜ liturgy (cf. *m. Meg.* 4:3); see Knohl 1983.

Most instructive for understanding the nature of Shemaᶜ is the *ʾEmet wĕyaṣṣib* prayer, which is recited immediately after the Shemaᶜ (no pause is allowed between the Shemaᶜ and *ʾEmet wĕyaṣṣib, m. Ber.* 2:2). As I have shown elsewhere (1976b, pp. 409–12), the *ʾEmet wĕyaṣṣib* constitutes the affirmation of the Shemaᶜ proclamation by the public and reflects the procedure known to us from the fealty oaths sworn to the emperor king. The loyalty oath consisted of two parts, an adjuration by the suzerain and the oath of the vassal. The Shemaᶜ, with its demand to love God, is the imposed obligation, whereas the *ʾEmet wĕyaṣṣib* is the loyalty oath, that is, the affirmation of the imposition of the yoke of the kingdom. In fact, the term "acceptance of the yoke" means the pledge given by the one who takes upon himself the yoke (for *qbl* in this sense cf. Lieberman 1952, p. 200).

The *ʾEmet wĕyaṣṣib* contains the following elements:

1. a formal affirmation of the demands of God the sovereign: "it is true, firm, established, and confirmed . . . this command upon us *(ʾmt wyṣb wnkwn wqym . . .)";*
2. a declaration about taking upon themselves the kingdom of God, "it is true, he is the God of the universe, our king . . . his kingdom . . . endures forever *(ʾmt ʾlhy ᶜwlm mlknw . . . wmlkwtw . . . lᶜd qymt)";*
3. a declaration of the validity of the obligation for coming generations, "Upon us, our children, our generations and for all the coming generations of the seed of Israel *(ᶜlynw, ᶜl bnynw wᶜl dwrwtynw wᶜl kl dwrwt zrᶜ yśrʾl ᶜbdyk)";* and

4. the exclusiveness of divine kingship, "our King . . . our redeemer . . . there is no God beside you *(mlknw . . . gwʾlnw . . . ʾyn ʾlhym zwltk).*"

The pattern of the pledge embodied in Shemaʿ and *ʾEmet wĕyaṣṣib* follows exactly the pattern of the loyalty oath to the Assyrian emperor as it appears in the vassal treaties of Esarhaddon, which were composed at the time that Deuteronomy was crystallized. In the *VTE* we find the adjuration of the suzerain, which corresponds to the Shemaʿ, and the oath of the vassal, which corresponds to *ʾEmet wĕyaṣṣib.* Thus we read in the adjuration of Esarhaddon, "You shall love Ashurbanipal, King [crown prince, see below] of Assyria, as you love yourselves. . . . You shall instruct your sons who will live in the future . . . you shall not set over yourselves another king, another lord" *(VTE,* lines 266ff.). This corresponds to the Shemaʿ passage with its statement of the unity of God, the demand of love, and the instruction of the children. A similar overlap exists between the *VTE* and the *ʾEmet wĕyaṣṣib.* The *VTE* reads, "as long as we, our sons and our grandsons live, the crown prince designate Ashurbanipal will be our King and our lord. We shall not place another king . . . over ourselves, our sons, our grandsons" *(VTE,* lines 494ff.). This corresponds to the *ʾEmet wĕyaṣṣib,* which also focuses on the exclusivity of God the king and the commitment for the future generation. The *ʾEmet wĕyaṣṣib* declaration in its present form is late, but its essence seems to go back to the period of the crystallization of the Shemaʿ liturgy.

6:10–19

After the proclamation of unity and the injunction about keeping loyalty to God (6:4–9) comes the warning about the erosion of faith that might occur after the entrance into the land, when the people would be exposed to foreign worship (v 14). The new, rich civilization that they are going fully to enjoy (vv 10b–11) will induce them to forget their God and his commandments (cf. 8:7–20) and to adopt the gods of the nations around them. Enjoyment and satiety, which may cause apostasy and abandonment of the true ways of YHWH, are ideas most characteristic of the literature of the eighth and seventh centuries, during which Deuteronomy came into being. Thus, Hosea states, "Your fathers seemed to me like the fig in its first season, but when they came to Baal Peor [cf. Num 25:1–9; Deut 3:29; 4:3] they turned aside to shamefulness" (9:10). In a style close to that of the present passage and of 8:11–14 (cf. 17:17, 20), Hosea refers to God's words, "I knew you in the desert in a land of drought. When they grazed they were sated, when they were sated they grew haughty and so they forgot me" (13:5–6). Similarly, we read in the Song of Moses, "he [YHWH] set him [Israel] atop the highlands to feast on the yield of the earth . . . so Jeshurun grew fat and kicked . . . he forsook the God who made him

. . . they aroused his jealousy *[yqn'hw;* cf. Deut 6:15] with foreign [gods] and vexed him with abominations" (Deut 32:13–16). The same idea is reflected in the prologue to this song, "When I bring them [with Targumim; MT *'by'nw]* into the land flowing with milk and honey that I swore to their fathers, and they eat, are sated, and grow fat and turn to other gods and worship them . . . breaking my covenant" (31:20).

Satiety usually invokes rebellion and mistrust in God, therefore the author warns them not to put YHWH to the test as they did in the desert (v 16; cf. Exod 17:1–7; Num 14:22). But there is a twist in the meaning of "test" here. Whereas the test at Massah, as described in Exod 11:2, 7, was to see whether God was able to provide their needs (cf. especially Exod 17:7), here the testing means also to try his patience by violating his commandments, in order to see whether he will react and punish. Testing God stands here (v 16) in opposition to keeping God's commandments (v 17). These two meanings of "testing" are attested in Ps 78, a didactic poem that has close affinities to Deuteronomy (cf. Junker 1953). Here we read, "and they tested *(wynsw)* God in their heart to demand food for themselves . . . saying, 'can God spread a feast in the desert?' " etc. (vv 18–19), and alongside this, "and they tested *(wynsw)* and rebelled against God most high, and did not keep his decrees" (v 56). Not keeping God's commandments means to test God; therefore one understands why the injunction to keep commandments in Deut 6:17 follows the warning not to test YHWH in 6:16. The concept of "testing" has thus been broadened to connote disobedience in general caused by temptations of all sorts. This concept has been further developed in the Jewish literature of the Second Temple period. Here we find that one tries God by yielding to temptations caused by Satan, who is the "evil spirit" *(yṣr hrʿ)* hidden in man.

In the Jewish literature of the Second Temple period mistrust in God is seen as motivated by Satan/Beliar(l), who was identified with the "evil spirit *(yṣr hrʿ)*" (cf. the *Testament of Asher* 1:8–9). Satan and the "evil spirit" were in turn considered to be the embodiment of idolatry. Submission to the evil spirit, in other words, to the power of Satan and Beliar(l), is like worshiping idols. Compare Rabbi Yanai's interpretation of the scripture in Ps 81:10, "You shall not have in your midst *(bk)* a foreign god and you shall not bow down to an alien god," which he renders, "the foreigner inside you you shall not make him king over you" *(y. Ned.* 9:1, 41a; for other references see Urbach 1979, pp. 473–75, 482). This idea has been used in the interpretation of Deut 6:10–19 that warns against following "other gods" (v 14) on the one hand, and the testing of God (v 16) on the other. (For the understanding of "other gods" as Satan and *yṣr hrʿ*, cf. the sources quoted in Urbach 1975, pp. 472–73.) It also comes to expression in the NT story about Jesus' rejection of the kingdom of Satan (Luke 4:1–13; Matt 4:1–11; cf. Mark 1:12–13). Jesus is tempted by Satan in the desert and is offered sovereignty over the world if he will submit and bow down to him. Jesus answers, "it is written, 'to YHWH your God you shall bow down and him only shall you worship' " (Deut 6:13; see the NOTES). Then Jesus is taken by Satan to the pinnacle of the Temple and is asked to throw himself from there if it is true that he is the son of God. Jesus then replies, "it is written, 'You shall not put YHWH your God to the test' " (Deut 6:16). All of this is based on a midrash on Deut 6:10–19. Testing God in Deut 6:16 is ascribed to Satan (cf. the story of Job), who tempts Jesus in the desert, as Israel was tempted there (cf. also Ps 95:8–9), whereas the verse about worshiping God alone in Deut 6:13 is interpreted as a demand to exclude Satan from divine worship. The idea of an existing dominion of Satan is known to us from the Qumran writings (1QS 1:16–18; 3:19–22; 1QM 13:11; 14:8–9). There we find the term *mmšlt blyʿl* 'the reign of Belial', whom the "sons of light" fight by keeping the laws, "all those who come into the order of the community should enter into the covenant to act according to everything which he [God] commanded, and not to turn back from following after him out of any fear, anxiety, or temptation which may arise under the *reign of Belial*" (1QS 1:16–18). Serving Satan/Belial in opposition to God appears in the apocalyptic *Ascension of Isaiah,* where it is said "that Manasseh (who put an idol in the Holy of Holies) forsook the service of the God of the fathers and served Satan and his angels and his powers" (2:2). There Satan is identified with Samael and Belial. (For Belial in the preceding sources see Flusser 1958 and Yadin 1955, pp. 211–13.) As indicated above, the idea of the rule of the evil spirit as opposed to rule of God also appears in rabbinic literature.

Deuteronomy 6:10–19, which demands complete devotion to YHWH alone, and which forbids one to follow foreign gods or to put YHWH to the test, is then most appropriate for such a polemic against Belial as is told in the NT passages. In the NT story, Satan tempts Jesus in the desert and is rebuffed on the basis of three verses from Deut 6: v 16, the prohibition of testing God; the exclusion of Satan from divine power, based on v 14 ("foreign gods"); and the prohibition of worshiping Satan implicit in v 13. The "worship *(ʿbd)*" in the latter verse is combined with the "bowing down *(hštḥwh)*" of Deut 5:9 (= Exod 20:5; cf. Matt 4:10; Luke 4:7) and seems to represent the rabbinic exegesis of "foreign gods" as referring to Satan and *yṣr hr*ʿ (see above).

6:20–25

As already indicated in the INTRODUCTION to this section, the beginning of the sermon in 6:4–25 and its end are concerned with the education of children (vv 7, 20–25). Here as well as in Exod 12:26–27 and 13:14 we find an instance of formal national education. The child asks, or is rather motivated to ask, about the meaning of the special laws and customs observed among the Israelites. The answer is that God has delivered us from Egypt, from the house of bondage, and in memory of this deliverance we celebrate the feast of Passover and keep the laws and customs enjoined by YHWH. As shown in the INTRODUCTION to this section, the instruction of the children by questions and answers occurs also in connection with the entrance into the land at Gilgal (Josh 4:6–7, 21–23).

The Exodus and the entrance into the land, the two gracious acts of the God of Israel, serve then as the basis of ancient Israelite education. Passover, the feast of the Exodus, is therefore the proper time to educate the children through the ceremonies that dramatize the Exodus. This educational procedure continues in Judaism until the present day. On the night of Passover the children have to be prepared to ask why this night is different from all other nights, and so on, and the answer given is Deut 6:20–25, "We were slaves," etc. *(m. Pĕsaḥ.* 10:4). The education of children by telling them the history of their ancestors who were freed from oppression is something peculiar to the Israelite nation, and for this reason the God of Israel is marked as the God who freed his people from Egypt (the opening of the Decalogue). Pagan nations, who marked their gods by their mythological features, educated their children through mythology. Thus we read in the Mesopotamian creation epic, "Let the father recite [the names of the God Marduk] and impart them to his son" *(ANET,* p. 72, epilogue of *Enuma elish).* In the Second Temple period the Passover was indeed marked as the time of freedom *(zĕman ḥerûtênu).* Compare the Passover liturgy (Singer 1915, p. 328).

One must indicate, however, that the release from Egypt in Deut 6:20–25 does not just motivate the Passover ceremony as in the other sources but serves also as motivation for the observance of the law in general. Furthermore, the Exodus is here combined with the entrance into the land, and both acts serve as the basis for the observance of God's laws. Thus, education in Deuteronomy is not linked to Passover alone but is a process going on throughout the year.

THE CONQUEST OF THE LAND; THE STRUGGLE WITH THE CANAANITES AND THEIR CULTURE (7:1–26)

7 [1]When YHWH your God brings you to the land that you come in to
occupy and he dislodges many nations before you—the Hittites, Girgashites,
Amorites, Canaanites, Perizzites, Hivites, and Jebusites, seven nations more
numerous and mightier than you—[2]and YHWH your God delivers them to
you, and you defeat them, you must doom them to destruction. You shall grant
them no terms and you shall not spare them. [3]You shall not intermarry with
them: do not give your daughter to his son and his daughter do not take for your
son; [4]for he will turn away your son from me so that they worship other gods;
then will YHWH's anger blaze forth against you and he will destroy you
quickly. [5]Instead, this is what you shall do to them: you shall tear down their

altars, smash their pillars, cut down their sacred trees, and burn their images in fire.

6For you are a holy people to YHWH your God; YHWH your God has chosen you to be his treasured people from among all the peoples on earth. 7It is not because you are the most numerous of peoples that YHWH desired you and chose you—indeed, you are the smallest of peoples; 8but it was because of YHWH's love for you and because he kept the oath he swore to your fathers that YHWH freed you with a mighty hand and released you from the house of bondage, from the power of Pharaoh king of Egypt.

9Know, therefore, that YHWH your God is the only God, the steadfast God who keeps his gracious covenant for those who love him and keep his commandments, to the thousandth generation, 10but who repays them who hate him to their face to destroy them; he is never late with the one who hates him—he repays him to his face. 11Therefore, observe the commandments, the laws, and the judgments with which I charge you today.

12Because you obey these judgments and observe them faithfully, YHWH your God will keep for you the gracious covenant that he made on oath with your fathers: 13He will love you and bless you and multiply you; he will bless the fruit of your womb and the fruit of your soil, your grain, wine, and oil, the increase of your herd and the lambing of your flock, in the land that he swore to your fathers to give you. 14You shall be blessed above all other peoples: there shall be no sterile male or female among you or among your livestock. 15YHWH will remove from you all sickness; all the evil diseases of Egypt, about which you know, he will not bring upon you, but he will put them upon all your enemies.

16You shall devour all the peoples whom YHWH your God delivers to you. You shall show them no pity. You shall not serve their gods, for that would be a snare to you. 17Should you say in your heart, "These nations are more numerous than we; how can we dispossess them?" 18Do not fear them. You have but to remember what YHWH your God did to Pharaoh and all the Egyptians: 19the prodigious acts that you saw with your own eyes, the signs and portents, the mighty hand and outstretched arm by which YHWH your God liberated you. Thus will YHWH your God do to all the peoples you now fear. 20YHWH your God will also send the hornet against them, until those who are left in hiding perish before you. 21You shall have no dread of them, for YHWH your God is in your midst, a great and awesome God.

22YHWH your God will dislodge those peoples before you little by little; you may not put an end to them quickly, lest the wild beasts multiply to your hurt. 23YHWH your God will deliver them to you, throwing them into great panic until they are wiped out. 24He will deliver their kings into your hand, and you shall make their names perish from under the heavens; no man shall stand up to you, until you have wiped them out.

25You shall burn the images of their gods with fire; you shall not covet the silver and gold on them and keep it for yourselves, lest you be ensnared thereby;

because it is an abomination to YHWH your God. 26You must not bring an abomination into your house, or you will be under ban like it; you shall make it detestable and abominable, for it is under ban.

TEXTUAL NOTES

7:2. *you defeat them (hḥrm tḥrym).* LXX: *afanismō afanieîs* 'you shall utterly destroy them'. This, together with other terms for destruction, is the common rendering of *ḥrm.* On other occasions, the LXX translates *ḥrm* with *anathema,* which means devotion by divine sanction. Thus at the end of chap. 7, in v 26, the LXX has *anathema;* and similarly, in 13:16, *hḥrm* is rendered *anathemati anathematieite* as if it were in Hebrew *hḥrm tḥrymw.* Similarly, the Aramaic Targumim usually translate *ḥrm* by *gmr/šṣy* 'destroy' *(Neof.)* but occasionally *šmtʾ* 'anathema (cursed)' (cf. *Tg. Ps.-J.* 7:26; 13:18), also *ʾpršʾ* 'devotion' (Lev 27:29). In Deut 7:2, *Tg. Ps.-J.* has both: "you will destroy them with the anathema of YHWH *(gmrʾ tgmrwn ythwn bšmtʾ d YHWH).*"

and you shall not spare them. Hebrew: *wlʾ tḥnm,* literally, "and you shall not be gracious toward them." The root of the verb is *ḥnn.* Rabbinic exegesis associated the verb with the root *ḥnh* 'to encamp' and understood the verse as a prohibition against allowing the Canaanites to own property in the land *(b. ʿAbod. Zar.* 20b). The *NJPS,* following Ehrlich, translates "give them no quarter." The archaic English idiom "to give quarter" means to grant clemency, which is in fact the meaning of the verse, but the translation alludes as well to exegesis based on the root *ḥnh* ('quarter' in the sense of lodging).

3. *You shall not intermarry. htḥtn* is a denominative from *ḥatan* 'son-in-law', and appears sometimes, as here, with preposition *bĕ* (compare Josh 23:12; 1 Sam 18:21, 23, 26; Ezra 9:14) and sometimes with the preposition *ʾlt* (1 Kgs 3:1; Gen 34:9); in 2 Chr 18:1 with *lĕ.*

4. *for he will turn away your son.* All the Targumim and Syriac have the plural: "they will turn *(ytʿyn).*"

from me. Some prefer to take the letter *yod* here as an abbreviation for YHWH, but this is unnecessary. See the NOTE to 7:4.

so that they worship. The Samaritan Pentateuch and the LXX have singular *(wʿbd),* which corresponds to "your son" in the previous clause; but see the NOTE.

6. *For you are a holy people to YHWH . . . to be his treasured people.* "To be to someone *(hyh l)*" means to gain a certain status in relation to somebody. Thus, for example, to be a woman *to* somebody *(lhywt lw lʾšh)* means to become his wife; cf. Gen 12:19; 16:13; etc. (in Akkadian: *ana aššūti).* Mark the difference in Aramaic between *ʾintu* -"status of wifehood" (Gen 12:19; 16:3) and *ʾittʾa* -"wife"; to be a son or daughter *to* somebody means to gain the status of a son, or daughter, in other words, to become an adopted son or daughter (Exod 2:10; Esth 2:7, 15; cf. 2 Sam 7:14; in Akkadian: *ana marūti);* see Paul 1978. By the

same token, "to be a people to God" (Exod 6:7; etc.) means to gain the status of a vassalship (see Weinfeld 1972a, p. 82 note). In Deut 7:6, it refers to a special privileged status (see the NOTE).

has chosen you (bk bḥr). The Samaritan Pentateuch, LXX, Targumim, and Syriac and some manuscripts read "and *(wbk)* has chosen you," as in 14:2.

treasured people. The LXX translates *periousion* 'superior'; the Aramaic Targumim translated *ḥbyb* 'beloved'. The Vg translates most correctly *peculium,* that which is set apart being of special value, which fits the original meaning of the term (see the NOTE).

7. *desired you (ḥšq).* Literally, "lusted after you" or "hung on you." Compare Gen 34:8; Deut 21:11; Ps 91:14; and for the physical sense "to stick, bind to," cf. Exod 27:17; 38:17, 28.

8. *released you (wypdk).* Literally, "ransomed you" (cf. Exod 13:13, 15; 21:8; 34:20; Lev 19:20; Num 18:15, 16, 17), but figuratively, "rescued" (2 Sam 4:9; 1 Kgs 1:29; etc.). Compare the verb *gʾl,* which basically means redeem or reclaim (Lev 25:25ff.; Jer 32:7–8) but is used figuratively as release and rescue from trouble (Gen 48:16 etc.) and actually parallels *pdh* (cf. Hos 13:14, Jer 31:11).

9. *steadfast (nʾmn).* The root *ʾmn,* like Akkadian *danānu,* implies both strength and validity; see Weinfeld 1982c, pp. 46–48.

(and keeps his) commandment. Several manuscripts, the Samaritan Pentateuch, the versions, Targumim, and *Qere* read plural: "commandments."

10. The suffix is singular *(pnyw, lhʾbydw)* after plural: "them who hate him *(lśnʾyw)*" is to be explained as distinctive: every one of them; cf. Exod 31:14 *(mḥllyh mwt ywmt),* Lev 17:14 *(kl ʾklyw ykrt),* Judg 1:34b; 7:4; Jer 22:46, see *GKC* §145, 1.

to his face. The MT has twice *ʾel (panayw),* while the Samaritan Pentateuch has *ʿal (panayw).* For the interchange of *ʾel* with *ʿal (panayw),* cf. Job 13:15 with 21:31. In the latter the idea is similar to that of the present verse: "who will upbraid him to his face? who will repay him *(yšlm lw)* for what he has done?"

the one who hates him (lśnʾw). The Samaritan Pentateuch has the same as in the first part of the verse—*lśnʾyw* in the plural—but see the TEXTUAL NOTE above.

12. *Because you obey. ʿeqeb* means "following after"; "in the footsteps of" *(ʿaqeb* 'heel'); "in consequence of" (cf. 8:20; Gen 22:18; 26:5; 2 Sam 12:6; Num 14:24; Isa 5:23; Pss 19:12; 119:33, 112). See the discussion of Naḥmanides on 7:12. Compare the expression *lrgl* 'following after' in Gen 30:30: "and God blessed you because of me" (literally, at my feet, *lrgly),* which is parallel there to *bgll* in v 27.

14. *there shall be no sterile . . . or among your livestock.* One would expect *lʾ yhyh lk . . . bk wbbhmtk,* but cf. 1:36 for a similar structure of a sentence: *wlw ʾtn ʾt hʾrṣ . . . wlbnyw* instead of *wlw wlbnyw ʾtn ʾt hʾrṣ.* See Driver 1902, ad loc. for other examples.

15. *about which you know.* 5Q Deut 1 I:1 (DJD 3.170) adds *wʾšr rʾyth* (over the line); compare the LXX: *has hērorakas kai hosa egnos.*

16. *You shall devour.* Literally, "eat up *(ʾkl),*" but with the meaning "to destroy." Compare Jer 10:25, "they have devoured *(ʾklw)* Jacob, devoured him *(ʾklhw)* and put an end to him *(wyklhw)";* see also Jer 30:16; 50:7. The LXX has "you shall devour the spoil *(skula),*" apparently under the influence of 20:14.

17. *these nations. (hgwym hʾlh).* Qumran: *hʾl* (5Q 1, *I* :3 [DJD 3.170]); cf. the MT in v 22; and cf. 4:42; 19:11.

how. (ʾykh). Qumran: *ʾyk* (5Q 1, *I* :4 [DJD 3.170]) and the Samaritan Pentateuch, which always has *ʾyk* instead of *ʾykh;* cf. 1:12; 12:30; 18:21; 32:30.

18. *you have but to remember. (zkr tzkr). zkr* means not merely "to remember" but "to keep in mind"; see the NOTE to 5:12.

19. *the prodigious acts that you saw.* 5Q 1 I:4: (DJD 3.170) adds *hywm* 'today' after *hmst* and before *ʾšr rʾw ʿynyk* 'that you saw with your eyes'.

by which. The relative particle *ʾašer* is used here elliptically: "where with/by which"; cf. Judg 8:15, *ʾšr ḥrptm ʾty* 'about which [= whom] you mocked me'.

22. *those. haʾel* instead of *haʾelleh;* cf. 4:42. The Samaritan Pentateuch has here and in other instances *haʾelleh* instead of *haʾel;* and so here 4Q Dt^{f}, 2–3 (White 1990, 164). see the TEXTUAL NOTE to v 17.

little by little. The repetition expresses a gradual process; compare 28:43 and see *GKC* §133, 3k3.

you may not (lʾ twkl). For this understanding of *lʾ twkl* as opposed to "you will not be able" see 12:17; 16:3; 17:15; 21:16; 22:3, 19, 29; 24:4; and cf. Gen 43:22; Exod 19:23; and the use of *lʾ ykhl* in the Aramaic documents (Muffs 1969, p. 36, n. 2).

23. *will deliver them to you.* MT: *(wntnm) . . . lpnyk,* 4Q Dt^{c} (Duncan 1989, Fig. 7) and LXX: *bydyk, lpny,* and *byd* alternate in meaning; it seems that Qumran and LXX are influenced by the next verse, which has *ntn . . . bydk.*

throwing them into great panic (hmm mhwmh). The *hmm* is pointed as if derived from *hwm,* and the same applies to the noun *mhwmh.* But the text in Exod 23:27 on which 7:23 is dependent has *whmty,* a form derived from *hmm;* cf. also *hmmny* in Jer 51:34 and 2 Chr 15:6, *hmmm.* See also the Rashbam's discussion of this verse.

24. *make their names perish (whʾbdt ʾt šmm).* The Samaritan Pentateuch has *wʾbdt (piʿel),* like 12:3.

no man shall stand up to you. MT: *bpnyk;* Samaritan and 4Q Dt^{f} (White, *ibid.* p. 164): *lpnyk. bpny* means "in the face of, with hostile intention," which is suitable for this content. *lpny* means "before," with no hostility implied *(BDB).*

until you have wiped them out (ʿd hišmidka ʾtm). Similarly 28:48; Josh 11:14; 1 Kgs 15:29; 2 Kgs 10:17. In all of these cases the form is infinitive *hiphʿil* with punctuation of *Hireq* instead of *Patah;* cf. also Num 21:35; Deut 3:3 *(hišʾir);* Lev 14:43 *(hiqṣot);* and Jer 50:36 *(hirgiʿa . . . hirgiz);* see also Ibn Ezra to this verse and *GKC* §53 1.

NOTES

7:1. *When YHWH your God brings you to the land.* Compare the same phrase in 6:10, both dependent on Exod 13:5, 13. See the NOTE to 6:10.

that you come in to occupy. This is characteristic phrase of Deuteronomy; see Weinfeld 1972a, p. 392.

dislodges. Hebrew: *wĕnašal,* used here and in v 22 in a transitive sense, as in Exod 3:5 and Josh 5:15 (both of which refer to the removal of a shoe). In Deut 19:5 and 28:40, the same verb is used intransitively. The former verse refers to the head of an ax becoming dislodged, while the latter refers to leaves falling off a tree. In 2 Kgs 16:6 the verb is used in the *piʿel* form: *wayĕnaššel ʾt hyhwdym mʾylwt* 'and he dislodged the Judeans from Elath'.

Hittites, Girgashites . . . seven nations. There are twenty-seven enumerations in the Bible of the peoples that inhabited the land before the Israelite settlement. Only three of these lists contain seven nations (this verse, Josh 3:10, and Josh 24:11). Far more common are six-name lists (eleven in all), which omit the Girgashites. T. Ishida (1979) has therefore proposed that the seven-name lists are based on the six-name lists, but the Girgashites have been added in order to reconcile the lists with the typology of seven nations.

The Girgashites are added in various positions in the lists, but otherwise the order of the lists is somewhat consistent. The last three nations are almost always the Perizzites, the Hivites, and the Jebusites. The first three nations vary in the order of their listing, but all three formed the main bulk of the pre-Israelite population in Eretz-Israel. The Canaanites mostly designated the coastal population associated with the Egyptian province of Canaan; the Amorites usually referred to the population of the hill country; while the Hittites referred to groups of fugitives from the Anatolian regions (see below) who later formed the neo-Hittite small kingdoms. These three components of the pre-Israelite population are well reflected in Ezekiel's words addressed to Jerusalem: "your origin and your birth are the land of the Canaanites; your father was an Amorite and your mother was a Hittite" (16:3, cf. v 45).

According to Ishida, in the early six-name lists the Canaanites are the first, reflecting the use of the term *Kinaḫḫu* for the Egyptian province of Syro-Palestine from the fifteenth century B.C.E. on (see above, in the NOTE to 1:7). In the later lists from the ninth century B.C.E. on, the Amorites are the first, reflecting the use of *Amurru* as the usual term for Syro-Palestine in the neo-Assyrian inscriptions of that period. In the latest six-name lists the order is the Hittites, the Amorites, and the Canaanites. This order occurs in the present verse, in Deut 20:12, in Josh 9:1, and in Josh 12:8, all of which are Deuteronomic or deuteronomistic passages, and they reflect the usage of the geographical-gentilic terms in neo-Assyrian inscriptions of the seventh century B.C.E. *Hatti* in these inscriptions is a common term for Palestine (cf. Josh 1:4, "all the land of the Hittites," in a Deuteronomic context, which overlaps the neo-Assyrian form, *māt Hatti gimriša* 'all the land of Hatti'; see references in Hawkins 1973, p. 153). *Amurru,* meaning 'west', is already an archaic term for the area; and the term *Kinaḫḫu* = *Knʿn* is virtually unknown.

The Hittites constituted an empire in Anatolia and Syria in the fifteenth and fourteenth century B.C.E. After the collapse of the Hittite Empire at the end of the thirteenth century B.C.E., when the "sea peoples" attacked the Anatolian and Syrian coast, there came down to Palestine hosts of refugees and immigrants consisting of various ethnic groups including Hittites, Jebusites, Hivites, and Girgashites, who settled in the densely populated areas in the hill country. They seized power in the few existing cities in the mountains such as Shechem, Gibeon, and Hebron; see B. Mazar 1986, pp. 35–48; and see the NOTE below on the Hivites.

The Girgashites were apparently from Karkiša, a place in Hittite Anatolia; see B. Mazar 1986, p. 43 n. 23. According to O. Margalith (1983–84), Karkiša is Gergis, mentioned in Herodotus 5.122 as occupied by the Teucrians; the Teucrians equal—in his opinion—the *ṯkr* who were dwelling in Dor on the Palestinian coast, as attested in the Wen-Amun Egyptian document of the eleventh century (Schachermeyer 1982, pp. 112–13). The Rabbis preserved a tradition that the Girgashites fled to Africa *(Lev. Rab.* [Margaliot 1953, 1960, p. 386]; cf. Levy 1969, pp. 76–77.

For the Amorites and the Canaanites, see the NOTE to 1:7.

The Perizzites appear sometimes in combination with the Canaanites (Gen 13:7; 34:30; Judg 1:4–5) and once with the Rephaim (Josh 17:15). It has been suggested that they represent a non-Semitic ethnic group, especially because they usually go together with the Hivites and Jebusites, who are considered to have been of Anatolian origin (see below).

The Hivites were found in Shechem, in the Tetrapolis of the Gibeonites (Gibeon, Beeroth, Kephira, and Kiriath-yearim: Gen 34:2; Josh 9:7; 11:19) and in Mount Lebanon, at the foot of Mount Hermon (Josh 11:3; Judg 3:3). According to B. Mazar (1986, pp. 39–40) they originated in the border region between the Hittite and Egyptian empires in the thirteenth century B.C.E. and moved from there to the south (cf. 2 Sam 24:4 and the cities in the hill country mentioned above). Mendenhall (1973, pp. 154–63) maintains that they were Luwians who came from Cilicia, which is called *Ḫuwe* in the Assyrian inscriptions.

The Jebusites were the inhabitants of Jerusalem (= Jebus) in the twelfth and eleventh centuries, until David's reign. They apparently migrated, like the Hivites, from the land of the Hittites. This claim may be supported by the fact that some of David's military commanders were Hittites: Uriah the Hittite (2 Sam 11:8ff.) and Ahimelek the Hittite (1 Sam 26:6). According to B. Mazar (1986, pp. 41–42) the name of the Jebusite who sold David the threshing floor where he built an altar to YHWH (2 Sam 24:18–25), Arawnah/Awarnah, is derived from Hurrian-Hittite *eweri,* which means 'Lord'. Further support for the Hurrian-Hittite origin of the Jebusites comes from the fact that the Jerusalemite priestly cult has many affinities with Hittite-Hurrian rituals (see Weinfeld 1983b).

more numerous and mightier than you. Compare v 17; 4:38, "greater and mightier"; 9:1; 11:23.

2. *doom them to destruction.* Hebrew: *hḥrm tḥrym,* infinitive absolute and imperfect of the verb *ḥrm* in the *hiphʿil* form. The root *ḥrm* in the Semitic languages has two connotations, forbidden and sacred (cf. *ḥarim* in Arabic); and compare the root *qdš,* which normally means "sacred" but is used in Deut 22:9 in the sense of "forbidden." In the context of war and punitive anti-idolatrous action, the verb in the *hiphʿil* is used to describe the consecration of the condemned to God, by dint of which they are doomed to total destruction (cf. Exod 22:19; Deut 13:16; Lev 27:29; 1 Sam 15:3). Usually the property of the banned is placed under the ban, that is to say, it is considered consecrated property (cf. Lev 27:28b; Num 18:14; 21:2–3; Josh 6:17–19; 1 Sam 15:3, 18; Mic 4:12), with the exception of the Deuteronomic/deuteronomistic legislator who allows the spoil of the banned Canaanites to be taken (Deut 2:35; 3:7; Josh 8:2). The religious nature of the institution of the *ḥerem* is most apparent in the Moabite inscription of Mesha, king of Moab, in which he tells of his massacre of the seven thousand Israelites after having consecrated *(hḥrm)* them to his god Ashtar-Kemosh *(KAI* 181:16–17). Similar practices are attested in the ancient world; cf. Lohfink 1986, 5.180–99. The verb *heḥerim* has in the meantime come to mean simply 'destroy'; see Isa 11:15; 34:2; Jer 25:9; 51:3; Mal 3:24.

The *ḥerem* originally followed a vow (e.g., Num 21:2–3) or a votive proclamation (Josh 6:17–19, cf. Judg 21:5: "a big oath"). This association is also reflected in the Second Temple period and in rabbinic usage, where *ḥerem* is understood as a communal vow for exclusion or extirpation (cf. Horbury 1985, pp. 19–38). There is a significant difference, however, between the First Temple *ḥerem* 'vow', which involved execution, and the Second Temple 'vow', which involved separation. Thus, for example, in Judg 21:5–11 nonattendance at the assembly is punished by execution, whereas nonattendance at the assembly in the time of Ezra is punished by separation *(hbdl;* cf. Isa 56:3; Ezra 9:1; Neh 9:2; 13:3) and confiscation *(ḥrm)* of property (Ezra 10:8). The latter is close to the Pharisaic *ḥerem,* which means exclusion from the community. As Horbury has shown (1985), however, in spite of the differences in the idea of the *ḥerem* between the First Temple and the Second Temple periods, there is a continuity in the concept of covenantal penalty (i.e., excommunication) from the biblical sources to the prerabbinic and rabbinic ones. The *ḥerem* vow was usually accompanied by an oath or curse (cf. Josh 6:26 in connection with the ban of Jericho and Judg 21:5), which involved divine sanction for the violation of the *ḥerem.* For covenantal curses bearing the character of excommunication in Deut 27:15–26, see Weinfeld 1983d, pp. 81–84.

As I indicate in the COMMENT to this chapter, the *ḥerem* of the Canaanites in Deuteronomy is conceived as an a priori decree, not dependent on any vow or oath, and bears thus a utopian stamp. The implementation of the *ḥerem* of the Canaanites in the deuteronomistic sources (Josh 10:28–43; 11:11–23) is wishful thinking, an attempt to adjust reality to the ideal norm, which was never implemented (cf. Judg 1:21–34; 1 Kgs 9:20–21).

grant them no terms. Literally, "you shall make no covenant with them *(lʾ tkrt lhm bryt)"*; cf. Exod 23:32; 34:12. It appears in a historical context in Josh 9:6 and 1 Sam 11:1, where it implies granting conditions (corvée) by the superior party to the inferior one. The Israelites make a covenant with the Gibeonites, imposing on them corvée duties (Josh 9:15, 21) while the people of Jabesh-Gilead, as the inferior party, ask the Ammonites to establish a covenant with them, namely, to let them survive on the condition that they serve them *(krt lnw bryt wnʿbdk,* 1 Sam 11:1). In all of these cases the expression is to "cut a covenant to *(krt bryt l)*" and not cut a covenant "with/between *(ʿm/byn),*" as in agreements with equal parties. Such agreements for corvée work are attested in Egypt and are called there *brt bḥ* 'covenant of corvée'; cf. Görg 1977, pp. 25–36; and cf. Weinfeld 1985a.

and you shall not spare them. Literally, "show them no grace"; compare v 16, "You shall devour all the peoples . . . show them no pity *(lʾ tḥws ʿynk ʿlyhm),*" and cf. also 28:50, "a fierce enemy . . . who does not regard the old and does not spare *(lʾ yḥn)* the young," which is to be compared with Isa 13:18, "[the Medes] who show no pity to the fruit of the womb and do not spare *(lʾ tḥws ʿynm)* the sons."

3. *you shall not intermarry with them.* Compare Gen 34:9 and see the COMMENT below.

do not give your daughter to his son and his daughter do not take for your son. Compare Exod 34:16; Judg 3:6. A negative attitude to mixed marriages is reflected in the patriarchal stories (Gen 24:3; 26:34–35; 27:46; 28:6, 8–9) and in the stories of the Judges (14:3). But there the motivation for the prohibition is nationalistic, while here and in the law of Exod 34:16 it is motivated by the danger of worshiping idols. In the period of Ezra and Nehemiah, when the danger of idolatry was over, the motivation is contamination of the holy seed (Ezra 9:2; Neh 9:12).

4. *he will turn away your son.* It is not clear who the subject is here, in other words, who will turn away the son (cf. Rashi and Ibn Ezra). It seems that the author has in mind the foreigner in general; for the phrase "turn away from YHWH *(sr mʾḥry YHWH),*" see 1 Sam 12:20; 2 Kgs 18:6; and compare 2 Kgs 10:29, "turn away from idols." In Exod 34:16 this concept is expressed by "they will lead astray your sons after their gods *(whznw ʾt bnyk ʾḥry ʾlhyhm).*" The verb *znh,* literally, 'whore after', is not used in the Deuteronomic sources, where *swr* is used instead.

from me. Moses, the speaker, is here merged with God, on whose behalf he speaks. Compare 11:14; 17:3; 28:20; 29:4–5; and Dillmann 1886, p. 273.

then will YHWH's anger blaze forth against you and he will destroy you quickly. Compare 6:14–15, and see the COMMENT. The change from singular to plural occurs twice in 7:4: "he will turn away *your* (sing.) son . . . so that *they* worship other gods"; and "YHWH's anger [will] blaze forth against *you* [pl.: *bkm]* and he will destroy *you* [sing.: *whšmydk].*" This stylistic change might have been influenced by 6:14–15—influenced in turn by the first commandment of the Decalogue and see the NOTE to 6:14–15—which also has the interchange of plural with singular: "Do not [pl.] follow other gods . . . lest the anger of YHWH *your* [sing.] God blaze forth against *you* [sing.] and he will destroy *you* [sing.] quickly." Compare 4:26; 11:17; 28:20.

5. *you shall tear down their altars, smash their pillars, cut down their sacred trees, and burn their images in fire.* Compare Exod 34:13, which, like the present pericope, opens with the adversative particle *ky* (cf. Exod 23:24b) and is also associated with the prohibition of intermarriage, concluding a covenant with the Canaanites and worshiping idols (cf. also Judg 2:3; Exod 23:24). The verbs for destroying the altars and the pillars are identical in both sources, *ntṣ* and *šbr,* respectively; but the verbs for cutting down the sacred trees are different: in Exod 34:13 *krt,* in Deut 7:5 *gdᶜ* (cf. 12:3). The use of *krt* for *ʾashera* seems to be more ancient; see Judg 6:24–32.

Exodus 34:13, which does not have the clause about burning images, reflects the original law that refers to the cultic practice of the high places, which mainly consisted of an altar, a pillar, and a sacred tree (cf. 16:21–22). The "images" are added by the author of Deuteronomy; cf. v 25 (and see the NOTE there) and 12:3. Exodus 34:13 is of pre-Deuteronomic origin and influences Deuteronomy (see Halbe, 1975, pp. 119f).

The plural style of this verse, which stands in contrast to the singular style of vv 1–4 and 6, is to be explained by the fact that the original prohibitions on which the author is dependent (i.e., Exod 34:13) were styled in the plural; cf. also 12:3.

sacred tree. The Ashera embodies the female element of divinity. The term is taken as a reference to a goddess (Judg 3:7; 6:25; 1 Kgs 18:19; 2 Kgs 21:3; 23:4, 7), compare *aṯrt,* the wife of El, the head of the pantheon in Ugarit. It may indicate a tree (Deut 16:21), or a wooden pole (Exod 34:13 et al.) as the verbs used in reference to its removal indicate: *krt* 'cut', *gdᶜ* 'hew down' (Deut 7:5), *śrp* 'burn' (Deut 12:3). As a function of her femininity the Ashera is responsible to fertility. Hence it need not surprise us that women play an important role in fostering Ashera worship. Maacah, the mother of king Asa, has an abominable image *(mplṣt)* made for the Ashera (1 Kgs 15:13) and during the syncretistic reign of Menasseh, women weave vestments for the Ashera (2 Kgs 23:7). Similar in character to the Ashera is the Canaanite goddess Anath, who is considered 'the Queen of Heaven' (cf. Porten 1964, 120) as the Mesopotamian goddesses Inanna and Ishtar (Weinfeld 1972b, 133–54) and compare Jer 7:18, 44:17 in connection with the worship of the Queen of Heaven. There is undoubtedly a correspondence between Ashera, Ashtoreth, and Anath as many have suggested (cf. Cross 1973, 28ff.).

Recent discoveries brought to light inscriptions from about 800 B.C.E. with the name *ʾšrh* next to Baal or YHWH. Thus, in Kuntillet ʿAjrud, eighty kilometers south of Kadesh Barnea, we read on a pithos: *brkt ʾtkm lYHWH Šmrn wlʾšrtw,* 'I have blessed you to YHWH Šmrn, and his Ashera' (Meshel 1978). There we also find *YHWH tmn wʾšrth,* 'YHWH of Teman and his Ashera'.

Further references to Ashera of YHWH were found in Khirbet el-Qom, about fifteen kilometers west of Hebron, from about 750 B.C.E. (Lemaire 1977), and most recently inscriptions with the name *ʾšrh* were discovered in Tel-Miqne = Ekron (not yet published).

Indeed the Asherim, along with the stone pillars *(maṣṣebot),* were popular in Israel and Judah (cf. Gen 21:33; 28:18; 35:4, 14; Exod 24:4; Josh 24:26) and were for the first time prohibited following the reform of Hezekiah (2 Kgs 18:4), compare Deut 16:21–22. (See Weinfeld 1984c, pp. 121–30); Day 1986, pp. 385–408.

6. *For you are a holy people to YHWH your God; YHWH your God has chosen you to be his treasured people from among all the peoples on earth.* This is the reason for the previous commandments about abstaining from contact with the Canaanites and their worship: Israel is of separate status to God, is set apart from other nations, and therefore should not behave like them. The verse is dependent on Exod 19:5–6: "if you will obey me . . . you shall be my treasured possession from among all the peoples . . . you shall be to me a kingdom of priests and a holy nation." But there is a significant difference in the concept of election between Exodus and Deuteronomy. In Exodus, the holiness expresses the special merit and privilege of Israel (compare Isa 61:6, "you shall be named the priests of YHWH," and see Moran 1962), whereas Deuteronomy, which adopted the idea of the merit and peculiar value of Israel (cf. 26:17–19), developed the notion and turned it into the basis for the duty to fulfill the obligations to YHWH. The high status bestowed on Israel is not just a merit but primarily a responsibility *(noblesse oblige);* compare also 14:2, 21 (see Weinfeld 1969, pp. 131–36). In post-Exilic times the election developed into a feeling of responsibility to serve as an example for other nations: Israel was chosen in order to bring light to the nations (Isa 49:6–7; cf. 41:8–9; 42:2; 43:10; 44:1–2; 45:4).

Another difference between Exodus and Deuteronomy is the appellation of the privileged people. In Exodus, Israel is called "a kingdom of [priests]and a [holy] nation" *(gôy* and *mamlākā),* terms that denote a political state (cf. 1 Kgs 18:10); while in Deuteronomy, Israel is named a "[holy] people *(ʿam qādôš),*" which marks an ethnic group bound by blood ties (see Speiser 1960).

has chosen you. "Chosen" is used here as a theological term for the first time in Deuteronomy (cf. 4:37; 10:15; 14:7) and coupled with love for Israel (cf. 7:8;

4:37; 10:15). The concept of God's election and love for Israel became an essential element of the Jewish liturgy of the Second Temple period connected with the Shemaᶜ declaration. The Shemaᶜ pericope, which demands "love of God" (Deut 6:5), is preceded by a benediction *(ʾahabah),* which praises God's love of Israel and his election (cf. *m. Ber.* 1:4, and for its recital in the Temple, cf. *m. Tamid* 5:1; *y. Ber.* 1:8 3c; *b. Ber.* 11b; and see Heinemann 1977, pp.xx), and thus love of Israel for God is presented as corresponding to love of God for Israel (see below, in the NOTE to v 8).

The theological concept of election was also applied by the author of Deuteronomy to the Temple, which has been called "the place that YHWH has chosen" (12:5, 14, 18, 26; 14:25; 15:20; 16:7, 15, 16; 17:8, 10; 18:6; etc.). It is also used in reference to the king and the chosen dynasty (17:15) and in the deuteronomistic school to David (1 Kgs 8:16; 11:34) and to the levitical priests (18:5; 21:5; cf. Jer 33:24).

his treasured people. The word *segullah,* which defines the privileged status of the people of Israel (cf. Exod 19:5; Deut 14:2; 26:18; Mal 3:17; Ps 135:4), refers twice to royal wealth (Eccl 2:8; 1 Chr 29:3) and marks the special treasure acquired by kings, namely, the privy purse. In rabbinic literature *siggel segullah* means 'accumulate a hoard for oneself' (cf. Latin *peculium* and hence *peculiaris,* English *peculiar),* a meaning well attested in Akkadian literature (cf. Greenberg 1951). Furthermore, in the Akkadian sources of the second millennium B.C.E. the term *sikiltum/sigiltum* is found as an epithet for a true believer in his god, as, for example, in a seal impression of Abban the king of Alalakh: "the servant of Adad, the beloved of Adad, the *sikiltum* of Adad" (Collon 1975, pp. 12–13). The same phenomenon is attested in the personal name Sikiltu-Adad (Goetze 1957, 13:47). The coupling of *sikiltum* in the seal of Alalah with other epithets such as "beloved *(narām)*" help us understand the Aramaic rendering "beloved *(ḥbyb)*" for *segullah.*

Most instructive for the understanding of *segullah* is a letter from the Hittite emperor to the last king of Ugarit, Ammurapi (end of the thirteenth century B.C.E.), wherein we hear the sovereign reminding his faithful vassal that he is his servant and his *sglt (KTU* 2.39:7, 12). The *sglt* and *segullah* belong then to the covenantal terminology, and they are employed to distinguish a relationship of the sovereign with one of his especially privileged vassals (see, recently, Loewenstamm 1983). *Segullah* connoting special preferable status comes clearly to expression in Exod 19:5. There we read, "you will be for me *segullah* from all the peoples for to me belongs the whole earth," which means that out of all the peoples who belong to YHWH only Israel was given the position of *segullah;* compare Deut 26:18–19, "a *segullah* . . . high above all the nations."

7–8. These verses warn Israel not to use the fact of being chosen and special in order to foster a superiority complex. It is not the number—the physical strength—of the people that makes them elected, but the love of God caused by his commitment to the Patriarchs. The same idea underlies 9:4–5, where the author warns the Israelites not to think that because of their virtues they have dispossessed the former inhabitants of the land. Indeed, the Rabbis understood the verse not in the physical sense of few versus numerous, but as humble versus proud: Israel was chosen because of its humility; cf. *b. Ḥul.* 89a and see *Tg. Ps.-J.*, "because you are humble of spirit and modest more than other peoples."

7. *indeed, you are the smallest of peoples.* This is to be understood against the background of the kingdom of Judah before its destruction in the sixth century B.C.E. and stands in contradiction to verses such as 1:10; 10:22; and 28:62 ("as numerous as the stars of the sky"), which are dependent on older sources reflecting the flourishing situation of the united kingdom (cf. the promises in Gen 15:5; 22:17; 26:4; Exod 32:13 and the descriptions of the Davidic and Solomonic kingdoms in 2 Sam 17:11; 1 Kgs 4:20).

8. *because of YHWH's love for you.* God's love for Israel, like God's election of Israel (see above, in the NOTE to v 6), is found in the Pentateuch only in Deuteronomy (4:37; 7:8, 13; 10:15; 23:5) and is also expressed there by the idea of paternal care (1:31; 8:5; 14:1). Both ideas, God's love and his paternal care, are well attested in Hosea (3:1; 9:15; 11:1, 4; 14:5). In one instance, they appear in combination (11:1–4; cf. Jer 31:2, 8, 19) and seem to be associated with the covenantal imagery in which the vassal is depicted as the son of the sovereign; cf. 2 Kgs 16:7 and see Munn-Rankin 1956, pp. 68–84; Weinfeld 1972a, p. 69n. One must admit, however, that in spite of the covenantal overtones, the love imagery in the description of the relationship between God and Israel has an affectionate connotation, especially in poetic texts such as Hosea and Jeremiah. Moreover, even in Deut 6:8 the affectionate connotation comes up when contrasted with the phrase "because YHWH hates us" in 1:27.

the oath he swore. See the NOTE to 1:8.

released you from the house of bondage. The verb *pdh* 'released', like *hwṣyʾ* 'freed' that precedes it, has judicial connotations, especially when connected with slavery; see the NOTE to 5:6. Its usage in the context of deliverance from Egypt is characteristic of Deuteronomy (9:26; 13:6; 15:15; 21:8; 24:18), while other sources prefer the use of *gʾl* (see the TEXTUAL NOTE) in the same context (Exod 6:6 [=the priestly source]; 15:13; Pss 74:2; 77:16; 78:35).

The change to singular in this clause is to be explained by the fact that it constitutes a (liturgical) frozen formula styled conventionally in the singular; compare 9:26; 13:6; 15:15; 24:18.

9–10. These verses constitute a passage of liturgical nature like the one in the second commandment of the Decalogue (see NOTE to 5:9–10) and in Exod 34:7; Num 14:18; and Jer 32:18–19. It comes indeed after a declaration that overlaps the opening of the Decalogue (v 8b).

9. *Know, therefore (wydʿt), that YHWH your God is the only God.* "To know" here means "to keep in mind," as in 4:39 (see the NOTE there). As there, this proclamation of faith precedes an exhortation to keep the law (v 11; cf. 4:40); compare also 8:5–6; 11:2–8.

the steadfast God. In other words, trustworthy and reliable; see the TEXTUAL NOTE.

who keeps his gracious covenant. Literally, "who keeps the covenant and the grace *(hbryt whḥsd),*" but this pair of words forms a hendiadys, that is to say, "a gracious covenant." The term denotes a pledge that involves a gift, such as the pledge given to the patriarchs concerning the grant of land; cf. v 12, "YHWH your God will keep for you the gracious covenant *(hbryt whḥsd)* that he made on oath with your fathers." The same expression is used in connection with the pledge given to David concerning his dynasty: "who keeps the gracious covenant *(hbryt whḥsd)* . . . which you kept to David your servant . . . what you promised to him: your line on the throne of Israel shall never end" (1 Kgs 8:23–25; cf. 3:6). Such pledges were given by Hittite and Assyrian kings to their loyal servants and are styled in a language similar to that of the verses just quoted. Thus we read, in a Hittite royal grant, "Middanamuwas was a man of grace to my father . . . and [King] Muwatalli was kindly disposed to him . . . and gave him Hattušas. My grace *(aššul)* was shown to him. I committed myself for the sons of Middanamuwaš and you will keep it and so shall the sons of my majesty and the grandsons keep for the sons of Middanamuwaš" (Goetze 1925, pp. 40–44). Similarly we read, in an Assyrian royal grant,

> I am Ashurbanipal . . . who does good *(epiš ṭabti)* . . . who always responds graciously to those who serve him . . . and keep the royal command *(nāṣir amat šarrutišu)* . . . PN a friend and beloved *(bel ṭabti bel dēqti)* . . . I took thought of his kindness and decreed his gift . . . anyone from the kings my sons . . . do good and kindness *(ṭābtu damiqtu)* by them and their seed; they are friends and beloved *(bēl ṭābti bēl damiqti)* of the king. (Postgate 1969, nos. 9, 10, 11, pp. 27–34)

Like the Hittite and Assyrian kings who, prompted by the kindness of their servants, commit themselves to do "good and kindness *(ṭābtu damiqtu)*" to the servants and their descendants, so YHWH commits himself to the Patriarchs and their offspring and to David and his descendants. This conception is reflected in the pre-Deuteronomic sources in the form of "does kindness *(ʿśh ḥsd)*" (Exod 20:6 = Deut 5:6) and "keeps kindness *(nṣr ḥsd)*" (Exod 34:7) to the future generations. These expressions too have their equivalents in the Akkadian language: *epiš ṭābti* 'does good' (cf. above) and *naṣir ṭābti* 'keeps good', in the context of keeping a promise. Similarly, the expression *rb ḥsd wʾmt* 'abundant in kindness and truth', which depicts God's fidelity to his promise, has its antecedents in Akkadian *Kittu ṭabuttu* 'truth and kindness', attested in a letter from Ugarit (cf. Moran 1963a, p. 174) and denoting an alliance. The hendiadys *hbryt whḥsd* also has its parallels in the covenantal terminology of the ancient Near East. The Aramaic treaty from Sefire is named "oath and kindness *(ʿdyʾ wtbtʾ)*" (Fitzmyer 1967, 2.B2, p. 80) and as in Deut 7:9 it is God who established "the oath and kindness" there. An identical phenomenon is found in Assyrian, *adê ṭābtu,* as well as in the Greek word *filotes kai horkia* 'friendship and oath' *(Iliad* 3.73, 94). See for all of this Weinfeld 1973a, pp. 190–96.

for those who love him and keep his commandments. Compare Exod 20:6 (=Deut 5:10). This refers to the Patriarchs and parallels the phrase in the above-quoted Assyrian grant, "who always responds graciously to those who serve him . . . and keep the royal command." Like the Patriarchs, who are named "lovers" of God, so the recipients of the royal grants in Assyria are called "friends and beloved *(bēl ṭābti bēl dēqti).*"

to the thousandth generation. A variation of the word "thousandths" in the Decalogue, Exod 20:6 (= Deut. 5:10).

10. *who repays them who hate him to their face to destroy them; he is never late with the one who hates him—he repays him to his face.* This is a radical deviation from the original liturgical-hymnic formula on which the passage is based (Exod 20:5 = Deut 5:9; Exod 34:6–7; Num 14:18). The author of Deuteronomy retains the first part of the hymnic formula, "keeping kindness to the thousandth generation," but changes altogether the clause about punishing the next generations for the sins of their ancestors. He does not accept the view that God visits the fathers' sins upon their descendants but, on the contrary, requites the sinner personally. This suits the principle of individual responsibility reflected in 24:16 (there applied to the human court) and with the line taken by the contemporaneous prophets (Jer 31:28; Ezek 18:2); see above, in the NOTE to 5:9. The polemic with the view of communal responsibility comes to expression in the words of Job 21:19, "Does God reserve his (the wicked's) punishment for his offspring? [for the question mark, cf. Tur-Sinai 1957, ad loc.]. Let him repay it to him that he may feel it."

In later post-Exilic times the praying congregation preserved both the old formula, which expresses communal responsibility, and the Deuteronomic formula, which propounds sheer individual responsibility, as for example in the inserted prayer in Jer 32:17–23 (see Rudolph 1958, ad loc.; and see Weinfeld 1972a, pp. 39–40). Here we read on the one hand, "shows kindness to the thousandth generation and repays *[mešallem;* cf. Deut 7:10] the sins of the fathers to the children after them" (v 18), and on the other, "O great and mighty God . . . whose eyes observe all the ways of men, so as to give every man according to his ways and with the fruits of his deeds" (v 19), which suits the Deuteronomic doctrine as well as Jeremiah's view (cf. the identical phrase in Jer 17:10 and 31:28). Thus a contradiction is revealed of which the compiler was unaware.

11. *Therefore, observe the commandments, the laws, and the judgments.* These are the practical conclusions of the sermonizing passage, which corresponds to 6:1. For such conclusions, compare 4:40, which, like 7:11, follows a declaration that opens with *wydʿt* 'know therefore' (4:39). Compare the conclu-

sion of the sermon in 1 Kgs 8:61, which comes after the monotheistic declaration there (v 60); and see above.

It seems that such conclusions were inserted by late editors who divided the Deuteronomic material for the liturgical recital, irrespective of the inner structure of the material. Thus chaps. 6–8 were divided into two: 6:1–7:11, which opens with "the command, the laws and judgments" and ends with the same; and 7:12–8:20, which opens with the reward for obeying the law *(ʿqb tšmʿwn)* and concludes with the punishment for not obeying the law *(ʿqb lʾ tšmʿwn).* Compare Hoffmann 1913. This division ignores the literary integrity of chap. 7; see the COMMENT below.

12–15. These verses describe the reward or blessing for obedience to the law; they are dependent on Exod 23:25–27; see the COMMENT below.

12. *Because you obey these judgments.* Compare the opposite at the end of chap. 8: "because you would not hearken to YHWH your God" (v 20); see the NOTE to v 11. For such phrases, which precede blessings or (if negative) curses, compare Exod 15:26; 23:22; Lev 26:14; Deut 11:12, 28:1, 15.

YHWH your God will keep for you the covenant. "Keep for *(šmr l . . .),*" like "remember for *(zkr l . . .)*" in connection with a pledge, means keep/remember on account of somebody; cf. Weinfeld 1970–72, pp. 187–88.

the gracious covenant that he made on oath. The covenant was based on oath (cf. Gen 21:21–22; 26:28; Deut 29:13; 2 Kgs 11:4; Ezek 16:8; 17:13), and the terms "covenant and oath" became a hendiadys in the Bible *(bryt wʾlh:* Gen 26:28; Deut 29:11, 13, 20; Ezek 17:18) and in Mesopotamia *(riksu u māmītu),* as well as in Greece *(horkos kai synthēkē);* cf. Weinfeld 1975b.

13. *He will love you.* See the NOTE to v 8.

and bless you and multiply you. Compare the promises to Abraham (Gen 22:17; 26:3–4, 24). Blessing means bestowing the power of fecundity and multiplication; cf. Gen 1:22, 28; 9:1–2; 28:3; 35:9–11; 48:3–4, and see Westermann 1974, pp. 192–94.

he will bless the fruit of your womb and the fruit of your soil . . . increase of your herd. . . . Compare the blessings and curses in 28:4, 11, 18, "the fruit of your womb, the fruit of your soil, and the fruit of your cattle." Similar curses and blessings occur in the oaths of the Greek amphictyonic leagues.

Thus in the oath taken by the members of the Greek amphictyony against Cirrha, which abrogated the sanctioned rules of the amphictyony, we find the clause "if anyone—whether city, man, or tribe [cf. Deut 29:13]—abrogates this oath . . . their soil will not bear fruit, their wives will not give birth . . . their livestock will not foal" (Aeschines, *Against Ctesiphon* 111). Similarly, in the Greeks' oath at Plateia before the war against the Barbarians (§7): "if I observe what is written in the covenant, then my city will be free of disease . . . my land will bear fruit . . . the women will give birth . . . and the cattle will give birth" (cf. Siewert 1972, p. 98). The latter is even closer to Deut 7:13–15 because it has not only blessings concerning fecundity of soil, women, and cattle but also blessings concerning health, as in Deut 7:15: "YHWH will remove from you all sickness." It also is to be compared with Exod 23:25–26, on which Deut 7 is dependent. There we read, "I shall remove illness from your midst, none will miscarry or go barren in your land." This genre of blessings and curses apparently has its origin in the tribal federation of the period of Judges; hence the similarity to the blessings and curses of the amphictyonic league in ancient Greece (for other similarities, see Weinfeld 1983d, pp. 79–84).

grain, wine, and oil. These terms, often used in Deuteronomy for the chief products of the land of Israel (11:14; 12:17; 14:23; 18:4; 28:51), are also marked in Hosea as YHWH's gifts to Israel (2:10, 24); cf. also Num 18:12; Jer 31:12; Joel 1:10; 2:19; Hag 1:11. In other sources we find the pair "grain and wine *(dgn, tyrš),*" cf. Gen 27:28, 37; Deut 33:28; Hos 2:11; 7:14; etc. Both *dgn* and *tyrš* are originally associated with divine names. Dagan is a well-attested deity in Syria (Ebla) and in Mesopotamia. In Ugaritic literature Baal is named the son of Dagan, and in the Phoenician history of Philo of Byblos we read that Kronos (= El) was the father of Dagan, the discoverer of grain and the plow. Dagon—as pronounced in Phoenician, with *o*—was also known as the god of the Philistines (Judg 11:23; 1 Sam 5:1–17; see Cassuto 1954, 2.623–24). *Trt* (= *Tyrwš)* is also attested in a god list from Ugarit *(Ugaritica* 5.3, no. 14A:9; cf. Astour 1966, p. 284).

The pair *dgn* and *tyrwš* corresponds to deified grain *(ᵈAšnan)* and deified beer *(ᵈSiraš)* in Mesopotamia (cf., e.g., *Ludlul bel nēmeqi,* 2.88–89, *BWL,* p. 44).

the increase (šgr) of your herd and the lambing (aštarot) of your flock. Like the pair "grain and wine" *(Dagan* and *Tiroš),* so also the herd (cattle) and the flock (sheep) are associated with names of divine nature. *Šgr* is attested as a deity in a sacrificial list from Ugarit *(Ugaritica* 5.3, 9, RS 9; see Astour 1966, p. 281) and in the inscription from Deir-ʿAlla we find *šgr* and *ʿštr* as a divine pair (cf. especially Weippert 1982, pp. 100–101).

Ištar/ʿaštoret, as the goddess of fecundity, was in charge of calving and lambing; compare the dictum in Babylonian wisdom literature, "Bow down to Ištar, the goddess of your city that she may grant you offspring, take thought of your livestock . . . the planting" *(BWL,* p. 108:13–14). In Israel the phrases *šgr, ʿštrt* are frozen poetic expressions devoid of any polytheistic meaning.

Interestingly, the sequence of grain, wine, cattle, and sheep in the context of divine blessing is found in the Phoenician Azitawadda's inscription from Karatepe: "let Baal bless Azitawadda . . . grain, wine, cattle, and sheep *(śbʿ, trš, ʾlpm, ṣʾn)" (KAI* 26 A.3 7, 9); for the pair *śbʿ tyrš* instead of *dgn tyrš,* cf. Prov 3:10; and see the discussion of Avishur 1975, pp. 13–14.

14. *You shall be blessed above all other peoples.* Compare 15:6; 26:19; 28:12–13.

there shall be no sterile male or female. Cf. Exod 23:26, "no woman in your land shall miscarry or be barren."

15. *YHWH will remove from you all sickness.* Compare Exod 23:25, "I will remove sickness from your midst."

all the evil diseases of Egypt, about which you know, he will not bring upon you. Compare Exod 15:26, "all the disease which I brought *(śmty)* upon the Egyptians I shall not put upon you for I am YHWH your healer"; see also 28:27 *(šḥyn mṣrym)* and 60 *(mdwy mṣrym),* an allusion to the plagues of Egyptians in the Exodus stories. It may also refer to the ailments common in Egypt; cf. Pliny, *Natural History* 26.1, 5: *Aegypti peculiare malum.*

but he will put them upon all your enemies. Compare 30:7, "YHWH your God will put all those curses upon the enemies and foes who persecuted you."

16. *You shall devour all the peoples whom YHWH your God delivers to you.* This brings us back to the main topic of the chapter: the destruction of the Canaanites. The first part of the verse is a kind of transition from the promises in vv 12–15 to the command in 16b. Verse 16a sounds indeed like a promise, though factually it has the meaning of an injunction. "Devour" here joins other verbs of destruction like *hḥrm* (v 2), *h'bd* (vv 20, 24), *klh* (v 22), and *hšmd* (v 24).

You shall show them no pity. Compare 13:9; 19:13, 21; 25:12; see also Gen 45:20; Isa 13:18; and it is common in Ezekiel. It has the same meaning as *l' tḥnm* in v 2.

You shall not serve their gods, for that would be a snare to you. See v 25 and compare Exod 23:33; 34:12; Judg 2:3b.

17–19. A military oration characteristic of the Deuteronomic school; see the COMMENT below.

17. *should you say in your heart . . . remember. . . .* A rhetorical device, which comes to uproot fear by recalling God's omnipotence. The same stylistics are used in the case of the opposite situation, when feelings of arrogance and self-confidence might occur: "and you say to yourselves, "My own power . . . [has] won this wealth. . . . Remember *(wzkrt)* that it is YHWH who gives you the power" (8:17–18); "do not say in your heart . . . YHWH has enabled me to occupy this land because of my virtues . . . remember *(zkr)* do not forget *('l tškḥ)* how you provoked" (Deut 9:5–7). The same pattern of mind appears in 6:10–12, where the danger is contemplated that wealth might cause the forgetting of YHWH. On these passages and their common stylistic structure, see Garcia-Lopez 1978, pp. 3–19.

These nations are more numerous than we; how can we dispossess them. This refers to the beginning of the chapter: "he dislodges many nations . . . seven nations more numerous and mightier *(rbym wʿṣmym)* than you"; cf. also 9:1. See Lopez 1978, pp. 6–7.

18. *Do not fear them.* This is a formula prevalent in the war oracles in Israel (compare 20:1–4) and in the ancient Near East. See Weippert 1981; and cf. the NOTE to 1:21 and the COMMENT below.

19. *prodigious acts that you saw.* Compare 29:2; see the NOTE to 4:34, and for the phrase "that you saw," see 4:9.

signs and portents. See the NOTE to 4:34.

mighty hand and outstretched arm. See the NOTE to 4:34.

20. *YHWH your God will also send the hornet against them.* Compare Exod 23:28 and Josh 24:12, as well as the warning of Isaiah: "On that day YHWH will whistle to the flies from the distant streams of Egypt and to the bees in the land of Assyria and they shall come and alight in the rugged wadis and in the clefts of the rocks and in all the thornbrakes, and in all the watering places" (7:18–19). The insects here serve as metaphors for invading armies; cf. Deut 1:44; Ps 118:12. Some commentators see also "the hornet" as a metaphor for a horror and panic or for plagues and pests (Ibn Ezra, Saadia, and modern authors and translators). It should not be excluded, however, that the image goes back to the use of insects as warfare agents, as attested in various ancient sources (see, e.g., Beck 1937 and, recently, Neufeld 1980).

until those who are left in hiding perish before you. The unhidden enemy will be destroyed by the Israelites themselves; see the COMMENT below. This is made clear by the opening of the sentence, "and *also (wgm)* the hornet." In Exod 23:28 the enemy as such (the Canaanites, the Hivites, and the Hittites) will be driven out by the hornet, not only the hidden ones.

21. *You shall have no dread of them.* The verb *ʿrṣ* 'dread' occurs as a pair with *yrʾ* in Deuteronomy (1:29; 20:3; 31:6) and in Isa 8:12, 13. There the pair was split: v 18, *yrʾ*; v 21, *ʿrṣ*.

your God is in your midst. Compare 6:15 and the NOTE thereto.

great and awesome. Compare 10:17, but there with the addition of *hgbwr* 'the mighty'. In other instances we find this pair of expressions referring to the wilderness (1:9; 8:15) and to God's deeds at the Exodus (10:21; cf. 2 Sam 7:23).

22. *YHWH your God will dislodge.* Compare v 1.

little by little. Compare Exod 23:30.

you may not put an end to them quickly, lest the wild beasts multiply to your hurt. Compare Exod 23:29, "I will not drive them out before you in a single year lest the land become desolate and the wild beasts multiply." The dependence on older sources creates a certain contradiction with the view of Deuteronomy proper: "you will dispossess and destroy them quickly *(mhr)*" (9:3). Compare the inconsistency in the description of the conquest in the editorial framework of the book of Joshua: in Josh 10:42, "all these kings and their land Joshua conquered at once *(pʿm ʾḥt),*" while in Josh 11:18, "over a long period [literally, many days] Joshua waged war with those kings." (For a discrepancy concerning the stay in Kadesh over a long period [literally, many days], cf. the NOTES to 1:46 and 2:1.) For an inconsistency concerning the size of the people, because of the dependence on old sources, cf. the NOTE to v 7. Rashbam explains the discrepancy between 7:22 and 9:3 in the following manner: 7:22 refers to the inability to exterminate the enemy quickly, whereas 9:3 refers to a speedy victory in war (see the commentary of Rashbam [Rosin 1881] to Deut 9:3). Nevertheless, there is a possibility that *mhr* in 9:3 is to be understood not as "quickly" but as "easily" (see the NOTE there), and there is then no contradiction between 7:22 and 9:3.

23. *YHWH your God will deliver them to you, throwing them into great panic until they are wiped out.* Exodus 23:27 has, "I will send forth my terror before you and will throw into panic all the people among whom you shall come and I will make them turn back." On the differences between the two sources see the COMMENT below.

24. *no man shall stand up to you.* Compare 11:25 and Josh 10:8; 21:42; 23:9 (in the last three instances with the verb *ʿmd* instead of *htyṣb).*

until you have wiped them out. Compare the end of the previous verse: "until they are wiped out." In the parallel passages of Exod 23 the result is expulsion *(grš)* and not extermination; see the COMMENT below.

25–26. This passage brings us back to the beginning of the chapter (vv 2–6), where the Israelites are warned not to engage in idolatrous practices because they are a holy people. Here they are warned not to be tempted by graven images and the gold and silver on them, lest they contract the *ḥerem,* which is abomination and the opposite of holy.

25. *You shall burn the images of their gods with fire.* This clause 25a is styled in the plural, while the surrounding verses are all in the singular. This stylistic digression is the result of the author's reference to a standard, fixed formula—actually a quotation—as found in v 6b; see my observations in the introduction Section 7.

The commandment about burning the images is attested only in the Deuteronomic law, and in accordance with that law the Chronicler corrected the historical data of 2 Sam 5:21. In 2 Sam 5:21 we read that David carried away the idols of the Philistines, while 2 Chr 14:12 has instead that David ordered the images to *be burned with fire,* which conforms verbally to the command here.

you shall not covet the silver and gold on them. The images were made of wood plated with gold or silver.

because it is an abomination to YHWH your God. The expression "abomination to YHWH *(twʿbt YHWH)*" appears only in two books of the Bible: in the book of Deuteronomy (7:25; 12:31; 17:1; 18:12; 22:5; 23:19; 24:4; 25:16) and in the book of Proverbs (3:32; 11:1; 10:20; 12:22; 15:8, 9, 26; 16:5; 17:15; 20:10, 23). A close analysis of the laws and dicta to which the rationale "abomination of YHWH" is appended shows that their common denominator is hypocritical attitude and false pretension. Hypocrisy and false pretension may appear in the social sphere—dealing perversely with one's fellow, man or woman (Deut 24:4; 25:16; Prov 3:32; 11:1, 20; 12:22; 20:10, 23)—and in the cultic sphere—dealing perversely with God, as, for example, sacrificing to him and provoking him at the same time (Prov 15:8; Deut 17:1; 18:9–11; 23:19; etc.). In the present case, the tolerance of idols in Israel is an abomination to YHWH because it misrepresents the true nature of the God of Israel. Identical expressions appear in the Egyptian Wisdom of Amenemope, "an abomination to the god Re," and there also it occurs in the context of hypocrisy (falsification of weights and measures); see Weinfeld 1972a, pp. 267–69.

26. *or you will be under ban like it.* Compare Josh 6:18, "but you must beware of that which is under ban lest you covet [= LXX, cf. 7:21] and take anything which is under ban, you will cause the camp of Israel to be under ban and you will bring calamity upon it."

you shall make it detestable and abominable. The Deuteronomic movement developed a whole series of derogatory expressions for idolatry: *šqṣ* 'destestable', *twʿbh* 'abomination', *glwlym* 'fetishes', *hbl/thw* 'vanity, nothingness'; Cf. Weinfeld 1972a, pp. 323–24. Idols as "detestable things *(šqwṣym)*" are alluded to in Hos 9:10, and the term was adopted by the Deuteronomic school (cf. Deut 29:16; 1 Kgs 11:5, 7; 2 Kgs 23:13, 24) and is attested in Jeremianic poetry (4:1; 13:27; 16:18) and prose (7:30; 32:34). In the priestly code the term *šqṣ* refers to forbidden and unclean animals (Lev 7:21; 11:10–13, 20, 23, 41, 42); compare Ezek 8:10 and Isa 66:17.

Compare the dictum in rabbinic literature: "whence that one is commanded to refer to idolatry with a nickname," it says, "*(šaqqeṣ tešaqqṣenu)* you shall make it detestable" (Deut 7:26; *b. ʿAbod. Zar.* 56a, *sipre Deut.* 61 [Finkelstein 1969, p. 127]; *t. ʿAbod. Zar.* 6:4 [Zuckermandl 1963, p. 469]; etc.).

COMMENT

Just as the former chapter, with the "catechistic" passages (6:4–9, 20–25) and the reference to the conquest of the land (6:10–15), draws from the Gilgal tradition reflected in Exod 13 and Josh 4 (see the COMMENT to 6:4–25), so chap. 7 draws from the Gilgal tradition as represented in Exod 23:20–33 and Judg 2:1–4. The latter ascribes the warnings against alliance with the Canaanites to the angel coming from Gilgal, while the former source, which deals with the entrance into Canaan and contains commandments against making a covenant with the Canaanites and worshiping their gods, refers to the angel who brings the people into the land and warns them (Exod 23:20–23).

Gilgal is indeed dominant in the Israelite tradition about the first contacts with the Canaanites. It is considered the pivotal point *(Haftpunkt)* of Joshua's conquest campaigns (Josh 3–5; 9:6; 10:6, 15, 43; 14:6; Judg 2:1; Mic 6:5; cf. Alt 1968) and was rightly seen as the scene of the crystallization of Israel's national ethos and culture (see Otto 1975). According to Josh 5 the newborn Israelites were circumcised in Gilgal, and the Passover was celebrated there for the first time after the entrance into the land (Josh 5:2–12). The monuments erected in Gilgal served to educate the children (4:6–7, 21–24) just as the Passover did (Exod 12:25–27; 13:8). The angel of YHWH who was to lead the Israelites into the land (Exod 23:20; 33:2; Num 20:16) stayed with the Israelites in Gilgal (Judg 2:1) and from there went to Jericho to assist Joshua in his military campaigns (Josh 5:13–15). As the one who was to bring the Israelites into the land and to expel before them the Canaanites (Exod 23:20; 33:2; Judg 2:3) the angel instructed the people not to make alliances with the Canaanites and not to worship their gods (Exod 23:21, 26, 32–33; cf. Judg 2:2–3), and furthermore he warned them against letting the Canaanites dwell in the land (Exod 23:33). This antagonistic policy regarding the Canaanites was apparently crystallized in the Gilgal sanctuary during the time of Saul, when Gilgal became the most important shrine (1 Sam 11:14–15; 13:8; 15:12, 21, 33). It was Saul who took a hard line vis à vis the native inhabitants of Canaan, as may be learned from the episode about the Gibeonites in 2 Sam 21:1–6 and especially from v 2, where it says that because of his zeal for the Israelites, Saul wanted to destroy the Gibeonites, a remnant of the Amorite stock. Indeed, the story about the covenant with the Gibeonites in Gilgal (Josh 9:3ff.) revolves around the alleged illegitimate conclusion of a covenant with the inhabitants of the land (vv 6–7, 15–16), which is prohibited in the laws of Exod 23:32; 34:12, 15; cf. Judg 2:2. The ban of Jericho in Josh 6:17–18, which is echoed in Deut 7:25–26 (see the NOTE above) fits perfectly with the time of Saul and seems to have originated in Gilgal. Thus the formulation of the ban *(ḥerem)* in Josh 6:21, banning "man and woman, young and old, ox and sheep and ass" is congruent with the formulation of Saul's ban of the city of Nob in 1 Sam 22:19: "man and woman, child and infant, ox and ass and sheep." To the same type of *ḥerem* belongs the ban of Amalek by Saul, which culminates in Gilgal (1 Sam 15:33) and about which it is said that the *ḥerem* is to encompass "man and woman, child and infant, ox and sheep, camel and ass" (1 Sam 15:3).

It seems indeed that the first stories about the national conquest of the land by the Israelites were formed during the time of Saul in Gilgal. The main scene of conquest in Josh 2–10 takes place in the area of Benjamin, the tribe of Saul (cf. Gilgal [chaps. 3–5]; Jericho [chap. 6]; Ai [chaps. 7–8]; Gibeon [chap. 9]; Beth Horon as far as Ayalon [chap. 10]), and it was King Saul who claimed the land for the Israelites in opposition to the claims of the Philistines over the land. The period of Saul is most appropriate for the crystallization of an anti-Canaanite ideology, in contrast to the Davidic–Solomonic era, when some sort of concilliation with the autochthonous nations took place. Note David's response to the Gibeonites in 2 Sam 21:3, 7f., and see 1 Kgs 9:20 (cf. recently Abramsky 1985).

The Gilgal attitude about the Canaanites is expressed by specific idioms as they occur in Exod 23:20–33; 34:11–16; Deut 7; Judg 2:1–3; and Josh 9. These idioms are

1. not to cut a covenant *(krt bryt)* with the Canaanites (Exod 23:33; 34:12, 15; Deut 7:2; Josh 9:6–7; Judg 2:2);
2. not to let them dwell in the midst of the Israelites (Exod 23:33: *l' yšbw*

bʾrṣk; cf. *yšb bqrb* about the Canaanites dwelling amidst the Israelites in Josh 9:7, 16; 16:10; Judg 1:25, 30);

3. not to intermarry with them (Exod 34:15–16; Deut 7:3; cf. Gen 34:9);
4. to break their altars, pillars, etc. (Exod 23:24b; 34:13; Deut 7:5; Judg 2:2); and
5. not to worship their gods (Exod 23:24a; 34:14; Deut 7:4; cf. 12:2–4).

The Deuteronomic author of Deut 7 is dependent on the Gilgal tradition of Exod 23, but he reworked it in accordance with his particular tendency. He adopted the motifs mentioned above—except motif number 3, which he took from Exod 34:15–16, see below—elaborated the blessings of Exod 23:25–26 (Deut 7:13–15), and enlarged the section about the conquest of the land (Exod 23:27–30) by adding a military oration in Deut 7:17–19 and some national patriotic notions (vv 23–24; see the NOTES). He omitted completely, however, the passage about the angel that appears in Exod 23:20–23; 33:2–3 and Judg 2:1–4. Like Hosea's criticism of the angel of Bethel (12:4–5), Deuteronomy rejects the view of angels as mediators (see the NOTE to 4:37) and denies the role of the angel at the Exodus (cf. Num 20:15–16) and at the conquest (see recently Weinfeld 1985c, p. 84), which suits the tendency to demythologization in the book of Deuteronomy. Just as Deuteronomy 6:4–25, which is dependent on the Gilgal tradition of Exod 13, dissociated the education of children from the Passover ritual to which it was originally connected, so the author of Deut 7 dissociated the role of the angel from the conquest tradition rooted in the Gilgal tradition of Exod 23. The apotropaic rites of the old Passover as well as the angelology connected with the Exodus and the conquest were not in line with the ideology of the Deuteronomic author, so he wrote them off. As indicated, the author of Deut 7 is also dependent on Exod 34:11–17, which comes especially to expression in the interdiction of intermarrying with the Canaanites (cf. Deut 7:3–4 with Exod 34:16). It seems, however, that this tradition is not of Gilgalite but of Shechemite origin. The prohibition of intermarriage that occurs in Exod 34:16 and is missing in Exod 23 is central in the Shechemite story of Gen 34, and the prohibition in Deut 7:3 actually overlaps the formulas in Gen 34:9, 16, 21 *(hthṭnw ʾtnw bntykm ttnw lnw wʾt bntynw tqḥw lkm).* By contrast, the command of not letting the Canaanites dwell amid the Israelites, which occurs in Exod 23, is missing in Exod 34. In fact, the interdiction of letting the Canaanites dwell in the land makes the command of intermarriage superfluous, because the fulfillment of the command means that Canaanite women are not available for marriage. This may explain why Exod 23, which follows the rigid Gilgalite tradition regarding the Canaanites, does not resort to the prohibition of intermarriage, while the more lenient Shechemite tradition—Shechem had a mixed population, cf. Judg 9—warns against intermarriage. Deut 7, however, combines both traditions. That Exod 34:11–17 has a Shechemite element may be learned from the fact that it contains a clause about the "zealous god" *(ʾel gannaʾ),* which also occurs in the Shechemite covenant in Josh 24:19.

Structure of Chapter 7

Deuteronomy 7 is a coherent chapter (see Lohfink 1963, pp. 167–88), basically built upon Exod 23:20–33, except that the passage about the angel in vv 20–23a was left out of Deuteronomy for ideological reasons (see above). Otherwise there is a thematic and verbal overlap between these two chapters:

1. Exodus 23:20–33 and Deut 7 both open and close with the warnings against an alliance with the Canaanites and their gods, and there are close parallels between the prologues (Deut 7:1–5 ‖ Exod 23:23aβ–24) and the epilogues of these two pericopes (Deut 7:25–26 ‖ Exod 23:32–33).

Exod 23	*Deut 7*
and brings you to the [land] of the Amorites . . . and Canaanites and I annihilate them. (v 23)	and he dislodges . . . the . . . Amorites, Canaanites . . . and YHWH your God delivers them to you, and you defeat them, you must doom them to destruction *(hḥrm tḥrym ʾtm).* You shall grant them no terms *(lʾ tkrt lhm bryt)* and you shall not spare them [give them no quarter = *JPS].* (vv 1–2)
I will deliver the inhabitants of the land unto your power and you will drive them *(wgrštmw)* out before you. You shall make no covenant with them *(lʾ tkrt lhm bryt)* and their gods. They shall not remain in your land. (vv 32–33)	you shall tear down their altars, smash their pillars *(šbr mṣbt)* . . . burn their images in fire. (v 5)
You shall not bow down to their gods . . . but shall destroy them and smash their pillars *(šbr mṣbt)* (vv 23–24) lest they cause you to sin against me; for you will serve their gods—and it will prove a snare for you *(lmwqš).* (vv 32–33)	You shall not serve their gods, for that would be a snare *(mwqš)* to you. (v 16)
	You shall burn the images of their gods with fire; you shall not covet the silver and gold on them . . . lest you be ensnared thereby *(twqš bw)* . . . for it is under ban. (vv 25–26)

Just as Exod 23:20–33 opens and closes with the injunctions not to worship the Canaanite gods and their cultic objects (vv 24, 33) so does Deut 7 (vv 4–5, 25–26). In Deut 7 the phrase "you shall burn the images with fire," which is peculiar to the Deuteronomic view (cf. 12:3; 2 Kgs 19:18), forms a kind of *inclusio* for the whole sermon (vv 5, 25).

2. The blessings that appear in Exod 23:25–26 following the fulfillment of the commands occur also in Deut 7, albeit in a more elaborate form (see the NOTES):

Exod 23	*Deut 7*
You shall serve YHWH your God and he *will bless* your bread and your water. I will *remove sickness* from your midst. No *woman* in your land shall miscarry or *be barren.* (vv 25–26)	Because you obey these judgments . . . YHWH . . . will love you and *bless you* . . . bless . . . the fruit of your soil. . . . there shall be no sterile male or female among you or among your livestock. YHWH will *remove* from you *all sickness.* (vv 12–15)

3. The victory over the Canaanite enemies is also paralleled in both sources:

Exod 23	*Deut 7*
I will send forth my terror before you and I will throw into panic *(whmty)* all the people . . . and make them turn back. I will send the "hornet" *(ṣrʿh)* ahead of you and it shall drive out before you the Hivites. (vv 27–28)	YHWH your God will deliver them to you, throwing them into great panic *(whmm mhwmh)* until they are wiped out. (v 23) YHWH your God will also send the hornet *(ṣrʿh)* against them. (v 20)
I will not drive them out before you in a single year, lest the land become desolate and the wild beasts multiply, I will drive them	YHWH your God will dislodge these peoples before you little by little; you may not put an end to

out before you little by little. (vv 29–30)

them quickly, lest the wild beasts multiply. (v 22)

The only passages in Deuteronomy that do not find their parallels in Exod 23 are vv 6–11 and vv 17–19. These are indeed expressly Deuteronomic sections, from the point of view of both contents and style. Verses 6–11 speak about the holy chosen people on the one hand, and the God "who keeps his gracious covenant *(hbryt whḥsd)*" on the other, themes rooted in the Decalogue tradition that is so prominent in the Deuteronomic paraenesis. For the election motif in connection with the Decalogue tradition, cf. Exod 19:5–6, and for the "keeping of grace" cf. Exod 20:6 (= Deut 5:10). In fact, the formula concerning the "impassioned God *(ʾel qannaʾ),*" which opens the credal declaration of the second commandment of the Decalogue (Exod 20:5–6 = Deut 5:9–10), is reflected in Deut 7:4b, "YHWH's anger [will] blaze forth against you and he will destroy you quickly." This idiosyncrasy *(ḥrh ʾp . . . hšmyd)* actually appears as a definition of the impassioned God *(ʾel qannaʾ)* in Deut 6:14–15, a passage influenced by the Decalogue (see the COMMENT there). It seems therefore that vv 4–5, which speak about idolatry (cf. *psl* in v 5b and in Exod 20:4 = Deut 5:7) and God's anger, triggered the whole passage of Deut 7:6–10, which amounts to a commentary on the Decalogue (see the NOTES, especially to vv 9–10).

Verses 17–19 are a kind of military oration characteristic of the Deuteronomic work; compare 1:29–33; 3:21–22; 9:1–6; 11:22–25; 31:1–6. These orations are punctuated by the encouraging formula "do not fear *(ʾal tyrʾ),*" which is known to us from Assyrian and Aramaic court prophecies. See, most recently, Weippert 1981, and for the military oration in the Deuteronomic literary creation, see Weinfeld 1972a, pp. 45–51.

The Ban of the Canaanites

The ban of the Canaanites, which is central in this chapter, is expressed here in the sharpest terms. The Canaanites are to be utterly exterminated. The verbs used for extermination not used in other Pentateuchal sources are *hḥrm* 'ban/exterminate' (v 3, cf. 20:17); *ʾkl* 'devour' (v 16); *klh* 'put an end to' (v 22); *hšmd* 'wipe out' (v 24); and *hʾbd* 'cause to perish' (vv 20, 26). By contrast, the verbs used in the previous sources for the expulsion of the Canaanites, *grš* (Exod 23:28, 29, 30, 31; 33:2; 34:11; Deut 33:27 [Song of Moses]; Josh 24:12, 18; Judg 2:3; 6:9) or *šlḥ* (Lev 18:24; 20:23), which is synonymous with *grš* (cf. Gen 3:23 *wyšlḥhw* with v 24 *wygrš* and the term for divorce in Deut 24:1, 3 compared with Lev 21:7, 14; 22:13), are never used in Deuteronomy, in order to avoid misunderstandings. According to the Deuteronomic law (20:16–17) the Canaanites are to be exterminated and not expelled; therefore, verbs that render "expulsion" are avoided consistently. When using old sources that have *grš*, the Deuteronomic author intentionally changes the verb into another in order to accommodate his own view. Thus, v 22, which is dependent on Exod 23:29–30, changes *grš* 'expel' to *nšl* 'dislodge' and *klh* 'put an end'.

Furthermore, whole clauses are paraphrased in order to accommodate the Deuteronomic view. Thus Exod 23:27, which stands behind Deut 7:23 and states,

> I will send forth my terror before you
> and will throw into panic *(whmty)* all the people . . .
> and make them turn back (Exod 23:27)

is changed into

> YHWH . . . will deliver them to you,
> throwing them into great panic *(mhmh)*
> until they are wiped out *(ʿad hšmdm)*. (Deut 7:23)

Instead of having the Canaanites "turned back *(ntn ʿrp)*" the Deuteronomic author has them "wiped out." He adds, moreover, that nobody will be able to stand against the Israelites until he be destroyed by them (v 24).

Similarly, in Exod 23:28 (cf. Josh 24:12), the hornet *(hṣrʿh)* is sent by God to drive Israel's enemy out of the land, whereas the Deuteronomic author when using this idea states that God will send the hornet to destroy the hidden survivors *(nšʾrym wnstrym)* of the enemy (7:20): the unhidden enemy will be—in his view—destroyed by the Israelites themselves.

Indeed, in the ancient sources it is God who drives out the Canaanites (Exod 23:22, 27f.; 33:2; 34:11; Josh 24:12; Judg 2:3; 6:9; Amos 2:9; Pss 44:3; 78:55; 80:9), while in the Deuteronomic sources exterminating the Canaanites is the task of the Israelites. Although it is done with the help of God (4:38; 6:19; 7:1, 22; 8:20; 9:3, 5; 11:23; 12:29; 19:1; 31:3), the actual performance of the task is placed upon the Israelites (2:34; 3:3, 6; 7:2, 16, 24; 20:17–18; Josh 8:1–2, 26; 10:28, 30, 32, 33, 35, 37, 39, 40; 11:11, 14). In fact one can discern a development in the Pentateuchal tradition concerning the removal of the Canaanites from the land of Israel. In the JE source, it is God who "drives out *(grš)*" the Canaanites by means of an angel or the hornet (Exod 23:22, 27–28, 29, 30, 31 [LXX]; 33:2; 34:11, 29). In the priestly source the Israelites are commanded "to dispossess *(hwryš)*" the inhabitants of the land (Num 33:52–55), whereas in the Deuteronomic source, the command is given "to exterminate *(hḥrym)*" them (7:2, 16, 24; 20:17–18). It is true, even in the JE source the expulsion of the Canaanites is implied, as, for example, in Exod 23:33, "they shall not dwell in your land"; and compare Judg 2:1–3, which is a reaction against the sin of the tribes of Israel in not dispossessing the Canaanites from their midst (Judg 1:21,

22, 23, 30, 31, 33; and see Weinfeld 1968b). Nonetheless, there is no explicit command to eliminate them, in contrast to the priestly and the Deuteronomic sources (cf. C. H. W. Brekelmans, *De Ḥerem in het Oude Testament,* 1959).

The reason for the expulsion or extermination of the Canaanites is twofold. In the JE and in the Deuteronomic sources the reason is religious: "they shall not remain in your land lest they cause you to sin against me, for you will serve their gods and it will prove a snare to you" (Exod 23:33; cf. 34:12, 15–16); "you shall ban them . . . lest they teach you to do all the abhorrent things that they have done for their gods and you shall sin against YHWH your God" (Deut 20:17–18). In the priestly sources the reason is political: "but if you do not dispossess the inhabitants of the land, those whom you allow to remain shall be stings in your eyes . . . and they shall harass you in the land which you live" (Num 33:55; cf. Josh 23:13, which is influenced by Num 33:55).

In reality, the Canaanites were neither expelled nor exterminated, as may be learned from Judg 1:21–33 and 1 Kgs 9:20–21), so that the whole question was a theoretical one, especially raised by the Deuteronomic movement. The Deuteronomic circle adopted the Gilgalite tradition of *ḥerem* but expanded it and applied it theoretically to the whole population of the land of Canaan. The original *ḥerem* referred to hostile cities and was implemented by means of votive proclamations (Josh 6:17; cf. Num 21:2–3; see also Judg 21:5), whereas Deuteronomy conceived *ḥerem* as an automatic decree that applied to the whole country and its inhabitants. This sort of *ḥerem* is not dependent on any vow or dedication, but is an a priori decree that belongs more to theory than to practice. The rabbis indeed could not conceive the removal of the Canaanites in such a cruel, radical manner and circumvented plain Scripture by interpreting Joshua's conquest as follows: "Joshua sent out three proclamations *(prostagma)* to the Canaanites: he who wishes to leave shall leave; he who wishes to make peace shall make peace; he who wishes to fight shall do so" *(Lev.* Rab. [Margaliot 1957, pp. 387–88; *y. Šeb.* 6:5, 36c). This kind of option for the Canaanites stands in clear contradiction to the commandments of Deuteronomy in 7:2 and 20:16–17 and actually reflects the tendency of Second Temple Judaism to depict the Israelite settlement according to the conquest procedures of the Maccabean period (1 Macc 13:43ff.) and in accordance with the prevalent views of the Israelite settlement as a perfectly legal process (see Weinfeld 1984a, 115–33).

THE LESSONS FROM THE WANDERINGS IN THE DESERT (8:1–20)

8 1You shall faithfully observe all the commandments that I command you today, that you may live and increase and come in and possess the land that

YHWH swore to your fathers. [2]Remember the long way that YHWH your God led you in the wilderness these past forty years, in order to chastise you, to test you by hardships to know what was in your heart: whether you would keep his commandments or not. [3]He chastised you and made you hunger and fed you with the manna that neither you nor your fathers had ever known, in order to teach you that man does not live on bread alone, but lives on anything that YHWH decrees. [4]The clothes upon you did not wear out, nor did your feet swell these forty years. [5]Bear in mind that YHWH your God disciplines you just as a man disciplines his son. [6]Therefore, keep the commandments of YHWH your God to walk in his ways and to fear him.

[7]When YHWH your God brings you into a good land, a land with streams, springs, and deeps issuing from plain and hill; [8]a land of wheat and barley, vine, figs, and pomegranates, a land of olives bearing oil and of honey; [9]a land where you will never eat food in poverty, where you lack nothing; a land whose rocks are iron and from whose hills you can mine copper. [10]When you have eaten your fill, you shall bless YHWH your God for the good land that he has given you.

[11]Beware lest you forget YHWH your God so that you do not keep his commandments, his judgments, and his laws, which I command you today, [12]lest when you have eaten your fill and have built fine houses to live in, [13]and your herds and flocks will multiply, and your silver and gold will be multiplied, and everything you own prospers, [14]beware lest your heart grow haughty and you forget YHWH your God—who freed you from the land of Egypt, from the house of slavery; [15]who led you through the great and terrible desert [with] flying serpents and scorpions, a parched land with no water in it, who brought forth water for you from the flinty rock; [16]who fed you in the wilderness with manna that your fathers had never known, in order to test you by hardships only to benefit you in the end—[17]and you say to yourselves, "My own power and the might of my own hand have won this wealth for me." [18]Remember that it is YHWH your God who gives you the power to get wealth, in fulfillment of the covenant that he swore to your fathers, as at this day.

[19]If you do forget YHWH your God and follow other gods to serve them or bow down to them, I warn you this day that you shall certainly perish; [20]like the nations that YHWH destroys before you, so shall you perish because you would not hearken to YHWH your God.

TEXTUAL NOTES

8:2. *these past forty years.* Hebrew: *zeh ʾarbaʿim šanah;* cf. 4b and see *GKC* §136d. The LXX omits it; it forms, however, with 4b an *inclusio* for the passage 2–4. See Lohfink 1963, p. 190 n. 10.

to know what was in your heart. Hebrew: *ldʿt ʾt ʾšr blbbk.* The Samaritan

Pentateuch and certain Hebrew manuscripts omit the direct object marker *ʾet;* cf., however, 2 Sam 3:25 and 14:20, which have *ʾet* with *kol ʾăšer,* as here.

whether you would keep his commandments. The latter word is written *mṣwtw* (singular), but read *(Qĕrê) miṣwotaw* in plural; cf. 7:9; 27:10.

3. *had ever known.* MT: *yadʿûn,* a third-person plural perfect with the addition of an anomalous *nun.* The form is found only here and in v 16 (same context as here), both before *aleph* in order to avoid hiatus; see *GKC* §44 el. The Samaritan Pentateuch reads the normal *yadʿû,* both here and in v 16.

that neither you nor your fathers had ever known. Literally, "that you did not know and that your fathers did not know." Most LXX manuscripts omit "that you did not know." But in v 16 below, where the MT lacks "that you did not know," many LXX manuscripts add the phrase.

4. *your feet swell.* MT: *weraglĕka loʾ baṣeqah,* literally, "your foot did not swell." The Samaritan and Syriac versions have the noun in the plural ("feet") with the singular verb.

5–10. These verses appear as a separate pericope in the Samaritan Pentateuch *(qiṣṣah)* and in 4QDeut m (All Souls Deuteronomy Scroll, Cross 1965, pl. 19, p. 20; cf. Stegemann 1967–69, pp. 222–23). It was apparently prepared for liturgical use, connected with the benediction after a meal that is mentioned in v 10 (see the NOTE to v 7, below).

5. Verse 5 starts a parashah in the Samaritan Pentateuch as well as in the Qumran scroll 4QDeut n, mentioned above.

in mind (ʿm lbbk). Cf. 15:9; Josh 14:7; 1 Kgs 8:18; 10:2; 1 Chr 22:7; 28:2; 2 Chr 1:11; 24:4; 29:10.

just as a man disciples. Samaritan, 4Q Dt^{j} (Duncan 1989, Fig. 21) add *kn (kʾ šr . . . kn),* which seems authentic; cf. Weinfeld 1972, 134–36.

6. *in his ways. (bdrkyw).* 4Q Dt^{j} (Duncan 1989, Fig. 21) and LXX^{l}: *"in all his ways" (bkl drkyw).* Cf. 10:12; 11:22; Jos 22:5 and LXX 19:9. In the Qumran scroll (4QDeut n (S. A. While 1990, 270) we read *wlʾhbh* 'and to love' instead of Masoretic *wlyrʾh* 'and to fear'. Compare Deut 10:12; 11:13, 22; 19:9; 30:6, 16, 20.

7. This verse begins a new line in 4QDeut n, which may support the interpretation of *ky* here as "when" rather than "for." See the NOTE to 8:7.

a good land Samaritan, 4Q Dt^{f} (White 1990, 167) and LXX have a plus: '(a good) and broad land *(ʾrṣ ṭwbh wrḥbh)*'. Cf. also 4Q 387 11 (Newsom 1988, 64); the phrase *ʾrṣ ṭwbh wrḥbh* appears in MT Exod 3:8. In the Jewish blessing after the meals the mention of *ʾrṣ ṭwbh wrḥbh* is obligatory (B. Ber 48b), which may indicate that this blessing contains a pre-Masoretic element.

8. *vine.* Samaritan LXX: *gpn* without *waw.*

figs. Samaritan LXX, Qumran (4QDeut n): *tʾnh* without *waw.*

a land of olives bearing oil. Hebrew: *ʾrṣ zyt šmn* (cf. 2 Kgs 18:32, *ʾrṣ zyt yṣhr).* For olives bearing oil compare "vine bearing wine *(gpn hyyn)*" in Num 6:4 and Judg 13:14.

9. *in poverty.* Hebrew: *miskenût,* an abstract noun derived from the adjective *misken* 'poor', attested four times in Ecclesiastes (4:13; 9:15 [twice]; 9:16) but nowhere else in the Bible. *misken* is a loanword from Akkadian *muškenu* (derived from *šukenu* 'to be subjugated'), a technical term used in the ancient Near East legal literature to refer to a person whose legal status is something between that of a slave and that of a full citizen, according to Speiser *(OBS,* pp. 332–43), a ward of the state. From this is derived the meaning "subject," hence "pitiable, underprivileged" or "poor." Similar meanings are attested in other Semitic languages, including Arabic, whence are derived Spanish *mesquino,* Italian *meschino,* and French *mesquin,* which mean 'mean, stingy'.

where you lack nothing. The LXX, Syriac, and Qumran (4QDeut n): "and where you lack nothing *(wlʾ tḥsr).*"

and from whose hills. Hebrew: *wmhrryh;* 4QDeut n (White 1990, 269), 5Q 1, 2:4 (DJD 3.169): *wmhryh.* The MT fits more the hymnic style (cf. 33:15; Num 23:7; etc.). In the Samaritan Deut, 33:15 has *hry* instead of MT *hrry.*

12. *lest.* Implicitly, this means "beware (v 11) . . . lest" you do all of the things mentioned in vv 12–17, which form one long dependent clause.

and have built fine houses to live in. Hebrew: *wyšbt.* The LXX has *en autais* and 5Q1, 2:6, DJD 3.171 (addition over the line): *(wyšbt) bm* 'and you will live *in them.*' Compare Josh 24:13 of a similar context: *wtšbw bhm* 'and you lived *in them*'.

13. *will multiply.* Hebrew: *yrbyn* instead of the regular *yrbwn* (like the Samaritan version). For such forms cf. Isa 17:12 *(yhmywn);* 21:12 *(tbʿywn);* 31:3 *(yklywn);* Pss 78:44 *(ystywn);* 122:6 *(yšlyw);* etc. See *GKC* §75u.

15. *[with] flying serpents and scorpions.* Hebrew: *naḥaš śarap w ʿaqrab,* without preposition. These either stand in a genitive relationship to an implied repetition of the noun *midbar* 'wilderness', in other words, "who led you through the great and terrible wilderness, [a wilderness of] flying serpents and scorpions," or they are "words of nearer definition standing in apposition" *(GKC* §128c). The LXX and Vg supply "in which are." The Targumim add "a place *(ʾtr)* of" ("place full of"). Compare the identical phrases in the Esarhaddon inscriptions (see the NOTE): "a place of *(ašar)* serpents and scorpions." The Hebrew for "flying serpents" is *nḥš śrp.* The Samaritan Pentateuch renders *nḥš śrwp* 'fiery serpents'. Compare also the Samaritan version of Num 21:8: *śrwp* instead of *śrp* in the MT.

16. *had never known.* See the NOTES at v 3.

17. *blbbk:* 5QDeut 1 2:9 (DJD 3.171) has *in your* (pl.) *heart, blbbkm* in the plural.

18. *in fulfillment of the covenant that he swore to your fathers.* Samaritan, LXX, and Qumran (5QDeut 1 2:11, DJD 3.171—according to the space left there, see note of J. T. Milik on p. 170) read, after *lʾbtyk,* "to Abraham, Isaac, and Jacob," as in 9:5.

19. A new section *(Petuḥah)* begins here in the MT, but not in the Samaritan Pentateuch or in 5QDeut 1 2:11 (DJD 3.171).

I warn you this day. Hebrew: *haʿidoti,* literally, 'call to witness', which is expressed by the addition in the LXX "of heaven and earth," as in the MT of 4:26 and 30:19. It seems that 5QDeut 1, 2:12 had a text identical to that of the LXX (cf. Milik in DJD 3.170).

20. *that God destroys.* The Samaritan Pentateuch has *mĕʾabbed (piʿel)* instead of *maʾabid (hiphʿil)* in the MT.

because. Hebrew: *ʿeqeb.* See the NOTE to 7:12.

NOTES

8:1. *all the commandments.* For the meaning of the term *miṣwah* see the NOTE to 5:28 and cf. 6:25; 11:8, 22; 15:5; 19:9; 27:1. The transition from singular in the first clause to plural in the rest of the opening verse is also characteristic of the closing sentences of this chapter; compare 19aβ–b with 19b–20. This change may allude to framing function of these verses, which indeed form a kind of *inclusio* for the chapter: promise at the beginning and threat at the end.

that you may live and increase. For this pair of concepts, see 30:16 *(wḥyyt wrbyt)* in the singular.

come in and possess the land. Compare 4:1, 5; 6:18 (in the singular); 7:1; etc. (see Weinfeld 1972a, p. 342 n. 2). The transition from the singular in the opening phrase, "all the commandments that I command *you*" to the plural in the continuance, "*you* shall observe," etc., is also found in the parallel of 6:17 (on the parallel, see the COMMENT), "Be sure [pl.] to keep the commandments . . . as he has commanded *you* [sing.]."

2. *that YHWH your God led you in the wilderness these past forty years.* Compare Amos 2:10, "I led you in the wilderness for forty years," and 29:5.

in order to chastise you. Compare vv 3, 16, in the sense of discipline, as in v 5. And compare Ps 119:71, "How good it is for me to have been chastised *(ʿunêti)* so that I learn your rules" and v 75, "I know your judgments are just, you chastised me rightly *(wʾmwnh ʿnytny).*"

to test you. Compare 6:16 and the NOTE there.

to know what was in your heart: whether you would keep his commandments or not. Compare 13:3; Judg 3:4; 2 Chr 32:31. The verse here is dependent on the manna episode in Exod 16:4, "That I may test them whether they will walk in my law or not." The manna functioned as a test for Israel's disposition regarding God (cf. the rebellious attitude in connection with the manna in Num 21:5) and as a test for the obedience of God's instructions. Compare Exod 16:19–20, 26–29 for the violation of the divine commandments in connection with the gathering of the manna.

3. *He chastised you and made you hunger.* The verb *ʿnh,* especially when

joined with *npš* 'soul', indicates fast and hunger; cf. Lev 16:29, 31; 23:27, 32; Num 29:7; Ps 35:13; Isa 58:3, 5; Ezra 8:21 *(hithpael);* Dan 10:12 *(hithpael).* Compare the noun *tᶜnyt* for 'fast' in Ezra 9:5 and in late Hebrew.

and fed you with the manna that neither you nor your fathers had ever known. It was a food unknown before. Compare Exod 16:15, "for they did not know what it was," but here dressed in rhetorical language typical of Deuteronomy; cf. also 13:7; 28:36, 64, and implying something never experienced before.

in order to teach you that man does not live on bread alone, but lives on anything that YHWH decrees. Some commentators see here a juxtaposition of bread with manna: the manna is given by God, unlike bread, which is prepared by man, but this is hardly what is meant here. The manna, though coming from heaven, is called "bread" (see Exod 16:2, 4, 32; Ps 105:40; Neh 9:15) and is also prepared by man (cf. Exod 16:23). Like bread, the manna comes to satisfy the need of men. The author rather wants to convey the idea that the existence of man depends not on food alone but on God's providence. A distinction should indeed be made between *ḥyh b* or *ḥyh mn* 'living on' (2 Kgs 4:1–7) and *ḥyh ᶜl,* which means existing or depending on (cf. Gen 27:40). Man *lives on* food consumed by him but *exists* on whatever God decrees. It is not bread alone that ensures man's existence, but God's providence. This is the lesson gained by the phenomenon of the manna. God is able to guarantee the existence of man even when nature does not. All of this goes well with the idea of the whole chapter that man should not rely on his power and wealth but on God (cf. Perlitt 1981). This sentence explains in fact the concept of "testing" in the present context. By causing deprivation and lack of food, God tests man to see whether he really puts his trust in him. This is indeed the way the Rabbis understood the testing here. Rabbi Eleazar of Modiᶜin says, "Whoever has what to eat today and says: what shall I eat tomorrow? is deficient of faith, as it is written: 'In order that I may test him [Exod 16:4]' " *(Mek. Mas. waYassaᶜ,* §2, p. 161).

The same attitude is reflected in the story about the testing of Jesus by Satan. After Jesus fasts for forty days, Satan tests him to see whether he will be able to turn stones into bread. Jesus replies by quoting this verse (Matt 4:1–4; Luke 4:3–4). Thus the "testing" in Deut 8:2, 16 is understood as being initiated by Satan, who represents evil (compare the "testing" of Satan in Job, chaps. 1 and 2). After this episode we find in the NT the episode about Satan's testing of Jesus by enticing him to fall from the roof of the Temple, to which Jesus reacts with the quotation of Deut 6:16, "you shall not test YHWH your God" (Matt 4:5–7; Luke 4:9–12). Associated with these two episodes is the third test concerning submission to Satan, which is rejected by Jesus, who relies on Deut 6:14 (Matt 4:8–10; Luke 4:5–8; see above, in the COMMENT on 6:10–19). As indicated in the COMMENT below, Deut 8 actually corresponds to Deut 6:10–19, and the "testing" in these two pericopes is presented ambiguously: man testing God in chap. 8 and God testing man in 6:16. Provision of food in the desert is the proper example for this. By asking for water in the desert, the people test God. Conversely, by giving manna God tests the endurance of the people.

on anything that YHWH decrees. Literally, "on that which comes out from the mouth of YHWH," meaning a decision that cannot be annulled. For this usage, *yṣʾ mpy X* in the sense of 'decree', cf. Isa 45:3; 48:3; 55:11, "so is the word that comes out from my mouth *(ʾšr yṣʾmpy),* it does not come back to me unfulfilled." The phrase here has some affinities to the Egyptian phrase in the Harris papyrus 44.6, "one lives from what comes out of his [God's] mouth" (cf. Brunner 1958, p. 428) but, as indicated, it is not limited to food but to the dependence of man's destiny on God's will.

4. *The clothes upon you did not wear out.* See 29:4; Neh 9:21; and compare in the Gilgamesh epic 11.244–46, "until he gets to his city [var. to his land], until he finishes his journey let not [this] cloak have a moldy cast *(šiba aj iddima),* let it be wholly new" (cf. Paul 1968, p. 119 n. 3.). *blh* is paralleled with *ʾkl ʿš* 'eaten by moth' in Isa 50:9 and Job 13:28 (concerning cloth), which makes the parallel with Gilgamesh's "moldy cast" even stronger.

nor did your feet swell. Compare Neh 9:21. In 29:4, "nor did your sandals wear out on your feet," and so the Aramaic Targumim here, "you were not barefooted." In fact, both Deut 8:4 and 29:4 express an identical idea: swollen feet cannot bear shoes on them (see Blau 1956).

5. *Bear in mind.* Literally, "know in your heart." Compare 4:39 and see the NOTE there.

that YHWH your God disciplines you just as a man disciplines his son. Hebrew *ysr* denotes training by chastising and punishing as a father does to his son (see 21:18; and cf. Prov 19:18; 29:17). For the didactic idea compare Prov 3:11–12, "My son, despise not the chastening of YHWH *(mwsr YHWH)* . . . for whom YHWH loves he corrects *(ywkyḥ),*" also Job 5:17, "Happy is the man whom God corrects, do not despise the chastening *(mwsr)* of Shaddai"; and Ps 94:12, "Happy is the man whom you YHWH chastise *(tysrnw yh)* and from your teaching you instruct him *(wmtwrtk tlmdnw).*" The noun *mwsr* derived from *ysr* means education in general (Prov 1:2, 8; 4:1; etc.) and is found in Deut 11:2, "your children, who neither experienced nor witnessed the *lesson (mwsr)* of YHWH your God." As in the educational human process, where punishment is actually correction that brings improvement in the future, so God chastised Israel in the desert for its future benefit (cf. v 16).

6. *Therefore, keep the commandments.* This verse rounds off the passage (vv 1–6) that started with the injunction to keep the commandments of YHWH: *tšmrwn lʿśwt* (v 1).

to walk in his ways. Compare 5:30; 10:12; 11:22; 19:4; 26:17; 28:9; 30:16. Following law and justice was conceived in the Bible as following God's ways; cf., for example, Gen 18:19, "they will keep the way *(drk)* of YHWH by doing justice and righteousness," and see Prov 2:8–9; 8:20; etc. Similarly, in the Mesopotamian sources the "way" of justice is frequently referred to (see Weinfeld

1985d, pp. 15–17). In Deuteronomy following the way of YHWH, or rather walking in his ways *(hlk bdrkyw)*, means to keep his commandments. The word *halakha* in rabbinic literature, which denotes the whole lore of Jewish practice, is also derived from *hlk* 'walk'. For general behavior defined as *way*, cf. Jer 5:4; compare also *drk* 'way' in Qumran (1Q5 9:21; 4:22; 8:10; etc.) and *hodos* 'way' in the NT (Acts 9:2; 19:9; 24:14; etc.); cf. Weinfeld 1985, pp. 15–17.

to fear him. Compare 6:13 and the NOTE there.

7. *When YHWH your God brings you into a good land.* This phrase opens a long conditional sentence (protasis), which ends with the consequential clause (apodosis) in v 11a, "Beware lest you forget." Although the word *ky* here is usually understood as 'for', the passage in 6:10–12 that opens with *ky ybyʾk*—"when YHWH your God brings you into the land," etc.—and ends with "beware lest" etc. (v 12), as in the present case, and actually parallels our pericope (see the COMMENT), shows that *ky* here has been understood as 'when' (cf. Lohfink 1963, p. 192); for *ky* with a participle in a temporal sense, see 2 Sam 19:8: *ky ʾnk ywṣʾ* 'if you do not go out'. In the Qumran scrolls v 7 indeed starts a new paragraph (4QDeut n [Cross 1965, pl. 19, p. 20]). Conversely, it is possible that within the laudatory passage of 8:7–10, which seems to be independent in nature (see the COMMENT), the *ky* of v 7 was understood as 'for', as in the opening of the identical laudatory passage in 11:10–12. The author who integrated the passage into the sermon, however, understood the *ky* as 'when'.

springs, and deeps. Compare Prov 8:14.

issuing from plain and hill. Compare 11:11, "a land of hills and valleys, it drinks its water according to the rains of heaven." Here the stress is on the subterranean water while there stress is laid on the rain from heaven. For the double blessing of waters, cf. 33:13.

8. *a land of wheat and barley. . . .* An almost hymnic description of the promised land blessed with its products. Compare in the *Letter of Aristeas* 112, "the land is thickly planted with multitudes of olive trees, with crops of corn and vegetables with vines . . . other kinds of fruit trees and dates do not count compared with these" (Charles 1913, 2.105–6). A striking parallel to this description is found in the Egyptian story of Sinuhe. Here we find the land of Yaa (in Qedem), where Sinuhe settled, depicted as "a good land . . . of figs and grapes. It had more wine than water, abundant with honey plentiful in oil . . . all kinds of fruits . . . barley and emmer" (Lichtheim 1973–76, 1.226). A smaller depiction, albeit preserved in a fragmentary state, is attested in the inscription of Panamuwa I of Yaudi in northern Syria (eighth century), who thanks his gods who gave him "a land of barley . . . a land of wheat . . . cultivate land and vineyard *(ʾrq śʿry ʾrq ḥṭy . . . ʾrq wkrm)*" *(KAI* 214:5–7). It seems that such laudatory descriptions of fertile land were common in Syria and Palestine for long periods. In spite of its rhetorical vein the description in Deut 8:8 reflects reality. In Ezek 27:17 we read that Judah and the land of Israel were exporting wheat of special kind *(mnyt)*, *png* (see below), honey, and oil. A

similar list of products is found in the Esarhaddon inscriptions, referring to income from the provinces in Syria: grain *(ḫašlatu),* honey, and *pinigu* (compare *png* in Ezek 27:17); see Borger 1956, p. 94, lines 21–26). For the export of wheat, oil, and wine from Palestine to Egypt during the Ptolemaic period, cf. Tscherikover 1932–33, pp. 229–30, 235, 242; cf. also idem 1959, p. 68.

In Tel Miqne (= Ekron) industrial oil complexes of the Iron Age (especially the seventh century B.C.E.) were discovered on a scale and level of sophistication previously unknown in the ancient world; see Gitin and Dothan 1985 and 1986.

honey. Dbš denotes basically thick syrup and means here "date honey," just like Arabic *dibs.* According to the Rabbis it refers here to palm dates: *tmrym (b. Ber.* 41b; *ʿErub.* 4b; *y. Bik.* 1, 3, 63d). In the recently discovered Aramaic Psalm in demotic script we find *tmr* 'date' paralleled with *mmtqym* 'sweets' (cf. Weinfeld 1985b, p. 181.)

Dates were grown in Jericho (cf. Deut 34:3; Judg 1:16; 3:13; 2 Chr 28:15; and see Pliny, *Natural History* 13.45), in the valley of the Jordan area near Tiberias and Beth Shean as well as in the plains of the wilderness (cf. Gen 14:7: *Ḥaṣṣon Tamar).* Dates of Eretz Israel were exported (see Felix 1968, p. 41), while bee honey was imported from Attica and from the Aegean islands (cf. Tscherikover 1932–33, p. 362).

9. *you will never eat food in poverty.* For *msknwt* 'poverty' cf. *mskn* 'poor' in Eccl 4:13; 9:15, 16, a loanword from Akkadian *muškenu* 'poor, destitute'. For the noun *miskenût,* cf. Akkadian *muškenūtu* 'poverty' *(CAD* 10.H.II, p. 276).

a land whose rocks are iron and from whose hills you can mine copper. The description is somewhat utopian but has roots in reality. Iron mines were existent in Transjordan, as may be learned from Josephus, who tells us about an iron mountain in the region of Moab opposite Jericho (Wars 4.454) and compare *m. Sukk.* 3:1: *hr hbrzl.* Copper mines were found in the ʿArabah and especially in the regions of Pûnon (Num 33:42–43) and Timna in Edom; cf. Abramsky, 1968, 5.644–62.

10. *When you have eaten your fill, you shall bless YHWH your God for the good land that he has given you.* This brings to culmination the glorious description of the rich land given to the people of Israel, and indeed this verse served as the basis for the proclamation of the grace after meals in Judaism. The grace after meals consists of three benedictions (cf. *m. Ber.* 6:8): a benediction for the food, a benediction for the land and for the Torah and the Covenant, and a benediction for the city of Jerusalem (a fourth benediction was added later). A threefold benediction after meals is ascribed by the book of Jubilees (22:6–9) to Abraham after the meal: thanks for the food on the earth, thanks for being saved from adversaries, and a prayer for the chosen nation and its inheritance (Charles 1913, 2.45). A threefold benediction after meals is also found in the *Didache* or the so-called *Teaching of the Twelve Apostles,* of the second century B.C.E.:

1. "We give thanks to you . . . for the knowledge and faith . . . etc."

which parallels the blessing for Torah and Covenant in the conventional Jewish blessing.

2. "You created everything . . . and gives food to men . . . ," which parallels the first blessing.

3. "Remember, Lord, your community *(ekklesia)* to deliver it from all evil . . . and gather it together from all the corners of the earth to your Kingdom." This overlaps the *Blessing for Jerusalem* and the Davidic dynasty in the conventional grace after meals. The 'Kingdom of God' mentioned here is actually prescribed in tractate *Berachot* 49a as a mandatory element in the grace after meals. Josephus also mentions the grace after meals of the Essenes *(Wars* 2.131). That the benediction after meals was based on Deut 8:10 may be learned from a Qumran text that contains Deut 8:5–10 *(All Souls Deuteronomy Scroll,* 4QDt n [White 1990, p. 269]; see Stegemann 1967–69, pp. 221–27). The copying of just this passage from Deuteronomy is enigmatic, and may be explained as serving a liturgical purpose. Indeed, the division of the passage into subunits in 4QDt n points in that direction. There is a space of one line between vv 8 and 9 which has puzzled the scholars (cf. Stegemann 1967–69, pp. 224–25). The explanation is provided in the rabbinic literature. In *m. Ber.* 6:8 we find a dispute between the rabbis concerning the benedictions after meals. According to Rabban Gamliel, one is obliged to pronounce the three benedictions even after eating fruits of the species mentioned in Deut 8:8, whereas according to the other sages the obligation to say the three benedictions is due only after eating bread. The latter view is based on the fact that the phrase "land where you may eat bread," etc. in v 9 opens a new paragraph and therefore the command to bless YHWH of v 10b refers to it, and not to all of the fruits mentioned in v 8. It seems then that the division in the Qumran passage in which v 9 starts a new section intends to stress the same principle, namely, that "the land where you may eat bread" in v 9 is linked to the blessing commanded in v 10 and not v 8, which enumerates all of the other species. The Qumranic passage of Deut 8:5–10 in 4QDeut n is then of liturgical nature and was copied only for the sake of instruction concerning the blessing after meals. Another scroll of the same nature is 4QDt j, recently published and investigated by J. Duncan (1990). There we also find Deut 8:5–10 next to Deut 5–6 (Decalogue and Shemaᶜ), 11:13–21 *(wehaya im šamōᶜa),* Exod 12–13 and Deut 32. All this material belongs to Jewish liturgical practice.

The Decalogue and the *Šemaᶜ* were recited daily in the temple (see above), and were put in the Phylacteries next to Exod 13 (the so called sections of *Qadesh,* vv 1–10, and *wehaya ki yebiʾ aka,* vv 11–16). Deut 8:5–10 reflects, as shown above, the grace after meals whereas Deut 32 is known as a liturgical text, recited by the Levites in the temple on the Sabbath (b. Rosh Hashana 31a; y. Megilla 3:6, 74b).

A text from Qumran which contains a blessing after meals in the house of the mourner that was until now unrecognized as such, is 4Q436 fr.2 (publication forthcoming). Here we find the following elements: (1) consolation for the mourner in the form of Isa 66:13, which appears in the conventional Jewish Blessing after meals at the mourner's house; (2) the eating from the fruit of the land; (3) the God who does good for the creatures (providing them with food); (4) the mention of the pleasant land *(ʾrṣ ḥmdh);* (5) the Torah and the Law; (6) the throne of Glory (which is associated with the Davidic throne in Jerusalem). All these elements are prescribed in the Rabbinic literature as mandatory.

11. *Beware lest you forget YHWH your God so that you do not keep his commandments.* Forgetting YHWH means ignoring his existence as well as his demands (cf. 6:12–14; 8:14, 19).

12. *lest when you have eaten your fill.* This phrase opens a long sentence, which ends up in v 17 with the apodosis, "then you will say to yourselves" etc.

and have built fine houses to live in. Compare 6:10–11. There is a difference in view between these two passages, however. In 6:10–14 the author refers not to the people's own achievements but to the beneficial things taken over by them from the native population: "cities that you did not build" etc. By contrast, in 8:11–18 the author speaks about the wealth acquired by the people themselves: fine houses were built, herds and flocks raised, silver and gold and all other things multiplied. Following this distinction there is a difference in the presentation of the apostasy in these two sources. In 6:10–14 the "forgetting of YHWH" means disobeying him because of affluence, while here it means ignoring his existence out of pride and reliance on one's own power. The idea as expressed here is reflected in Hos 8:14: "Israel has forgotten his maker and built temples and Judah multiplied fortified cities."

13. *and your silver and gold will be multiplied.* Compare in the king's law, "neither shall he multiply to himself silver and gold" (17:17), followed, as here, by the motivation, "lest his heart grow haughty" (17:20). The silver and gold actually were multiplied by God, but Israel ascribes it to his own power. The same idea is expressed in Hosea, "I who multiplied the silver on her and gold, which they used for Baal . . . she would go after her lovers forgetting me."

14. *lest your heart grow haughty and you forget YHWH your God.* Compare 2:10–15; also Hos 13:6, "they were filled and their heart grew haughty, therefore they forgot me *(śbʿw wyrm lbm ʿl kn škḥwny).*" It seems that the whole notion of "forgetting YHWH" through reliance on one's own power was widespread in northern Israel, especially in Hosea, and this influenced Deuteronomy (see Garcia Lopez 1979, pp. 61–65; Weinfeld 1985c, pp. 84–89).

This idea had also been propagated in Assyria. Thus we read in an Assyrian text regarding Tirhakah, king of Egypt, that "he forgot the might of the god Aššur . . . and trusted in his own strength" (Streck, 1916, 2.6, i:56–57).

who freed you from the land of Egypt, from the house of slavery. A phrase taken from the Decalogue (Deut 5:6); compare 6:12.

15. *who led you through the great and terrible desert.* Compare 1:19.

[with] flying serpents and scorpions, a parched land with no water in it.

Compare the inscriptions of Esarhaddon concerning his campaign to the Arabian territory of Bazu: "a waterless region . . . a place of serpents and scorpions *(ašar ṣumāmi . . . ašar ṣeru u aqrabu)*" (Borger 1956, p. 56, iv:54–56. See also Isa 30:6 on the way to Egypt, "through a land of trouble . . . viper and the flying serpent." In Esarhaddon's campaign to Egypt we hear Esarhaddon speaking about snakes with deadly breath and yellow flying serpents (Borger 1956, p. 112, RS. 5–7). Herodotus also speaks about flying serpents in the Sinai desert and South Arabia (2.75; 3.109). One is of course reminded of the story about the fiery serpents *(śrpym)* in Num 22:6.

For illustrations of winged serpents in ancient Egypt, see Keel 1977, p. 77.

who brought forth water for you from the flinty rock. Compare Exod 17:6; Num 10:8, 11. Deuteronomy adds *ḥalamiš* in order to enhance the impression of the rock's hardness. *Ḥalamiš* equals Akkadian *elemešu,* which means a brilliant precious stone (compare *ḥšml* in Ezek 1:4, 27) that is the hardest naturally occurring substance. Compare Greek *adamas* 'diamond' (hence English adamant). For *ḥalamiš* in association with precious stones, cf. Job 28:9. The word appears elsewhere in poetry (cf. Deut 32:13; Ps 114:8; Isa 50:7; Job 28:9).

16. *who fed you in the wilderness with manna . . . in order to test you . . . only to benefit you in the end.* Testing by hardship for the sake of a better future *(ʾaḥarit)* is a prevalent idea in sapiential literature; cf. Job 8:7; 42:12; Ps 37:37–38; Prov 23:18; 24:14, 20; etc. See Weinfeld 1972a, pp. 316–17.

17. *and you say to yourselves.* This takes us back to 14a; see the COMMENT below.

My own power and the might of my own hand have won this wealth for me. *ḥyl* here has the sense of wealth (cf. Gen 34:29; Num 31:9; Isa 8:4; 10:14; Jer 15:13; Job 5:5; 31:25), and the verb *ʿśh* with reflexive *l* denotes 'acquire' (cf. Gen 12:5; 31:1); see especially Ezek 28:4, "by your wisdom and understanding you have gained riches *(ʿśyt lk ḥyl)* and you have acquired *(wtʿś)* gold and silver in your treasuries."

18. *Remember that it is YHWH your God.* The construction "when you say to yourselves *(ʾmr blbb)* . . . remember *(zkr)*" is characteristic of the Deuteronomic speeches (see 7:17–18; 9:4–7a; cf. Garcia Lopez 1978a, pp. 485–86.

in fulfillment of the covenant. Literally, "in order to erect/establish the covenant," which is typical of the priestly literature (cf. Gen 6:18; 9:9, 11; 17:7, 10, 19; Exod 6:4; Lev 26:9). In the Deuteronomic literature we find "erecting/establishing the word *(hqym dbr)*" as in Deut 9:5; 1 Kgs 2:4; 8:20; 12:15; but also the combination "establishing/erecting the *words of the covenant*" (2 Kgs 23:3; Jer 34:18).

as at this day. Compare 2:30 and the NOTE there.

19. *If you do forget.* The opposite of the "remembering" enjoined in v 18.

I warn you this day that you shall certainly perish. This type of threat is always styled in the plural (see 4:26; 30:19).

20. *because you would not hearken. ʿqb lʾ tšmʿn* rounds off the section, which started in 7:12 with "if you hearken" (see the NOTE to 7:11).

COMMENT

This chapter constitutes a sermon that underscores God's providence and care over Israel. In the first part of the sermon (vv 1–6) the author recounts how Israel was sustained and guided in the desert by God. This is described here as an educational process: the trek in the desert with all the sufferings is conceived as a test for the Israelites. The people were subjected to all sorts of difficulties in order to see whether, in spite of the hardships, they would follow the will of God and keep his commandments (v 2). Furthermore, by subjecting the people to hunger and by feeding them with manna, God taught the Israelites that man does not live on bread alone (v 3). Through the suffering in the desert God disciplined the people as a man disciplines his son (v 5; compare Prov 3:11–12; Job 15:16–17) for his benefit in the future (v 16).

The second part of the sermon, which envisages the people thriving in the land (vv 7–20), urges them to draw the moral of the trek in the wilderness and not to forget its lesson. When they enter the land they ought to remember that it was God who gave them the land and that it was not acquired by their own strength and power (vv 17–18).

By way of juxtaposition of the desert and the fertile land, the author is drawn into a glorious description of the promised land (vv 7–9). It is depicted here not just as "a land of milk and honey" as in the previous sources, but as a rich land in every respect: it is a land of grain, wine, and fruits as well as of natural resources such as iron and copper.

Chapter 8 actually overlaps the sermon in 6:10–19, which contains the same motifs as chap. 8 albeit in a less elaborate manner. Thus the testing in the desert and the exhortation to keep the law that appear in chap. 6 in the second part of that sermon (vv 16–19) occur in chap. 8 at the beginning (vv 1–6) with the difference that in chap. 6 the testing is by the people, and therefore carries a negative sense, while in chap. 8 the testing is by God and is therefore of constructive nature. As indicated in the COMMENT on 6:10–19, this ambiguous view of testing is anchored in the Exodus narratives, especially in the episodes of the manna and the water (see the NOTE to v 3).

The second part of chap. 8 corresponds to the first part of the sermon in chap. 6:10–19 and is even structured similarly. Both open with the formula "when YHWH your God brings you into the land" (compare 6:10 with 8:7). Next comes the description of the richness of the land (compare 6:10b–11 with 8:7b–9), which ends with the phrase "you eat your fill *(wʾklt wśbʿt)*" (compare 6:11 and 8:10). Afterward comes the warning not to forget YHWH (compare 6:12 with 8:11). Both sermons culminate with the threat of annihilation in the event that they worship foreign gods (compare 6:14–15 with 8:19–20).

Both sermons urge the people to remember and not to forget YHWH, who freed them from the house of bondage in Egypt (6:12 compared with 8:14), a phrase taken from the opening of the Decalogue. According to N. Lohfink (1963, p. 192), 8:7–18 is dependent on 6:10–15, but this can hardly be proved.

The two main themes around which chap. 8 revolves are—as already indicated—the desert on the one hand, and the land on the other. Both of these themes are described in detail by means of elevated prose, as, for example, "a land with streams, springs, and deeps issuing from plain and hill; a land of wheat and barley, vine, figs, and pomegranates, a land of olives bearing oil and of honey; . . . a land whose rocks are iron and from whose hills you can mine copper" (vv 7b–9). The same applies to the description of the desert: "who led you through the great and terrible desert . . . who brought forth water for you from the flinty rock; who fed you in the wilderness with manna" (vv 15–16). In the latter description, hymnic participial style is used, as, for instance, in Ps 104:2–4, 10, 13–14.

In the opinion of F. Garcia Lopez (1977, pp. 481–522), these hymnic descriptions were adopted by the author from old tradition and were used by him in order to build his arguments about the reliance on God. This may explain the difficulties of the integration of the hymnic passages in the overall construction. Thus, for example, the urge to bless YHWH for the land in v 10b is hard to understand in the context of the warning in v 11. Nevertheless, it is a proper culmination for such a laudatory passage as vv 7–10. Similarly, vv 14b–16, which contain a hymnic description of the redeeming God, seem to disrupt the connection between 14a and 17. One should admit, however, that in spite of the difficulties of integrating the underlying elements of the chapter, the chapter as a whole constitutes a coherent unit because it is structured in chiastic fashion, as N. Lohfink (1963, pp. 194–95) has shown:

A. v 1: paraenetic frame
    B. vv 2–6: wandering in the desert
        C. vv 7–10: the richness of the land
            D. v 11: the central idea (not to forget YHWH)
        C′. vv 12–13: the richness of the land
    B′. vv 14b–16: wandering in the desert
A′. vv 19–20: paraenetic frame

The central idea of the chapter, to remember the past and to keep in mind God's providence, is boldly expressed by the recurring expressions "forget *(škḥ)*" and "remember *(zkr)*" (vv 2, 11, 14, 18, 19).

THE SIN OF THE PAST (9:1–10:11)

9 [1]Hear, O Israel! You are about to cross the Jordan to come in and dispossess nations greater and mightier than you: large cities with walls sky-high; [2]a people great and tall, the Anakites, of whom you have known, of whom you have heard, saying: "Who can stand up to the Anakites?" [3]Know then this day that none other than YHWH your God is crossing at your head, a devouring fire; it is he who will wipe them out, he will subdue them before you, you will dispossess and destroy them quickly, as YHWH promised you. [4]And when YHWH your God drives them out from your path, say not to yourselves, "YHWH has enabled me to occupy this land because of my innocence and because of the guilt of these nations YHWH is dispossessing before you. [5]It is not because of your righteousness and your rectitude that you will be able to occupy their country, but because of the wickedness of these nations YHWH your God is dispossessing before you, in order to establish the word that YHWH swore to your fathers, Abraham, Isaac, and Jacob.

[6]Know, then, that it is not for any virtue of yours that YHWH your God is giving you this good land to occupy; for you are a stiff-necked people. [7]Remember, never forget, how you provoked YHWH your God to anger in the wilderness: from the day that you left the land of Egypt until you reached this place, you have been continuously rebellious with YHWH.

[8]At Horeb you so provoked YHWH that YHWH was angry enough with you to have destroyed you. [9]When I had ascended the mountain to receive the tablets of stone, the tablets of the covenant that YHWH had made with you, and I stayed on the mountain forty days and forty nights, I neither ate bread nor drank water. [10]And YHWH gave me the two tablets of stone inscribed by the finger of God, with the exact words that YHWH had spoken to you on the mountain, out of the fire, on the day of the assembly.

[11]At the end of those forty days and forty nights, YHWH gave me the two tablets of stone, the tablets of the covenant. [12]And YHWH said to me, "Hurry, go down from here at once, for your people whom you freed from Egypt have acted wickedly; quickly they strayed from the way that I commanded them; they have made themselves a molten image." [13]YHWH said to me, "I see that this is a stiff-necked people. [14]Let me alone and I will destroy them and blot out their name from under heaven, and I will make you a nation mightier and larger than them."

[15]I started down the mountain, while the mountain was ablaze with fire, the two tablets of the covenant in my two hands. [16]I saw how you had sinned against YHWH your God: you had made yourselves a molten calf; you had been quick to stray from the path that YHWH had commanded you. [17]Thereupon I

gripped the two tablets and flung them away with both my hands, smashing them before your eyes. [18]I lay prostrate before YHWH as at the first—eating no bread and drinking no water forty days and forty nights—because of the great wrong you had committed, doing what displeased YHWH to vex him. [19]For I was in dread of YHWH's fierce anger against you, which moved him to wipe you out. And that time, too, YHWH listened to me. [20]Moreover, YHWH was angry enough with Aaron to have destroyed him; so I also interceded for Aaron at that time. [21]As for that sinful thing you had made, the calf, I took it and put it to the fire; I crushed it to bits, grinding it well to dust, and I threw its dust into the brook that comes down from the mountain.

[22]Again you provoked YHWH at Taberah, and at Massah, and at Kibroth-Hattaavah.

[23]And when YHWH sent you on from Kadesh-Barnea, saying, "Go up and occupy the land that I am giving you," you flouted the command of YHWH your God; you did not put your trust in him and did not obey him.

[24]As long as I have known you, you have been rebellious against YHWH.

[25]When I lay prostrate before YHWH the forty days and forty nights that I lay prostrate, because YHWH was determined to destroy you, [26]I prayed to YHWH and said, "O Lord YHWH, do not annihilate your people and your inheritance, whom you released in your greatness and whom you freed from Egypt with a mighty hand. [27]Give thought to your servants, Abraham, Isaac, and Jacob, and pay no heed to the stubbornness of this people, its wickedness, and its sinfulness. [28]Else the country from which you freed us will say, 'It was because of the inability of YHWH to bring them into the land that he had promised them, and because he hated them, that he brought them out to have them die in the wilderness.' [29]Yet they are your very own people, whom you freed with your great might and your outstretched arm."

10 [1]At that time YHWH said to me, "Carve out two tablets of stone like the first, and come up to me on the mountain; and make an ark of wood. [2]I will write on the tablets the commandments that were on the first tablets, which you smashed, and you shall deposit them in the ark."

[3]I made an ark of acacia wood and carved out two tablets of stone like the first; I took the two tablets with me and went up the mountain. [4]YHWH wrote on the tablets as at the first writing, the Ten Commandments that he addressed to you on the mountain out of the fire on the day of the assembly; and YHWH gave them to me. [5]Then I left and went down from the mountain, and I deposited the tablets in the ark that I had made, and there they remain, as YHWH had commanded me.

[6]From the wells of Bene-Jaakan the Israelites marched to Moserah. Aaron died there and was buried there; and his son Eleazar became priest in his stead. [7]From there they marched to Gudgod, and from Gudgod to Jotbatah, a land of streams of water.

[8]At that time, YHWH separated the tribe of Levi to carry the Ark of

YHWH's Covenant, to stand before YHWH and to serve him, and to bless in his name, as is still the case. [9]Therefore Levi has no portion nor inheritance along with his brethren. YHWH is his inheritance, as YHWH your God spoke to him.

[10]I had stayed on the mountain, as I did the first time, forty days and forty nights; and YHWH listened to me that time also: YHWH agreed not to destroy you. [11]And YHWH said to me, "Arise for journeying before the people, that they may invade and occupy the land that I swore to their fathers to give them."

TEXTUAL NOTES

9:1. *Hear.* In *Tg. Ps.-J.* to this chapter, all direct address to Israel is in the second-person plural, even where the MT has second-person singular.

2. *a people great and tall.* Hebrew: *ʿm gdwl wrm.* The LXX has *megan kai polun kai eumēke* 'great and numerous and tall' like the MT in 2:10, 21: *gdwl wrb wrm,* where next to it we find the Anakites, as we do here; cf. also 1:28 and the NOTE there (see the discussion in R. Weiss 1981, p. 104).

3. *a devouring fire.* Driver (1902) considers this phrase to be an adverbial accusative meaning "as a devouring fire" in the form of "a devouring fire." It seems more likely, however, that the phrase "a devouring fire" stands in apposition to "YHWH your God." The LXX and Peshitta translate, "he is a devouring fire." Compare *Tgs. Ps.-J.* and *Onq.*, "His word [i.e., He] is a devouring fire." *Targun Neofiti* and the Vg each use two verbs to translate Hebrew *ʾoklah* 'devouring'. *Neof.*: *ʾklh wmtʾklh* 'devouring and self consuming'; compare *Tg. Ps.-J.* to 4:24 and Exod 24:17: *ʾš ʾklh ʾš* 'fire, devouring fire' (= self-consuming fire); Vg: *devorans atque consumens.*

you will dispossess and destroy them. The LXX omits "dispossess."

destroy them. MT: *whʾbdtm.* Samaritan text: *wʾbdtm;* compare the TEXTUAL NOTE to 8:20.

4. *when . . . drives . . . out.* MT: *bhdp.* Samaritan text: *bhdyp* ($\sqrt{ndp}$). Compare 6:19 and the TEXTUAL NOTE ad loc.

from your path. MT: *mlpnyk.* Samaritan text: *mpnyk;* cf. 7:22, where the MT has *mpnyk* and the Samaritan text *mlpnyk,* as the MT here.

5. *your God.* Omitted in some Hebrew manuscripts, the Samaritan text, and the LXX.

to establish [the word]. Hebrew: *lhqym,* literally, 'to raise up'. Compare the opposite: *hpyl dbr* 'let the word fall' in 1 Sam 3:19; cf. Josh 21:43; 23:14; 1 Kgs 8:56; 2 Kgs 10:10; see Weinfeld 1972a, p. 350.

word. Hebrew: *dabar,* in the sense of "oath." LXX: *diathēke* 'covenant' (compare 8:18b). *dabar* actually connotes covenant; cf. Akkadian *awatu/amātu,* Sumerian *enim,* Hittite *memiyaš,* Greek *rhētra,* all of which mean literally 'word' but are used in the sense of 'covenant' as well (see Weinfeld 1975b, 2.257).

YHWH swore. YHWH is omitted in the Samaritan text, some LXX manuscripts, and Peshitta.

7. *never forget.* Samaritan text, Peshitta, and Vg: "and never forget."

from the day. Hebrew: *lmn (hywm).* For this pleonastic form, *lmn* instead of *mn,* see 4:32 and the NOTE there.

you left. In the MT the verb is *yṣʾt,* second-person singular; in the Samaritan text, LXX, and Peshitta it is second-person plural. Because the verb "you came" that follows is in the plural in all texts, it is likely that the MT should be emended to *yṣʾtm,* the final *m* having been lost through haplography.

you have been continuously rebellious. Hebrew: *mamrîm hĕyitem.* The construction *hyh* plus participle is the past continuous.

with. Hebrew: *ʿm,* that is to say, "in dealing with"; see Driver 1902, ad loc.

9. *I had ascended . . . and I stayed.* Literally, "When I ascended . . . and I stayed." The first clause is a temporal clause, separated from the main clause by *waw*-consecutive; see *GKC* §111b. Driver 1902, ad loc. also considers the possibility that the first clause is meant to modify v 8, while "and I stayed" begins a new idea. But there is no reason to ignore the verse division, because the construction above is well attested. Compare also v 23 below.

I neither ate bread nor drank water. Literally, "I ate no bread and drank no water."

10. *with the exact words.* Hebrew: *wʿlyhm kkl hdbrym,* literally, 'and upon them as all the words'. Some Hebrew manuscripts read *kl* 'all' for *kkl* 'as all', which is smoother. The LXX, Vg, Peshitta, and *Tg. Neof.* likewise ignore the preposition *k-,* but this most probably reflects simply the exigencies of translation.

to you. MT: *ʿmkm,* literally, 'with you'. Samaritan text: *ʾlykm* 'to you', as in the MT at 10:4.

on the mountain, out of the fire, on the day of the assembly. Some LXX manuscripts omit "on the mountain," others omit "out of the fire," and still others omit "on the day of the assembly." "On the mountain" is omitted, apparently through oversight, from the *NJPS.*

11. *tablets of stone.* Omitted in the Samaritan text.

12. *that I commanded them.* Hebrew *ṣwytm* is read *ṣiwwitîm* but could be vocalized *ṣiwwitam* 'you commanded', as rendered by the LXX in the parallel verse of Exod 32:8. Indeed, the latter rendering would fit the tone of the verse in which the people are dissociated from YHWH: "your people whom you brought out . . . whom you commanded." On the tendency of the Masoretes to correct such readings, which ascribe the commanding to Moses, see Geiger 1928, pp. 329–30.

a molten image. Samaritan text: *ʿgl mskh* 'a molten calf', as in Exod 32:8. Compare v 16 and the TEXTUAL NOTE there.

13. *YHWH said to me.* The LXX reads, "I have told you once and again saying, ['I see,' etc.]," in order to circumvent the difficulty of having twice

"YHWH said to me" (vv 12, 13) without interruption between the two; this is also the reason for adding "further" in *JPS.*

14. *Let me alone.* Hebrew: *herep mimmeni,* literally, 'loosen [your grip] from me'. Compare Judg 11:37; 1 Sam 11:3; 15:16; Ps 46:11; and cf. the parallel text Exod 32:10, where *hannîḥāh lî,* literally, 'let me rest, let me be', is used instead. Peshitta prefaces the verse with *hšʾ* 'now', under the influence of Exod 32:10. *(wʿth)* The Aramaic Targumim, here and in Exod 32:10, are disturbed by the gross anthropomorphism implied in the Hebrew text, which indicates that Moses is physically preventing YHWH from carrying out his will. They translate, therefore, "Stop praying to me"; and see the NOTE to this verse.

a nation mightier and larger. LXX adds "great *(gdwl)*"; cf. 26:5.

15. *I started down.* MT: *wʾpn wʾrd.* Samaritan text: *wʾpnh wʾrdh.*

16. *I saw how.* Hebrew: *wʾrʾ* [Samaritan text: *wʾrʾh]whnh,* 'I saw, and behold'. LXX, Vg, and Peshitta: "I saw that."

calf. Omitted in some LXX manuscripts, which read simply "a molten [image]." Compare v 12, in which the MT and LXX omit "calf," while the Samaritan text adds it.

been quick to stray. Literally, "strayed quickly." "Quickly" is omitted in some Samaritan and LXX manuscripts; cf. 4:26, and v 3 above.

17. *I gripped.* MT: *wʾtpś;* Samaritan text: *wʾtpśh.* The Vg omits "I gripped" because it is inappropriate at this point, when Moses has been gripping the tablets for some time and is about to release his hold.

18. *as at the first.* LXX: "again, as before."

the great wrong (ḥṭʾtkm). The Samaritan text, LXX, Vg, Peshitta, and *Tg. Ps.-J.* read *ḥṭʾtykm* 'your sins'; but see v 21, where the "sin" refers to the physical object, that is, the calf.

19. *YHWH listened.* Some Hebrew manuscripts add "your God," as do some LXX manuscripts. Other LXX manuscripts add "our God"; still others add simply "God."

20. *YHWH was angry enough.* The words *YHWH mʾd* are omitted in LXX^{B}.

I . . . interceded. MT: *wʾtpll;* Samaritan text: *wʾtpllh.*

at that time. Vg: *similiter* 'in that manner, likewise'; see, however, the NOTE to this verse.

21. *sinful thing.* MT: *ḥṭʾtkm,* literally, 'your sin'. Samaritan text: *ḥṭʾtykm* 'your sins'; cf. v 18. Here, however, a single, concrete object is referred to, and the plural is therefore less appropriate.

I took. The verb *lqḥty* 'I took' is in the perfect tense, rather than the expected imperfect with *waw*-consecutive, *wʾqḥ.* The verb should therefore be understood as a pluperfect, "I had taken"; see *GKC* §106f. This action thus took place before the intercessions of vv 18–20, a sequence that accords with the description in Exod 32:20, 31ff.

The verbs in the verse are in the simple form in the MT; they are in the usual lengthened form in the Samaritan text *(wʾśrph, wʾkth, wʾšlykh).*

I crushed it to bits, grinding it well. Hebrew: *wʾkt ʾtw ṭḥwn hyṭb,* literally, 'I crushed it, grinding thoroughly'. The LXX and Peshitta translate with two finite verbs, as I do. The Vg omits *ṭḥwn. Targumim Ongelos* and *Pseudo-Jonathan* translate *ṭḥwn* as *bšwpynʾ* 'with a file'. *Targum Neofiti* translates *ṭḥwn* as *zqyq* 'fine'.

22. *Again you provoked.* Hebrew: *maqṣipîm hĕyyitem.* See the TEXTUAL NOTE to v 7 ("you have been continuously rebellious").

23. The syntax is the same as that of v 9. See the TEXTUAL NOTE and references there.

(you flouted the) command. Hebrew: *pi,* literally, 'mouth'. The Hebrew expression is idiomatic. The versions translate "word" or "command."

24. *against.* Hebrew: *ʿm.* See the TEXTUAL NOTE to v 7.

as I have known. MT: *dʿty.* Samaritan text: *dʿtw* 'as he has known'. LXX: *hēs egnōsthē humin* 'that he was made known to you', reflecting the Samaritan reading.

25. *the forty days and forty nights (ʾṭ ʾrbʿym* etc.). For duration of time marked by *ʾet,* cf. Exod 13:7, *mṣwt yʾkl ʾt šbʿt hymym* 'shall be eaten seven days'; and Lev 25:22, *wzrʿtm ʾt hšnh hšmynt* 'and you shall sow the eighth year'.

26. *O Lord YHWH.* LXX: *kurie, kurie, basileū tōn theōn* 'O Lord, lord, king of gods'. A similar title, *śr ʾlym* 'prince of gods', is found in 1QH 10:8, where "gods" are to be understood as angels; and see the discussion in Holm-Nielsen 1960, pp. 173–74. The LXX's version was apparently influenced by the contemporary liturgy.

greatness. Hebrew: *gdlk.* LXX: "your [some manuscripts add: *great]* power"; cf. v 29 and Exod 32:11b.

with a mighty hand. Samaritan text and LXX: "with your mighty hand," as in 3:24; cf. the discussion in R. Weiss 1981, p. 111.

27. *Give thought to.* Hebrew: *zĕkor le,* literally, 'remember to'. See Weinfeld 1971–72a, pp. 96f., for this construction with the verb *zkr.*

Jacob. The LXX adds, "to whom you yourself swore"; cf. Exod 32:13.

the stubbornness. Hebrew: *qĕšî,* a form otherwise unattested; cf., however, in Qumran literature: 1QS 4:11, 5:5, 26; 6:26. Samaritan text: *qšh.*

its sinfulness. MT *ḥṭʾtw,* literally, 'its sin'. LXX, *Tg. Onq.,* and *Tg. Ps.-J.:* "their sins."

28. *the country.* MT: *hʾrṣ.* Samaritan text: *ʿm hʾrṣ* 'the people of the country'. All of the versions likewise supply "people" or "inhabitants," but the MT is idiomatic; see the NOTE to this verse.

because of the inability. Literally, "for lack of power." "For lack of" in MT is *mbly;* compare 28:55; Isa 5:13; Hos 4:6; Ezek 34:5; in the Samaritan text *mblty,* as in Num 14:16.

to bring them. MT: *lhbyʾm.* Samaritan text: *lhbyʾ ʾtm.*

29. *whom you freed.* The Samaritan text and some Greek manuscripts add "from Egypt."

with your great might. Some LXXβ add "and your strong arm," as in v 26; compare Exod 32:11.

10:1. *stone. Targum Pseudo-Jonathan* translates *mrmwrʾ* 'marble'. According to another rabbinic tradition, the tablets were sapphire *(Lev. Rab.* 32:22).

4. *to you.* MT: *ʿlykm.* Some Hebrew manuscripts and the Samaritan text have here *ʿmkm,* literally, 'with you'; cf. 5:4 and 9:10.

on the day of the assembly. Most LXX manuscripts omit. Compare the TEXTUAL NOTE to 9:10.

5. *and there they remain.* Hebrew: *wyhyw šm,* literally, 'and there they were'. Vg: *hueusque ībī sunt* 'and they are there until now'. *Targum Pseudo-Jonathan: whww tmn ṣnyʿyn* 'and they were hidden there'. The Samaritan text completely rewrites vv 6–7, in order to harmonize this account with that of Numbers:

> *wbny yśrʾl nsʿw mmsrwt wyḥnw bbny yʿ*qn. *mšm nsʿw wyḥnw hgdgdh mšm nsʿw wyḥnw byṭbth ʾrṣ nḥly mym. mšm nsʿw wyḥnw bʿbrwnh. mšm nsʿw wyḥnw bʿṣywn gbr.mšm nsʿw wyḥnw bmdbr ṣn hyʾ qdš. mšm nsʿw wyḥnw bhr hhr wymt šm ʾhrn wyqbr šm wykhn ʾlʿzr bnw tḥtyw.*

> And the Israelites marched from Moseroth and encamped in Bene-Jaakan. From there they marched and encamped in Gudgod; from there they marched and encamped in Jotbatah, a land of running brooks. From there they marched and encamped in Ezion-Geber; from there they marched and encamped in the Wilderness of Zin, that is, Kadesh. From there they marched and encamped in Mount Hor; there Aaron died and was buried, and his son Eleazar became priest in his stead.

We are obviously dealing with two different traditions in Numbers and the MT Deuteronomy (see the NOTE to this verse). Harmonistic commentators (Rashi, Keil quoted in Driver 1902, ad loc.) attempted to harmonize the accounts by claiming that the Israelites retraced their steps, visiting the places twice, in a different order each time. According to Ibn Ezra, Beeroth-Bene-Jaakan of Deuteronomy is not the Bene-Jaakan of Numbers, but is to be identified with Kadesh, and Gudgod is not Ḥor-Hagidgad but a region encompassing Zalmonāh, Pûnōn, Ōbōt, and Jōtbatāh. *Targum Pseudo-Jonathan* connects these verses with vv 8–9: The Israelites attempted to retrace their steps and return to Egypt, journeying from Bene-Jaakan back to Moserah, whereupon the Levites waged a civil war against their brethren, preventing the return to Egypt. The battle was so bloody that the mourning was equal to the mourning at Aaron's death at Mount Hor. The Levites were rewarded for their dedication by being called into God's service (cf. Ginsberg 1959, 3.330–34).

8. *to stand.* Some Samaritan manuscripts, Qumran (2QDeut 12:2, DJD 3.61) manuscripts, Vg, and Peshitta read "and to stand."

before YHWH. Vg: "before him."

to serve him. LXX: "to serve" (without "him"); cf. 18:5.

to bless in his name. Peshitta: "to bless the name of the Lord."

9. *YHWH your God.* Omitted in most LXX manuscripts.

10. *I had stayed.* The pluperfect is indicated by the use of the perfect tense here, instead of the imperfect with *waw*-consecutive. See *GKC* §106f. Moses' stay took place before his descent from the mountain in v 5, and before the events narrated in vv 6–9 (which are in any event probably an interpolation; see the NOTES).

as I did the first time. Hebrew: *kayāmîm hāri'šōnîm,* literally, 'as the first days'. Omitted in LXX. Vg: "as before."

agreed not to destroy you. In the MT, "you" is in the singular; in the LXX it is plural.

11. *Arise for journeying.* Hebrew: *qwm lk lmsʿ,* literally, 'arise, go to march'. The infinitive *lĕmassaʿ* 'to march' is formed with an *m*-prefix as in Aramaic. Compare, with the same verb, Num 10:2. For further examples, see *GKC* §145e.

the people. The Samaritan text adds *hzh* 'this [people]'; So also the LXX.

NOTES

9:1. *Hear, O Israel.* Compare 5:1; 6:4; 20:3.

You are about to cross the Jordan. Compare 2:18, in connection with crossing the border of Moab. The word *hywm* 'today' here is not to be taken literally, it means rather time period. For *ywm* in the general sense of time see Weinfeld 1986b, pp. 343–45.

greater and mightier than you. Compare 4:38; 11:23; 7:1 *(rbym wʿṣwmym).*

large cities with walls sky-high. Compare 1:28.

2. *a people great and tall, the Anakites.* Compare 1:28.

of whom you have known, of whom you have heard. Compare Isa 40:28, "have you not known, have you not heard" and Isa 48:8. See also the LXX and Qumran versions to 7:15: "of which you have known, and which you have seen." One should complement here: "[heard] saying: 'who can stand.' "

Who can stand up to the Anakites. A proverbial saying concerning the giants who inhabited the area before the settlement of the Israelites; see the NOTES to 1:28; 2:10–11. For proverbial sayings of this kind, cf. Pss 147:17, "who can stand his icy cold"; 89:49; Prov 30:4; Job 38:41; etc.

3. *Know then this day.* Compare 4:39.

YHWH your God is crossing at your head. Compare 31:3.

a devouring fire. Compare 4:24.

you will dispossess and destroy them quickly. The word *mhr* here does not necessarily mean "speedily," which would contradict 7:22; but, as A. Ehrlich has recognized (1909, ad loc.), it means "easily," as in Eccl 4:12, "a threefold cord is not easily (lʾ *bmhrh)* broken."

as YHWH promised you. Compare Exod 23:23, 27, 31.

4. *drives them out.* For the verb *hdp* in this context, cf. 6:19.

say not to yourselves. This should be taken together with the exhortation in v 7 "[but] *remember,*" etc.; compare 7:17–18 and see the NOTES there.

because of my innocence, and because of the guilt of these nations. Verse 4b is usually seen as a doublet of v 5b, especially because the direct speech of the people in v 4a is changed awkwardly into indirect speech in 4b: "before you *(mpnyk)*" instead of "before me *(mpny).*" But, as Ehrlich (1909, ad loc.) suggested, the second-person suffix *-k* of *mpnyk* is a result of misplaced *ky,* which actually introduced v 5: *ky lʾ bṣdqtk;* and v 4b originally continued the direct speech, which ends with "before me *(mpny).*"

The claim that v 4b is missing in the LXX is incorrect; it is missing only in the Vaticanus. In fact, clauses a and b are both needed in this verse for the sake of argument: Israel's virtues compared with the Canaanites'. As N. Lohfink (1963, pp. 201–9) has shown, *ṣdqh* and *ršʿh* here are rendered "innocence" and "guilt," respectively, and have to be understood as in 25:1, "they will acquit the innocent and condemn the guilty *(whṣdyqw ʾt hṣdyq whršyʿw ʾt hršʿ).*" The point made is that Israel should not think that its confrontation with the Canaanites is a judicial one: God declared Israel innocent, whereas the Canaanites were condemned by him as guilty. It is true that because of their guiltiness the Canaanites were dispossesed (v 5), but this does not mean that the Israelites are innocent. God's decision to give the land to the Israelites is not the outcome of a judicial case in which one party is innocent and the other one guilty; it is rather the result of the gracious promise of God to the Patriarchs. The Israelites themselves are not clear of guilt, as is shown in the long sermon that starts with v 7.

The *ṣdqh* here has nothing to do with the *ṣdqh* in 6:20. There it says that the keeping of the law will be to the people's merit or credit (cf. the NOTE there); here the author speaks about unjustified feelings of self-righteousness, not about merit.

5. *It is not because of your righteousness.* This exhortation belongs to a series of exhortations against pride in the sermons of Deuteronomy. In 7:7 we find a warning against boastfulness as a result of physical greatness, in 8:17 against reliance on one's own power, and in 9:5 against self-righteousness. All of these serve to uproot feelings of superiority that might be stimulated by election (7:7), affluence (8:17), or inheritance of new land (9:5).

but because of the guiltiness of these nations. For the sins of the Canaanites, that caused their dispossession, see Gen 15:16; Lev 18:20; 20:23; Deut 18:12; 20:18, etc.

in order to establish the word. In other words, to fulfill the oath/covenant; cf. 8:18 and the NOTE there.

6. *you are a stiff-necked people.* In other words, stubborn and rebellious; see vv 13, 26; cf. Exod 32:9; 33:3, 5; 34:9; Deut 10:16; 31:27; Jer 7:26; 17:23; 19:15; etc. Stiff-necked is the opposite of "turn the ear *(hṭh ʾzn)*" by bending the neck in order to listen; cf. Jer 17:23; 19:15; Zech 7:11; Neh 9:29. See Couroyer 1981.

7. From the middle of this verse, starting with the words "from the day that you left the land of Egypt" (see the TEXTUAL NOTE), the style changes from singular to plural address, which continues to the end of the story of the rebellion in vv 22–24. Change of address usually indicates a shift to a new mode of speaking, and this time it is from exhortation in 9:1–7a to history. Verses 9–21 constitute a historical survey of the sin of the golden calf, which is provided with a framework, vv 7b–8 at the beginning and vv 22–24 at the end. Verses 7–8 form together with vv 22–24 a kind of *inclusio.* Verses 7–8 open with the provoking *(qṣp)* of YHWH and rebellion *(mrh)* at Horeb, while vv 22–24 end with provocation *(qṣp)* and rebelling *(mrh),* at the other stations in the desert including Kadesh, the place of the sin of the spies. The section consisting of vv 7–24 concludes with the proclamation, "As long as I have known you, you have been rebellious against YHWH" (v 24), which—as observed in the COMMENT—reflects the pessimistic view about Israel's history prevalent after the fall of Samaria. The historical survey reminds us of the historical survey in chaps. 1–3, and there are even affinities in style; compare, for example, v 7b, "until you reached this place," with the end of 1:31. That survey is also styled in the plural.

you have been continuously rebellious with YHWH. Compare the conclusion of the pericope in v 24: "As long as I have known you, you have been rebellious against YHWH." This points not only to the behavior of the Israelites in the desert but alludes to the Israelites worshiping the golden calves during the monarchy (see the COMMENT).

8. *At Horeb you so provoked YHWH.* This opens a list of places where they provoked God, starting with the most important basis of the revelation—Horeb—and continuing in vv 22–23 with Taberah, Massah, Kibroth-Hattaavah, and Kadesh-Barnea. Mark the stylistic affinities: "and at Horeb *(wbHrb)*" (v 8), "and at Taberah *(wbTabʿerah),*" "and at Massah *(wbMassah),*" "and at Kibroth-Hattaavah *(wbQiberot hataʾwah),*" "and when . . . sent from Kadesh-Barnea" (v 22). From the beginning of the trek in Horeb to the station of Kadesh-Barnea on the border of land (cf. 1:2, 19) the people provoked God.

9–21. The story here is dependent on the (Elohistic) source in Exodus, hence the verbal correspondence with that source, as will be seen in the following NOTES. The Deuteronomic author added phrases and definitions that suit his tendency.

9. *When I had ascended the mountain to receive the tablets of stone, the tablets of the covenant that YHWH had made with you.* This clause opens a long sentence that is contained in vv 9–10. It complements v 8 by describing the circumstances of YHWH's anger. Verses 9–10 are dependent on the Elohistic tradition of Exod 24:12–14, 18b and 31:18b. For 9a compare Exod 24:2, "Ascend to me *(ʿlh ʾly)* to the mountain . . . and I will give you the tablets of stone *(lḥt hʾbn),*" only that Deuteronomy added to the "tablets of stone" the definition: "the tablets of the covenant *(lwḥt hbryt)*" (cf. v 11; 4:13; 1 Kgs 8:9), just as the priestly source defines the tablets as "the tablets of the *ʿedût (lḥt hʿdt),*" cf. Exod 31:18; 32:15; 34:29. But *ʿedût* in the priestly literature constitutes the symbol of divinity (cf. 2 Kgs 11:12) and his majesty (the winged disk of the cherubim?), which also denoted the oath of the majesty, as shown recently by S. Dalley (1986, p. 92). This broad meaning of *ʿedût* explains the priestly terms "the tabernacle/tent of the *ʿedût*" (Exod 38:21; Num 9:15), "the curtain of the *ʿedût*" (Exod 27:21; 30:6; Lev 24:3), as well as the "ark of the *ʿedût*" (Exod 25:22) and "the tablets of the *ʿedût*" (Exod 31:18; 32:15; 34:29). The Deuteronomic author, who was reserved toward physical symbols of divinity (see the INTRODUCTION §10–12), defines the Ark and the tablets in the spiritual, covenantal sense: "the ark of the covenant" (10:8; Josh 3:6) and the "tablets of the covenant."

and I stayed on the mountain forty days and forty nights. This is dependent on Exod 24:18b, "I neither ate bread nor drank water." This sentence also occurs in Exod 34:28 in the episode of the second tablets, but Deuteronomy, which turned the forty days and forty nights into a principle of division for the whole pericope (see the COMMENT), apparently did not make distinctions between the various occasions of forty days and forty nights: all of them were accompanied by fasting.

10. *two tablets of stone inscribed by the finger of God.* These words are dependent on Exod 31:18b, "tablets of stone inscribed with the finger of God." The "finger of God," in contrast to the "hand of God," indicates some extraordinary performance; compare Exod 8:15 and Ps 8:4, where the creation of the moon and the stars is called "the work of your fingers," in contradistinction to v 7, where the "work of your hands *(mʿśh ydyk)*" refers to the general works of nature (cf. Ehrlich 1909, at Exod 8:15).

For the tradition of two tablets, its iconography through generations, and the distribution of the commandments on them, see Ṣarfati 1990.

the exact words that YHWH had spoken . . . out of the fire, on the day of the assembly. The Deuteronomic description of the revelation; cf. 4:10–12; 10:4; 18:16.

11. *At the end of those forty days . . . YHWH gave me the two tablets of stone.* This is not just a doublet of v 10, where it was already said that YHWH gave to Moses the two tablets, but instead its recapitulation in order to stress the

fact that on the very day that the tablets of the covenant were given, the people violated the covenant and Moses was asked to descend to the people.

12. Compare with Exod 32:7–8:

Deut 9:12	*Exod 32:7–8*
Hurry, go down *from here at once (qwm rd mhr mzh),* for your people whom you freed *(hwṣ't)* from Egypt have acted wickedly.	Hurry down *(lk rd)* for your people whom you brought out *(h'lyt)* of the land of Egypt have acted wickedly.

The differences are (1) in pathos: Moses is asked to descend *at once;* and (2) using the verb "free *(hwṣ')*" from Egypt, as in the Decalogue (see the NOTE there) and not "bring up *(h'lh),*" as in the older sources.

at once. This does not leave time for intercession, in contrast to Exod 32:11–14, where Moses intercedes before descending.

your people [acted wickedly]. God wants to dissociate himself from his people and therefore says to Moses, "your people [i.e., not mine]whom you liberated from Egypt," which is the only place in which Exodus is ascribed to Moses. This tendency is reflected in the next verse (13), where we find the term "this people *(h'm hzh),*" which is a contemptuous designation of Israel; see, e.g., Isa 6:9; 8:6, 12; 9:16; etc. Moses, however, in his intercession insists on the reverse: "your people and your inheritance" (vv 26, 29). This debate about Israel, being God's people or not, comes boldly to expression in the original narration of the sin of the golden calf in Exod 32–33. See, for example, the arguments about God's personal participation in the leading of the people in Exod 33:12: "You say to me: lead *this people* . . . but see this nation is *your people.* And he [God] said: *my presence will lead.*" For a discussion of this topic, see Muffs 1978).

they strayed from the way. Compare the NOTE to 8:6.

quickly. That is to say, right after their commitment not to worship idols.

molten image. The word *mskh* is derived from *nsk* 'molten metal' and, according to Exod 32:2, the calf was prepared from the golden rings of the people; compare also the definition of the golden calf as *'lhy zhb* 'god of gold' in Exod 32:31. The molten image could refer to the plating of the image, the core of which could be of wood or inferior metal; compare Isa 30:22, "And you will treat as unclean the silver overlay of your images and the golden plating *(mskh)* of your idols." For *mskh* and all its connotations see Dohmen 1984.

The details about the worship given in the parallel account in Exod 32:8, "they bowed down to it and sacrificed to it, saying: 'This is your God,' " are not of special interest for the Deuteronomic author, who is generally indifferent to technical ritual procedures (see the INTRODUCTION §12), so he omitted them.

13. *YHWH said to me.* The repetition of "YHWH said to me" (cf. v 12) is also attested in the Exodus version of the story; cf. Exod 32:7, 9. For this phenomenon at other places, see, e.g., Gen 16:10, 11.

14. *Let me alone.* For this expression compare Judg 11:37; 1 Sam 11:3; 15:16. God anticipates as it were the intervention by Moses, as befits a prophet whose function is prayer and intercession for the afflicted; cf., e.g., Gen 20:7; Exod 8:4, 24–25; Jer 7:16; 11:14; 15:1; etc.; see Muffs 1978. Thus the saying of God, "let me alone," paradoxically leaves open the way for Moses to ask for mercy; see the Targumim and *Midr. Šem. Rab. Tiśa'* §42.9; cf. Cassuto 1967, ad loc. and Moberly 1983, p. 50.

[I will] blot out their name from under heaven. Compare 7:24, "you shall make their names perish *(h'bd).*" The expression "blot out the name" is characteristic of the Deuteronomic literature (see Deut 25:6; 29:10; 2 Kgs 14:27) and is attested in the northwest Semitic inscriptions *(KAI* 26 A 3:12; C 3:14) and in the Assyrian inscriptions (see Weinfeld 1972a, pp. 107–8). In Exod 17:14 we find the expression "blot out memory *(mḥh zkr),*" and Deut 25:14 is dependent on it.

I will make you a nation mightier and larger than them. In Exod 32:10: "I will make you a great *(gdwl)* people" and in Num 14:12: "greater *(gdwl)* and mightier than it." Deuteronomy uses the term "great *(gdwl)*" in a spiritual sense (4:7, 8) and avoids therefore its usage when it applies to physical size, as in the present verse.

15. *while the mountain was ablaze with fire.* A Deuteronomic rhetorical phrase; cf. 4:11, 5:20. The fire symbolizes the presence of God (cf. 4:24, 36), and the author wants to say by this that while the people violated the covenant the revelation was still going on.

17. *I gripped the two tablets . . . smashing them before your eyes.* In Exod 32:19 the "gripping" and the smashing "before their eyes" is missing. Deuteronomy wants to make clear that the breaking of the tablets was an intentional act and not a spontaneous one, as it might appear from the text in Exodus. "Breaking a tablet" in the ancient Near Eastern tradition connoted cancellation of the validity of a document; compare the Akkadian expression *ṭuppam hepû* (cf. Akkadian Dictionaries). The violation of the commandments, validated by the covenant, made the covenantal document void, and the breaking of the tablet-document was the proper sign for it. This was correctly understood by Ibn Ezra in his commentary to Exod 32:19: "Moses broke the tablets which were in his hands like a document of testimony *(šṭr ʿdwt),* and thus he tore up the certificate of conditions *(šṭr htn'ym)* and this before the eyes of all Israel as it is written: 'I broke them before your eyes' (Deut 9:17)." See above, in the INTRODUCTION to the Decalogue.

18. *I lay prostrate.* Compare Ezra 10:1. This liturgical term *(htnpl)* is also reflected in the expression *npl tḥnh* 'make fall a petition' (Jer 36:7; 37:20; 38:26; 42:2, 9; Dan 9:20). In other old sources supplication is rendered by "fell on his

face *(npl ʿl pnym)"*; see Num 16:22; 17:9–10; 20:6. (For a discussion cf. Gruber 1980, pp. 131–36.) In the rabbinic literature the term for supplication is *npyḷt ʾpym* 'falling on the face'; cf. Elbogen 1931, pp. 74–76.

as at the first. This phrase may refer to the period of time mentioned in 9:9,11, but it seems that the reference is also to the *first* prayer before the descent, which is not mentioned here, but is in Exod 32:11–14. This interpretation may be supported by v 19b, "And *at that time, too,* YHWH listened to me," implying that the present prayer, after the descent, was accepted, like the first one before the descent. Although the author of Deuteronomy did not mention that first prayer, it might have been presupposed either by the author himself or by the editor. If this is correct, we may count three periods of forty days: one for the reception of the first tablets of the covenant, at the end of which the first prayer was presented (Exod 32:11–14); the second designated for supplication (Deut 9:18, 25–29; Exod 32:31–34); and the third dedicated to the reception of the second tablets and to the final petition and forgiveness (Exod 34:1–9, 27–28; Deut 10:10). Compare *S. ʿOlam* Rab. 86 and *Midr. Tanhuma ki tśʾ* 31. See also Naḥmanides to this verse and Luzzatto 1871, newly edited by P. Schlessinger, 1965, pp. 522–23; and Hoffmann 1913, ad loc.

to vex him. See the NOTE to 4:25.

19. *And that time, too, YHWH listened to me.* The only plausible explanation for this phrase is that is refers back to the first intercession mentioned in Exod 32:11–14; see the NOTE to "as at the first" in v 18, and cf. Hoffmann 1913, ad loc. The alleged allusions to the intercessions in Exod 14:15; 15:25 (Ibn Ezra); Num 11:2; 12:13f.; 14:13–20; 21:7–9 (Driver) look forced.

20. *YHWH was angry enough with Aaron . . . so I also interceded for Aaron at that time.* This passage constitutes an independent unit, as may be learned from the accompanying formula *bʿt hhyʾ*; cf. Loewenstamm 1968–69, pp. 101–2. It has been added in the Samaritan Pentateuch to Exod 32:10 and is found in the Qumran text of Exod 32:10–30 (4Q *paleoEx* m); cf. Skehan 1955. The fact that the text was discovered in Qumran proves that the Samaritan Pentateuch was based in this case on older traditions; see Tov 1985, p. 14.

21. This verse, which tells us about the destruction of the golden calf, the making of which was the gravest sin in Israel's history, reflects the procedure of destruction of idols in ancient Israel. It serves indeed as a kind of model for iconoclasm in the future. A comparison of this verse with its parallel in Exod 32:20 reveals that Deut 9:21 is an elaborated and revised version of Exod 32:20 and conforms with the deuteronomistic descriptions of breaking and shattering idols in the Books of Kings. Let us analyze first the procedure of destruction: the most prominent parallel to the verse in this respect is the Ugaritic description of the destruction of Môt, the god of death. The account of Môt's destruction has survived in two versions in the Ugaritic literature. The first is a complete text, which tells us how Anat destroyed Môt. The second, a broken text, relates how

Môt, having returned to life, recounts his suffering at the time of his killing. The first version *(KTU* 1.6 ii:30–36) reads as follows: *tiḫd bn ilm mt bḥrb tbqʿnn, bḫtr tdrynn, bišt tšrpnn, brḥm tṭḥnn, bšd tdrʿnn, širh ltikl ʿṣrm* 'she seized Môt, son of Il, cleaved him with a sword, winnowed him with a sieve, burned him in fire, ground him with a millstone, scattered him in a field, his flesh the birds ate." The second fragmentary text *(KTU* 1.6 v:12–15) reads as follows: *ʿlk pht šrp bišt, ʿlk [pht ṭḥ]n brḥm, . . . ʿlk pht drʿ]bym* 'because of you I have suffered burning by fire, because of you I have suffered grinding by millstone, . . . because of you I have suffered scattering in the sea." The common images and identical verbs in the description of the destruction of Mot and that of destroying the golden calf are: *takl,* eat; *lqḥ* = *ʾḫd,* take; *šrp,* burn; *ṭḥn,* grind; and *drʿ,* scatter (in the sea), in one version, and being eaten by birds on the other. The Exodus version might have preserved the image of "being eaten" while the Deuteronomic version may have preserved the image of "being scattered in the sea." It seems that both accounts, the Ugaritic about Môt and the biblical about the golden calf, are not to be taken literally, for their purpose is to describe total destruction without regard for the factual applicability of the actions involved (burning and grinding). Otherwise it is hard to explain, for example, in the Ugaritic account, that after burning and grinding something would be left for the birds to eat (see Loewenstamm 1980b; Begg 1985).

An accumulation of measures taken for the liquidation of hostile beings is found also in Egyptian, Mesopotamian, and Hittite sources. (For references see Begg 1985, 215–21.) It is also found in the description of the extirpation of idolatry in the account of the Josianic reforms in 2 Kgs 23:6, 15. Furthermore, as in the biblical account so in the Assyrian royal inscriptions, we find descriptions of liquidation of cultic objects by burning, smashing, and consigning to water (Begg 1985, pp. 222–29).

Now let us compare the version in Deut 9:21 with that of Exod 32:20. The formulation of the destruction of the calf in Deuteronomy is more verbose and elaborate, which is characteristic of Deuteronomy and the Deuteronomic school. The main differences enumerated in the following paragraphs.

A. Exodus 32:20 tells us simply that Moses took the calf *(wyqḥ ʾt hʿgl),* while Deuteronomy 9:21 adds to the calf a theological definition: "that sinful thing you had made *(wʾt ḥṭ ʾtkm ʾšr ʿśytm ʾt hʿgl lqḥty).*" The word *ḥṭʾt* 'sinful thing' is used by the Deuteronomist in reference to the golden calf (1 Kgs 12:30; 13:34; 14:16; 15:3, 26, 30, 34; etc.) and is the typical expression for the sin of Jeroboam *(hṭʾt yrbʿm)* that caused the downfall of the Northern Kingdom (1 Kgs 14:15–16; 2 Kgs 17:22).

B. Exodus 32:20 reads, "he ground *(wyṭḥn)* until it was crushed fine *(ʿd ʾšr dq),*" while Deuteronomy has "I crushed it to bits, grinding it well to dust *(wʾkt ʾtw ṭḥwn hyṭb ʿd ʾšr dq lʿpr).*" Such a way of destroying idolatrous objects—crushing them to dust—is found in the account of the Josianic reform in 2 Kgs 23:6, 15: "he burned it [the Asherah] . . . and crushed it to dust *(hdq lʿpr).*"

C. Exod 32:20 tells us that Moses scattered the ground calf upon the water, while Deut 9:21 has, "and I threw *(wʾšlk)* its dust into the brook *(hnḥl).*" The Deuteronomic formulation conforms verbally with the descriptions of the elimination of idolatrous objects in the Josianic reform: "He [Josiah] threw their dust [of the illicit altars] into the brook of Kidron *(whšlyk ʾt ʿprm nḥl qdrwn)*" (2 Kgs 23:12) and "He threw its dust [of the Asherah] on the grave *(wyšlk ʾt ʿprh)*" (2 Kgs 23:6). A similar procedure is ascribed to King Asa's reform: we read that Asa burned the abominable image *(mplṣt* prepared for the Asherah) in the brook of Kidron (1 Kgs 15:13). Moses' throwing the dust of the calf into the brook in Deut 9:21 seems then to be a reflection of cultic reforms in Judah and especially the cultic reform of Josiah.

D. The difference in the formulation of the disposition of the golden calf between Exodus and Deuteronomy has to do also with the function of the water into which the ground calf is thrown. In Exod 32:20 the ground calf is scattered upon the water and the water is then given to the Israelites to drink, whereas in Deut 9:21 the water is destined to carry off the dust of the golden calf because a brook, "which flows down from the mountain," will rapidly carry away the gold dust thrown into it and drinking it would be impossible. It is clear, then, that in this matter Deuteronomy deviates completely from Exodus. What is the meaning of the deviation? Exod 32:20b is to be understood as an ordeal. The people who sinned in the worship of the golden calf were tested, like the woman in Num 5:11–31 (cf. *b. ʿAbod. Zar.* 44a), and those who proved wrong were punished, like the woman suspected of faithlessness. As Ibn Ezra (to Exod 32:20) saw, the persons killed by the Levites (Exod 32:26–28) were those who proved wrong in the ordeal. Furthermore, from Deut 33:8–9 we might deduce that the Levites themselves underwent the ordeal and proved innocent: "Let your Thummim and Urim be with your faithful one, whom you tested at Massah, challenged at the waters of Meribah; who said of his father and mother: 'I do not know them'; his brother he disregarded, ignored his own children."

The testing of the Levites can best be understood on the basis of the ordeal that Moses administered to the people in order to discover the guilty ones. The Levites apparently proved to be innocent, and they were the ones chosen by Moses to execute the guilty ones, even their own relatives (Exod 32:27; Deut 33:9). The author of Deuteronomy, who does not admit sacral media into his judicial system (cf. Weinfeld 1972a, pp. 233–34), intentionally omitted the detail about the ordeal, though in other details he followed the Exodus source, on which he depended (cf. Begg 1985, pp. 239–51). Although he mentions the appointment of the Levites in 10:8, he dissociates this event completely from the episode about the Levites executing the sinners, as presented in Exod 32:26–29. In the latter tradition it was the killing of the sinners that brought about their nomination for their sacral posts (cf. *mlʾ yd* in 32:29, which means 'consecrate'). In fact Deuteronomy, in this account of the golden calf, avoids all of the punishments of the people mentioned in the Exodus account, such as 32:28, 35 (see Hoffmann 1913, p. 109).

22. *at Taberah.* Compare Num 11:1–3.

and at Massah. See 6:16 and Exod 17:1–7.

and at Kibroth-Hattaavah. Compare Num 11:4–34.

22–24. These verses correspond to vv 7–8 and form together with them a kind of framing device for the historical survey in vv 9–21 (see the NOTE to vv 7–8).

23. *And when YHWH sent you on from Kadesh-Barnea.* The verb "send" here looks peculiar, but the author wants to allude to the spies who were sent to explore the land (cf. 1:22; Num 13:2), and it was the spies who "have taken the heart out of" the Israelites (1:28). The whole verse looks like an epitome of the episode of the spies in Deut 1:19b–32; compare *ʿlw wršw* 'go up and occupy' with 1:21, *ʿlh rš; wtmrw ʾt py YHWH ʾlhykm* 'and you rebelled against the command of YHWH', with the same phrase in 1:26b; and *wlʾ hʾmntm lw* 'you did not trust him' with 1:32, "you do not trust YHWH your God *(ʾynkm mʾmynm bYHWH ʾlhykm).*"

24. *you have been rebellious against YHWH.* Compare v 7b and 31:27b.

As long as I have known you. The Samaritan text and the LXX read *"he* knew you *(dʿtw),*" but 31:27, *"during my lifetime . . .* you have been rebellious" seems to support the Masoretic version.

25–29. These verses are told in retrospect, referring to the intercession mentioned in v 18, but there the historical facts were recounted and the author did not want to interrupt the story by quoting the prayer of Moses. After the story was rounded up by the *inclusio* (vv 22–24, which correspond to vv 7–8, see above), the author annexed the prayer (vv 26–29). For such procedure in ancient texts see Daube 1947, pp. 74–101.

The prayer draws on the older sources of Exodus and Numbers; compare Deut 9:26, 29 with Exod 32:11b; Deut 9:27a with Exod 32:13a; and Deut 9:28 with Num 14:16 and Exod 32:12. But the Deuteronomic author peppered this prayer with liturgical formulas characteristic of Deuteronomy and the Deuteronomic school (see Weinfeld 1972a, pp. 32–45). Thus the pair *ʿam naḥělah* 'people and inheritance', which occurs in 9:26, 29, is attested in the deuteronomistic prayer ascribed to Solomon (1 Kgs 8:51) and in a sermon of liturgical nature (Deut 4:20). Similarly, "redeem [from Egypt] *(pdyt)*" (9:26) is a typical Deuteronomic expression (cf. 7:8; 13:6; 15:15; 21:8; 24:18; 2 Sam 7:23), as is the idiom "with great might and outstretched arm *(bkḥ gdwl wbzrʿ nṭwyh)*" (9:29; cf. 2 Kgs 17:36; Jer 32:17; 27:5). The Deuteronomic idiom "strong hand and outstretched arm *(yd ḥzqh wzrʿ nṭwyh)*" (cf. Weinfeld, 1972a, p. 329) has been split in two: 9:26 *(yd ḥzqh);* 9:29 *(zrʿ nṭwyh).*

25. *I lay prostrate . . . the forty days and forty nights that I lay prostrate.* This style "idem per idem" is found in 1:46 and in 29:15; see the NOTE to 1:46.

26. *O Lord YHWH.* This form of address is typical of the opening of prayers; cf. 3:24 and the NOTE there.

do not annihilate your people and your inheritance. ʾal tašḥet is a formula rooted in petitions to human leaders or to God. Thus in the petition of the wise woman of Abel-Beth-Maacah in 2 Sam 20:19–20, "Why should you destroy *(blʿ)* YHWH's inheritance? Joab replied: 'Far be it from me to destroy or to annihilate' *(šḥt).*" For *blʿ* and *hšht* as parallels, see Lam 2:8.

The formula "do not annihilate *(ʾal tašḥet)*" serves as a title to several petition prayers in the Psalms: 57:1; 58:1; 59:1; cf. also 75:1. Note that in Deut 9:26 and in 2 Sam 20:19–20 the annihilation is applied to "the inheritance of YHWH *(nḥlt YHWH).*" For the concept of *nḥlt YHWH* 'the inheritance of YHWH' see above, in the NOTE to 4:20.

whom you released. Typical of Deuteronomy; see the NOTE to 7:8.

whom you freed from Egypt with a mighty hand. Compare Exod 32:11b, "whom you freed from the land of Egypt with great power *(kḥ)* and mighty hand." The usual pair in Deuteronomy is "mighty hand and outstretched arm *(yd ḥzqh wzrʿ nṭwyh)*" (see the NOTE to 4:34), but here the pair is split: at the beginning of the prayer "mighty hand" (v 26) and at the end "outstretched arm" (v 29). In order to create a pair of divine attributes, however, the author added in vv 26 and 29 another pair of components, "greatness" and "might," respectively: "whom you released in your greatness *(bgdlk)*" (v 26), "whom you freed with your great might" (v 29). In 11:2 we find all three components together: "his greatness, his mighty hand, his outstretched arm."

27. *Give thought to your servants.* Compare Exod 32:13. The verb *zkr* (literally, 'remember') with the preposition *lĕ* means to think in favor of someone; cf. Ps 132:1; Jer 2:2; Pss 25:7; 136:23; 2 Chr 6:42; and see Weinfeld 1973a, pp. 193–96. *zkr lĕ* overlaps the phrase *šmr lĕ* 'keep to someone', which also refers to the Patriarchs in 7:9; see the NOTE there. The favorable thought is motivated by God's promissory oath to the Patriarchs following their obedience and trust (Weinfeld 1970–72, pp. 184–89).

pay no heed to the stubborness of this people, its wickedness, and its sinfulness. The wickedness of the people may in fact justify their destruction; therefore Moses invokes the merits of their ancestors, who serve as protectors of their descendants. Interceding with the ancestors on behalf of their children was a common phenomenon in ancient Israel and in the ancient Near East. Intercession was called in Akkadian "to keep fatherhood *(abūta ṣabātu/aḫazu)*"; cf., e.g., in a Mari letter, "Just as I interceded [kept your fatherhood, *abūtki aṣbutu]* for you so shall the god Šamaš intercede for my business" (ARM 10.156:30–33; see Artzi and Malamat 1971, p. 183); cf. also *BWL,* p. 132 line 99; *ṣābitu abūti enše ṭābi eli Šamaš* 'he who intercedes [literally, keeps fatherhood] on behalf of the weak is pleasing to Šamaš'; *VTE,* p. 59 line 418, "May Ninlil . . . not intercede [literally, keep fatherhood, *iṣbata abūtkun]* for you." The same phrase is attested in a curse in the Qumran *Manual of*

Discipline (1QS 2:9): "May there be no place for you at the mouth of any intercessors [who keep the ancestors, *ʾwḥzy ʾbwt]*"*;* see Wernberg-Møller 1957, p. 53n. 26, who quotes Syriac *ʾḥd ʾbwtʾ* 'to intercede'. In rabbinic literature the term for intercession is "to invoke the merit of the fathers *(zkwt ʾbwt)*"*;* cf. Urbach 1979, pp. 495–510. As in the quoted Akkadian, Hebrew, and Aramaic passages, so in the midrashic literature we find the phrase "*to keep* the merits of the ancestors *(tpś zkwt ʾbwt)*"*:* when Moses prayed on behalf of Israel he interceded with the ancestors (literally, kept the merits of the fathers, *tpś zkwt ʾbwt):* "Give thought to your servants Abraham, Isaac, and Jacob" (Exod 32:13 = Deut 9:27); see *Midr. Pesiq. R.* (Ish-Shalom 1880, 4.13b).

28. *Else the country from which you freed us will say.* Rather, the inhabitants of the country will say; cf. Gen 41:57; 1 Sam 17:46b; 2 Sam 15:23; the Samaritan text reads *ʿam hʾrṣ* 'the people of the land' and similarly the versions: LXX, Syriac, Targumim, and the Vg.

because of the inability of YHWH to bring them into the land that he had promised them . . . he brought them out to have them die in the wilderness. Compare Exod 32:12. Appealing to the fame of God and his reputation is a common motif in the national prayers; compare the parallel invocation in Num 14:15–16, "the nations who have heard of your fame will say: 'because of the inability of YHWH to bring the people into the land that he had promised them he slaughtered them in the wilderness.' " The passage continues, "let the power of the Lord be shown in its greatness" (v 17). In other instances the prayer appeals to God's great name, which could be affected by not helping his people; see, e.g., Josh 7:7–9: "Joshua said . . . O Lord, what can I say after Israel has turned tail before its enemies? When the Canaanites and all the inhabitants of the land hear of this, they will turn upon us . . . and wipe out our name . . . and what will you do about your great name?" In other prayers we hear a direct address: "do . . . for the sake of your name," cf. Pss 25:11; 79:9–10: "Help us, O God our deliverer for the sake of the glory of your name, save us and forgive our sin for the sake of your name. Let the nations not say: 'where is their God' "; compare Pss 109:21; 115:1–2: "Not to us, O YHWH, but to your name bring glory . . . let the nations not say: 'where now is their God.' " See also the prayers in Jer 14:7 ("do for the sake of your name"), 21. Ezekiel's theology is based on this principle of God's reputation among the nations; cf. 20:44; 36:22; 39:13, 25; etc., see Greenberg 1983, 1.384.

This motif, together with the motifs of invoking the father's merits (see the NOTE to v 27) and the recital of the gracious qualities of God (Exod 34:6–7; Num 14:18), became the three pillars of the Jewish prayers for forgiveness *(sĕlichot)* prevalent until the present day:

1. *ʾl mlk ywšb ʿl ksʾ rḥmym* 'God king who sits on the throne of mercy', which includes the list of the gracious qualities of God in Exod 34:6–7 and Num 14:18;

2. *my šʿnh lʾbwtynw* 'God who answered the prayer of our ancestors', which invokes the merits of the fathers; and
3. *ʿśh lmʿn šmk* 'do for the sake of your name'.

Compare Elbogen 1934, pp. 221–31.

29. *Yet they are your very own people.* This serves as an *inclusio* with the phrase "your people and inheritance *(ʿmk wnḥltk)*" in the opening of the prayer in v 26. The *inclusio* is reflected also in the phrase in v 26, "whom you released in your greatness and whom you freed from Egypt with a mighty hand." It corresponds to the conclusion of the prayer in v 29, "whom you freed with your great might and your outstretched arm."

10:1–5. This account about the hewing of new tablets and the making of the Ark is partly dependent on Exod 34:1–4, but not wholly: the making of the Ark is not mentioned there. The account about making the Ark has apparently been suppressed in Exodus in favor of the priestly account, according to which the Ark was made by Bezalel after Moses' return from the mount (Exod 37:1–9) and not before his ascent, as Deuteronomy has it (9:3). An indication of the existence of an Ark tradition in the JE source may be hidden in Exod 33:7, where it says that Moses pitched the tent "for it *(lw),*" which may refer to the Ark.

The Ark with the cherubim above it was considered to be the throne of the deity and consisted of two parts: the divine seat represented by the cherubim, cf. the epithet "enthroned on the cherubim *(yšb hkrbym)*" (1 Sam 4:4; 2 Sam 6:2 = 1 Chr 13:6; 2 Kgs 19:15 = Isa 37:16); and the footstool represented by the Ark (cf. Haran 1959, pp. 30–38, 89–94). As Haran has shown, the cherubim with the cover *(kapporet),* which constitute the divine seat, have to be separated from the Ark, which plays the role of the footstool. Being the footstool of the God, the Ark was most appropriate as a depository for the tablets of the covenant. In the ancient Near East, written treaty oaths were put at the feet of gods (see Korošec 1931, pp. 100–101). The Deuteronomic author, however, for ideological reasons (see the INTRODUCTION Sec. 12) completely ignores the function of the Ark as the divine throne and therefore does not refer to the cherubim and the *kapporet* at all. For him the Ark functions as a container of the tablets of the covenant and nothing more (see 1:42, in comparison with Num 14:44, and see the NOTE there). See also the Deuteronomic statement in 1 Kgs 8:9, "There was nothing inside the ark but the two tablets of stone . . . the tablets of the covenant [LXX] . . . which YHWH made with the Israelites after their departure from the land of Egypt." In contrast, in the pre-Deuteronomic literature the Ark appears mainly as a sign of the presence of the deity, not merely as a receptacle of the tablets. Being the symbol of the divine presence, the Ark accompanied the Israelites in their movements (Num 10:35, 36; 14:44) and in their wars (Josh 3–6; 1 Sam 4:3, 6f.; 2 Sam 11:11). After the

Davidic period nothing is heard of the Ark any more, and we do not know anything about the circumstances of its disappearance. The prophecy in Jer 3:16 that the ark "will not be remade" seems to imply that the Ark was nonexistent in those days. M. Haran (1963) suggested that it was removed by Manasseh, who put in its place a sculptured image of the Asherah (2 Kgs 21:7).

1. *At that time.* As already indicated (in the NOTE to 1:9), this phrase introduces an independent unit and might be an excerpt from an old source.

Carve out two tablets of stone like the first. This sentence repeats Exod 34:1a.

and come up to me on the mountain. This uses the verbiage of Exod 24:12a, which refers to the first ascent; cf. also Deut 9:9a.

2. *I will write on the tablets the commandments that were on the first tablets, which you smashed.* This repeats Exod 34:1b.

3. *I made an ark of acacia wood.* Compare Exod 25:10. This type of wood was used also for other cultic objects of the Tabernacle (passim). The acacia tree *(šiṭah)* was common in the land of Israel; compare the various names with the component *šiṭah:* Beth-Hashita (Judg 7:22), Abel-Hashitim = Shiṭim (Num 25:1; 33:49; Josh 2:1; 3:1; Mic 6:5); Nahal-Hashitim (Joel 4:18). Various types of acacia grow in the Sinai peninsula and in Egypt, and they were used as building materials in these areas. In Egypt the acacia *(šnḏt)* was considered a holy tree; see Helck, 1972, 1.113; and on the Shitah tree in general see Felix 1968, pp. 96–98. According to the priestly account, the Ark was overlaid with gold (Exod 25:11; 37:2), about which nothing is said in Deuteronomy.

and [I] carved out two tablets of stone like the first. Compare Exod 34:4a.

I took the two tablets with me and went up the mountain. Compare Exod 34:4.

4. *YHWH wrote on the tablets as at the first writing.* Compare Exod 34:28b, but there it might be understood that Moses wrote, "and he was there with YHWH forty days and forty nights . . . and he wrote upon the tablets the words of the covenant, the ten commandments." But, as Driver remarked (1911, p. 374), Exod 34:28b may have once stood in a different context, in which the word "he wrote" would refer to YHWH, as in Deut 10:1–4 and in Exod 34:1.

The author of Deuteronomy is eager to stress that the new tablets, which represent the new covenant, would not differ from the original ones. The tablets are the same as the first ones (vv 1, 3), and the inscribed words are identical with the words of the first tablets (v 4). These words are the Ten Words/Commandments revealed to the people "out of the fire on the day of the assembly"; compare 5:19–21; 9:10; 18:16.

5. *and there they remain.* Compare 1 Kgs 8:8b, "and there they remain to this day." But there we find a supplementary note: "there was nothing inside the ark but the two tablets of stone which Moses placed there at Horeb, when YHWH made [a covenant] with the Israelites at their departure from the land

of Egypt." This note may have a polemic tendency, that is, to refute priestly traditions, which ascribed to the Ark other sacred functions, such as representing the divine throne (see above) in which all kinds of sacramental objects were placed (cf. Exod 16:34; Num 17:25; and Heb 9:4).

6–9. *Itinerary.* These verses, in which Israel is spoken about in the third person and not in the second person, as is usual in the speech of Moses, interrupt the account of the Ark with its tablets (vv 1–5) and the passage about the Levites, the bearers of the Ark (vv 8–9). It seems to be an excerpt of the Elohistic source from which Deuteronomy drew its traditions. It was inserted here because of the information about Aaron and Eleazar, who were the first Levites consecrated to priesthood. For Aaron as Levite in a nonpriestly source see Exod 4:14, and for Eleazar in a nonpriestly account see Josh 24:33.

The itinerary, which parallels in general the itinerary in Num 33:30–34 (= priestly source), differs from that text at several points. For one, the itinerary is styled in the style of JE (*mšm nsʿw* 'from there they marched'; cf. Num 21:12–13) and not in the style of the priestly source, which has the stereotype *wysʿw . . . wyḥnw* 'they set out . . . and encamped' (cf. Num 33:1–49). Also, the order of the encampments is different: in Num 33 the order is Moserah, Bene-Jaakan, Hor-Hagidgad, and Jotbatah, whereas in Deuteronomy the order is Bene-Jaakan, Moserah, Gudgod, and Jotbatah. There are also slight variations in the names of the places (see below). Finally, according to the Deuteronomic account Aaron died and was buried in Moserah, whereas according to the priestly account he died and was buried in Hor-Hahar (Num 33:37–38; compare 20:22–29). It is obvious that this itinerary is independent of the priestly itinerary in Num 33. It is similar to the itinerary of the JE source, which is less stereotypic than the itinerary in Num 33. Thus we find here Bĕeroth Bĕnê-Jaakan 'wells of the children of Jaakan', whereas in Num 33:31, 32, Bĕnê-Jaakan appears without "wells." Similarly, Jotbatah is defined in v 7 as "a land of streams of water," which is lacking in Num 33:33–34. Such characterizations of the encampments are typical of the JE itineraries (see Exod 15:22, 27; 17:1b) and of the Mesopotamian itineraries as well. See, for example, in the annals of Tukulti Ninurta II (890–884 B.C.E.), "I crossed the river. . . . The second day . . . not filling my belly with the bitter water. From the river I departed, I kept in the desert. . . . in the region of Margani I found streams . . . wells of much water; I spend the night there. . . . I drew near to Dur-Kurigalzu, I spent the night. From Dur Kurigalzu I departed" (*ARAB,* pp. 128–29).

6. *Bene-Jaakan.* In Gen 36:27 we find the name ʿAqan for a Hurrian clan, for which 1 Chr 1:42 has Jaakan, and it seems that the two are to be identified; the letter Jod of Jaakan might be a result of dittography, so that the original reading in Num 33:31–32 and Deut 10:6 would have been *bĕnê ʿAqan.* (The reading "Jaakan" in 1 Chr 1:42 was then influenced by Num 33:31–32 and Deut 10:6.) According to B. Maisler (1938, p. 49) the suffix *-an* in ʿAqan/Jaakan shows its Hurrian origin.

Moserah. Aaron died there and was buried there. According to the priestly itinerary, Aaron was buried in Hor-Hahar (Num 20:28; 33:38), seven stations after Moserah (Num 33:31–37). The site of Moserah is unidentified.

and his son Eleazar became priest in his stead. Eleazar, who is mentioned frequently in the priestly literature (Exod 6:23; Num 20:25–28; 27:18–23; 31:13–54; 32:1–28; Josh 14:1; etc.), had a long tradition in ancient Israel; cf. the account of his burial in Josh 24:33, a nonpriestly source. Eleazar played an important role in the tradition of Šiloh (see Weinfeld 1988, pp. 274–75).

7. *From there they marched.* A formula characteristic of the JE source; cf. Num 21:12, 13.

Gudgod. In Num 33:32 "Hor-Hagidgad," which may point to a wadi of Gudgod. But the LXX and several Hebrew manuscripts read "the mount of Gidgad *(har haGidgad).*" The site is unidentified. For proposed identifications see Loewenstamm 1954, *EM* 2.431.

Jotbatah, a land of streams of water. It is probably to be identified with modern Ṭabeh, an oasis about seven miles south of Eilat (Elath) on the western shore of the Gulf of ʿAqaba. In Byzantine times an island in this region was known by the name Jotabe, which controlled the sea traffic to Elath. This island is to be identified with Jazirat Farʿun, a small island about three miles south of Ṭabeh. The Midianite sherds that were discovered on Jazirat-Farʿun (Rothenberg 1967, pp. 3–41) prove that the place was settled at the end of the second millennium B.C.E. (cf. Aharoni and Rainey 1979, pp. 199–200). The name Jotabe was apparently given to the island because of the oasis Ṭabeh = Jotbatah nearby (see B. Mazar 1975b, pp. 47–48).

The "streams of water *(nḥly mym)*" may refer here to the brooks and pools of the oasis; cf., e.g., Exod 15:27 (the oasis with "twelve springs of water *[ʿynt mym]*"); compare the description of the exiles coming back from the northland and led to "streams of water *(nḥly mym)*" in Jer 31:8 (cf. Isa 41:18). The phrase *ʾrṣ nḥly mym* 'a land with streams . . .' in Deut 8:7 occurs also next to *ʾrṣ ṭwbh* 'good land'. A similar play on words appears in 10:7, where Jotbatah (the root of *ṭwb)* is associated with "a land of streams of water."

8–9. Another independent pericope about the Levites, who were designated to carry the Ark that is spoken of in the passage vv 1–5. According to Exod 32:29 the Levites were consecrated at Horeb after their struggle with the worshipers of the golden calf; vv 8–9 here seem to presuppose the events as presented in Exod 32, though the details about the punishment of the people are not given here (see the COMMENT below).

8. *At that time.* This phrase introduces a separate account; see v 1.

separated (hbdyl) the tribe of Levi to carry the Ark . . . to serve him, and to bless in his name. Compare 21:5, "for YHWH your God has chosen *(bḥr)* them [the Levites] to minister to him and to bless in the name of YHWH"; cf. 18:5; Jer 33:24; Ps 105:26; 1 Chr 15:2.

The use of the verb "separate *(hbdyl)*" instead of "choose *(bḥr)*" is characteristic of the priestly literature. Compare Lev 20:26 in connection with the election of Israel: "and I separated you from all the peoples to be mine," and in connection with the Levites, cf. Num 8:14; 16:9; 1 Kgs 8:53. For the consecration of the Levites see Num 3:5ff., 40ff.

to carry the Ark. In the priestly literature the task is assigned to the Levites as distinguished from the priests, in particular to the Kohathites (Num 3:31; 4:15; cf. 1 Chr 15:2, 15, 26; etc.). In Deuteronomy, in which no distinction is made between priests and Levites, the carrying of the Ark is assigned to priests and Levites, "the tribe of Levi" as here or "the priests the son of Levi" (31:9) or the "Levites" in 31:25. For the priests carrying the Ark, see Josh 3:3, 6, 8 (and passim); 6:6 (and passim); 1 Kgs 8:3, 6; cf. 1 Sam 6:15; 2 Sam 15:24; 1 Kgs 2:26.

the Ark of YHWH's Covenant. This expression occurs mostly in Deuteronomic passages or in passages influenced by its phraseology; cf. Deut 31:9, 25, 26; Josh 3:3, 6, 8, 14, 17; 4:9, 7, 18; 6:6, 8; 8:33; 1 Kgs 3:15; 6:19; 8:1, 6 = 2 Chr 5:2, 7; Jer 3:16; 1 Chr 15:25, 26, 28, 29; 16:6, 37; 17:1; 22:19; 28:2, 18.

The usual expression was the Ark of YHWH (or God) (Josh 3:13; 4:5, 11; 6:6, 7, 11, 13; 7:6; 1 Sam 3:3; 4:6, 11; 17–22; chaps. 5–6 (passim); 7:1; 2 Sam 6 (passim); 15:24b, 25, 29), and in several instances it can be shown that the word "covenant" was added. Thus in Josh 3:14, 17 the extraordinary syntax *(nśʾy hʾrwn hbĕryt; nśʾy hʾrwn bĕryt)* makes it clear that the original text did not have *bĕryt,* as in 3:15 and 4:10. Similarly, *bĕyt (ḍiathēkē)* does not appear in the LXX in 1 Sam 4:3–5, and this reflects the genuine text (cf. McCarter 1984, Textual Notes, p. 103). A comparison of 2 Sam 6:12, 13, 15, 16; 7:2 with its parallels in 1 Chr 15:25, 26, 28, 29; 17:1 also shows that the Chronicler has added *bĕyt* in all of these verses. On the whole problem see Seyring 1891, pp. 114–21; Driver 1902, pp. 122–23; Japhet, 1977, pp. 89–91.

It was the Deuteronomic school that was eager to define the ark as "the Ark of the Covenant" (see below). One should admit, however, that the "Ark of the Covenant" appears also in pre-Deuteronomic passages (Num 10:33; 14:44; Judg 20:27; 1 Sam 4:3, 4, 5; 2 Sam 15:24a), therefore it cannot be said that the Ark of the Covenant is a Deuteronomic invention. Furthermore, as indicated above, the notion of the Ark as a receptacle of Covenant is very ancient (see the Notes to 10:1–5), and seeing the Ark solely in its covenantal function belongs to the specific ideology of Deuteronomy (see above). This ideology motivated the scribes to add to the phrase "the ark of YHWH" the word "covenant [of YHWH]."

The priestly term *ʾaron haʿedût* (Exod 25:22; 26:33–34; 30:6, 26; etc.) is not synonymous with *ʾaron habĕrit,* rather, it means "the ark of the majesty"; see above, in the Note to 9:9. The priestly author does not allude anywhere to the Decalogue as a covenantal document, in contrast to the author of Deuteronomy.

to stand before YHWH and to serve him. "To stand before" means to serve; cf. 1:38; 17:12; 18:7; Judg 20:28; 1 Kgs 10:8; 12:8; 17:1; 18:15; 2 Kgs 3:14; 5:16;

Ezek 44:15; 2 Chr 29:11; similarly, in Akkadian *uzuzzu ina pāni* means 'to serve' (see Weinfeld 1982c, p. 42). For the combination of "standing" and "serving *(ʿmd. šrt),*" see Deut 17:12; 18:5; and compare v 7 there: "he may serve *(wšrt)* in the name of YHWH his God like all his fellows the Levites who stand there *(hʿmdym)* before YHWH"; cf. also Num 3:6; 16:9; Ezek 44:11b; 2 Chr 29:11. Unlike Deuteronomy, which entitles the whole tribe of Levi to serve before YHWH, the priestly code makes a distinction between the priests and the Levites. The priests serve God directly: they stand before YHWH and serve him (Ezek 44:15: "they shall approach me to serve me *(lšrtny)* and stand before me"), whereas the Levites are subordinate attendants who do not "stand before YHWH" and serve him but "stand before" the Aaronite priests and serve them: "make him [the tribe of Levi] stand before Aaron the priest and let him serve him" (Num 3:6; compare Num 8:26; 18:2; 2 Chr 8:14). The Levites, according to the priestly literature, also serve the congregation; cf. Num 16:9, "he separated *(hbdyl)* you . . . to stand before the congregation *(hʿdh)* to serve them" (compare Ezek 44:11b; 2 Chr 8:14). According to that literature, they also performed menial tasks for the people, such as slaughtering and flaying (Ezek 44:11; 2 Chr 29:34; 35:6), guarding the tabernacle and carrying its objects (Num 1:50, 4:9, 12; 8:23–26).

and to bless in his name. Compare 21:5. The functions of the Levites—"to serve God and to bless in his name"—are assigned in 1 Chr 23:13 to the Aaronites, in accordance with the priestly code; see Num 6:22–27 and compare Lev 9:22. In 2 Sam 6:18 and 1 Kgs 8:14, 55 (in the latter, without *bšm YHWH* 'in the name of YHWH') we find the king performing this function. In the monarchic period kings in fact conducted cultic celebrations (1 Sam 13:9; 14:34; 2 Sam 6:17; 1 Kgs 12:32; 13:1; cf. Ezek 45:17, 22f.; 46:2, 9, 12), as in Mesopotamia and in the Hittite and Ugaritic rituals (see Weinfeld 1983b, pp. 116–23). But in the legal normative literature, which has its roots in the premonarchic period (see Noth 1966, pp. 1–107), the king has no function in the cult.

9. *Therefore Levi has no portion nor inheritance along with his bretheren.* Compare 18:1–2; 12:12b; 14:27b, 29; Josh 13:14, 33; 18:7.

YHWH is his inheritance. Compare Deut 18:2; Josh 13:14, 33. This means that the sacred dues made to YHWH belong to him; compare Num 18:19–20, referring to Aaron.

as YHWH your God spoke to him Compare 18:2b. Such divine statement is indeed found in Num 18:20 (= priestly source), where God says to Aaron, "I am your portion and inheritance among the Israelites." But there it refers to the Aaronites, whereas in Deuteronomy it refers to the whole tribe of Levi (cf. 18:1, "the whole tribe of Levi"). It seems that the phrase "the whole tribe of Levi" has a polemical thrust (see Milgrom 1976, pp. 11–12) and comes as a reaction against the preference shown to the Aaronite clan. Deuteronomy knows the practical distinction between the officiating priests and the nonofficiating

Levites (see 18:3–5 versus 18:6–8); but, in contrast to the priestly code, which makes this distinction a key to status and revenues, Deuteronomy makes the whole tribe of Levi eligible to service and prebends.

10–11. These verses bring us back to the main topic, the renewal of YHWH's relationship with Israel after the grave sin of the golden calf. It is not clear, however, whether the "forty days and forty nights" mentioned in 10:10 are the same as in 9:18 and 25, the forty days of prayer after his descent from the mount with the tablets that he broke. It seems that they refer to the forty days during which Moses received the second tablets, which, according to Exod 34:1–9, were accompanied by a liturgy of forgiveness (vv 6–9). See the NOTE to 9:18.

10. *I had stayed on the mountain.* There seems to be a distinction between 9:9b, where Moses is said to "stay *(yšb)*" (cf. Deut 1:46) on the mountain for the acceptance of the tablets, this verse, where he is said to "stand *(ʿmd)*" on the mountain for prayer. For *ʿmd* 'stand in prayer' see Gen 18:22; 19:27; Jer 18:20; Ps 106:20; and note the term *ʿmydh* for the official prayer in Judaism (cf. *Sipre Dĕbarim* §26 [Finkelstein 1969, pp. 39–40 and the references there for the rabbinic literature, p. 39 line 9]).

YHWH listened to me that time also. Compare the same phrase in 9:19b, which refers to Moses' first intercession before the making of the second tablets and the Ark. Here it refers to the second intercession after the reception of the second tablets and their placement in the Ark (compare Exod 34:1–9).

11. *Arise for journeying before the people.* This line is possibly dependent on Exod 32:34, "Go now, lead the people," and 33:1, "set out from here you and the people . . . to the land but there the angel is to drive out the Canaanites before the Israelites" (32:34; 33:2; cf. Exod 23:20). Here the angel is not mentioned at all (cf. the INTRODUCTION and the COMMENT below).

COMMENT

This sermon, like the previous ones, is concerned with the entrance of the Israelites into the land of Canaan (mark seven times the root "inherit *(yrš)*" in 9:1–6), but, unlike the others, it does not contain warnings against apostasy and violation of the law in the future but rather relates to the sins of the past. The sermon serves to uproot feelings of pride and self-righteousness: the Israelites should not think that they were given the land because of their righteousness and perfection; it was given to them because of the promise of God to the Patriarchs (vv 5–6). In contrast, their behavior in the past does not entitle them to the gift of the land, for they were constantly provoking God and defying him.

The gravest provocation to God was the worship of the golden calf, which constituted a violation of the first commandments of the Sinaitic revelation, which enjoin exclusive loyalty to YHWH and prohibit the worship of idols (Deut 5:6–10). These commandments were violated right after Israel's commitment to keep them. In fact, the main part of this section is devoted to this crime and its rectification. The commission of this crime caused the annulment of the covenant of God with Israel and hence the breaking of the tablets of the covenant by Moses (see the NOTE to v 17). Only after Moses' intercession did God agree to write new tablets and thus renew the relationship with the people (9:25–10:4). This finally enabled Moses to lead the people on their march to the promised land (Deut 10:11).

Still, it was not only the sin of the golden calf that angered God; there were other sins that showed the defiance and wickedness of the people (vv 22–23). The rebelliousness of the people at Massah (Exod 17:7), at Qibrot Hataʾwah (Num 11:31–34), and at Tabʿerah (Num 11:1–3), as well as the sin of the spies (cf. Deut 1:19–39) were all testimony to the stubbornness and sinfulness of the people. Israel has in fact been rebellious: from the day they left Egypt (v 7) and until this very day (vv 7, 24).

The sin of the golden calf was the dominant one, however, and it actually reflects here the historical sin of the northern Israelites, who were worshiping the golden calves (cf. 1 Kgs 12:28–29 and especially Hos 8:5–6; 10:5; 13:2). The exile of the northern Israelites was indeed seen by the Deuteronomic historiographer as a punishment for this sin (cf. 1 Kgs 14:15–16; 2 Kgs 17:16; etc.). The stubbornness and the wickedness of the northern Israelites is described in the Books of Kings in terms similar to those of Deut 8 and 9; see, for example, 2 Kgs 17:13, "they did not obey, they stiffened their necks like their fathers who did not have faith in YHWH their God . . . they made molten idols for themselves—two calves" (cf. 9:13, 27). Although 2 Kgs 17:7–23 was written sometime later than Deut 9:1–10:11 it reflects the same ideology and belongs to the same literary school. Furthermore, the view expressed here that the people were rebellious *from the beginning till today* is prevalent also in the admonitions to Judah composed by the same school. Thus we read, concerning the sin of Manasseh, king of Judah, "I will bring a disaster on Jerusalem and Judah . . . because they have been vexing me *from the days that their fathers came out of Egypt to this day*" (2 Kgs 21:12–15). Similar statements are found in the prophecy of Jeremiah (7:25), which was edited by the Deuteronomic scribes (see Weinfeld 1972a, p. 31), and in Ezekiel (see, e.g., chap. 20).

The Worship of the Golden Calf

The bull or the calf was a divine symbol of strength and fertility in the ancient Near East. Plenty of emblems and statuettes of bulls in a cultic context have been found in the Levant. The cult of the Apis bull in Egypt is well known, but the cult was even more widespread in other areas of the Fertile Crescent and especially in the areas of Anatolia and Syria.

In Ugarit the epithet of El, the head of the pantheon, is *ṯrʾl* 'bull god', and according to the view of H. Torczyner (1925, 277–80), this epithet was applied to the golden calf in Israel and is attested in Hos 8:6, which is to be read, "for who is 'bull god' *(ky my šrʾl),* it is no god, a craftsman made it, the calf of Samaria will be broken in fragments" (cf. *NEchB).*

In the Hittite religion the worship of the bull is iconographically well represented. Thus we find on a grand relief from Alaca Hüyük of the fifteenth century B.C.E. a royal couple making an offering before an altar and a horned bull (cf. *ANEP* ² no. 616). The Hittite weather god was mostly represented by a tin-plated or silver-plated bull (see Gurney 1977, pp. 25–26), and in a Hittite text depicting a god we read, "the city of Maletta; a bull of wood tin plated, standing on all fours, this is the Weather-god of Maletta" (Güterbock 1964, p. 55 n. 6). Furthermore, a bronze bull figurine unique in its dimensions and style was recently discovered in northern Samaria. The exploration of the site of the discovery unraveled a whole cultic installation consisting of an open cult place including a circle of stones constructed at the top of the hill; within it was a large stone *(maṣṣebah)* with a pavement before it (cf. A. Mazar 1982). Another significant find is the iconography of the cult stand from Taʿanakh (Lapp 1969, pp. 42–44), where on the top register we find a young bull and above it a winged sun disk, which represents the deity (see, recently, Hestrin 1987, pp. 74–75).

It seems that the account about the cult of the golden calf established at Bethel by Jeroboam on the one hand (1 Kgs 12:28–29), and the account about Aaron's making the molten calf (Exod 32:4) on the other, point toward an old northern Israelite tradition—anchored in Bethel—about the Aaronic priesthood being involved in the golden calf cult. There is significance to the fact that the sons of Jeroboam, Nadab and Abijah, bear the same names as the sons of Aaron who offered alien fire before YHWH (Lev 10:1; see Aberbach and Smolar 1967, pp. 134 and 139). That the divine symbol of a bull was associated with Bethel may be learned from Gen 49:24, where the term *ʾabyr Jacob* 'the bull of Jacob', applied to the God of Israel, is coupled with *ʾbn Israel* 'the stone/rock of Israel', in other words, the *maṣṣebah,* of Bethel. For the bull/ram imagery in connection with the God of Israel cf. Num 23:22; 24:8.

One should, however, be aware of the fact that applying a symbol of a bull to the God of Israel does not necessarily mean that the people believed that the bull represented YHWH himself. According to some scholars (Obbink 1929; Albright 1968, p. 172), the calf was considered the pedestal upon which YHWH was enthroned and thus was parallel in function to the "cherubim" in Jerusalem. Bull pedestals of the god Baal-Hadad are also attested in the Hittite and Syrian iconography (see, e.g., *ANEP,* nos. 500, 501, 531). It was in the framework of the Jerusalemite polemic against the north after the reform of Jeroboam (2 Kgs 12:28–29) that the calves were depicted as gods, hence the appellation "your gods" (2 Kgs 12:28, Exod 32:8); the reason for the use of the plural is the introduction of Dan in the narrative about Jeroboam.

One should admit, however, that the divine symbol can easily be confused with the divinity itself (cf. Jacobsen 1987); hence the objection to the veneration of divine symbols (cf. 2 Kgs 18:4) and especially the veneration of the calves. This objection was particularly voiced by Hosea (8:5–6; 10:5; 13:2) and was later presented by the Deuteronomic historiographer as the historical sin of Israel (cf. above); see also Ps 106:19–20: "they made a calf at Horeb and bowed down to a molten image. They exchanged his glory for the image of a bull that eats grass" (cf. Neh 9:18).

It should be added here that although in principle there was no difference between the calf as a pedestal and the cherubim as a pedestal, in practice there was a big difference between the two. The cherubim were not exposed to the public, whereas the calves were. Putting the statue in the open means displaying the deity for public worship, as is actually described in the stories about the worship of the golden calves: "they bowed down to it and sacrificed to it, saying: 'these are your gods, O Israel' " (Exod 32:8; cf. 1 Kgs 12:28). The display of the statue of the god for public adoration is indeed attested in the Hittite religion. Thus we read in a Hittite text, "In former times the statue of god was kept in the inner chamber so that the people could not see it, now it stands on a pedestal in the open" (KUB 42 100 iii:36f.; see Beckman 1982, p. 437).

Structure of 9:1–10:11

This section opens with an announcement about the crossing of the Jordan in order to inherit the land (9:1–2) and ends with the command to Moses to march at the head of the people in order to inherit the land (10:11). The entrance into the promised land was turned by the author into a problem of religious education: the elimination of feelings of self-righteousness and the consciousness of sin.

This section in fact constitutes an edifying speech, which opens with the exhortation to Israel (vv 3–7) not to nourish feelings of superiority (cf. 7:7) following the inheritance of the land, because the inheritance of the land is an act of grace by God and not a reward for righteousness (cf. above). On the contrary, Israel provoked God constantly and does not deserve the grace. This is what the author intends to stress in the next paragraph of his speech (vv 8–24), which centers on the breach of the covenant caused by the worship of the golden calf.

The next paragraph is dedicated to the renewal of the covenant (9:25–10:5). It opens with a prayer of intercession by Moses (vv 25–29), which made possible the renewal of relations between God and Israel. This is followed by the making of the new tablets and their deposit in the Ark (10:1–5); then comes an itinerary (10:6–7), which is a digression because it interrupts the continuity between vv 1–5, which contain information about the Ark, and vv 8–9, which tell us about the Levites who were appointed to carry the Ark. The appointment of the Levites indeed is the outcome of their pious behavior during the sin of the golden calf; see Exod 32:25–29. Deuteronomy 10:10–11 relates to the final propitiation of God, following which Moses is commanded to lead the people to the promised land.

On the whole, the section of 9:8–10:11 constitutes a juxtaposition of the illegitimate cult of the golden calf (9:8–24) with the establishment of the legitimate cult (10:1–9). This juxtaposition corresponds to the layout of the traditions in the book of Exodus, where we find the story about the erection of the tabernacle (chaps. 35–40) right after the story about the sin of the golden calf (chaps. 32–34). Whereas the priestly redactor in Exodus is interested in the cult of the tabernacle, however, the author of Deuteronomy is interested in the tablets of the covenant and in the Ark of the Covenant as educational media, and is not interested in the cultic institutions as such (see the INTRODUCTION).

This section revolves around the concept of the miraculous "forty days and forty nights" spent by Moses on the mount of God. The forty days and forty nights actually create the division of the section into five units:

1. 9:9–10 deals with the "forty days and forty nights" needed for the reception of the first tablets of the covenant by Moses.
2. 9:11–17: the end of the forty days and forty nights marks the violation of the covenant.
3. 9:18–21, the intercession of Moses during the second forty days and forty nights.
4. 9:25–10:5: forty days of the atonement for the sin and the renewal of the covenant through the building of the Ark of the Covenant and the making of the second tablets.
5. 10:10–11 contains the conclusion of the narrative mentioning the atonement during the forty days and the preparation for the journey to the promised land (cf. Lohfink 1963, pp. 207ff.).

The recurrence of the expression "forty days and forty nights" points toward the liturgical-intercessory nature of the whole section under discussion. Indeed, the source upon which this section is based, namely, Exod 32–34, revolves around three intercessions of Moses concerning the sin of the golden calf and the restoration of God's presence following Moses' prayers. The first intercession comes upon Moses' hearing from God about the sin and about the will of God to exterminate the people: Moses prays and God renounces the punishment (Exod 32:7–14). But this does not mean that the sin was forgiven. The second one occurs the morning after his descent and after he had seen the crime: Moses expresses his wish to ascend to God again and to ask for forgiveness. After a discussion with Moses about forgiveness, God agrees to let the people go to the promised land, though not without punishment (32:30–35). But God is not ready yet to restore his presence within Israel; he would rather send his emissary, the angel, who will lead the people into the land (32:34, 33:2–3). In order to draw the presence of God into the camp, Moses sets up the tabernacle outside the camp so that he could speak "face to face *(pnym ʾl pnym)*" with God. But this is only an incentive for the restoration of the "face," that is, the presence of God to the camp of the Israelites in their moving to the promised land (Exod 33:12–17). Finally, the next step will be to entreat YHWH for the revelation of his "glory *(kbwd),*" following which God appears before Moses in his capacity as a compassionate and gracious God who forgives sin (34:6). This is all done while the new tablets are kept in Moses' hands and the covenant is renewed (33:18–34:10).

Although Exod 32–34 is not of homogeneous nature and apparently underwent a complex process of redaction, as has been seen by many commentators, it preserved a basic degree of unity, literary and theological (cf. recently Moberly 1983), and this unity is also reflected in the Deuteronomic account. In Deut 9:8–10:11, as in Exodus, Moses' intercessions are recounted three times the first in 9:18–20, the second in 9:25–29, and the third in 10:10. Nonetheless, there is a difference between Exodus and Deuteronomy in the order and nature of the prayers, as well as in the liturgical setting involved. In Exod 32–34 the first prayer is presented by Moses before his descent from the mountain (32:11–14), while in Deuteronomy it occurs after his descent (9:18–20). From the point of view of contents the prayer in Deut 9:25–29 overlaps partially that of Exod 32:11–14 but comprises also elements from the prayer in Num 14:16. By contrast, the liturgical formulas of Exod 34:6–7, which are echoed in the prayer of Num 14:18, are completely absent in Deuteronomy. The same applies to the theophany, which stands at the background of the prayers in Exod 33 and 34 (cf. 33:21–23; 34:5) and Num 14 (cf. vv 10, 14) but is missing in Deuteronomy.

Deuteronomy, like Exodus, has interest in the restoration of God's relationship with Israel, but whereas in Exodus this relationship is renewed only after a series of heavy punishments (32:20b, 27–28, 35; 33:5), in Deuteronomy nothing is heard of punishments. Yet another difference: the renewal of the relationship in Exodus is expressed by the erection of the Tabernacle (Exod 33:7–11) and by the revelation of God's "presence *(pnym)*" (33:11, 14) and "glory *(kbwd)*" (33:18, 22–23), which is the priestly term for God's presence. Deuteronomy, however, sees the restoration of the presence of God in Israel only through the covenant as represented by the Ten Commandments written on the two tablets. By the same token, the angel who appears so prominently in Exodus (32:34; 33:3) is completely ignored in Deuteronomy, which is against angelology (cf. Introduction sec. 13)

THE PREPARATIONS FOR THE ENTRANCE INTO THE PROMISED LAND (10:12–11:32)

10 12And now, O Israel, what does YHWH your God demand of you? Only
this: to fear YHWH your God, to walk in all his ways, to love him, and to serve
YHWH your God with all your heart and soul, 13to observe YHWH's commandments and laws, which I command you today, for your good. 14Lo, the
heavens and the heavens of heavens belong to YHWH your God, the earth and
all that is on it! 15Yet only your fathers YHWH desired and set his love on
them, so that he chose you, their descendants after them, from among all
peoples—as is now the case. 16Circumcise the foreskin of your hearts and stiffen
your necks no more. 17For YHWH your God is the God of gods and the Lord
of lords, the great, the mighty, and the awesome God, who shows no favor and
takes no bribe, 18but upholds the cause of the orphan and the widow, and loves
the stranger, providing him with food and clothing. 19You shall love the
stranger, for you were strangers in the land of Egypt.

20You must fear YHWH your God: only him shall you worship, to him shall
you cleave, and by his name shall you swear. 21He is your glory and he is your
God, who wrought for you those great and awesome deeds which your eyes have
seen. 22Your ancestors went down to Egypt seventy persons in all; and now
YHWH your God has made you as numerous as the stars of heaven.
11 1Love, therefore, YHWH your God, and you shall keep his charge, his laws,
his rules, and his commandments at all times.

2You shall know this day that it is not your children, who neither experienced nor witnessed the lesson of YHWH your God—his greatness, his mighty
hand, his outstretched arm; 3his signs and his deeds that he performed in Egypt
against Pharaoh king of Egypt and all his land; 4what he did to Egypt's army, its
horses and chariots; how YHWH caused the waters of the Sea of Reeds to flow
over them when they were pursuing you, thus destroying them to this day;
5what he did for you in the wilderness until you arrived in this place; 6and what
he did to Dathan and Abiram, sons of Eliab son of Reuben, when the earth
opened her mouth and swallowed them and their households, their tents, and
every living substance that followed them in the midst of all Israel—7but it was
with your own eyes that you saw all the great deed(s) that YHWH performed.

8You shall keep all the commandments that I command you today, so that
you may have the strength to come in and occupy the land that you are about to
cross into and occupy, 9and so that you may prolong the days upon the land that

YHWH swore to your fathers to give to them and to their descendants, a land
flowing with milk and honey.
10For the land that you are about to come into and occupy is not like the
land of Egypt from which you have come, where you sow your seed and water it
with your feet like a vegetable garden; 11but the land you are about to cross into
and occupy, a land of hills and valleys, it drinks its water according to the rains
of heaven. 12It is a land that YHWH your God cares for, the eyes of YHWH
your God are always on it, from year's beginning to year's end.
13If, then, you obey the commandments that I command you this day, to
love YHWH your God and serve him with all your heart and soul, 14I will give
the rain for your land in season, the early rain and the late. You shall gather in
your grain, your wine and oil. 15I will give grass in the fields for your cattle and
you shall eat and be satiated. 16Beware lest your heart be seduced and you turn
away to serve other gods and bow to them. 17For YHWH's anger will flare up
against you, and he will shut up the skies and there will be no rain and the land
will not yield its produce; and you will perish quickly from the good land that
YHWH is giving you.
18You shall put these my words upon your heart and your soul and you shall
bind them as a sign on your hand and as a frontlet on your forehead, 19and
teach them to your children—reciting them when you stay at home and when
you are away, when you lie down and when you get up; 20and inscribe them on
the doorposts of your house and on your gates—21so that your days and the days
of your children may be multiplied in the land that YHWH swore to your
fathers to give to them, as long as there is a heaven over the earth.
22For if you surely keep all the commandments that I command you, to love
YHWH your God, to walk in all his ways, and cleave to him, 23YHWH will
drive out all these nations from before you: you will dispossess nations greater
and mightier than you. 24Every spot on which your foot treads shall be yours;
your territory shall be from the wilderness and the Lebanon, from the river—the
Euphrates—to the western sea.
25No man shall stand up to you: YHWH your God will put your dread and
fear of you over all the land in which you set foot, as he promised you.
26See, this day I set before you blessing and curse: 27blessing, if you obey the
commandments of YHWH your God that I command you this day; 28and
curse, if you do not obey the commandments of YHWH your God, but turn
aside from the way that I command you this day and follow other gods, whom
you have not known. 29When YHWH your God brings you into the land that
you are about to come into and occupy, you shall pronounce the blessing at
Mount Gerizim and the curse at Mount Ebal. 30Are they not beyond the
Jordan, beyond the west road that is in the land of the Canaanites who dwell in
the ʿArabah—in front of Gilgal, by the oaks of Moreh?
31For you are about to cross the Jordan to come in and occupy the land that
YHWH your God is giving to you. When you have occupied it and are settled

in it, [32]take care to observe all the laws and rules that I have set before you this day.

TEXTUAL NOTES

12. *to walk (llkt).* Two Hebrew manuscripts, Greek Minuscules, Syriac, and Vg read: *wllkt* 'and to walk'; cf. MT 19:9.

13. *to observe (lšmr).* The Samaritan text, Syriac, and Vg render *wlšmr* 'and to keep'.

YHWH's commandments. Qumran (8Q3 [phylacteries], DJD 3.152, 154; 8Q4 [mezuzah], DJD 3.158, 160), the Samaritan text, LXX, and Syriac read: YHWH "your God *(ʾlhyk),*" which seems to be genuine in view of the fact that *miṣwot YHWH* in Deuteronomy come always with *ʾlhyk(m);* cf. 4:2; 6:17; 8:6; 11:27, 28; 28:9, 13.

for your good. See the Textual Note to 6:24.

15. *Yet (raq) only.* Compare the Textual Note to 4:6. Qumran (8QFr 19 [phylacteries], DJD 3.154) renders instead of *raq: ʿl kn* 'therefore'.

[YHWH] desired. Hebrew: *ḥšq,* literally, 'attached'. Compare the Textual Note to 7:7.

16. *God of gods.* These words are translated by *Tg. Onq.* and *Tg. Ps.-J.* as "God of judges," which is influenced by rabbinic tradition; cf. *Mek. Exod* 21:6; 22:7, 27 (Horowitz 1928, pp. 252, 268, 302, 317).

Lord of lords. The MT has the majestic plural *ʾdny* (Qumran: 4Q, 138 Phyl. K, *DJD* 6.68 has singular: *ʾadôn).* Compare Gen 42:30; Isa 19:4; etc; and see *GKC* §126i.

18. *the cause of the orphan.* Qumran (4Q 138 Phyl. K, *DJD* 6.68) XQ Phyl 1–4, Yadin 1969, p. 71) and LXX: "the cause of the stranger *(gr =proselytos)* and the fatherless," but this is superfluous because the stranger occurs in the second part of the verse. The reading was influenced by the triplet *gr ytm wʾlmnh* common in Deuteronomy; see the Note to v 18.

20. *him shall you worship.* Hebrew: *ʾtw.* Qumran (4Q Phyl. K, *DJD* 6.68) and Samaritan text: *wʾtw* 'and him', as in 6:13.

him shall you cleave. Hebrew: *wbw tdbq.* Qumran (8Q Phyl. fragment 16, DJD 3.152) has *tqrb,* which was influenced by the Targumic renderings: *Onq., ttqrb, Ps.-J., tqrbwn* 'come near [to the fear/worship of YHWH].'

those . . . awesome. Hebrew: *hnwrʾt hʾlh.* Qumran (8Q Phyl. fragment 12, DJD 3.152), Syriac, and the Armenian version omit *hʾilh* 'those'.

22. *seventy persons in all.* Hebrew: *běšibʿîm nepeš.* The *be-* prefix is the *beth essentiae* and is literally rendered, "as seventy persons"; see *GKC* §119i.

11: 1. *you shall keep his charge, his laws, his rules, and his commandments.* The Samaritan text reverses the order: commandments *(mṣwtyw)* before rules *(mšpṭyw);* cf. 8:11; 30:16; and the deuteronomistic passage in 1 Kgs. 2:3.

2. *who neither experienced nor witnessed.* Hebrew: *ʾšr lʾydʿw wʾšr lʾ rʾw,*

literally, 'which they have not known and which they have not seen'. According to A. Ehrlich (1909, ad loc.) we encounter here a chiastic structure. The *knowing* refers to the "lesson *(mwsr)*" while the *seeing* refers to the "greatness *(gdl).*" But both "knowing" and "seeing" connote experience, and they frequently interchange, especially, in the Deuteronomic literature, when they describe the marvelous deeds of God; compare Josh 24:31, "the elders . . . who had experienced [literally, known = *ydʿ]* all the deeds that YHWH had done for Israel," with its parallel in Judg 2:7, "who had experienced [literally, had seen = *rʾh]* all the deeds . . . that YHWH had done for Israel." For a thorough discussion of *ydʿ* and *rʾh* in the thinking of old Israel, see Seeligmann 1977).

2. *his mighty hand and his outstretched arm. (ydw hḥzqh wzrʿw hnṭwyh)* 4Q Phyl. K*(DJD* 6.68) and the Samaritan text have *wʾ t zrwʿw hnṭwyh ʾt ydw hḥzqh.* the Qumran *(ibid),* Samaritan and other versions have "and *(wĕ)*" before *ʾt ydw.*

3. *his signs and his deeds.* Hebrew: *ʾt ʾ ttyw wʾt mʿśyw.* The LXX renders "his signs and his portents *(ʾt ʾttyw wʾt mwpṭyw),*" following the Deuteronomic stereotype (4:34; 6:22; 7:19; 26:8; 29:2; 34:11), but this is hardly original. As indicated in the NOTE to this verse, "the deed that God did *(mʿśh . . . ʾšr ʿśh)*" serves as an *inclusio* for the hymnic passage in vv 3–7.

king of Egypt. These words are missing in the Samaritan Pentateuch and certain Greek manuscripts.

6. *and swallowed them.* Qumran (Phyl. A, K, DJD 6.50, 68) and the Samaritan text add here *wʾt kl hʾdm ʾšr lqrḥ* 'and all the men of Korah', taken from Num 16:32. This can hardly be original, for—as is shown in the NOTE below—Korah belongs to the priestly stratum of the story, which is not represented in Deuteronomy.

7. *the great deeds that YHWH performed.* The LXX adds "for you as at this day *(hymīn semeron)*" (= Hebrew *lkm hywm hzh),* apparently wanting to create a correspondence to v 4, where Egypt is described as "destroyed to this day," this allegedly in contrast to what God did for the Israelites, which lasts "until this day." Qumran (4Q Phyl. K, DJD 6.69) adds, after *ʾšr ʿśh, ʾtkmh* 'with you'.

the great deed(s). MT, Samaritan, Tg.Ps.-J, Tg.Onq.: *hgdl* in singular. 4Q Dt[j,k1] (Duncan 1989, Figs. 22, 28), LXX, Tg.Neof., Peshitta, Vg.: *hgdwlym* in plural. For the semantic and phonetic identity of *mʿśh/mʿśy* in Biblical Hebrew and in Qumran, see E. Qimron, *The Hebrew of the Dead Sea Scrolls, HSS* 29, Atlanta Scholars Press, 1986, 100.

8. *so that you may have the strength to come in and occupy the land.* The LXX reads, "that you may live and multiply *(wrbytm* is under the obelus in uncial LXX) and enter and occupy the land *(hina zēte kai polyplasiasthēte kai eiselthete kai klēronomesete ten gen),*" exactly like 8:1, *lmʿn thywn wrbytm wbʾ tm wyrštm ʾt hʾrs.* Compare Syro-Palestinian version: *dtḥwn wtstgwn lswgy* (Goshen-Gottstein 1973, p. 43). Qumran has two versions: 4Q Phyl. K *DJD* 6.69) reads, *lmʾn tḥzqw wʾbrtmh wbtmh wyrštmh ʾt hʾrṣʾ, so that you may have the strength to cross and enter and occupy the land';* 8Q *(DJD* 3.155) has: *lmʾn*

tḥywn wyṭbw ymym 'that you may live and [your] days be well'. 4Q Dt[kl] (Duncan 1989, Fig. 28) *wrḃẏtṁ.*

that you are about to cross into. Hebrew: *ʾšr ʾtm ʿbrym šmh.* Samaritan and Vg have *bʾym šmh* 'enter into' instead of *ʿbrym šmh* 'cross into' (for the interchange of *bʾ* and *ʿbr,* see R. Weiss 1981, p. 82). Qumran and LXX render "you cross the Jordan" (Phyl. A, K, DJD 6.50, 69; 4Q Dt[kl] [Duncan 1989, Fig. 28]). The expansion of *ʾt hyrdn* is influenced by passages like 4:26, 11:31, 30:18, and 31:13.

9. *that you may prolong the days.* Literally, "that you may lengthen [your] days." In one of the Qumran variants: "that your days may be multiplied *(wlmʿn yrbw ymykm)*" (8Q, DJD 3.155), as in MT 11:21.

to give to them and to their descendants. The Samaritan text omits "to them *(lhm).*"

10. *For the land that you are about to come into.* MT: "which you [sing.] enter *(ʾth bʾ)*". 4Q Dt[kl] (Duncan 1989, Fig. 28), Phyl. A, K *(DJD* 6.50, 69); 8Q *(DJD* 3.155) has plural, as does the Samaritan text *(ʾtm bʾ ym)* as well as in the Peshitta, Tg.Neof. and Vg.

(not like the land of Egypt) from which you have come. The MT has plural *(ʾšr yṣʾtm mšm)* but may be read in the singular, supposing dittography of the letter *mem.* Qumran (4Q 138, Phyl. K, DJD 6.69) reads singular: *šr yṣʾth mšmh.*

11. *the land you are about to cross into.* Hebrew: *ʾtm ʿbrym.* Qumran (4Q 138, Phyl. K, DJD 6.69) reads "the land that you enter into *(ʾtmh bʾym šmh)*"; compare the TEXTUAL NOTES to vv 8 and 10 concerning the interchange of *ʿbr* and *bʾ.*

according to the rains of heaven. Lamed of rule and proportion, as later Hebrew *lepi* 'in accordance with'; cf. 32:8 *(lmspr);* Isa 11:3; 32:1 *(lmšpṭ lṣdq);* etc.

12. *from year's beginning.* MT: *mršyt hšnh.* Qumran varies: 4Q [Deut kl (Duncan 1989, Fig. 28), 4Q Phyl. K *(DJD* 6.69) read, *(mršyt) šnh* (= nonemphatic), while 8Q *(DJD* 3.155) has, like the MT, *hšnh.*

to year's end. Hebrew: *ʾḥryt šnh* (nonemphatic). The Samaritan text and some Hebrew manuscripts use *hšnh.*

14. *I will give rain.* The Samaritan text, LXX, and Qumran (8Q4, DJD 3.159) have here and in v 15 "he will give *(wntn)*"; cf. also the Syro-Palestinian version (Goshen-Gottstein 1973, p. 43:to vv 14, 15 *[wytl]).*

for your land. The Samaritan text has the singular *(ʾrṣk),* followed by the LXX.

15. *I will give (wntty).* The LXX, Codex Alexandrinus, and some other Greek manuscripts read "and you will give *(wntt).*" 4Q Phyl A: *wntn* 'he will give' *(DJD* 6.50).

and you shall eat and be satiated (wʾklt wśbʿt). In the LXX this phrase joins the next sentence as a prelude to the warning in v 16. Compare the Syro-Palestinian version (Goshen-Gottstein 1973, p. 43): *wkd tkwl wtsbwᶜ ʾstklw* etc.

'and when you shall eat and be satiated beware' etc. Compare *Midr. sipre:* " 'and you shall eat and be satiated, beware' . . . be careful lest you rebel because one rebels against god out of affluence" (Finkelstein 1969, p. 92).

17. *(you will perish) quickly (mhrh).* Samaritan text: *mhr,* as in the other instances in the MT of Deuteronomy (4:26; 7:4, 22; 9:3, 12, 16; 28:20).

18. *these my words.* Hebrew: *dbry ʾlh* without emphatic article because of the suffix, in contrast to *hdbrym hʾlh* in 6:6; cf. Ehrlich 1909, ad loc. and *GKC* §126y.

on your hand (ydkm). The Samaritan text, Syriac, and some Greek manuscripts have plural "on your hands *(ydykm)";* cf. 6:8.

19. *at home (bbytk).* Samaritan text, LXX: "in the house *(bbyt)";* cf. 6:7.

20. *and inscribe [sing.] them.* The LXX, Syriac, and *Tg. Ps.-J.* use the plural.

(on the doorposts) of your house. The Samaritan text, LXX, Syriac use the plural; cf. 6:9 and the NOTE there.

22. *if you . . . keep.* Hebrew: *(ky ʾm) šmr tšmrwn,* as in 6:17. LXX: *akoē akousēte* [= *šmʿ tšmʿw]* 'if you obey', as in v 13. The phrase *šmr tšmrwn* in 6:17 is translated by the LXX properly: *fulasson fulaxe,* but here the translator wants to link this section (vv 22–25) linguistically with the previous one (vv 13–21) in order to indicate that by obeying the commandments the people will not only gain fertility and longevity but will also conquer the land in its ideal borders. But this reading cannot be original, for *šmʿ tšmʿ* should be followed by *ʾel,* as in v 13, and not by *ʾet,* as here.

that I command you. The Samaritan text, LXX, and Syriac have added "today *(hywm)*", as the MT in vv 13, 27, 28.

23. *from before you.* MT: *mlpnykm.* The Samaritan text has the singular: *mlpnyk.*

than you. MT: *mkm.* Again, the Samaritan text has the singular: *mmk.*

24. *Every spot.* Hebrew: *kl hmqwm* (with an article); cf. Gen 20:13; Exod 20:24; also 4:2:*kl hʾyš.* Joshua 1:3, which quotes this verse, omitted the article: *kl mqwm.*

from the river. The Samaritan text, LXX, and Syriac read "and from *(wmn)* the river." Some manuscripts, the LXX, *Tg. Ps.-J.,* and *Tg. Neof.* read "the great river *(hnhr hgdwl),* river Euphrates," as in Gen 15:18; Deut 1:7; Josh 1:4.

25. *(stand) up to you.* Hebrew: *bpnykm.* Samaritan text: *lpnykm,* cf. 9:2 *(lpny);* Josh 1:5 *(lpnyk),* but 7:24: *bpnyk,* for which the Samaritan text has *lpnyk.*

27. *blessing, if you obey.* Hebrew: *ʾašer* = *ʾim* 'if'; cf. Lev 4:22. *ʾašer* and not *ʾim* (as in the next verse) is especially appropriate here, because it implies a wish that the people may obey (Ehrlich 1909, ad loc.)

30. *Are they not.* Hebrew: *hlʾ hmh;* Samaritan text: *hlwʾ hm.*

the oaks. Samaritan text: LXX: "the oak *(ʾlwn)*" in the singular, as in Gen 12:6 (see the NOTE).

Moreh. MT: *mrh.* Samaritan text: *mwrʾ.* Syriac and *Tg. Ps.-J.: mmrʾ.* But *mmrʾ* belongs to the Hebronite tradition (Gen 13:18) and was introduced here by association with plural *ʾelonêy,* which occurs in the verse here. The plural *ʾelonêy* is usually combined with *mmrʾ* (Gen 13:18; 14:13; 18:1) and not with *mrh.*

NOTES

10:12. *And now, O Israel.* The word *weʿatah* 'and now' marks a transition from history (9:7–10:11) to the moral religious lesson that is to be drawn from it (compare 4:1 and the NOTE there, and the COMMENT to the present section).

what does YHWH your God demand of you. Compare Mic 6:8, *mh YHWH drš mmk* 'What does YHWH demand of you?' and the answer there is, doing justice, loving kindness, etc. Although the answer here is somewhat different—fearing, loving, and serving God, keeping his commandments, etc.—there is no difference in substance. In the continuation the author of 10:12 speaks about God doing justice and loving the destitute, which is to be imitated by the people (vv 18–19).

Questions concerning the true nature of the divine will are already attested in the first half of the second millennium in a prophetic letter addressed to Zimri-Lim, king of Mari (A 2731): "Am I not Adad, Lord of Halab. . . . I never demand anything of you. When a wronged man or woman cries out to you, stand up and do justice to him. This is what I demand from you" (cf. Lafont 1984, pp. 9–11, lines 52–55; also Anbar 1975, pp. 517–18; Malamat 1980, p. 73; Weinfeld 1982b.

to fear YHWH your God. Compare 5:29; 6:13; see Weinfeld 1972a, p. 332.

to walk in all his ways. Compare 5:30; 11:22; see Weinfeld 1972a, pp. 333–34.

to love him. Compare 6:5; 11:1, 13, 22; etc.; see Weinfeld 1972a, p. 333. For the combination of fear and love, see the NOTE to 6:13.

to serve YHWH your God. Compare 10:20; 11:13; 13:4; see Weinfeld 1972a, p. 332.

with all your heart and soul. Compare 4:29; 6:5; 11:13; and see Weinfeld 1972a, p. 334 for other references. On the phrase and its cognates in ancient Near Eastern covenantal texts, cf. the NOTE to 6:5 and the COMMENT to 6:4–9.

13. *to observe YHWH's commandments and his laws, which I command you today, for your good.* Compare the identical formulation in 4:40; "Observe his laws and commandments, which I enjoin upon you this day, that it may go well with you." Compare also 5:30 and 6:24.

14–15. God's dominion over heaven and earth makes him sovereign over all creatures, and he may pick up and choose whomever he wants to be his chosen and beloved one, in this case the Patriarchs of Israel and their descendants. The same pattern—God's dominion is universal and therefore he has the right to elect whomever he desires—is found in several places in the Bible. In the prayer of Nehemiah that has much in common with this passage (see the COMMENT) we read, "You made the heavens, the heavens of the heavens . . . the earth and everything upon it . . . you are YHWH, the God who chose Abraham" (9:6–7).

Another type of election that has the same motivation—sovereignty and therefore the right to choose—is found in connection with choosing foreign kings for dominion on earth. Thus we read in connection with Nebuchadnezzar, "It is I who made the earth, the men and beasts who are on the earth, by my great might and my outstretched arm and I give it to whomever I deem proper. I herewith deliver all these lands to my servant, King Nebuchadnezzar of Babylon" (27:5–6); and in connection with Cyrus, king of Persia, "It was I who made the earth and created man upon it; my own hands stretched out the heavens and I marshalled all their host. It was I who roused him [Cyrus] for victory and who straightens all roads for him, he shall rebuild my city and let my exiled people go" (Isa 45:12–13).

The same pattern appears in connection with picking up an individual and giving him a special privilege:

> To YHWH belongs the earth and all that it holds
> the world and its inhabitants
> for he founded it upon the ocean . . .
> who may ascend the mountain of YHWH
> who may stand in his holy place?
> he who has clean hands and a pure heart (Ps 26:1–4)

In this case God chooses the individual who may ascend his mountain and his holy place.

14. *Lo. hen* is a particle employed for the purpose of emphasis, for calling special attention of the hearer; cf. Muraoka 1985, pp. 137–40; Kogut 1986.

the heavens of heavens. Compare 1 Kgs 8:27; Pss 68:34, 148:4; Neh 9:6; 2 Chr 2:5. According to ancient Mesopotamian views there are three superimposed heavens (cf. Lambert 1975, 4.411–12), but in the Jewish apocryphal literature we find seven firmaments; cf., e.g., Ginzberg 1959, vol. 1 p. 10, n. 22 (cf. 2 Cor 12:3, "third firmament").

15. *Yet only your fathers YHWH desired and set his love on them, so that he chose you, their descendants after them, from all peoples.* Compare 4:37 and 7:7; also Jer 31:2; Mal 1:2. The concept of election and love of Israel by God serves as the basis of the second benediction before the Shemaʿ liturgy, the so-called Ahabah benediction (Singer 1915, pp. 47–48; cf. Elbogen 1931, pp. 20–21), which concludes with, "who has chosen his people Israel in love *(hbḥr bʿmw Ysrʾl bʾhbh).*" In such a manner love of Israel by God (expressed in the Ahabah benediction) rounds off the love of God to Israel expressed in the Shemaʿ passage (v 5). God's love of Israel and its election constitute the central motif of the Sabbath and festival prayers: "You have chosen us from all the peoples, loved us,

taken pleasure in us, and exalted us above all tongues; you have sanctified us by your commandments and brought us near to your service and have given us the Sabbath for rest." (That this was the original formulation of the Sabbath prayer has been shown by Wieder 1981b.)

Such prayers for Sabbath and festival from Qumran were recently published (1982) by M. Baillet in DJD 7: "blessed be the god of Israel who has chosen us from all the nations . . . [and given us days] for rest *(mnwḥh)* and pleasure *(ʿng)*" (4Q 503:24–25, p. 111). This liturgy may be traced back to the prayer of Neh 9, where, after the mention of god's universality (v 6), the concept of election is brought up (v 7) and the giving of the Torah and Sabbath to Israel is hallowed (vv 13–14). Election and love of Israel are here expressed by God's sanctifying the people through giving them the Torah and the Sabbath. This is clearly reflected in the blessing before the recital of the Torah: "Blessed are you . . . YHWH our god, King of the universe, who has chosen us from all the peoples and has given us his torah" (Singer 1915, p. 212). Thus election is not privilege but obligation.

In other words, *as is now the case.*" Compare the NOTE to 2:30.

16. *Circumcise the foreskin of your hearts.* The election of the fathers and especially the election of Abraham, which was sealed by the covenantal sign of circumcision (Gen 17), triggered the idea of circumcision here. The Deuteronomic author, however, interpreted circumcision in a figurative manner: not circumcision of flesh but circumcision of heart, in other words, of spirit and soul. Compare 30:6, where God is the one who will circumcise the people's hearts after the restoration. The same idea formulated in the same manner is found in Jer 4:4, where the people are asked to "be circumcised to YHWH and to remove the foreskin of their hearts *(hmlw lYHWH whsrw ʿrlwt lbbkm).*" Deuteronomy 10:16 is also reflected in the *Manual of Discipline* of the Qumran sect: "to circumcise in the community the foreskin of the mind and the stiff neck *(lmwl byḥd ʿwrit yṣr wʿwrp qšh)*" (1QS 5:5), but here the heart *(lb)* has been changed to mind *(yṣr)*: for *yṣr* instead of *lb* in rabbinic literature, see the NOTE to 6:5. Compare also 1QP *Hab.* 11:13, "Its interpretation *(pšr)* is the priest . . . who did not circumcise the foreskin of his heart *(kyʾ lʾ ml ʾt ʿrlt lbw),*" etc.

The Aramaic Targumim *(Onq.* and *Ps.-J.)* paraphrase this verse by omitting the words for circumcision *(mwl)* and foreskin *(ʿrlh).* They rendered, "you shall remove the folly *(ṭpšwt)* of your heart"; cf. also these Targumim to Deut. 30:6 and compare the Targum to Jer 4:4, "and remove the wickedness *(ršʿ)* of your heart." *Targum Neofiti* I to this verse combined both the Masoretic version and the Targumic renderings: "circumcise the folly *(ṭpšwt)* of your heart." The omission of the words "circumcision" and "foreskin" by *Tgs. Onq.* and *Ps.-J.* bears a polemical character: against the notion that circumcision of the heart comes instead of physical circumcision (cf. Le Déaut 1981). The concept of spiritualization is also expressed in Ezek 11:19; 36:26, where God restores the people by giving them a new heart and new spirit; cf. Weinfeld 1976a, pp. 33–35. An uncircumcised heart, like an uncircumcised ear (Jer 6:10) and uncircumcised lips (Exod 6:12, 30), means an organ that is incapable of absorbing feelings and impressions from the outside; compare the fattened heart in Isa 6:10 (cf. Ps 119:70), and there also sealed eyes and heavy ears.

stiffen your necks no more. Compare 9:6, 13, 27; and the NOTE to 5:6.

17–18. These verses contain hymnic attributes characteristic of royal imagery; see the NOTES that follow.

17. *For YHWH your God is the God of gods and the Lord of lords.* A hymnic liturgical formula; cf. Ps 136:2, 3 and Dan 2:47. In Dan 2:47 the second epithet is paraphrased: "the Lord of kings *(mrʾ mlkyn),*" not "Lord of lords" as in Deut 10:17 and Ps 136:3. The Targumim and the Peshitta to this verse translate, like Dan 2:47, "the Lord of kings *(mrʾ mlkyn)*" instead of "Lord of lords." The epithet "Lord of kings *(mrʾ mlkyn)*" is actually found in a letter of a Philistine king to Pharaoh *(KAI* 266:1.6, and see Porten 1981, pp. 36–39) and is attested as a title in Phoenician *(ʾdn mlkm),* applied by Eshmunazar of Sidon to the Persian king *(KAI* 14:18). In Akkadian this title appears as *bēl šarrāni* and was most characteristic of Esarhaddon and Ashurbanipal, the Assyrian kings (cf. Seux 1967, p. 56). The title "Lord of Lords" found in the verse here, however, is also applied to Assyrian emperors *(bēl bēle)* next to the title "King of kings *(šar šarrāni)*" but was characteristic of times prior to Esarhaddon and Ashurpanipal (cf. Seux 1967, p. 55). "King of kings" is found in Ezek 26:7; Ezra 7:12; and in Dan 2:37 applied these to earthly kings (Nebuchadnezzar and the Persian kings), hence the need for a higher title for God, which developed in later Judaism: "King of the kings of kings *(mlk mlky hmlkym)*" (Eccl 51:34; see the book of Ben 1973, p. 65 and *m. Sanh.* 4:5; *ʾAbot* 3:1, 4:32).

the great, the mighty, and the awesome. A liturgical formula (cf. Neh 9:32) that opens the Jewish Amidah prayer, and its introduction into the prayer is ascribed to the men of the great synagogue *(anšei kĕnesset hagĕdolah).* Compare *b. Yoma* 69b; also 7:21, "great and awesome *(gdwl wnwrʾ).*" These epithets are royal epithets applied to the divine king; thus we find in Ugarit the title of the suzerain *mlk rb (CTA* 64:11, 13, 26 = *KTU* 3.1), which equals the title *šarru rabû* in Akkadian, Hebrew *mlk gdl* (2 Kgs 18:28 = Isa 36:4), and Aramaic *mlk rb* (Ezra 5:11; Dan 2:10: *mlk rb wšlyṭ);* compare Ps 48:3, *qryt mlk rb* 'the city of the great king' and see the discussion of Greenfield 1967, pp. 118–19. The epithets "great and awesome *(gdwl wnwrʾ)*" are applied to God as king in Ps 47:3: "for YHWH most high *(ʿlywn)* is awesome *(nwrʾ),* a great king *(mlk gdwl)* over all the earth."

The title *gbwr* 'mighty [warrior]' is also a kingly epithet; compare Akkadian *qardu* 'hero or warrior', which is applied to both king and god alike (see *CAD,* s.v. *qardu).* For God as king and warrior cf. Ps 24:8, "who is the King of glory? YHWH valiant and mighty *(ʿzwz wgbwr),* YHWH mighty in battle *(gbwr mlḥmh)";* compare Isa 42:13, and see also Exod 15:3.

who shows no favor and takes no bribe. A human judge is similarly commanded not to show partiality by taking bribes; cf. 1:16–17; 16:19; 27:25. Although God has chosen Israel he does not discriminate in judgment between his people and other peoples; therefore he grants justice to the stranger (v 19). For the term *nś᾿ pnym* 'lift up face' in the sense of showing favor, see Gen 19:21; 32:20; Deut 28:50; Job 32:21; the equivalent phrase in Akkadian is *pānam wabālu* (cf. *CAD,* B s.v. *abālu,* p. 18).

18. *but upholds the cause of the orphan and the widow, shall love the stranger, providing him with food and clothing.* For the triplet of stranger, orphan, and widow, cf. Exod 22:20–21; Deut 14:29; 16:11, 14; 24:17, 19, 20–21; 27:19. The phrase *ʿśh mšpṭ* in this context does not mean to sit in judgment and adjudicate the case but to administer justice by helping the poor and the needy, which is one of the main functions of the ruler in the ancient Near East; cf., for example, the description of the king's function in Ugarit: "he will uphold [literally, judge] the cause of the widow, will do justice to the orphan *(ydn dn almnt. yṯpṭ ṯpṭ ytm/ qṣr npš)" (KTU* 1.19.I:23–25; 1:17 v: 7–8; 1.16 v: 45–47). For "judging" in the sense of administering justice and helping the weak and the poor, cf. Isa 11:4; Jer 22:15–16; Ps 72:1, 2; Prov 29:14; etc., and see Seeligmann 1967, pp. 273f. This is especially clear when judging is coupled with kindness and mercy *(ḥsd and rḥmym),* as for example in Jer 9:23; Mic 6:8; Hos 12:7; and Zech 7:9–10. The same applies for Akkadian "judging *(dīn dânu).*" For all of this see Weinfeld 1985d, pp. 21–25.

Verse 18 has to be attached to the end of v 17b: God does not show partiality in judgment and does not discriminate between the rich and the poor, the resident and the alien (cf. 1:16–17, also 2 Chr 19:7). Men should therefore imitate God and love the alien too (v 19). It is remarkable that this line of thought—avoiding partiality and therefore caring for the stranger—is attested in the legal codes of the Tetrateuch. Thus we read in the covenant code, "*Keep far from a false charge* . . . do not take bribes . . . *do not oppress the stranger* for you know the feelings of the stranger having yourself been strangers in the land of Egypt" (Exod 23:7–9); and in the Holiness Code, "When a stranger resides with you in your land you shall not wrong him. The stranger . . . shall be to you as one of your citizens and you shall love him as yourself, for you were strangers in the land of Egypt" (Lev 19:33–34). All of this is linked there to "*you shall not pervert justice*" (Lev 19:35).

Similar associations of partiality and relations to the stranger are to be found in the Hittite instructions to the King's commands to the border guards *(bēl madgalti):* "One should not favor a superior . . . should not take bribes . . . do whatever is right . . . if a widow has a case judge it and set it right . . . a stranger who resides in the Land provide him fully with seeds, cattle and sheep (von Schuler 1957, pp. 36f.; see for a discussion Weinfeld 1977a, pp. 76–80). For God as king upholding the cause of the stranger and the weak, compare Ps 146:7–10, "YHWH upholds the cause of the wronged *(ʿśh mšpṭ lʿšwqym),* gives food to the hungry . . . YHWH loves the righteous . . . YHWH watches over the stranger, he gives support to the orphan and the widow . . . YHWH shall reign forever."

19. *You shall love the stranger, for you were strangers in the land of Egypt.* This was placed here by association with the previous verse, which states that YHWH loves the stranger; compare Lev 19:33; also Exod 22:21; 23:9; Ps 146:9; and see the NOTE to v 18. Strangers *(gerim)* were vulnerable because of being deprived of protection from the side of clan and family, hence the constant injunctions not to molest them (cf. Exod 22:20–22; 23:9; Lev 19:33; Deut 1:16; 24:14, 17; 27:19) and to support them (Deut 14:29; 16:11, 14; 24:19, 20; 26:11, 12, 13).

20. This verse resumes the singular address that was disrupted by vv 16–19, styled in the plural. But this shift does not justify the view that vv 16–19 are a late intrusion (pace Minette de Tellesse 1962, p. 37). The irregularity in forms of address is also characteristic of other parts of the book and is especially salient in 4:1–40, which is similar in nature to this section (see the COMMENT); cf. Mayes 1981, p. 208. Verse 20 repeats the command of vv 6:12 with the addition of the clause "you shall cleave [or, hold fast] to him" found in 11:22; 13:5; and 30:20; cf. also 4:4 and the Deuteronomic passages in Josh 22:5; 23:8; 2 Kgs 18:6 (Hezekiah). In Gen 2:24; 34:3; 1 Kgs 11:2 this verb expresses affectionate love of a man for a woman, but only in the Deuteronomic literature is it used as an indication of the relation of Israel to God; cf. Weinfeld 1972a, p. 333, par. 5.

21. *He is your glory . . . who wrought for you those great and awesome deeds.* compare Exod 15:11, "awesome in glory *(nwrʾ thlt)* doing wonders *(ʿśh plʾ)*" in connection with the marvelous deeds of the Exodus. The "great and awesome deeds *(gdlt wnwrʾwt)*" are characteristic of Deuteronomy and Deuteronomic literature (2 Sam 7:23 = *Dtr);* cf. Weinfeld 1972a, pp. 37–38. The two components "great" and "awesome" occur sometimes as noun and adjective *(mwrʾ gdl/mwrʾym gdlym),* Deut 4:34: 26:8; 34:12. This pair of expressions actually corresponds to the doing of wonders *(ʿśh plʾ)* in the Song of the Sea just quoted and in Ps 77:14; compare also Ps 78:11–12, "they forgot his deeds and the wonders that he showed them, he wrought wonders *(ʿśh plʾ)* in the sight of their fathers."

For god as Glory *(thlh)* of men cf. Jer 17:14 (in connection with healing) and Ps 109:1 (God as savior).

which your eyes have seen. Compare 4:9; 7:19; 29:3; and the passage in 11:2–7.

22. *Your ancestors went down to Egypt seventy persons in all.* Compare Gen 46:26; Exod 1:5 (= the priestly source). Seventy is typical of an administrative body of judicial nature. Thus we find seventy elders who form the judicial body at the side of Moses (Exod 24:1, 9; Num 11:16; compare Ezek 8:11); seventy submissive kings (Judg 1:7); seventy sons of Gideon who was the first to be offered kingship (Judg 8:30); and seventy princes ("kings' sons") of King Ahab

(2 Kgs 10:1). Similarly we read in a Hittite royal grant about the seventy sons of the king's palace (cf. Riemschneider 1958, p. 355, line 54) and in the inscription of Bar-rakib, King of Yaudi (eighth century B.C.E.) as head of seventy brothers who were killed with King Barṣur *(KAI* 215:2–3). The table of nations in Gen 10 contains seventy nations that correspond to seventy sons of Athirat, the consort of El *(KTU* 1.4 VI:46), compare Deut 32:8 (cf. Fensham 1977). In the Second Temple period the supreme council of the Jews, the Sanhedrin, consisted of seventy persons. It seems that a national/kingly council consisting of seventy persons was a reality in the ancient Near East. In this specific context, however, the seventy come to indicate the meager number *(mty mʿṭ;* cf. 26:5) of the Israelites coming down to Egypt from which sprout the mighty and populous mass (see 26:5; Exod 1:5, 7), a miraculous phenomenon like the other wondrous phenomena of the Exodus.

as numerous as the stars of heaven. Compare 1:10; 28:62; Gen 15:5; 22:17; 26:4; Exod 32:13; an imagery rooted in the period of the United Monarchy (cf. above, in the NOTES to 7:7 and 1:10), which is not to be taken literally; contrast 4:38; 7:17; 9:1; 11:23; and see Driver 1902, ad 7:7: "the representation of Israel's number and power appears to vary in different passages, according to the thought which the writer at the time desires to express."

11: 1. *Love (therefore) YHWH your God.* This is actually the concluding verse of the section that starts in 10:12 and ends with 11:1. Deuteronomy 10:12 opens with the demand to fear YHWH and to love him, while the concluding verses of this section, 10:20–11:1, also start with the demand to fear YHWH (v 20) and end with the demand to love him.

You shall keep his charge. The phrase *šmr mšmrt* appears often in the priestly code in the sense of "guard duty for," especially in connection with the Tabernacle (cf. Num 1:53; 3:7, 28, 38; 8:26, 35; 9:19, 23; 31:30, 47) but also in the sense of guarding against violation of taboos (sexual, Lev 18:30; impurity and defilement, Lev 22:9; see Milgrom 1970, 1.8–16). In Deuteronomy and in the Deuteronomic literature (Deut 11:1; Josh 22:3; 1 Kgs 2:3) and in later sources (Zech 3:7; Mal 3:14) *šmr mšmrt* has the meaning of fulfilling duty in the general sense; cf. also Gen 26:5, which might reflect a late editorial addition. The Akkadian equivalent *maṣṣartu naṣāru* has an identical range of meanings: (1) to watch/guard; (2) to care for; (3) to perform the duty for the king or the Temple; etc. (see *CAD* M I, vol. 10, s.v. *maṣṣartu).*

2–9. The passage is written in historical retrospect and styled in the plural, like the section 9:8–10:11.

2. *you shall know this day that it is not your children, who neither experienced nor witnessed the lesson of YHWH your God.* Some commentators (cf. Rashi and Ibn Ezra, ad loc.) see here the beginning of a long sentence with a series of relative particles: "what he did" (vv 3, 4, 5, 6: *ʾšr ʿśh),* which terminates in v 7: "but it was you who saw with your own eyes," etc. (compare the *JPS* translation). One should admit, however, that this rendering fails to take account of

the accusative *ʾet,* which is to be preceded by a verb such as "not to your children *do I speak.*" Other commentators (cf. *RSV)* consider the words "not with your children who neither experienced nor witnessed *(ky . . . lʾ rʾw)*" to be a parenthesis and view the phrase "the lesson of YHWH *(mwsr Y.)*" as the object of *wydʿtm* 'and you shall know'. The disjunctive cantillation sign *(Zaqeph Qatan)* on *raʾû* may support such a reading. But even with this solution one misses a verb in the parenthesis: "not with your children . . . (am I *speaking* or *making covenant')";* compare 5:3, "not with our fathers that YHWH made this covenant" (see below on the correspondence of 11:2 to 5:3). It is possible that after a long series of clauses (2b–6) a verb connected with "not your children" has been omitted by mistake.

Similarly to the phrase in 5:3, "not with our fathers that YHWH made this covenant, but with us, the living, all of us here today," the author here wants to stress that it is the present generation who stand before God, the same generation as saw the miracles of Exodus, and not their sons, who did not experience the Exodus and the Sinaitic revelation. Yet there is a tendency in Deuteronomy to blur the gap between the generations and to see Israel as a corporate personality throughout all of its generations (cf. 29:13–14); thus a conflict is created between the wish to single out the generation of Exodus on the one hand and the wish to see Israel as a continuum throughout all the generations on the other (see the NOTE above for 5:2–3, and cf. Y. Hoffman 1982–83).

the lesson of YHWH. Hebrew: *mwsr,* derived from *ysr* 'to chastise/discipline' (4:36; 8:5; Prov 19:18; 29:17), signifies education (Greek *paideia;* cf. Prov 1:2, 8; 3:11; 4:1; Job 5:17) sometimes achieved by corporal punishment (Prov 22:15; 23:13; Jer 2:30; 5:3; 30:14). Compare the root *lmd* 'teach/learn' the original meaning of which is 'to train'; also *mlmd hbqr* 'ox-goad' in Judg 3:31 and the verb *lmd* in Jer 31:18; Hos 10:11; Cant 3:8; 1 Chr 25:7. The pictograph that represents the letter *lamed* in the ancient Hebrew script is an ox-goad.

his greatness. Compare 3:24.

his mighty hand. . . . Compare 4:34.

3–7. This passage sounds like a hymnic-liturgical paean; mark the repetition of the phrase *ʾšr ʿśh* in vv 3, 4, 5, 6, 7. Compare the hymnic descriptions of the blessed land (repetition of *ʾrṣ)* and the leading of the people in the desert (8:7–9; 14b–16), on which see the COMMENT to chap. 8.

3. *his signs.* Compare 4:34; 6:22; 7:19.

his deeds that he performed. Compare v 7, "the great deeds that YHWH performed," which creates an *inclusio* for the hymnic passage in vv 3–7. Compare also Exod 34:10, "the deed of YHWH which is awesome *(mʿśh YHWH ky nwrʾ)* which I perform for you," and Judg 2:10, "the deed which he performed for Israel *(hmʿśh ʾšr ʿśh lyśrʾl).*"

against Pharaoh king of Egypt and all his land. This refers to the plagues of Egypt; cf. 6:22, "YHWH wrought before our eyes great and grave signs and portents . . . against Pharaoh and all his household," and Neh 9:10, "and you performed signs and portents against Pharaoh, his servants, and all the people of his land."

4. *what he did to Egypt's army, its horses and chariots; how YHWH caused the waters of the Sea of Reeds to flow over them.* The destruction of the Egyptians at the Sea of the Reeds is expressed in various literary descriptions in different manners: Exod 15:4–5 uses *yrh bym* 'has cast into the sea'; *ṭbʿw* 'drowned'; *thmt yksymw* 'the deeps covered them'; *yrdw bmṣwlwt kmw ʾbn* 'they went down into the depths like a stone'; 15:10 has *ṣllw kʿprt bmym ʾdyrym* 'they sank like lead in the mighty waters'. Exod 14:27–28 says, *wynʿr . . . btwk hym* 'and hurled them in the sea'; *wyksw . . . lkl ḥyl prʿh, lʾ nšʾr bhm ʿd ʾḥd* 'and they covered . . . Pharaoh's entire army, not one of them remained'. The later hymn descriptions are dependent on the sources of Exodus and none of them relies on this verse. Compare the following scriptures: "and the sea covered *(ksh hym)* their enemies" (Ps 78:53, compare Exod 14:28); "and the water covered their foes, none of them was left" (Ps 106:11, compare Exod 14:22); "he hurled Pharaoh and his army into the sea of the Reeds" (Ps 136:15, compare Exod 14:22); "you throw their pursuers into the depths, like a stone in the raging waters" (Neh 9:11, compare Exod 15:5, 10).

thus destroying them to this day. JPS: "destroying them once and for all." Naḥmanides and Ibn Ezra understand it as referring to the later fate of the Egyptian kingdom: "they became a lowly kingdom *(whyth mmlkh šplh)*" (Ezek 17:14). D. H. Hoffmann (1913, ad loc.) interprets it as "completely, without return (to power)." Compare Exod 14:13, "for the Egyptians whom you see today you will never see again," which implies that the strength possessed by the Egyptians in the past will never return to them again.

5. *what he did for you in the wilderness.* Compare 8:15–16.

until you arrived in this place. Compare 1:31; 9:7.

6. *and what he did to Dathan and Abiram.* God saved Israel not only from the enemies outside but also from the enemies within. These were also destroyed in a miraculous way: the earth swallowed them up; cf. Num 16. This verse is verbally dependent on the JE source, with only small deviations:

Num 16:32	*Deut 11:6*
The earth opened her mouth and swallowed them and their households and all the men of Korah and all their possessions.	when the earth opened her mouth and swallowed them and their households, their tents, and every living substance that followed them.

The differences are, first, the appearance of the verb *pṣth* 'opened' in Deuteronomy, which is not used in the parallel verse in Num 16:32; second, the addition of the "tents" mentioned in other verses of this episode in Numbers (16:26, 27b); third, the absence of Korah and his men in Deuteronomy (they are added by the Samaritan text and Qumran; see the TEXTUAL NOTE); and, finally, the reading "living substance that followed them *(hyqwm ʾšr brglyhm)*" in Deuteronomy instead of "all the possessions *(kl hrkwš)*" and "all that belongs to them *(kl ʾšr lhm)*" in Num 16:30, 32, 33.

Korah is not mentioned in Deuteronomy because Deuteronomy follows the JE tradition, concerned with the rebellion of Dathan and Abiram directed against the leadership of Moses in general. In contrast, the Korah rebellion, which was directed against the religious-cultic authority of Moses and Aaron, belongs to the priestly strand of the Pentateuch (see also Num 26:9–11; 27:3 [= priestly source]), which is not represented in Deuteronomy.

opened her mouth. For *pṣh ph* cf. Gen 4:11; Num 16:30; Judg 11:36; Isa 10:14; Ps 22:14; Job 35:16; Lam 2:16; 3:46.

living substance. Compare Gen 7:4, 23. It denotes the thing that subsists or exists; compare Latin *substantia* (from *subsisto)* 'that which stands', and "existence," which is derived from *ex-sisto.* In Late Hebrew *qayyam* (from *qum 'stand')* signifies the existing thing.

that followed them. Literally, "at their feet." For this idiom for "following" see Gen 30:30, "and YHWH blessed you following me *(lrgly)*" (cf. 30:27); Exod 11:8; 1 Sam 25:27.

in the midst of all Israel. The faithful Israelites escaped the fate of the rebels; compare Num 16:33b–34, "and they perished from the midst of the assembly, and *all Israel* around them fled," etc.

7. *but it was with your own eyes that you saw.* Compare 3:21; 4:9; 7:19; 10:21; 29:2.

the great deeds that YHWH performed. Compare Judg 2:7 = Josh 24:31; also Judg 2:10 (= Dtr); and see the NOTE to v 3.

8. *You shall keep all the commandments.* For the meaning of *miṣwah* here and at 5:31; 6:25; and 7:11, see above, in the NOTE to 5:28.

that I command you today. This phrase is in the singular though embedded in a passage (vv 8–9) styled in the plural. The phrase in the singular is more prevalent in Deuteronomy than the plural one. The first time it appears in the plural in the book of Deuteronomy is 11:13 (4:2 has the phrase without "today"). The Samaritan text has the plural here, cf. the TEXTUAL NOTE.

that you may have the strength to come in and occupy the land. Compare 31:7, "be strong *(ḥzq wʾmṣ)* and courageous for you shall come . . . into the land," also 31:6 and Josh 1:6(= Dtr). For a different reading see the TEXTUAL NOTE.

9. *and so that you may prolong the days upon the Land.* Implicit are the words "as a nation"; cf. 4:40; 5:29 (Hebrew); etc. See Weinfeld 1972a, p. 345.

that YHWH swore to your fathers to give to them and to their descendants.

For the various formulas concerning the recipients of the promise of the land and of the land itself (the Patriarchs or their children), see Brettler 1982.

a land flowing with milk and honey. As Ehrlich (1909, ad loc.) has observed, this phrase triggered the next two verses, which describe the blessed nature of the promised land.

10–12. Following the concluding phrase of the previous section, "a land flowing with milk and honey," the author was inspired to give a fuller description of the blessed land, similar to the descriptions in 6:10–11 and 8:7–9, but here the land of Israel is contrasted with the rainless Egypt. In Egypt one must use physical labor in order to water the field, whereas in Israel the land is made fruitful by the rain sent by God. This comparison is fanciful and sounds illogical. A peasant would prefer a field provided with irrigation than a field depending on rain, which may occasionally be withheld (cf. v 17). Indeed, elsewhere in the Pentateuch Egypt is represented as a most fertile land. In Gen 13:10 Egypt is described as "the garden of YHWH *(kgn YHWH kʾrṣ mṣrym),*" compare Exod 16:3; Num 16:13; 20:5. The comparison should therefore be taken theologically and not realistically: the rain from the heaven symbolizes divine providence; in other words, the land of Israel is watered by God himself while other lands are watered by proxy: "people lie on their beds and God makes the rain fall down" *(Sipre Deut* §38 [Finkelstein 1969, p. 74], and cf. Buber 1950, pp. 41–50).

The Egyptians developed a theology of an opposite nature. According to their view, the barbarians and the animals depend on the Nile from heaven, while for the Egyptians the Nile emerges from the underground (cf. Lichtheim 1973–76, 2.99). For getting rain, however, Israel is dependent on God. If Israel follows the will of God, it will be provided with rain in all seasons, in the autumn and in the spring; but if it does not follow his commandments, rain will be withheld and the earth will not yield its crop (vv 13–17).

10. *like the land of Egypt . . . where you sow your seed and water it with your feet like a vegetable garden.* For watering the fields in Egypt one had to use hands and feet: lifting the buckets from the river by means of a machine *(shaduf);* or turning water wheels by foot (see the discussion of Smith 1918, ad loc.). Others understand the watering by foot to mean channels dug with the foot in which water would flow and water the crop. Such means of irrigation were used in Israel only for small vegetable gardening (cf. Isa 1:30; for *gan yaraq* cf. 1 Kgs 21:2). Recently L. Eslinger suggested (1987) that "to water with your feet" is a euphemism for using *urine* (cf. *mēmē raglēhem* [kere] in 2 Kgs 18:27 = Isa 36:12) for watering. We then encounter here, according to his view, a sarcastic contrast of Israel's hills and valleys drinking the water of heaven to the Egyptian system of watering, which is like watering gardens with urine.

11. *a land of hills and valleys, it drinks its water according to the rain of heaven.* Unlike Egypt, which is flat, rainless, with only the Nile incessantly

flowing through a monotonous landscape, the land of Israel has hills and valleys (from which brooks spring forth; cf. 8:7), soaking water from heaven.

12. *a land that YHWH your God cares for.* The LXX translates the verb *drš* here with *episkopeo* 'inspect/watch over'; cf. Isa 62:12, "you shall be called, cared for/watched *(drwšh)* . . . not forsaken"; see also Jer 30:17 (in the negative sense), "they called you outcast, that Zion for whom no one cares *(drš ʾyn lh)";* compare also Job 3:4.

the eyes of YHWH your god are always on it. Compare Prov 15:3, "the eyes of YHWH are everywhere watching good and evil men"; see also Zech 4:10. For eyes of YHWH on *(ʿyny b)* with the purpose of punishment, cf. Amos 9:8, "the eyes of my Lord Yahweh are upon the sinful kingdom; I shall destroy it from the surface of the earth." The idiom *ʿyny YHWH ʾel x,* compared to 11:12 by S. R. Driver (1902, ad loc.) has a different nuance: turn to or pay attention to; cf. Ps 33:18, "the eyes of YHWH *are turned to (ʾel)* those who fear him"; compare Ps 34:16.

from year's beginning to year's end. The fate of the land and its crops is destined every New Year for the whole coming year. This tradition has been preserved in Judaism *(m. Roš. Haš.* 1:2) but is also attested in the Hittite and Babylonian cultures; cf., e.g., in a Hittite text about the festival of the beginning of the year: "To the weather god . . . pronounce the life of heaven and earth, pronounce [the life] of the crop" (Otten 1956), and see Weinfeld 1983b, pp. 116–176).

13–21. According to the Masoretic division, this section stands as a parashah by itself and constitutes the second part of the Shemaʿ liturgy *(m. Tamid* 5:1). Thematically, however, vv 13–17 join vv 10–12: the bountiful rains of heaven described in vv 10–12 are conditioned by the observance of God's commandments, whereas vv 18–21 with their edifying overtones create an *inclusio* with 6:4–9 (see the NOTE to that section) and form a kind of framework for the block of material in 6:4–11:21. Verses 22–32, by contrast, are concerned with the entrance into the promised land (vv 22–25) and the ceremonies connected with it (vv 26–32).

13. *If . . . you obey (šmʿ tšmʿw) the commandments . . . to love . . . and serve.* Compare the beginning of the next parashah in v 22, "if you surely keep all the commandments *(šmr tšmrwn)* . . . to love," etc., but the difference between the two is in the kind of reward: in vv 13–21 the reward is the produce of the land, whereas in vv 22–25 the reward is the conquest of the land in its ideal borders.

the commandments that I command you this day. In Deuteronomy it is Moses who commands the people; compare 7:11; 11:8; etc., and see Weinfeld 1972a, pp. 356–57. But in view of vv 14 and 15 *(wenatati)* "I will give rain/grass" (see the TEXTUAL NOTE), it is not impossible that the one commanding here is God. One has also to take into account that Moses as a prophet and as a mediator speaks on behalf of God, and his words may appear as the words of God himself; cf. the NOTE to 7:4.

with all your heart and soul. Compare 4:29; 6:5; 10:12; etc.

14. *I will give the rain.* The discourse of Moses shifts imperceptibly from Moses to God (see the NOTE to v 13). The Samaritan text and the LXX, as well as Qumran here and in the following verse, read "he will give *(wntn)*" (see the TEXTUAL NOTE), but these might be corrections of the difficult "I will give" in the mouth of Moses; see the NOTE to v 13.

the rain for your land in season, the early rain and the late. Compare 28:12; Lev 26:4; Exod 34:26. Jeremiah 5:24 may have been influenced by this verse: "YHWH who gives rain *(gšm)* the early *(ywrh)* and the late *(mlqwš)* in season *(bʿtw).*" Compare also Joel 2:23, "[God] has given you the rain *Moreh* [= *Ywrh]* in justice, the early rain *(mwrh)* and late rain *(mlqwš).*" The early rain in Eretz Israel starts in October or November, whereas the late rain *(mlqwš)* falls in March and April.

You shall gather in your grain, your wine and oil. The verb *ʾsp* signifies not just collecting and gathering but mainly ingathering, i.e., bringing into the house. *ʾsp,* like the later Hebrew *kns,* means both to gather and to bring into (make enter) the house; cf. Deut 22:2; Gen 42:17; Num 12:15; Josh 2:18; 20:3; Ps 104:22; Judg 19:15; 2 Sam 11:27; and especially the idiom *nʾsp ʾl ʿmyw* (Gen 25:17 etc.), which means entering the ancestor's grave. The season of ingathering the crop is indeed called *ʾasip* (cf. Exod 23:16; 34:22). For grain, wine, and oil *(dgn, tyrwš, yṣhr),* see the NOTE to 7:13.

15. *I will give grass in the fields for your cattle.* Some Greek manuscripts read "you will give *(wntt).*"

you shall eat and be satiated. Affluence causes rebellious behavior; compare 6:11, *wʾklt wśbʿt,* which also comes before "Beware [lest you forget] *(hšmr lk [pn tškḥ])*" (v 12). The same is found in 8:10, 11: *wʾklt wśbʿt,* etc., *hšmr lk (pn tškḥ).* Compare also 8:12–17 (see the NOTE there) and 31:20.

16. *Beware lest your heart be seduced.* Compare Job 31:9 (in connection with fornication) and 27 (in connection with idolatry and astral worship): "If I ever saw the moon and my heart be secretly seduced *(wypt bstr lby)* and my hand touched my mouth in a kiss."

and you turn away. Compare 1 Sam 12:21 *(wlʾ tswrw)* and the more elaborate expression "to turn aside from the way *(sr mn hdrk)*" in Deut 9:12, 16; 11:28; 31:29; Judg 2:17; 1 Kgs 22:43.

serve other gods and bow to them. Compare 8:19, 29:25; see Weinfeld 1972a, p. 321.

17. *YHWH's anger will flare up against you.* Compare 6:15; 7:4.

and he will shut up the skies and there be no rain. Compare 28:23; Lev 26:19; 1 Kgs 8:35. The latter seems to be dependent on the present verse: *wʿṣr ʾt hšmym wlʾ yhyh mṭr* (Deut 11:17), and *bhʿṣr šmym wlʾ yhyh mṭr* (1 Kgs 8:35).

and the land will not yield its produce. Compare Lev 26:2, 20.

and you will perish quickly from the good land. Compare 4:26; 28:20; Josh 23:13, 15, 16b (the latter clause, which does not appear in the LXX, seems to be a verbal reproduction of Deut 11:17 and was apparently added by a late Hebrew scribe; see Holmes 1914, p. 28). Both threats that occur in this verse—shutting up the skies from giving rain and perishing from the land—are attested in the curses of the ancient Near Eastern treaties. For the first compare *VTE* lines 528–31, "Just as rain does not fall from a brazen heaven, so may rain and dew not come upon your fields and pastures" (see Weinfeld 1972a, p. 117 and see the NOTE to 28:23). For the second threat, compare the Hittite treaty of Šuppiluliuma, "may your offspring perish from the land *(zērka ištu erṣeti lihalliqa)*" (Weidner 1923, no. 1 RS. 65, pp. 34–35) and *VTE* lines 538–39, "may your name, your seed, and the seed of your sons and your daughters perish from the land" (TA KUR *lihliq, halaāqu* equals Canaanite–Hebrew *ʾbd;* cf. EA 288, where *halqat* is glossed by *abadat);* also *VTE* lines 543–44, where the same curse is pronounced with the variation "from the face of the earth *(pāni ša qaqqari),*" which is to be compared with Hebrew *ʾbd mʿl pny hʾdmh* (see 6:15; 28:63; Josh 23:13; 1 Kgs. 9:7; 13:34). In all of these instances the threat involves deportation and exile; for *ʾbd* in this sense of wandering and going into exile, see 26:5, "a wandering Aramaean *(ʾarami ʾobed),*" compare Isa 27:13; Jer 27:10, 15.

quickly. Compare 4:26; 28:20.

the good land. Compare 1:35.

18–20. This passage parallels 6:6–9, except that it is styled in plural but for 19b (cf. the NOTE to this verse). This section seems to form an *inclusio* with 6:6–9, making Deut 6:4–11:21 appear to be a continuous, comprehensive sermon.

18. *You shall put these my words upon your heart.* This parallels 6:6, "These words . . . shall be on your heart," and see the NOTE there on the parallel of this expression in a Hittite covenantal text.

and you shall bind them as a sign. . . . Compare 6:8 and the NOTE there.

19. *and teach them to your children—reciting them.* Compare 6:7, "You shall inculcate them to your children and you shall recite them *(dibber bam)";* see the NOTE to 6:7.

when you stay at home. Literally, "when you [sing.] stay in your [sing.] house." The change to singular may indicate that v 19b was a known formula or a stock phrase styled in the singular, as is Deut 6:7a. On the meaning of the verse and its parallel in Prov 6:22, see the NOTE to 6:7. In the parallel passage of 6:5–9 the command of binding the words as a sign, etc. (v 8), occurs next to the command of writing the words on the doorposts (v 9), while here the teaching of the children (v 19) interrupts these two commands. The order in 6:5–9 seems to be the one that is genuine; compare Prov 3:3; 7:3, where "binding" the commands appears next to writing them and, as shown in the NOTE to 6:8, the metaphor of binding the words or wisdom to the body (cf. also Prov 6:21) has affinities with Deut 6:5–9.

21. *so that your days . . . be multiplied.* This idiom (Hebrew: *rby ymym)* is characteristic of the wisdom literature; cf. Prov 4:10; 9:11; Job 29:18. Otherwise Deuteronomy uses "to lengthen days *(h'ryk ymym)*"; cf. 4:26, 40; 5:30; 11:9; etc. (see Weinfeld 1972a, p. 345, 1).

as long as there is a heaven over the earth. Literally, "as the days of heaven over the earth," that is to say, as long as the heaven endures above the earth *(kymy šmym ʿl h'rṣ);* compare Ps 89:30, "I will establish his descendants [= dynasty] forever . . . as long as the days of heaven *(kymy šmym).*" Compare the letter of King Adon of Ashkelon (or Ekron) to Pharaoh *(KAI* no. 266:3; cf. Porten 1981), "[let the days of Pharaoh lengthen] like the days of heaven *(kywmy šmy').*" See also Job 14:12, in a negative formulation, "When the heavens are no more *(ʿd bly šmym)*" and Ps 72:5, "as long as the sun endures, as long as the moon, generation after generation"; and, in a negative formulation, in the same Psalm (72:7): "and well-being *(šlwm)* abound until the moon is no more," that is, as long as the world exists (cf. also Ps 72:17). For an analysis of these formulas and their ancient Near Eastern background see Paul 1972.

22–25. These verses contain a military oration of the sort found in 1:29–30; 2:24–25; 3:21–22; 7:17–24; 31:1–6; cf. Weinfeld 1972a, pp. 45–51.

22. *For if you surely keep all the commandments.* This recapitulates the statement of v 8, "You shall keep all the commandments *(kl hmṣwh)*" (see the NOTE there); but whereas there the keeping of the law is motivated by the inheritance of the good land and enjoyment of its produce (see vv 9, 10–12, 13–21), here the reward for keeping the law is victory and military success. Compare 11:8, "that you may . . . occupy the land *(wyrštm 't h'rṣ)*" with 11:23, "you will dispossess nations greater and mightier than you *(wyrštm gwym gdlm wʿṣmm mkm).*"

to love YHWH your God, to walk in all his ways, and cleave to him. Compare 6:12; 8:6; 10:12, 20; 13:5.

23. *YHWH will drive out all these nations from before you.* Compare 4:38; Exod 34:24.

you will dispossess nations greater and mightier than you. In Deuteronomy the verb *yrš* in *qal,* like the causative *hiph ʿil,* connotes dispossession by extermination; see 2:12, "the descendants of Esau dispossessed them, wiping them out *(yyršwm wyšmydwm)*" compare 2:21, 22; 12:2, 29; 18:14; 19:1; 31:3); cf. Lohfink 1983. In this verse divine dispossession is intertwined with the human one: God causes the dispossession and the Israelites implement it. For the combination of the divine and human factors in Israelite historiography, cf. Seeligmann 1963, p. 385.

24. *Every spot on which your foot treads shall be yours.* Compare Josh 1:3, which is dependent on this verse and where the author refers to Deut 11:24 explicitly: "every spot on which your foot treads I give to you, *as I promised Moses.*"

from the wilderness and the Lebanon, from the river—the Euphrates—to the western sea. Joshua 1:3–4, which is dependent on this verse (see the previous NOTE), is slightly different: "from the wilderness and the Lebanon to the great river, the river Euphrates—the whole Hittite dominion—and to the Great sea where the sun sets." Unlike Deut 11:24, which has "from" *(mn)* twice and "to *(ʿd)*" once, Josh 1:4 has "from *(mn)*" once and "to *(ʿd)*" twice. Besides, Josh 1:4 has an additional definition: "the whole Hittite country," which is an Assyrian term designating the Syro-Palestine area; cf. Weinfeld 1983d, pp. 98–99.

In both sources, however, Lebanon is not preceded by "to *(ʿd),*" therefore no justification can be given for adding it, as some have suggested (e.g., Dillmann 1886, ad loc.); Lebanon is seen in both as an intermediary spot, between the south (wilderness) and the northeast (Euphrates): compare Deut 1:7, "the land of the Canaanites, and the Lebanon, as far as the Great River, the river Euphrates" (cf. the discussion of Saebø 1974, pp. 18–20. For the delineation of the borders compare Exod 23:31, "I will set your borders from the Sea of the Reeds to the sea of the Philistines and from the wilderness to the River [= Euphrates]." Such ideal borders, for which only great natural obstacles such as oceans, rivers, mountains, and deserts serve as boundaries, are known to us from Hittite and Assyrian royal inscriptions. Thus we read in one of the Hittite treaties, "I made the Euphrates my rear line and Mount Lebanon my border" (KBO I 1 rev. 16 = Weidner 1923, p. 22), and see especially the inscriptions of Adad-Nirari III (810–783 B.C.E.): "From the mountains to the great sea in the east . . . from the Euphrates to the great sea where the sun sets" *(ANET²,* p. 281; cf. recently Tadmor 1973, p. 148, lines 11–12). For such ideal delineations of borders in the Bible and in the ancient Near East, see Weinfeld 1983d, pp. 97–99.

the wilderness. This term refers to the desert in the south and the east of the land of Israel; compare Exod 23:31, "from the wilderness to the River."

the western sea. Literally, "the hinder sea *(hym hʾḥrwn),*" that is, the Mediterranean Sea, cf. 34:2; Joel 2:20; Zech 14.8. In the two latter references "the hinder sea" stands in opposition to "the front sea *(hym hqdmwny,*" that is, the Dead Sea to the east; cf. also Ezek 47:18. The natural orientation was eastward, and thus "the front" indicated the east, the right hand being the south *(ymn > teiman),* the left one the north (cf. Gen 14:15; Josh 19:27), while the hinder side is the west (cf. Job 23:9).

25. *No man shall stand up to you.* Compare 7:24 and the NOTE there.

YHWH your God will put your dread and fear of you over all the land in which you set foot. Compare 2:25, but there it is *pḥd wyrʾh* instead of *pḥd wmwrʾ.* In the older sources the expression is *pḥd wʾymh,* see, e.g., Exod 15:16 (with the verb *npl);* compare also *ʾymh* in Exod 23:27; Josh 9:9b *(nplhʾymh, nmgw kl yšby hʾrṣ)* is dependent on Exod 15:15–16 (chiastic order).

as he promised you. Compare Exod 23:27, "I will send forth my terror *(ʾymty)* before you," cf. *Sipre Deut.* §52 (Finkelstein 1969, p. 119).

26–32. The blessing and the curse offered here for Israel's choice are linked to the ceremony at mounts Gerizim and Ebal, which is to be performed at the entry into the land. This ceremony actually serves as a kind of envelope for the Deuteronomic code: 11:26–32 appears as a prologue to the law and 26:16–27:26 as an epilogue. The ceremony is interwoven with Moses' proclamation about Israel "becoming a people this day" (26:16–19; 27:9–10). This proclamation indicates that the establishment of Israel as the people of God took place at the plains of Moab before the crossing of the Jordan. The establishment of the people of God was ratified by a ceremony that consisted of erecting monumental inscribed stelae (27:1–4, 8), building an altar and sacrificing on it (27:5–7), and the pronouncement of blessings and curses, which comes right after Moses' farewell address at the plains of Moab. According to Deuteronomy, the establishment of Israel as God's people took place not at Sinai, as presented by earlier sources (Exod 19:5–8; 24:3–8), but at the entry of the people into the promised land (27:3–4, 9–10).

Such foundation ceremonies are attested in the Greek traditions about settlement in a new territory. New settlers used to perform ceremonies accompanied by the following acts: blessings and curses, the inscription of divine instructions on stelae for the new settlers, the erection of pillars of stone and monuments at the conclusion of the journey, the building of an altar (which for centuries was visited by pilgrims), and the offering of sacrifices on the occasion of the foundation ceremonies (cf. Deut 27:6–7; also Josh 8:31; see Weinfeld 1988). All of these occur in the description of the ceremony at mounts Gerizim and Ebal in Deut 26:16–27:26 (cf. Josh 8:30–35).

Alongside the Shechemite foundation tradition recounted in Deut 27 and Josh 8:30–35, we find a Gilgal foundation tradition attested in Josh 3–5. According to this tradition (about the Gilgal cycle of traditions, see Comment to chap. 7), the Israelites erected stone monuments at the crossing of the Jordan at Gilgal, and instead of a written covenant we find there the ceremony of circumcision—considered the sign of covenant in Gen 17—and the celebration of the Passover, the oldest ritual connected with the Exodus. It seems that these two rival foundation traditions were amalgamated in v 30 here.

Nevertheless, the blessings and the curses as presented by the Deuteronomic author here have to be understood in the theological sense: at the entry into the land Israel was given the choice between the blessing, which is *life* and *good*, and the curse, which is *evil* and *death* (cf. 30:15, 19); as Deut 30:19 puts it, "you choose life," which means the observance of God's commandments.

Verses 26–32 form a coherent unit, as may be learned from the fact that the passage opens with the phrase "I set before you today *(ʾnky ntn lpnykm hywm)*" and concludes with the same phrase (v 32).

26. *See . . . I set before you.* For such a construction, opening with "see," that is to say, "behold," cf. 1:8 (see the NOTE there); 21; 2:24, 31; 4:5; 30:15.

28. *but turn aside from the way.* Compare v 16; 9:12, 16; 31:29 (see the NOTE to 6:12).

follow other gods. Literally, "go after"; cf. 6:14 and the NOTE there.

whom you have not known. In other words, "you have not experienced"; cf. 13:3, 7, 14; 28:64; 29:25; and in the Song of Moses, 32:17, "gods they have never known *(ʾlhym lʾ ydʿwm)*" and see also Hos 13:14, "besides me you have never known a god *(wʾlhym zwlty lʾ tdʿ)*" (cf. Weinfeld 1972a, p. 324).

29–30. These verses, which are styled in the singular within a plural context, are concerned with the ceremony of foundation (cf. Deut 27; Josh 8:30–35; and see Introd. sec. 5) and thus stand out in their context, which is concerned with the choice between the blessing, which means life, and the curse, which means death (cf. 30:19). The commandments carry with them blessings if fulfilled and curses if not fulfilled.

29. *When YHWH your God brings you into the land.* This is an old formula connected with the Gilgal traditions about the entry into the land (cf. 6:10; 7:1; Exod 13:5, 11; and see above, 328 ff), but here it is applied to the Shechemite tradition, which rivals the Gilgalite one (see M. Weinfeld, 1988).

the blessing at Mount Gerizim and the curse at Mount Ebal. Gerizim is the mountain of blessing, apparently because of its lying on the south, which is the right-hand side *(ymn/teiman;* see above, in the NOTE for v 24), while Mount Ebal is on the north, which is on the left-hand side, and the sinister symbolizes bad fortune. Mount Gerizim is more fertile than Mount Ebal. The writer or speaker is facing east (see above, in the NOTE to v 24).

30. Verse 30 is a topographical gloss, apparently necessary for the Judahites who were not familiar with the location of northern sites; compare the gloss in Judg 21:19 concerning the location of Šiloh.

Are they not beyond the Jordan. Compare the gloss that also opens with the word *halô,* "is it [the bed of Og] not in Rabbah of the Ammonites." For an analysis of the word *halô* and its usage as factual communication see van Selms 1937.

beyond the Jordan. Taken from the standpoint of Moses the speaker; compare 3:20, 25; contrast 3:8.

beyond the west road. Literally, "the way of the sun setting." Apparently this alludes to the main road, passing from Transjordan to Shechem through the plain east of Shechem. "The western road" stands in opposition to "the eastern road," which passed through Transjordan (cf. Num 20:17).

in the land of the Canaanites who dwell in the ʿArabah. The ʿArabah of the Canaanite is the plain of the Jordan south of Chinneret (Josh 11:2; 12:3) through which the western road twisted before it reached the Shechemite mountains. The road, which starts at the ford of Adam (cf. Josh 3:16), leads through Wadi Farʿah to Tirzah (Tell al-Farʿah) and Shechem and was the best road connecting Mount Ephraim with Transjordan (cf. Aharoni and Rainey 1979, pp. 34, 60; see also Kaufmann 1959 pp. 131–32).

in front of Gilgal. This seems to refer to the well-known site of Gilgal near Jericho (Josh 4:19; 5:9ff; cf. Mic 6:5) and, as Driver (1902, p. 133) observed, "the words are being meant to indicate that from the point of view of one looking westwards from a site at foot of Nebo, Ebal and Gerizim would be 'in front of' this well known spot in the Jordan valley opposite." It should be added that—as indicated above—Gilgal was mentioned here intentionally in order to bring together the two rival traditions about a foundation ceremony. At both places stones were erected to commemorate the event of passing the Jordan and the entry into the promised land (cf. Deut 27:1–8; Josh 3–5); see L'Hour 1962, pp. 168–84). I dispense thus with the various identifications of Gilgal here that have been raised by commentators (cf., e.g., Driver 1902, pp. 133–34; Smith 1918, pp. 153–54).

by the oaks of Moreh. The Samaritan text and the LXX have the singular here; see the TEXTUAL NOTE. It is apparently an oracular tree (or grove) mentioned in Gen 12:6; compare *ʿelon meʿonnim* 'the oak of the soothsayers' near Shechem in Judg 9:37 and the *"elah* at Shechem" in Gen 35:4, as well as *"allah* in the sanctuary of YHWH" at Shechem, mentioned in Josh 24:26. It is possible that the author of Deuteronomy, who prohibits the plantation of sacred trees at the Temple (16:21), intentionally changed "the oak" into "oaks" in order to indicate that it was not a sacred tree standing there for worship but a grove or a small wood serving some aesthetic or practical purpose (for shade or the like). The Samaritan text added at the conclusion of the verse the phrase "in front of Shechem *(mwl škm)*" in order to neutralize the phrase "in front of Gilgal." The Rabbis reacted against this by accusing the Samaritans of forgery *(Sipre Deut* §56 [Finkelstein 1969, pp. 123–24]).

31. *For you are about to cross the Jordan.* The translation ("for" for *ky)* is supported by the LXX *(gar),* by the Targumim *(ʾrwm, ʾry),* and by the Syriac *(mṭl).* But the Samaritan Pentateuch has a new beginning here, marked by *qiṣṣa* 'end of section' after v 30, and thus makes vv 31–32 start the law of the unification of worship in chap. 12. According to this division of the text, we are to translate the word *ky* at the opening of v 31 as temporal: "when you cross the Jordan," like Num 33:51 and 35:10 (cf. Rofé 1972). Although such division looks plausible it is not decisive. As indicated above in the introductory note to vv 26–32, the phrases "I set before you this day" *(ʾnky ntn lpnykm hywm)*" in v 26 and v 32 form an *inclusio* for the passage of vv 26–32; therefore it is justified to consider it to be a unit by itself (cf. Lohfink 1963, pp. 233–36). One should admit, however, that vv 26–32 serve as a link between the prologue of chaps. 1–11 and the law in chaps. 12–26 (see Mayes 1981, p. 217) and the two last verses may be then considered as a conclusion and an opening at the same time.

Comment

This section constitutes a complex homily like the one of 4:1–40 (see above). Here 10:12 opens, like 4:1, with the address *we ʿatah Israel* 'and now, O Israel'.

In both cases the address marks a shift from a historical survey (chaps. 1–3 and 9:7–10:11, respectively) to an exhortation to keep the laws (4:1–40; 10:12–11:21). Both homilies close with the assurance that Israel will thrive in the promised land if the people observe the law. As I have indicated above, chap. 4 has its Sitz im Leben in liturgy, and the same can be said about this section.

It comes right after the description of sin, confession, and forgiveness (9:9–10:11), which constitutes by itself an important element in liturgy (compare Neh 9) and contains doctrines embedded in the liturgical-homiletic sermons of the Deuteronomic author. Thus the notion of the universal God found in 4:35, 39 occurs here in 10:14, 17 and in Neh 9. Mark especially the phrases "the heaven of heavens" (belonging to God) in Deut 10:14 and in Neh 9:6 on the one hand, and the divine titles "the great, the mighty, and the awesome *(hgdl, hgbr, whn wrʾ)*" in Deut 10:17 and Neh 9:32 (cf. 7:21; Neh 1:5; Dan 9:4) on the other. The notion of election found in 4:37—"he loved your fathers and chose their descendants after them *(ʾhb ʾt ʾbtyk wybḥr bzrʿw ʾḥryw)*"—is expressed here by the same terms: "he loved your fathers and chose their descendants after them" (10:15; compare Neh 9:7–8). Indeed, both the stress of God's universality and the election of Israel became the main pillars of Jewish liturgy as developed in the Second Temple period (cf. above in the COMMENT to chap. 4).

Another liturgical feature in this homily and in the other related homilies is the description of miraculous events that accompanied the Exodus and the wanderings in the desert. The plagues, the "wonders," and "the mighty hand" revealed by God in Egypt found in the present homily (10:21–22; 11:2, 7) and in 4:34; 6:21–22; 7:15–19; and 26:8 occur also in the prayer of Neh 9:10ff. and in the conventional Jewish liturgy (cf. the Geʾullah benediction after Shemaʿ *(t., Ber.* 2:1 and see Elbogen 1932, p. 22).

The blessed land that is mentioned in 11:8–12 also belongs to the Deuteronomic liturgical pattern (cf. 4:21–22, 38; 8:7–10; 26:9; also Neh 9:24; Ps 105:44). Another stereotypical liturgical formula found in this section is "the God of gods and the Lord of lords *(ʾlhy hʾlhym wʾdny hʾdnym)*" (10:17; cf. Ps 136:2–3; Dan 2:47, *ʾlh ʾlhyn wmrʾ mlkyn;* see the NOTE to 10:17). The prayer in Neh 9:6–12 contains in fact the elements found in Deut 10:14–11:7: the universal dominion of God (Neh 9:6; cf. Deut 10:14, 17); the election of the Patriarchs (Neh 9:7–8; cf. Deut 10:15); the miraculous events in Egypt (Neh 9:9–12; cf. Deut 10:21–22; 11:2–7); and the confession (Neh 9:16–35, which corresponds to Deut 9:7–10:11).

As a homily Deut 10:12–11:32 incorporates a variety of liturgical elements, but they appear sporadically and do not present an organized liturgical piece. Various kinds of ideas are introduced into the homily by way of association. Thus the mention of the election of the fathers in 10:15 triggered the idea of circumcision which, according to Gen 17, marked the covenant with Abraham, though this was transformed here—due to the tendency of spiritualization, see note—to circumcision of the heart (cf. 30:8). By the same token the liturgical titulature of God in 10:17 drew the author to insert other "humanistic" attributes of God, the sovereign: 'the god who upholds the cause of the fatherless and the widow and loves the stranger, providing him with food and clothing' (10:18). The latter idea in turn brought him to the injunction about 'loving the stranger' which is found also in Exod 23:9, Lev 19:34.

The passage 10:20–11:9 constitutes a sort of a poem devoted to the divine miraculous deeds connected with the Exodus (4:34; 6:22–23; 7:18–19; 8:2–5, 14–18; 26:6–9) (cf. above) and closes with the entrance to the blessed land which is also typical of deuteronomic liturgy (see above). The land theme inspired the author by way of association to the comparison of the land of Israel with Egypt. Unlike Egypt, which is not dependent on rain from heaven, the land of Israel is dependent on rain and thus is depending on God and especially cared by him. However, this is conditioned by obeying the law of God, should the Israelites disobey God, the sky will be shut and there will be no rain and the land will not yield its produce and the Israelites will perish quickly from their land (vv 13–17, compare 4:25–27).

The section concludes with a passage (vv 18–20) which parallels 6:6–9. Both passages command the Israelites to put "these words" (i.e. the *miṣwah* = *Hauptgebot,* see note to 6:4ff.) upon the heart, to impress them upon the children, to put them as signs upon the hand and the forehead and to write them on the doors of the houses and the gates. Thus 6:4–9 and 11:18–20 form an inclusio for the "main words" included in the *miṣwah* of 6:4–11:20. It is significant that the two pericopes 6:4–9 (Shemaᶜ) and 11:13–21 *(whyh ʾm šmᶜ)* constitute the daily credal liturgy in the Jewish worship and were recited by the priests of the Second Temple together with the Decalogue *(m. Tamid* 5:1.).

Verses 22–32, which form a conclusion to the prologue of Deuteronomy, are concerned with the entrance into the promised land (vv 22–25) and with the foundation ceremony at mounts Gerizim and Ebal, accompanied by blessings and curses (vv 26–32). These are linked with the epilogue of the book (chaps. 27–31), which treat broadly the foundation ceremony (see the INTRODUCTION) and the blessings and curses (chaps. 27–30) on the one hand and the entrance into the promised land (chaps. 31) on the other.

Sources

♦

Sigla and Sources

Dtr	Deuteronomistic editors of the Historiography of Joshua-Kings.
E	Elohistic Source
J	Jahwistic Source
JE	Jahwistic-Elohistic Source (combination of J and E)
MT	Masoretic Text
P	Priestly Code

Ancient Near Eastern Sources

Die El-Amarna Tafeln, ed. J. A. Knudtzon, Leipzig, 1908–15.
The Babylonian Laws, eds. G. R. Driver and J. C. Miles, Oxford, 1952.
Die Hethitischen Gesetze, ed. J. Friedrich, Documenta et Monumenta Orientis Antiqui, Leiden, 1959.

Rabbinic Sources

Genesis Rabba, ed. J. Theodor and Ch. Albeck, Jerusalem, 1965.
Lamentations Rabba, ed. S. Buber, Vilna, 1899.
Leviticus Rabba, ed. M. Margaliot, Jerusalem, 1953–60.
Maimonides, *Sefer ha-Mitswot*, ed. H. Heller, Jerusalem, New York, 1946.
Mekhilta de Rabbi Ishmael, trans. J. Z. Lauterbach, 3 vols., Philadelphia, 1933–35.
Mekhilta de Rabbi Ismael, eds. H. S. Horowitz and I. A. Rabin, Frankfurt, 1928.
Mekhilta de Rabbi Simeon bar Yochai, eds. J. N. Epstein and E. Z. Melamed, Jerusalem, 1955.
Midrash Haqqadol, ed. S. Fish, London, 1947.
Midrash Shemuel, ed. S. Buber, Krakau, 1893.
Midrash Tanaaim, ed. D. Z. Hoffmann, Berlin, 1908.

Midrash Tehillim (Shocher Tov), ed. S. Buber, Wilna, 1891.
Pesikta Rabbati, ed. M. Ish-Shalom, Vienna, 1880.
Pesikta de Rav Kahanna, ed. Y. Y. Mandelbaum, Newark, 1987.
Sipre to Deuteronomy, ed. E. Finkelstein, New York, 1969.
Targum Jonathan, ed. A. Sperber, Leiden, 1959.
Targum Jonathan ben Uziel (= Ps Jon), ed. D. Rieder, Jerusalem, 1974.
Tosephta, ed. M. S. Zuckermand, Jerusalem, 1963.

Commentators

Abravanel's Commentary to the Pentateuch, Jerusalem, 1964.
Ibn Ezra's Commentary to the Pentateuch, ed. A. Weiser, Jerusalem, 1976.
S. D. Luzzatto's Commentary on the Pentateuch, ed. P. Schlesinger, Tel Aviv, 1965. (Orig. Padua, 1871).
Rabbi Shemuel ben Meir, *Commentary to the Pentateuch,* ed. D. Rosin, Breslau, 1881.
Ramban's Commentary to the Pentateuch, (= Naᶜhmanides), ed. H. D. Shevell, Jerusalem, 1969.
Rashi, *A Commentary on the Pentateuch,* ed. A. Berliner, Frankfurt, 1905.

Apocrypha and Pseudepigrapha

The Apocrypha and Pseudepigrapha of the Old Testament, ed. R. H. Charles, 2 vols., Oxford, 1913.
The Book of Ben Sira, Text, Concordance, and an Analysis of the Vocabulary, The Academy of Hebrew Language, Jerusalem, 1973.